Visions of the Future in Germany and America

Germany and the United States of America
The **Krefeld Historical Symposia**

Previous titles published in this series by Berg include:

German and American Constitutional Thought: Contexts,
Interaction and Historical Realities
Edited by *Hermann Wellenreuther*

Confrontation and Cooperation: Germany and the United States
in the Era of World War I, 1900–1924
Edited by *Hans Jürgen Schröder*

German and American Nationalism:
A Comparative Perspective
Edited by *Hartmut Lehmann and Hermann Wellenreuther*

Visions of the Future in Germany and America

Edited by
Norbert Finzsch
and
Hermann Wellenreuther

BERG

Oxford • New York

First published in 2001 by
Berg
Editorial offices:
150 Cowley Road, Oxford, OX4 1JJ, UK
838 Broadway, Third Floor, New York, NY 10003-4812, USA

Published with the aid of a financial grant from the Ministerium für
Kultur und Wissenschaft des Landes Nordrhein-Westfalen

Berg is the imprint of Oxford International Publishers Ltd.

Library of Congress Cataloging-in-Publication Data

Visions of the future in Germany and America / edited by Hermann
Wellenreuther and Norbert Finzsch.
    p. cm.
Includes bibliographical references and index.
    ISBN 1-85973-521-5 (Cloth)
1. Utopias. 2. Millennialism. 3. United States--Social conditions.
4. Germany--Social conditions. I. Wellenreuther, Hermann. II.
Finzsch, Norbert.
    HX806 .V57 2001
    335'.02--dc21   2001004385

British Library Cataloguing-in-Publication Data

A catalogue record for this book is available from the British Library.

ISBN 1 85973 521 5 (Cloth)

Typeset by JS Typesetting, Wellingborough, Northants.
Printed in the United Kingdom by Antony Rowe, Chippenham,
Wiltshire.

Dedicated to past religious, political, literary and ecological visions of the future in America and Germany. Twenty-eight scholars from the United States and Germany explored the meaning of eschatological and utopian thoughts and concepts propagated and pursued during the last three centuries.

Contents

Contents

Contents

Introduction

Norbert Finzsch

> Harmony and understanding
> Sympathy and trust abounding
> No more falsehood or derisions
> Golden living dream of visions
> Mystic crystal revelations
> And the mind's true liberation
> Aquarius, Aquarius[1]

In literature, utopian societies, if portrayed as functioning and presentable ones, demand spatial and chronological isolation.[2] Therefore, the presentation of fictional utopias requires one traveler as an observing subject that condenses experience and represents the author's dominant perspective. Social life in utopian narrative is usually prone to a certain reductionism in order better to represent the idealized harmonious relations that are supposed to exist in an enhanced environment. Since the traveling newcomer comes into this ideal world as an utterly uninstructed and uninformed person, he or she has to be enlightened in long discourses by mentors. What I describe here has been established as common traits of utopian

---

1. "Aquarius," lyrics by Galt MacDermot, music by James Rado and Gerome Ragni, performed by Fifth Dimension, 1967.
2. It can be questioned whether the dichotomy of utopias of space ("Raumutopien") and utopias of time ("Zeitutopien") is a valid one. Whereas the older research on utopias established a causal link between the disappearance of the spatial utopia owing to the "discovery" of the world and a subsequent emphasis on the utopias of time, modern research did away with this hierarchy and emphasized the coexistence of both models in Western thinking. Utopias of time rather seem to have been accepted by the lower clerus and the underclasses, while utopias of space seem to have been favored by humanists and better educated people with access to the centers of power like Thomas More and Francis Bacon.

literature, whether we consider Thomas More's *Utopia* (1516) or Edward Bellamy's *Looking Backward* (1888).[3]

It is not my intention to perform the role of mentor that is needed for the typical newcomer in an utopian nowhere. Rather, I would like to position the reader of this book in the sense that she or he understands what we were doing when we assembled in Krefeld in May 1999. This year marked the end of the twentieth century, and whether this end is an arbitrary one is beyond the point – like any sign it can be arbitrary and binding at the same time. The "end of the century" as a metonymical signifier does not always occur at the very end of the hundred years that are marked by the double digit zero. Historians have often argued that there are "long" and "short" centuries. In American history much can be said in favor of the nineteenth century starting in 1814 with the Peace of Ghent and the end of the Napoleonic Wars that affected the young nation in multiple ways. The end of the nineteenth century is placed arbitrarily either in the year 1898 with the Spanish–American War

---

Utopias of space also have the advantage (from the perspective of those in power) of being less subversive since they do not require political implementation. Sven-Aage Jørgensen, "Utopisches Potential in der Bibel: Mythos, Eschatologie und Säkularisation," in Wilhelm Voßkamp, ed., *Utopieforschung: Interdisziplinäre Studien zur neuzeitlichen Utopie*, 3 vols. (Frankfurt/Main, 1985), vol. 1, 375–401, 376–380. Richard Saage, "Zum Stand der sozialwissenschaftlichen Utopieforschung in der Bundesrepublik, Part 1": *Neue Politische Literatur* 38(2) (1993), 221–238. Part 2, *Neue Politische Literatur* 39(1) (1994), 55–97. Recent research seems to indicate that with the exploration and colonization of America the ancient dream of an ideal world regained topicality. The paradisiacal concept of the reconciliation between culture and nature developed into an important aspect of the American dream. From the seventeenth century, a specifically American version of the harmony of man and world, subject and object, has been envisioned by English as well as American writers. Both the comedy *Eastward Hoe* (1605) and Michael Drayton's ode "To the Virginian Voyage" (1606) describe Virginia as a region where a perfect nature magically anticipates the cultivation of settlers. See Jochen Achilles, "Die Paradiesvorstellung von der Versöhnung des Menschen mit der Natur: Literaturgeschichtliche Betrachtungen zu einem Aspekt des amerikanischen Traumes," *Amerikastudien/American Studies* 35(2) (1990), 203–218.

3. Jonathan Auerbach claims that *Looking Backward* is foremost not a utopian novel, but the expression of middle-class fears and anxieties. This is in my under-

and America's subsequent imperialistic thrust or in the year 1917 with its entrance into World War I. Similar and equally arbitrary epochs can be formulated when we look into German history. In a way the nineteenth century started either in 1789 or in 1814 – depending on the point of view taken by historians. These two examples just show how much defining temporal borders depends on the underlying understanding of the essence of an epoch, the deep structure of an era, that hidden meaning which sums up what a century was all about.

At the end of epochs and eras human beings tend to reflect about the shape of things to come. They either rejoice or worry about a future that is unknown to them until it unravels in front of them. This may or may not be a part of the human condition, but the way in which concerns about the future are expressed, is dependent on historical specificity and can and must therefore be put in historical context. The 1999 Krefeld symposium was therefore dedicated to visions of the future in America and Germany.

The "future," as a point in time that one has not reached yet, but that is destined to come and then is left behind, is, historically speaking, a relatively new idea, because it depends on the idea of an independent, unidirectional, and equidistanced time, as defined by Sir Isaac Newton in 1687: "Absolute, true, and mathematical time, of itself, and from its own nature, flows equally without relation to anything external."[4] Time concepts and visions of the future are

---

standing not necessarily a contradiction to an utopian interpretation of Bellamy's novel. Jonathan Auerbach, "'The Nation Organized'": Utopian Impotence in Edward Bellamy's Looking Backward, *American Literary History* 6(1) (1994), 24–47. Auerbach's view is somewhat put in jeopardy by Vincent Geoghegan, "The Utopian Past in Edward Bellamy's *Looking Backward* and William Morris's *News from Nowhere*," *Utopian Studies* 3(2) (1992), 75–90; Hans Ulrich Seeber, "Thomas Morus' *Utopia* (1516) und Edward Bellamys *Looking Backward* (1888): Ein funktionsgeschichtlicher Vergleich," Wilhelm Voßkamp, ed., *Utopieforschung: Interdisziplinäre Studien zur neuzeitlichen Utopie*, 3 vols. (Frankfurt/Main 1985), vol. 3, 357–377, 357.

4. Isaac Newton, *Mathematical Principles of Natural Philosophy and His System of the World* (Berkeley, CA 1934), 6. The first edition appeared 1687 with Pepys as Isaac Newton, *Philosophiae Naturalis Principia Mathematica* (London, 1687).

related and interdependent and one cannot speak of the future without some relation to time, be it (a) a circular, reiterative time, (b) a limited and clearly defined time between genesis and apocalypse, (c) an endless, abstract physical time without beginning or end, or (d) a time/space continuum in which time is just another dimension of space and vice versa. In some societies different concepts of time do coexist with others. Sometimes concepts of temporality oscillate between their secular and religious versions. The same Isaac Newton, quoted above because of his modern concept of time, was a very typical specimen of a scientist who worked as a theologian at the same time. On the one hand he designed a modern concept of time and space, on the other hand he believed firmly in the second coming of Christ, the apocalypse and the end of time.[5]

Newton's double time is not so far removed from modern reality. Millions of Americans and Germans alike do adhere to an apocalyptic view of the world that is seated deeply within Christian traditions and beliefs.[6] Whereas German society is a largely secular one, Christian beliefs and traditions still reside at the very center of popular culture in the United States.[7] These beliefs tend to form a solid block of convictions and ideologies in which specific visions

5. Isaac Newton, *Observations upon the Prophecies of Daniel and the Apocalypse of St. John* (London, 1733).

6. Frank and Fritzie Manuel rightfully claim, that "the profusion of Western utopias has not been equaled in any other culture," which, according to Sven-Aage Jørgensen, is the result of Judaism and Christianity. The Manuels underline the link between utopian thinking and Christianity by claiming that "[w]hen plain belief in religious paradise became attenuated, utopia came into being" (Sven-Aage Jørgensen, "Utopisches Potential in der Bibel: Mythos, Eschatologie und Säkularisation," in Wilhelm Voßkamp, ed., *Utopieforschung: Interdisziplinäre Studien zur neuzeitlichen Utopie*, vol. 1, 375–401, at 375); Frank E. and Fritzie P. Manuel, *Utopian Thought in the Western World* [Cambridge, MA, 1979], 1; 112; Michael Barkun, *Disaster and the Millennium* (New Haven, CT, 1974).

7. The ideological background of American utopian communities from the religious and secular groups of the eighteenth century to the hippie communes of the 1960's are largely based on religion rather than political ideologies. This view is supported by Laurence Veysey, "Ideological Sources of American Movements," *Society* 25 (2) (1988), 58–61; Diane L. Barthel, *From Pietist Sect to American Community* (Lincoln, NE, 1984).

of the future play an important role. Events and historical phenomena like the end of the Cold War or the founding of the state of Israel are perceived as omens of the dawning of time.[8] For a substantial minority of Americans, the future is symbolized by the Last Judgement at the end of the Millennium and the subsequent reign of Christ on earth.[9] The minority of Germans who believe in a future that is limited to the remaining years before Armageddon may be less outspoken, visible or dominant in the discourse about the future, but they nevertheless exist within a largely secularized society.[10] This means that there is a temporality in both American and German societies that is uncoupled from modern visions of time and future. These segments of society could be said to adhere to premodern concepts of time.[11] These premodern versions of time

---

8. Michael Barkun, *Disaster and the Millennium* (New Haven, CT, 1974). See the apocryphal Ezra, who, in referring to the apocalypse, wrote: "All periods and years will be destroyed, and thereafter will neither exist month nor day, nor hours" (Ezra 4:26,27, quoted in Jeannine Marie King, "A New Millenium: Memory and Apocalypse in African-American Literature," Dissertation, University of California, Berkeley, 1999, 3). The whole complex of chronology and temporality in the American context is treated in Norbert Finzsch and Michaela Hampf, "Y2K-Madness und andere Millenarianismen: Eine historische Betrachtung zum Ende des Jahrtausends," in Annette Simonis and Linda Simonis, eds., *Zeitwahrnehmung und Zeitbewußtsein der Moderne* (Bielefeld, 2000), 153–195.

9. Revelation 20, 1–6.

10. The reasons for the secularization are many. Among them is Germany's tradition of "bible critique" in the eighteenth century in which biblical texts were perceived as texts in the first place, in the sense that they had been written by human authors and displayed rhetorical and stylistical tropes. See Robert Lowth and his influence in Germany. Robert Lowth, *Praelectiones de Sacra Poesi Haebraeorum* (Göttingen, 1758); Johann Gottfried von Herder, *Vom Geist der ebraeischen Poesie: Eine Anleitung für die Liebhaber derselben, und der ältesten Geschichte des menschlichen Geistes* (Dessau, 1782).

11. Premodern visions of the future included communistic experiments like the Münster Anabaptists. In their communism they tried to reproduce the utopia in Genesis 2,17; 3,16–24, a world without death, work, want, and urge. In Thomas Müntzer's *Confession* of 1525 one finds the telling sentence: "Omnia sunt communia, and everyone should receive according to his demands. Whatever prince, count or nobleman does not want to act accordingly should be executed by the sword or hanged [my translation, N.F.]" (Thomas Müntzer, *Schriften und Briefe. Kritische Gesamtausgabe* [Gütersloh, 1968], quoted in G. List, *Chiliatische Utopie und radikale Reformation* [Münster, 1973], 138).

and future may be rejuvenated and brought to the surface of discourse in times of crisis and change.[12]

Premodern time and premodern visions of the future denote concepts that are limited in twofold ways. They include understandings of the future that go back to medieval concepts in which time (*tempus*) was part of the divine creation. Time was always secular time since it was part of God's creation, while eternity was timeless.[13] It was limited to the epoch between creation and Eternal Judgement and would perish with the world at the end of time.[14] Thus time differed strictly from eternity, and visions of the future were by and large confined to this timeless eternity. But beyond this medieval time there was a premodern concept of time that combined both a secular and a divine time and a secular and divine future.[15] In America at least, with its waves and layers of immigrants arriving from largely rural backgrounds in the seventeenth, eighteenth, and nineteenth centuries, religious expectations and political hopes for betterment were stirred and brought into the dominant discourse.[16]

12. Paul Boyer, "Bible Prophecy Belief in Contemporary American Culture," *Anglican and Episcopal History* 67 (4) (1998), 448–466; Charles B. Strozier, "The Apocalyptic in America," *Psychohistory Review* 22(2) (1994), 159–191.

13. Hans-Werner Goetz, "Zeitbewußtsein und Zeitkonzeptionen in der hochmittelalterlichen Geschichtsschreibung," in *Zeitkonzeptionen, Zeiterfahrung, Zeitmessung: Stationen ihres Wandels vom Mittelalter bis zur Moderne*, Trude Ehlert, ed. (Paderborn), 12–32.

14. Augustine was adamant in his conviction that there could be no time outside of creation. Augustine also claimed that the Millennium had started with Christ's birth and that therefore one could expect the *parousia* ("second coming of Christ") and the Final Judgement to happen within the existing temporal frame (St. Augustinus, Bishop of Hippo, *Confessions* [London, 1993], book 10, ch. 30, p. 230).

15. Johann Valentin Andreae (1586-1654) depicted in Christianopolis (1619) an ideal state in which science is tightly bound to the fundamental religious truths of the inhabitants: Andreas Urs Sommer, "Religion, Wissenschaft und Politik im Protestantischen Idealsstaat: Johann Valentin Andreaes Christianopolis," *Zeitschrift für Religions- und Geistesgeschichte* 48(2) (1996), 114–137.

16. The first religious utopians in America were, of course, the Puritan immigrants. James Ross Holstun, "Puritan Utopias of the Interregnum" (Ph.D.-thesis, University of California, Irvine 1983); James Holstun, *A Rational Millennium: Puritan Utopias of Seventeenth-Century England and America* (New York, 1987). In

African-American churches, combining a vision of the future that
brought liberation both from slavery and oppression in the near
future and salvation from want and sin in another world influenced
American visions of the future. For African American denominations
the end of time and the apocalypse meant the end of racism,
exclusion, sorrow and pain and were therefore sought and expected
with impatience, even in twentieth century America.

In nineteenth-century America, the emergence of hundreds of
socialist or communitarian communities[17] with a variety of political,
sexual and religious utopias is sometimes ridiculed when looked
upon from a twentieth-century perspective, but Icarians, Oneidas
Fourier phalanxes and other communities and sects were definitively
a trait of mainstream American culture between 1800 and 1900.[18]

---

the nineteenth century there emerged one communal experiment after the other.
Schenck, a member of a German fraternity, arrived in Galveston, Texas, in April
1840. His group planned to establish a utopian community patterned after Etienne
Cabet's Icarian colony, established in 1840: H. T. Edward Edward, ed., "A letter
from Friedrich Schenck in Texas to His Mother in Germany, 1847," *Southwestern
Historical Quarterly* 92(1) (1988), 145–165. After 1900 utopias took on a different
form, even in the United States. Planned communities in North America often
emerged in the form of a cooperative socialist movement. Eventually, many of the
values of the ailing utopian communities were realized in the Finnish community
in Superior, Wisconsin, the center of a flourishing regional network of local
cooperatives: Carl Ross, "The Utopian Visions of Finnish Immigrants, 1900–30,"
Scandinavian Studies 60(4) (1988), 481–496.

John H. Bracey, Jr. and August Meier, "Black Ideologies, Black Utopias:
Afrocentricity in Historical Perspective," *Contributions in Black Studies* 12 (1993–
1994), 111–116.

17. There existed 180 American communitarian experiments between 1800
and 1887: Lyman Tower Sargent, "Utopian Literature before Bellamy," ATQ 3(1)
(1989), 135–146.

18. I can only give a small sample of the huge recent literature. The classical
study on Oneida is Louis J. Kern, *An Ordered Love: Sex Roles and Sexuality in Victorian
Utopias. The Shakers, the Mormons, and the Oneida Community* (Chapel Hill, NC,
1981); Robert S. Fogarty, *All Things New: American Communes and Utopian Movements,
1860–1914* (Chicago, 1990); Carl J. Guarneri, *The Utopian Alternative: Fourierism in
Nineteenth-Century America* (Ithaca, NY, 1991); Carl J. Guarneri, "Reconstructing
the Antebellum Communitarian Movement: Oneida and Fourierism," *Journal of
the Early Republic* 16(3) (1996), 463–488; Spencer Klaw, *Without Sin: The Life and*

Unforgotten are the many millenarian sects and churches that evolved out of the "burned-over district" in New York, the arena of a religious mass movement, called the Second Great Awakening.[19]

Although one could argue that Germany had its own kind of Great Awakening, first in the form of the Reformation, but later in Pietism, communitarianism in Germany was never as important as it was in the United States. What Germany did have, though, was its fair share of political utopianism, but that never resulted in a large-scale and extended period of experimentation with utopian communities. What is interesting in the context of ecological movements in the 1980s is that rural communities of the post-World War I period often had elements of an ecologist ideology.[20] The *Genossenschaften*, although perceived as an integral part of an infant non-capitalist economy, never separated from the powerful and influential social-democratic movement and had, on the whole, more the character of self-help organizations than of utopian communities.[21] On the

---

Death of the Oneida Community (New York, 1993); Diana Marie Garno, "Gendered Utopia: Women in the Icarian Experience, 1840–1898" (Ph.D.-thesis, Wayne State University, TX, 1998); Robert P. Sutton, *Les Icariens: The Utopian Dream in Europe and America* (Urbana, IL, 1994); Janet Fischer Palmer, "The Community at Work: The Promise of Icaria" (Ph.D.-thesis, Syracuse University, 1995); Richard Francis, *Transcendental Utopias: Individual and Community at Brook Farm, Fruitlands, and Walden* (Ithaca, NY, 1997); Donald E. Pitzer, ed., *America's Communal Utopias* (Chapel Hill, NC, 1997); Fitzhugh W. Brundage, *A Socialist Utopia in the New South: The Ruskin Colonies in Tennessee and Georgia, 1894–1901* (Urbana, IL, 1996).

19. Michael Barkun, *Crucible of the Millennium: The Burned-Over District of New York in the 1840's* (Syracuse, NY, 1986).

20. There is not much recent research on the German agrarian settlement movement. For settlements and rural communities see Anne Feuchter-Schawelka, "Siedlungs- und Landkommunebewegung," in Diethart Kerbs and Jürgen Reulecke, eds., *Handbuch der deutschen Reformbewegung, 1880–1933* (Wuppertal, 1998), 227–244; Christoph Conti, *Abschied vom Bürgertum: Alternative Bewegungen in Deutschland von 1890 bis heute* (Reinbek, 1984); Ulrich Linse, *Ökopax und Anarchie: Eine Geschichte der ökologischen Bewegungen in Deutschland* (München, 1986); Gustav Heinecke, *Frühe Kommunen in Deutschland. Versuche neuen Zusammenlebens. Jugendbewegung und Novemberrevolution 1919–1924* (Herford, 1978).

21. There were only 428 agrarian communities (farmers' associations) in Germany in 1914, in which farmers cooperated in the production and processing

other hand, neither socialism/communism nor fascism became an important political force to be reckoned with in the United States in the sense that socialist, communist or fascist movements developed into mass parties. That was an exceptionalism that was reserved for Germany.[22]

Germany, on the other hand, did experience its share of apocalyptic experiments and traumata. The connection between visions of the future and German fascism is too obvious. A future world, dominated by an "Aryan master race," a world after a "final solution" at the cost of millions of human beings slaughtered in concentration camps and killed in worldwide wars of annihilation, looks like the embodiment of a dystopia to us, but surely stood for a paradise in the eyes of protofascist supporters of eugenics and Nazi ideologies.[23]

---

of food, compared to almost 20,000 credit associations. See Michael Prinz, in Diethart Kerbs and Jürgen Reulecke, eds., *Handbuch der deutschen Reformbewegung, 1880–1933* (Wuppertal, 1998), 251–264, p. 258.

22. Some scholars have argued that the German youth movement of the late nineteenth and early twentieth century, as part of a larger German reform movement, did indeed include an utopian element. See Winfried Mogge, "Jugendbewegung," in Diethart Kerbs and Jürgen Reulecke, eds., *Handbuch der deutschen Reformbewegung, 1880–1933* (Wuppertal, 1998), 181–196; Otto Neuloh and Wilhelm Zilius, *Die Wandervögel: eine empirisch-soziologische Untersuchung der frühen deutschen Jugendbewegung* (Göttingen, 1982); Rosemarie Schade, *Ein weibliches Utopia: Organisationen und Ideologien der Mädchen und Frauen in der bürgerlichen Jugendbewegung 1905–1933* (Witzenhausen, 1996). It is important, however, to insist that these movements never created working communities of people who lived, worked, or settled together for an extended period of time. The notable exception, Kuhle Wampe, a workers' settlement near Berlin, acquired fame only because it figured prominently in a movie coproduced by Bertold Brecht: Wolfgang Gersch and Werner Hecht, *Kuhle Wampe: Protokoll des Films und Materialien* (Frankfurt am Main, 1969); Helmut Korte and Reinhold Happel, *Film und Realität in der Weimarer Republik: Mit Analysen der Filme "Kuhle Wampe" und "Mutter Krausens Fahrt ins Glück"* (Munich and Vienna, 1978).

23. As Peter Weingart has argued convincingly, there is only a thin line between eugenics and preventive medicine: Peter Weingart, "The Thin Line between Eugenics and Preventive Medicine," in Norbert Finzsch and Dietmar Schirmer, eds., *Identity and Intolerance: Nationalism, Racism, and Xenophobia in Germany and the United States* (Washington, DC, Cambridge and New York, 1998), 397–412. Along the same lines: Götz Aly and Christian Pross, *Der Wert des Menschen: Medizin in*

For them, the Third Reich was identical with the Millennium ("Tausendjähriges Reich") and thus was just a necessary step on the road to a perfect world.[24] Albert Speer, the Führer's chief architect, even designed a "futurist" architecture, in which the design of buildings was based to a large extent on the aesthetics of the ruins they would present in a thousand years.[25] Some historians even argue that the Nazis' policy of extermination had a utopian kernel.[26]

Apart from Nazism Germans did have alternative visions of the future. Socialism was one of them, as can be seen from the fact that there once existed a "first socialist state on German soil," the GDR.[27]

Deutschland 1918–1945 (Berlin, 1989). Eugenics and scientific racism were by no means limited to the Nazis in Germany. There existed in Weimar Germany a eugenic discourse across the spectrum of almost all political parties, excluding the Communist Party. See Benoît Massin, "Anthropologie und Humangenetik im Nationalsozialismus oder: Wie schreiben deutsche Wissenschaftler ihre eigene Wissenschaftsgeschichte?" in Heidrun Kaupen-Haas and Christian Saller, eds., *Wissenschaftlicher Rassismus: Analysen einer Kontinuität in den Human- und Naturwissenschaften* (Frankfurt am Main and New York, 1999), 12–64; Anette Herlitzius, *Frauenbefreiung und Rasseideologie: Rassenhygiene und Eugenik im politischen Programm der "Radikalen Frauenbewegung" (1900–1933)* (Wiesbaden, 1995); Jochen-Christoph Kaiser, Kurt Nowak, and Michael Schwartz, eds., *Eugenik, Sterilisation, "Euthanasie": Politische Biologie in Deutschland 1895–1945. Eine Dokumentation* (Berlin, 1992); Paul Weindling, *Health, Race and German Politics between National Unification and Nazism, 1870–1945* (Cambridge and New York, 1989).

24. On *parousia*, eschatology, and the millennium in Christianity see *Religion in Geschichte und Gegenwart*, vol. 5, pp. 130–132. On Nazi utopias Jost Hermand, *Old Dreams of a New Reich: Volkish Utopias and National Socialism* (Bloomington, IN, 1992); Jost Hermand, "Zwischen Superhirn und grüner Siedlung: Faschistische Zukunftsvisionen," *Zeitschrift für Religions- und Geistesgeschichte* 40(2) (1988), 134–150.

25. Johanne Lamoureux, "La Theorie des Ruines d'Albert Speer ou l'Architecture 'Futuriste' selon Hitler," *RACAR* 18(1–2) (1991), 57–63.

26. Michael Zimmermann, "Utopie und Praxis der Vernichtungspolitik in der NS-Dikatur: Überlegungen in vergleichender Absicht," *Werkstatt Geschichte* (13) (1996), 60–71.

27. This is by no means to say that socialist utopias were confined to Europe or Germany. As early as 1802 American socialists envisioned a socialist future. *Equality – A Political Romance* was a text, published in installments during 1802 in

Socialist utopias, in which an individual could be "hunter, fisher or critical critic"[28] according to his/her demands without ever being stuck to that profession, may be perceived as the historical recurrence of the "garden of Eden" theme portrayed in Genesis.[29] In an interesting reversal of Genesis, however, in which the paradise was closed for rebellious human trespassers with death and work as undesired side-effects, modern "secular" communism was achievable, among other things, through organization, work, and revolution, although in the case of the GDR, revolution was played down considerably,[30] and the "competition of systems" between the

---

The Temple of Reason, a Philadelphia journal. It represents the first socialist work in American history. The tract tells the story of an utopia, called Lithconia according to its founder John Lithgow, whose inhabitants share in an egalitarian community where property-holding, legal institutions, and lawyers have ceased to exist. Children are property of the state, thus liberating women from daily drudgery: Michael Durey, "John Lithgow's Lithconia: The Making and Meaning of America's First 'Utopian Socialist'Tract," *William and Mary Quarterly* 49(4) (1992), 675–694. Eighty years later, Albert Chavannes, a Marxist utopian, published a monthly journal *The Sociologist* and two utopian novels, *The Future of the Commonwealth* (1892) and *In Brighter Climes* (1895). In his visions of "Socioland," communism principally supplied the social models for utopia. Chavannes' Marxist thinking never won a lot of supporters, because of the predominance of Edward Bellamy's utopian approach: Jon Roper, "Utopianism, Scientific and Socialistic: Albert Chavannes and 'Socioland'," *Journal of American Studies* 23(3) (1989), 407–421.

28. Karl Marx and Friedrich Engels: *Die deutsche Ideologie, in: Marx/Engels Works MEW*, vol. 3, 33.

29. Darby Lewes, "Middle-Class Edens: Women's Nineteenth-Century Utopian Fiction and the Bourgeois Ideal,": *Utopian Studies* 4(1) (1993), 14–25.

30. Alexander Brandenburg, "Utopischer Sozialismus, Arbeiterkommunismus, Marxismus: Ein Tagungs- und Literaturbericht," *Internationale Wissenschaftliche Korrespondenz zur Geschichte der Deutschen Arbeiterbewegung* 24(2) (1988), 192–212, sums up the history of early utopian socialism in Germany; Ramnath Narayanswamy, "Utopia and Determinism in Marx, Lenin and Stalin," *China Report* 22(2) (1986), 129–140; Lothar Knatz, *Utopie und Wissenschaft im frühen deutschen Sozialismus. Theoriebildung und Wissenschaftsbegriff bei Wilhelm Weitling* (New York, Frankfurt/M. 1984).

capitalist West and the socialist East increasingly replaced utopian Marxist perspectives.[31]

These few passing remarks may suffice to awaken the reader's interest in the present volume. The idea of pursuing the visions of the future of course had to be parceled up in such a way that one could follow the discourses on the future envisioned in different discursive formations without losing track of the overall connections between the discursive dispositives. We singled out five areas in which the imaginative creation of the future would be especially important: religion, foreign policy, utopian communities, utopian state concepts, and science fiction in popular culture.

Accordingly, this book is organized in five parts that are the equivalent of the conference's five topical sections. In consonance with our preliminary discussions during the planning period of the 1999 conference, we decided that religious utopias and theological visions of the future had to be at the very beginning of our comparative reflections on visions of the future. The first session was therefore dedicated to the theme of transatlantic millenarianism from the seventeenth to the twentieth century, and historians of religion and culture gave presentations that are printed here, although somewhat amended and extended. A. Gregg Roeber's discussion of pietism and Methodism shows how both communities struggled with an American environment after they had been transplanted to American soil. Roeber, among other things, raises the question whether antinomian pietist movements led to successful millennial or futuristic visions, and his answer is that they did not. Typically both pietist and Methodist communities shared convictions that contributed to various social reform movements in later centuries, but these religious convictions continued to recede further within the individuals and thus contributed to the demise of a theological vision of the future among Methodists and pietists in North America. William R. Hutchison approaches the comparative paradigm from

31. Rainer Gries, "Virtuelle Zeithorizonte: Deutsch–deutsche Geschichtsbilder und Zukunftsvisionen Ende der fünfziger Jahre," *Comparativ* 4(3) (1994), 9–28; Gerald Diesener, "Schon einmal am Wendepunkt: Im 'Neuen Deutschland' 1959," *Comparativ* 4(3) (1994), 29–48.

another angle by focussing on American religious concepts of the future and European responses to them in the nineteenth and early twentieth centuries. Foremost among those concepts was the idea of reform and Hutchison discusses at length the problem of the "Americanization" of different European denominations, churches and communities that were connected with the reform impulse. What first comes to mind when one addresses the problem of Americanization is the Catholic Church, mostly because this label has been used first and extensively in connection with the Church's modernist struggle during the late nineteenth century, but Hutchison shows how both Judaism and Protestantism alike went through a phase that could be dubbed "Americanization.". The Americanized versions of worship were then transplanted to a European environment and stirred controversy there. Their common traits were optimism, activism and the development of foreign missions, showing that discourses are in fact not limited by arbitrary geographic or mental frontiers. The mission controversy for instance is intimately connected with American conceptions of culture and politics and brought the charge of world cultural domination upon American missions by Europeans.

Visions of the future cannot be invented unless there is a dreamer and a dream about how life and afterlife are supposed to be. Grant Wacker discusses major American millenarian dreams and dreamers in the twentieth century, when he addresses the Pentecostal vision of the future. This denomination developed into the second largest Christian aggregation, only to be surpassed by the Roman Catholic Church, within less than one hundred years. Pentecostal Christians believe, among other things, in the Lord's imminent physical return or *parousia*, discussed earlier in this introduction. In dealing with the Second Coming of Christ, Wacker demonstrates that utopias and dystopias can exist within the same frame of reference: The believer's hope will turn out to be the unbeliever's doom, according to Pentecostal beliefs.

David Ellis rightly emphasizes in his comment to the first session's contributions the similarities between the different groups addressed in the papers of A. Gregg Roeber, William R. Hutchison and Grant Wacker. Among the commonalties between the denominations

13

under review he stresses the emphasis on this-wordly achievement, the high degree of tolerance, the difficulty of social reproduction, the importance of 'bad' examples, and what one can learn about modern subjectivity as expressed in these groups. In his comment, Aaron Fogleman reflects on "The Failure and Success of Millenarianism in American Religious Culture". In contradiction to Roeber's article, while Fogleman concedes that there have been many failures to realize millennial dreams by pietists in America, it is important to note that so many denominations and communities kept trying. Additionally, according to Fogleman, it remains paramount, when studying American religious culture, to link the migrating and pious and others to futurism and millennialism, thus sanctioning a session dedicated to religious themes at the very beginning of our symposium.

The second session was dedicated to "Visions of the New World Order". *Utopia*, Thomas More's influential masterpiece, depicted a world that represented a New World in the sense of a spatial utopia. One would be mistaken to claim that utopian visions of foreign policy are chiefly utopias of space, but it is striking to observe how often foreign policy combines concepts of space with a political agenda. Paul T. Burlin demonstrates in his contribution "The US Quest for a Global Pax Americana: Myths and Realities" the longevity of American concepts of world order that are based on the notion that the American nation enjoys an exceptional status among the nations of the world. This exceptionalism entitled the United States to a special role in world affairs by demanding the spread of the American system of democracy and free enterprise all over the world – according to Henry Luce and others. Burlin then shows convincingly how the notion of American exceptionalism emerged with the migration of the Puritans to American shores and continued throughout the eighteenth, nineteenth and twentieth centuries, when it acquired an economic subtext that became more dominant as the twentieth century grew older. Gunther Hellmann approaches the problem of a world order from the German side by looking into the problem of "*Weltpolitik* or Self-Containment: Germany's Global Ambitions". Hellmann rightly states the problematic nature of German "visions" in the twentieth century, which usually spelled disaster. By focussing on Germany's role in international politics after unification he succeeds in bringing together Germany's new model of "international civility" with the long shadows of past discussions about German visions and ambitions. In her comment Beverly Crawford reminds us that what has been dubbed the "American Century" seems to have come to an end. With Germany's democratization after 1945 and its ascent to power, there comes a need for growing responsibility. German political rhetoric strongly reminds one of the language used by Woodrow Wilson and Crawford rises the question whether this kind of language could be termed "utopian" or whether utopian rhetoric just masks the pursuit of power. Ralph Dietl questions the underlying assumption in Burlin's paper that American foreign policy has always been and still is shaped by an unwavering faith in America's divine mission. Instead he emphasizes the radical break with diplomatic traditions shaped by the Founding Fathers of the American democracy. Thus, the American export of democracy after 1917 was simply a strategy to secure America's disengagement from the European continent without jeopardizing American National Security.

The third session, "Utopian Communities in the Nineteenth and Twentieth Centuries" concentrated on social experiments in American and German society. James B. Gilbert presented "Social Utopias in Modern America," in which he undertook the difficult task of summing up the multiple utopian movements in modern America. He stressed the continuities of intentional utopian communities in North America that go back to millennial Christianity. In looking for the continuum it is hard to separate the secular from the sacred, as Gilbert demonstrates abundantly. He also underscores the continuities by comparing actual social movements and the vast (belletristic) literature that originated in the United States between 1880 and 1910. Paul Nolte covered the German aspect of utopian movements by discussing "Broken Utopias: Visions of the Social Order in Modern Germany." In expounding the notions of society, state and community in a comprehensive history of concepts (*Begriffsgeschichte*), Nolte explained the German need for order and harmony as the effects of the rapid diversification of a modernizing society in nineteenth century Germany. In his comment, titled "Thoughts on the National Peculiarities of Talking about Utopias," Martin Geyer, addressing the differences between James Gilbert's and Paul Nolte's papers, stresses the notion that German history in the twentieth century appears above all as a flight into utopian irrationality and anti-modernism, a yearning for *Gemeinschaft* instead of modern values of *Gesellschaftlichkeit* (liberty, pluralism, and individualism). According to Martin Geyer, Paul Nolte demonstrates how German utopian thinking has lost its innocence, unlike its American counterpart.

In her comment to Dietl's and Gilbert's papers, titled "Comparative Views on Social Utopias in Germany and the United States", Ursula Lehmkuhl takes on the task of comparing the complicated ways in which the German and the American society dealt with utopian communities in the past. Referring to Paul Nolte's argument that, as a rule, in Germany utopias of a better world are not to be attained from within society, but rather by revolutionary change, Ursula Lehmkuhl explains that in Germany, in contrast to the United States, what is needed in order to achieve these utopias is a "theory" rather than millennial interpretations of Scripture. The vast differences between American and German concepts of communitarianism and utopia notwithstanding, Lehmkuhl then proceeds to ask, whether a global civil society could be envisioned as a feasible utopia of the twenty-first century in either society. According to her, visions of the future in German and American social theories tend towards a common concept, a possible result of the Americanization of Germany.

It was appropriate that the fourth session's topic was "The Future Society Envisioned" and thus the previous discussion could be continued without an interruption. Dietmar Schirmer, in his paper entitled "Beyond the Nation? A Grand Category Revisited" dealt with a category of towering importance in the political discourses of both societies, yet a concept that he called into question not only because of the centrifugal effects of globalization. Schirmer's hypothesis is that the nation-state represents a historical contingency that will eventually pass and that passing is already emerging as we witness the "de-hierarchization of state–society relations and de-territorialization of social relations". Schirmer next proposes a methodological fusion between functionalism, which he deems theoretically powerful but methodologically deficient, and social action theory, thus reformulating the emergence of nations and nationalisms as an effect of society's conversion from segmented to functional differentiation. Leon Litwack, in his contribution "Future Blues: Race Relations in the United States," takes a very different approach, both in content and style, by focussing on the "American Dilemma". Using blues lyrics as sources, he portrays past American race relations in rather grim terms and implicitly predicts a future, that is even less promising, an earnest reminder that, globalization notwithstanding, racism is a definite future force to be reckoned with, both in the United States and in Germany. Maria Mitchell takes up a similar topic in her discussion of "*Volksgemeinschaft* in the Third Reich: Concession, Conflict, Consensus." Although the utopian notion of *Volksgemeinschaft* was torn by contradictions, it was eventually a "successful" concept in so far as it helped to unite Germany's population behind the genocidal scheme of annihilation of undesirables by, among other things, the "racialization" of social differences. Whereas Schirmer's and Litwack's contributions were rather broad in their scope, Olaf Stieglitz's study on "Youth and the Nation's Future during the New Deal Era" aligned itself more closely with Maria Mitchell's paper, which centered on the 1930s. The desperate exclamation "We may be losing this generation" expresses American concerns about the future of their youth during the New Deal era, a period of American history that lends itself to cautious comparisons with Germany's Nazi period, especially when one considers the militarized work programs for youths that existed in both the United States and totalitarian Germany.[32] Stieglitz

32. Let me say again, as I have stated earlier, that explicit comparison does not mean that both periods in the national histories were one and the same thing. See Norbert Finzsch, "Reconstruction and 'Wiederaufbau' in German and American Perspective: Some Remarks on the Comparison of Singular Developments, 'Sonderweg' and Exceptionalism," in Norbert Finzsch and Jürgen Martschukat, eds., *Different Restorations: Reconstruction und "Wiederaufbau" in the United States and Germany: 1865–1945–1989*, The Krefeld Historical Symposia: Germany and the USA, 3 (Providence, RI and Oxford, 1996), 1–24; "Comment [Blood, Ethnicity and Comparative History]," in Hartmut Lehmann and Hermann Wellenreuther, eds., *German and American Nationalism: A Comparative Perspective* (Oxford and New York 1999), 453–473.

underlines the utopian vision of the Civil Conservation Corps, albeit a defensive utopia, as he calls it. Dirk Moses, in his synoptic comment on all four papers of this session, titled "Biblical Narratives in German and American National Utopias" again takes up the first session's topic in addressing the religious aspect of political ideologies and visions of the future. In his analysis of nationalism in both the United States and Germany, Moses sees two variations of the religious exodus theme at work, a homogenizing liberal universalism and an exclusionary ethnic particularism.

In his contribution, Heiko Stoff finally tackles the complex question of a comparison between the New Deal and Nazi Germany. "What Distinguishes the American New Deal from the German *Volksgemeinschaft*?" he asks in his commentary. He corners that question by outlining the things that both societies had in common: Nazi Germany's racist community and America's New Deal were both situated in a historical setting that one can describe as the "bio-power" (Michel Foucault) of disciplining the individual and regulating the population. Yet the specific forms of biopower in both countries differed immensely. The differences lay in the fact that Nazi Germany came about as a retro-defense of producerism, whereas New Deal America represented the vanguard of consumerism.

The fifth and final session addressed the "soft underbelly" of historiography, cultural studies. It was the conveners' firm conviction that, although cultural studies are still regarded as a less than serious undertaking by some historians (especially in Germany), this approach is important in order to understand the full impact of utopian thinking in America and Germany alike. Without going into the controversy whether history should be a *Geisteswissenschaft*, a social science or a *Kulturwissenschaft* too deeply, it is obvious that visions of the future have had a great impact on everyday culture or mass culture in film, fiction, and literature.[33] The session was

33. Cultural Studies are an Anglo-American invention that is widely debated in Great Britain and the United States. In Germany its discussion is limited to a tiny political spectrum left of the mainstream. See Ben Agger, *Cultural Studies as Critical Theory* (London and Washington, DC, 1992); Russel A. Berman, *Cultural*

somewhat too widely dubbed "Science Fiction, Social Construction, and New Realities," but the participants struggled bravely with the difficult and widespread subject and came up with some very interesting results. Ole Frahm's contribution "Different Drafts of a Future Horizon: *Weird Science* versus *Nick, der Raumfahrer*" deals with fundamentally different concepts of the future in popular culture, i.e. in comic strips around 1950, an important venue for the popularization of futuristic visions in America and Germany.

Another popular, if not populist, concern with the future is the notion of an apocalyptic collapse through an ecological catastrophe. Susan Strasser deals with this idea in her paper "Environment and Apocalypse", going back to Ovid's story of Daedalus and Icarus, although the idea of the eco-apocalypse is clearly connected to industrial modes of production. Strasser then deals with the rich American popular scientific literature that evolved in the early 1960s, whose predecessors go back to Thoreau. An American historian, Susan Strasser has to remain silent on the vast German literature dealing with the ecological catastrophe.[34]

Studies of Modern Germany: History, Representation, and Nationhood (Madison, WI, 1993); David Buckingham and Julian Sefton-Green, *Cultural Studies Goes to School: Reading and Teaching Popular Media*, Critical Perspectives on Literacy and Education (London and Bristol, PA, 1994); Lawrence Grossberg, ed., *Cultural Studies*, (New York, 1992); Reiner Lehberger and Bernd-Peter Lange, eds., (Paderborn, 1984); Informationen zur Sprach- und Literaturdidaktik 41. *Cultural Studies: Projekte für den Englischunterricht*. Ioan Davies, *Cultural Studies and Beyond: Fragments of Empire* (London and New York, 1995); Patrick Fuery, *Cultural Studies and the New Humanities: Concepts and Controversies* (Melbourne and New York, 1997); Richard Lee, *Cultural Studies as Geisteswissenschaften? Time, Objectivity, and the Future of Social Science*, (Binghamton, NY, 1997).

34. Ecological utopia goes back to German romanticism and had its first climax during the anti-modern *Lebensreform* movement around the turn of the nineteenth century, which roughly corresponds with American reform movements at the end of the nineteenth century. This movement included, among other movements, both vegetarianism and nudism. See Eva Barlösius, *Naturgemäße Lebensführung: Zur Geschichte der Lebensreform um die Jahrhundertwende* (Frankfurt and New York, 1997). See also Maren Möhring's forthcoming dissertation on German nudism (Munich, 2001). I refrain from listing the more than 200 German books that deal with ecological aspects of the future in general and the many books that envision an

Susan Winnett then explains the relationship of "Gender and the Narrative of Science Fiction" by comparing four movies, the 1939 film *The Wizard of Oz*, the movies *Alien* (1979), *Aliens* (1986), and finally *Contact* (1997). Winnett demonstrates the implicit and explicit intertextuality of the recent films with *The Wizard of Oz* and detects in all four movies a literal or figurative curtain which is pulled back to expose male embodiments of authoritative science as fraud. Science fiction thus becomes a literary genre in which speculation about gender is possible and productive – as demonstrated in this essay. Luigi Cajani concluded not only this session but the whole conference with his general and comparative remarks in "Apocalypse How? Or the Visions of Future between Fear and Hope," in which he describes the shift from utopian optimism to dystopian fear of

---

eco-dystopia. It may suffice to look at the following titles. Contrary to Strasser's findings regarding the United States, religious apocalypse and ecological catastrophe are not incomensurable in German culture. See for instance [Anonymous], *Macht euch die Erde untertan? Schöpfungsglaube und Umweltkrise* (Wurzburg, 1981); Jürgen Moltmann, *Gott in der Schöpfung: Ökologische Schöpfungslehre* (Munich, 1985); Alfons Auer, *Umweltethik: Ein theologischer Beitrag zur ökologischen Diskussion* (Düsseldorf, 1984); Rudolf Bahro, *Bleibt mir der Erde treu!: Apokalypse oder Geist einer neuen Zeit* (Berlin, 1995); Sigurd Bergmann, *Geist, der Natur befreit: Die trinitarische Kosmologie Gregors von Nazianz im Horizont einer ökologischen Theologie der Befreiung* (Mainz, 1995); Otto Bischofberger, *Umweltverantwortung aus religiöser Sicht* (Freiburg, 1988); Philipp Schmitz, *Ist die Schöpfung noch zu retten?: Umweltkrise und christliche Verantwortung* (Würzburg, 1985). Other important titles are Chingiz Aitmatov and Günther Grass, *Alptraum* [sic] *und Hoffnung: Zwei Reden vor dem Club of Rome* (Göttingen, 1989); Carl Amery, *Die ökologische Chance: Das Ende der Vorsehung. Natur als Politik* (Munich, 1985); Hoimar von Ditfurth, *So lasst uns denn ein Apfelbäumchen pflanzen: Es ist soweit* (Hamburg, 1985); Irenäus Eibl-Eibesfeldt, *Der Mensch, das riskierte Wesen: Zur Naturgeschichte menschlicher Unvernunft* (Munich and Zurich, 1988); Walo F. Eppenberger and Robert Kopp, eds., *Endzeit?* (Basle, 1986); Herbert Gruhl, *Ein Planet wird geplündert: Die Schreckensbilanz unserer Politik* (Frankfurt/M., 1975); [Anonymous], *Grenzen der Menschheit: Vorträge gehalten auf der Tagung der Joachim Jungius-Gesellschaft der Wissenschaften, Hamburg am 2. u. 3. Okt. 1973,* Veröffentlichung der Joachim Jungius-Gesellschaft der Wissenschaften Hamburg (Göttingen, 1974); Hans Jonas and Wolfgang Schneider, *Dem bösen Ende näher: Gespräche über das Verhältnis des Menschen zur Natur* (Frankfurt/M., 1993); Klaus Klasing, *Apokalypse auf Raten: Respektlose Gedanken über den Fortschritt* (Munich, 1971); Konrad Lorenz, *Die acht Todsünden der zivilisierten Menschheit* (Munich, 1973).

ultimate destruction in Western culture taking place after the unleashing of nuclear power at the end of World War II.

By looking at the utopian impulses in two societies, we discovered similarities and differences, sometimes in places where we had not expected to find them. It is impossible to do justice to all aspects of utopian thinking in one society, let alone in a comparison of two societies as complex as the American and the German ones. Even if we failed to tackle all of the problems at once, during the conference and in this volume, it was worth trying. We all left Krefeld, in the words of Erich Angermann, "confused on a much higher level."

Part 1
Transatlantic Millenarianism from the Seventeenth to the Twentieth Century

1
The Migration of the Pious: Methodists, Pietists, and the Antinomian Character of North American Religious History

A. Gregg Roeber

Between 1718 and 1721, Valentin Ernst Löscher wrote his classic critique of the movment known as "Pietism." His *Vollständiger Timotheus Verinus: oder, Darlegung der Wahrheit und des Friedens in denen bißherigen Pietistischen Streitigkeiten* . . . offers a useful point of departure in assessing the migrations of the pious from northern and central Europe to North America and their visions of the future. Although various free church groups from the continent, and Methodists from the British Isles, contributed to the later texture of North American "experiential religion," we need to begin by examining the pious visions of the future elsewhere. We could usefully share Löscher's puzzlement about why so many of the "pious" were attracted to visions of the future that rejected the confessional churches' view of piety, a view Löscher was at some pains to defend.

As he surveyed the astonishing variety of Böhmists and Schwenkfelders in Silesia and Saxony, of spiritualist and pietist-inspired cells in Celle and Württemberg, of affinities of German spiritualist groups to the antinomian strains in English Quakerism, Löscher discerned some commonalities. Among the "special characteristics" of what he called "Pietistic Evil," millennialism ranked fifth for Löscher, far behind more serious errors such as indifference to doctrine, contempt for the sacraments, denigration of the pastoral office, and confusion of justification with a zeal for practical piety. He wrote too early to catch the significance of migrations, but he could well have added to his list a common discontent with Europe's religious past, a disbelief in the ways believers could encounter God offered by the everyday manifestation of European Christianity in socio-economic, political, and devotional prayer life.[1]

At no time did the regional and theological diversity of the migrating pious sort itself out into one, coherent "vision" of a future. We also know that this diversity of subjective, emotive, "experiential" Protestantism found a receptive soil in North America. Recent scholarship reveals that Stuart England was more heavily sewn with antinomian cells and groups, and that this influence found deeper roots in New England soil than the surface appearance of the "Antinomian Crisis" of 1636 suggested. Even John Winthrop's son may well have been a covert member of the radically subjective theology that Löscher, writing nearly a century later, viewed with alarm.[2] Among English-speakers, as David Lovejoy wisely observed years ago, migration managed to encompass visions of "utopia, asylum, escape of religion, the linking of religion with profit, and recognition of a general duty to expand Christianity . . ."[3] In assessing the continental pietists, and later British Methodists, however, we actually find relatively little by way of explicitly chiliastic or millen-arian disputes. Whatever controversies the French Prophets aroused in Britain at the outset of the eighteenth century, this kind of "enthusiast" vision rarely emerged from the migrations of the pious from the continent.[4]

Despite their diverse regional backgrounds and distinct theological emphases, moderate to radical continental pietists migrating to North

---

1. I cite here the English translation, *The Complete Timotheus Verinus*, trans. James L. Langebartels and Robert J. Koester (Milwaukee, WI, 1998); 144–148 on millennialism. Löscher actually treats 14 characteristic evils of pietism in his work.

2. David R. Como, "Puritans and Heretics: The Emergence of an Antinomian Underground in Early Stuart England," unpublished Ph.D. thesis, Princeton University, 1998.

3. David S. Lovejoy, *Religious Enthusiasm in the New World: Heresy to Revolution* (Cambridge, MA, and London, England, 1985), 16.

4. On the concern over "inspirationists" in England, and the role of the French Prophets, see Michael Heyd, *"Be Sober and Resonable": The Critique of Enthusiasm in the Seventeenth and Early Eighteenth Centuries* (Leiden, New York, Cologne, 1995), 168–190.

America shared a common theological tendency. In Löscher's mind, they represented a recurring and perhaps timeless flight from the continuity of God's presence in the church throughout history, and into the absorption with the self and its yearning for immediate access to a personally reassuring God. Even if one cannot posit a fully developed "modern" individual personality in many of the communal experiments that emerged in the seventeenth century, at least some degree of individual assurance and privileged insight marked even the communal experiments. Radical individualists did, in fact congregate together, whether at Quedlinburg, or at Conrad Beissel's Ephrata, in Pennsylvania.

This recurring problem deserves serious reflection from the outset. After all, later generations of pietists tended to point back to Luther himself and the centrality of an "experience" or "breakthrough" as critical to the "grasping" of the truth that one was saved by grace alone, through faith alone. How could hoped-for individual trans-formation – sanctification was the preferred Lutheran term – remain linked to public proclamation of the Word, reception of objective sacraments, administered by a divinely instituted pastoral Office? Luther feared, and for good reasons, that those caught up in a rush to sanctification, freed from the burden of "the law," would fall into an error of universal and immediate grace, vertically tied to personal access to the Spirit. Such persons, Löscher agreed two centuries later, would be tempted by the intensity of their pious insights to reject an incarnational theology whose manifestation lay in a continuous view of history and God's working in it.

In fairness to the radical antinomians, they could point to very ancient Christian doubts about historical continuities. Marcion of Pontus had denied that the Jewish scriptures had anything to say to Christians. Although orthodox Christianity found its voice in Irenaeus of Lyons's famous rejection of "supercessionism" in his essay *Against the Heresies*, Marcion's disjunctive view of history, and hence of creation and redemption, was never completely routed from the churches. The Reformation's assault on the historical continuities of the western Church and appeals to a supposedly "pure" apostolic age rekindled a kind of historically disjunctive "primitivism" that had enormous socio-economic and political, but also deeply spiritual appeal to anyone unhappy with the realities of European church life.[5]

A very impressive connection to constructing a future of "utopian" dimensions this side of the Second Coming hence could not emerge from the radical pious who migrated to North America. To remarkable diversity, we must add, as a deeper reason for the absence of clear vision, the implications of the theological point noted above. Pietists, of whatever stripe, tended toward absorption with the personal theological "breakthrough" or "insight" of Luther about the centrality of discovering justification that is personally appropriated. They paid a heavy price for this fixation, which built upon the deep-seated suspicion of the pre-Reformation past. Admittedly, many of the first generation of Protestant theologians had struggled to tie their insights to the ancient patristic witnesses, and to insist upon their movement as one of restoration, not revolution. But again, in fairness to the radicals, not only Luther but Calvin and other "magisterial" Protestant writers seemed to invite a deeply individualist stance toward the history of the faith. For Luther, "bound only to Christ the Teacher, the Christian is free in evaluating the Fathers . . . [he] freed the Fathers from tradition. At long last it was possible for them to be mistaken." Calvin, Zwingli, and other major figures were likewise inclined toward a polemical and highly selective use of mostly the western, not eastern patristic authors.[6]

---

5. On the ancient battles, see variously, James L. Kugel and Rowan A. Greer, *Early Biblical Interpretation* (Philadelphia, PA, 1986); Joseph T. Lienhard, S.J., *The Bible, the Church, and Authority: The Canon of the Christian Bible in History and Theology* (Collegeville, MN, 1995), 9–23; on the appeal of primitivism among Protestants in general, see Richard T. Hughes and C. Leonard Allen, *Illusions of Innocence: Protestant Primitivism in America, 1630–1875* (Chicago, IL, 1988). The present essay omits from consideration how Roman Catholic mysticism and its migrants to the New World grappled with these themes; nor do I treat here Russian Orthodox missions in Alaska and their struggle to bind personal pieties to public liturgy.

6. See Manfred Schulze, "Martin Luther and the Church Fathers," 573–626, citation at 623, 625; Irena Backus, "Ulrich Zwingli, Martin Bucer and the Church Fathers, 627–660; Johannes van Oort, "John Calvin and the Church Fathers," 661–700, all in Irena Backus, ed., *The Reception of the Church Fathers in the West: From the Carolingians to the Maurists*, 2 vols. (Leiden, 1997).

Pietism, of whatever stripe, identified not only with Luther's defiant stance toward Rome, his doubts about the scriptural canon, and his selective use of the patristic past. It also arose in the wake of the religious wars in whose catastrophic aftermath not only the Roman Church, but magisterial versions of Lutheran or Reformed churches failed to connect interior spiritual thirst to the public prayer life of shattered communities. Thus, whether they were fleeing from overt persecution and saw themselves as a saved "remnant" – as one could argue was true for Dutch Labadists, for instance – or, as with the majority of Lutherans, Reformed, and Moravians, were bent on avoiding the more annoying aspects of both civic and church regulations, a discontinuous view of the past informed visions of the future among almost all pietist migrants.

By the early nineteenth century, this inherited disjunction predestined to incoherence a vision of communities, or systematic engagement with the political and socio-economic realities of the New World. Instead, confrontation with the availability of personal property, the institution of slavery, and the general suspicion of authority they had inherited tended to concentrate pietist visions of the future on fairly modest "reforms" which we can recognize as the first stirrings of the later emphasis on "benevolence." Communal experiments and mission activity that promised visions of a transformed life among the Moravians in their contact with African-Americans and the Delaware both foundered. German Reformed Pietism found an eventual home in Johann Philip Otterbein's United Brethren, a movement that settled on a deeply interiorized piety akin to Methodism, but lacking in the latter's hopes for social regeneration.[7] In the case of Halle's Lutheran pietism, the transformation of society based on a future replete with educational institutions that would produce pious and productive individuals and whole communities, failed to take root. Methodists, whether British or continental, found a receptive audience in various New World communities on the edges of an increasingly prosperous

---

7. James Tanis, "Reformed Pietism in Colonial America," in Ernest Stoeffler, ed., *Continental Pietism and Early American Christianity* (Grand Rapids, MI, 1976), 34–73.

and consumer-oriented society. But modest, not radical, visions of future transformation emerged.

I

Many commentators have noted the influence the so-called "German Theology" of Johannes Tauler and later mystics exercised upon Luther himself. But Luther, as Löscher documented, while admitting the early influence of this theology upon his thinking, later denounced it as pernicious.[8] The persistence of mystical-antinomian religion suggested to magisterial Protestant critics two equally disturbing characteristics: Those inclined to this understanding of Christianity were often quite fervent, more so in fact than the passive and often unresponsive adherents of the confessional churches. Second, these intensely religious souls persisted in their erroneous insistence upon personal experience, despite the efforts of the orthodox, lay and clerical, to point out the uncertainty of such insights. In various corners of the Reich, and in the Netherlands, speculative theologians such as Valentin Weigel in Saxony, Jakob Böhme, and even Johann Arndt, the latter arguably at least somewhat more orthodox in his Lutheranism, struggled to see actualization in both an interior faith and ethical behavior of the central teaching on justification. The acute dilemma remained, however: how to awaken this interior faith and behavior without relapsing into institutionalized formalism, the legalism which had finally paralyzed the Roman Church and necessitated the Reformation in the first place, or sliding into radical spiritualist subjectivity.

---

8. *Timotheus*, 13. For a general overview of the later influence of the mystical tradition which also suggests a long-term quietist outcome, see Andrew Weeks, *German Mysticism from Hildegard of Bingen to Ludwig Wittgenstein: A Literary and Intellectual History* (Albany, New York, 1993), 133–201. For a nuanced view of Luther's appropriation of selected aspects drawn from "German mysticism", see Heiko A. Oberman, "*Simul Gemitus et Raptus*: Luther and Mysticism," in Oberman, *The Dawn of the Reformation: Essays in Late Medieval and Early Reformation Thought* (Grand Rapids, MI, 1992), 126–154.

Before we can assess a "migration of the pious" that manifested itself in the eighteenth century among early Methodists and both German and Dutch-speaking continental radical pietists, we need to recall that the channels for radical-antinomian migration had been shaped in the seventeenth century. The story of New England's struggle with its Antinomians has been told often enough. But in early New Netherland and in New Sweden, not only laity, but also clergy of questionable orthodoxy kept alive the theology of "immediate access" to God. Reformed Pietism surfaced early at Bohemia Manor by 1683, attracting some Dutch-speakers from New York. These Dutch Reformed gravitated toward preachers influenced by Jean de Labadie and the Frisian circles of pietism, just as the late seventeenth-century Swedes on the Delaware listened to Peter Schaeffer and Lars Tollstadius, and sang the hymns of Anders Rudman – all representatives of the pietist emphasis on interior conversion and experiential religion. Among the small Lutheran minority in New York, Johann Fabritius, the earliest pastor known among them, arrived via Amsterdam in 1669 after being expelled for his radical spiritualist ideas from a pastorate in Sulzbach. His Silesian background and his absorption of a radical reading of Johann Arndt and Tauler during studies in Rostock with Joachim Lütkemann marked Fabritius, and probably his congregation in New York, as proto-pietists long before the major migrations of the pious commenced.[9]

---

9. Martin Brecht, "Die deutschen Spiritualisten des 17. Jahrhunderts," 205–240 at 229–230 in Brecht, et al., eds., *Der Pietismus vom siebsehnten bis zum frühen achtzehnten Jahrhundert*, vol. 1 of *Die Geschichte des Pietismus* (Göttingen, 1993); Randall H. Balmer, *A Perfect Babel of Confusion: Dutch Religion and English Culture in the Middle Colonies* (New York, 1989), 22–25; A. G. Roeber, "The Origins of Whatever Is Not English among Us': The Dutch-speaking and the German-speaking Peoples of Colonial British America," in Bernard Bailyn and Philip D. Morgan, eds., *Strangers within the Realm: Cultural Margins of the First British Empire* (Chapel Hill, NC, 1991), 220–283, at 222–223; 231–232; I am also indebted to Evan P. Haefeli, "The Origins of American Religious Freedom: Churches and Politics in the Middle Colonies, 1609–1714" (dissertation in progress, Princeton University) for permission to read and cite some of his findings for New York.

The predominant characteristic of North American Protestantism, lay or clerical, in the seventeenth century seemed to emerge from concerns about the problem of evil – a classically Calvinist anxiety that flowed naturally from that theological tradition's departing point: the utter sovereignty and justice of God. This concern produced zealous and earnest congregations in New England, while the more laconic Dutch in New Netherland seemed to separate into those more comfortable with the mainstream Reformed preachings of the clergy, and those "seekers" who would, by the late seventeenth century, greet the arrival of the Labadist-influenced pietists. Not only at Bohemia Manor, but in Quaker-dominated West Jersey and Pennsylvania, an explicitly antinomian cast colored early Christianity in those regions, a coloration markedly deepened by the arrival of mystics like Johann Kelpius on the Wissahickon.

By the time the Halle pietists noted the possible harvest of souls in the New World, they wisely connected themselves to Dr. Thomas Bray and the emerging SPCK. But Anton Wilhelm Böhme, Halle's man in London, fell under condemnation by the Wittenberg faculty. Robert Barclay and the English Quakers, the Wittenberg theologians noted, would feel at home in Böhme's mix of Schwenkfelder, Weigelian and spiritualist errors. Dismissed from Waldeck, Böhme moved to England in 1701. A resurgent Anglicanism may have thought of Lutherans as "half papists", as Böhme anxiously informed Samuel Urlsperger in 1714. Böhme's worry about being cast as a half-cousin of Rome, however, reflected his indifference toward outward structures and ceremonies. He insisted that "interior" Christianity manifested in works of charity defined "real Christianity" and he still maintained that "Christ must win a model within us."[10]

---

10. Arno Sames, *Anton Wilhelm Böhme 1673–1722: Studien zum ökumenischen Denken und Handeln eines Halleschen Pietisten* (Göttingen, 1990), 21–28; quotation from the *Responsum Theologicum und Juridicum* (Frankfurt and Leipzig, 1715), 38, cited at 28. Sames's conclusion (154) that Böhme's mysticism led to a general confessional indifference seems incontestable, despite the younger Francke's insistence that clergy sent abroad to Tranquebar (and later North America) hold to the confessional symbols of the Lutheran church.

The historian who seeks to ponder visions of the future among the religious seekers in North America must naturally be aware of these debates and mutual recriminations, as well as this seventeenth-century background. But the more critical question still remains as to why so many of the more radically "pious" found their way to North America and what future they envisioned there. If the trajectory of American religion in the eighteenth and nineteenth centuries finally affirmed the supremacy of an emotive-individualist understanding of Christianity, this success reflects the triumph of an antinomian cast to much of North American Protestant Christianity. Certainly, by the time Jonathan Edwards attempted a restatement of Calvinist theology which could be reconciled to the general "awakening" of religious sentiment, it was the latter that triumphed. His theological program, and that of his successors in the New England Divinity movement, largely failed as a regenerative movement within the Reformed tradition. Moreover, as the astute historian of that movement has pointed out, inherent difficulties lay ahead for a tradition which attempted to engage in "disinterested benevolence" where such activity was "frequently tied to quests for personal sanctification."[11] So, when J. H. C. Helmuth published in the 1790s a set of sermons laying out the objective means of grace via Lutheran preachers, the sacraments, and public confessional standards, his vision of the future failed to carry the day among early nineteenth-century Lutherans who turned easily to "inward" visions of pietist holiness.[12]

One explanation that has been offered for the alienation of so many of the migrating pious turns on the concepts of social discipline and social marginalization. The latter is unconvincing, the former perhaps more so. No village-level study of religious revitalization anywhere in the North Atlantic world has succeeded

11. Joseph A. Conforti, *Jonathan Edwards, Religious Tradition, & American Culture* (Chapel Hill and London, 1995), 86.

12. On Helmuth's sermons and attempt at articulating an orthodox future, see Roeber, "J.H.C. Helmuth, an Interpreter of Lutheranism in the Early Republic," *Interpreting Lutheran History: The Lutheran Historical Conference, Essays and Reports* 17 (1999), 1–19.

in linking economic or social deprivation or marginalization to the sporadic "revivals" of religion. Adherents ranged from the genuinely poor to members of the aristocracy. The alienation of ordinary believers from Lutheran pastors as the latter came to be identified with the secular powers' interest in social discipline may be more instructive. The persistence of popular attachment to the rituals and emotive satisfaction of medieval piety at the village level in areas ostensibly Lutheran has been documented repeatedly. Rather than seeing here an affirmation of Luther's own incarnational theology and deep attachment to a theology of sacramental presence, however, Lutheran pastors and superintendents became increasingly didactic and schematic in their attempt to systematize theological insights that probably fit more easily into the mystagogical categories of Eastern Orthodoxy than western scholasticism. The flight of ordinary believers back into the warmth of the "German Theology" was one result; the studied refusal to use auricular confession and to commune regularly was another. These memories survived the migration of the pious continentals to the New World.[13]

Jon Butler has forced us to ask whether ordinary believers, rather than clerical leaders, ever really absorbed and "carried" orthodox creedal expressions of Lutheran or Reformed Protestantism. Butler suspects not, and credits what limited success these churches enjoyed in eighteenth-century America to a clerical leadership and economic

---

13. Susan Karant-Nunn, *The Reformation of Ritual: An Interpretation of Early Modern Germany* (London and New York, 1998), see the entries under "social discipline"; the above also summarizes a deeply revisionist attack of Finnish theologians on the view of Luther constructed by Karl Holl and the German theologians of the twentieth century; for a summary of that literature, see, in German, Gottfried Martens, *Die Rechtfertigung des Sünders: Rettungshandeln Gottes oder Historisches Interpretament* (Göttingen, 1992); in English, see Carl E. Braaten and Robert W. Jensons, eds., *Union with Christ. The New Finnish Interpretation of Luther* (Grand Rapids, MI, 1998); for a summary of the impact of Holl and other twentieth-century Luther scholars, see Bernhard Lohse, *Martin Luther: An Introduction to His Life and Work*, trans. Robert C. Schultz, (Philadelphia, PA, 1986), 199–237. I summarize some of the "social discipline" literature as it applies to Lutheran practices and the role of pastors in Roeber, "Official and Non-Official Piety and Ritual in Early Lutheranism" *Concordia Theological Quarterly* 63 (April, 1999), 119–143.

and political ties that linked them to European sponsors and patrons. But if the predisposition toward the radically pious had been so successfully laid down already in the seventeenth century, one wonders why any version of quasi-orthodox theology survived at all in eighteenth-century North America. Alienation among the migrating pious was real; it was never the whole story.[14]

II

Early Methodism, as Nathan Hatch pointed out some years ago, indulged more radical visionary possibilities than the more sedate version of evangelicalism it later became in nineteenth-century America found tolerable.[15] The interpretation of dreams, the visionary and sometimes apocalyptic genre of the early Methodist circuit riders' preaching, did much to answer emotive anxieties about what seemed the classical Protestant question: how do I find access to a gracious God? Doris Andrews' survey of colonial Methodism traced the German–Irish dimensions of the migration to port cities like Baltimore and Philadelphia. The artisan occupations, and the prior German and Irish social and economic setting, lead one naturally to assume that visions of the future among these people rested largely upon hopes for better times, both in this world and in the next. Certainly, early Methodists in Ireland were violently set upon by large mobs, but these were as often as not also composed of ordinary people loyal to the established Church, not groups of the middling sorts or the well-to-do. The reduction of early Methodism's visions to that of social marginalization borders on caricature.[16]

14. For my assessment of this problem, see Roeber, "The Religious Problem of the Eighteenth Century," in Renate Wilson, Hartmut Lehmann, and Hermann Wellenreuther, eds., *In Search of Peace and Prosperity: Essays on the* (University Park, PA, 2000), 115–138.

15. Nathan Hatch, "The Puzzle of American Methodism," *Church History* 63 (1994), 175–189.

16. S. J. Connolly, *Religion, Law, and Power: The Making of Protestant Ireland 1660–1760* (Oxford, 1992), 185–186; Doris Andrews, "Popular Religion and the

Early Methodism drew upon Anglicanism for its clergy, its adherents from members of the various societies for moral improvement, Old Dissenters, and selected groups of immigrants, including Moravians. W. R. Ward, John Walsh, and Bernard Semmel, to name but a few, have uncovered a far more complex picture of early Methodism which has overturned the last remnants of the Halévy thesis. The reservoir of socio-economic and political resentments that might have taken Britain through the throes of social and political revolution were not, in fact, tapped by Methodist appeals to better times in a new millennium. Instead, Ward points out, Methodism had actually declined by the late 1740s as the threat of Jacobite revolution faded for the last time. Undoubtedly, the impoverished towns of industrial England did receive Wesley's message, but it was the slow work in the "dark corners" of the land, and not spectacular revivalism that we now know characterized Methodism's impressive rise on both sides of the Atlantic.

We cannot simply lump together Methodists, Moravians, German Lutheran Pietists, and Reformed Labadists, as if they shared identical theological, socio-economic, and therefore, common futurist visions. Wesley himself tended to think that those seeking a quiet piety would gravitate toward the Moravians, including their communal town experiments. British Methodism resonated with the poor, who could obtain the immediate assurance of justification without "works" which their socio-economic condition left them in no good position to perform anyway. Ruth Bloch succinctly summarized millennial themes in late eighteenth-century American thought by noting that the Calvinist tradition of Congregationalists, Presbyterians and Baptists produced the millennialists; Quakers, Anglicans, Lutherans, Methodists, and the German-Dutch Reformed were far less inclined toward such visions.[17]

Revolution in the Middle Atlantic Ports: The Rise of the Methodists, 1770–1800" (Ph.D dissertation, University of Pennsylvania, 1986).

17. Ruth Bloch, *Visionary Republic: Millennial Themes in American Thought, 1756–1800* (Cambridge, London and New York, 1985), xiv, 134–5; Bloch notes that American Methodists did not copy John Wesley's fascination with the Württemberg chiliast Johann Albrecht Bengel; on the Bengelian conventicle in Philadelphia's

Methodists, as with the German Lutheran and Reformed Dutch, evinced less emphasis on "revivals" of religion than did the theme of inner assurance seeking perfection that manifested itself in comparatively modest socio-economic improvements. While no single reason can account for this theme, the composition of early Methodist, and to a degree, German-pietist groups is still suggestive. Certainly, among Methodists, disproportionate numbers of women, children, and eventually African-Americans comprised the congregations, leading one to wonder if these pious were not fairly self-possessed in their realistic assessment of what could be hoped for in their contemporary socio-economic and political condition. Modest campaigns to restrain the use of alcohol, coupled with women's insistence on the reforms of asylums and orphanages, and, among the African Methodist Episcopal churches, a determination to achieve at least a modest level of recognition of free black integrity in northern communities, reflected these convictions. Interior assurance implied a slow vision of an improving future, not access to immediate raptures that translated into utopian socio-economic existence.[18]

Thus, the truly visionary Methodism of dream interpretation and "hot revivalism" that survived the Atlantic crossing and flourished, albeit briefly, may not simply have undergone "embourgeoisification" in the United States. The pious who responded to the call for a "methodical piety" eventually built upon the transformation of the interior life emphasized by an "enthusiast" leadership, to connect this inward assurance in concrete, incarnated outward signs of "benevolence." Yet, well into the nineteenth century, many among

---

Lutheran community, see Roeber, *Palatines, Liberty, and Property: German Lutherans in Colonial British America* (Baltimore, 1998, rev. ed.), 254; for an attempt to draw connections among the welter of Protestant pious in Pennsylvania, see Liam O'Boyle Riordan, "Identities in the New Nation: The Creation of an American Mainstream in the Delaware Valley, 1770–1830" (Ph.D. dissertation, University of Pennsylvania, 1996).

18. Richard J. Cawardine, *Evangelicals and Politics in Antebellum America* (New Haven and London, 1993), 14–17; 31–32.

North America's Methodist communities shared with Moravians and many German Lutheran pietists a distinct aversion to overt political activity as the forum within which to realize their religious convictions. The vision of a future that later analysts would come to describe in terms of "private benevolence" sprang from these remarkably common-sense assessments of how little confidence the pious had placed in political leaders or wholesale legislative assaults upon impiety.

The growth of Methodism among the African-American population of Philadelphia, a theme that has been repeatedly examined since D. E. B. DuBois' pioneering study of a century ago, confirms the overall picture of this strand of the migrating pious.[19] Whatever the motives and nature of Richard Allen's foundation of the African Methodist Episcopal Church, his departure from St. George's segregated parish and the founding of Bethel, the free black community of Philadelphia found in a separate Methodism a vision of self-respect and a modicum of personal control over both worship and the governance of a faith community. Milton Sernett, Gary Nash and Julie Winch have all commented that the impetus for a separate African congregation predated the departure from St. George's, and that this impetus led not to Methodism, but to the Episcopal church of St. Thomas, dedicated even before the founding of Allen's Bethel African-Methodist Episcopal church. Yet, near contemporary segregation of blacks in Baltimore's Methodist churches also led these historians to wonder if competition for scarce employment may not have propelled the move toward separate congregations. In fact, as Winch points out, it was the need to organize their own charitable relief societies, despite some patronage from wealthy white Methodists, that best explains the modest but important vision of urban blacks in the late eighteenth century. Not unlike the German-language pietists, the African pious who had migrated under duress, tended toward the establishment of churches, schools, and relief societies in the effort to construct a

---

19. W.E.B.DuBois, *The Philadelphia Negro* (Philadelphia, PA, 1899).

culturally intact context within which heartfelt religion could find practical expression.[20]

Social marginalization, the favorite theme of a generation ago, has failed to deliver much clarity on what to make of the migrations of the pious and their visions of the future. On both sides of the Atlantic, radical antinomian and mystical movements seem to have ebbed and flowed almost irrespective of the socio-economic and political contexts of early modern Europe and North America. And we have been reminded that while some of the working class in the emerging cities of North America embraced the Methodist movement, others found universalism just as attractive.[21] Undoubtedly, in addition, African-Americans embrace of Methodism pointed to a persistent and unresolved flaw in pietist visions which only with great difficulty found room for African-American participants. Some historians noted African-American "contributions" to the story of the pious, particularly concentrating at times on messianic visions of the future. Not only DuBois, but also more recent scholars have pointed to the existence of an enforced separate African-American Methodist community as a persistent challenge to pious visions of a socially just future.[22]

Rather, Methodism's early radicalism lay in the highly internalized and individualized appropriation of a selective view of the Christian

---

20. Milton C. Sernett, *Black Religion and American Evangelicalism: White Protestants, Plantation Missions, and the Flowering of Negro Christianity, 1787–1865* (Metuchen, NJ, 1975), 117–120; Gary B. Nash, *Forging Freedom: The Formation of Philadelphia's Black Community, 1720–1840* (Cambridge, MA, 1988), 120–126; Julie Winch, *Philadelphia's Black Elite: Activism, Accommodation, and the Struggle for Autonomy, 1787–1848* (Philadelphia, PA, 1988), 4–12.

21. Ronald Schultz, "God and Workingmen: Popular Religion and the Formation of Philadelphia's Working Class, 1790–1830," in Ronald Hoffman and Peter J. Albert, eds., *Religion in a Revolutionary Age* (Charlottesville, VA, 1994), 125–155.

22. See Wilson J. Moses, "African American Historiography and the Works of Benjamin Quarles," *The History Teacher* 32 (November, 1998), 77–88; and for his critique of the messianic dimensions of "visionary" African-American traditions, Moses, *Black Messiahs and Uncle Toms: Social and Literary Manipulations of a Religious Myth* (University Park, PA, 2nd ed., 1992).

past. Nowhere did this tendency manifest itself more strikingly than in the rise of black women preachers who, in contrast to their white counterparts, did not remain within the commonly accepted restrictions upon female authority to preach imposed by early Methodism in Britain and North America. Black Methodist women were deeply involved in connecting the promptings of individual spiritual conviction to assaults upon slavery, as the preaching careers of Jarena Lee and Zilpha Elaw illustrated.[23]

While evangelical Methodist piety seems at first glance rather far removed from universalism, Löscher would not have found the two movements all that alien from one another. Both emphasized the predominance of God's love and universal "benevolence," the term Perry Miller chose to characterize the entire sweep of early nineteenth-century American religion. The speed with which Methodism transformed itself from a marginal visionary movement that spoke to the anxieties and encounters with real socio-economic evils by its adherents, to one of the most respectable representations of "bourgeois" Christianity would also have been understood by Löscher. For the orthodox Lutherans this move reflected the fundamental error of the Wesleys: their endorsement of an Arminian understanding of human agency in its relationship to the deity, and an overweening confidence in the privileged status of subjective judgement in matters spiritual.

Thomas Jenkins has demonstrated how leading nineteenth-century American theologians managed to sentimentalize and romanticize the very concept of God. His findings suggest that access to a comfortable Deity may have lain near the heart of a wide variety of future visions that crossed all socio-economic boundaries. Personally accessible, particularly well-disposed toward experimental communities of wanderers from the corrupt and oppressive religious climate of Europe, the God of the migrated pious − of remote or recent vintage − seems to have been domesticated with relative ease. Yet the major exponents of a benevolent Deity were not the leaders

---

23. Marilyn J. Westerkamp, *Women and Religion in Early America, 1600–1850: The Puritans and Evangelical Traditions* (London and New York, 1999), 104–130.

of the recently disembarked immigrants, but rather mainline theologians of the denominations whose adherents had arrived long before the German pietists or their Methodist cousins.[24]

II

A great and central puzzle in the history of North American Protestantism remains in the fact that many of the early arrivals genuinely believed in a God of wrath and judgement, took seriously the doctrine of Original Sin and the possibility of damnation, sought out teachers and theologians who would not utter mere pious banalities; and sang, generation after generation, a hymnody whose vision of the future did not mesh easily with premillenialist visions of the heavenly kingdom to be found on the shores of the New World. Perhaps significantly, however, little overt connection between visions of a future tied the migrating pious to the political upheavals and warfare of North America in quite the same way this worked for the New England descendants of the English Puritans. The latter, whose collective memory and self-identity as standard-bearers of an earthly Zion was reawakened by the Seven Years War, inherited a very different religious vision. The migrants from the continent shared none of that past, and hence could catch only glimpses of such imagined futures.[25] Indeed, it may not be an exaggeration to suggest that the predisposition toward individual experience and validation of religious truth – the antinomian danger that had always troubled the original Puritan experiment – had finally erupted by the 1740s in the way "paper money enthusiasts . . . welcomed the evangelicals." While no one would risk assuming a direct causal link between these mid-century affinities, the primacy of reflected choice, based on personal experience, does suggest why a deepening commercial-consumer society could also produce a Protestant faith

24. Thomas E. Jenkins, *The Character of God: Recovering the Lost Literary Power of American Protestantism* (New York and Oxford, 1997), 19–55.

25. Fred Anderson, *A People's Army: Massachusetts Soldiers and Society in the Seven Years' War* (Chapel Hill, NC, 1984), 213–221.

whose adherents pointed to "a free, reasoning self in adjudicating competing claims to authority, rival assertions of value, contested efforts to set boundaries on behavior, belief, motion, and choice."[26]

Whether one takes as examples the success of William Otterbein among the German Reformed, or the phenomenal response to David Henkel's strenuous orthodoxy among German Lutherans, many late eighteenth-century North Americans with familial roots in a migration of the pious did not endorse visions of a sentimental or romantic God. Neither were they necessarily engaged in visions of constructing a millennialist future that easily meshed with that emerging from the New England experience in religion, politics, and commerce. Moreover, in their encounters with the American Indian peoples, European theologians by the late eighteenth century still spoke of "Gospel Agency" in the process of "civilizing" pagan peoples. But they spoke in such guarded terms that their pessimism contrasts sharply with the optimistic visions of conversion which the first arriving pious penned about the future of Christianity among the American Indian populations of North America.[27]

The German Moravians, by far the most successful European proclaimers of a Protestant Christian Gospel to the Indians, had intentionally avoided didactic approaches to the thorny issue of justification and assurance that so bedevilled European Christians. For their pains, they, too, were lumped with "enthusiasts" by suspicious British observers, who could make little sense of their mix of mystical, Lutheran, and Hussite theologies.[28] Like their

---

26. See variously, H. Shelton Smith, *Changing Conceptions of Original Sin* (New York, 1955); Jon Pahl, *Paradox Lost: Free Will and Political Liberty in American Culture, 1630–1760* (Baltimore, MD, 1992); for the overview of renewed debates on whether religious "revivals" of the eighteenth century can be tied to political identity, see Philip Goff, "Revivals and Revolution: Historiographic Turns since Alan Heimert's *Religion and the American Mind*," *Church History* 67 (1998), 695–721. The quotation is from T. H. Breen and Timothy Hall, "Structuring Provincial Imagination: The Rhetoric and Experience of Social Change in Eighteenth-Century New England," *American Historical Review* 103 (1998), 1410–1439, at 1437.

27. On the revival of "Gospel Agency," see Joseph R. Lucas, "Conquering the Passions: Indians, Europeans, and Early American social Thought, 1580–1840," Ph.D. dissertation, The Pennsylvania State University, 1999.

28. On British reaction, see Lovejoy, *Religious Enthusiasm*, 206–214.

Roman Catholic competitors, the German Moravians had followed Zinzendorf's insistence since the 1740s that the Indians first be brought to appreciate the love of God, and "the wounds of the Lamb," and only by slow stages should the more careful distinctions between "justification" and "sanctification" be broached.[29] Moravian visions of the future, initially for their own communities as well as for the converted Delaware, persisted in the more apolitical, communal systems of support that eventually succumbed to a pragmatic vision of the future anchored in common-sense engagement with agriculture and trade. The Gnaddenhutten Massacre of March 8, 1782 effectively removed the horizon upon which such a future could be realized.

Although the Moravians had at least temporarily, in North Carolina, managed to bridge some racial barriers in their communities, their adjustment to slavery proved their undoing. Elders found by the late eighteenth century that younger German-American Moravians were drawn away not only by the emotive preaching of Methodist revivalists, but equally by the acceptance among American Methodists of segregated congregations. Whatever vision of a future that ignored race had shimmered before the early Moravians, it had wavered and vanished by 1800.[30]

Among none of these groups, therefore, can one find very solid roots for the later trumpet calls for a "Christian republic" or legislating the connection between inner assurance, acts of mercy, and the reform of entire societies. To be sure, German Lutherans in Philadelphia could petition their government to prohibit secular theatre as a nursery of vice; in response to a general consensus of many of these pietist-inspired groups, Pennsylvania by the 1790s

29. See the discussion of Zinzendorf's instructions on this point in Hermann Wellenreuther and Carola Wessel, eds., *Indianermission in der Amerikanischen Revolution: Die Tagebücher von David Zeisberger 1772 bis 1781* (Berlin, 1995), 56–63, Zinzendorf's citation at 57.

30. Jon F. Sensbach, *A Separate Canaan: The Making of an Afro-Moravian World in North Carolina, 1763–1840* (Chapel Hill, NC, 1998), 178–217; for the Methodists, see William Cortland Johnson, "To Dance in the Ring of all Creation: Camp Meeting Revivalism and the Color Line, 1799–1825," Ph.D. dissertation, University of California-Riverside, 1997.

sought to restrain the habits of the vicious by legislation. Fear of Presbyterian dominance in the political and the religious life of the Commonwealth, however, explains the sharply divided religious atmosphere in the state where so many of the pious had settled. Grander visions of an evangelical future came from other corners of the new republic.[31]

Just as German-speaking Moravians, deeply indebted to pietist emphases upon interior regeneration and emotive spirituality, foundered in the quest to build transracial communities in the face of the allure of property and slave labor, so too did Halle-inspired Lutheranism fail in its future vision in North America. While historians have rightly noted the flirtation with orphanages supposedly modeled on Halle's by George Whitefield, the thrust of Halle's future vision really lay elsewhere. The orphanage at Halle itself, after all, functioned primarily as a showplace to attract donors and supporters from among the German nobility. The real thrust of the Foundations lay in the educational system, which envisaged the training, especially of young men, for both practical self-help and deep interior piety as the transforming agents for a future hope for better times.[32]

The failure of the younger pastors such as J. H. C. Helmuth, Johann Christoph Kunze, and Friedrich Schmidt, to convey the centrality of this vision to congregants from the Reich's south-western regions revealed again the limits of pietism's capacity to anchor its emphasis upon interior transformation to redeeming the real world via socio-economic institutions engaged with the expanding market world of the eighteenth century. Among the German Reformed, as among the Lutherans, the parochial school served as an institution for the inculcation of the German language,

31. On the brief romance of Pennsylvanianas with legislating Christian morality and creating a Christian republic, see Roeber, "The Long Road to *Vidal v Philadelphia*: Charity and State Formation in Early America," in Christopher Tomlins and Bruce Mann, eds., *The Many Legalisties of Early America* (Chapel Hill, 2000, forthcoming).

32. See Roeber, "J.H.C. Helmuth, Evangelical Charity, and the Public Sphere in Pennsylvania, 1793–1800," *The Pennsylvania Magazine of History & Biography* CXXI (1997), 77–100.

and hence, the survival of hymnody, catechization, and Luther's translation of the Bible. In neither instance did a vision of the future rise to the challenge of seminary training of future pastors and teachers; both traditions would not face up to this challenge until the third decade of the nineteenth century.

In fairness to the migrated pious, they remained highly conscious of their status as relative latecomers. Theologically, as well as practically, they saw the value of respecting other people's visions of the future as equally plausible "opinions." But mere opinion, of course, dissolved faith as conviction as surely as it loosened tight communion of the saints into mere "associationalism," the "voluntarism" for which America became so famous in the nineteenth century. For the migrated pious, no less so than for embattled Anglican orthodox theologians, "opinion [became] the freedom of the spirit to seek Christ . . . [and became] enthusiasm once again."[33] If the history of one's own collective religious past became simply one among many acceptable versions, what definitive future could possibly be articulated? Uncertain pasts, themselves created in a flight from various unacceptable religious realities in Europe, fashioned a compromised language unsuitable for crafting a common future. That future could only remain pregnant with opinions, but barren of certainty.

Some latter-day observers have noted that a resulting indecisiveness may explain the lack of connection between realized socioeconomic "progress" and the religious hopes for better times the pietists represented. If "underdevelopment" is really a "state of mind," the poverty of pietism, revealed in its inability to take institutionalized form, may have been, in the last analysis, a theological poverty. That impoverishment can be traced back to the uncertainty with which the migrating pious faced the "real" world of Europe from which they came.[34]

---

33. J.G.A. Pocock, "Within the Margins: The Definitions of Orthodoxy," in Roger D. Lund, ed., *The Margins of Orthodoxy: Heterodox Writing and Cultural Response, 1660–1750* (Cambridge, MA, 1995), 33–53, citation at 50.

34. Lawrence Harrison, *Who Prospers? Underdevelopment is a State of Mind* (New York, 1999).

The ability to "institutionalize" a vision of religious engagement with the socio-economic realities of life lies, of course, in part in the vision of a "corporate" or "body" of believers. The integrated parts of the "body", whether politic or religious, and the remedies for disorders therein were contested, even among the pious. Methodists following Wesley's *Primitive Physic,* for example, would not have regarded the body and its workings in the same way as did continentals who were often treated with the conviction that "lifestyle and dietetics . . . [should be understood] by the subordination of health and physical function and dysfunction to the active agency of the soul."[35] We lack any serious study of the Methodist and pietist concepts of the "body" in North America comparable to Robert St. George's careful study of the body's "image" in New England's believing communities. But his conclusion, with due caution noted given very different continental theologies, is still worth pondering. A deep tradition of antinomianism bequeathed on New England a 'mixed' body with a 'multiplicitie' of opinions defining both orthodoxy and heterodoxy . . . the repertoire of radical millenarianism, fueled by the cross-class appeal of New Light enthusiasm during the Great Awakening and the identicality of bodies in science and commerce, combined to make a new kind of homegrown social leveling during the first half of the eighteenth century."[36] While various alienated groups sometimes sought to understand both self and future in visions and dreams within an ostensibly "leveling" context, that attempt at sketching a future declined, not only among Methodists, but also among radical pietists from the continent (with the exception of utopian communalists) in the course of the nineteenth century.[37]

35. Renate Wilson, "The Traffic in Halle Orphanage Medications: Medicinals, Philanthropy, and Colonial Mission," *Caduceus: A Humanities Journal for Medicine and the Health Sciences* 13 (1997), 6–22, at 8.

36. Robert Blair St. George, *Conversing by Signs: Poetics of Implication in Colonial New England Culture* (Chapel Hill, NC, 1998), 203.

37. Mechal Sobel, "The Revolution in Selves: Black and White Inner Aliens," in Ronald Hoffman, Mechal Sobel, and Fredrika Teute, eds., *Through a Glass Darkly: Reflections on Personal Identity in Early America* (Chapel Hill, NC and London, 1998), 163–205.

Such tensions cannot be replicated precisely among early Methodists; among congregations from the Amish and Moravians to Lutheran and Reformed, however, envisioning a corporate future for believers jostled with settlement patterns that reflected attempts to preserve familial cohesion.[38] But the collapse of communal experiments, from Ebenezer in Georgia to Pennsylvania's Ephrata and beyond, revealed the dissolvent qualities of choice employed by self-conscious individuals. Bafflement at, or dissent from, the emerging patterns of individual ownership could easily be dismissed as misinformed or deluded "opinion," especially by younger believers increasingly open to seeking personal "assurance" from revivalist "new measures." Even with the passing of the mass revivals of "born-again" experiences from the mainstream of American religious life, the pietist legacy remains in New Age spiritualism.[39]

In a strange way, the migrating pious ended by being unable to affirm the godliness of the New World. The various subsequent experiences of a "private" nature, or of utopian communal experiments also, all remained unstable because the adherents' own pasts consisted of a flight from an old world also lacking in a presence of the divine in which they could confidently see the manifestation in everyday life and the events of the natural world. Pietism's paradox lay in its capacity to release energies that did, quite probably, contribute to various social reform movements in later centuries. Yet, in the end, visions of a future kingdom continued to recede further within the seekers whose restless migrations have so marked the history of Christianity in North America.

38. The most convincing documentation of the attempt to preserve a coherent settlement is Aaron Spencer Fogleman, *Hopeful Journeys: German Immigration, Settlement, and Political Culture in Colonial America, 1717–1775* (Philadelphia, PA, 1996), 80–99.

39. See, for example, Robert Wuthnow, *After Heaven: Spirituality in America since the 1950s* (Berkeley, CA, 1998), 188–198; for more extensive reflections on the later legacy of German-American religion, see Roeber, "The Future of German-American Religions in North America," in Frank Trommler and Elliot Shore, eds., *The Future of German-American History* (New York, forthcoming, 2001).

2
American Dreams and European Responses, from the 1840s to the 1920s

William R. Hutchison

In 1925, a young – later quite famous – Swiss theologian named Emil Brunner offered a succinct definition of "religious American-ism." He defined it as "the evolutionistic optimism of world-betterment."[1]

No surprise there. Anyone remotely related, then or now, to the study of such matters would know that Americans have been noted through most of their history for optimism and activism. While the "evolutionistic" label would not have been affixed before the advent of Darwinism, the other elements in Brunner's description had been common ones for at least a century. Ralph Waldo Emerson, himself no slouch when it came to optimism, in the 1840s had expressed a good deal of innocent merriment about the various reform assemblages of that time. There were, he reported, almost more schemes for world betterment than there were schemers:

> What a fertility of projects for the salvation of the world! One apostle thought all men should go to farming, and another that no man should buy or sell . . . another that the mischief was in our diet, that we eat and drink damnation. . . . Others attacked the system of agriculture, the use of animal manures in farming, and the tyranny of man over brute nature. . . . Even the insect world was to be defended . . . and a society for the protection of ground-worms, slugs, and mosquitoes was to be incorporated without delay . . .[2]

1. Emil Brunner, *Reformation und Romantik* (Munich, 1925), p. 26.
2. Ralph Waldo Emerson, "New England Reformers," in Joel Porte, ed., *Essays and Lectures*, (New York, 1983), 591:592.

Another trait of the Americans, almost as well known as their optimism about the future, has been their capacity for stirring controversy in Europe. What I shall attempt in this essay is a brief inquiry – or, really, a reconnaissance – into the points of intersection between the first of these American characteristics and the second; that is, I shall examine several examples of European conflicts over "Americanization" – in this case conflicts that had to do with the supposed influence of American religion – and will try to see where hyperbolic or otherwise distinctive "visions of the future" figured in such conflicts – if they did so at all.

Visions of the Future among the Catholic "Americanists"

For historians of American religion who usually find it necessary to begin with Protestant examples (since those tend to be proto-typical), it is refreshing to be able to begin elsewhere. Catherine Albanese's textbook in American religious history manages to place Judaism ahead of Protestantism in her chronological account, but only on the (as she acknowledges) somewhat dubious ground that there were Marranos on Christopher Columbus' ships. But no such sleight of hand is necessary here: The so-called Americanist Contro-versy in the Roman Catholic Church is better known, and far more thoroughly chronicled, than those in any of the other religious bodies that pursued a transatlantic career.

The Americanist Controversy of 1897–9 was one culmination – another was the nearly concurrent "Modernist Controversy" – of long-simmering disputes about the degree and manner of the Church's adaptation to modernity. At issue was, in fact, the very possibility of accommodation to changes in the intellectual atmos-phere, or in political and social conditions, in the late nineteenth-century West. The struggle began to acquire its name when, just as the decade opened, Father William Elliott published his biography of Isaac Hecker, the American founder of the Paulist order of priests. The story of Hecker's efforts and seeming success in adapting Catholic practice to American conditions suggested to many

European conservatives that "American" traits such as individualism and anti-traditionalism bore significant responsibility for similar adaptationist trends in Europe. Concerns of that kind were greatly intensified by the appearance in 1897 of a French-language edition of the Hecker biography, and even more by a new introduction written by Félix Klein, a young priest and professor of marked modernist inclinations. At the end of two years of voluminous and highly acrimonious controversy, Pope Leo XIII issued the Papal letter known familiarly as "the Encyclical against Americanism."

Whatever the true extent of American involvement in a controversy that featured many indigenous-European elements, it is clear that American leaders and ideas did play a role. So, certainly, did images and perceptions of American religion and culture. The question here is how American "visions of the future" figured in this mix of real and alleged influences, if they did at all.

There are two ways to answer that question, and I think both are important. The more general answer really relates to the "style" of the Americans. Their style was optimistic, enthusiastic, and this-worldly; and such a style readily suggested the religious individualism and activism that Roman authorities found excessive and that conservative Catholics all over Europe found infuriating. The Americans, or at least those given voice by the more liberal of the American prelates, were thought to be out of balance – too much preoccupied with variously defined "good works," too little given to prayer and contemplation and religious observance. And all this, in turn, seemed to play itself out as an enthusiasm for the present and future that either excluded or diminished reverence for the past – for tradition.

The other answer is a very specific one, and it can be stated quite briefly: The Americans were understood to be telling the Roman Catholic Church at large that *America is the future.*

Were the critics who heard that euphoric message hearing correctly? Was it really that blatant? Often it was. During the Americanist Controversy and for at least two generations afterward, Catholic spokesmen and historians – especially the American ones – were inclined to deny this. "Americanism," they argued, was a "phantom heresy" – either because the various liberal tendencies were greatly and maliciously exaggerated by ultra-conservatives, or because the offending liberal ideas were actually Continental – mostly French – in origin and not "American" at all.[3] But recent historians of the controversy have demonstrated beyond any reasonable doubt that "America is the future" was indeed a subtext or assumption in the thought and actions of the more liberal American prelates. The work of these same historians has prompted us to go back and read the actual utterances of Catholic liberals such as Hecker, John Ireland (Archbishop of St. Paul), and other alleged Americanists, and has shown that such utterances were not aberrational or even rare.[4]

If one were asked to choose the *locus classicus* or key document for this Catholic version of American future-mindedness, there would in fact be a number of reasonable candidates such as Hecker's *The Church and the Age*, which was published in 1887, the year before his death. But most historians, I think, would fix on a sermon bearing the same title that Archbishop Ireland preached six years later at a service celebrating the twenty-fifth anniversary of the episcopal consecration of James Cardinal Gibbons, Archbishop of Baltimore. One of Ireland's biographers refers to him as "startlingly frank . . . a magnetic speaker, militant and yet conciliatory."[5] What Ireland was willing to be frank about in this sermon was not only an affirmation that America is the future, but also the "flip side" of that affirmation – *Europe is the past* – and a warning to Rome and the Church at large: The Church must join the future; and that means that Rome had better take note of its American advance guard and reform the Church according to the model the Americans were presenting.

Ireland began by proposing that "the age," though filled with solemn challenges, was preeminently full of hope, and was determined upon change. The watchword of humanity, he said, is "let all

---

3. Félix Klein, *Americanism: A Phantom Heresy* (Atchison, KS, 1951).

4. See especially Thomas Wangler, "The Birth Of Americanism: 'Westward the Apocalyptic Candlestick," *Harvard Theological Review* 65 (1972), pp. 415–436; and R. Scott Appleby, *'Church and Age Unite'; The Modernist Impulse in American Catholicism* (Notre Dame, IN, 1992).

5. Richard J. Purcell, in the *Dictionary of American Biography*.

things be new." To make all things new was "humanity's strong resolve."

The Church's mission, in that charged atmosphere, was what it had always been: to conquer the world for Christ; in that regard one could take comfort in an absolute fixity. But the conquest of a rapidly changing world required that "the Church must herself be new, adapting herself in manner of life and in method of action to the conditions of the new order, thus proving herself, while ever ancient, to be ever new, as truth from heaven is and ever must be."[6]

But this renewal, Ireland argued, was not occurring. "The Church and the age are at war. I voice the fact with sorrow."

Who or what was to blame for this? He did blame the age, which he characterized as materialistic, naturalistic, contemptuous of the past and its institutions, dismissive of the claims of the supernatural. But he also blamed the Church, and in his lengthy reprimand of the blindness, rigidity, and outright reactionary stubbornness of contemporary Catholicism, Ireland's "frankness" and "militance" nearly drowned out his attempts to be "conciliatory." And he left no doubt at all that he placed the blame for reaction and inaction upon European Catholicism and the Roman authorities. The latter had been "too slow to understand the new age and too slow to extend to it the conciliatory hand of friendship . . . to Christianize its aspirations and to guide its forward march." Although prescient leaders like Jean-Baptiste Lacordaire (pastor at Notre Dame de Paris) had proclaimed the duties of the hour, "timid companions" had abandoned such prophets. "Reactionaries accused them of dangerous liberalism . . . and they were forced to be silent."[7]

Seemingly too excited to wait any longer, Ireland rose to his peroration in mid-speech: What the Church at any time was, certain people hold she must ever remain. They do her much harm, making her rigid and unbending, incapable of adapting herself to new and changing surroundings. . . . What! The Church of the living God . . . the great, freedom-

6. John Ireland, *The Church and Modern Society: Lectures and Addresses*, 2 vols. (New York, 1903), I, p. 107.
7. Ibid., pp. 109, 110.

loving, truth-giving, civilizing Catholic Church – this Church of the nineteenth century afraid of any century! . . . I preach the new, the most glorious crusade. Church and age! Unite them in the age of humanity, in the name of God.[8]

What followed, although we might expect it to sound anti-climactic, was not such, especially if one is interested in the Americanists' conviction that their own brand of Catholicism defined the future. In the later sections of the speech Ireland devoted his attention to two of the several contemporary churchmen, worldwide, "by whom salvation [would be] brought to Israel." One was Leo himself, who had, after all, promulgated the encyclical *Rerum Novarum* just two years earlier. "Leo, I hail thee, pontiff of thy age, providential chieftain of the Church in a great crisis of her history!"[9]

The other, of course, was Cardinal Gibbons, whose anniversary was being celebrated. And it is in the course of Ireland's paean of praise for Gibbons that we encounter outright assertions of what has been latent throughout the oration. For the Roman Catholic Church and its people America is and must be the future:

A special mission is reserved to the American Cardinal. In America, the Church and the age have fairest field to display their activities, and in America more speedily than elsewhere is the problem of their reconciliation to be solved. . . . My whole observation of the times . . . convinces me that the Church has now her season of grace in America.[10]

Ireland's expressions of confidence in Leo XIII as the future liberalizer of the Church may have been a trifle overblown, but these expressions were sincere; the Americanists showed repeatedly that they did feel such confidence. As Thomas Wangler writes, they made Leo into a liberal Catholic – and an Americanist to boot! "They repeatedly claimed that Leo saw America as the 'future.'"[11]

---

8. Ibid., pp. 113, 115.
9. Ibid., p. 123.
10. Ibid., pp. 127–128, 130.
11. Wangler, "Growth of Americanism," 431 and 431–436 *passim*.

But if Leo saw America and "Americanism" as representing a desired future for the Church, clearly his most influential advisers did not. The latter listened with greatest sympathy, throughout the lengthy and acrimonious debate of the late 1890s, to those who discerned an implicit – and frequently an explicit – "modernism" in the enthusiasms of Ireland and his American colleagues. In 1899 came the encyclical *Testem Benevolentiae*, which was addressed to Leo's fellow liberal (!) Cardinal Gibbons, and which then and since has been known by its nickname, "the Encyclical against Americanism."

In this letter Leo condemned roundly, though also tactfully, "the opinions which some comprise under the head of Americanism." Those opinions, although the kindly Pontiff professed to believe that "the bishops of America would be the first to repudiate and condemn" them, sounded remarkably similar to what Ireland and the others had preached at home and abroad throughout the late 1880s and the early 1890s. (Ireland, alarmed by French Modernism, had "changed his tune" – or, better, his "tone" – by the end of the decade; but others had not.)[12] Here is Leo's succinct definition of the doctrines and tendencies he deplored:

> that, in order the more easily to bring over to Catholic doctrine those who dissent from it, the Church ought to adapt herself somewhat to our advanced civilization, and, relaxing her ancient rigor, show some indulgence to modern popular theories and methods. Many think that this is to be understood not only with regard to the rule of life, but also to the doctrines in which the *deposit of faith* is contained.[13]

Ay, there was the rub. Whether one found the "Americanist heresy" to be that or merely some kind of harmless practical accommodation depended upon the degree to which one saw theological and doctrinal "modernism" therein. Whichever it was, however, the element of future-mindedness loomed large.

---

12. Appleby, *Church and Age*, 86–88.

13. Quoted in John Tracy Ellis, ed., *Documents of American Catholic History* 2 vols. (rev. ed. Chicago, IL, 1967), II, 546, 539.

"Here is our Zion": American Jewish Visions of the Future

In March 1841, when Congregation Beth Elohim in Charleston, South Carolina, completed a new building, Gustav Poznanski preached the dedicatory sermon. Although the sermon itself has never been found, one part that the Charleston *Courier* printed verbatim was remembered throughout the nineteenth century as an especially noteworthy expression of the same sentiment we have encountered in the rhetoric of the Catholic liberals. Poznanski, who was *hazan* and spiritual leader of Beth Elohim, sounded like a Jewish John Ireland as he declared that America represented the future – not only for the world at large, but also quite specifically for the Jewish people: "This synagogue is our *temple*, this city our *Jerusalem*, this happy land our *Palestine*, and as our fathers defended with their lives *that* temple and *that* city and *that* land, so will their sons defend *this* temple, *this* city, and *this* land . . ."[14]

In Catholic renditions of this kind of enthusiasm, Europe was almost always the foil. For Jewish leaders and publicists (virtually all of them Reform Jewish) who voiced the same affirmation, the foil or alternative was usually not Europe. It was Palestine. Here, for example, is Max Lilienthal, pastor in Cincinnati and a founder of its Hebrew Union College. In an 1868 address, he averred that "we Israelites of the present age do not dream any longer about the restoration of Palestine and the Messiah crowned with a diadem of earthly power and glory. Here is our Zion and Jerusalem; Washington and the signers of the glorious Declaration . . . are our deliverers . . ."

What follows immediately in that speech deserves special emphasis, because it bears directly on the question of American future-mindedness – in fact deserves to rank as a classic illustration of the way in which that strand of "Americanism" could weave itself into the fabric of a transatlantic or international religious community:

14. Quoted in W. Gunther Plaut, *The Growth of Reform Judaism* (New York, 1965), 9.

The time when their doctrines [those of Washington *et al.*] will be recognized and carried into effect is the time so hopefully foretold by our great prophets. When men will live together united in brotherly love, peace, justice, and mutual benevolence, then the Messiah has come indeed, and the spirit of the Lord will have been revealed to all his creatures.[15]

So the party line among American Reform spokesmen – reiterated well into the 1920s – held that America's founding principles not only define what Judaism must become; those principles sketch the lineaments of the Kingdom foretold in biblical prophecy. The further question for us, however, is whether this set of ideas created controversy abroad, or at least was recognized there as distinctive and either potentially or actually influential. The answer, so far as I can discover, is that this Jewish Americanism, while it figured in no controversies comparable in scale to the one in European Catholicism (which is scarcely surprising, considering the modest "scale" of European Jewry itself), did contribute to perennial disputes and discussions concerning Jewish adaptation to modernity. And in those discussions, American Reform Judaism did serve as the model for radical or extreme forms of adaptation.

In the Jewish community of Great Britain, for example, a Lithuanian-born minister named Israel Mattuck, educated at Harvard College and an ordinand of the Hebrew Union College of Cincinnati, ranked for over forty years (1911–1954) as the most radical – if also one of the most respected – leaders of British Judaism. Like most other Reform spokesmen, Mattuck eschewed and advised against traditional practices that modern Jews could not accept. But he went farther than nearly all of his British or German colleagues – altering liturgies, abandoning the traditional sequence of prayers, opening his pulpit to women (notably to the formidable Lily Montagu), and preaching the equal "chosenness" of all peoples.[16]

15. Max Lilienthal, "The Platform of Judaism," in David Philipson, *David Lilienthal, American Rabbi: Life and Writings* (New York, 1915), 457.

16. Michael A. Meyer, *Response to Modernity: A History of the Reform Movement in Judaism* (New York, 1988), 220–221.

From the very beginning – almost from the moment of Mattuck's opening of London's "Liberal Jewish Synagogue" in February of 1911 – his reforms and advocacies were identified as American.[17] Not only that, but Mattuck's detractors pointed out that his brand of radical Judaism was *not* radical in America, but rather was quite common there and widely accepted. In other words, Mattuck's markedly reformist ideas were not, in the American context, the aberrations of some kind of renegade; they *were* American Reform Judaism.

Whether or not British Jews found this alarming – and most did – the American or American-trained liberals were quite ready to agree that, back home, the Mattuck positions were broadly representative. Leon Harrison, an Englishman who had become pastor of the Reform congregation in St. Louis, put the case bluntly in an interview for the London *Jewish Chronicle*. Whereas Orthodoxy, he said, could exert "no vital influence" on American Judaism or its future, the ideas of Mattuck were virtually centrist. The *Chronicle* put it this way: "Although in this country Mr. Mattuck's platform is considered the extreme of Reform, Dr. Harrison assured our representative that he was quite in accord with [that platform], and he regarded himself as being a moderate Reformer."[18] As for Mattuck, he referred to himself repeatedly (though without any hint of personal pride) as a missionary for the only kind of Judaism that would persuade Jews not to defect to Christianity or secularism. "Anyway," he told the *Chronicle*, "that has been the experience in America, and I do not see that it will not apply here."[19]

As Mattuck's congregation prospered but also stirred a steady barrage of criticism, and as visitors from the American Reform community came and went, the *Chronicle* did its best to provide an open forum, if not to hide entirely its own serious reservations about American Reform. But in July 1912, in the wake of Harrison's visit, the editors cried "Enough!" Behind their careful critiques,

---

17. 17 Mattuck and the newer liberalism are discussed and debated steadily in the *Jewish Chronicle* of London, especially throughout the years 1911 and 1912.

18. *Chronicle*, July 12, 1912.

19. *Chronicle*, March 8, 1912.

apparently, had lain objections too fundamental to be called merely reservations. Harrison, they wrote, had put the case for Reform "as conceived in the United States, at its highest and best"; but what that highest and best amounted to was "our great faith drained of its very life-blood." American Reform might better be called "Deform." Jews in all ages, the editors acknowledged, have had to adapt to the surrounding majority culture. But they also have insisted upon maintaining their traditions and traditional practices, and by virtue of this steadfastness have frequently been able to outlast the civilizations that have tried to assimilate or eliminate them.

By contrast, the "one ideal" of American Reform appeared to be "assimilation to Americanism and conformity with American aspirations." Everything truly sacred to the Jew must give way to "the exigencies of American civilization and the demands of American 'hustle.'" It is far better, the editors wrote, to endure the terrible difficulties involved in maintaining Jewish language and practices in an alien environment than to "adopt the *manqué* Judaism – the neurotic, decadent, degenerate Judaism – presented by so-called American Reform." Jews need not flounder hither and thither "in what must at most be a doubtfully successful quest for – Americanization."

The editors plainly saw Mattuck, Harrison, and other spokesmen as sincere, eloquent and effective (too effective) in their projection of a future defined by America and American Reform. But they insisted that Judaism must reject such projections and instead look to "a future compatible with our doctrine, our practice, and our tradition":

> "Our future, as he 'visions' it, Dr. Harrison compares to prophetic ideals. But the prophets would not have given a 'thank you' for the universality of a faith which was to be such an amalgam as . . . is obviously emerging out of the religious melting pot into which it has been thrown."[20]

20. *Chronicle*, July 12, 1912.

William R. Hutchison

Protestants and the Future

In many respects, the Protestant forms of American religious influence, and of friendly and unfriendly European responses, are strikingly similar to the Roman Catholic one that historians have known about, and also to the one I have delineated – I believe for the first time – in relation to Judaism. In one European Protestant context after another, we find American peculiarities (real or alleged) held up, in about equal measure, as models to be imitated or as dangerous tendencies to be feared and scorned. And in virtually all the Protestant instances, from British Quakers alarmed by American evangelical influences, to German and other pietists worried about the Social Gospel, the most common and pervasive subject of praise or blame is one or another version of religious activism. "American-ism" stood, not surprisingly, for the same range of attributes that were under debate in Catholic and Jewish contexts (and, indeed, in many secular ones).

The questions then become: Were the Americanist controversies in European Protestantism at all comparable in scope and importance to the famous one that raged among Catholics? Second, to what extent, if at all, was an identifiably American "vision of the future" at play in the discussions and disputes that occurred in Protestant settings?

With respect to the first question, I find that several kinds of intra-Protestant argument over American influence were as persistent and/or as consequential as the controversy within Catholicism. Both American revivalism and American forms of social activism drew attention and occasioned often-bitter disputes in various European settings for at least a century after the 1820s. And in two areas of joined European–American enterprise, foreign missions and the ecumenical movement, Americanist controversies arose which, *mutatis mutandis*, actually outdid the Roman Catholic dispute in both scope and severity.

Disputes over missionary methods and strategies, which I have treated extensively in other writings,[21] pitted Continental Protestants,

---

21. See, for example William R. Hutchison, *Errand to the World: American Protestant Thought and Foreign Missions* (Chicago, II, 1987), chs. 5 and 6.

especially Germans, against the Anglo-Americans, preeminently the Americans. From the 1880s on, Anglophone missionaries and mission organizations were criticized both for revivalistic activism (an undue "individualism" on both sides of the missionary encounter) and for the social gospel activism of those missionaries who, critics thought, had lost interest in preaching and conversion altogether. In addition, and increasingly during this era, the Americans and their British abettors were accused of a scarcely disguised preoccupation with forms of world cultural domination that could not be passed off as sheerly (or even mainly) religious in nature.

Well before the 1920s, the terms *Amerikanismus* and *Aktivismus* were being used synonymously. The resentments reflected in such usages, I have argued, were deeply enmeshed – as effects but also as causative factors – in the tensions and imperial rivalries that surrounded the war of 1914–1918. And the arguments they symbolized, however one judges them on their merits, are especially relevant to the subject of this essay. They involved "American" visions of the future that for decades, or even centuries, had dismayed nearly as many Old World observers as they had inspired.[22]

Any adequate, fully contextual, treatment of American missionary "visions" would offer a substantial sampling of the vast literature of American future-mindedness that helps explain the confidence of mission ideologists who predicted "the evangelization of the world in this generation." Here I must be content to recall your attention to some of the rhetoric in the Reverend Josiah Strong's landmark volume of 1885, *Our Country*. In a chapter significantly (for our purposes) entitled "The Anglo-Saxon and the World's Future," Strong had sounded forth – repeatedly and at an especially high decibel level – the note we have heard in the writings of the non-Protestant enthusiasts; i.e., AMERICA *IS* THE FUTURE! Strong wrote that

---

22. I use the term "observers" quite advisedly. Well into the twentieth century, those like the Reverend Sydney Smith who thought the Americans not worth observing, formed an important constituency, perhaps a majority. ("In the four quarters of the globe," Smith asked rhetorically in 1820, "who reads an American book? Or goes to an American play? . . . etc." *Edinburgh Review*, vol. 6 [January 1820], 79–80.)

it is chiefly to the English and the Americans that we must look for the evangelization of the world . . . [but] America is to have the great preponderance of numbers and of wealth, and by the logic of events will follow the scepter of controlling influence. . . . The Americans may reasonably look forward to a time when they will have produced a civilization grander than the world has ever known. . . I believe it is fully in the hands of the Christians of the United States, during the next ten or fifteen years, to hasten or retard the coming of Christ's kingdom in the world by hundreds, and perhaps thousands, of years.[23]

The missionary Watchword being promulgated at this same time – "the evangelization of the world in this generation" – embodied a number of the elements in Strong's vision. His chauvinism was usually not in evidence. American leaders of the Student Volunteer Movement, the organization most thoroughly identified with the Watchword, were nearly as intent upon winning European adherence to their outlook and methods as they were upon winning the world for Christ; and even if they had believed as firmly as Strong did in an American cultural imperialism (the evidence, for example in the writings of Robert E. Speer, is that they did not), they would have eschewed Strong's blatant chauvinism. Yet surely it is justifiable to interpret their ardent advocacy of the Watchword as arising out of a vision not unlike Strong's. It is, furthermore, not only justifiable but quite important to recognize that European critics of an "American style" in missions placed the Watchword in this broader – and to them quite menacing – context.

A number of missionary leaders wrote extensively about the Watchword and its implications for their enterprise, but the key document is John R. Mott's manifesto of 1900, which took the motto for its title. Mott, a preeminent organizer, an inspiring if not

---

23. Josiah Strong, *Our Country: Its Possible Future and Its Present Crisis* (modern edition Cambridge, MA, 1963), 201, 206, 211–212, 218. For many other examples of this way of thinking, see the seminal study by Ernest Lee Tuveson, *Redeemer Nation: The Idea of America's Millennial Role* (Chicago, IL, 1968); and James H. Moorhead's "The American Israel: Protestant Tribalism and Universal Mission," in W. R. Hutchison and Hartmut Lehmann, eds., *Many Are Chosen: Divine Election and Western Nationalism* (Minneapolis, MN, 1994), 145–166.

charismatic personality, and a father figure for several generations (irony intended) of young Protestant missionaries, was not among the more effective literary stylists in the mission leadership. His *Evangelization of the World in this Generation* reads as a kind of handbook — a catalogue of scriptural, historical, and other warrants for the program of speedy world conquest. Thus the "vision of the future" in Mott's book emerges not as part of a philosophical discussion, nor even as an integrated, dynamic, argument, but instead as a litany of testimonies, one after the other, to "The Possibility of Evangelizing the World within a Generation as Viewed by Leaders in the Church."

Mott's chapter under that title, giving new meaning to the term "pedestrian," walks the reader through thirty-six testimonies to the efficacy of the Watchword in the course of its thirty-six paragraphs. Although several of these date from the early or middle years of the nineteenth century, most are the utterances of Mott's contemporaries or immediate predecessors. In their vision of a very-near future within which the entire world will be evangelized, a good many imply a definition of "evangelization" that Mott himself carefully avoided — a definition that equates that term with "conversion." And some of those whom Mott was willing to endorse alluded quite explicitly to successful mass conversion, to a veritable, wholesale, coming of the Kingdom. Thus he quoted from an 1877 report of the General Conference of the Protestant Missionaries of China: "Ought we not to make an effort to save China *in this generation?* . . . We want China emancipated from the thralldom of sin *in this generation.*"[24] Most of those cited, however, adhered strictly, and often in careful detail, to the more limited definition that, as Mott insisted, had always applied to the term "evangelization." For such advocates, "evangelization in this generation" did not mean that all the world would be converted; it meant that everyone everywhere must and would hear the Word. Thus, in the painstaking phrases of the editor of a Scottish mission journal, "if the Church would realise her relations to her enthroned Lord . . . there would

24. John R. Mott, *The Evangelization of the World in This Generation* (New York, 1900), 135.

be little difficulty, within one generation, in covering the whole open field of heathendom with centres of evangelisation sufficiently near each other to diffuse the gospel over the intervening spaces." More eloquently and poignantly, the Archbishop of Canterbury explained that "the aim . . . is that the Name of Christ shall be made known to all the nations of the world . . . that before those who are now living shall altogether pass away, there shall not be one spot on the earth where the name of Christ, and the Cross of Christ, and the Love of Christ, and the Love of God the Father is not known.[25]

That the watchword originated by the Americans should have provoked opposition and hostility among others devoted to the mission enterprise may seem surprising – especially when its meaning had been so carefully delimited and its aims could be stated in the warm and seemingly traditional phrasings of the Archbishop. And indeed, neither the Watchword nor the tone of optimism and urgency that pervaded it was resisted everywhere in Europe. Even Germans of pietist background, among whom the most serious opposition arose, frequently were able to say merely that "this is their way, though it is not our way." (As one German theologian wrote in the 1920s, American activism was simply "nicht unser Beruf.") But the American and Anglo-American approach was also subjected to a steady barrage of vehement criticism from the time of the Continental Mission Conferences, in the last third of the nineteenth century, until well into the 1920s. Gustav Warneck, the great mission historian of Halle, was only the most articulate and colorful of the many who sought to calm the hotheaded Anglo-Americans with "sober German words" about the proper conduct of foreign missions. Warneck, contrasting the Watchword's admonition unfavorably with that contained in Holy Scripture, wrote that Christ "bids us 'go' into all the world, not 'fly'"; and that Jesus likened the Kingdom of Heaven to a farmer's field, not to a hothouse. In a paper sent to the New York Missionary Conference of 1900 (Warneck and a number of other Germans had refused to attend), he lashed out at the Anglo-American preoccupation with numbers

25. Ibid., 156, 157.

and publicity and quick results. Employing language so strong that the editors of the conference volume censored it, Warneck railed against "pious rhetoric endeavoring to startle by exaggeration," "a self-righteous adherence to preconceived theories," and catchwords that were "romantic will o' the wisps . . . more apt to confuse than to enlighten."[26]

Already, at the turn of the century, indictments of haste and over-optimism were interlarded with charges that an earthly Kingdom under American sponsorship would be a good deal more earthly – more cultural and political – than the one contemplated in biblical sources. Warneck, calling again in his playful but serious way for semantic precision, pointed out that Jesus had not commanded his followers to "go . . . and teach English to all nations." But such indictments, naturally enough, became more frequent and more bitter after June 1919. In that later tragic era, the young Heinrich Frick, *Privatdozent* at Giessen, stands out as the most vehement of those who lashed out against an alleged Anglo-American imperial-ism. For Frick, the war, the Versailles settlement, and the confiscation of German mission properties all demonstrated that the Anglo-Americans had indeed, all along, intended to flood the world not with Christian conversions and lovingkindness but rather with their crude and materialistic culture. The Edinburgh missionary confer-ence of 1910 and the Versailles conference of 1919 had been "in their innermost meaning . . . products of the same spirit: namely, of the Americanism in modern evangelical missions."[27]

Although the critique of American "visions of the future," and even more of American impatience about getting to that future, by no means disappeared during the 1920s, it did become more complex and controverted. The overall impression, in fact, is that by 1925 the stereotyping of the Anglo-Americans as reckless social gospelers had become so widespread and automatic – hence so unfair – that it was producing its own reaction. A leading German

26. This characterization of the Warneck complaint is taken, some of it verbatim, from Hutchison, *Errand to the World*, 133–135.

27. Heinrich Frick, *Die Evangelische Mission: Ursprung, Geschichte, Ziel* (Bonn, 1922), 392.

ecumenist, René Heinrich Wallau, thought Frick had in large part misunderstood the Americans. The latter, he wrote, are realists; they are intensely practical. ("Der Amerikaner steht ganz und gar auf dem Boden der Wirklichkeit. Er träumt nicht.") They deal with the world as it is with the intention of bringing that world to Christ; and this, said Wallau, is an emphasis we Europeans need, not one we should treat disdainfully.[28] Another German commentator, reflecting on the charges and countercharges surrounding the Stockholm conference of 1925 (which explored the social mission of the churches), remarked wryly that if Wichem, the great German prophet of modem social Christianity, had reappeared at Stockholm, he would have been denounced as a dangerous Americanizer.[29] And when Heinrich Frick himself, during his first visit to the United States, began praising American activism and critiquing the "inward-ness" of the German churches, one knew that something was happening – that a process of "second thoughts" was under way.[30] Within a few years, as cutting-edge thinkers and activists on both sides of the Atlantic – Tillichs, Niebuhrs and, yes, Brunners and Fricks – struck alliances in the 1930s and after, one could say that the Protestant "Americanist Controversy" was over. *Aktivismus* became much less of an issue, or at least became a very different issue.

Some Rough-hewn Conclusions

I opened by remarking that Emil Brunner's characterization of the American style as optimistic and activistic would not surprise anyone. And it would perhaps be fair to say that there's very little "news" in my answer to the question posed near the beginning of this essay: Did American future-mindedness enter into European disputes over

---

28. René Heinrich Wallau, *Die Einigung der Kirche vom Evangelischen Glauben aus* (Berlin, 1925), 248–249.

29. Adolph Deissman, *Die Stockholmer Bewegung* (Berlin, 1927), 94.

30. Frick, "Amerikanische Reiseneindrücke," in *Christliche Welt*, 1925–1926. See especially his second installment, "Echo auf Stockholm," December 12, 1925.

the benefits and dangers of American religious influence? The answer is that it surely did, especially (and here's the part that is *not* surprising) when the influence in question represented the more liberal strains or movements in American religion. Wherever the subject of controversy was instead focused on such things as revivalism, "sectarianism," or pentecostalism − as it usually was, for example, in Scandinavia − American "visions of the future" were less directly in contention.

Even in European dialogues about these non-liberal American influences, however, the various tropes or assumptions of American futurism were usually not far away − just off-stage, or perhaps speaking *sotto voce* from the prompter's box. And wherever American evangelicals or their protégés busied themselves, as they so regularly did, promoting sabbatarianism or getting Europeans to sober up, the celebrated American "optimism of world-betterment" could become quite explicit in an evangelical context.

That, however, would be the subject for another essay − for a longer and perhaps more colorful essay than this one. In the present context, one that features the more liberalizing influences, a couple of further observations are in order. One of these is that the various Americanist controversies differed in important ways. The other is that they were strikingly similar.

In the Catholic controversy, "Americanism" was to some extent a counter in an essentially intra-European dispute. But it seems to me that this was less true in the Reform Jewish instance, and scarcely true at all in the great Protestant dust-up over foreign missions. Yet the several controversies, those we know about and others that we can learn about from work in archives and somewhat esoteric printed source,[31] also had much in common. For example, Wangler

---

31. Americanist controversies like the one among English Jews would seem to merit treatment in the secondary literature but, like most other matters of comparative history, have not made it into that literature. I learned about the Jewish discussion because my research assistant, Michael Kress, spent dozens of hours mining such sources as the London *Chronicle*. While doing somewhat similar work in Swedish sources (for a paper some years ago on Fredrika Bremer), I learned about a number of little-recorded influences of (and controversies over) Theodore

and others have shown conclusively that Catholic Americanism was not a "phantom heresy"; Ireland and others *really were* preaching the gospel of activism at home and abroad; the American(ist) prelates were not simply pawns in a European chess game. This was true in other cases as well.

Which leads to a final point concerning similarities; though perhaps an obvious point, it should be mentioned: Americanist controversies in overseas religious communities were similar because they were arguments about much more than religion. As the German–American differences over missions show especially well, they were arguments about the baneful effects of Amenca s cultural influence and growing geopolitical power.

Parker and other American liberals or radicals. Some of my European forays have been, to date, less productive than that; but in other instances − for example, that of Dutch Calvinists in Holland and America − I have at least seen a prima facie case for further exploration.

3
Present Tenses of the Everlasting Life: Pentecostal Visions of the Future

Grant Wacker

Just after supper on Monday April 9, 1906, a handful of black saints gathered in a cottage in Los Angeles to seek the baptism of the Holy Spirit. Soon one, then another, then nearly all found themselves shouting and singing in the mysterious cadences of Asia, Africa, and the South Sea Islands. The worshipers believed that their ability to speak unstudied languages confirmed that they had received the coveted experience of Holy Spirit baptism described in the New Testament *Book of Acts*. Word raced through the African-American community. In the next few days the rapidly growing band scraped together funds to lease a vacant African Methodist Episcopal Church in a run-down section of the city at 312 Azusa Street. The following Tuesday the Lord chose to advertise the mission's existence through a most hapless instrument, a Los Angeles *Times* newspaper reporter, who may have been simply walking home from work. "The night is made hideous . . . by the howlings of the worshipers," he wrote. "The devotees of the weird doctrine practice the most fanatical rites, preach the wildest theories and work themselves into a state of mad excitement." Predictably the devotees of the "weird doctrine" saw things differently. In their minds anyone with a pure heart and an open mind could see that the long-awaited worldwide revival had finally begun.[1]

---

1. Quotation from Los Angeles *Times*, April 18, 1906, 1. The title of this essay is adapted from Frederick B. Meyer's classic, *The Present Tenses of the Blessed Life* (New York: Fleming H. Revell, 1892), a work pentecostals eagerly appropriated as one of their own. Some of the sentences in this and the following paragraph replay sentences in my "The Functions of Faith in Primitive Pentecostalism," *Harvard Theological Review* 77 (1984), 353, and "Searching for Eden with a Satellite Dish:

Whether the pentecostal insurgence really started among these blacks at Azusa, as commonly supposed, or among whites in divine healing services in Topeka, Kansas, a half-dozen years earlier, or among North Carolina hill folk in the 1890s, as various scholars have contended, there can be little dispute that the Holy Ghost stirring has mushroomed into one of the most powerful religious upheavals of the twentieth century. By 1999, according to demographers David W. Barrett and Todd Johnson, nearly 450,000,000 souls considered themselves pentecostals or charismatics, making them the largest aggregation of Christians on the planet outside the Roman Catholic Church. Almost certainly those numbers swelled in the telling, perhaps wildly so, yet other studies consistently showed that within a hundred years of its beginnings the pentecostal-charismatic movement claimed an immense following, both at home and abroad.[2] Equally remarkable, perhaps, was the persistence of the essential doctrines and practices of the pentecostal revival from the time of its emergence just after 1900 through the end of the 1990s. More on that later.

What did Holy Ghost folk believe? Besides the emphasis on tongues (which distinguished them among radical evangelicals), they also stressed the necessity of a heartfelt conversion experience, divine healing and, of course, the Lord's imminent physical return. This last event would be followed by the consummation of history in the battle of Armageddon, the Millennium, and Final Judgment. This last point brings us to the subject of the present essay.

Primitivism, Pragmatism, and the Pentecostal Character," in Richard T. Hughes, ed., *The Primitive church in the Modern World* (Urbana: University of Illinois Press, 1995), 138–139.

2. David B. Barratt and Todd M. Johnson, "Annual Statistical Table on Global Mission: 1999," *International Bulletin of Missionary Research* 23 (January 1999), 24–25. Of course some pentecostals are Catholics, but there is no easy way to sort them out. The primary and secondary literature on the worldwide pentecostal movement is vast. For a summary of some of the key texts see Augustus Cerillo, Jr. and Grant Wacker, "Bibliography and Historiography of Pentecostalism in the United States," Stanley Burgess, ed., *New International Dictionary of the Pentecostal and Charismatic Movements* (Grand Rapids: Harper Collins Zondervan, forthcoming 2000).

Rather than trying to trace the formal structure of millenarian ideas that undergirded early pentecostals' thinking about the future (a topic already well-explored in other works[3]), I wish instead to focus on the ramifications of such thinking for daily life. One ramification involved a sense of doom just ahead, especially for those who discounted the pentecostal message. Another ushered in an exhilarating sense of hope, especially for those who embraced the full gospel message, as partisans put it. Finally this hope prompted saints to a frenzy of expansionist activity. In principle of course it should not have been so, for the Bible pictured the end times drama unfolding outside history, independent of human wishes or cooperation. But in practice pentecostals proved unwilling to leave themselves out of the most exciting story ever told. For a band of "despised nobodies," as one of their leaders had put it, it was a handsome destiny indeed.[4]

Doom

At first blush a pervasive sense of doom seemed the most conspicuous result of millenarian thinking on daily life. By doom I mean not so much a specific set of ideas as an abiding sense of cataclysmic changes soon to come. In its eerie light life's edges grew sharper and its colors darker. Occurrences that most folks considered ordinary acquired grim meaning.

The sheer ominousness of converts' view of events just ahead immediately arrests our attention. For example the front cover of every copy of the *Everlasting Gospel,* a monthly issued by the quasi-pentecostal healing community in Shiloh, Maine, proclaimed that "THE HOUR OF HIS JUDGMENT IS COME . . . THE LAST SOLEMN MESSAGE OF THE AGE. . . . the day of vengeance of

---

3. See for example D. William Faupel, *The Everlasting Gospel: The Significance of Eschatology in the Development of Pentecostal Thought* (Sheffield: Sheffield Academic Press, 1996).

4. *Victory!,* April 1909, 1.

our God."[5] And solemn it was too. In the nation's heartland Charles Fox Parham, the Holy Ghost revival's main theological architect, repeatedly declared that the age of salvation had nearly passed. The "'Gospel of The Kingdom' [has] spent its force," he warned. Now a "Heaven-born soldiery are treading their way to the various battlefields to spread the flames." "A reign of terror will ensure . . . The end draweth nigh."[6] Soon the gutters of the land would splash with blood.[7] Surveying world affairs in the winter of 1916, Memphis pastor L. P. Adams advised his people that the previous year had exceeded all years of human history for the number of wars, earthquakes, famines, pestilence, commotions, and disasters on sea and land. "The background is indeed dark," he scowled. "Time is speeding us on, and we stand at the closing of the 6,000 years of the world's history."[8] The passage of weeks only darkened Adams' outlook. Six months later the young pastor found the prospect of things immediately to come "so tremendously awful before our eyes, that the mind almost staggers."[9] In the midst of the supposedly roaring 1920s William Booth-Clibborn, pentecostal grandson of Salvation Army founders William and Catherine Booth, judged that in the preceding decade the human race had witnessed "five different colossal calamities, the greatest each of its kind in all history." Those catastrophes included the Great War, the Russian Revolution, global plagues of Spanish flu, worldwide famines, and the earthquake in Kansu China.[10]

Though the spiritually blind imagined progress in human affairs, pentecostals perceived deeper forces at work. Students at the Rochester Bible and Missionary Training Institute in upstate New York learned for example that the present downward course of

5. See almost any issue. This one is taken from January 1, 1901, 1, logo under the title.

6. The first quotation is from *Apostolic Faith* [KS], January 1916, 1, the second is from February 1913, 8–9, both unsigned but presumably by Charles Parham, the editor.

7. *Apostolic Faith*, September 1914, 1–4.

8. L. P. Adams, in *Grace and Truth*, January 1916, 2.

9. L. P. Adams, in *Grace and Truth*, June 1916, 1.

10. William Booth-Clibborn, in *Glad Tidings* [SF], April 1927, 2–3.

history would continue, the chasm between the classes and the masses would deepen till the world burst into flame with revolution, and science would continue to create weapons accelerating the suicide of the human race.[11] For many years influential periodicals bearing the name *Midnight Cry* streamed from independent presses at both ends of the continent, Seattle and New York City. The same apocalyptic language could be heard in England, where the editor of *Confidence* announced that the pentecostal movement sought not only "[t]o bring restoration of the apostolic gifts," but also "[t]o preach the Gospel to the world as a last call of the Lord . . . To sound the midnight cry."[12]

And then there was the overwhelming sense of urgency. The very first number of the Azusa Mission's *Apostolic Faith* said it all: "Time is short."[13] "When the trumpet sounds," the mission's leader warned shortly afterward, "it will be too late to prepare."[14] Evangelist H. M. Turney in San Jose, California, judged the current revival without doubt the "last call that the world will receive before He comes."[15] One nameless zealot stirred a Memphis meeting by proclaiming, "'Jesus is coming,'" while a cohort shouted out, "'Pentecost! Pentecost! Last message! Last Message! Get under the blood! No time to lose!'"[16] In the mountains of eastern Tennessee the second issue of the *Evening Light and Church of God Evangel* trumpeted the same solemn news: "The end is near and we have no time to parley or reason with the devil."[17] When the Great War swept Europe the urgency deepened, yet the cessation of fighting in the fall of 1918 brought no let-up in saints' premonition of the nearness of the End. Just days after the signing of the Armistice the *Christian Evangel*, published by the infant Assemblies of God in Springfield, Missouri, grimly warned that the "real tug of war for the nations . . . is still to

11. R. S. Craig, in *Trust*, November 1915, 15.
12. A. A. Boddy, in *Confidence*, April 1913, 74.
13. *Apostolic Faith* [CA], September 1906, 1.
14. W. J. S. [William J. Seymour], *Apostolic Faith* [CA], January 1907, 2.
15. H. M. Turney, in *Apostolic Faith* [CA], January 1907, 1.
16. L. P. Adams, in *Present Truth*, December 1909, 7.
17. *Evening Light and Church of God Evangel*, March 15, 1910, 1, almost certainly by A. J. Tomlinson, the editor.

come. . . . The night cometh when no man can work."[18] In pentecostals' eyes even technology heralded the imminent closing of history. Writing in 1912, evangelist Florence L. Burpee suspected that steam cars and automobiles represented the "chariots" discerned by the prophet Nehemiah as he looked forward to the climax of history.[19]

With the nations stumbling toward Armageddon, it is hardly surprising that pentecostals resorted to martial rhetoric to describe their present and future relation to the outside world. A sampling of letters posted to periodical editors revealed deep-seated attitudes. "We are still on the firing line for God";[20] "This leaves us still in the battle at Seymour";[21] "All the artillery of hell was turned on us."[22] For some the crisis of the times elicited bravura: "We are flying our colors and are still in the battle."[23] Dispatches from the Glad Tidings Mission in New York City similarly declared that evangelist William H. Durham was pouring "fiery shot and shell into the ranks of the enemy, dealing death to sin and striking terror to everything that savored with compromise."[24] Others betrayed only grim determination. So it was that Hawaii missionaries "H. M. Turney and Wife" would dutifully report that they had "opened fire upon the enemy" as soon as they arrived on the island.[25] Still others took the long view. Charles Parham advertised his annual Apostolic Faith convocation in Baxter Springs, Kansas, as a "gathering of the battle scarred heroes of the cross." No wonder they were battle scarred. What the world needed, declared Parham, was men who could "wield the jawbone and smite the enemies of the cross."[26]

---

18. E. N. Bell, in *Christian Evangel*, December 14, 1918, 1.

19. Florence L. Burpee, in *Word and Work*, May 1912, 369.

20. G. F. Patton, in *Apostolic Faith* [KS], April 1925, 17.

21. J. H. Bennett, in *Christian Evangel*, May 9, 1914, 8.

22. Maria B. Woodworth-Etter, in *Acts of the Holy Ghost* (Dallas: John F. Worley Printing, 1912), 171.

23. W. E. Krise, *Apostolic Faith* [KS], February 1913, 16.

24. *Midnight Cry*, March–April 1911, 8.

25. H. M. Turney and Wife, in *Apostolic Faith* [CA], February–March 1907, 1.

26. *Apostolic Faith* [KS], August 1927, p. 3, unsigned but almost certainly by editor Charles Parham.

Not to be outdone, the 1920 annual convocation of the black United Holy Church noted that in the preceding year that body had been "victorious in every battle" – yet warned that there was "still much land to be taken, and greater victories to be won."[27] Even Quaker pentecostals took up arms, albeit verbal ones. "[T]he 'sham battle' is over, the real fight is on," wrote one.[28] Against a background of "sharp cannonading," "frequent skirmishes," and "heavy siege[s]," Quaker leader Levi Lupton described his evangelistic forays in language that would have stirred the troops on San Juan Hill.[29]

This military rhetoric undoubtedly stemmed from multiple sources. It represented the climate of the age, a time when the memory of bloody Civil War battles remained fresh enough that Presidential aspirant Teddy Roosevelt still could use *Onward Christian Soldiers* as a campaign theme song. It also represented the very real verbal and physical harassment that early pentecostals endured, even if they brought a good measure of it on themselves. And it betokened the stock vocabulary of the radical evangelical tradition as a whole. But above all it expressed saints' abiding sense of imminent worldwide cataclysm.

Finally we should note pentecostals' special fascination with the torments of hell–fire soon to come – for others. Here we must be careful. Since time immemorial Christians of all stripes had conjured up lurid visions of the fate of the lost, and pentecostals' radical evangelical parents certainly contributed their fair share to that fiery imagery. Still, most Holy Ghost writers (with several important exceptions[30]) found this line of speculation especially congenial and applied it to the unredeemed with unflinching ferocity. Many went out of their way to highlight the inevitability of eternal punishment

27. *Minutes of the 26th Annual Convocation of the United Holiness Church, 1920,* 1.

28. Lillian Thistlethwaite, in *Apostolic Faith* [KS], November 1912, 4.

29. Levi Lupton, in *New Acts*, August 9, 1906, 6.

30. Charles Parham and his immediate followers formed the main advocates of conditional immortality. Charles H. Pridgeon and his Pittsburgh Bible Institute represented a modified universalism (hell's duration is limited). Robert Mapes Anderson, *Vision of the Disinherited: The Making of American Pentecostalism* (New York: Oxford University Press, 1979), 159.

for all non-Christians (by which they really meant all non-evangelical Protestants) in their official statements of faith.[31] Some actually listed it as a doctrine equal in importance to salvation and Holy Spirit baptism.[32] More striking than the official statements, however, were the visions about hell that peppered the early periodicals' pages. One Effie Cooper's out-of-body experience proved typical. "As I looked, oh, horror of horrors, there was an ocean of fire. . . . It was so hot there was a vapor looking a little like steam, everywhere. Oh, the misery and suffering. Words utterly fail me."[33] Florence Crawford, founder of Portland's The Apostolic Faith, similarly described a vision in which she saw a "great lake of fire. O, it was awful! . . . The flames would lap up and fork over. The Lord showed me it was an everlasting lake of fire that would burn with brimstone forever."[34]

The palpable reality of hell in the pentecostal mind flowed from their distinctive ability to mix ecstasy with ideology. Simply put, visions, reinforced by Scripture, functioned as polemical weapons in themselves. Consider Effie Cooper's and Florence Crawford's visions noted above. For Cooper the dream targeted saints' harshest enemies, the mainline preachers, who told their hearers "how joyful heaven is" but never remembered to tell them "how awful hell is."[35] For Crawford the dream targeted rival evangelists who went around deluding the people with the heresy of "nohellism."[36] To be sure, Holy Spirit-filled saints poured an exceptional share of their resources into the evangelization of the lost. But damnation for the recalcitrant never moved very far from the center of their attention

31. See for example "WHAT THE MOVEMENT TEACHES," in *Apostolic Faith* [TX], October 1908, 6–7, esp. p. 7; William J. Seymour, *Doctrines and Discipline*, 54; *Showers of Blessings*, May 1915, 9.

32. See for example L. P. Adams, in *Grace and Truth*, June 1916, 3, sum of their doctrinal emphases with key Bible proof texts.

33. Effie Cooper, in *Glad Tidings* [SF], March 1928, 9.

34. Presumably by editor Florence Crawford, in *Apostolic Faith* [OR], September 1908, 4.

35. Effie Cooper, in *Glad Tidings* [SF], March 1928, 9.

36. Presumably by editor Florence Crawford, in *Apostolic Faith* [OR], September 1908, 4.

either. Historian Shirley Nelson once said that Holy Ghost believers found it "easier to cast out demons than learn to live with them."[37] So too saints found it easier to consign their real and imagined adversaries to everlasting damnation than to live with them.

Yet who should be surprised? For pentecostals anyone with a clear eye could see that the world was hurtling to its doom. Convinced that "a terrific battle" was being fought between two great powers, "the Hosts of the Almighty, and Satan and the hosts of evil,"[38] saints looked for the imminent fiery end of history with as much certainty as most folk looked for the daily rising and setting of the sun.

Hope

The rhetoric of doom, though real, frequently receded into other tones, other languages. At the end of the day, hope for the future seemed always to accompany and, more often than not, overwhelm doom. Hope made doom less frightening because it placed doom in a larger framework of providential design. More importantly hope represented more than intellectual assurance of God's governance. It intimated glorious anticipation welling up from the depths of the emotions.

To begin with, saints knew that Christ would soon reign and that they would reign with Him. It is hard to imagine a message better suited to inspire the faithful. "This is a world-wide revival, the last Pentecostal revival to bring our Jesus," proclaimed the premier issue of the Azusa Mission's *Apostolic Faith*. "The church is taking her last march to meet her beloved."[39] The pentecostal revival betokened the end of times to be sure but, as a later issue of the same periodical made clear, it also betokened the "greatest revival

---

37. Shirley Nelson, *Fair Clear and Terrible: The Story of Shiloh, Maine* (Latham, NY: British American Publishing, 1989), 429.

38. Seeley D. Kinne, in *Evening Light and Church of God Evangel*, March 15, 1910, 4.

39. *Apostolic Faith* [CA], September 1906, 4.

the world has ever had"[40] – "the greatest miracle the world has ever seen."[41] A mission in Akron, Ohio, excitedly reported that the "burden of everyone that has received their personal Pentecost is, *'Jesus is coming soon.'*"[42] The Massachusetts weekly *Word and Work* likewise proclaimed that its sole purpose was to spread the "Good News of the Soon Coming of our Lord" – not, it is worth noting, the historic Good News of salvation in Christ, but the Good News of the imminent consummation of history.[43]

The promise of the Rapture of the saints from the earth before the terrible suffering of the battle of Armageddon – a staple of fundamentalist eschatology – in particular fired believers' imagination. Over and over, letter-writers spoke of their anticipation of being caught up to "meet the Lord in the air."[44] For many the expectation that they would be literally, physically whisked off the face of the earth remained an ever-present prospect. No one captured that electric tension better than Azusa leader William J. Seymour: "The time is short when our blessed Jesus shall return to this earth, and snatch away His waiting bride."[45] Evangelist Elizabeth Sisson, a delegate to the organizing meeting of the Assemblies of God in 1914, actually left instructions at home about what should be done with her personal effects lest she be "caught up" in the Rapture while away.[46] The 1912 annual encampment of the Churches of God in Christ in Eureka Springs, Arkansas, could barely proceed because of the intensity of the anticipation among many that they were about "to be caught up to meet Jesus in the air."[47] Enthusiasts

---

40. *Apostolic Faith* [CA], October 1907, 4.

41. *Apostolic Faith* [CA], October 1907, 1.

42. Pearl Brown, posted from Akron, in *Apostolic Faith* [CA], January 1907, 1.

43. Ad for *Word and Work* in *Bridal Call*, April 1918, 2.

44. *Apostolic Faith* [CA], October 1907, 1.

45. Brother [William J.] Seymour, in *Apostolic Faith* [CA], June–September 1907, 4; see also Seymour, *Apostolic Faith* [CA], January 1907, 2; Tomlinson, *The Last Great Conflict* (New York: Garland Publishing, 1985, original 1913), 111; *Trust*, February 1915, 9; Walter Riggs, *New Acts*, January 4, 1906, 4; E. N. Bell, in *Christian Evangel*, October 19, 1918, 5.

46. *Minutes of the General Council of the Assemblies of God . . . 1917*, 20.

47. *Word and Witness*, August 20, 1912, 1.

routinely closed letters with such lines as, "Yours waiting for the wedding in the air,"[48] or "Yours in the Coming One."[49] In that context one can readily sense the exhilaration one missionary clearly felt as he exploded with the realization, "we, ourselves, shall never see the grave!"[50] Sometimes anticipation of the Rapture grew so intense that it encroached on the fantastic. One preacher looked forward to flying past the atmospheric heaven, past the starry heaven, and on into the "heaven of heavens – the place where God is."[51] What such dreams may have lacked in theological orthodoxy they gained in potency to inspire.

The early periodicals conveyed a sense of thrilling events taking place almost too fast to report, like a television newsroom on election night. Under the banner, "Italians and Indians Receive The Holy Ghost," the *Apostolic Faith* announced – one can almost hear the wire service machines clattering in the background – "reports are coming in from nearly every quarter of the globe of how the latter rain is falling."[52] In this framework social marginality, real or perceived, served less as a limitation than as a springboard for action. "However little is our band, and however ignorant and simple are we," declared Mok Lai Chi, pastor of the Apostolic Faith Mission in Hong Kong, "the Lord has been pleased to set us apart, one after another, to go forth proclaiming His soon coming."[53] At the tiny Household of God mission in Pasadena, California, the leader breathlessly told of emissaries – endowed, not incidentally, with the power to raise the dead – fanning out to take the word to Oakland, to Palestine, to India. Alas, the Lord's return, he added almost glumly,

---

48. A. W. Orwig, in *New Acts*, July–August 1907, 6.

49. Addie A. Knowlton, in *New Acts*, June 1907, 8.

50. Tom Hezmalhalch, in *Apostolic Faith* [CA], June–September 1907, p. 4. See Anderson, *Vision of the Disinherited*, 80, for numerous additional indications of pentecostal anticipation of the imminent second coming.

51. A. J. Tomlinson, in [Church of God] *General Assembly Minutes 1906–1914: Photographic Reproductions of the First Ten General Assembly Minutes* (Cleveland, TN: White Wing Publishing House, 1992), 142.

52. *Apostolic Faith* [CA], May 1908, 4.

53. Mok Lai Chi, in *Pentecostal Truths*, April 1909, 2.

would be delayed until those distant places had heard the pentecostal message.[54]

Given all that needed to be accomplished, time counted. That plain fact required rigorous husbanding of one's time in order to focus on the task at hand. Scurrying from one mission to another up and down the California coast, evangelist Frank Bartleman dashed off a note to himself: "My time is not my own. . . . 'The King's business requires haste.'"[55] So it was everywhere. Church of God Overseer A. J. Tomlinson boasted that he worked tirelessly, "at late hours of the night while the millions . . .were taking their rest." He had no choice. "An unseen impelling" had "pressed it" on him.[56] Tradition held that Tomlinson habitually ran, not walked, home for lunch in order to save time.[57] Given the ripeness of the harvest, Tomlinson knew that he "dare not falter" before the task at hand.[58] Indeed much of the asceticism for which pentecostals gained notoriety is best explained not as prudery but as an instinctive sense that conventional mores consumed precious moments better spent elsewhere. The great sin of women's cosmetics, Quaker pentecostal Levi Lupton judged, was the "wasted hours they spent in adorning themselves."[59] Soda water and chewing gum similarly drew a rebuke from the General Superintendent of the Assemblies of God, not because they were intrinsically wrong, but because they squandered God's money and wasted minutes, making a partisan a "soda fountain bum or a gum sot."[60]

How then should Holy Spirit-filled Christians spend their time? The answer seemed plain. "Thrust in now," Lupton exploded. "First and last and all the time," the true Christian must "bend to the one

54. William F. Manley, in *Household of God*, September 1906, 6–9.

55. Frank Bartleman, *Azusa Street: The Roots of Modern-day Pentecost*, ed. Vinson Synan (Plainfield, NJ: Logos International, 1980; originally titled, *How "Pentecost" Came to Los Angeles – How It Was in the Beginning*, 1925), 47.

56. Tomlinson, *Last Great Conflict*, p. viii.

57. Roger Glenn Robins, "Plainfolk Modernist: The Radical Holiness World of A. J. Tomlinson," Ph. D. diss., Duke University, 1999, 395.

58. Tomlinson, in *Evening Light and Church of God Evangel*, March 1, 1910, 1.

59. Levi Lupton, in *New Acts*, January 4, 1906, 7.

60. E. N. Bell, in *Christian Evangel*, June 29, 1918, 9.

end – the salvation of men and the hastening of the Lord's return."[61] The problem with the kind of religion that passed itself off for real Christianity in most places, charged Missouri pastor Howard Goss, was that it represented a "defeatist religion." Its message was: "'just do the best you can, and hope for the best after death."[62] Saints wanted none of that. "I am still on the war path," one convert declared more than a little breathlessly, "with the eternal glow and GO in my soul."[63] The "GO" seemed more important than the "glow." Levi Lupton spoke for most: "all of God's true people are feeling keenly the weight of each step," carried special meaning.[64] Saints were God's agents, and since God remained in charge, they had nothing to lose. As a later era would say, they could afford to go for broke. Indeed they could afford to do nothing else.

Expansion

These points bring us finally to expansion, the cluster of actual and prescribed practices that defined daily life.

Here we must be careful. When converts speculated about the grand scheme of things, where they had come from and where they were going, they seemed prone to say that the journey had been hard. Some had fallen by the wayside, many more had grown cold and lost their first love. Indeed, before the first decade was out one evangelist would grouse that he did not intend to attend any more camp meetings because the "force of the first message of this Movement [has] largely been spent, and the energies [have been] consumed in haggling and contending over the spoils of early conquest."[65] When Chicago fire-eater William Durham visited the Los Angeles missions in 1912 he felt forced to record "with grief"

---

61. Levi Lupton, in *New Acts*, December 14, 1905, 1, and in *New Acts*, June 1905, 7.

62. Howard A. Goss, *The Winds of God: The Story of the Early Pentecostal Days (1901–1914) in the Life of Howard A. Goss, As Told by Ethel E. Goss* (New York: Comet Press Books, 1958), 149.

63. Elizabeth Lee, in *New Acts*, March 8, 1906, 6.

64. Levi Lupton, in *New Acts*, July–August 1907, 6.

65. W. M. Allison, in *Apostolic Faith* [KS], December 25, 1910, 7.

that many were "departing from the first order of things."[66] Sadly, things seemed to grow worse as the years wore on. By 1918 ordinary folks were beginning to remember the "good old camp meeting times of ten years ago . . . when there were hungry souls praying through to God."[67] Soon a small cottage industry came into existence devoted to the excoriation of the "coldness and indifference among God's baptized saints."[68] Houston pastor John G. Lake even wondered whether they were about to witness the "dying of Pentecost as other lesser revelations of God have come to the world, fluttered and sputtered for a few years, and then disappeared?"[69] Looking back from the vantage point of 1927, historian Frank Bartleman growled that the movement was "like the little chicken who has dropped the worm. It is still running and the other chickens are chasing it. But the worm is gone. We have lost the vision."[70] By 1932 things seemed even worse. New York City pastor Marie Brown lamented that Holy Ghost Churches now looked little different from other Protestant churches. Typically spending only five or ten minutes at the altar, and acting as if the Holy Spirit were a "*toy* to be amused with," Brown sadly conceded that her confederates had lapsed into "Sleepy Virgin time."[71]

But the great irony of course was that none of these comments was meant to be taken literally. Seriously, yes; literally, no. All represented bugle blasts calling the troops to new triumphs. In their heart of hearts pentecostals knew that the Lord had chosen them and them alone to lead a vast movement of global spiritual conquest. No storefront meeting place seemed too small or too impoverished to send out missionaries to all parts of the continent and, soon, to all parts of the world. "[T]he blessed work is spreading so rapidly," breathlessly reported the British *Confidence*, "that I suppose there

66. William Durham, in *Pentecostal Testimony*, January 1912, 8.

67. Brother Pittman, *Pentecostal Holiness Advocate*, April 18, 1918, 13.

68. Mrs. R. G. Staple, in "Believing and Receiving or Doubting and Retreating," Christian Workers Union tract, June 1923, 1.

69. John G. Lake to Charles Parham, March 24, 1927, 3, Assemblies of God Archives, Springfield, Missouri.

70. Frank Bartleman, *Pentecost or No Pentecost*, tract, 1928, 2.

71. Mrs. Robert A. Brown, in *Glad Tidings Herald*, November 1932, 2.

are few large towns where there are not one or more Missions."[72] Within a year of the Azusa Mission's founding in Los Angeles in 1906 native language newspapers were thriving in Norway, Germany, China, Japan, Palestine, and Brazil.[73] By 1909 zealots had planted missions in at least fifty foreign countries.[74] The chapter titles of one of the earliest insider historical accounts of the movement, Stanley H. Frodsham's 1926 *"With Signs Following": The Story of the Latter-Day Pentecostal Revival,* breathlessly recounted the movement's global spread: "The First Shower of Latter Rain at Topeka, Kansas," "Early Days in Los Angeles," "The Revival Spreads Northward and Eastward," "The Pentecostal Flame in Canada," "The Pentecostal Outpouring in the British Isles," "The Work in Norway and Denmark," "A Continuous Pentecostal Revival in Sweden," "The Pentecostal Work in Holland," "Pentecost in Germany," "Revival in Russia and Other European Countries," "Showers of Latter Rain in India," "Signs Following in China and Japan," "A South African Glimpse," "A Great Pentecostal Outpouring in Central Africa," "The Beginning of a Great Work in Egypt," "The Rain Falls in South America," "God's Visitation in Venezuela."[75]

By any reasonable measure of such things, the rhetoric of global conquest vastly outstripped the reality. As early as 1901 a Harvard-trained leader of the tiny (quasi-pentecostal) Shiloh compound in Maine boasted that Shiloh stood as a great "enginery for belting the earth" with "THE TRUTH."[76] Though none of Charles Parham's students carried the pentecostal message farther than his wee Bible school on the Kansas plains, he boasted that his institution's

72. [Probably James or Ellen Hebden], in *Confidence,* July 1908, 7, Assemblies of God Archives, Mattersey Hall, UK.

73. *Apostolic Faith* [OR], July & August 1908, 1; *Apostolic Faith* [TX], October 1908, 2. More generally see Gary B. McGee, *This Gospel Shall Be Preached: A History and Theology of Assemblies of God Foreign Missions to 1959* (Springfield, MO: Gospel Publishing House, 1986), ch. 5.

74. Faupel, *Everlasting Gospel,* 15, n. 6.

75. Stanley H. Frodsham, *"With Signs Following": The Story of the Latter-Day Pentecostal Revival* (Springfield, MO: Gospel Publishing House, 1926). I omitted the titles of chs. 2, 5, 20–25.

76. N. H. Harriman, in *Everlasting Gospel,* March 31, 1901, 136.

sole purpose was to "fit men and women to go to the ends of the earth to preach."[77] Within three years of the Los Angeles revival pentecostal speakers were crowing about the way that the movement had already "circled the globe."[78] One asserted that never in history "did a revival of God fly round the world as this one has."[79] Another impetuously judged that the full gospel message had "stirred the religious world from center to circumference."[80]

This expansionist vision, global in aspiration if not in actual scope, represented more than geographical expansion. It also betokened priority of origin, size, and influence. Soon local pentecostal groups all over the country fell into the habit of describing their convocations as the first or the biggest or the best of its kind.[81] Many routinely hailed their local meetings as national or international in scope.[82] Hyperbole reigned. "Mammoth," "immense," and "mighty" became the adjectives of choice to describe everything they set out to do.[83] The Holy Spirit never moved imperceptibly or slightly but always in a "mighty outpouring"[84] or in a "cyclonic manifestation"[85] or in "mighty shocks of power."[86] A scant twenty-nine months after the first missionaries departed American shores, saints in India started laying plans for a "World's Pentecostal Conference."[87] In 1920 the

77. [Charles Fox Parham], *The Life of Charles F. Parham: Founder of the Apostolic Faith Movement*, compiled by His Wife [Sarah E. Parham] (Garland Publishing, NY: 1985, original 1930), 51.

78. *Apostolic Faith* [OR], July & August 1908, 1; William H. Piper, in *Latter Rain Evangel*, March 1909, 7.

79. *Upper Room*, June 1909, 5.

80. J. W. Welch, Introduction, to Lawrence, *Apostolic Faith Restored*, 7.

81. See for example *Apostolic Faith* [KS], January 1913, 11; L. P. Adams, in *Grace and Truth*, October 1915, 3.

82. For one of countless examples see *Weekly Evangel*, March 30, 1918, p. 8, ad for the second "WORLD WIDE MISSIONARY CONFERENCE."

83. See for example *Apostolic Faith* [KS], June 1925, 1; *Apostolic Faith* [KS], April 1928, 8; L. P. Adams, in *Present Truth*, December 1909, 1.

84. Sister [Ellen] Hebden, in *Apostolic Faith* [CA], April 1907, 1.

85. Bartleman, *Azusa Street*, 125.

86. John G. Lake, "Diary," October 1907, Assemblies of God Archives, Springfield, Missouri.

87. Max Wood Moorhead, *Cloud of Witnesses to Pentecost in India*, November, 1908, 24.

Chicago-based *Pentecostal Herald* greeted its readers with a six-inch front page headline, "WORLD'S GREATEST PENTECOSTAL CONVOCATION: A Nation Wide Union Revival Meeting: Evangelists with World-Wide Reputation will speak."[88] A tongues message given at a Quaker camp meeting in Alliance, Ohio, in 1907, affirmed (in vernacular translation) that henceforward the spiritual headquarters of the pentecostal movement would reside in Ohio, from which it would "extend to all parts of the world."[89] Visting the same camp meeting several months later, evangelist Frank Bartleman recorded that believers who had attended the holiness revivals in Wales and in India in 1904 and 1905 found the Ohio revival the "deepest of all."[90] Yet one suspects that few were impressed. They had heard it all before.

From their radical evangelical forebears pentecostals inherited and amplified a variety of techniques for sustaining this kind of frenetic global consciousness. One was prayer chains, which bade churches and foreign mission stations around the world to join in supplication for the revival's success at exactly the same time of the day.[91] The inconvenience and unreliability of electronic communication in the early twentieth century may have actually enhanced rather than minimized the sense of world solidarity by forcing partisans to rely on ideal (and therefore unlimited) linkages of prayer. Zealots also sustained global consciousness through mail networks. The *Minute Book* of the oldest pentecostal work in Britain, the Church of God in the remote village of Kilsyth, Scotland, revealed a world in itself. The record for December 28, 1908, a page taken almost at random, registered contributions posted to evangelist Levi Lupton in the United States, to missionary Mrs. Cowan in Japan, to orphanage director Pandita Ramabai in India, and to the Quarrier Homes orphanage nearby.[92]

---

88. *Pentecostal Herald*, June 1920, 1.
89. A. J. Rawson, in *New Acts*, April 1907, 3.
90. Frank Bartleman, in *New Acts*, July–August 1907, 2.
91. See for example *Christian Evangel*, November 1914, 3.
92. Church of God, Kilsyth, Scotland, *Minute Book*, December 28, 1908.

Periodicals constituted by far the most important technique for sustaining national and world consciousness. They created the impression that pentecostals were triumphing everywhere. Holy Ghost papers routinely published long lists of approved — and sometimes disapproved — evangelists, churches, camps, books, and even other periodicals.[93] The papers typically set aside a column or two, or even a page or two, for reports from pentecostal out-stations in far-away places. Typical was the first page of the January 1909 issue of Portland, Oregon's *The Apostolic Faith*, which carried announcements of the activities of fire-baptized workers and missionaries in China, Egypt, Germany, Holland, India, Ireland, New Zealand, Scotland, Sweden, Syria, and the Transvaal — along with letters from missions in various parts of the United States serving non-English speaking constituencies (such as the Finnish mission in San Jose).[94] These accounts normally highlighted the rapid progress of the work, though they occasionally admitted slow progress in the face of the "dense ignorance and superstition of the masses."[95] Correspondents' single-minded focus on the scorecard of converts won, or almost won, helped focus readers' attention on the spiritual needs of the world at large.

Expansionist fervor stemmed from several sources. One of course involved the long tradition of Christian missions, rooted in the Great Commission and other biblical injunctions to spread the Gospel. A sense of social marginality undoubtedly played a role too. Though this mood waxed and waned, in its full moon phase it tempted saints to translate perceptions of immediate misfortune into dreams of long-range fortune. The globalist momentum in pentecostals' ecstatic experiences also surfaced in testimony accounts of the baptism event. As noted, those accounts commonly indicated that the Lord had lifted new-born saints into the heavens, and from that vantage point they could survey the terrible lostness of the heathen

---

93. See for example *Confidence*, July 1908, p. 7; *Apostolic Faith* [TX], October 1908, 5.

94. See for example monthly column on "PENTECOST OVER THE GLOBE," in *Apostolic Faith* [OR] January 1909, 1.

95. Edith E. Baugh and B. C. Lu from India in *Trust*, June–July 1915, 25.

world. Above all the sense of inevitable global triumph emerged from the feeling of chosenness, the sense that the Holy Spirit had elected to reside within – not metaphorically, but literally, physically within – the believer's human body. When respected pentecostal leaders on both sides of the Atlantic could, without a trace of irony, describe their compatriots as sparkling "diamonds" in the Lord's crown,[96] or as stalwarts who had "gone through the furnace of affliction and come out pure gold,"[97] or as the "elite of the Universe,"[98] or simply as "hand-picked fruit,"[99] outsiders surely knew it was time to seek cover. In one sense pentecostals proved as parochial as the next person, for the world they visualized in experiences of this sort was a world of their own construction. But the more important point is that they soared beyond their immediate self-interests to embrace peoples and cultures not their own. And who should be surprised? Was not the earth theirs for the taking? Whatever else the pentecostal message meant, it meant Good News – wanted or not – for the rest of humankind. Memphis, Tennessee, pastor L. P. Adams captured the joyousness of these prospects with brilliant succinctness. Like many perfectionist Christians before him, Adams felt certain that Scripture proved "our intimate and absolute union with . . . Christ." Unlike most perfectionist Christians, however, he felt equally certain that the cash value of that intimate and absolute union was that "we shall be like Him," not some time in the future, "but here, and now, as He is, so are we in this world."[100]

It remains a truism that all social movements change over time, but sectarians who take their identity from their angularity with the surrounding culture typically change more slowly than the surrounding culture. They find new ways to keep on doing the same old (angular) things.[101] This pattern of cultural persistence in

96. Mrs. J[ulia?] W. Hutchins, in *Apostolic Faith* [KS], September 1905, 1.

97. *Apostolic Faith* [OR], January 1909, 2.

98. T. M. Jeffreys, in *Confidence*, quoted in *Upper Room*, July 1910, 8.

99. *Latter Rain Evangel*, October 1908, 9.

100. L. P. Adams, in *Grace and Truth*, June 1916, 2.

101. See for example Herbert G. Gutman, *Work, Culture, and Society in Industrializing America* (New York: Vintage Books/Random House, 1977, original 1966), 15–19.

the face of social modernization proved true of pentecostals as they enveloped the globe after World War II. It would require another paper – a book, really – to document and nuance the tenacity of the models of belief and behavior described in this essay, especially in non-Western contexts. But test borings into *Charisma & Christian Life*, by far the largest-circulation pentecostal-charismatic periodical of the 1990s, suggest that the underlying forms continue to thrive.[102] Students of the recent global expansion of pentecostalism, such as theologian Harvey Cox, historian Mark Hutchinson, and sociologists David and Bernice Martin, say much the same.[103] At the end of the century, as at the beginning, pentecostals see themselves soaring free, envisioning a future as vast in scope as it is glorious in complexity. Not since Mormon visionary Joseph Smith received a revelation of the essential God-likeness of redeemed human nature had a body of Christians been so confident of their calling and so aggressive about putting it to work.

102. The themes discussed in this essay – doom, hope, expansionism – come to light in virtually any issue of *Charisma & Christian Life*, in the articles, in the slant given to news items and, above all, in the advertisements for books, schools, institutes, and upcoming conferences. Terms like "power team," "victory explosion," "spiritual warfare," "revival fire," "countdown to the 21st century" abound. Especially apropos in the present context are the surveys, country by country, of the progress of the pentecostal movement in the annual January "HOLY SPIRIT AROUND THE WORLD" issue. *Charisma & Christian Life* claims a monthly international readership of 600,000.

103. Harvey Cox, *Fire from Heaven: The Rise of Pentecostalism and the Reshaping of Religion in the Twenty-first Century* (Reading, MA: Addison Wesley Publishing, 1990); David Martin, *Tongues of Fire: The Explosion of Protestantism in Latin America* (Cambridge, MA: Basil Blackwell, Inc., 1990); Mark Hutchinson and Ogbu Kalu, eds., *A Global Faith: Essays on Evangelicalism and Globalization* (Sydney: Center for the Study of Australian Christianity, 1998); Douglas Petersen, *Not by Might nor by Power: A Pentecostal Theology of Social Concern in Latin America* (Oxford: Regnum, 1996); David and Bernice Martin, *Betterment from on High: The Life Worlds of Evangelical Believers in Chile and Brazil* (forthcoming).

Comment on Part One: Visions of the Future and Visions of the Self: God, the Individual, and Subjectivity in Utopian Theology[1]

David L. Ellis

Professors Hutchison, Roeber, and Wacker have presented us with fascinating accounts of very different religious groups. Despite their considerable differences, what strikes me about these groups are certain similarities in their views on transforming themselves and the world around them – whether one calls such views utopian, millenarian, progressive, or Americanist. I would like to discuss five points which highlight characteristics common to these otherwise radically different groups: an emphasis on this-worldly achievement, a high degree of tolerance, the difficulty of social reproduction, the importance of "bad" examples, and what we can learn about modern subjectivity as expressed in these groups. Finally, I would like to offer some important categories, or rather questions, to keep in mind when dealing with the notion of utopia, a topic which defies simple definition.

First, although each of the religious groups discussed evinced utopian elements, their utopias were rather tightly bound to this-worldly concerns. In the case of the "Americanists" Professor Hutchison treats, the explanation for this is relatively straightforward. Americanism *qua* Americanism was remarkable for its "optimism and activism,"[2] for its attempt to realize the Kingdom of God here and now, or at least here and very soon. One may well wonder where Catholics, Jews, and Protestants had suddenly got the confidence to challenge centuries of their more contemplative faith

---

1. The references to the papers of this session will be by name of author and page number.
2. Hutchison, p. 49.

traditions, but the defining characteristic of the American spirit was, as Emerson observed, the "fertility of projects for the salvation of the world!"[3] In this light, we can understand why the Jewish pastor Max Lilienthal perceived the Founding Fathers as "deliverers" who had led Jews into the "Zion" of the United States,[4] and Archbishop John Ireland of St. Paul (much like some of his Protestant counter-parts) demanded that "the Church must herself be new, adapting herself in manner of life in method of action to the conditions of the new order." The case of the other groups, however, is far more problematic. Many of the newly immigrated pious that Professor Roeber examines came from pietistic or free church traditions with a strong emphasis on inferiority, self-examination, and reflection. For some, especially those of Lutheran, Reformed, and Moravian background, the Protestant tendency toward an "individualist stance"[5] loosed from the tradition of the Church Fathers led them into generally inward utopias.[6] But even so, other German Lutherans, Reformed Dutch, and Methodists clearly "evinced ... the theme of inner assurance seeking perfection that manifested itself in comparatively modest socio-economic improvements." In other words, faith traditions whose roots lay in the Protestant claim of "salvation through faith alone"[7] sought evidence or perhaps the outworking of that salvation in the fruits of good works. Faith traditions whose genesis lay in the individual's immediate experience of God looked first for proof and perhaps increasingly for sustenance to the individual's accomplishments and contributions to social reforms in campaigns to limit the consumption of alcohol, to improve asylums and orphanages, and to underpin the self-respect of northern black congregations.[8] Meanwhile, the pentecostal and

---

3. Cited in Hutchison, p. 49.
4. See Hutchison, p. 56, p. 53, p. 62.
5. Roeber, p. 28 and p. 29.
6. See Roeber, pp. 27–28 and p. 29.
7. Roeber, p. 37 and p. 27.
8. Roeber, p. 37. "Yet, well into the nineteenth century, many among North America's Methodist communities shared with Moravians and many Lutheran pietists, a distinct aversion to overt political activity as the forum within which to realize their religious convictions" (pp. 37–38).

charismatic "Holy Ghost folk" Professor Wacker analyses were not interested in an Americanist "evolutionistic optimism of world-betterment"[9] for the simple reason that they expected Jesus to return at any moment. Schemes of gradual social improvement have little appeal for those who anticipate the immediate consummation of world history. The Holy Ghost folk concentrated on activities of a mostly interior spiritual nature, such as their personal conversion, divine healing, speaking in tongues, and consideration of Jesus' return.[10] Yet, they also entered into a "frenzy of expansionist activity," eagerly seeking new converts across the globe.[11] Professor Wacker underlines the paradox their activity represented when he observes that "in principle of course it should not have been so, for the Bible pictured the end times drama unfolding outside history, independent of human wishes or cooperation."[12] In other words, for both Professor Wacker and Professor Roeber's subjects, although their theology and tradition stressed the inward experience of the divine, their actions reveal people impelled to contribute to the realization of their utopia in the external world.

Second, although each of the groups discussed appeared certain that it possessed not only correct but also more accurate insights into God's plan and divine truth, they still displayed in practice a high degree of tolerance. Many factors help to explain that tolerance, including the fact that many of these groups had had themselves been relatively recent victims of marginalization in Europe. However, we might also speculate that their tolerance was in part related to the way these groups imagined their utopias and their fulfillment. Their utopias involved a certain ideal which could be worked toward but not realized in one's lifetime (in the case of the Americanists), or the subjective, often highly emotionally charged experience of the divine (in the case of Wacker's and many of Roeber's subjects). Both instances represent a movement somewhat away from the more

9. Emil Brunner's description of "'religious Americanism,'" cited in Hutchison, p. 49.

10. Wacker, p. 71.

11. Wacker, p. 71.

12. Wacker, p. 71.

certain (and staid) world of traditional religious institutions, dogma, and doctrines, and toward less well-charted and more subjective religious territory. At the risk of reading too much into the papers, we may say that most of the groups depended on modern, autonomous, reasoning and experiencing selves to accept or not accept received religious truths and traditions. What in previous generations may have been accepted on *authority* now had to be *scrutinized* and/or *experienced* before being fully approved. Such innovations consciously or unconsciously added to the importance of human effort and subjectivity. There were, then, few well-worn paths on this comparatively unexplored religious frontier. That must have made the participants' journey all the more exciting and fresh (as even a cursory look at their rhetoric reveals). But it must have also made it more difficult to discern when others were heading off in a "wrong" direction, adding to the impetus for tolerance but also detracting from the experience of unity. Given this relative lessening of the role of doctrine and discipline, it is little surprise that those groups which had hierarchical religious structures to fall back on (such as the Catholics) did better at staying together, at least externally. Those with less hierarchical structures, notably the free church Protestants, saw a flowering of new denominations. Yet, even those splits were, in comparison with past religious divides, relatively peaceful. And, in support of the first observation, such splits often involved issues, such as slavery and alcohol, more closely related to the practice or application of religion than to issues, such as salvation, which Protestants had traditionally regarded as their doctrinal core.

As we have seen, as doctrine, dogma, and discipline lost some of their relative power to motivate and unify each group, the projection of the group's ideals or their interior experience rose in importance. This change in style (and perhaps in substance) meant that the groups also had to alter their means of social reproduction, of passing on their essence to converts and to the next generation. One might have expected the Americanists to have done better than their somewhat more inwardly focused competitors. To mention only two advantages, their optimistic, hands-on approach was in tune with popular culture, and they also captured commanding positions in many mainline seminaries. And yet, over time, pentecostals, charismatics, and Professor Roeber's diverse subjects generally had more success in attracting new followers and keeping old ones. Past scholarship has often focussed on social, cultural, economic, and political explanations for this trend. The twentieth century has presented many challenges to the Americanists' utopian optimism, including the Great Depression, fascism, communism, two world wars, numerous instances of genocide, the Cold War, and the complacency of postwar prosperity. In addition, the American "character" which Americanists were supposedly in harmony with may have fundamentally changed. Some of the non-Americanist groups, however, seem to have thrived in spite of these and other, earlier challenges. The descendants of many of Professor Roeber's immigrants became less marginalized as they learned English and/ or moved from small, tightly knit communities to be eventually tolerated and absorbed in an Anglo-dominated, increasingly urban mainstream. Professor Roeber himself points to an interesting link in the 1700s between "a deepening commercial-consumer society" and "a Protestant faith whose adherents pointed to 'a free, reasoning self in adjudicating competing claims to authority.'"[13] Professor Wacker notes that pentecostals and charismatics proved particularly adept at using and improving old techniques, such as the newsletter, to propagate and unite their faith.[14] The twentieth-century calamities that beset Americanism only helped fuel the fervor, drama, and sense of urgency felt by Holy Ghost folk.[15] All three papers, however, rightly focus primarily on how the *theology* of these groups motivated their adherents. This space is too short to accommodate a satisfactory discussion of the diverse theologies of the dozen or so groups the presenters have anyway so expertly handled. It may therefore be more profitable to focus instead on the importance of bad examples to both the theologies and social reproduction of these groups, and to discuss what we might conclude about the relationship between the groups and expressions of modern subjectivity.

13. Roeber, p. 42.
14. Wacker, p. 83.
15. See Wacker, pp. 71–76.

Despite their general tolerance, most of these groups made extensive use of the bad examples of others. There are at least three reasons that help to explain why bad examples were so important. First, bad examples famously serve as a means to negative integration. Second, pointing out what you oppose is a quicker and initially easier way to establish group unity and identity than communicating to others the unique personal experiences of the divine (in the case of the Holy Ghost folk and Professor Roeber's Protestants). Third, the use of bad examples reinforced a sort of social gospel mentality wherever it established itself, notably among the Americanists.

It is worth noting that the bad examples the groups chose were usually *not* their old religious or denominational foes. Instead of bashing Jews or baiting Catholics or the like (though doubtless some of that continued), the groups profiled themselves against four main evils. Some of the groups, but particularly and paradoxically the antinomian elements in Professor Roeber's study, focused on specific sinful practices, such as alcoholism, or the "world" in general. All of the groups also identified large portions of their denomination's own religious past as archaic. Many antinomian strains of Protestantism, pentecostals, and charismatics tended to view contemplative traditions and doctrine negatively if they seemed to hinder direct contact with God. Americanists tended to view negatively contemplative traditions, dogma, and doctrine if these stood in the way of a dynamic response to the present. The citations in Professor Hutchison's paper also reveal that Americanists rhetorically portrayed Europe and Israel as the embodiment of ossified religious life. Finally, most of the groups also warned against bad examples within their own ranks, foes who were all the harder to identify once the doctrine and dogma declined in relative importance. Professor Wacker explains that such efforts among Holy Ghost folk often "represented bugle blasts calling the troops to new triumphs."[16] The cost of condemning these four sorts of bad examples was to leave the groups who crafted the rhetoric not only isolated but self-isolated, cut off from important parts of their own traditions and alienated from the world around

16. Wacker, pp. 73–74.

them. And because of the specific nature of their visions of the future,[17] that left these groups partly dependent for the realization of their utopias not only on the efforts of their hands in reform efforts and/or evangelization, but also on the efforts of their minds to imagine in the first place utopias which needed their efforts for completion. Members of such groups were isolated, internally marginalized, and dependent on their own subjectivity: in a word, modern.

What, then, can we learn about the nature of modern subjectivity found in such diverse groups? First, that this subjectivity reflected remarkable confidence, for many of those who crafted these utopias that needed or were fundamentally influenced by their own efforts were often boldly stepping away from their traditions. That left more conservative elements condemning Reform Judaism, for instance, as "*manqué* Judaism."[18] Similarly we have seen that pentecostals, charismatics, and some antinomian Protestants had a way of reintroducing the importance of their efforts despite their own theology's tendency to downplay the importance of human agency in fulfilling a divine plan. Second, that subjectivity, as practiced by antinomian Protestants and Holy Ghost folk, could simultaneously create discontinuities and preserve or create compensating continuities. We have seen that most of these groups were alienated from parts of their own faith traditions, hierarchies, and institutions. However, their subjective and individual experience of the divine gave them continuity with God and the more subjective, emotional parts of their own selves. One might even argue that this tension has been present in Judaism and Christianity since their inceptions. Their scriptures, after all, contain both prophetic traditions which reveal that God has a divine plan He allows to unfold continuously in history and yet also stories of miracles and other interventions which show God actively inserting Himself in the affairs of individual humans and humanity. Third, the subjectivity of those in

17. This does not apply to those of Prof. Roeber's groups which continued to regard the contemplative traditions, doctrines, and dogmas with their old importance.

18. Hutchison, p. 59.

these groups allowed them to compartmentalize their lives. Some of the people discussed in the papers had glimpses of imagined futures, but apparently easily went back to everyday life and set about achieving practical tasks or reforms. The pentecostals and charismatics, for instance, were quite able to speak in tongues or prophesy at one moment and organize such mundane activities as performing their workaday jobs or distributing newsletters the next. That leads to a fourth observation, that such subjectivity must have made liberal use of paradox, allowing those who practiced it to balance both an all-encompassing worldview more typical of the premodern world with acceptance of modern, fragmented, compartmentalized life. Fifth, this sort of subjectivity also helped to maintain a tension between chronological and diachronic perceptions of time. Those outside these groups might perceive the passage of time differently, but members of these groups could simultaneously follow events either in this-worldly or in other-worldly time. The fact that some around them did not see either the gradual or imminent fulfillment of a utopia appears not to have shaken their faith one bit.

Finally, sharp readers will have observed that neither this paper nor those it examines contained a definition of utopia. Rather than defining the concept of utopia in so general a way as to apply to all the topics treated at this conference, it may be more helpful to offer several specific questions that may be of use in considering widely varying visions of the future.

1 Do believers consider their utopia as something real, to be achieved in this world, or as something ideal, which may be fulfilled in the next world (if at all)?
2 Where is the utopia found? Will it prevail universally, or only among a chosen few? Is it inclusive, or exclusive? Will it be comprised of an imagined or an actual community?
3 If the utopia will actually be achieved, how will it be so? Will it come about through evolutionary or revolutionary change?
4 Who are the actors who will achieve the utopia? Will God, material forces, history, *Geist*, or humans be the prime means to

attaining the utopia? Must individuals consciously and voluntarily strive for its completion?

5 Does the utopia reflect primarily premodern, modern, or post-modern elements? How unified is the worldview?

6 Do those who strive for the utopia tend to practice political religion, religious politics, or something else?

7 Is the utopia gendered?

8 How is the fervor for or vision of the utopia transmitted or socially reproduced?

9 Is the utopia primarily positive, with a fairly detailed program, or is it negative, with a fairly detailed list of bad examples that will be avoided?

Comment on Part One: The Failure and Success of Millenarianism in American Religious Culture

Aaron Fogleman

Since the early colonial period America has been a place where immigrants and American-born religious peoples have sought refuge, holiness, and a chance to build God's community the way they knew it was meant to be built, often with hopeful, millennial visions of the future. Focussing on the "migrating pious" of the early period, A. G. Roeber rightly points out that there were many failures in early America by those who would seek a better future, including the Salzburg Lutheran settlement at Ebenezer, Georgia, the German mystic cloister at Ephrata, Pennsylvania, the Moravians and their Native American mission, and others who failed in their quests to build and maintain godly communities. Many other pietists who were less communally oriented, like the Halle pietists in the mid-Atlantic colonies, as well as other Lutheran and German Reformed leaders in the late eighteenth century and the Methodists, never established successful utopian, millennial goals for America. Roeber raises the question whether antinomian pietist movements could or did lead to significant, successful millennial or futuristic visions, and his answer is that they did not. The migrating pious were unable to affirm the godliness of the New World and became more concerned with the past than the future. A primitive, backward-looking mentality emerged in these groups, instead of a futuristic, millennial one, as the pietists emphasized individual access to God instead of the fate of the community. (Indeed, individualism and "benevolence" are a part of Roeber's property-oriented interpretation of revival, awakening, and pietism in early America.[1]) Thus

---

1. See A. G. Roeber, "Germans, Property, and the First Great Awakening: Rehearsal for a Revolution?" in Winfried Herget and Karl Ortseifen, eds., *The*

visions of a future kingdom receded within the seekers, whose restless migrations have marked American religious history.

In response to Roeber I will incorporate pietist movements, visions of the future, and other aspects of American culture in later periods, some of which were discussed by Grant Wacker and William Hutchison, and argue two points. First, while there have been many failures to realize millennial dreams by pietists in America (some more antinomian than others), what is perhaps more important to American religious culture is not that they failed, but that so many kept trying and many experienced at least some success before failing. Second, it remains important when studying American religious culture to link the migrating and pious and others to futurism and millennialism. Evangelical pietism, which I understand in a broad, transatlantic sense to include Germans and non-Germans, as well as radical communitarian spiritualists and "mainstream" church reformers who tried to make both the individual and society more godly, has indeed been connected to futurism and millennialism of some sort throughout much of American history.[2] The emphasis on individual access to God and a pessimistic view of the future of worldly society which Roeber points out is significant, but primitivism and withdrawal does not characterize all of these groups, and millennialism, especially premillennialism, remained important to many. In the end evangelical pietism, including the radical antinomian variety, was connected to futurism and millennialism even though a comprehensive reform of society never took place. Further, most pietist movements remained activist and engaged in society instead of withdrawn and disconnected.

In the colonial era there were many other failures in addition to those mentioned by Roeber. These include well known cases like the Puritan "City on a Hill," which finally declined, and the Holy

---

Transit of Civilization from Europe to America: Essays in Honor of Hans Galinsky (Tübingen, 1986), 165-184, and A. G. Roeber, *Palatines, Liberty, and Property: German Lutherans in Colonial British America* (Baltimore, MD, and London, 1993).

2. Definitions of pietism and evangelicalism vary. I prefer a broad, transatlantic perspective like that promoted by C. R. Ward, *The Protestant Evangelical Awakening* (Cambridge, 1992).

Experiment, which didn't remain holy for very long. Then there were the small-scale attempts, like the small group of Puritan farmers who tried to build a covenanted utopian community at Dedham, Massachusetts, in the 1630s, or the premillennialist vision of Johannes Kelpius of Transylvania, who led a group of Germans to pristine Pennsylvania in 1694 in order to avoid God's imminent judgement. Kelpius' Rosecrucians built a tabernacle in the wilderness outside of Germantown and placed a telescope on its roof to observe the heavens raining down destruction on wicked Europe, and they also hoped to observe the Second Coming itself. Kelpius' community failed and its members dispersed, largely because Jesus and the Tribulation didn't come in 1700 as they were supposed to. Kelpius' vision did not last too long, but the community at Dedham retained its covenant and followed at least some of its points for decades.[3] Further, two communities Roeber does discuss, namely the Salzburger refugee community at Ebenezer and the Ephrata cloister, lasted for decades as well, before losing their special, communal character.[4] And, in addition to their Native American mission, which was the most successful of the century in the British colonies before it finally failed, the Moravians (the quintessential hopeful optimists of the period) made a major attempt to recapture Christian unity in the land where diversity, schism, and conflict seemed most prominent – Pennsylvania during the Great Awakening. Ignoring traditional boundaries of gender, as well as local and confessional church authority, the Moravians first tried to align the numerous

---

3. On Dedham see Kenneth A. Lockridge, *A New England Town: The First Hundred Years: Dedham, Massachusetts, 1636–1736* (New York, 1970). On Kelpius see Elizabeth W. Fisher, "'Prophesies and Revelations': German Cabbalists in Early Pennsylvania," *Pennsylvania Magazine of History and Biography* 109 (1985), 299–333; Klaus Deppermann, "Pennsylvanien als Asyl des frühen deutschen Pietismus," *Pietismus und Neuzeit*, 10 (1982), 190–212; Julius F. Sachse, *The German Pietists of Provincial Pennsylvania* (Philadelphia, PA 1895).

4. On Ebenezer see Renate Wilson, "Halle Pietism in Colonial Georgia," *Lutheran Quarterly* 12 (1998), 271–301, and Renate Wilson, "Public Works and Piety in Ebenezer: The Missing Salzburg Diaries of 1744–1745," *Georgia Historical Quarterly* 77 (1993), 336-366. On Ephrata see E. G. Alderfer, *The Ephrata Commune: An Early American Counterculture* (Pittsburgh, PA, 1985).

radical and other religious groups in Pennsylvania into a coherent, functioning organization. When that failed they sent out a hundred men and women preachers to the tens of thousands of German-speaking and other settlers (and sometimes slaves), first in Georgia and then in the mid-Atlantic colonies. The Moravians claimed many early successes, especially among the Lutherans and German Reformed, but their optimistic, ecumenical, mystic-spiritualist message, which included beliefs that Jesus and the Holy Ghost were female, women could preach, and married believers received a blessing while having sex, awakened the fears of European authorities and local religious leaders in the colonies, especially when this strange, ecumenical challenge to confessional boundaries appeared to be gaining many followers. European authorities sent pastors and polemics to America to counter this Moravian threat, and many American settlers responded. After a violent campaign lasting for years in the mid-Atlantic colonies, other Germans defeated the Moravian vision for America.[5] All these cases and more reflect hopeful pietist visions of migrants leaving persecution and/or a world gone wrong in order to find a better world and a better future in America. And they all ultimately failed.

But failure is not always as negative as it might at first appear: Religious experiments almost always fail eventually. What is important is that so many groups tried and experienced some success. Indeed by the mid-eighteenth century America had established a reputation among many in central Europe as a place where immigrants could go and find large quantities of land (after it was taken from the people who already lived there), as well as

5. On Moravian involvement in the Pennsylvania ecumenical synods of 1742 see Peter Vogt, "Zinzendorf und die Pennsylvanischen Synoden 1742," *Unitas Fratrum: Zeitschrift für Geschichte und Gegenwartsfragen* 36 (1994), 5–62; Charles H. Glatfelter, *Pastors and People: German Lutheran and Reformed Churches in the Pennsylvania Field, 1717–1793*, vol. 1: *The History* (Breinigsville, PA, 1981), 68–81; John J. Stoudt, "Count Zinzendorf and the Pennsylvania Congregation of God in the Spirit: The First American Oecumenical Movement," *Church History* 9 (1940), 366–380. On Moravian preaching efforts and the religious conflict that followed see Aaron Spencer Fogleman, *Jesus Is Female: The Moravian Challenge in the German Communities of British North America*, forthcoming.

"freedoms" and a weak (if any) state and established church. Many came to see America as a special place, which they contrasted with old, decadent Europe – a place where a more godly society perhaps could be built. It was also clear by the late colonial era that an activist, enthusiastic, experiential style of religion could not only exist but flourish in the colonies, which was not always the case in Europe. In other words, the attempts of the migrating pious to affirm the godliness of the New World helped shape the religious culture that did develop there, and the link to millennialism and futurism was alive and well among the pious in eighteenth-century America, in spite of the failures.

Millennialism and futurism soared in the nineteenth century among evangelical pietists. Energizing this movement were not issues of property and benevolence but rather a burning desire of individuals to get right with their God and reform themselves, their community, and their country before it was too late – or to hasten the Second Coming. After 1815 it became clear to many that both the republic and evangelical religion had a bright future in America as a wave of postmillennial perfectionism and enthusiasm affected both. Revivalism was increasing, Methodists, Baptists, and others finally succeeded in converting almost all of the slaves (which the missionaries saw as a positive development, though the results for the slaves themselves were mixed), anti-slavery societies emerged (early on in both the North and the South), and the pagan Indians were driven past the Mississippi, since few really wanted to Christianize them anyway and most Native Americans themselves were hardly interested. Also, Roman Catholic empires and colonies were falling in the West. Many more utopian, millenarian movements like first the Rappites and then the Owenites at New Harmony began (and failed), and some, like the premillennial Millerites, achieved enormous success until faced with the same perplexing problem that Johannes Kelpius had faced a century and a half earlier, namely that Jesus did not come when he was supposed to. Others, like the Mormons, struggled early before achieving astounding success. Hopeful millennialism permeated the dynamic new African-American Christian culture – in some ways perhaps the most "antinomian" of all – as Christian slaves often associated their own emancipation with the Second Coming and hoped both would happen soon. Indeed, immediately after the Civil War, African-Americans may have been the most optimistic evangelical Christians in America, as they achieved at least part of their long awaited millennial religious goals.

An enthusiastic, activist, millenarian religious style permeated American culture in the late nineteenth century as well, as the horrors of the Civil War faded. For the first time the American religious landscape became not a curiosity or an opportunity for Europeans but a threat, at least to some Catholic, Protestant, and Jewish leaders, as William Hutchison has shown. (Hutchinson persuasively connects these developments to the rise of the United States as a world power.) While it is clear that atheism and agnosticism began to gain legitimacy in America in the late nineteenth century[6] and that there were many other grounds for pessimism, Grant Wacker shows how backward-looking "primitivism," "antinomianism," emotionalism, and an emphasis on individual conversion in the Pentecostal movement were indeed connected to futurism, millennialism, and *hope*. Members of this movement, one of the fastest growing in America at the time, certainly had a pessimistic view of the state of society and where things were headed, but their belief in Christian hope and activism kept them from withdrawing. This brings us back to Roeber's question about whether antinomian pietist movements could or did lead to significant, successful millennial or futuristic visions. Perhaps the answer is that they could and sometimes did, rather than that they did not. In fact, I would extend Wacker's analysis to include the Dispensationalists as well.[7] Together these hopeful fundamentalists – the one antinomian and the other strictly Scripturalist – did their maths and deduced that the end was coming soon, but knew that someone else (not them) was going to have to face the Tribulation,

6. See James Turner, *Without God, Without Creed: The Origins of Unbelief in America* (Baltimore, MD, 1985).

7. On the Dispensationalists and other Scripturalist aspects of the Fundamentalist movement see George M. Marsden, *Fundamentalism and American Culture: The Shaping of Twentieth-Century Evangelicalism, 1870–1925* (New York and Oxford, 1980).

Antichrist, and the Lake of Fire. Anyone who got right with God would be safe. Then and now these premillennial fundamentalists continued earlier traditions and lamented the decline of society, yet maintained a vibrant futuristic world view which was (is), indeed, the "hope" of all true believers. To them the Apocalypse meant a transition to new beginnings (this was part of the "Good News") rather than a gloomy end. Moreover, this emphasis on individual salvation and access to God did not lead to failure and withdrawal, but rather enthusiastic proselytizing – spreading the Good News of the believer's hope, as well as doing something about the evils of the world. Indeed, they probably would have done more if they could have gained more political power.

In the late twentieth century American religious movements and ways have affected Europe more than European religious culture has affected America – a marked contrast from the early period. (Perhaps Hutchinson has documented the beginnings of this shift.) Enthusiastic, activist, sometimes millennialist movements like the Mormons, Baptists, Pentecostals, Scientologists, and others have made deep inroads and threatened traditional religious culture in central Europe and elsewhere. This parallels the rise of other American cultural influences in Europe, and it is difficult to say what this trend might lead to.

Rather than minimalizing the impact of the "migrating pious" in the colonial era because of their failure to find or build perfection in America, I would argue that the early immigrants and their failures established a hopeful, millenarian, activist religious style which has continually shaped and reshaped American religious culture from the seventeenth to the twentieth century. Futurism has been a strong trend among the pious in America, even as they tried and failed to achieve perfection themselves or predict when Christ would come and do the job for them. Perhaps Roeber is right to emphasize that the migrating pious of the early period failed to perfect a godly society in America and thus turned to individual access toward God, but millennialism – ultimately premillennialism for the most part – remained, as did the loud public message of those premillennialists to get as many individuals as possible right with God before it was too late and to remove what evils they could in a diverse, pluralistic society which insisted on a formal separation between church and state. This activist style has sometimes impressed European religious leaders and sometimes threatened them, but it has almost always interested them. Since the colonial era they have admired American religious enthusiasm and growth, but ultimately feared its consequences.

Part 2
Visions of the
New World Order

1

The US Quest for a Global Pax Americana: Myths and Realities

Paul T. Burlin

> The New England Puritans were certain that a broken
> covenant would not go unpunished. . . . But is it not
> possible that our punishment for breaking the covenant
> is to be the most developed, progressive and modern
> society in the world?[1]
>
> Robert N. Bellah

Robert N. Bellah's statement, although written several decades ago, remains an excellent starting point for a historical discussion of issues related to national identity and designs for world order, premised as it is on the perception of a continuous pattern of belief which runs from early American history to the present. The ironic twist which throws into question the state and nature of contemporary American society virtually compels a re-examination of some basic American values and beliefs. The symbolism inherent in the ending of a century and a millennium simply makes such a re-examination all the more timely.

What follows is a brief discussion; first, of the American belief in the nation's exceptional status, and second, of the history of that belief in buttressing and rationalizing American involvement with the external world. Then the contrasting interpretations of two of the most important American diplomatic historians, George F. Kennan and William Appleman Williams, are brought to bear on the subject. Finally, as both of the historians are scathing critics of American culture and society and call for changes in how the nation

---

1. Robert N. Bellah, *The Broken Covenant: American Civil Religion in Time of Trial* (2nd. ed., Chicago, IL, 1992), 143.

conducts its affairs at home and abroad, the concluding section of the essay makes some tentative suggestions in that regard. Specifically, it argues that American culture could benefit from a heavy infusion of a sense of the tragic and an awareness of the inherent limits of human existence, sentiments articulated eloquently by some Latin Americans. It is suggested that such sentiments might well serve to counter the unhealthy belief in life without limits, a belief that ultimately extends to empire.

It should also be noted at the outset, in order to preclude misunderstanding, that the call for a relative shift of American attention and resources away from external matters and toward domestic affairs, is not a plea for "isolationism." Isolationism is an ambiguous term at best, and unfortunately it has been appropriated in the United States by the foreign policy elite in such a manner and to such an extent that any proposal for retrenchment, no matter how minuscule, is labelled "isolationist" and images of Chamberlain and Munich are brought to bear, immediately precluding further discussion.[2] Needless to say, this has not helped to foster a wide-ranging debate as to the appropriate role for the United States to play in the world in the future. It is hoped that, in some small way, what follows below might help stimulate such a debate.

In a relatively short time the curtain will come down on what has often been referred to as the "American Century." Perhaps first coined by Senator Albert Beveridge, as vociferous and unabashed an imperialist as one can find in all of American history, the adage of the "American Century" has become synonymous with America as the architect of world order. As Beveridge wrote almost one hundred years ago:

> The most promising sign of the times at the dawn of the twentieth century is American advance. This is to be the American century. American influence will dominate the world. The American People will

---

2. It should also be noted that the argument of this essay if not explicitly, then certainly by implication, is diametrically opposed to American "unilateralism," another meaning sometimes associated with the term "isolationism." Retrenchment and multilateralism are not incompatible. The first might well take the form of the second.

be the most powerful force throughout the entire period of which the twentieth century is the beginning . . . American supremacy on land and sea is by far the most promising sign of the times. This circumstance is as much a blessing for the world as it is for us.[3]

Whether or not Beveridge originally coined the phrase, its most renowned iteration came in early 1941 through the pen of Henry Luce, the son of American missionaries to China and the influential founder of one of the most powerful media empires ever constructed, at least to that point in time. Luce was chagrined that "isolationist" sentiment might well continue to inhibit the exercise of American power in the world just as it had throttled the efforts of Woodrow Wilson at the end of the previous European conflagration. Impatient for the United States to assume its rightful place as the first among nations, Luce argued that the American system of democracy and free enterprise could only continue to exist if it were expanded throughout the world. The country needed to seize the opportunity, enter the war in a fully conscious and committed fashion, and then proceed to structure the postwar world to its own liking. As Luce put it, Americans needed: "to accept wholeheartedly our duty and our opportunity as the most powerful and vital nation in the world and in consequence to exert upon the world the full impact of our influence, *for such purposes as we see fit and by such means as we see fit.*"[4] It was, of course, axiomatic to Luce, as it had been with Beveridge, that what was good for the United States was also necessarily good for the world as a whole. Although he died in 1927, Beveridge's imperial spirit very much haunted Luce's editorial.[5]

3. Albert Beveridge to Henry Hall, January 8, 1901, Beveridge Papers, Container # 130, Library of Congress, Washington, DC. For more on Beveridge's views regarding America's rightful role in the world, see Albert J. Beveridge, *The Meaning of the Times and Other Speeches* (1st ed. 1908, New York, 1968), and John Braeman, *Albert J. Beveridge: A Biography* (Chicago, IL, 1971).

4. Henry Luce, "The American Century," *Life*, February 17, 1941, 63. (emphasis added)

5. On the similarities between Beveridge and Luce, see W. A. Swanberg, *Luce and His Empire* (New York, 1972), 21, 29, 181. On Beveridge's overall perspective on American foreign policy and purposes in the world, see Braeman, *Albert J. Beveridge.*

It is fair to say that in many respects Henry Luce got his wish. The United States did enter the war, albeit through the Pacific, and it did take concrete steps to design and then to implement a new world order. It did this well before the slaughter ended and the guns fell silent.[6] That the United States continues to see itself as the principal and rightful architect of world order is amply evidenced by current American rhetoric and actions.[7]

While it is true that other nations besides the United States can certainly point to imperialism and schemes for world order in their pasts, the experience of any nation is rendered intelligible only from the perspective of historical specificity. In the case of the United States, the belief in "American exceptionalism" has had a great deal to do with its visions of world order, both past and present. Henry Luce is a case in point. Near the conclusion of the famous editorial quoted above he wrote:

> Other nations can survive simply because they have endured so long – sometimes with more and sometimes with less significance. But this nation, conceived in adventure and dedicated to the progress of man – this nation cannot truly endure unless there courses strongly through its veins from Maine to California the blood of purposes and enterprise of high resolve.[8]

The idea that America is somehow exceptional or unique among nations with a special burden to bear in terms of "purposes and enterprise of high resolve" has a very long history.[9] With roots in the Protestant Reformation as interpreted by the English Puritans, the meaning of the migration to and founding of what was to become the United States was originally conceived in rigorously biblical terms. It was John Winthrop, the first governor of the Massachusetts Bay Colony, who early on articulated the meaning

6. Gabriel Kolko, *The Politics of War: The World and United States Foreign Policy, 1943–1945* (New York, 1968), 242–313. Robert A. Divine. *Second Chance: The Triumph of Internationalism in America During World War II* (New York, 1967).

7. Hardly a day goes by when there is not some reference emanating from Washington or elsewhere in the country regarding the sole remaining superpower's responsibility for the shape of world order or the conduct of world affairs.

of the "Great Migration." He did this in the form of a lay sermon to his fellow shipmates even before they made landfall on the rocky shores of New England. As Winthrop and other Puritans had it, the "errand into the wilderness" was the portentous opening act to what would be nothing less than the redemption of all of human-kind.[10] America was to be as a "city upon a hill" for all to see and for all to emulate.[11] While this collective self-perception could, of course, beat a short and hasty path to arrogance, that was not necessarily foreordained; for as scholars have pointed out, at least some of the Puritans, perhaps many of them, were well aware that "chosen" status in no way predetermined a righteous and godly outcome to their collective endeavor. As heirs of Calvin, the best of them were acutely aware of their shortcomings and of the real prospect for failure.[12]

8. Luce, "The American Century," 65.

9. The literature concerning American exceptionalism is huge. For a representative sample, see *Is America Different? A New Look at American Exceptionalism,* ed., Byron E. Schafer (Oxford, 1991); David M. Wrobel, *The End of American Exceptionalism: Frontier Anxiety from the Old West to the New Deal* (Lawrence, KS, 1993); Seymour M. Lipset, *American Exceptionalism: A Double-Edged Sword* (New York, 1996); C. Vann Woodward, "The Aging of America," *The American Historical Review* 82 (1977), 583–594, and Woodward, "The Fall of the American Adam," *The New Republic* 185 (December 2, 1981), 13–16; Michael Kammen, "The Problem of American Exceptionalism: A Reconsideration," *American Quarterly* 45 (March 1993), 1–43; Garry Wills, "The American Adam," *The New York Review of Books* 44 (March 6, 1997), 30–33; & James M. McPherson, *Drawn with the Sword: Reflections on the American Civil War* (New York, 1996), 3–23.

10. Loren Baritz, *City on a Hill: A History of Ideas and Myths in America* (New York, 1964), 3–45, especially, 17–18. Also see Perry Miller, *Errand into the Wilderness* (Cambridge, 1956), 1–15, and Robert N. Bellah, *The Broken Covenant: American Civil Religion in Time of Trial,* 2nd. ed. (Chicago, IL, 1992), 1–35. For a vigorous scholarly dissent regarding the redemptive motives of the early Puritan migrants, see Theodore Dwight Bozeman, *To Live Ancient Lives: The Primitivist Dimension in Puritanism* (Chapel Hill, NC, 1988), esp. 81–119.

11. John Winthrop, "A Modell of Christian Charity," in *Winthrop Papers* 2 (Boston: Massachusetts Historical Society, 1929), 282–284. The biblical reference to the "city upon a hill" metaphor is found at Matt. 5:14.

12. Edmund S. Morgan, *The Puritan Dilemma: The Story of John Winthrop* (Boston, MA, 1958), and Bellah, *The Broken Covenant,* 37–44.

The sense of divine mission and unique status carried on through the colonial era and into the antebellum period. In her discussion of the Revolutionary Era, historian Dorothy Ross writes:

> Protestant Americans had available in the history of New England a Christian paradigm to which the establishment of the new nation could be assimilated. Reformation prophecy allowed the millennium to be seen as a progressive historical period into which the reformed world was about to enter, and the Puritan errand had moved the scene of that hope to the New World. When independence was won, fervent Protestants identified the Republic with the advent of the millennial period, which was to usher in the salvation of mankind and the end of history. America thus represented a radical break in history and a radical breakthrough of God's time into secular history.[13]

Within several decades, this sense of divine mission and purpose was rearticulated in numerous reform movements and then in the phenomenon of "Manifest Destiny." Coined by John O'Sullivan, a Democratic publicist, "Manifest Destiny" was the ideological underpinning of antebellum continental expansion as well as sacred mission beyond its finite confines. As with the Puritans, the redemption of the entire world was the real issue. O'Sullivan wrote:

> The far-reaching, the boundless future will be the era of American greatness. In its magnificent domain of space and time, the nation of many nations is destined to manifest to mankind the excellence of divine principles; to establish on earth the noblest temple ever dedicated to the worship of the Most High-the Sacred and the True. For this blessed mission to the nations of the world, which are shut out from the life-giving light of truth, has America been chosen; and her high example shall smite unto death the tyranny of kings, hierarchs, and oligarchs, and carry the glad tidings of peace and good will where myriads now endure an existence scarcely more enviable than the beasts of the field.[14]

13. Dorothy Ross, "Historical Consciousness in Nineteenth Century America," *The American Historical Review* 89 (1984), 909–928, here 912.

14. Quoted in Anders Stephanson, *Manifest Destiny: American Expansion and the Empire of Right* (New York, 1995), 40.

With a mission to people the continent, and to expand the realm of democracy, by the late 1840s what Jefferson had referred to as an "empire for liberty" had reached the Pacific shores.

As the nineteenth century ebbed, American imperialism reached into the Caribbean and out across the Pacific to Hawaii and to the Philippines beyond. It was immediately following a trip to the Philippines, after all, that Albert Beveridge began to hold sway in the Senate and elsewhere on what today would be called the "geopolitical" significance of the Spanish–American War and its aftermath. And of course, Americans generally saw their role in the Philippines, and less formally in China, as qualitatively different from what they perceived as the sordid practices of the aggressive, self-serving Europeans. As the First Philippine Commission reported to Washington after its fact-finding tour of the Islands in 1899:

> Our control means to the inhabitants of the Philippines internal peace and order, a guranty (*sic*) against foreign aggression and against dismemberment of their country, commercial and industrial prosperity, and as large a share in the affairs of government as they shall prove fit to take. When peace and prosperity shall have been established throughout the archipelago, when education shall have become general, then, in the language of a leading Filipino, his people will, under our guidance, "become more American than the Americans themselves."[15]

It is, of course, Woodrow Wilson who is generally regarded as the most articulate and influential of twentieth-century apostles of American global mission and design for world order. That he thought of the United States as a nation of a different order with a unique mission is, perhaps, nowhere better articulated than in his insistence at the outset of American armed participation in the First World War that the United States was not an "Ally," but an "Associate Power," and in remarks Wilson made in England before the start of the Versailles Peace Conference. On that occasion, he said:

15. U.S. Philippine Commission. "Preliminary Report of the Philippine Commission," *Report of the Philippine Commission*, 4 vols. (Washington, DC, 1900), I, 184.

You must not speak of us who come over here as cousins, still less as brothers; we are neither. Neither must you think of us as Anglo-Saxons, for the term can no longer be rightly applied to the people of the United States. Nor must too much in this connection be attached to the fact that English is our common language . . . No, there are only two things which can establish and maintain closer relations between your country and mine: they are community of ideals and interests.[16]

Needless to say, the nature of those ideals and interests were as defined by Wilson himself in contradistinction to those held by the Europeans.[17]

Although Wilson lost his fight for American participation in the League of Nations, his vision of world order, as articulated in his war aims address of January 1918, had a profound affect on American policy-makers as the world was once more engulfed in bloody, global conflict. While there was no total consensus among the foreign policy elite of the United States as to the design the post-second World War world should take, there is little doubt that the heirs to Wilson largely held sway. As Emily Rosenberg writes: "The nationalists or 'isolationists' believed that the United States should retract its far-flung economic interests and repudiate globalism, expansionism and militarism. The nationalist critique of globalism, which had garnered considerable support in the 1930s, faded during the war and was almost completely discredited in the postwar period."[18]

---

16. Quoted from Lloyd C. Gardner, *Safe for Democracy: The Anglo-American Response to Revolution, 1913–1923* (New York, 1984), 2–3. Also see Arthur S. Link, *Wilson The Diplomatist: A Look at His Major Foreign Policies* (Chicago, IL, 1963), 97–98; and Herbert Hoover, *The Ordeal of Woodrow Wilson* (New York, 1958), 12–13, 93.

17. Gardner, *Safe For Democracy*; N. Gordon Levin, Jr., *Woodrow Wilson and World Politics* (New York, 1968); Arno J. Mayer, *Political Origins of the New Diplomacy, 1917–1918* (New York, 1970).

18. Emily S. Rosenberg, *Spreading the American Dream: American Economic and Cultural Expansion, 1890–1945* (New York, 1989), 191–192. For a "defense" of Wilson which argues that if the post-World War II, Cold War globalists were children of Wilson, then they were illegitimate, see Thomas J. Knock, "Kennan versus Wilson," in John Milton Cooper, Jr. and Charles E. Neu, eds., *The Wilson Era: Essays in Honor of Arthur S. Link* (Arlington Heights, IL, 1991), 316.

The internationalist consensus which developed with the Second World War and the subsequent Cold War, committed the United States to a globalism that continues to the present day. Stephen Ambrose writes:

> During World War II Henry Luce of *Life* magazine spoke for most political leaders as well as American businessmen and soldiers when he said that the twentieth century would be the American Century. The politicians looked for areas in which American influence could dominate; the businessmen looked for profitable markets and new sources of raw materials; the military looked for overseas bases. All found what they wanted as America after World War II inaugurated a program of expansion that had no inherent limits. Americans who wanted to bring the blessings of democracy, capitalism, and stability to everyone meant just what they said – the whole world, in their view, should be a reflection of the United States.[19]

What is perhaps most notable in all this is the national faith's remarkable immunity to the vicissitudes of history. The 1970s and their aftermath are a case in point. There was considerable concern expressed during the decade regarding the country's future. A good example in this regard is the Wall Street financier, Felix Rohatyn. In a book which was a compilation of previously published essays titled *The Twenty Year Century* (an explicit, but ironic reference to Luce), Rohatyn argued that the United States was headed for precipitous economic decline if the country did not take stock of its situation and initiate more rational economic policies. According to Rohatyn, the United States could regain a competitive productivity edge and a broadly based comparative advantage only if the American people began to save and invest more of their income, and if American corporate managers began making business decisions on the basis of a long- instead of a short-term calculus. The times demanded sacrifice and delayed gratification, difficulty and pain.

---

19. Stephen E. Ambrose, *Rise To Globalism: American Foreign Policy, 1938–1976* (rev. ed. New York, 1976), 21.

Although this was tantamount to calling for a cultural sea change, that was, nevertheless, Rohatyn's prescription.[20]

Others joined the refrain. Lester Thurow, Dean of the Business School and the Massachusetts Institute of Technology was notable in this regard. *Zero Sum Society*, followed by *Zero Sum Solutions*, were two popular books that had a prophetic ring not unlike Rohatyn's. While the solutions might differ, a good number of Americans began to argue that the country was in trouble and that its place as the world's preeminent political and economic power was threatened.[21]

The discussion of the eclipse of American power and the decline of American civilization in this period is, on the face of it, not surprising. It followed on the heels of the collapse of the Bretton Woods gold-based, fixed exchange system; defeat in Vietnam; the resignation of a disgraced President; an "energy crisis"; stagflation, record high interest rates and the Iran hostage debacle. These events, and the apparent unwillingness or inability of the political establishment and the American people to do much about them, led President Jimmy Carter to give his famous (in some circles, infamous) "malaise" address. Calling on his fellow citizens to tone down their materialistic expectations, to tighten their belts, and to redirect their moral compass, the President tried to cajole the country into accepting the dictates of his proposed energy program.[22]

The somber message, particularly from Carter, was not something that set well with many Americans. This is perhaps best evidenced by Ronald Reagan's 1980 victory over the beleaguered President. With a reassuring smile and the slogan that it was "morning in America," Reagan rode into office promising to rearm the country in its crusade against the "Evil Empire" and, in the process, also to

20. Felix G. Rohatyn, *The Twenty-Year Century: Essays on Economics and Public Finance* (New York, 1980). Rohatyn, who is a partner at Lazard Frères, was a frequent contributor to *The New Review of Books* during this period and the general theme of his articles in that publication was very much the same.

21. Lester Thurow, *Zero Sum Society: Distribution and the Possibilities for Economic Change* (New York, 1980) and Thurow *Zero Sum Solutions: Building a World Class American Economy* (New York, 1985).

22. For Jimmy Carter's so-called "malaise" address, see *The New York Times*, July 16, 1979.

restore the American people's faith in themselves as the best hope of humankind. It appeared to many Americans that the United States remained the Promised Land as the congenitally optimistic candidate, then President, adopted the much touted supply-side economics which demanded sacrifice of absolutely no one![23] The American faith in its mission and place was reasserted once again in an unabashed fashion. The continuity was maintained.

Piling up a mountain of new debt in the 1980s as a result of yawning deficits that stemmed in large part from the huge military build up and tax cuts, the United States spent its way out of recession and into George Bush's "New World Order," as the Soviet Union collapsed, unable to compete in the latest round of the arms race.

There was not much "New" about the version of world order that the Gulf War underwrote. It is true that it was easier to amass a United Nations' coalition with the states of the former Soviet Union in disarray; however, the policy of maintaining a delicate balance of power among the countries of the Middle East in order to insure the continuous flow of inexpensive oil was hardly an innovation.[24] As things currently stand, notwithstanding discussion about the emergence of a "multi-polar" world, the United States continues to see itself as principal architect and enforcer of the dictates of a beneficent world order.[25]

This continuity of faith and belief regarding the American place and purpose in the world has been well articulated by Robert Bellah

---

23. It should be pointed out that while Carter's tone was somber and glum, particularly when compared to Reagan's, the "malaise" address made clear that the country could regain its self-assurance, presence in the world, and the future if the American people would simply mend their ways. For an analysis of their differences in style, see Garry Wills, *Reagan's America: Innocents at Home* (New York, 1987), 198, 383–385. Wills draws on a religious typology of William James to argue that Carter had the "sick soul" temperament and that Reagan, was the "healthy-minded" type. For a detailed discussion of these types, see William James, *Varieties of Religious Experience: Study in Human Nature* (New York, 1960), 77–162.

24. See Simon Bromley, *American Hegemony and World Oil* (Cambridge, 1991), and George Philip, *The Political Economy of International Oil* (Edinburgh, 1994).

25. George Bush and Brent Scowcroft, *A World Transformed* (New York, 1998), esp. 565–566.

in his first book about American civil religion. Commenting on the sentiments of a young Herman Melville who argued that the United States was comprised of a "peculiar" and "chosen people" that represented "the political Messiah" whose "national selfishness [is] was unbounded philanthropy," Bellah wrote:

> In such a passage we can see the link between the notion of the American Israel, which was already in the mind of John Winthrop in the early 17th century, and Henry Luce's recent idea of "the American Century," or John Foster Dulles' easy identification of the "free world" with those nations willing to do the bidding of the American government.[26]

What is one to make of all this then, this "rise to globalism" and the patterns of belief by which Americans have understood that rise?[27] The answers provided by historians, particularly American diplomatic historians during the past half-century, have been along two broadly critical interpretative paths, conventionally labelled "realist" and "revisionist." The former is associated with the work of Hans Morgenthau and George F. Kennan, although there is by now a large number of quite distinguished historians who share their essential orientation.[28] While "revisionist" is a slippery term, its most recent usage typically applies to the work of William

---

26. Bellah, *The Broken Covenant*, 38–39.

27. It is always a risky proposition to speak of "America" or "Americans" as a generalized whole. The historical, demographic, and cultural diversity of the country is a reality that cannot be ignored. On the other hand, notwithstanding some of the differences that exist between groups within the United States, it is still possible to discuss a dominant cultural perspective which is no doubt held by a majority of the American people. In addition, what all Americans have in common is an interesting and important issue in itself, but not one that has been of much interest lately.

28. Hans Morgenthau, *In Defense of the National Interest: A Critical Examination of American Foreign Policy* (New York, 1950); George Kennan, *American Diplomacy* (1st expanded edition 1951, repr.: Chicago, IL, 1984); Norman A. Graebner, ed., *Ideas and Diplomacy. Readings in the Intellectual Tradition of American Foreign Policy* (New York, 1964); Graebner, *America as a World Power: A Realist Appraisal from Wilson to Reagan* (Wilmington, DE, 1984). For analysis and historiographical discussion

Appleman Williams, his students, and those who have continued to mine the interpretative vein opened by them.[29]

At the core of the realist thesis articulated by Kennan, for example, is the assertion that Americans, or at least the Americans who followed in the wake the Federalist Founders, did not understand power. Ignoring the fact that for the first hundred years of the country's existence, the United States was not only protected by the expanses of the Atlantic and Pacific Oceans, but by the power of the British Royal Navy, Americans were able to devote themselves to the development of the continent and to indulge their fantasies and delusions about the efficacy of isolationism. As the nineteenth century drew to a close, and with it the relative decline of British power, so the argument goes, the United States stepped out upon the world scene as a nascent power still harboring naive and distorted ideas about how the world really worked. Drawing on its sense of uniqueness and mission, the country was inclined to resort to "moralistic" and "legalistic" cliches championing high-sounding

---

regarding Kennan, his diplomacy and the realist perspective, see Barton Gellman, *Contending with Kennan: Toward a Philosophy of American Power* (New York, 1984); David A. Mayers, *George Kennan and the Dilemmas of US Foreign Policy* (New York, 1988); and Anders Stephanson, *Kennan and the Art of Foreign Policy* (Cambridge, MA, 1989). On Graebner see Jerald A. Combs, "Norman Graebner and the Realist View of American Diplomatic History," *Diplomatic History* 11 (1987), 251–264.

29. Notable contributions by some of Williams' students include Lloyd C. Gardner, *Economic Aspects of New Deal Diplomacy* (Boston, MA, 1971); Gardner, *Pay any Price: Lyndon Johnson and the Wars for Vietnam* (Chicago, IL, 1995); Walter LaFeber, *The New Empire: An Interpretation of American Expansion 1860–1898* (Ithaca, NY, 1963); LaFeber, *The Clash: U.S.–Japanese Relations throughout History* (New York, 1997); Thomas J. McCormick, *China Market: America's Quest for Informal Empire 1893–1901* (Chicago, IL, 1967); McCormick, *America's Half-Century: United States Foreign Policy in the Cold War* (Baltimore, MD, 1989); Edward P. Crapol, *America for Americans: Economic Nationalism and Anglophobia in the Late Nineteenth Century* (Westport, CT, 1973). For a complete bibliography of Williams' publications, see Henry W. Berger, ed., *A William Appleman Williams Reader* (Chicago, IL, 1992). For a collection of articles written by former students for Williams, see Lloyd C. Gardner, ed., *Redefining the Past: Essays in Diplomatic History in Honor of William Appleman Williams* (Corvallis, OR, 1986).

policies that resonated with an emotional and ill-informed democratic populace, but which bore no rational relationship to the realities that defined world affairs.

Thus, to Kennan, for example, the Spanish–American War was an example of the difficulty of implementing a rational, consistent foreign policy in the context of political institutions often held hostage by the vagaries and absurdities of partisan politics and a self-serving press. On the other hand, the Open Door Notes, defined by some as one of the "lodestones" of American history, were seen by Kennan as essentially an accident both unreflective and unproductive, although the American public was easily led to the conclusion that they had saved China from the sordid European imperialists and had struck "an American blow for an American idea."[30]

Kennan reserved his most severe criticism, however, for Woodrow Wilson and, by implication, the entire liberal internationalist thrust of twentieth-century American foreign policy. From Kennan's perspective, much of the horror and tragedy of the twentieth century had its roots in the crisis which led to World War I and to the peace which followed it. As a matter of fact, to a large extent, Kennan's post-diplomatic career as a historian has focussed on the meaning of the "Great War."[31]

30. For the "lodestone" reference, see James C. Thomson, Peter W. Stanley, and John Curtis Perry, *Sentimental Imperialists: The American Experience in East Asia* (New York, 1982), 121. For Kennan's early, and remarkably consistent, views on the Spanish–American War and the Open Door Notes, see *American Diplomacy*, 3–37, esp. 11, 37.

31. In addition to his numerous articles and essays dealing with a wide range of topics, Kennan's most important historical works have dealt with the Russian Revolution and its aftermath, and with the evolution of the international order from the unification of Germany to 1914. World War I, of course, is the implicit or explicit epicenter of these works. On the importance of World War I to Kennan's view of twentieth-century history, see John Lamberton Harper, *American Visions of Europe: Franklin D. Roosevelt, George F. Kennan, and Dean G. Acheson* (Cambridge, 1994), 226–229. For a complete list of Kennan's books, and a partial list of his articles, see Mayers, *George Kennan and the Dilemmas*, 376–378.

The importance of that catastrophe in Kennan's thought was clearly set forth in his Walgren Foundation Lectures given in 1951. Speaking shortly after he had left the State Department, and concerned about the evolving Cold War and the Soviet Union's threat to American security, the former diplomat, now historian, was decidedly negative in his assessment of what had been gained from the carnage of the two World Wars. And insofar as he saw the Second World War as the almost inevitable result of the First, he wrote:

> Eclipsed for many of us by the fresher and more vivid recollections of World War II, this first World War has become in many respects a forgotten factor. Yet all lines of inquiry, it seems to me, lead back to it. . . . [But] I would submit that a significant narrowing of the choices of the generations from 1920 to 1950 began with the outbreak of violence in 1914; . . .[32]

And while Kennan states quite explicitly that he was not unsympathetic to "the depth and bitterness" of Woodrow Wilson's problems, he argues that the President's policies throughout the war and, in particular, at Versailles, served largely to compound the tragedy.[33]

For it was Wilson who went to Versailles with the vision of establishing a new world order that was, according to Kennan, unmindful of the balance-of-power realities that must undergird any lasting peace. In fact, as other scholars have pointed out, Wilson specifically rejected the idea that a balance of power was the key to peace, and argued that its inherent failings were one of the principal causes of the war itself. With this analysis, of course, Wilson was not alone, but he was the one in the position of power who sought most strenuously to substitute a new world order based on the principles of self-determination and collective security instead of a re-established, but revised, balance-of-power and sphere-of-influence approach. Of the Versailles peace that he believed was the major cause of the next war, Kennan wrote almost a half century ago:

32. Kennan, *American Diplomacy*, 56–57.
33. Ibid., 63.

And this was the sort of peace you got when you allowed war hysteria and impractical idealism to lie down together in your mind, like the lion and the lamb; when you indulged yourself in the colossal conceit of thinking that you could suddenly make international life over into what you believed to be your own image; when you dismissed the past with contempt, rejected the relevance of the past to the future, and refused to occupy yourself with the real problems that a study of the past would suggest.[34]

Although Kennan's most influential critique of American foreign policy was published in 1951, in the subsequent expanded edition of that book, he makes it clear that his views have remained essentially unchanged. Notwithstanding his important and problematic role in the beginnings of the Cold War, for the past fifty-odd years Kennan has consistently argued for a delimited and selective American involvement overseas – an involvement which focusses only on the few areas that he deems crucial to American security.[35]

The essence of the Kennan critique, then, is that Americans are very naive about how the world really works, and they are inclined to fashion a foreign policy that is irrational in that it is not characterized by a calculated adjustment of efficacious means to sound, realistic, external ends. According to Kennan, the errors in US foreign policy (and here, of course, he would include the "moralistic" and "legalistic" schemes for world order) largely stem from "attempts to strike noble postures and to impress ourselves."[36]

Nothing could be further from this interpretation of America's involvement with the world than that articulated by William Appleman Williams and the other "revisionists." According to Williams, whose early book, *The Tragedy of American Diplomacy*, has been as influential in its own way as Kennan's *American Diplomacy, 1900–1950,* American foreign policy, while not devoid of irrational

---

34. Ibid., 69.

35. See, for example, George F. Kennan, *The Cloud of Danger: Current Realities of American Foreign Policy* (Boston, MA, 1977), esp. 3–26, 228–234; Kennan, *Around the Cragged Hill: A Personal and Political Philosophy* (New York, 1993), 180–231.

36. Kennan, *American Diplomacy*, 169.

elements, is more accurately characterized as a remarkably consistent, shrewd, and sophisticated attendance to the requirements of the nation's political economy. The rational adjustment of means to ends is, according to Williams, precisely what American foreign policy (including its designs for world order) is all about. Where Kennan, for example, perceived naivete, moralism, and delusional perception, Williams saw the entire sweep of twentieth-century American foreign policy as the conscious pursuit of an Open Door World that American policy makers (and the broader elite) perceived as absolutely (and realistically) essential to stave off periodic economic crises and the political and social instability that would necessarily attend them.[37]

And again, Woodrow Wilson goes to the heart of the matter.[38] For Williams, Wilson was the most sophisticated of American architects of empire. To see him simply as a naively moralistic and easily beguiled innocent is, for Williams, to miss the central meaning of the United States in the twentieth century. Influenced by the intellectual consensus which developed in the 1890s regarding the enhanced need for exports and overseas investments to insure continued prosperity through a new frontier to replace the closed, continental one, Williams argued that Wilson was an extremely savvy and assertive trustee of the political economy he inherited. Williams wrote:

> But Wilson has a central importance as one who practically and symbolically integrated all the elements of empire as a way of life. He called for (and began to build) a navy second to none, vigorously supported the expansion of American economic strength, repeatedly intervened (militarily as well as politically) to reform and educate societies that he considered wayward or backward, and boldly undertook to

37. William Appleman Williams, *The Tragedy of American Diplomacy* (2nd rev. ed., New York, 1972), 59, 66–67. For a suggestion that Williams' book was as a point-counterpoint to Kennan's *American Diplomacy, 1900–1950*, see Paul M. Buhle and Edward Rice-Maximin, *William Appleman Williams: The Tragedy of Empire* (New York, 1995), 109.

38. On the central place Wilson occupies relative to any interpretation of twentieth-century American diplomacy, see Knock, "Kennan Versus Wilson," 303.

institutionalize the Open Door Policy on a global scale. . . . To effect that purpose he led the nation in World War I in the righteous conviction that the deployment of American police power was necessary to usher in a millennium of democratic progress based on the acceptance and observance of the principles and practices of American marketplace political economy.[39]

Williams' point, among others, is that Wilson's program, although idealistic in the sense that his reach was high, was, at the same time, based on a hardheaded assessment of the real (practical) needs of the American political economy. The same was true of the League of Nations. The historian wrote:

Wilson and his supporters advocated joining the League of Nations on the grounds that its system of collective security to preserve the fundamental features of the status quo offered the best method of keeping the world safe for the Open Door Policy. Given that framework, American power consolidated behind the integrated program of reformist and economic expansion would produce perpetual welfare for the United States and the world.[40]

The important point here is that Williams' assessment of the nature and roots of the Wilsonian program is fundamentally at odds with that provided by Kennan and the others of the "realist" perspective.

If Kennan and Williams' interpretations of American foreign policy and schemes for world order are different in fundamental ways, it is interesting that they also share certain things in common. First, both men were born and raised in the Midwest, Kennan in Wisconsin and Williams in Iowa, although they stand a generation apart.[41] One might well argue that the diverse intellectual paths they took are a direct result of their different responses to the same populist and progressive political traditions for which that section

39. William Appleman Williams, *Empire as a Way of Life: An Essay on the Causes and Character of America's Present Predicament Along With a Few Thoughts About an Alternative* (New York, 1980), 134.

40. Williams, *The Tragedy of American Diplomacy*, 110–111.

41. Kennan was born in 1904. Williams was born in 1921 and died in 1990.

of the country is known.[42] In addition, insofar as both favored, albeit for quite different reasons, a withdrawal from spreadeagled globalism, they both reflect an "isolationist" tendency again often associated with the midwestern part of the United States.[43]

The similarities go further. At least at one level, the critiques of American society foisted by Kennan and Williams share a common sensibility. While Kennan is very much a conservative, political, and social elitist who harbors profound doubts about the common people and mass democracy, and Williams was a democratic socialist with a deep faith in both, the two historians nevertheless were utterly appalled by the same characteristics of late twentieth-century American society. Pollution and the desecration of nature, the arms race and the military-industrial complex, materialism and consumerism, as well as the inimical power of the corporate and media empires to manipulate public opinion and tastes, were all shared, vocal concerns of Kennan and Williams.[44]

Succinctly stated, putting America's own house in order was an overarching concern of both historians and they agreed on the nature, if not the cause, of a good deal of the mess! Linking his advocacy of withdrawal to his perceptions about the decadence of

42. On Kennan's temperament as a "dissident," a trait which may well have led to his dissent from the ethos of progressive, Midwestern Wisconsin, see Mayers, *George Kennan and the Dilemmas*, 9. On Kennan's conservatism, see 48–63, 317–332. Also see Gellman, *Contending with Kennan*, 7. For a different perspective on Kennan's Midwestern upbringing which emphasizes his father's interest and immersion in German culture, and the large German immigrant population in Milwaukee, Wisconsin, where the future diplomat and historian grew up, see Harper, *American Visions*, 135–143.

43. "Isolationism" is another one of those terms with which one must be very careful as it has carried a number of different meanings. Certainly neither Kennan nor Williams advocated an absolute withdrawal from the affairs of the external world. Neither was an apostle for American unilateralism. On the other hand, Kennan's interest in delimiting American overseas involvement, and Williams' desire to transform the American political economy to further the pursuit of the open door at home, and thereby to obviate the need for its pursuit abroad, share a certain affinity.

44. On something of a convergence between Kennan and Wilson and Kennan and those historians writing in the Williams' tradition, Knock, "Kennan Versus Wilson," 319.

modern American society, Kennan stated in an interview: "My main reason for advocating a gradual and qualified withdrawal from far-flung foreign involvement is that we have nothing to teach the world. We have to confess that we have not got the answers to the problems of human society in the modern age."[45] Barton Gellman reiterates this perspective when he states that, in Kennan's view, "a society's internal health is logically precedent to its relationship with the external world. The role of American power in international life cannot be sensibly discussed until its role at home is clear."[46]

One is reminded here of Williams' appeal to Americans that they rethink their imperial way of life; or as he once wrote:

> The unhappy truth of it is that American radicals, along with American liberals and conservatives, have always lusted for saving the world. We have no tradition of leaving other people alone in order to find ourselves. We have always defined *our* purpose as bringing *them* to *our* level. What nonsense, what arrogance, what lack of any sense of ourselves! We have failed to imagine, let alone realize, any conception of how to live.[47]

Although Williams attributes America's global sprawl to the underlying dynamics and requirements of the country's capitalist political economy, and Kennan has never formulated his critique in such terms, they share an aversion to the way the country has evolved, particularly in the twentieth century.[48]

With both of these influential critics of American diplomacy and American society advocating a fundamental reassessment and restructuring of the United States at home and abroad, their appeal really should not be ignored. And here it is appropriate, perhaps, to begin with the premise, raised by so many environmentalists, to the

45. "A Conversation with George Urban," in Daniel P. Moynihan, ed., *Encounters with Kennan: The Great Debate* (London, 1979), 25. Also see Harper, *American Visions*, 204–205.

46. Gellman, *Contending with Kennan*, 140.

47. William Appleman Williams, "Radicals and Regionalism," *Democracy* 1 (October 1981), 94 (emphasis in original).

48. Gellman, *Contending with Kennan*, 139–157. Also see Kennan, *Around the Cragged Hill*, 111–179

effect that current trends of resource use, pollution, and global disparities of wealth portend disaster for the planet. Environmental degradation has been a consistent theme of Kennan and, to a lesser extent, Williams as well. And insofar as the United States is the preeminent political and economic power in the world, and is a massively disproportionate user of non-renewable resources, it is more than appropriate for the country to embark upon a serious and broad-based discussion about a new human ecology and mode of existence.[49] Williams articulated this need clearly near the end of his book *Empire as a Way of Life*. Hoping to convince a broad public that imperialism and empire had been inherent in American history from the outset, he likewise sought "to encourage a searching dialogue among ourselves about the character of our culture."[50]

For such an enterprise to have even a remote chance of bearing any fruit, the discussion should probably begin with a thoroughgoing critique of the idea of American exceptionalism. In its most pernicious form, this idea undergirds the belief, often an unconscious one, that America can escape from history and the common lot of humanity; or as Dorothy Ross puts it, "Embedded in exceptionalist ideology is a distinctive, pre-historicist historical consciousness that removes America from the vicissitudes of time."[51] By the same token, perhaps one of the quintessential American traits is the notion that one can start over, begin anew, leave the past behind. Francis Fitzgerald put this quite well when she wrote "That individuals could start over again, and if necessary reinvent themselves, is one of the great legends of American life."[52]

49. On global environmental degradation see William Cronon, ed., *Uncommon Ground* (New York, 1995); J. Baird Callicott and Fernando J. R. da Rocha, *Earth Summit Ethics: Toward a Postmodern Philosophy of Environmental Education* (Albany, NY, 1996); D. A. Brown and John Lemons, eds., *Sustainable Development: Science, Ethics, and Public Policy* (Dordrecht, 1995).

50. Williams, *Empire as a Way of Life*, 200.

51. Quoted from Stephanson, *Manifest Destiny*, 13. For a discussion regarding the "escape from history," see Paul T. Burlin, "American Exceptionalism and the Late Twentieth Century Escape From History," *The Maine Scholar* 10 (Autumn 1997), 79–99.

52. Francis Fitzgerald, *Cities on a Hill: A Journey Through Contemporary American Cultures* (New York, 1986), 23.

While this belief that history can be left behind probably lies at the root of much of the innovation and creativity the nation has exhibited over its history, it also inspires some of the arrogance and existential hubris so evident in the country as well. For a corollary to the belief in exceptionalism, it would seem, is the equally problematic idea that there are no limits to what human existence realistically affords. This faith in unlimited progress, usually defined in material terms, not only bears a direct relationship to the environmental crisis and American expansion abroad, but has also seriously undermined the ability of many Americans to imagine the nature, meaning and purpose of human existence in a different way.[53]

Of course, there have been Americans who have questioned the belief in unlimited progress and the optimism it entails, most notably American novelists. In addition, there was considerable debate in recent years about whether the country was in decline. That debate, however, one largely confined to the intellectual community, seems to have evaporated in the wake of the collapse of the Asian economy and the relative immunity from its fall-out that the United States has thus far enjoyed. The ability of Americans to continue to see themselves as beyond the vicissitudes of time appears essentially endless.

The Civil War was, without a doubt, the most catastrophic and traumatic event in American history. And yet even that massive historical upheaval did not in a permanent way undermine the broad cultural belief in unlimited progress. The eminent historian from the South, C. Vann Woodward, once held great hope for his region to serve as an antidote to the blithe and morally shallow optimism associated with the triumphant, industrial North. He wrote:

> How much room was there in the tortured conscience of the South for the national self-image of innocence and moral complacency? Southerners

---

53. Williams, *Empire as a Way of Life*, 4–9. For a provocative and critical look at the idea of progress in American history and society, see Christopher Lasch, *The True and Only Heaven: Progress and its Critics* (New York, 1991). For a comment on Kennan's profound skepticism regarding progress, see Harper, *American Visions*, 229–230.

have repeated the American rhetoric of self-admiration and sung the perfection of American institutions ever since the Declaration of Independence. But for half that time they lived intimately with a great social evil and the other half with its aftermath. . . . An age-long experience with human bondage and its evils and later with emancipation and its shortcomings did not dispose the South very favourably toward such popular American ideas as the doctrine of human perfectibility, the belief that every evil has a cure, and the notion that every human problem has a solution. For these reasons the utopian schemes and the gospel of progress that flourished above the Mason Dixon Line never found very wide acceptance below the Potomac . . . [54]

For Woodward, the South's history separated it from the dominant culture of the victorious Yankee North, and linked it closely to the historical experience of the vast majority of humankind. It might be possible to argue that the history of the country as a whole had generally been one of success and immunity from the painful experiences of the balance of the globe. The South, however, had experienced ignominious defeat, colonial occupation during Reconstruction, along with a deep sense of sin, guilt, tragedy, and failure. These were the more common lot of humankind, and they necessarily nourished a more "realistic" assessment of the human condition.

Woodward's dissent from the idea of America as exception stemmed from his deep intellectual, emotional, and spiritual roots in the South. On the other hand, as he has candidly admitted, the region has never lived up to his expectations of it as a wise counsel for the nation as a whole. Instead, in many ways the South has been the most uncritical champion of unfettered capitalism and the bright future it supposedly heralds. The South also supported the long war in Vietnam more strenuously and broadly than any other region.[55] As Robert Bellah has noted, the defeated South came to identify with the North in many ways and adopted some of the

54. C. Vann Woodward, *The Burden of Southern History* (rev. ed., New York, 1969), 28.

55. Ibid., 138, 160–162, and C. Vann Woodward, "The Aging of America," *The American Historical Review* 82 (1977), 591.

victor's most notable cultural values and beliefs.[56] This is, of course, precisely the opposite of what Woodward had hoped. Instead of the country as a whole listening to the South, the former converted the latter, or so it would appear.

And if America might have learned something of value from the tragic history and experience of the South, the same can be said for other peoples and cultures. And yet it would seem that, as a result of belief in America as exception, Americans listen to no one. If one is perpetually the vanguard of history, from whom could one conceivably learn?[57]

Nevertheless, listening to others could very well be the most important element of any "national dialogue" about the country's future. And while Americans could, no doubt, learn much of value from a wide variety of peoples and cultures, there is probably no better place to begin the process of listening and conversation than with the peoples of Latin America.[58] After all, we share a common

---

56. Bellah, *The Broken Covenant*, 145.

57. It would seem that one must distinguish here between "listening" to others for purposes of analysis, and "listening" to others for the purposes of societal change. There is, after all, a rich "foreign traveler" literature which Americans do pay attention to. Alexis de Tocqueville's work is, of course, the most notable in this regard. But his work, as well as that of other foreign commentators, is read for insight about the workings of American society, not for insight into how the country might be changed.

58. This is not to suggest that Canadians have nothing from which the people of the United States could learn. There is as profound an ignorance in the United States about Canada as there is about Latin America. Nevertheless, the cultural and power differences which exist between the United States and Latin America, coupled with the history of US intervention there, all suggest that there would be much to gain were Americans able to marshall the humility and wisdom to listen to those whom they have generally deemed "inferior."

An interesting case of looking south concerns African-Americans and Brazil. At one time, in some quarters of the African-American community, Brazil was held up as an example of a "racial paradise," at least in comparison with the United States. Although the presumed heavenly quality of Brazilian race relations soon was found to be an illusion, it is fair to say that something important was learned. On African-Americans' perceptions of Brazil, see David J. Hellwig, ed., *African–American Reflections on Brazil's Racial Paradise* (Philadelphia, PA, 1992).

locale and our histories have been intertwined, if not generally in the most sanguine of ways.[59] And there is a great deal to be said morally for a people of a country such as the United States engaging in a cultural dialogue, as one among equals, with other peoples whom they have long sought to control and have generally perceived as inferior.

This suggestion to look south as a part of a process of national soul searching and reflection would strike Kennan as ill-advised.[60] Lawrence E. Harrison who, unlike Kennan, has spent a considerable

---

Furthermore, all Americans, as a part of the process of rethinking the future, need to have an honest discussion regarding the central paradox of American history, the coupling of freedom and slavery. The enduring legacy of racism in the country, the deviation from the "American Creed" from the outset, needs to be addressed as a key part of imagining the future. On the coupling of slavery and freedom, see Edmund S. Morgan, *American Slavery-American Freedom: The Ordeal of Colonial Virginia* (New York, 1975).

And finally, if it is worthwhile to look south for insight, it would be equally important to examine the variety of perspectives, values, and sensibilities that exist between groups within the United States. Is it likely, for example, that a group which spent most of its time on the American continent in slavery is going to have exactly the same values and perspectives as people who did not? Along these lines see, for example, W.E.B. Dubois, *The Souls of Black Folk* (New York, 1989), 51–62, for a skeptical and ironic perspective on "progress" in American history.

59. For early insight regarding the need to see American history in a broader context that includes both Anglo and Latin America, see Herbert E. Bolton, *Wider Horizons of American History* (Notre Dame, IN, 1967), esp. 1–54. The portion of the book cited here is Bolton's Presidential Address delivered at the annual meeting of the American Historical Association in 1932.

60. Not particularly knowledgeable nor interested in Latin America, Kennan visited the region in 1950 and then wrote a very critical and damning report about what he saw there. Viewing contemporary Latin American affairs as a function of a catastrophic history of colonialism and genocide, Kennan argued that the cultural divide between that part of the world and the United States was so immense as to be unbridgeable. Therefore, he counseled essentially ignoring the area. Subsequently he has reiterated that the region was inconsequential from a geopolitical perspective and therefore not deserving of much attention. See *Foreign Relations of the United States 1950*, vol. 2, "Report on Latin America," 598–624, George F. Kennan, *Memoirs 1925–1950* (Boston, MA, 1967), 476–483, Kennan, *Cloud of Danger*, 66–67. On Kennan's constitutional aversion to "Latin" cultural traits, see Harper, *American Visions*, 146, 150–152, 202.

amount of time in Latin America, but shares Kennan's assessment of the culture of the region, would chime in likewise. As a matter of fact, Harrison argues that the backwardness of Latin American countries is a function of cultural values stemming from the Iberian Roman Catholicism imposed on that region by its European conquerors. By the same token, he argues that Protestant values are at the root of much of the prosperity and success of Canada and the United States. Rather than the United States listening to and contemplating what it might learn of value from Latin America, Harrison argues the reverse. If Latin America is to progress, and he equates progress with economic growth, then profound cultural change is necessary on the part of the countries which comprise that region. He writes: "If fundamental cultural differences principally explain the North–South divergence in the Hemisphere, then convergence depends largely on cultural change in Latin America – the reinforcement of those values that lie behind the success of Canada, the United States, Western Europe, and now several East Asian countries."[61]

What is suggested here, however, certainly in the United States (if not in the industrial world as a whole), is that there is need for a profoundly critical look at some of the very values that Harrison is so eager that Latin Americans adopt. If it is true that the earth's environment cannot support the expansion of something approximating the American way of life, then the growth formula bodes ill for all concerned. Second, even if one brackets and ignores the

---

61. Lawrence W. Harrison, *The Pan-American Dream* (Boulder: CO, 1991), 4. Also see Harrison, *Underdevelopment as a State of Mind: The Latin American Case* (Lanham, MD, 1985). Of course, one needs to be careful here. Given the horrible conditions of poverty that exist in many places in Latin America, it would be inappropriate to romanticize about the region. Nevertheless, Harrison's call for Latin America to adopt wholesale, Protestant cultural values is also problematic. And while his brief against dependency theory may well have some merit, he again is remarkably uncritical about the values and beliefs he sees as the keys to "progress" and "success." One looks in vain for any sensitivity to the "price" that "progress," defined in largely material terms, exacts. There are, of course, echoes here of the long debate initiated by Max Weber regarding the relationship of Protestantism to capitalism.

environmental issue for the sake of discussion, and looks beyond the question of material abundance, there is ample evidence that American society and culture are in a bad state. Continued serious problems of racism, crime, poverty, urban blight, and the decline of family and community are clearly evident. More fundamentally, there is also ample evidence of a spiritual emptiness at the core of modern America. In other words, it can certainly be argued that American culture is neither something worth emulating, nor something worth exporting.

If it is fair to say that the export of American values and ways of organizing life is problematic, then withdrawal, contemplation, and discussion should really be the order of the day. And to this discussion, some Latin Americans do have much to contribute. The Mexican poet and essayist, Octavio Paz, who won the Nobel Prize for Literature in 1990 and who died last year, is a case in point. Paz, who was very familiar with the United States, having studied and worked in the country, published a long essay in 1950 titled *The Labyrinth of Solitude*.[62] Although the book has become a classic expression of a search for Mexican identity, part of that search involved reflection on the differences between the cultures of the United States and Mexico. In a particularly revealing passage, Paz wrote:

> Man is alone everywhere. But the solitude of the Mexican, under the great stone night of the high plateau that is still inhabited by insatiable gods, is very different from that of the North American, who wanders in an abstract world of machines, fellow citizens and moral precepts. In the Valley of Mexico man feels himself suspended between heaven and earth, he oscillates between contrary powers and forces, and petrified eyes, and devouring mouths. Reality – that is, the world that surrounds us – exists by itself here, has a life of its own, and was not invented by man as it was in the United States. . . . Nothing could be further from this feeling than the solitude of the North American. In the United States man does not feel that he has been torn from the center of creation

---

62. James. G. Lesniak, ed., *Contemporary Authors,* New Series Revision (Detroit, MI, 1991), 32, 328–331.

and suspended between hostile forces. He has built his own world and it is built in his own image: it is his mirror.[63]

What Paz suggests, here and elsewhere, is that there is a "givenness" in the "Mexican" sensibility regarding the nature of reality and human existence which stands in stark contrast to that in the United States. Human beings pale before the harsh and forbidding nature of existence. In the United States, on the other hand, reality is manipulated by human beings to meet their needs and aspirations. There is great faith in human competence.

This perception of fundamental cultural difference at what might be called the "ontological level" is echoed by the Mexican–American writer and social commentator, Richard Rodriguez. A controversial figure in some circles because of his opposition to bilingual education and affirmative action, Rodriguez is a very insightful cultural critic. He argues that Mexicans emphasize the tragic and Americans the comic. Although Rodriguez's parents were successful immigrants to the United States by any reasonable standard, his father was quick to point out to his son that most of what he (the father) accomplished by way of securing a middle-class standard of living was a mere chimera devoid of substance and any real meaning.

According to the father "nothing lasts a hundred years" and he believed that the culture of optimism and hubris of the United States would break his young son's heart. Raised by parents of a culture rooted in the dark and tragic history of Mexico, Rodriguez was taken aback the first time he heard "A Mighty Fortress is Our God" pouring forth from a Presbyterian Church in California where he grew up. His later comment was that "we did not sing like that in church!"[64] The uplifting power of the hymn sharply contrasted

63. Octavio Paz, *The Labyrinth of Solitude and Other Writings* (New York, 1985), 19–20. For a discussion of Paz and several other Mexicans who share certain commonalities of perspective, see Michael A. Weinstein, *The Polarity of Mexican Thought: Instrumentalism and Finalism* (University Park, PA, 1976).

64. *A World of Ideas with Bill Moyers: A Victim of Two Cultures*, Princeton, N.J., Films for the Humanities and Sciences, Inc., 1994, 60 minutes. Also see Richard Rodriguez, *Days of Obligation: An Argument with My Mexican Father* (New York, 1993).

with the sensibility attuned to suffering, pain, and defeat he experienced as part of his immigrant culture, steeped as it was in a Mexican sense of the inherently tragic limits of human existence. Both Paz and Rodriguez discuss the central importance of death in Mexican culture; and death, after all, is the ultimate denier of human pretensions. As Rodriguez puts it, "Mexico's lesson is death and that's a very wise lesson, America needs more death in its culture. I think we could learn from Mexico in that sense."[65]

That lesson is, of course, lost on many Americans.[66] In the United States there is the often absurd, and extremely costly, effort to deny death through the technological extension of the end of life, generally without much regard to its quality. And for the very affluent, there is the Alcor Foundation and its promise of deep-freeze immortality![67]

If all this seems a bit far removed from American designs for world order, that really is not the case. The point here is that the worldview that at some level denies the limits imposed by death, is the same worldview that inspires and sustains "empire as a way of life." At its deepest level, perhaps, that is what Williams' critique of American society and foreign policy is all about. A way of life

65. *A World of Ideas.*

66. Interestingly, notwithstanding Kennan's revulsion during his 1950 trip to Latin America, he noted in his *Memoirs* that the region might be "humanity's best hope for the future." He then went on to argue that human existence is by its very nature tragic, but that the manifestation of that nature was "less apocalyptic" in Latin America than elsewhere, particularly in the north with its stockpiling of nuclear weapons. Kennan went on to say that drawing on the great fund of precept and experience and custom that has been created in the Christian West to reconcile man with God and with the requirements of a civilized condition. . .the South American continent may prove some day to be the last repository and custodian of humane Christian values that men in the European motherlands and in North America – overfed, overorganized, and blinded by fear and ambition – have thrown away. (Kennan, *Memoirs 1925–1950*, 483–484)

67. The Alcor Life Extension Foundation, an organization dedicated to cryonics, the services of which are currently available. The Foundation can be located on the Internet at http://www.alcor.org/01b.html. On the ethical and public policy issues raised by the technological prolongation of life, see Daniel Callahan, *Setting Limits* (New York, 1987).

predicated on continual marketplace expansion throughout the globe is, by its very nature, a way of life that refuses to recognize any limits. The phenomenon of globalization, and the Clinton Administration's insistence that all markets must be open, is simply the most recent chapter in this long saga. While the United States should play some delimited international role in the future, much more is to be gained by quiet and sustained national contemplation and discussion of ways Americans should conduct themselves at home and abroad – ways which are more commensurate with the overarching limits that set the parameters of sustainable life.

And on that note, the argument comes full circle back to Bellah's point in the opening quotation. If the idea of divine judgment for the sins of arrogance and pride are not compelling, then there is the prospect of an uninhabitable planet which ought to inspire a second look at "empire as a way of life." And for the discussion to be worthwhile, all sorts of ideas, and a wide range of voices, should be entertained.

At one point in his career, for example, Williams argued for the breakup of the United States into a confederation of regionally based entities. This scheme was predicated on his belief that there is an inverse relationship between the scale of human institutions and the degree of authentic citizen participation in them. Kennan voiced similar views as to the merits of decentralization.[68] Their proposals are cited here simply as an example of the depth or scale of ideas that should be a part of any worthwhile discussion.

It is also important to emphasize that this need not become yet another conjuring of "the city on the hill." Other peoples need to have similar conversations from which all can learn. Whether or not the United States will be able to serve as a useful example of a truly democratic, humane, and sustainable society at some time in the future must remain, at least for the time being anyway, an open question. What is clear, however, is that the United States cannot

---

68. William Appleman Williams, "Radicals and Regionalism," 87–98; id. *America Confronts a Revolutionary World: 1776–1976* (New York, 1976), 183–185, 192–200. Kennan, *Around the Cragged Hill,* 142–144, 149–151.

continue to conduct its affairs, at home and abroad, as it has during the course of this ebbing century.

Reply to Commentators

I clearly created some confusion relative to the issue of "isolationism." While I have tried to clarify my position by revising somewhat the introductory part of the essay, let me add here that I am certainly not proposing a total withdrawal on the part of the United States and, even more strenuously, I am not recommending that the United States pursue a policy of unilateralism, a stance also associated with "isolationism." Without getting into specific foreign policy issues, let me give one example of what I think the United States faces today.

In the past twenty to thirty years, it is fair to say that medicine has been transformed by advances in pharmacology. Nevertheless, with an aging population in the United States, the government-sponsored medical insurance program (Medicare) for aged and retired individuals covers virtually none of the costs of prescription drugs. This is a national disgrace.

That a prescription drug program would severely compound the existing financial problems faced by Medicare goes without saying. However, these costs need to be viewed within the overall context of the national budget, which still allocates an enormous proportion of resources to the military to maintain the country's ability to project its power and its purposes virtually anywhere in the world. From my perspective, this is simply not acceptable, but it is an allocation of resources based on the needs of the country's interminable globalism.

In addition, retrenchment need not result in unilateralism. I would argue, in fact, that it should be coupled with a renewed commitment to international organizations and multilateralism. The country's recent history relative to its dues to the United Nations is for many of us from the United States a profound embarrassment.

As to the positive role that the United States has played in the twentieth century, it is in some ways undeniable. One of the things

I was most impressed with during the conference was the degree to which history is so utterly inescapable to Germans, or at least to those Germans who participated in the conference. I am referring here in particular to the comments of several German participants regarding their perception of the United States as welcome liberator from the horrors of the Third Reich and as the principal author of the political and social transformation that took place during the post-Second World War occupation.

I would argue that it is one thing to claim that American policy has not been all bad, that the history of the American empire compares favorably with that of others; nevertheless, it is quite another matter to suggest that it is anything other than imperial, or that the type of social and economic life it supports is sustainable, or worthy to be sustained, as a vision for the twenty- first century

Professor Crawford's comment that a usable past is partly a function of power is quite well put, I think. She stated that because America has won so many wars, it could afford, for example, to marginalize and forget, indeed, define out of existence, the genocide it practiced in the western portion of the continent during the nineteenth century. Now, undeniably, historiography during the last twenty to thirty years has brought some of those marginalized and discomforting aspects of American history to the fore. Nevertheless, I think it fair to say that American history as one of empire-building, and American history as one of almost continual environmental degradation, and both of these as a function of a broadly shared worldview which denies virtually all limits: these perspectives still remain very much at the margin in the United States. They are on the margin of the academic community and they are even more marginalized in the broader society and culture.

As to Professor Dietl's comments, it is difficult to know where to begin as they are so much at odds with the argument I present. Nevertheless, if I understand his position correctly, we both do share a view as to the importance of ideology in foreign policy, although he draws on a different historical strand, a perspective informed by the recent scholarship on the role of republicanism in the late colonial and early national periods. I actually find his discussion of this strand in relation to Woodrow Wilson to be quite interesting.

However, I remain convinced of the role of exceptionalism and mission in Wilson and his heirs' visions for world order. And finally, as to my own experience with empire in the Peace Corps, and as to the question of Dirk Moses to which I failed to respond adequately during the session, those of us in Micronesia during the late 1960s and 1970s were certainly encouraged to see our role in exceptionalist terms, as being something other than it was, that is, a form of "soft core" imperialism.

I could not disagree more regarding Professor Dietl's contention that Wilson's messianic rhetoric was simply propaganda designed to convince a reluctant population to go to war in Europe. Here I would go back to the very scholarship of republicanism that Professor Dietl cites, and particularly to Gordon Wood, one of its most important proponents. In an article many years ago Wood argued that the historical actors of the revolutionary and early national periods were more "victims" of their exaggerated rhetoric than they were the manipulators of it.[69]

This insight, of course, was the departing point for Bernard Bailyn's profound revision of the way many historians, including Wood, now think of that important period. It was Bailyn's re-reading of revolutionary pamphlets, and taking their rhetoric seriously and not as propaganda as the previous progressive historians had done, that led to so many of the new insights about the period over the past quarter-century. I think Bailyn and Wood's insight about the relationship of human beings to their rhetoric is important, and I believe it applies to Wilson as well. Certainly propaganda exists at times in history, but it seems to me that the burden of proof lies with those alleging it.

As to Professor Dietl's apparent suggestion that interests, more than ideals or ideology, have driven American foreign policy, I would simply say (and I think he may agree to some extent about this) that the two are not mutually exclusive. In my view, a perspective of a world without limits, where everything is possible, is exactly

69. Gordon S. Wood, "Rhetoric and Reality in the American Revolution," in Frank Otto Gatell and Allen Weinstein, eds., *American Themes: Essays in Historiography* (New York, 1968), 55–79.

the kind of perspective that serves to buttress and to reinforce the foreign policy of a country that sees its health as a function of an open world economic order. The two go hand in hand.

In closing, I want to go back to the question of an American vision for the twenty-first century. The American historian, Ronald Steel, says quite well what I am proposing relative to this. He says:

As the architects of the American Century did nearly a half century ago, we must reinvent American foreign policy for another postwar world. This means forging not only the mechanics and the superstructure, but the very terms of our relationship with other states – and beyond that, with ourselves. Perhaps most crucial is the restructuring of the compact we Americans have with one another – our sense of who we are as a people, what we stand for, and how we can best live among others. For as long as most of us can remember, foreign policy has dominated our national agenda. Our domestic needs have consistently been sacrificed to it. We have turned security against foreign challengers into a shibboleth. But we have neglected the threats to our own security that come from within.[70]

70. Ronald Steel, *The Temptations of a Superpower* (Cambridge, MA, 1996), 22–23.

2

Beyond *Weltpolitik*, Self-Containment and Civilian Power: United Germany's Normalizing Ambitions

Gunther Hellmann[1]

Introduction: Visions, Ambitions, and Order

For many the mere thought of associating Germany with "visions," "ambitions" and "order" is a nightmare, and even more so when this is done in the context of world politics (or even *Weltpolitik*). Since much of history has shown that German visions and ambitions about the creation of any type of *order* – world order in particular – have, more often than not, spelled trouble or even disaster, this is a difficult terrain for any author. Accordingly I have defined my task here in a rather restricted sense. In what follows I will concentrate on German debates about the role of the country in international affairs since unification in 1990. Moreover, given that much of the trouble and disaster which German visions and ambitions have caused historically had to do with the exercise of power in general and the use of force in particular, I will focus on these issues. Such a focus, it seems to me, is also well chosen because since unification many German visions have been circulating which seemed to suggest that a new and German model of international civility was finally making its

1. This essay was originally prepared for the Krefeld Historical Symposium 1999 'Visions of the Future in Germany and America', 13–17 May 1999. For assistance in preparing this essay, especially with regard to collecting and presenting public opinion data, I am grateful to Roland Bathon, Daniel Gaus, Ulrich Gross, Heiko Knobel, and Kemal Oezden. For comments and suggestions I thank Beverly Crawford and the participants at the Krefeld Symposium. Thanks also to the Institute of German Studies, especially Charlie Jeffery, for advance publication as a working paper and for assisting in checking my English and in translating the tables.

way into a world at large which was still dominated by 'traditional' great powers.

In this essay I will argue that, almost from the start, this well-intentioned self-image was an ill-conceived founding myth of united Germany which neither corresponded to the realities on the ground nor to the ambitions of the Germans themselves. The 'new' Germany which entered the world stage in 1990 was the old FRG in many ways. In its own self-image the old 'Bonn Republic' (as the Federal Republic before unification is nowadays called) had become a 'civilian' power because it had learned from its own history and the world's history more broadly. I argue, however, that it had been the power which it was because, more than anything else, the Allies wanted it to be that way. The still emerging 'Berlin Republic' similarly remains a power shaped by circumstance and choice, i.e. a power shaped by the environment in which it is located, by the aspirations of its leadership and people, and by the demands of other states.

If the German self-image of an avantgarde-type civilian power would have been accurate in 1990, the Germany of March 1999 fighting a war alongside its NATO allies almost exclusively on (at least questionable) human rights grounds probably would have to be ranked as a failure. If, however, the Germany of 1990 was no more (and no less) a power shaped by circumstance and choice than *any* of its partners in NATO and the European Union, today's Germany is equally no less (and no more) a 'normal' (or 'abnormal') country thus shaped. In other words, by most standards of 'civility' today's Germany is no more (and no less) 'civilian' than any of its allies. Therefore, if the transformation process which German foreign policy has experienced during the last nine years – a process which, as I will try to show, was remarkable indeed – is aptly regarded as a 'normalization' process, it is a process of 'normalization' which *any* country experiences at *any* time.

In addressing the question of Germany's global visions and ambitions I had to figure out some way of relating visions and ambitions. 'Vision' normally relates to the question what world we want to live in, i.e. a desirable future state of the world. 'Ambition' normally relates to the question of how we can get there, i.e. what we can and should do in order to realize this desirable future state of the world. In trying to relate these two concepts empirically I have decided to examine not only academic or political visions but also what beliefs the political elites and the public more broadly held with regard to the future. The rationale behind this methodological strategy was that for visions to be actually moving policy they had to be grounded in broader beliefs of decision-makers and the people on whom they depend, the voters. As a result, I have been looking at three things: (1) explicit visions and ambitions outlined in political speeches and academic books; (2) two prominent foreign policy decisions in 1990/91 and 1999 which should enable us to check the nexus between vision and ambition (here: concrete political steps towards a desired future); and (3) extensive data from public opinion polls among foreign policy elites and the German public more broadly.

In arguing that Germany has gone through a process of 'normalization' I will proceed as follows. As a start I will first recount Germany's role during the Gulf War. This crucial episode coinciding with German unification in 1990 reveals that the country was caught largely unprepared for what was to come in January and February 1991. Still, even at that time decision-makers were seriously (if only briefly) considering sending German troops alongside the anti-Saddam coalition. The reasons for considering such a decision *and* for finally deciding against had nothing to do with *either Weltpolitik* in the tradition of the *Kaiserreich* or the Third Reich *or* with a presumed mistrust among Germans themselves that their country had somehow to 'contain' itself *or* with a more fundamental change of the country towards a new type of 'civilian power.' Rather, in addition to securing safe ratification of the 'Two-plus-Four' treaty (which was only completed in March 1991) it was a specific West German foreign policy tradition, the tradition of exercising 'restraint,' which prevailed over some of the more ambitious designs by the American allies in particular.

The Gulf War experience setting off a new world order where similar regional conflicts and civil wars were starting to proliferate had a sobering and lasting effect on German minds. Far from sharing some of the more visionary 'internationalist' designs of a segment of German intellectuals and academics the German public slowly but steadily adjusted to the new realities of an increasingly conflictual world. An even accelerated speed of adjustment was noticeable among the foreign policy elites more broadly. As a result, nine years after the Gulf War Germany's 'normalization' process has carried the country in a direction which few observers had expected in 1990. In security matters – be it regionally or globally – the 'new' Germany still envisioned itself as reluctant a power as the old one. Yet given that the environment of its alliance had changed dramatically during these years Germany has increasingly become the 'normal' ally its partners had hoped for. Irrespective of whether *this* process of 'normalization' is applauded or criticized, it is something with which Germany as well as its allies have to live. In security matters Germany is having a harder time living with it than its allies. In European matters (defined more narrowly in the context of the European Union) the opposite is the case. As Germany's *European* visions fade, Germany's EU partners will increasingly be faced with 'normal' German ambitions – ambitions much more similar to their own. I doubt that they will like it. In the end, therefore, a shade of nightmare might reappear at a very distant horizon – but, as yet, it is only a shade.

A Defining Moment: German Unification, the Gulf War and *Ultima Irratio*

Nineteen-ninety through 1992 were the formative years of Germany's 'new' foreign policy. At the time of unification (i.e. between September and December 1990) the political rhetoric about Germany's global visions and ambitions was filled with sentences redeploying certain key terms in varying contexts. What was least surprising for the experienced observers of German foreign policy was that these visions were primarily couched in terms of 'Europe' and 'responsibility'. Hans-Dietrich Genscher's interpretation of the preamble of the Basic Law – according to which a united Germany would 'aspire to serve peace around the world as a member with equal rights in a united Europe' – probably best expressed how

Germans wanted to see themselves and be seen by others. Although his more far-reaching claims about the 'identity' of Germany's national and European interests (which Genscher had so forcefully expressed just the day before the Wall came down a year earlier[2]) no longer showed up, his judgement that a unified Germany carried significantly more 'European' and 'global responsibility' was widely shared. Against the dual background of both 'the greater weight of united Germany' in international politics and 'the question of the peoples of Europe, how we will use this increased weight,' the conduct of a 'policy of the good example' ('Politik des guten Beispiels') or, alternatively, a 'policy of responsibility' ('Verantwortüngspolitik') sounded good to German ears, especially when contrasted with notions of 'power politics' ('Machtpolitik') associated with German foreign policy prior to the Federal Republic.[3] As to the specific areas of Germany's 'greater responsibility' (or 'special responsibility') Genscher listed seven points: (1) the 'unique link between Germany and France'; (2) developments in Central and Eastern Europe, especially with regard to a 'European policy of stability in which military factors will play an ever decreasing role'; (3) the relationship with the Soviet Union and (4) Poland; (5) the 'deepening and institutionalization of the CSCE process,' especially with regard to the fact that 'a new relationship between the members of the two military alliances (NATO and Warsaw Pact, G.H.) opens the way for new cooperative structures in Europe'; (6) a 'strengthening of the transatlantic relationship' based on a new relationship between the European Union and North America; and (7) a 'new world order' based on the hope of building 'a new culture of international coexistence.'[4]

2. Cf. *Deutscher Bundestag*, Stenographischer Bericht, 11. Legislaturperiode, 173. Sitzung (8. November 1989), pp. 13050D and 13051D (subsequently cited as *DBT* 11/173, 8.11.1989).

3. 'Erklärung der Bundesregierung zum Vertrag über die abschließende Regelung in bezug auf Deutschland durch den Bundesminister des Auswärtigen, Hans-Dietrich Genscher, am 20. September 1990', *DBT* 11/226, 17803D and 17804C.

4. *Ibid.*, 17805A–17807A. See also 'Rede des Bundesministers des Auswärtigen, Hans-Dietrich Genscher, vor der 45. Generalversammlung der Vereinten Nationen

However, a closer reading of both public debates about this new German role as well as concrete foreign policy decisions reveal that both Genscher and his coalition partners as well as the opposition parties had more concrete (and sharply differing) ideas as to where Germany ought to be heading. In hindsight one could even argue that these debates clearly foreshadowed the changes that were to come in subsequent years. Against the background of the 'Two-plus-Four' talks (which were only completed in mid-September), the 1990/91 Gulf War marked the most disturbing international event from a German perspective because it forced Germany even before unification had formally been completed (on October 3, 1990) to spell out in very concrete detail how it would define its role in such a conflict.

As to the contrast between rhetoric and action two phases can be distinguished: (1) the final phase of 'Two–plus–Four' leading up to unification (during this phase the conflict in the Gulf steadily escalated, culminating in the November 8 announcement by President Bush that the US-led coalition would prepare for an offensive military option); (2) mid–November 1990 through February 1991 (during this period German hostages held in Iraq were released and the first all-German elections took place in early December, with the new *Bundestag* meeting for its first sessions starting in mid-January 1991).

---

am 26.9.1990' (Auswärtiges Amt 1995: 708). The fact that Genscher's rhetoric did not fully convince foreign observers neither surprised nor deterred Genscher in sticking to it. Marsh (1995: 167), for instance, then a British journalist covering Germany, later said that Genscher was the quintessential master in spelling out a 'seraphic vision of a Germany diligently exercising its new found responsibilities in pursuit of universal brotherhood.' Geipel, an American expert on Germany, similarly judged that 'to take the German elite at its word is to drown in the latest conventional wisdom' (Geipel 1993: 19).

Visions of Civilian *Weltpolitik* and the Blessings of Constitutional Constraints

It was only three weeks after the Caucasus summit in July 1990 (where Chancellor Kohl and Soviet President Gorbachev settled the outstanding issues relating to unification) that German decision-makers were faced with new foreign policy realities. Iraq's invasion and occupation of Kuwait in early August occurred at a time when the foreign policy establishment was preoccupied with wrapping up the 'Two-plus-Four' negotiations. Yet behind the scenes decision-makers at the highest level were deliberating an unprecedented move: to send the *Bundeswehr* to the Gulf in support of the anti-Saddam coalition.

Shortly after the Iraqi invasion the American administration had informally approached the military attaché at the German embassy in Washington to ask whether Germany would be ready to send troops to the Gulf.[5] Within a week Defense Ministry circles in Bonn hinted publicly that a deployment of the German Navy would indeed be conceivable and that it could even start within seven to ten days. Among the main reasons for this major departure from previous practice, these unnamed sources pointed to the 'new situation' which had emerged owing to the 'new thinking on security' and the participation of the Soviet Union in the anti-Saddam coalition.[6] Moreover, Hans Stercken (a CDU member and chairman of the Bundestag's Foreign Affairs Committee) argued that 'we should not in advance count ourselves out of involvement . . . if through readiness we can avert the danger of escalation.'[7]

5. See Inacker, (1991: 84). Based on background interviews. Inacker reports that the official request was made in a letter from US Secretary of Defense Cheney to Defense Minister Stoltenberg dated August 20, 1990. For a more detailed analysis of German decision-making regarding the Gulf War see Hellmann (1997: 165–194).

6. See 'Streit um Bundeswehreinsatz am Golf. Hardthöhe schließt Präsenz außerhalb des NATO-Gebiets nicht aus', *Süddeutsche Zeitung* (August 10, 1990), 2; see also *DPA* report from Bonn (August 9, 1990), *FBIS-WEU-90-154* (August 9, 1990), 3.

7. See *DPA* report from Hanover (August 8, 1990), *FBIS-WEU-90-154* (August 9, 1990) 3.

Chancellor Kohl himself hinted that Germany would be willing to send troops, if a multilateral cover could be provided thereby making it difficult for Germany to shun its obligations.[8] However, a broad coalition of politicians – including members of Kohl's party[9] – opposed any such thought, arguing that the German constitution prohibited any deployment of the Bundeswehr outside NATO territory. Although constitutional experts differed as to whether this was indeed the proper interpretation of the Basic Law, there had been a long-established *political* consensus among all the major parties to interpret the constitution restrictively.[10] Foreign Minister Genscher in particular rejected any deployment of the Bundeswehr outside NATO territory adding – in a pointed counter to Chancellor Kohl – that it would even be impossible for German troops to participate in a UN peacekeeping mission unless the Basic Law was changed.[11]

---

8. According to Italian Foreign Minister Gianni de Michelis, Kohl had informed the Italian Government in mid-August that Germany might consider sending troops not only to the Mediterranean, but also to the Persian Gulf if the WEU at its meeting on August 21 decided to send ships to the Gulf; see 'Deutsche Minensuchboote in den Golf?', *Frankfurter Allgemeine Zeitung* (August 15, 1990), 2.

9. See 'Streit um Bundeswehreinsatz am Golf', *Süddeutsche Zeitung* (August 10, 1990), 2.

10. See the debate between Dieter Blumenwitz, 'Die Politik kann frei entscheiden,' and Hans-Peter Schneider, 'Der Verteidigungsauftrag ist eng auszulegen,' *Süddeutsche Zeitung* (August 22, 1990), 8. As Harald Müller (1992: 139) put it, before 1990 there existed 'an unequivocal interpretation of ambiguous legal language'. Inacker (1991: 28–30) reports that in May 1982 the Federal Government under Chancellor Schmidt asked for a constitutional opinion from the Justice Ministry as to whether or not the Bundeswehr could participate 'out of area.' This was apparently done against the background of the Iran–Iraq war and the possibility of Western intervention in case of an escalation of the conflict. The legal opinion turned out to advise against the use of the Bundeswehr 'out of area,' evading, however, the sensitive issue whether the Bundeswehr could participate within the framework of the UN.

11. See 'Keine Mehrheit für Marine-Einsatz im Golf', *Süddeutsche Zeitung* (August 16, 1990), 1 and 'Genscher gegen Einsatz deutscher Kriegsschiffe im Persischen Golf', *Der Tagesspiegel* (August 16, 1990), 1. Referring to the still ongoing negotiations in the 'Two-plus-Four' context, the Chancellor argued that 'one cannot claim international solidarity for oneself and then refuse when others ask

These conflicting views were reconciled in two meetings on August 20. First the Chancellor met with the Foreign and Defense Minister in the morning, agreeing not to send any troops to the Persian Gulf and to stick to the traditional interpretation of the Basic Law.[12] Then Genscher and Stoltenberg appeared before a joint meeting of the Bundestag Foreign and Defense Committees explaining the position of the Federal Government.[13] Whereas

---

for international solidarity from us. This is my very clear position.' Asked whether he could imagine the use of the Bundeswehr in the Gulf conflict within the framework of a UN contingent, he said: 'If it comes to a clear vote by the United Nations I can imagine a number of possibilities.' See *DPA* report from Bonn (August 16, 1990), *FBIS-WEU-90-160* (August 17, 1990), 10; for background see also K. Feldmeyer and G. Bannas, 'Streit in der Bonner Koalition über Bundeswehreinsatz am Golf,' *Frankfurter Allgemeine Zeitung,* (August 16, 1990), 2; G. Bannas, 'Bonn sucht nach einer Einigung im Streit um Golfeinsatz', *Frankfurter Allgemeine Zeitung* (August 18, 1990), 4 and 'Bundeswehr unter UN-Kommando?,' *Die Welt* (August 18/19, 1990), 1.

12. In his memoirs Genscher (1995: 902) pointed out that 'the status of the "Two–plus–Four" talks called for restraint,' a reference to his judgement that it would sharply contradict the provisions of the treaty (and send disturbing signals to Moscow) if Germany would send troops to the Gulf at this point in time. The draft treaty which had already been agreed to in its core aspects, committed Germany to conduct its foreign policy in such a way 'that only peace will emanate from German soil' ('daß von deutschem Boden nur Frieden ausgehen wird'); see Article 2 of the 'Two–plus–Four'-Treaty, 'Vertrag über die abschließende Regelung in bezug auf Deutschland, 12 September 1990,' *Bulletin. Presse- und Informationsamt der Bundesregierung,* No.109 (September 14, 1990), 1153–1156. For background on the importance of this aspect from the Soviet point of view see the memoirs of Eduard Schewardnadse (1991: 233–267, esp. 248). Chancellor Kohl probably accepted this reasoning in spite of his conviction that Germany was morally obliged to help the United States. In a telephone conversation on September 6 with President Bush the Chancellor said that given the solidarity which Germany had always received from the United States in the past, he personally felt particularly troubled ('. . . daß es ihn persönlich sehr belaste') that the Germans could not do more at this point in time (Teltschik 1991: 358).

13. See K. Feldmeyer, 'Die Bundesmarine wird sich nicht an Aktionen im Golf beteiligen', *Frankfurter Allgemeine Zeitung* (August 21,1990), 4. Genscher for his part said shortly afterwards that he did not share the views of those whom he characterized as being 'keen to participate under any circumstances in an international conflict.' (See 'Unsere Bundeswehr ist für Einsätze unter der UN-Charta

Stoltenberg supported the decision reached he also stated his reservations vis-à-vis the current interpretation of the Basic Law. In the evening Kohl finally met with the leaders of the major parties. In these talks the leaders of the governing coalition parties (CDU, CSU, and FDP) and the opposition party (SPD) expressed their support for the decision reached between Kohl, Genscher, and Stoltenberg earlier. They also agreed to work to amend the constitution to allow future military participation in UN actions. However, they left unsettled whether they would pursue such a change before or after the elections scheduled for December.[14]

The outcome of this precedent-setting episode had some of the typical hallmarks of a bureaucratic and political compromise. Genscher, the Foreign Ministry, and the FDP on the one hand strictly opposed any direct military involvement. Rather than participating militarily they wanted to limit Germany's role to political support and direct financial assistance to those Middle East countries most affected by the embargo.[15] Stoltenberg, the Defense Ministry, and large parts of the CDU and CSU, on the otherhand, were prepared to go much further in terms of direct military support.[16] However, in the end they did not push very hard and

gut geeignet. Interview mit Hans-Dietrich Genscher,' *Süddeutsche Zeitung*, August 25/26, 1990, 7.)

14. See Feldmeyer, n. 13, and U. Bergdoll, 'Kein Einsatz der Bundeswehr am Golf', *Süddeutsche Zeitung* (August 21, 1990), 1. As it turned out it took four more years (and a decision of the Federal Constitutional Court in July 1994) to settle these differences. According to the court's decision the Basic Law allowed for Bundeswehr out-of-area participation in the context of international organizations irrespective of whether these were based on the principle of collective security or collective defense. See 'Urteil des Bundesverfassungsgerichts über die Verfassungsbeschwerden gegen internationale Einsätze der Bundeswehr', *Europa Archiv* 49: D428 ff.

15. For a detailed discussion of Germany's overall financial, military-technical, and logistical contributions to the anti-Saddam coalition see Hellmann (1997: 167–172). All in all this amounted to some DM 18 billion (or almost one third of Germany's annual defense budget).

16. Inacker (1991: 115) reports that military planners in the Defense Ministry had developed a scenario for deploying one division of the Bundeswehr to the Persian Gulf in the fall of 1990.

broader political considerations prevailed. Given the FRG's history, it would indeed have been unprecedented if the Kohl government had decided to send German troops abroad without securing the broadest possible consensus, i.e. including (at least) the SPD opposition. One of Chancellor Kohl's closest advisers, the Minister in the Chancellor's Office Rudolf Seiters, was probably also speaking for Helmut Kohl when he said in an interview shortly before August 20 agreement that the deployment of Bundeswehr troops to the Persian Gulf should not become a subject of partisan controversy.[17]

Controversy, however, continued and even intensified after President Bush's November 8 announcement that the US-led coalition would prepare for an offensive military option.[18] This was especially visible in the rhetoric of the Greens and the SPD. Throughout the preceding months, both parties had accused the governing coalition of once again aiming at a new great power role for Germany. Given the fact that the first all-German elections at the national level in early December had already been set by August, members of the Bundestag opposition (the SPD and the Greens) were increasingly demanding that Germany's 'new role as a world power' should take center stage in the upcoming election campaign.[19] The 'internationalist' policies advocated by the Greens here marked the strongest contrast to the politics of governing coalition.[20] Interestingly enough, deputies of the Greens, such as Antje Vollmer, appeared to take it for granted (and welcome it) that

---

17. Seiters made this point in an interview which was published two days before the August 20 meeting between the party leaders, see 'CSU: FDP muß ihre Haltung ändern', *Süddeutsche Zeitung* (August 20, 1990), 2. Asked in an opinion poll in August 1990 whether they would support or oppose a change of the Basic Law in order to enable the Bundeswehr to participate in out-of-area operations, 53 percent of Germans objected with 32 percent in support and 15 percent undecided (Noelle-Neumann and Köcher, 1993: 1085).

18. See excerpts from President Bush's news conference at the White House on November 8, 1990 (in Sifrah and Cerf 1991: 228–229).

19. See Antje Vollmer, *DBT* 11/220 (August 9, 1990), 1740D. Vollmer was a leading deputy of the Green Party.

20. The only party rivalling with the Greens for true "demilitarization" rhetoric was the Party of Democratic Socialism, the former SED (PDS 1990: 49–53).

Germany would henceforth again be conducting *Weltpolitik* since, as she pointed out, 'the European world, in spite of all scepticism and resentment, . . . no longer fears this new role of the Germans.'[21] In outlining the presumed reasons for Europe's confidence vis-à-vis the Germans, Vollmer pointed to two major factors: According to her, Europe no longer feared the Germans because her own generation (the so-called '1968 generation') had 'thoroughly civilized and humanized' German society, which before had been character-ized by crude anti-communism, self-aggrandizement ('Wir-sind-wieder-wer-Gegröle'), and narrow-mindedness ('spießig und muffig').[22] This legacy in her view carried a clear message for a 'civilian' international future of the Germans: A new Germany once again conducting *Weltpolitik* had 'the opportunity, never again to shed the experience of the dictatorship of the left and the right from its historical baggage. Given that baggage, one has to proceed more slowly.'[23] The party programme of the Greens, which was formulated on the basis of difficult compromises and long sessions,[24] spelled out in detail what this civilian future implied. Since the 'climate of peace' was 'favorable,' Germany's new slow-moving *Weltpolitik* amounted to pursuing a strategy of 'unilateral disarma-ment' in conjunction with a policy of 'demilitarization' which would − 'actively, not meekly' − aim at the creation of a 'new order of peace' through 'bloc subversion' on the one hand and 'bloc tran-scending cooperation' on the other. The ultimate goal was to create 'a world without military blocs and a society without weapons and

21. 'Bei Ihren weltpolitischen Ausflügen erleben Sie, Herr Bundeskanzler . . ., daß wir Deutschen jetzt tatsächlich − das ist das Neue − Weltpolitik machen dürfen und daß offenbar die Welt nichts dagegen hat' (*DBT*, 11/220 [August 9, 1990], 17402A).

22. Ibid., p. 17402A–D.

23. Ibid., p. 17402D.

24. See Ludger Volmer (1998: 383–90). Volmer, who currently serves as deputy ('Staatssekretär') under Foreign Minister Joschka Fischer in the coalition govern-ment between SPD and Bündnis 90/Die Grünen, is generally counted as a member of the more 'left'-leaning faction within the party. His detailed history of the debates on foreign policy among the Greens was published shortly before he assumed his official position.

armies' (Die Grünen 1990: 18, 20–1). The activist 'internationalist' impulse of this policy was balanced by an emphasis on 'a policy of self-restraint' complemented by 'an opening of the FRG vis-à-vis international control mechanisms as well as effective binding of the FRG in multilateral contexts which assure additional international control and restrictions of German power' (Die Grünen 1990: 20–1). The internationalist agenda propagated by the Greens thus combined *Weltpolitik*-activism *and* self-containment of German power.[25]

Although the SPD was more circumspect in choosing its language, the overall thrust of its vision pointed in a similar direction. At the time when Antje Vollmer was calling for a substantive definition of 'world power' in terms of 'civility' in August, she had directly addressed herself to the SPD candidate for the chancellorship, the Prime Minister of Saarland, Oskar Lafontaine. In Vollmer's view, Lafontaine's preoccupation with internal unification issues appeared to 'evade the new international tasks of a German world power.'[26] A few weeks later Lafontaine responded by saying that 'the term world power' would be inappropriate. Instead, he suggested that Germany should display 'a lot of restraint.' Like the Greens, Lafontaine also saw 'new opportunities' regarding Germany's international role which 'should be used to take over leadership roles' ('Vorreiterrollen') in the fields of disarmament and controls over arms exports rather than 'talking us with utmost speed into a change of the constitution in order to send German troops to the Gulf.'[27] Such remarks became even more pointed after President

---

25. For background to the decision making process leading up to these formulations (especially with regard to the differences between a more radical faction among the Greens which were calling for an end to Germany's NATO membership – 'Wir müssen raus aus der NATO' – and a more moderate faction led by 'Joschka Fischer and his faithful followers' which was advocating a 'fundamental change of course towards a Pro-NATO position') see Volmer (1998: 386–389).

26. *DBT*, 11/220 (August 9, 1990), 17402D.

27. *DBT*, 11/226 (September 20, 1990), 17809C–17810C. In the same session, Gerald Häfner, a deputy of the Greens supported this position, saying that those 'who, after German unity, cannot think of anything better than German units,

Bush's announcement in early November. After former Chancellor Willy Brandt had secured the release of hostages held in Baghdad, he implored the Kohl government to stick to diplomatic means and economic sanctions 'in order to reach, in every conceivable way, a political solution.' Germany 'must not lag behind anybody in its efforts for peace,' Brandt said, because war, in his view, was 'the *ultima irratio* of politics.'[28]

'And I fear that this is only the beginning of a new development . . .': The Politics of Avoiding War and Evading Alliance Commitments

Although these debates provided first hints as to the difficulties the foreign policy elites had in spelling out visions and ambitions for united Germany in dealing with the unexpected realities of war, it would be misleading to take this sample of views as evidence that the crisis in the Gulf attracted much attention in its early phase. Rather, as the Bonn correspondent of the Washington Post reported in early November, with the election campaign moving into final gear the situation in the Persian Gulf went 'virtually unmentioned.'[29] Yet, with the elections decided and the *ultima irratio* approaching quickly in early January, the debate heated up and the international community saw the German elites engaged in a frantic effort to

---

play with fire', ibid., 17825C. The SPD's election programme for the period 1990–1994, which was approved by a party congress in late September 1990, outlines the following additional foreign policy objectives: 'drastic disarmament' including a 50 percent reduction in the strength of Bundeswehr as well as – 'in the medium term' – of the defense budget more broadly; a ban on weapons exports; the withdrawal of all nuclear weapons from German soil; and the redistribution of 'at least DM 1 billion' from the defense budget to the development aid budget. The programme also stated that the SPD 'opposes the deployment and additional military tasks of NATO and the WEU outside the jurisdiction of the alliance' (SPD 1990: 21–22).

28. *DBT*, 11/235 (November 15, 1990), 18842B and 18843C.

29. M. Fisher, 'In Bonn and Tokyo, Gulf Crisis Is Better Left Unmentioned,' *International Herald Tribune* (November 5, 1990), 1 and 4.

somehow arrest what Genscher had called the 'war automatism.'
Genscher's reaction on January 10, 1991 to the upcoming visit of
UN Secretary General Perez de Cuellar to Baghdad ('In such a
critical situation one must give diplomacy the chance to preserve
peace'[30]) probably best summarized the mood in Bonn and beyond:
It was simply unimaginable for Germans (including the highest
political leadership) that the crisis in the Gulf could further escalate.
The issue was not framed in terms of 'effectiveness' of *force versus
sanctions*. Rather, the dominating issue was whether there would be
war or more diplomacy – and faced with *that* choice the Germans
certainly preferred the latter.[31] It should not have come as such a
surprise, therefore, that Germany was paralysed after the beginning
of the air war. 'We are very decisively against surrendering to a
mechanism of war. We are in favour of sanctions' and: 'Rather 1,000
days of negotiations than one day of war' – these statements by
Joschka Fischer and Heidemarie Wieczorek-Zeul probably best
expressed what most Germans felt.[32]

---

30. Genscher Interview with *Hesse Radio*, cited in *DPA* report from Frankfurt
(January 10, 1991), *FBIS-WEU-91-007* (January 10, 1991), 14–15.

31. In a telephone survey conducted right before the expiration of the deadline
on January 17, 1991 79 percent of Germans were in favor of continued diplomatic
efforts and more than 80 percent 'prefered a political solution' to the crisis if a war
would 'cost the lives of 1,000 US soldiers' (see '79 Prozent der Bundesbürger für
weitere Verhandlungen', *Der Tagesspiegel* (January 16, 1991), 7). According to another
survey 25 percent favored an advance by the allied troops; see *DPA* report from
Frankfurt January 10, 1991, *FBIS-WEU-91-008*, (January 11, 1991), 11.

32. 'Kaum ist die Einheit da, schickt man deutsche Soldaten zur Front. Interview
mit Joschka Fischer', *Frankfurter Rundschau* (January 9, 1991), 6. It is a 'grave matter,'
Fischer criticized, that 'we have to live through a mechanism of war preparations
which almost reminds me of Sarajevo and the ultimatum which was issued then'.
Rather than engaging in 'geopolitics with military means' – as the Kohl government
presumably did – Fischer advocated a policy of sanctions. Given the 'solidarity of
the international community of states' he thought that sanctions provided for a
'clear alternative,' 'an opportunity to restore international order and the respect of
sovereignty and human rights through peaceful means.' (At the time of the interview
Fischer was head of the parliamentary group of the Greens in the state parliament
of Hesse. It is important to recall that in 1990 'Sarajevo' was still a metaphor for
the accidental break-out of war as in 1914 and not yet a metaphor for a beleaguered

Given that Germany was at the sidelines with regard to the preparations for a military offensive, the debate about war versus diplomacy was less consequential than the more immediate issue of how Germany would respond to requests for alliance support. For more than four decades Germany had profited from the security guarantees offered by its allies. As it became ever more likely that the war in the Gulf would escalate, Germany for the first time ever was faced with the eventuality that its own support would be called for. In contrast to the decision not to send troops to the Gulf because of constitutional constraints vis-à-vis 'out of area' operations, Turkey's request for alliance support in case of an Iraqi attack could not as easily be refused.

On December 20, 1990 the Turkish government filed a request for assistance by its NATO allies. As a result NATO's Defence Planning Committee decided in early January to send the Allied Mobile Force's air component to bases in southeastern Turkey. Given the fact that a NATO ally was calling for help and since this rapid reaction unit was highly integrated and included some 200 Bundeswehr soldiers and 18 German fighter jets (apart from similar Belgian and Italian contingents) the German government would have had a very hard time to justify not participating. On the first day of the new year the German government decided to send the Bundeswehr

---

city shelled at will from the surrounding hills, as in the mid-1990s.) Although the German public was as hesitant as Fischer to escalate the war, a large majority of Germans (81 percent) thought that the use of force against Saddam Hussein was 'correct' after the air war had begun in mid-January. Still, three quarters of those questioned rejected any direct military involvement by Germany (with only 20 percent in favor); see *ADN* report from Tübingen (January 22, 1991), *FBIS-WEU-91-014* (January 22, 1991), 22. The public, however, did not share Fischer's optimism regarding the use of sanctions. Only one in three thought that sanctions were of any use (see *DPA* report from Frankfurt [January 10, 1991], *FBIS-WEU-91-008* [January 11, 1991], 11). For Heidemarie Wieczorek-Zeul's statement see *DPA* report from Hamburg January 12, 1991, quoted in *FBIS-WEU-91-009* (January 14, 1991), 25–26 (Wieczorek-Zeul, who is currently serving as minister for international development, then was SPD Deputy in the Bundestag and Deputy Chairman of the Social Democrats).

to Turkey in order to 'deter aggression,' as the government spokesman said.[33] However, the opposition parties as well as some senior representatives of the governing coalition were arguing that an Iraqi attack on Turkey would *not* automatically lead to German assistance to Turkey under Article 5 of the Washington Treaty because, as some critics argued, allied air strikes from Turkish soil under the mandate of the UN Security Council would in effect amount to *offensive*, not *defensive* operations. If Iraq were to retaliate, as one might expect, this could not be taken to trigger assistance obligations under Article 5 of the Washington Treaty.[34] Joschka Fischer, among others, made the criticism that the deployment of German troops 'to the front' marked a 'qualitative change' in post-World War II history. For the first time German soldiers were called to 'war service' ('Kriegsdienst') rather than mere 'military service' ('Militärdienst'). 'And I fear that this is only the beginning of a new development. For the first time we have to deal with geopolitics with military means by our government rather than the defense of one's own country. To this we as Greens say very clearly "No".' Asked whether it wouldn't be demanding too much from Chancellor Kohl if he were to stand 'head-on' against the Americans and the British, Fischer said: 'Kohl is chancellor and significant as such: he has democratic legitimacy.'[35]

The official government statement was also ambiguous as to how to define eventualities. In announcing the decision to deploy the Bundeswehr, the spokesman of the Federal Government had left open whether the Bundeswehr units would automatically assist Turkey if the Iraqi air force were to launch air strikes on Turkey in response to allied air strikes from Turkish soil. He merely said that

---

33. See *DPA* report from Bonn, January 2, 1991, *FBIS-WEU-91-0023* (January 3, 1991), 12. For background to the decision see Inacker (1991: 108–109).

34. For a sample of statements along these lines from respresentatives of the opposition as well as the governing coalition parties see C. Gennrich, 'Bonn will durch Entsendung von Alpha-Jets den Irak abschrecken,' *Frankfurter Allgemeine Zeitung*, 4 January 1991, 2; *ADN* report from Bonn, 4 January 1991, *FBIS-WEU-91-003* (January 4, 1991), 5; 'Keine Mehrheit für Bundeswehr-Einsatz,' *Süddeutsche Zeitung* (January 23, 1991), 2.

35. See Frankfurter Rundschau, n. 32.

the Bundeswehr would only fight 'in the event of a *clear aggression* against the alliance partner Turkey.'[36]

To sum up: The political rhetoric and the actions taken during the course of the final phase of German unification and the escalation of the Gulf War clearly show that uniting (and united) Germany was largely unprepared for these new developments. The overwhelming majority of Germans certainly didn't like what they were seeing: its own political leadership seriously (if only briefly) considering breaking with past practices by sending the Bundeswehr to the Gulf in the context of the UN-authorized and US-led anti-Saddam coalition; an ally which had stood at Germany's side for four decades during the height of the Cold War now asking for reciprocal support in case of an attack; a dictator refusing to consider any 'diplomatic solution'; an American President at peace with himself while ordering the use of force; and, finally and most awkwardly, Iraqi chemical warheads produced with German know-how in the hands of 'a Hitler' determined to terrorize the Jewish state.

German legacies of *Machtpolitik* and *Weltpolitik*, self-images of the FRG as a 'civilian power' and 'trading state,' moral obligations of 'Auschwitz never again' in general and support for the state of Israel in particular – all these factors which dominated public debates about Germany's new international role in subsequent years were here fused in an intricate web of 'multilemmas.' The Hitler–Saddam analogy in particular struck a sensitive nerve.[37] If there was *any* analogy which ought to have mobilized 'the German fighting spirit'[38] it should have been a reminder of Hitler's legacy – and indeed it

36. See *DPA* report from Bonn, January 2, 1991, *FBIS-WEU-91-002* (January 3, 1991), 12 (emphasis added), and G. Bannas, 'Bundeswehrflugzeuge in die Türkei?,' *Frankfurter Allgemeine Zeitung* (January 3, 1991), 2.

37. See W. Safire, 'The Hitler Analogy,' *New York Times* (August 24, 1990), reprinted in Sifrah and Cerf (1991: 210–212); see also 'Vergleich Hitler-Hussein gerügt. Vor allem Juden in USA sind empört über Präsident Bush', *Frankfurter Rundschau* (November 5, 1990), 2.

38. J. Hoagland, 'German Wobbling Puts the Trans-Atlantic Partnership at Risk', *International Herald Tribune* (January 30, 1991), 6.

did. Like few other debates before or after, this one captured the minds of German intellectuals[39] – and in many ways it foreshadowed subsequent debates about the use of the Bundeswehr in the Balkans. To the astonishment of many observers, however, the dividing line was not between left and right but rather among left intellectuals.[40] Although prominent writers and academics rejected the Saddam–Hitler analogy as an 'apples and oranges' comparison,[41] a surprising number of well-known left-leaning intellectuals vehemently spoke out 'in favour of this war.'[42] Yet with the war ending rather quickly and with 'internal unification' just about to start, the first months of the first democratically legitimized all-German parliament since 1932 certainly didn't look like a propitious time for spelling out visions beyond the very general acknowledgement to shoulder 'greater responsibility.' Still, as the subsequent years showed, Germany's Gulf War experience had a lasting effect in that it initiated the 'normalizing' nation to the sobering realities of a new world order which contrasted sharply with Hans-Dietrich Genscher's hopes for 'a new culture of international coexistence' and which also seemed to run counter to the expectations raised by the rhetoric of a 'policy of the good example.'

39. See 'Ein amerikanischer Jude und eine deutsche Friedensrede. Ein Briefwechsel unter den linken Freunden Andrei Markovits und Jürgen Hoffmann, aus dem eine Grundsatzdebatte wurde', *Frankfurter Rundschau* (February 16, 1991), 6.

40. See G. Hofmann, 'Wenn die Linke normal sein will. Nicht der Pazifismus, sondern das Bekenntnis zum Krieg fällt auf,' *Die Zeit*, no. 8 (February 15, 1991), 5; and K. Hartung, 'Ein zweites München für Saddam Hussein?,' *tageszeitung* (January 19, 1991), reprinted in *Golf-Journal zum Wüstenkrieg* (Frankfurt: Tageszeitungsverlagsgesellschaft "die taz" 1991), 60–61.

41. So the German author Günter Grass in an interview with the newspaper *tageszeitung* (February 16, 1991), 68. See also J. Habermas, 'Wider die Logik des Krieges', *Die Zeit*, no. 8 (February 15, 1991), 40.

42. See especially W. Biermann, 'Kriegshetze, Friedenshetze,' *Die Zeit*, no. 6 (February 1, 1991), 51 and H.M. Enzensberger, 'Hitlers Wiedergänger,' *Der Spiegel*, no. 6 (February 4, 1991), 26–28.

Redefining *Ultima (Ir-) Ratio* in the 1990s: Foreign Policy Adjustments between *Realpolitik* and *Idealpolitik*

On March 24, 1999, just eight years after the Gulf War had ended, the first German government exclusively formed by parties which self-consciously describe themselves as 'left' in an 'internationalist' tradition ordered German soldiers to wage war with its NATO allies against the regime of Slobodan Milosevic. For the first time since the end of World War II German soldiers were sent on a combat mission – and the tragic irony was that this precedent-setting decision brought them back to the Balkans where their fathers had fought the last great war. Yet the contrast both Germany's abstention during the Gulf War in 1991 and Hitler's aggression during World War II couldn't have been starker. Whereas back then German soldiers were the outcasts (for either waging a brutal war of aggression or for standing aside while others fought against a dictatorial regime), they now were joining their partners in a war as a 'normal ally.'[43] Given that NATO's air raids were clearly outside the jurisdiction of the alliance and given, moreover, that a UN mandate could not be furnished, the sole basis of legitimacy was provided by reference to human rights.[44] Nothing better symbolized how much Germany had changed since unification and the debates at the time of the Gulf War. Many of the actors which back then

43. Cf. 'Rede von Bundeskanzler Gerhard Schröder anläßlich der 35. Münchener Tagung für Sicherheitspolitik am 6. Februar 1999 in München,' *Bulletin. Presse und Informationsamt der Bundesregierung No. 8* (February 22, 1999), 91.

44. Experts of international law even questioned that one could speak of 'legitimacy' in this case because the UN Charter's two exceptions to the use of force (a) individual and collective self-defense and (b) authorization by the UN Security Council under chapter 7 of the UN Charter) obviously didn't apply. Asked whether NATO's air raids therefore marked a 'Fall of man in terms of international law' ('völkerrechtlicher Sündenfall'), Bruno Simma, an internationally renowned expert of the UN Charter, assented adding, however, that 'NATO has done everything to keep the transgression within the limits of venial sin'; see 'Die Nato-Bomben sind eine läßliche Sünde'. Interview mit Brunno Simma zur völkerrechtlichen Beurteilung der Luftangriffe,' *Süddeutsche Zeitung* (March 25, 1999), 5.

vehemently opposed an escalation of the war (even though the UN Charter had provided a rather solid legal justification in comparison to the Kosovo operation of March 1999) now not only supported NATO's attack but also the participation of the Bundeswehr.

What had happened between January 1991 and March 1999 to account for this dramatic turn-around, and what does this tell us about Germany's redefinition of its 'self,' its global ambitions, and its visions of world order today? In the following section I will argue that the seeds of change were visible as early as 1991. The image of Germany as a 'big Switzerland' which was widely circulated in 1991 was misleading from the very start as to the receptivity of the German public in general and the foreign policy elites in particular for the socializing pressures of Germany's international as well as domestic environment. Still, it would be similarly misleading to assume that Germany's new 'self' could either be adequately captured by the dichotomy *Weltpolitik or* 'self-containment' or by an alternative 'civilian' symbiosis of *Weltpolitik and* 'self-containment,' as Antje Vollmer and the Greens suggested in 1990. Rather, what best describes Germany's new role in international relations today is, so to speak, a *translation of 'normalization' into German* by spelling out the multiple meanings of the term in the political and historical context of the country.

Measured against an imaginary standard of a 'typical' mid-size democracy within the so-called 'OECD world,' Germany, in spite of its 'abnormal history' (Richard von Weizsäcker), is increasingly *becoming* more than a mere 'normal' country.[45] And if it is still useful

---

45. 'Normality' and 'normalization' are sensitive but often-used terms in German political discourse, especially as far as post-unification foreign policy is concerned; for illustrations and references see Hellmann (1999: 837–847). If one listens into political debates in other countries, in contrast, one gets the impression that there couldn't be anything more abnormal than not qualifying one's own country as 'normal.' For an impressive spectrum of leading politicians describing their countries as having become 'normal' by the mid-1990s (at the latest) see 'The same as you an' me', *The Economist* (October 29, 1994), 20 (the countries cited are Japan, China, Russia, Italy, Spain, Poland, Czech Republic, Slovakia and Israel; Germany is not listed and Canada's prime minister, Jean Chrétien, is quoted as the only political leader abhorring 'normalism': 'Canada is not a normal country . . . . It is an

to distinguish empirically between powers that do and powers that do not belong to a class of 'major' or 'great' powers – and nothing in the way that the so-called 'contact group' handled the Kosovo war speaks against this distinction – Germany has again joined ranks with the other great powers politically and militarily. The Bundes-wehr was sent into combat by its political leadership after a process of intense consultation in order to do with the other allied armies what great powers always felt compelled to do: to (re-)establish international order according to their own design. In contrast to 1990 when Germany was *allowed* to (and *wanted* to) go 'civilian,' it now felt – for moral reasons domestically and political reasons internationally – that it *had* to dress up militarily as all of its allies did. In short, Germany finally looked *no more and no less* 'civilian' than any of them, a power conducting as good or bad a 'policy of the good example' as any of them.

Civilian Internationalism and Swiss Myths

The seeds of this change were sown in late 1990 and early 1991 when unification and the Gulf War marked the conception of the yet to be conceived 'Berlin Republic.' In surveying public opinion in the immediate aftermaths of unification as to how the Germans wanted their country to position itself in the world, one poll received particular attention. Asked what country they perceived to be a model for Germany to emulate, 40 percent of Germans put Switzerland at the top of their list, clearly outdistancing the runners-up.[46] The image of a country in pursuit of welfare and happiness in

---

extraordinary country'). Given that my primary objectives are analytical (rather than political) I will try to be as specific as possible when I speak of Germany as a 'normal' or 'normalizing' country.

46. See 'Deutschland 2000. Der Staat, den wir uns wünschen,' *Süddeutsche Zeitung Magazin*, no. 1 (January 4, 1991), 8–15, here pp. 8–9. Only 2 percent of Germans in East and West named the United States and a mere 10 percent mentioned Japan. Switzerland was followed by Sweden with 29 percent. A similar poll conducted in August 1991 found 55 percent of West Germans and 57 percent of

an idyllic environment and very much detached from the troubles of the world around – this image, reminiscent of the stereotypical German garden, well-groomed and stuffed with garden gnomes (*Gartenzwerge*), apparently seemed quite appealing to Germans.[47]

Although academic analyses were both more differentiating and less idyllic, and, moreover, dismissive of the 'neutrality' which the Swiss example suggested, the underlying 'civilian' thrust of the image was generally supported. In a widely cited article which appeared in the prominent pages of *Foreign Affairs* about the time the poll was conducted, Hanns Maull argued that Germany and Japan represented 'prototypes of a promising future' for international affairs, i.e. prototypes of 'a new type of international power' which he called 'civilian power' and which he thought the United States had to emulate as well in order to live up to the challenges of an increasingly interdependent world marked by 'intense conflicts over the distribution of its costs and benefits [of interdependence, G.H.]' and confronted with 'such new challenges as political instability and crises in Eastern Europe or the Third World, terrorism, drugs or environmental dangers' where 'military force is likely to be largely irrelevant' (Maull 1990). According to Maull (1990: 92f.), becoming a 'civilian power' implied three things:

(a) the acceptance of the necessity of cooperation with others in the pursuit of international objectives; (b) the concentration on non-military, primarily economic, means to secure national goals, with military power

---

East Germans similarly favouring Switzerland followed by Sweden (41 percent of West Germans and 50 percent of East Germans), the US (36/22), England (24/17), France (22/22) and Japan (10/15) with the rest of the countries lagging far behind; see Noelle-Neumann and Köcher (1993: 955). See also Chr. Bertram, 'Der Riese, der ein Zwerg sein möchte,' *Die Zeit*, no. 18 (April 26, 1991), 12–13.

47. The 'dwarf' or 'gnome' image used to be a recurring theme in the foreign policy discourse of the early 1990, although the connotations were most often even less favorable than in the case of the *Gartenzwerg*. Former Foreign Minister Klaus Kinkel, who was well known for not shying away from undiplomatically strong language said in 1992 that Germany sometimes looked like an 'impotent dwarf,' quoted by Heinrich (1993: 20). See also Peters (1997: 361–388).

left as a residual instrument serving essentially to safeguard other means of international interaction; and (c) a willingness to develop supranational structures to address critical issues of international management.[48]

The general thrust of these visions was shared by a distinct segment among German academics and the foreign policy elites which one might call 'internationalist' – experts who now either make up or are closely related to the current German government.[49] In its more ambitious (or idealist) version this view held that Germany's new international responsibility could be concentrated on 'the values of peace-maintenance, safeguarding of nature, human rights, and the elimination of poverty,' thereby aiming at 'a national policy in the international interest' (Volmer and Fues 1993: 71; see also Senghaas 1993: 491). None of this was meant to imply that the nation-state would simply disappear or that a 'world state' ('Weltstaat') could (or should) be created. Yet, the 'world of states' ('Staatenwelt'), according to this view, was gone for good and nation-states would henceforth 'only be sovereign with regard to their competence for chaos; with regard to their competence for solutions, they will depend on transnational and supranational structures in the future' (Fischer 1994: 232. See also Czempiel 1994a: 1–14 and Habermas 1991: 105–10). The implications for Germany's global ambitions were clear: Germany had to beware that it is 'an inter- and transnationally cooperating democracy and market economy

48. As to the specific illustration of this concept in the German context see also Maull (1992: 269–278, 1993: 53–72, and 1993a: 934–948). In developing his 'paradigm' of a 'civilian power,' Maull specifically referred to the similarities with the ideal-type of a 'trading state' which was developed by Richard Rosecrance (1986); as to Rosecrance's application of his concept to Europe after 1990 see Rosecrance (1993: 127–145). However, in contrast to Rosecrance's 'primarily economic orientation' Maull (1990: 93, n. 2) wanted to stress the normative 'civilian' aspect of his paradigm.

49. This paragraph draws on arguments developed in a different context (Hellmann 1996: 12–16). In contrast to the internationalists I distinguished four additional schools of thought in post-unification foreign policy discourse until the mid-1990s: the pragmatic multilateralists, the europeanists, the euroskeptics and the normalization nationalists.

which is integrated in Europe and obliged to act "collegially" rather than "directorially'" (Rittberger 1992: 215). Sharing greater 'responsibility' and taking over 'leadership roles' did not mean, however, playing the role of a global policeman or firefighter in a 'territorial' or 'great power world.' Rather, in self-consciously choosing a strategy of self-restraint and in 'refusing to project power or apply the (traditional) instruments of power, be they military, economic, or ideological' the aim was to take over the lead as a promoter of preventive conflict management and, if need be, of a "'benevolent hegemon" in the sense of supporting the strengthening of civil, joint (*solidarisch*), and ecologically sustainable structures.'[50] To be sure, none of this was meant to imply that the use of force was excluded under any circumstances. There would, of course, still be situations in which force as *ultima ratio* might be unavoidable. However, even in these cases 'the crucial question will be, whether we succeed in developing effective and legitimate forms of multi-lateral sanctions ('Zwangsmaßnahmen') or whether the recourse to force follows traditional nation-state thinking' (Maull 1993a: 71).[51]

At first glance these visions initially also seemed to resonate among the German public more broadly. Even in the aftermath of the Gulf War a majority of Germans thought that Germany should not change the Basic Law in order to enable the Bundeswehr to participate in UN operations such as the Gulf War (see tables 1 and 2). Second, Germans in general seemed to be sympathetic vis-à-vis the internationalist impulse of their political leadership as far as 'civilian' or 'humanitarian' tasks were concerned, but very hesitant as to military missions. When asked, for instance, what they considered to be the most important tasks of German foreign policy,

---

50. These last two quotes are from Statz (1993: 184, 193); for additional arguments in favor of playing 'civilian' leadership roles see also Maull (1993: 69) and Wolf (1995: 62–63).

51. For different views among internationalists on the conditions under which force could still be necessary see Lutz (1993: 90–94, 125–128), Schmillen (1993:36–44) – Schmillen today serves as head of office of Foreign Minister Fischer, Czempiel (1994: 39); J. Fischer, 'Wir müssen für den militärischen Schutz der UN-Zonen sein,' *Frankfurter Rundschau* (August 20, 1995), 10.

Table 1. Germans Opposing a Change of the Basic Law

Question: Chancellor Kohl demanded to change the Federal Law after the parliamentary elections in order to allow for deployment of German troops for UN-activities. Do you agree? (A parallel survey worded it ". . . in order to allow for the deployment of German troops within UN-activities aimed at peacekeeping. . ." (in percent)

Bundeswehr to be deployed for UN-activities	Old Länder		New Länder	
	October 1990	February 1991	October 1990	February 1991
I agree	24	36	19	16
I disagree	55	49	53	66
Don't know	21	15	28	18
Sum	100	100	100	100

Addition: deploy for peace keeping	Old Länder		New Länder	
	October 1990	February 1991	October 1990	February 1991
I agree	26	37	27	33
I disagree	55	49	42	54
Don't know	19	14	31	13
Sum	100	100	100	100

Source: Survey of the Institut für Demoskopie Allensbach in March 1991 (Noelle-Neumann and Köcher 1993: 961).

strong majorities in 1991 were in favor of global improvements of environmental conditions (75 percent of West Germans and 77 percent of East Germans thought that this was 'very important'), the prevention of the proliferation of nuclear weapons (77/75) and global arms control (65/66). In contrast, among the least important tasks Germans ranked the preservation of a military balance with

Table 2. German Opposition to Bundeswehr Participation in UN-Missions

Question: 'Assuming a similar conflict to the one in the Gulf arises somewhere else in the world: If on the orders of the United Nations allied troops were to be deployed again, should German soldiers participate or not?' (in percent)

March 1991	Old Länder	New Länder
German troops should. . .		
. . . take part in UN-activities	39	19
. . . not take part in such activities	42	65
Don't know	19	16
Sum	100	100

Source: Noelle-Neumann and Köcher 1993: 962.

the Soviet Union (15/17), the defense of an ally (19/22), and the defense of 'weak' states against external aggression (27/33; see table 3). Similarly, whereas almost 60 percent in both East and West in 1991 supported the position that Germany ought to 'take over more responsibility in world politics' (rather than exercise restraint 'because of Germany's political history and earlier *Machtpolitik*'; see table 4), 36 percent of West Germans (and 37 percent of East Germans) 'in this context' opposed the view that Germany ought to play an increasing role 'in the solution of international conflicts' (only 32 percent (24) were in favor; see table 5). Moreover, when asked more specifically, in 'what framework' Germany could participate in the solution of international conflicts, the view that Germany ought to participate in 'humanitarian measures' (86 percent of West Germans, 92 percent of East Germans) clearly outdistanced the position that Germany ought to send the Bundeswehr 'in the context of UN-blue-helmet operations, i.e. without a military mission' (60/48 percent); only a tiny proportion spoke out in support of the position that the Bundeswehr ought to participate in 'military UN-missions such as the Gulf War' (26/14; see table 6). Also, when asked whether

Table 3. The Most Important Tasks of German Foreign Policy (multiple responses, in percent)

Problems	Weighted index		Very important		Relatively important		Relatively unimportant		Not important at all		Don't know		No response		Sum	
	East	West	E	W	E	W	E	W	E	W	E	W	E	W	E	W
Open up foreign markets to secure jobs in Germany	1014	984	52	48	33	38	10	9	2	2	3	3	0	0	100	100
Protection of economic interests in Germany	1014	984	35	33	45	51	12	10	3	2	5	4	0	1	100	100
Secure sufficient energy supply	1014	984	47	56	38	33	10	6	2	2	3	2	0	0	100	100
Defence of the security of our allies	1014	984	19	22	35	42	29	24	9	6	7	5	0	0	100	100
Prevention of the spread of nuclear weapons	1014	984	77	75	14	15	4	2	2	5	3	2	0	0	100	100
Promotion and defence of human rights in other states	1014	984	45	53	38	34	10	8	3	2	4	3	0	0	100	100
Improvement of global ecological conditions	1014	984	75	77	20	18	3	2	0	1	2	2	0	0	100	100
Protection of weaker states against external aggression	1014	984	27	33	41	44	20	15	7	2	6	6	0	0	100	100
Preservation of the military equilibrium against the USSR	1014	984	15	17	21	26	28	28	30	20	7	8	0	1	100	100

	1014	984														
Global arms control	1014	984	65	66	24	21	5	6	3	4	3	3	0	0	100	100
Strengthening of the United Nations	1014	984	41	38	38	39	11	13	4	5	6	5	0	0	100	100
Improvement of living conditions in the Third World	1014	984	48	50	38	39	8	8	2	1	4	3	0	0	100	100
Support of the introduction of democracy in other states	1014	984	21	36	42	42	18	11	10	3	9	7	0	0	100	100

Source: Infratest 1991: 93–106.

171

Table 4. Playing a More Active Role in World Politics

Question: 'Unification highlighted the issue of Germany's role in world politics. Accordingly, there are two contradictory viewpoints. Which one do you agree with?' (in percent)

October/November 1991	East Germany	West Germany
Weighted index	1014	984
– Some say, that Germany should continue to restrain itself because of its political past and former *Machtpolitik* in world affairs.	40	41
– Others say, a unified Germany should play a more active role and take on more responsibility in world politics.	59	59
– No comment	1	0
Sum	100	100

Source: Infratest 1991: 107–108.

Table 5. Hesitations about Getting Involved in International Conflicts

Question: 'In regards to the above it is often expected that Germany will take a more active part in resolving international conflicts. Do you agree?' (in percent)

	East Germany	West Germany
Weighted index	1014	984
– Agree	24	32
– Disagree	37	36
– Depends	36	28
– Don't know	3	4
– No comment	0	0
Sum	100	100

Source: Infratest 1991: 109–110.

Table 6. A Preference for Shouldering 'Civilian' Tasks in International Conflicts

Question: 'Within which framework could you envisage Germany participating in resolving international conflicts?' (multiple answers, in percent)

	East Germany	West Germany
Weighted index	633	628
– Participation in humanitarian aid	92	86
– Participation in economic blockade	46	57
– Financial support of UN interventions	46	53
– Deployment of Bundeswehr units within UN-peacekeeping operations but without military tasks	48	60
– Deployment of Bundeswehr units for military UN-interventions, i.e. like in the Gulf	14	26
– no comment	1	1
Sum	248	283

Source: Infratest 1991: 111–112.

they wanted to see defense expenditures reduced, increased, or kept at about the same level, almost two-thirds of West Germans (and 84 percent of East Germans) were in favor of spending cuts in March 1991, while only 2 percent of West Germans (and 1 percent of East Germans) supported an increase in spending (see table 7). Finally, more than two-thirds of Germans in East and West supported 'drastic cuts' in the strength of the Bundeswehr in September 1991 (see table 8).

In spite of the fact that these responses seemed to support the widely shared view that Germans were content with playing an activist, yet largely 'civilian' global role, other data from about the

Table 7. Cutting Defence Spending

Question: 'Generally asking: Should we increase defence expenditures, should we keep them at today's level, or should we decrease them?' (in percent)

March 1991	Old Länder	New Länder
We should . . . defence expenditures:	Population total	Population total
. . . increase	2	1
. . . keep same	30	12
... decrease	62	84
... don't know, no comment	6	3
Sum	100	100

Source: Noelle-Neumann and Köcher 1993: 1048.

Table 8. Reducing the Size of the Bundeswehr

Question: 'The amount of troops in the Bundeswehr is to be reduced drastically, many Bundeswehr garrisons are to be closed down. Do you think it is a good idea to decrease the size of the Bundeswehr now or should we await developments in the East?' (in percent)

September 1991	Old Länder	New Länder
It is a good idea, that the Bundeswehr will be decreased in size.	66	79
Await developments in the East	26	14
Don't know	8	7
Sum	100	100

Source: Noelle-Neumann and Köcher 1993: 1055.

same time indicated that Germans did not differ significantly from other nations as to how they defined their role in international politics. First of all, when questioned as to their views regarding the overall positioning of Germany in international affairs, a majority of Germans supported positions which could more easily be described as 'isolationist' rather than 'internationalist,' a position which sounded Swiss indeed. For instance, 51 percent of Germans in East and West in 1992 supported the view that as a result of Germany's EU membership 'too much gets lost of what is character-istic about Germany.' Even more significantly, the same poll found that 59 percent of Germans thought that Germany should 'not care about world politics' but concentrate instead on the problems within Germany itself; also, a surprising 60 percent of Germans thought that their country would be 'strong enough to care for itself' (see table 9). Second, even in 1990 (i.e. when hopes were still high that a 'peace dividend' could be gained as a result of a 'new world order') more than 80 percent of Germans held the view that it would be normal for a sovereign nation to have its own army (see table 10). In equal numbers Germans supported the view that their country had to have a 'well-functioning army simply because of its political location between East and West,' a position which even received *increasing* support *after* 1990, when the political slogan about united Germany being 'encircled by friends' was widely circulating (see table 11).[52] Also, whereas a majority of Germans thought that there

---

52. This support was obviously welcomed by the military leadership of the Bundeswehr; see the remarks by Klaus Naumann (1993). According to Naumann the Bundeswehr represented 'a constitutive element of the state even without a concrete threat.' The majority of the Germans assented. Another survey from 1993 found that almost 70 percent of Germans considered it 'normal' for a sovereign country to have its own army (including an astonishing 68 percent of the electorate of the Greens). Moreover, some 50 percent favored having a 'strong military' even in the absence of a military threat to Germany (Holst 1995, Tables 1, 2). For some some German observers propagating the principle of 'conflict prevention before conflict resolution' ('Konfliktvermeidung vor Konfliktbekämpfung') this was nothing but an illustration of the 'wretched Whilhelminian spirit' resurfacing within the army of united Germany (Mutz 1994: 225); the former quote is from Bastian (1993: 83).

175

Table 9. Defining Germany (and what it should do for itself and others)

Question: 'This list contains statements about different political topics. Please indicate, if you (1) fully agree, (2) rather agree, (3) rather disagree, (4) disagree completely with these statements.' (in percent, G = Federal Republic (total), O = East Germany, W = West Germany)

	Fully agree			Rather agree			Rather disagree			Disagree completely			no comment		
	G	O	W	G	O	W	G	O	W	G	O	W	G	O	W
Germany loses too many of its specific characteristics through EU membership.	21	20	21	30	30	30	35	39	35	12	11	12	2	1	2
Germany should not care for world politics, but rather concentrate on its internal problems.	27	35	25	32	30	32	27	23	28	13	10	14	1	1	1
Germany is strong enough to take care of itself.	24	28	23	36	33	36	27	28	27	12	10	13	1	1	1
Germany has to decide on its future freely and independently of any external influences.	24	30	23	33	28	34	27	28	26	15	12	16	1	2	1

Source: Infratest 1992: 84–87.

Table 10. Sovereignty and the Normality of Having an Army
Army as an integral part of a sovereign nation (in percent)

	Answers	1989	1990	1991 East	West
To have an army is part of a sovereign nation.	Yes			80	81
	No			17	16
	Don't know			3	3
Every independent state needs armed forces so it cannot be blackmailed politically.	Yes	85	85	82	85
	No	13	15	17	14
	Don't know	2	–	1	1

Source: Survey of the Institut Marplan in 1991, quoted in Sicherung des Friedens (Überparteilicher Arbeitskreis von Christen zur Förderung von Frieden in Freiheit), vol. 12, no. 6 (June 1992), p. 6.

was indeed room for 'certain cuts' in defense spending, an *increasing* number after 1990 supported the position that defense spending should equal that of other nations 'in the East and in the West' (see table 12). Third, even in the immediate aftermath of the Gulf War Germans were not as hesitant about the use of force in international affairs as some of the surveys seemed to indicate which I have been referring to above. When asked in February 1991 whether Kuweit should have been left in the hands of Saddam Hussein or whether 'it was right to fight this war' 56 percent of West Germans (but only 36 percent of East Germans) thought that the war was justified (15 percent of West Germans and 22 percent of East Germans thought that Kuweit should have been abandoned, 29 (42) percent were undecided; see table 13). One year later almost 50 percent of Germans in the West supported the position that Germany should 'after all participate in UN peace keeping operations' since Germany

Table 11. Germany's Geopolitical Location and the Need for a Well-Functioning Army

Question: 'I will read you some statements about the Bundeswehr. Please indicate, if you fully agree, agree somewhat, disagree somewhat or disagree completely. The Federal Republic needs well functioning armed forces because of its political location between East and West.' (in percent)

	WPL89	WPL90	WPL91	WPL92	WPL93
− Fully agree	39.3	31.3	32.9	38.5	40.5
− Agree somewhat	38.0	43.5	42.6	42.6	40.1
− Disagree somewhat	15.1	15.7	17.0	13.5	15. 0
− Disagree completely	7.5	9.6	7.5	4.4	4.5
− Invalid	1.2	0.7	0.5	1.5	1.2
Total	100.0	100.0	100.0	100.0	100.0
N	1918	1924	2096	1949	2000

This data originate from a database, which was created for a research project by Hans Rattlinger and added to the publication as an electronic database. WPL90 stands for the annually repeated survey by Emnid on behalf of the Bundesministerium für Verteidigung about the 'defence-political situation'; the data here is for 1990; for exact data see Rattinger, Behnke, and Holst (1995: 60–61).

could no longer 'shun its responsibility' while others were risking their lives (see table 14). Also, and even more significantly, when the conflict in ex-Yugoslavia escalated during 1991 and 1992, Germans were becoming ever more determined not to stand aside. In August 1992 50 percent of West Germans (and 40 percent of East Germans) were in favor of sending the Bundeswehr to the Balkans 'in the framework of UN peacekeeping troops.' An additional 12 percent of West Germans (and 8 percent of East Germans) even

Table 12. Cutting Defence Spending (as Other Countries do too)
Question: 'Three men talk about our military situation (WPL92
and WPL93) and about the suitability of a reduction in spending
for the Bundeswehr. Their viewpoints are indicated below. What
opinion do you agree with most?'
The first says, 'I think the situation right now is dangerous. The
Federal Republic should increase defence expenditure.'
The second says, 'We have to spend as much as other countries in
the East and West spend per head of population.'
The third says, 'I think, considering today's situation we could
decrease spending for the Bundeswehr.' (in percent)

	WPL81	WPL84	WPL89	WPL90	WPL91	WPL92	WPL93
1. Increase expenditures	18.8	9.5	3.6	3.8	4.0	4.8	5.3
2. Same as other countries	54.5	52.5	41.6	30.1	30.9	31.9	41.8
3. Decrease expenditure	26.7	37.9	54.8	66.0	65.1	63.2	52.9
Invalid	2.2	1.2	1.2	1.2	1.0	1.3	1.1
Total	100.0	100.0	100.0	100.0	100.0	100.0	100.0
N	1753	1806	1918	1924	2096	1949	2000

Source: (Rattinger, Behnke, and Holst 1995).

supported the deployment of German troops as part of a peace-
enforcing operation (see table 15).

What conclusion can be drawn from these data about the overall
outlook of the German public in the immediate aftermath of
German unification and the Gulf War? The image of Germany as a
big Switzerland shying away from what most of Germany's partners
considered to be its increased 'responsibility' in European and global
affairs was misleading from the very start. To be sure, whenever
Germans were offered to choose between non–military and military
instruments in pursuit of international objectives they certainly
preferred the former. Support for global environmental protection
and emergency help in humanitarian catastrophes were definitely

Table 13. A Just War against Saddam Hussein

Question:'Should Kuwait have been left to Iraq, in order to prevent a war or was it right to fight this war?' (in percent)

February 1991	Old Länder	New Länder
	Population total	Population total
— Kuwait should have been left to Iraq in order to prevent war.	15	22
— It was right to fight the war.	56	36
— undecided	29	42
Sum	100	100

Source: Noelle-Neumann and Köcher 1993: 1087.

more appealing than sending troops. It is questionable, however, whether the broader public in other 'Western' states would have reacted very differently. What is surprising, therefore, is not so much that in the immediate aftermath of unification a certain hesitation was noticeable with regard to the use of force, but rather that even then substantial numbers of Germans were speaking out in favor of such 'traditional' (or 'non-civilian') instruments as armies and the use of force. Thus, the seeds for a process of 're-socialization' into international politics along the lines of other middle-sized or great powers within the West (and in contrast to the expectations of the ideal-type of a 'civilian power') were visible from the very start.

None of this is to say that Germans were intent at reviving the dubious traditions of *Machtpolitik* or *Weltpolitik* of the German Reich as some observers speculated at that time.[53] Rather they were

53. For arguments along these lines drawing, in particular, on 'the German character' see Thatcher (1993: 791); L. Bellak, 'Why I fear the Germans', *New York Times* (April 25, 1990), A29; D. Lawson, 'Saying the Unsayable about the Germans. Interview with Nicholas Ridley,' *The Spectator* (July 14, 1990), 8–10. For good overviews of the historical analysis of the *Weltpolitik*-tradition during Bismarck's time as well as the Third Reich see Hildebrand (1994) and Recker (1990).

Table 14. Shouldering Responsibility for Peace?

Question:'Two people are talking about whether Germany should participate as UN peacekeeping forces. Which opinion would you agree with?' (in percent)

March 1992	Old Länder Population total	New Länder Population total
'Germany has finally to participate as UN peacekeeping troops, the so-called blue helmets. We cannot shirk our responsibilities and leave it to others to risk their lives.'	45	26
'Considering our history we should not take part as UN peacekeeping troops. We should use our economic and political influence rather than soldiers.'	37	57
Undecided	18	17
Sum	100	100

Source: Noelle-Neumann and Köcher 1993: 1094.

responding positively (if, at least initially, still hesitantly) to what they perceived to be justified demands by their allies to help in bringing about 'stability' in Europe and the world according to Western designs. Given the multilateral and integrationist tradition of the old Federal Republic and its foreign policy impulse of 'avoiding international loneliness' (Bertram 1994: 91), the new situation and the demands from friends and allies called for far-reaching changes in Germany's outlook and engagement in international affairs. The German public did realize these demands as early as 1990/91 – and it was ready to respond positively (and

Table 15. Germany and UN peacekeeping

Question: 'How should the Bundeswehr participate in military activities in Yugoslavia: troops within UN military intervention, only within UN peacekeeping forces (blue helmets), or should Germany refrain altogether?' (in percent)

August 1992	Old Länder	New Länder
Bundeswehr should take part . . .		
. . . as troops in UN military intervention	12	8
. . . within UN peacekeeping forces	50	40
Bundeswehr should not participate at all	28	42
Undecided	10	10
Sum	100	100

Source: Noelle-Neumann and Köcher 1993: 1095.

increasingly so) as subsequent years showed (I will discuss this in more detail below).

Pragmatic Multilateralism in Elite Perceptions

This acute sense for what Germany's allies expected after unification was even more noticeable among foreign policy elites. Moreover, as a detailed survey from 1991/92 shows, the views prevailing among these elites as to how Germany should respond were fully in line with these expectations. In 1991 and early 1992 Dietmar Schössler, Reiner Albert, and Frank Kostelnik conducted a survey among more than 400 policy-makers, Bundeswehr officers, researchers of thinks tanks and academics as to their views about European and global security.[54] I will draw extensively on this survey here for three

54. Schössler, Albert and Kostelnik (1992). Of those invited to participate in the survey 423 responded. Among the respondents those with a military background (almost 200) were clearly in the majority. However, there were also large numbers

reasons. First, to my knowledge this is the most extensive survey among security specialists ever conducted in the 1990; since we know from extensive research that the political elites have much more leeway in shaping the views of the public more broadly (and in setting the agenda in foreign and security policy) than in domestic politics, the views of these elites are particularly important if one is searching for indicators of foreign policy change. Second, the detailed results of this survey have not been published in full although one more analytical publication by the authors relies on these data (Schössler, Albert, and Kostelnik 1993). Third, the data collected clearly underline the argument developed here that even in the immediate aftermath of the Gulf War the intellectual climate in Germany was neither one of a renaissance of *Machtpolitik* (as critics from the left charged) nor one of *Machtvergessenheit* (as critics from the right did). The views expressed were far from envisioning a future of peace and stability. Rather, if one examines these views in detail it is astounding how far removed they were compared to both the political slogans from an 'internationalist' left ('make peace without weapons') and the critique of an alleged 'Angst vor der Macht' (Schöllgen 1993) from 'Realist' critics. German experts were fully aware that Germany's allies expected the country to participate across 'the whole spectrum' of political and military tasks (see table 16). They were also willing to respond positively. Against the background of these results it is far *less* surprising how quickly Germany's policies have changed during the past nine years with regard to peace-keeping or even peace-enforcing missions in multilateral contexts.

First, the vision among the elites about the future in Europe and beyond were anything but rosy. Overwhelming majorities among the experts questioned held the view (1) that a revival of national identities would lead to more international instability (90 percent);

---

of policy-makers or party representatives (87, including the Party of Democratic Socialism, the former SED), researchers and academics (67), and members of transnational organizations such as the *Deutsche Atlantische Gesellschaft* (33), and experts on foreign policy working for the industry and the trade unions (26).

Table 16. The Allies and their Expectations vis-à-vis Germany

Question:'If one takes a look at the German debate from "outside" Germany – what expectations does the West (the allies) have towards enlarged future German responsibilities?' (in percent)

	Total
Interviewees	N=423
A: The allies expect German participation in everything	73.0
B: The allies primarily expect Germany to take on responsibilities within the UN	14.9
C: The allies expect primarily participation in UN peacekeeping activities	3.3
D: The allies expect primarily a financial and economic relief of their responsibilities in international politics	13.7

Source: Schössler, Albert, and Kostelnik 1992: Question # 79.

(2) that war will remain an instrument of politics in the hands of aggressors (97 percent); and (3) that the use of force would have to remain an instrument to fight aggressors if all other means have failed (96 percent; see table 17). Second, although they were not wholly pessimistic as to the hopes for creating a new and 'satisfactory order' in Europe, two-thirds of the experts thought that even if such an order could be created, it would 'constantly be endangered by crises' (see table 18). The elites did sympathize with the broader public's preference for 'civilian' policies in that a clear majority (60 percent) spoke out in favor of using the military in 'police' functions if possible (see table 19). However, more than three quarters thought that in spite of nuclear weapons the use of military power would still be necessary for the realization of political objectives under certain conditions (see table 20). When asked as to where they thought that military power would play an *increasing* role, the experts ranked Asia and Africa at the top (45 and 42 percent respectively) and Europe and the Soviet Union at the bottom (14/10) of their

Table 17. International Instability, Aggressors, and the Instrument of Warmaking

Questions about the international political situation (in percent)

	Total
Interviewees	N=423
1. Stability: 'Does the renaissance of a national identity towards the issue of regional integration and security structures have consequences for the stability of international relations?'	
− Increased stability	7.1
− Decreased stability	89.6
− No consequences	3.3
2. War as politics: 'Do you think that in the future, aggressors will continue to see the use of war as successful political instrument?'	
− Yes	96.9
− No	2.4
− No comment	0.7
3. Resistance against war: 'If all other instruments fail, should the military option be considered in order to resist aggressors in the future?'	
− Yes	95.8
− No	3.3
− No comment	0.9

Source: Schössler, Albert, and Kostelnik 1992: Questions # 12, 141, 142.

list (48 percent thought that the role of military power would stay about the same in Europe, 36 percent held that view with regard to the Soviet Union; and 36 percent thought that the role of military power would decrease in Europe (49 percent thought so with regard to the Soviet Union; see table 21). In other words, the experts thought that Europe, including the Soviet Union, would become a much safer place militarily in comparison to both the time before

Table 18. A Crisis-Ridden New World Order

Question: 'The situation in Europe today is marked by insecurity and instability. Do you think, that it will be possible to create an agreeable and satisfying long-term European order?' (in percent)

	Total
Interviewees	N=423
A: An order guaranteeing long-term peace and stability can be achieved.	34.8
B: A new order might be achieved, but it will constantly be endangered by crises.	63.8
C: Any order will disintegrate again.	0.7
No comment	0.7

Source: Schössler, Albert, and Kostelnik 1992: Question # 44.

Table 19. The Military as Constabulary Forces

Question: 'Within the changed international security situation, there is an increasing debate over the changed functions of military power. An important hypothesis suggests that we should conceive of future military activities primarily in terms of constabulary force tasks. What is your opinion? Should military forces primarily be viewed as constabulary forces, which should be deployed according to the principle of proportionality?' (in percent)

	Total
Interviewees	N=423
A: Yes, deploy accordingly.	59.8
B: No, as previously.	36.9
No comment	3.3

Source: Schössler, Albert, and Kostelnik 1992: Question # 52.

Table 20. The Uses of Military Power

Question: 'Since nuclear power was invented, there is a theory that military power can no longer be used to achieve political goals. Against this theory there is the fact that there have been 300 to 400 armed conflicts since 1945. What is your opinion?'

	Total
Interviewees	N=423
A: 'Considering certain restraints, controlled military intervention can help to achieve political goals.'	26.5
B: 'A limited use of conventional military power in order to achieve political goals is still possible today.'	50.1
C: 'Considering today's accumulation of nuclear weapons, there is no correlation between military tools and political goals. Therefore military intervention can no longer be considered as a means of achieving political goals.'	5.4
D: 'Even in a deployment of purely conventional military forces, there is no justifiable relationship between military tools and political goals.'	21.7

Source: Schössler, Albert, and Kostelnik 1992: Question # 51.

1989 and in comparison to other regions. Third, in spite of the fact that the experts thought that force would henceforth play a *decreasing* role in Europe and the Soviet Union more than 98 percent supported the view that 'the Europeans' should take over 'more responsibility for peace,' and among those more than 80 percent thought that NATO should provide the main framework to do so (see table 22). Asked more specifically how this increased responsibility should be realized, more than 80 percent supported the view that *all* means 'including military power' should be applied (only 16 percent wanted these instruments to be limited to 'diplomatic and economic means' (see table 23). Fourth, whereas a large number among foreign policy experts was sympathetic to ideas about

Table 21. The Importance of Military Power in Different Continents

Question: 'How do you view the future role of military power?' (in percent)

	In Africa	In Asia	In Europe	In the Soviet Union	In Latin America
Small role	13.5	5.9	35.7	49.4	24.3
No change in importance	41.1	45.6	47.5	35.7	56.3
Importance will grow	41.6	44.9	13.7	10.2	16.1
No comment	3.8	3.6	3.1	4.7	3.3

Source: Schössler, Albert, and Kostelnik 1992: Question # 72.

strengthening all-inclusive European security institutions such as the CSCE, they remained skeptical as to whether political stability could be provided solely or even primarily on this basis. In 1991/ 92 almost 53 percent supported the view that 'existing structures such as the OSCE' should be extended in order to form an 'effective all-European' security framework (only 27 percent thought that the 'transatlantic structures should be extended to Eastern Europe'; see table 24). However, when asked specifically as to which view best described their own assessment of the CSCE almost two-thirds among foreign policy experts thought that 'because of structural deficiencies' the CSCE would not be able to provide for a 'stable order of peace on its own' (see table 25). Moreover, a similarly large proportion (65 percent) subscribed to the view that NATO should play 'an important role' even within a 'bloc-transcending order of peace' since it is 'in fact the only functioning security institution' (see table 26). Also, when the experts were asked to describe NATO's role against the background of a 'new world order of peace,' more than three quarters supported the position that NATO structures should either 'take conflicts out of area into consideration' (52

Table 22. European Responsibility for Security within a Euro-Atlantic Framework

Question: 'Should Europeans take on more responsibility in the field of security policy? Which answer do you agree with most?' (in percent)

	Total
Interviewees	N=423
A: 'Europeans should take on more responsibility for peace.'	6.9
B: 'European should take on more responsibility for peace within the Western alliance.'	33.1
C: 'Europeans should take on more responsibility for peace within the Western alliance, preferably, however, within the UN.'	47.5
D: 'Europeans should only take on more responsibility for peace within the framework of the UN.'	10.4
E: 'Europeans should not take on more responsibility for peace.'	1.2
No comment	0.9

Source: Schössler, Albert, and Kostelnik 1992: Question # 4171.

percent) or even 'primarily reshape its structures' with respect to this new world order (25 percent; see table 27). Fifth, foreign policy experts were almost unanimous in their assessment that German unification 'raised the question of extended international responsibility for Germany' (95 percent supported this position, see table 28). Moreover, almost 50 percent thought that Germany's 'extended responsibility' had to be defined 'primarily in global terms' (44 percent thought that a regional focus on Europe should receive priority, see table 29). When asked more specifically as to how Germany should reorient its security policy almost 80 percent subscribed to the position that Germany should help in strengthening a European pillar within NATO, whereas only 29 percent

Table 23. Exercising Responsibility Based on All Means, Including Military Means

Question: 'According to you, how should this enlarged responsibility be put into practice?' (in percent)

	Total
Interviewees	N=423
A: With all political and defence instruments available, including the use of military power	81.6
B: With restricted political and defence instruments, i.e. mostly with diplomatic and economic instruments	16.3
No comment	2.1

Source: Schössler, Albert, and Kostelnik 1992: Question # 4172.

Table 24. Strengthening "All-European" Security Structures

Questions: 'Structural changes were initiated by the August coup in the Soviet Union, the conflict between Croatia and Serbia, the formation of CSCE institutions and the changes in NATO. How do you view these changes in regards to the necessity of creating a new European security system?' (in percent)

	Total
Interviewees	N=423
A: 'The changes thus far are sufficient to maintain peace and stability.'	3.8
B: 'The Atlantic–West European structures should be extended to Eastern Europe.'	27.0
C: 'Existing structures (i.e. CSCE) should be expanded to become effective structures for the whole of Europe.'	52.9
D: 'A new European peace order calls for completely new structures.'	15.6
No comment	0.7

Source: Schössler, Albert, and Kostelnik 1992: Question # 46.

Table 25. CSCE as Useful, but "Structurally Deficient" Security Institution

Question: 'Which one of the following points are you most likely to agree with?' (in percent)

	Total
Interviewees	N=423
A: 'The problems of the Cold War can be overcome and the formation of a new stable European order will be possible within the CSCE.'	15.1
B: 'The CSCE cannot serve as sole promoter of a stable peace order because of structural deficiencies. Therefore it needs to be supplemented by other institutions.'	63.4
C: 'The CSCE is not really a structurally significant collective security institution, and even "supplements" through other institutions will not change this.'	19.6
No comment	1.9

Source: Schössler, Albert, and Kostelnik 1992: Question # 4121.

thought that Germany should do 'everything to build an all-European security system in order to supersede military alliances' (here multiple responses were possible; 63 percent even supported a view which seemed to imply that NATO should be the sole institutional context for realizing Germany's security interests; 7 percent thought that Germany should aim at a '"europeanization" of Germany's security policy' as an alternative to NATO and only 2 percent were in favor of leaving NATO; see table 30). Finally, the experts were confronted with the question whether they thought that the Bundeswehr's traditional 'Atlantic spirit' or 'NATO-mindedness' would change as a result of unification and the developments in Eastern Europe. Almost half of the respondents thought that the Bundeswehr would develop a 'European identity' in the course of European integration, and another 33 percent thought that nothing would change in that regard. Only 16 percent

Table 26. NATO as the "Only Functioning" Security Institution

Question: 'Which statement about NATO do you agree with?' (in percent)

	Total
Interviewees	N=423
A: 'NATO should play an important role as the only functioning security institution, even within a bloc-transcending peace order.'	65.3
B: 'NATO should be kept for now, but it should lose its importance in the process of establishing a European security structure.'	24.8
C: 'NATO should immediately transform itself into a broad collective security system.'	9.2
No comment	0.7

Source: Schössler, Albert, and Kostelnik 1992: Question # 410.

Table 27. NATO's New Responsibilities for a "New World Order of Peace"

Question: 'After the end of the Gulf War much has been talked about a new order for world peace. In your opinion, should NATO adapt to the demands of military security within a new world order?' (in percent)

	Total
Interviewees	N=423
A: 'NATO should concentrate on security within its own area.'	22.0
B: 'NATO should also consider conflicts outside its area within its structures.'	52.2
C: 'NATO should actively participate in the new peace order and above all organize its structures accordingly.'	24.6
No comment	1.2

Source: Schössler, Albert, and Kostelnik 1992: Question # 516.

Table 28. Extended Responsibility

Question: 'Do you agree that German unification raised the question of extended international responsibility for Germany?' (in percent)

	Total
Interviewees	N=423
Yes	95.0
No	4.3
No comment	0.7

Source: Schössler, Albert, and Kostelnik 1992: Question # 771.

Table 29. Global Responsibility

Question: 'Is this extended role to be primarily understood as a regional (European) one or as a global role?' (in percent)

	Total
Interviewees	N=423
A: Extended German responsibility is primarily regional	44.0
B: Extended German responsibility is primarily global	49.0
No comment	6.8

Source: Schössler, Albert, and Kostelnik 1992: Question # 772.

expected the Bundeswehr to develop a new identity of its own and emphasize 'national interests' (see table 31).

In sum, the foreign policy elites were even more determined than the German public more broadly to quickly and pragmatically adjust to a new world order which (in their view) revealed many characteristics of the old one.[55] In brief, although the world that

55. For a more detailed discussion of this position, which I have called 'pragmatic multilateralism' in another context see Hellmann (1996: 5–8); that discussion also includes references to prominent representatives of this school of thought.

Table 30. Euro-Atlantic Orientation of Germany's 'New' Security Policy

Question:'There are different conceptualizations according to which Germany can guarantee the security of its new role in the changed situation. This changed situation also led to debates about new orientations in German security policy. In your opinion, which ones are appropriate ways to deal with this new situation?' (multiple answers, in percent)

	Total
Interviewees	N=423
A: 'As military power will not play a big role in the future, it should be minimized and security policy should be concentrated on diplomatic means.'	5.4
B: 'The Federal Republic should leave NATO and become a neutral state.'	2.1
C: 'Germany should do everything for the creation of a pan-European security system, in which military alliances would disappear.'	29.1
D: 'Germany should try to Europeanize European defence by creating a purely European security system as an alternative to NATO.'	6.9
E: 'Germany should help to strengthen European responsibility and the European pillar in NATO.'	79.2
F: 'Germany should stay fully integrated in NATO, because this is the only proven way to guarantee security.'	63.1

Source: Schössler, Albert, and Kostelnik 1992: Question # 73.

German security experts saw in 1991 was one which was highly interdependent it was at the same time made up of a sea of increasing (rather than decreasing) instability with only a few islands of stability formed by alliances such as NATO and *supplemented* by inclusive (rather than exclusive) security institutions such as the CSCE.

Table 31. 'European Identity' of the Bundeswehr

Question: 'The Bundeswehr has been integrated in NATO since its foundation. Generations of officers have forged tight contacts with their NATO comrades. One could say that the Bundeswehr is permeated by an 'Atlantic spirit' and 'NATO-mindedness'. Do you think this will change with German unification and the changes in the Soviet Union and in East and Central Europe?' (in percent)

	Total
Interviewees	N=423
A: 'No, the consciousness of the Bundeswehr will not change.'	33.1
B: 'The Bundeswehr will create its own identity and promote national interests.'	16.1
C: 'The Bundeswehr will develop a "European identity" as Europe becomes more integrated.'	46.3
D: 'Considering transnational cooperation, the Bundeswehr will orient itself more towards France.'	2.4
E: 'The Bundeswehr will orient itself more towards the East.'	1.2
No comment	0.9

Source: Schössler, Albert, and Kostelnik 1992: Question # 75.

According to this majority view order – in the sense of predictable, stable, and peaceful relations among states in general and the major powers in particular – was an equally valuable and scarce resource. Therefore, the threat and use of force was considered to be both necessary and legitimate as an *ultima ratio* to (re)establish order given the conflict-ridden nature of international politics and the repeated occurrence of war. Moreover, the major powers (united Germany now being included) had both a special interest and a special obligation to see that order was kept (or re-established). As a result, Germany had to come to terms with the fact that its more visible role in international politics had to be 'commensurate with its political and economic weight as well as the expectations of its allies' (Meiers 1995: 96). If it was 'normal' for a great power to be 'responsible' for (re)creating international order – even if only in a 'co-leadership' role (Haftendorn 1994: 150) – and if this, at times, also necessitated the use of force, then it was also part of the 'normalization' of German foreign policy to shed whatever restrictions existed to participating fully in these activities (see also table 32).[56]

None of this implied that there was a need for a wholesale reinvention of German foreign policy. On the contrary, many prominent foreign policy experts argued that there was much to learn from the successes of the first 40 years of the Federal Republic. Since *Einbindungspolitik* – as the old FRG's diplomatic strategy of multilateralism and integration had come to be known within Germany – had turned out to be 'a more cost-efficient variant to a strategy based on narrowly defined national interests' (Haftendorn 1994: 140), and since Germany was perceived *not* be in a position to deal with *any* of the major problems in its immediate environment or even globally on its own,[57] sticking with multilateralism and integration seemed to be the only reasonable strategy for the 'new' Germany as well. If Germany was to be in position to choose freely among international institutions, there was a clear preference for (global or regional) 'omnilateral' (Bull and Watson 1984: 434) security institutions such as the United Nations and the CSCE (OSCE). However, given that the majority of the experts were rather skeptical as to whether a more peaceful new order could be built by relying solely on these institutions, other more exclusive (or merely 'multilateral') clubs – such as those made up by the Western democracies, like the European Union and NATO – were deemed

---

56. For prominent examples of German foreign policy experts supporting this view see vol. 1 of the 4-volume project by the Deutsche Gesellschaft für Auswärtige Politik on Germany's 'new' foreign policy (Kaiser and Maull 1994), especially Kaiser (1994: 9–10), Stürmer (1994: 44–51), and Nerlich (1994: 157–163).

57. According to Stürmer (1994: 61) "for Germany, the ability to act ('Handlungsfähigkeit') is, first and foremost, synonymous with its ability to be a reliable Western ally ('westliche Bündnisfähigkeit')".

Table 32. The Basic Law and the Participation of the Bundeswehr in Military Operations

Question: 'A further point of argument in public debate is the deployment of the Bundeswehr outside the NATO area. A change of the Basic law (constitution) has been discussed in order to widen the possibilities of Bundeswehr deployment. What is your opinion on this matter?' (in percent)

	Total
Interviewees	N=423
A: 'The constitution should not be changed and the mission of the Bundeswehr should stay confined to the NATO area.'	7.8
B: 'Changing the constitution is not necessary because the *Grundgesetz* only prohibits the fighting/planning of attacks, it does allow for participation in all activities which are in accordance with international law.'	44.0
C: 'Changing the constitution should only allow for peacekeeping operations.'	4.5
D: 'Changing the constitution should allow for peacemaking operations as well as peace-enforcement operations (Ch. VII UN-Charter).'	14.6
E: 'A change of the constitution should allow comprehensively for joint missions in all systems of collective security in which Germany is a member.'	28.6
No comment	0.5

Source: Schössler, Albert, and Kostelnik 1992: Question # 78.

equally or even more significant. The fact that they carried less legitimacy in terms of international law was balanced by the judgement that they would be more effective.

The 'New' Germany: Still a Reluctant Power, but Increasingly a Normal Ally and a Self-Confident Nation

The views of foreign policy elites and the German public in general which I have summarized here for the first two years after unification thus reveal a clear trend to live up to the expectations of the allies that Germany should take over more international responsibility. The fact that 'responsibility' here was defined to a significant extent in terms of security in general and the use of military means in particular was seen by most of Germany's allies as a sign of 'geopolitical maturation' (Asmus 1992: 41) Within Germany, however, critics interpreted these changes as a degeneration (or perversion of the term 'responsibility') because Germany now seemed to (once again) 'militarize' (rather than 'demilitarize') its foreign policy.[58] Thus, as usual, the *perceptions* of change among security experts were *converging*, whereas the *assessment* of these changes was increasingly *diverging*. While representatives of the community of 'security experts' welcomed the fact that Germany was finally becoming 'once again a "normal country"' taking over 'normal responsibility' as 'our Western allies had already requested during the Gulf War,'[59] representatives of the community of 'peace researchers' saw a 'new' Germany characterized by 'arrogance and a craving for recognition' ('Übermut und Geltungsdrang') instead of the 'sense of proportion, sensitivity and restraint' ('Augenmaß, Fingerspitzengefühl, Zurückhaltung') characteristic of the 'old' FRG (Mutz 1994: 228).

---

58. For a critique of definitions of 'normality' and 'responsibility' in military terms see Mutz (1994: 220–228). According to Mutz, 'responsibility' had degenerated to 'nothing but an appeal to get rid of scruples vis-à-vis the use of military power' (1994: 225). For a recent statement in favor of 'demilitarization and civilianization' of German foreign policy see the section 'Entmilitarisierung und Zivilisierung – die Schlüssel der Friedenspolitik' in the election programme of Bündnis90/Die Grünen for the 1998 federal elections (Bündnis90/Die Grünen, 1998).

59. R. Scholz, 'Deutschland auf dem Weg zur internationalen Normalität', in *Der Mittler-Brief*, No. 1/1994, 5 (quoted according to Mutz 1994: 220). In the late 1980s Scholz, a member of the CDU, had been serving a German Defense Minister.

Whatever the *judgements*, the *perceptions* of change were right on the mark. Whether it was hailed that Germany was 'again' becoming as 'normal' as its Western allies or whether it was castigated for 'again' becoming as 'abnormal' as other great powers ('normality' here being defined as corresponding to a stringent *normative* standard (Mutz 1994: 221), the experts seemed to agree as to the *direction* of this '(ab)normalization' process. In the eyes of the normalization-sympathizers, Germany was 'coming of age'; becoming more 'self-confident' (and assertive);[60] feeling less inhibited ('befangen') by its pre-World War II legacy;[61] able 'to live up to' the 'legitimate expectations' of its allies; and ready to 'make a contribution' in order to 'preserve peace.' In the eyes of the abnormalization-critics, in contrast, Germany was again 'militarizing' its foreign policy; returning to a 'security policy of re-confrontation' (Mutz 1994: 227); determined once again to conduct *Großmachtpolitik* and – in the form of a Wilhelminian Berlin Republic of the left – retreating to

60. The most direct and authoritative statement recently made along these lines was by Chancellor Gerhard Schröder in his first major address to the Bundestag. Schröder said:

We are proud of this country, its landscape and culture, the creativeness and will to achieve of its people. We are proud of the older generation that rebuilt the country after the war and gave it its place in a Europe at peace. We are proud of the people in the eastern part of Germany who threw off the communist yoke and brought down the Wall. That is the self-confidence of a nation that has come of age, that feels neither superior nor inferior to anyone ('"Weil wir Deutschlands Kraft vertrauen . . .", Regierungserklärung von Bundeskanzler Gerhard Schröder vor dem Deutschen Bundestag am 10.11.1998', *Bulletin*, no. 74 (11.11.1998), 910, emphasis added; quoted in the translation of 'The Berlin Republic. A Survey of Germany,' *The Economist*, 6 February 1999, 21)

In my judgement the distinct connotations of the German term *Selbstbewußtsein* (which Schröder used) is not adequately transported by 'self-confidence' alone; rather the meaning of the term is best conveyed as a mixture of self-confidence and assertiveness.

61. Cf. P. Bahners, 'Total Normal. Vorsicht Falle: Die unbefangene Nation,' *Frankfurter Allgemeine Zeitung* (November 3, 1998), 43; W.A. Perger, 'Wir Unbe-fangenen,' *Die Zeit*, no. 47 (November 12, 1998), 7; 'Total normal?', *Der Spiegel*, no. 49 (November 30, 1998), 40–48.

a dubious past with 'the fatal smack of false continuities' (Habermas 1995: 187).[62]

The trends in public opinion during the past nine years support the perceptions of change which underlie the hopes (or fears) expressed by the experts as the (ab)normalization trends which were visible already in 1991/92 have mostly accelerated: Pride in being a citizen of a large and influential country has increased steadily (see table 33). The same holds (at an even accelerated speed) for taking over 'more responsibility' (see table 34). At the same time opposition against sending the Bundeswehr in support of UN peacekeeping missions steadily dropped (see table 35) as pessimism increased that wars in general can be prevented (see table 36). Following the same logic more and more Germans believed that it is important to have an army (see table 37) and to keep NATO intact as a functioning alliance (see table 38). Still, there were no signs of *Weltpolitik* self-aggrandizement. To be sure, when asked whether they wanted their country to get a permanent seat in the UN Security Council, a majority of Germans said yes. However, since 1990 this majority has been slowly decreasing (see table 39).[63]

62. In a review of Richard Rorty's book 'Achieving Our Country' (which was published in German under the title 'Stolz auf unser Land'), Habermas indirectly criticized not only the 'snappy nationalist brag' of Chancellor Schröder but also the fact that after the 1998 election victory of the SPD and the Greens 'normality' had now been seized by a 'nationalist left'; see J. Habermas, 'Rortys patriotischer Traktat. Aber vor Analogien wird gewarnt', *Süddeutsche Zeitung* (February 27/28, 1999). It is important, however, to note the crucial differences between Chancellor Schröder and Foreign Minister Fischer in terms of their emphasis on 'normality' and national 'lack of inhibition' ('Unbefangenheit') on the one hand (Schröder) and 'Europeanness' and 'constitutional patriotism' ('Verfassungspatriotismus') on the other (Fischer); for perceptive observations about these differences see 'Es gibt doch Alternativen. Interview mit Jürgen Habermas,' *Die Zeit*, no. 42 (October 8, 1998), 12–15, and Bernard-Henri Lévy, 'Ein paar Versuche, in Deutschland spazieren zu gehen, Part I and II,' *Frankfurter Allgemeine Zeitung* (February 17, 1999), 50 and *Frankfurter Allgemeine Zeitung* (February 18, 1999), 46.

63. This is even more surprising in view of the fact that Germany's material and, to some extent, ideational commitment to the UN has increased during the 1990s. For a detailed analysis see Knapp (1999: 10 (table 1) listing Germany's (steadily increasing) assessed contributions to the regular UN budget throughout the decade.

Table 33. Pride in Being Large and Influential

Question: 'After unification Germany has become a big and influential country in the world. Do you approve of this or do you worry about this development?' (in percent)

	October 1990			1993	1994	1995
	Old Länder	New Länder	Germany total	Germany total		
Approve	51	53	51	50	52	54
Worry	23	24	23	28	20	21
Undecided	26	23	26	22	28	25
Sum	100	100	100	100	100	100

Source: Noelle-Naumann and Köcher 1997: 1098.

Table 34. Steadily Increasing Support for Taking over 'More Responsibility'

Question: 'Should Germany take on more responsibility in the world or should we hold back?' (in percent)

	1991 September	1991 December	1992 June	1993 March	1994 October
Germany should take on more responsibility.	31	23	28	37	41
Germany should hold back.	56	59	55	49	46
Undecided	13	18	17	14	13
Sum	100	100	100	100	100

Source: Noelle-Naumann and Köcher 1997: 1099.

Table 35. Opposition Against Bundeswehr Participation in UN Peacekeeping Steadily Drops

Question: 'The United Nations have international peacekeeping forces which monitor armistices in different regions of the world. It has been suggested that Bundeswehr soldiers should participate in these peacekeeping forces. Below, two opinions are mentioned. Who do you agree with?' (in percent)

	Total July 1996	West Germany 1988	1993	1995	1996	East Germany 1993	1995	1996
'I am against such deployment of the Bundeswehr. It is not Germany's task to send troops to regions of crisis around the world. Considering our past we Germans especially should hold back in these questions.'	31	44	31	29	28	43	52	44
'I don't agree. A country of Germany's importance cannot shirk its international responsibilities. As members of the UN we have to be prepared to take on international responsibility, as it is expected of us.'	53	36	54	54	56	42	29	42
Undecided	16	20	15	17	16	15	19	14
Sum	100	100	100	100	100	100	100	100

Source: Noelle-Naumann and Köcher 1997: 1144–1145.

Table 36. Increasing Doubts that Wars Can be Prevented

Question: 'Do you think that wars can be avoided or that wars are in humans' nature?' (in percent)

| | West Germany | | | East Germany |
	1981	1988	1997	1997
Wars can be avoided	55	61	51	63
Wars are in humans' nature	33	31	37	25
Undecided	12	8	12	12
Sum	100	100	100	100

Source: xxx.

Table 37. It is Useful to Have the Bundeswehr . . .

Question: 'Looking at things from a practical point of view, do we actually need a Bundeswehr or could we do without it?' (in percent)

| | West Germany | | | | East Germany | | |
	1984	1990	1991	1996	1990	1991	1996
Need Bundeswehr	75	57	62	66	47	57	61
Could do without	15	32	27	21	42	32	23
Undecided	10	11	11	13	11	11	16
Sum	100	100	100	100	100	100	100

Source: Noelle-Naumann and Köcher 1997: 1123.

Thus, while Germany still displays many signs of a 'reluctant power' (Meiers 1995) it has increasingly become a 'normal ally.'[64] The contrast between the Gulf War in 1990 on the one hand and NATO's strikes against Serbia in the summer of 1995 and again in March 1999 on the other is particularly instructive here. When asked in March 1991 whether Germans would support the participation

---

64. See Gerhard Schröder's statement, n. 60.

Table 38. . . . and Important to Keep NATO

Question:'Two people are talking about NATO, the western alliance. Who do you agree with most?' (in percent)

| | West Germany | | | | East Germany | | |
	1990	1991	1994	1995	1991	1994	1995
'Now that there is no danger from Eastern Europe and the former Soviet Union, NATO has lost its importance as a military alliance.'	27	23	14	13	42	21	26
'NATO has to continue as a strong alliance so as to be prepared for eventualities. You don't know how things will develop in the former Soviet Union.'	54	62	72	75	39	64	57
Undecided	19	15	14	12	19	15	17
Sum	100	100	100	100	100	100	100

Source: Noelle-Naumann and Köcher 1997: 1136.

of the Bundeswehr in UN operations similar to the Gulf War only one third was in favor (see table 2). In 1995, however, more than 50 percent of the German public welcomed NATO strikes (support among the elites in East and West was almost unanimous, see table 40). Similar numbers thought that it was 'right' for Germany to participate actively in these strikes (see table 41). Support was even stronger after the escalation of the war in Kosovo in March 1999.

Table 39. A Permanent Seat in the UN Security Council would be nice (but with time passing ever fewer Germans think that Germany should aim for it)

Question: 'Have you ever heard about the Security Council of the United Nations?'
If 'heard about it': 'The permanent members of the United Nations' Security Council are the United States, Russia, China, France and Great Britain. Do you think that united Germany should also receive a permanent seat in the Security Council, or is it of little importance?' (in percent)

	October 1990		Population (total)			
	Old Länder	New Länder	1992 July	1993 July	1994 Oct.	1996 July
Have heard about the Security Council	88	90	94	93	90	90
Never heard of it	11	10	6	7	10	10
No comment	1	X	X	X	X	X
Sum	100	100	100	100	100	100
Persons, who have heard of the UN Security Council United Germany should also receive a seat.	64	67	64	59	58	56
This is not very important	22	21	18	24	21	18
Undecided	14	12	12	10	11	16
Sum	100	100	100	100	100	100

Source: Noelle-Naumann and Köcher 1997: 1100.

In the survey from October 1990 the question was asked slightly differently: 'Have you heard of this: "The permanent members of the UN Security Council have power of veto and can block decisions. Do you think that unified Germany should also receive a permanent seat on the UN Security Council or is this of little importance?"' See Noelle-Naumann and Köcher (1993: 963).

Table 40. Support for NATO´s Airstrikes on Serbian Troops in 1995

Question: 'For the first time NATO flew heavy airstrikes in Bosnia. Do you approve or disapprove of this action?' (in percent)

September 1995	West	East	Elite West	Elite East
Approve	56	31	94	84
Disapprove	28	52	4	12
Undecided	16	17	2	4
Sum	100	100	100	100

Source: Noelle-Naumann and Köcher 1997: 1147.

Table 41. Support for German Participation in NATO's Airstrikes in 1995

Question: 'Do you think it is right that Germany participate in NATO's airstrikes in Bosnia, or should Germany not take part?' (in percent)

September 1995	West	East	Elite West	Elite East
Should participate	50	25	92	83
Should not participate	38	64	6	14
Undecided	12	11	2	3
Sum	100	100	100	100

Source: Noelle-Naumann and Köcher 1997: 1147.

Sixty-four percent of West Germans (but only 38 percent of East Germans) were in favor of airstrikes against Serbian troops in late March, in spite of the fact that a UN mandate could not be furnished, and still higher numbers of West Germans supported the participation of German Tornados in these strikes (here again East Germans were much more reluctant, with only 30 percent in favor, see table 42). Another poll from late March 1999 found that 52 percent of

Table 42. German Support for NATO Airstrikes against Serbia in 1999, including German *Tornados* (in percent)

March 1999	West Germany		East Germany	
	Yes/ Right	No/ Wrong	Yes/ Right	No/ Wrong
'Do you approve NATO airstrikes against Serbian positions in Yugoslavia?' (yes/no)	64	33	39	58
'Is the participation of German *Tornado*-planes in NATO airstrikes right or wrong?' (right/wrong)	69	41	30	58
'In case of an emergency, would you approve the deployment of NATO ground forces in Kosovo?' (yes/no)	33	63	23	74

Source: Emnid-Umfrage on behalf of *Der Spiegel*, no. 14, 1 April 1999 (online-Version).

Germans were in support of German participation even if 'German soldiers would be killed in combat'; still more surprisingly, 46 percent of Germans thought it 'apt' for the United States 'to intervene militarily in conflicts which do not directly affect their national security'. Also, whereas a clear majority of Germans (58 percent) thought that Germany's participation in NATO's airstrikes 'corresponds to the current role of united Germany in world politics', only one fifth thought that this would strengthen Germany's self-confidence (see table 43).

Whether in shifting its views the public was merely following the agenda set by the political elites during the preceding nine years or whether, in enlarging the scope of Germany's international

Table 43. Readiness to Risk the Lives of German Soldiers, Pro-Americanism, and Acceptance of Germany's New Role without Arrogance (in percent)

March 1999	**Germany (total)**	
	Yes	**No**
'Is Bundeswehr participation to be continued if German soldiers should die in combat?'	52	36
'The United States intervenes in conflicts using military power even if these conflicts do not necessarily endanger their national security. Does the role of the United States give them the right to do so?'	46	45
'Do you believe that participation in the airstrikes corresponds with unified Germany's role in world politics?'	58	32
'Do you think, that Bundeswehr participation in the airstrikes against Yugoslavia strengthens the self-confidence of Germans?'	19	67

Source: Forsa-Umfrage on behalf of *Der Stern*, no. 14, 31 March 1999, p. 52.

military engagements, the political leadership was anticipating these shifts in public mood and acting accordingly is not of interest here. The main point simply is that *Germany has changed almost as dramatically between the fall of 1990 and the spring of 1999 as its environment has changed*. The Gulf War was a new type of international conflict for *any* country involved. In terms of being 'prepared' for it, however, Germany certainly was lagging farther behind than most. Of course, the adjustment process took time, with the normalization-sympathizers bemoaning the slowness of pace and the abnormalization-critics castigating both the speed and the direction of the process. Still, in all likelihood, few observers would question the conclusion that *Germany has come a very long way in a rather short period of time.* This conclusion is especially noteworthy in view of the fact that many of the same people who were among the most outspoken critics of both the American conduct during the Gulf War and the Kohl government's cautious, even timid signals of support vis-à-vis the anti-Saddam coalition are now among those who are either vehemently defending NATO's military operation and the Bundeswehr's participation in it or keeping quiet. This is even more striking if one takes into account the *similarities* and the *differences* between the Gulf War and the Kosovo War. In 1990 the German left overwhelmingly spoke out *against* a war which the UN had 'authorized,' a war, moreover, which certainly was 'legitimate' by any standard of international law given that a member state of the UN was threatened with extinction. In 1999 the first government in German history solely formed by parties which define themselves as 'left' couldn't have been more of a reliable ('normal') ally in carrying out NATO's first fully-fledged military campaign in its history. For the first time since the end of World War II a German cabinet sent German troops into war, and for the first time ever a social democratic defense minister had to give the order. Moreover, this government of the left did so not only without being able to refer to a UN mandate but having to justify, in addition, that the military operations of the alliance (which many a Green once wanted to abolish) were directed against a sovereign state which (justifiably or not) was rejecting an intervention in its 'internal affairs' based on human rights grounds.[65]

Most of those German respresentatives now being truly 'responsible' for these decisions would probably hesitate to interpret their

---

65. If one were to leave aside the legal aspect that Kuweit was a recognized entity in terms of internal law while Kosovo is not, it probably could be argued that the violations of human rights which Saddam Hussein's troops committed against the Kuweitis were only marginally less severe than the ones committed by the troops of Slobodan Milosevic against the Kosovo Albanians. Yet in 1990 the German left was rather unmoved by the plight of the Kuweiti people, seeing instead predominantly a war where 'blood' had to be spilled for 'oil.'

Table 44a. Germany's 'Special' History

Question: 'Is there something in our history, which distinctly distinguishes us from other countries, I mean something that can really be called a peculiarity of German history. Does that exist?' (in percent)

Yes, exists	West Germany	East Germany
1989	59	–
1990	–	67
1992	59	60
1993	64	62
1995	61	62
1996	69	68

Source: Noelle-Naumann and Köcher 1997: 503.

Table 44b. A Very Special History: the Holocaust, Many Wars and a Nation Divided and Reunited

Questions to persons, who believe that there is something special in German history: 'What is special about our history, what distinguishes our history from that of other countries?' (in percent)

	West Germany		East Germany	
	1989	1996	1990	1996
1. The Third Reich, National Socialism, Hitler	52	44	4	13
Among which:				
(a) explicit reference to Nazi crimes (extermination of the Jews)	13	20	1	4
(b) explicit reference to expulsion, destruction, death	2	1	1	1

2. Many wars in Germany history, World War II	23	29	36	33
Among which:				
(a) The Germans started the wars.	6	5	17	18
(b) The Germans lost the wars.	3	2	2	1
(c) The carrying out of the war by German officers	X	1	1	2
3. Unification	X	20	X	40
4. Germany is/was a divided country, Berlin Wall	11	15	36	37
5. exceptional achievements (poets, philosophers, scientists, inventions, etc.)	4	6	3	3
6. characteristics (industriousness, love of order, etc.)	5	4	13	5
7. reconstruction after the war	6	5	1	1
8. names of famous persons were mentioned	2	1	X	X
9. reference to German history before the Weimar Republic (empire (Kaiserreich) etc.)	7	1	1	1
Other	4	9	12	9
Don't know	4	4	5	5

Source: xxx.

behavior as a case of 'learning.' The same probably holds for many International Relations specialists who in the past two decades have developed an extensive research agenda on 'learning' in international affairs and foreign policy.[66] Yet this is precisely what I would argue: During the past nine years Germany in general and the German left in particular has 'learned' some very hard lessons about international politics. The point here, though, is *not* that some idealists

---

66. For an overview see Levy (1994: 279–312); for extensive theoretical treatment as well as detailed illustrations of this research programme see Breslauer and Tetlock (1991).

have (finally) come to understand that international politics is driven by certain 'eternal laws' of power and national interest, as the realists suggest. Rather, the point is that *any* type of (political) action has to be conducted in an environment which (more often than not) confronts decision-makers with 'problematic situations.' These problematic situations call for solutions that have to rely on both experience *and* innovation.[67]

A large part of the 'problematic' aspect of Germany's new environment consisted in the fact that the desired 'all-European order of peace' ('gesamteuropäische Friedensordnung') has not materialized beyond those regions containing countries that will (sooner or later) be included in the exclusive clubs of the European Union and NATO. Seen from a German perspective, today's Europe is in significant ways much less 'all-European' and certainly less 'peaceful' than the old Cold War order was.[68] At the same time Germany's 'problem' has been worsened (or at least been 'reshaped') in that after 1990 its partners have started pushing ever harder for a German 'contribution' to ordering Europe. As a result it has become ever more difficult for Germany to stand aside.

In foreign policy (as in any other field of human action) being 'responsible' always meant being 'responsive' – responsive to what

67. The epistemological position and the theory of action underlying these propositions draw heavily on the tradition of American pragmatism and such classical writers as William James, John Dewey (who has coined the concept of 'problematic situations'), and George Herbert Mead, but also extending to the present work of authors such as Richard Rorty, Hilary Putnam and (in part) Jürgen Habermas. I develop these propositions in more detail in a larger project on German foreign policy currently under way. For introductory overviews of the tradition of pragmatism see Menand (1997: xi–xxxiv); Rescher (1995: 710–713); Bernstein (1995: 54–67); and Joas (1992: 7–65). For more recent prominent contributions see Rorty (1989, 1998); Putnam (1995); and Habermas (1996: 715–741). Two authors who have spelled out the consequences of this position for sociology (and the theory of action in particular) and the academic discipline of history are Joas (1992) and Hawthorn (1991).

68. For an early expression of pessimism as to a European order of peace see Mearsheimer (1990: 5–55). Mearsheimer's analysis is still very much contested. However, even though his scenario has not materialized as he expected, the European order of security looks much less promising at the end of the decade than at the beginning.

Table 45. Hitler and the 'Moral Obligation' to Support the Anti-Saddam Coalition

Question: 'Just some time ago someone said, "We Germans have a special moral responsibility to help overthrow the aggressor Saddam Hussain. If the whole world had not fought together against Hitler, Germany would have never been freed."
Do you think that because of this we have a particular moral duty to support the Americans, or do you disagree?' (in percent)

February 1991	Old Länder	New Länder
We have a particular moral duty to support the Americans.	47	32
I disagree	34	43
Undecided	19	25
Sum	100	100

Source: Noelle-Neumann and Köcher 1993: 1088.

Table 46. The Lesson of (West) German History: Fight Dictators

Question: 'Two people are talking about the lessons the Germans should have learnt from their history. Who do you agree with most?'
One says: 'Looking at the harm the world war caused we Germans should have learned never to participate in a war again.'
The other says: 'I don't agree. German history shows how dangerous a dictatorship can be. If there is no other way we have to fight against a dictator.' (in percent)

February 1991	Old Länder	New Länder
Germans should never again participate in a war	36	58
A dictator must be fought against	50	38
Undecided	14	4
Sum	100	100

Source: Noelle-Neumann and Köcher 1993: 1088.

other significant actors demand, responsive to what your own (material *and* ideational) interests suggest, and responsive to the demands and limits set by your voters. The responses called for by German decision-makers today are different than they were ten years ago. During the old days of the 'Bonn Republic' Germany was asked to do mainly two things: (1) be a responsible ally in that it did not rock the boat of an alliance steering the (only seemingly) quiet waters of a semi-stable and bipolar European security order by pushing ahead too far with its own 'all-German' agenda; (2) be a responsible 'motor' (in 'co-leadership' with France) of European integration in the western half of Europe. The fact that the Bonn Republic was largely living up to these expectations helped significantly in bringing down the old order, thereby enabling the Germans in East and West to realize their 'all-German' ambition of 'self-determination' *in concert with* their allies and former opponents. As a result, Germany has been not only one of the big winners of the radical transformations in Europe at the turn of the decade from the 1980s to the 1990s. It subsequently has also realized many of its ambitious goals of reshaping its immediate environment according to its own design by opening up NATO and the EU to its Eastern neighbours. The price for these desired changes has been German reciprocation in shouldering a larger part of the costs of the institutional transformations of both NATO and the European Union. In this sense the 'new' Germany is as '(ab)normal' as the old FRG: (1) It has excelled at adapting the old strategy of 'attritional multilateralism'[69] in order to reshape its new environment according to its own goals. Yet as before 1990, Germany has experienced that the allies are no less apt at 'attritional diplomacy'. As a result Germany has been forced to live up to the demands of the allies on which it depends (as ever) politically and economically. (2) The new Germany is as (ab)normal as the old one also in another respect. The legacy of *Machtpolitik* which had crucially shaped Germany's strategy of *Einbindungspolitik* during 40 years of post-World War II West German

---

69. This term was coined by Timothy Garton Ash (1994: 71), who defined attritional multilateralism as 'the patient, discreet pursuit of national goals through multilateral institutions and negotiations.'

foreign policy had taught mainly three lessons best summarized under the heading of 'restraint'; never go it alone, never be out in front, and always keep German soldiers as invisible (in their being 'German') as possible. The dual legacies of *both Machtpolitik and Einbindungspolitik* are still being felt today. With very few exceptions,[70] Germans are still moving only in crowds, mostly behind some ally out front and almost always with German uniforms disappearing in a sea of NATO olive. Given that NATO olive now is more often shown at trouble spots in the Balkans (rather than at the intra-German border) German unifom colors are appearing there too. But up to this point it is *not Weltpolitik* self-aggrandizement but precisely the *dual* legacy of *both 'Machtpolitik' and 'Einbindungspolitik'* why German uniforms are reappearing. In other words, for what we can tell thus far it is *not* 'arrogance and a craving for recognition' (Mutz 1994: 228) which drives the German government to send the Bundeswehr along with its NATO allies; rather, it is precisely for *normative* reasons (reasons which, of course, are disputable and disputed) and the effects of the socializing pressure of its environment that Germany's military *normality* has changed.[71]

Conclusion: Revisioning Germany

During the last nine years Germany has learned some hard lessons about international politics. It was hard for Germans to learn these lessons because few really *wanted* to learn them. At the same time it was easy because it would have been difficult based on the old

70. For a detailed analysis for one of the most often cited exceptions after unification see Crawford (1996).

71. The German public and, presumably, the political elites as well have a clear sense of what is 'special' about Germany's history. Throughout the 1990s increasing majorities testified to the country's historical 'specialness' (see table 44a). The Holocaust and the many wars initiated by Germany stand out as being 'special'; the division of the country and German unification in 1990 are ranked next in line (with more emphasis in East Germany placed on the latter, see table 44b). At least as far as the (dominating) West Germans are concerned, the lesson to be drawn from that special history are equally clear: Germans have a 'moral obligation' to fight dictators (see tables 45 and 46).

Federal Republic's foreign policy tradition *not* to learn them. These lessons learned are neither captured by the dichotomy *Weltpolitik or* 'self-containment' nor are they captured by an alternative 'civilian' symbiosis of *Weltpolitik and* 'self-containment', as the Greens suggested in 1990. Rather what probably best describes Germany's new role in international relations today is a translation of 'normalization' into the specific political and historical German context by spelling out the multiple meanings of the term itself.

In aspiring to be regarded as 'normal' in some respects and very 'special' in others any country has to make its own choices. Some of these choices are rather abstract. They relate to the long-term aspirations of a country, its visions. Most, however, are very concrete, involving core values, material interests, and historical experience in specific problematic situations. The 'visionary thing' (George Bush) feeds into these concrete choices as well. It is not, as Helmut Schmidt, the quintessential pragmatic 'doer' ('Macher') among Germany's postwar chancellors, once said, that if you are having visions you should consult your doctor. Rather, as his successor has shown, the visionaries sometimes are the true realists.[72] Western Europe's integration would not have proceeded as far as it did (for good or ill) had Kohl not been obsessed with his vision of creating an ever more closely integrated union. Without Kohl Europe would, most likely, still be a 'Euro-free' zone dominated by the Deutschmark. It is significantly, but not exclusively, in this regard that German visions and ambitions have reshaped both the county itself and the continent during the past nine years.

However, in order not to idealize these recent developments in German foreign policy I will also mention one important downside of this normalization process *beyond Weltpolitik*, 'self-containment', and 'civilian power'. As Germany has learned some hard lessons about international politics during the past nine years, Germany's

72. This has been a standard line in Kohl's speeches during the past few years. His legacy in these terms (including a reference to 'the visionaries' being 'the true realists') is summarized in his first speech in the Bundestag after his resignation; a condensed version of this speech was reprinted *Frankfurter Allgemeine Zeitung* (July 2, 1999), 8.

allies soon may also have to learn some hard lessons themselves. In Germany's policy towards European integration (as in no other area) Germany's domestic discourse about 'national' interests has markedly shifted during the past decade (and particularly during the past three or four years) from a position of supranationalism and inhibition ('Befangenheit') based on both Germany's postwar enthusiasm for European integration and its pre-World War II legacy of *Machtpolitik* to a more self-centered, assertive, and more 'national' position (see figure 1).[73] Some of the early repercussions of this 'normalization' shift have already been felt around Europe during the end game of the negotiations of the Amsterdam treaty. In all likelihood *this* trend of (ab)normalization will also accelerate. In 1994 Hans-Peter Schwarz (1994: 92) predicted that Germany's European policy was bound to become 'more selfish, more calculated and cost-conscious, less flexible and primarily fixed on a rather narrowly defined national interest. Similarly, one of the state secretaries of both Foreign Minister Kinkel and Fischer said in 1997 that Germany's European policy had, almost by necessity, become 'more British.'[74]

None of this means that Germany is about to go 'wild' again. Many of the 'taming' effects of German integration in Western institutions will probably persist (Katzenstein 1997). But other images may be somewhat misleading: the image of Germany as not living up to its presumed leadership responsibilities in Europe because of a powerful grip of collective memory (Markovits and Reich 1997) and the image of Germany as imploding under the burdens of 'anti-imperial overstretch' (Hamilton 1994: 17). In significant respects the metaphor of Germany becoming 'more British' adequately captures recent developments in Germany's *European* policy. When Schröder said in the early days of his chancellorship that Germany 'is contributing more than half' of the money which 'Europe squanders' ('verbraten')[75] he was, in stark

---

73. I discuss this in more detail in Hellmann (2000).

74. See P. Hort, 'Die deutsche Europa-Politik wird "britischer"', *Frankfurter Allgemeine Zeitung* (November 30, 1997). It was State Secretary Friedrich von Ploetz who offered this judgement.

75. Gerhard Schröder quoted according to E. Lohse, 'Ministerpräsidenten wollen Steuerreform zustimmen,' *Frankfurter Allgemeine Zeitung* (December 9, 1998), 1.

contrast to his predecessor, expressing a new type of German *resentment* vis-à-vis the project of European integration increasingly felt among the German public more broadly. Surveys clearly underline this trend: Throughout the 1990s Germans saw ever fewer benefits and ever more costs associated with European integration (see table 47); at the same time opinion turned around as to whether Germany should play a leadership role in order to pursue its interests

Table 47. Increasing Costs and Decreasing Benefits of European Integration

Question: 'Does Germany's membership of the European Union have more advantages or disadvantages, or do you think they even out?' (in percent)

	More advantages	More disadvantages	Evens out	Don't know, no comment	Sum
West Germany					
1979	15	25	46	14	100
1984	13	36	39	12	100
1990	24	27	40	9	100
1991	22	27	41	10	100
1992	16	36	37	11	100
1993	17	39	34	10	100
1994	18	32	41	9	100
1995	19	22	48	11	100
1996	13	36	40	11	100
East Germany					
1990	35	7	36	22	100
1991	24	13	38	25	100
1992	14	21	40	25	100
1993	15	27	37	21	100
1994	12	30	42	16	100
1995	12	27	41	20	100
1996	10	34	36	20	100

Source: Noelle-Naumann and Köcher 1997: 1158.

(see table 48); finally, and most interestingly, an early 1999 poll found that more than 80 percent of Germans welcomed the fact that 'Schröder was presenting himself more self-confidently and assert-ively in Europe' than his predecessor (see table 49). Even Foreign

Table 48. In Pursuit of German Interests in Europe: Leadership Replaces Restraint

Question: 'Two people are talking about the position unified Germany is to have in the future in Europe. Who do you agree with most?' (in percent)

	West Germany		East Germany	
	1990	**1996**	**1990**	**1996**
'We should rather hold back. It is sufficient to be economically strong. We do not also have to play a leading political role.'	57	33	62	42
'Unified Germany is economically the strongest country in Europe. Therefore Germany has to take on a leading role in Europe, otherwise our interests will not be sufficiently considered in a unified Europe.'	30	52	28	41
Undecided	13	15	10	17
Sum	100	100	100	100

Source: Noelle-Naumann and Köcher 1997: 1154.

The same message also appeared during the 1999 election campaign to the European Parliament. One large campaign poster carrying Chancellor Schröder's picture sent the following message to German voters: 'We do not expect gifts from Europe. But the same should also hold vice versa' ('Wir erwarten von Europa keine Geschenke. Aber umgekehrt sollte es genauso sein').

Table 49. An Increasingly Self-confident and Assertive Germany in Europe (in percent)

January 1999	Yes	No
'In 1999 the Federal Republic is 50 years old. Should Germany now present itself more self-confidently and assertively than previously?'	68	25
'Schröder behaves more self-confidently and assertively in Europe than Kohl. Do you approve?'	82	12
'Should Germany take on a leading role in Europe?'	31	61

Source: Survey by Infratest/dimap, January 1999 on behalf of 'Sabine Christiansen' (http://www.sabine-christiansen.de/03011999.htm).

Minister Fischer seems to imply that Germany has to stand up for its interests. While he denies that the Kosovo experience will tempt Germany to 'speak up' in international institutions, he expressed his 'wish' that Germany will 'speak more effectively' there – obviously implying that even Helmut Kohl's heir apparent in terms of Germany's Euroenthusiasm is hoping to maximize German influence in Europe.[76]

Thus, while Germany is becoming a more normal ally globally (which most of its partners welcome), it is at the time also becoming a more normal – i.e. more self-centered and assertive – big player regionally in European affairs (which most others will probably increasingly resent). Whether Europe (and Germany itself) will be better off as a result of both (ab)normalization processes remains to be seen.

76. '"Nicht lauter, aber wirksamer sprechen". Interview with Joschka Fischer,' *Frankfurter Rundschau* (July 10, 1999), 8. For an interesting research project on German foreign policy since unification examining, among others, a realist-inspired influence maximization hypothesis see Baumann, Rittberger and Wagner (1998).

References

Asmus, R. (1992), *Germany in Transition: National Self-Confidence and International Relations (Rand Notes N-3522-AF)* (Santa Monica: The Rand Corporation).

Auswärtiges Amt (ed.) (1995), *Außenpolitik der Bundesrepublik Deutschland. Dokumente von 1949 bis 1994*, herausgegeben aus Anlaß des 125. Jubiläums des Auswärtigen Amtes (Köln: Verlag Wissenschaft und Politik).

Bertram, Chr. (1994), 'Germany's New International Loneliness', in A. Baring (ed), *Germany's New Position in Europe: Problems and Perspectives* (Oxford and Providence, R.I.: Berg Publishers).

Bull, H. and Watson, A. (1984), 'Conclusion', in H. Bull and A. Watson, eds, *The Expansion of International Society* (Oxford: Clarendon).

Czempiel, E.-O. (1994a), 'Gewalt in der Gesellschaftswelt: Die Rolle des Militärischen in der Außenpolitik der neuen Bundesrepublik', *Blätter für deutsche und internationale Politik* 39: 36–43.

—— (1994b), 'Vergesellschaftete Außenpolitik', *Merkur* 48: 1–14.

Fischer, J. (1994), *Risiko Deutschland: Krise und Zukuft der deutschen Politik*. (Köln: Kiepenheuer und Witsch).

Die Grünen (1990), *Das Programm zur 1. gesamtdeutschen Bundestagswahl* (Bonn: Die Grünen).

Habermas, J. (1991), *Vergangenheit als Zukunft* (Zürich: pendo).

—— (1995), '1989 im Schatten von 1945. Zur Normalität einer künftigen Berliner Republik', in J. Habermas, *Die Normalität einer Berliner Republik* (Frankfurt/Main: Suhrkamp).

—— (1996), 'Rortys pragmatische Wende', *Deutsche Zeitschrift für Philosophie* 44: 715–741.

Haftendorn, H. (1994), 'Gulliver in der Mitte Europas: Internationale Verflechtung und nationale Handlungsmöglichkeiten', in K. Kaiser and H.W. Maull (1994).

Hamilton, D.S. (1994), *Beyond Bonn. America and the Berlin Republic* (Washington, D.C.: Carnegie Endowment for International Peace).

Infratest (1991), *Die Welt der Deutschen im Wandel. Eine repräsentative Befragung der Bevölkerung in Deutschland ab 14 Jahren. Tabellen Band 1. Teil: Ost-West-Vergleich. Eine Untersuchung von Infratest in Auftrag von The Rand Corporation, Santa Monica, and USIA, Washington, D.C.* (Berlin: Infratest Burke).

—— (1992), *Die Welt der Deutschen im Wandel, Band II. Eine repräsentative Befragung der Bevölkerung in Deutschland ab 18 Jahren. Tabellenband. Eine Untersuchung von Infratest in Auftrag von The Rand Corporation, Santa Monica, and USIA, Washington, D.C.* (Berlin: Infratest Burke).

Katzenstein, P.J. (ed.) (1997), *Tamed Power. Germany in Europe* (Ithaca: Cornell University Press).

Knapp, M. (1999), *Enhancing Global Commitment? The Policies of Germany and Japan towards the United Nations,* Studien zur Internationalen Politik Nr. 1 (Hamburg: Universität der Bundeswehr).

Markovits, A.S. and Reich, S. (1997), *The German Predicament. Memory and Power in the New Europe* (Ithaca: Cornell University Press).

Marsh, D. (1995), *Germany and Europe: The Crisis of Unity* (London: Mandarin).

Maull, H.W. (1990), 'Germany and Japan: The New Civilian Powers', *Foreign Affairs* 69: 91–106.

—— (1992), 'Zivilmacht Bundesrepublik Deutschland: Vierzehn Thesen für eine neue deutsche Außenpolitik', *Europa Archiv* 47: 269–278.

—— (1993a), 'Großmacht Deutschland? Anmerkungen und Thesen', in K. Kaiser and H. W. Maull, eds., *Die Zukunft der europäischen Integration: Folgerungen für die deutsche Politik* (Bonn: Europa Union).

—— (1993b), 'Zivilmacht Bundesrepublik? Das neue Deutschland in der internationalen Politik. Ein Gespräch mit Hanns W. Maull', *Blätter für deutsche und internationale Politik* 38: 934–948.

Meiers, F. J. (1995), 'Germany: The Reluctant Power', *Survival* 37: 82–103.

Mutz, R. (1994), 'Militärmacht Deutschland? Die Bundeswehr auf der Suche nach ihrer Zukunft', in F. Solms, R. Mutz, G. Krell, eds., *Friedensgutachten 1994* (Münster: Lit Verlag).

Noelle-Neumann, E. and Köcher, R. (eds.) (1993), *Allensbacher Jahrbuch der Demoskopie 1984–1992* (München: K. G. Saur).

—— (1997), *Allensbacher Jahrbuch der Demoskopie 1993–1997* (München: K. G. Saur). Rittberger, V. (1992), 'Nach der Vereinigung: Deutschlands Stellung in der Welt', *Leviathan* 20: 207–229.

Schössler, D., Albert, R. and Kostelnik, F. (1992), Eurosipla '90: Grundfragen des Europäischen Sicherheitssystems in den 90er Jahren, Mannheim: Mannheimer Zentrum für Europäische Sozialforschung (mimeo).

—— (1993), *Deutschland, die NATO und Europa. Die sicherheitspolitische Lage im Spiegel von Elite-Gruppen-Meinungen. 1. Forschungsbericht zum EURO SIPLA-Projekt*, (Münster: Lit Verlag).

Schwarz, H.-P. (1994), *Die Zentralmacht Europas. Deutschlands Rückkehr auf die Weltbühne* (Berlin: Siedler).

Senghaas, D. (1993), 'Was sind der Deutschen Interessen?', in S. Unseld, ed., *Politik ohne Projekt? Nachdenken über Deutschland* (Frankfurt/Main: Suhrkamp).

Volmer, L. (1998), *Die Grünen und die Außenpolitik – ein schwieriges Verhältnis* (Münster: Westfälisches Dampfboot).

—— and Fues, T. (1993), 'Schlußfolgerungen für eine neue Außenwirtschaftspolitik Deutschlands', in K. Fuchs, P. von Oertzen, and L. Volmer (1993).

Comment on Part Two: Foreign Policy Utopias of Great Powers Revisited: A Comparison of Germany and the United States

Beverly Crawford

Ten years ago, most observers predicted that an era of peace would follow in the wake of the Cold War's end, and the new millennium would open onto a "new world order" – a democratic, inter-dependent, and peaceful world. Indeed it is still fashionable to predict an era of "globalization" in which the nation state – the source of the most gruesome wars of history – would rapidly come to an end. Francis Fukuyama even wrote that with the collapse of communism, the "end of history" was at hand. And just as a wave of democratization was sweeping the globe from Eastern Europe to Latin America, Michael Doyle and his colleagues convincingly demonstrated that democracies do not go to war with each other. Indeed, his finding is one of the most robust in the political science literature on international politics.

Thus the "American Century" seemed to come to an end with the achievement of the very goals that Woodrow Wilson proclaimed for American foreign policy when he asked Congress to declare war on Germany in 1917: to "make the world safe for democracy." And even though it took two wars and a long period of military occupation, Germany itself became "safe for democracy." Indeed Germany – under US occupation – was probably the most promi-nent case of political and economic transformation in the postwar period. What was required of Germany in 1945 is what is required of post-communist and post-authoritarian states today: nothing less than the destruction of illiberal and traditional economic, political, and social practices and the creation of a liberal society, polity, and economy. And as Germany's power grows, its leaders believe that it too will become a model for the world to emulate.

Indeed, the policy goals of an increasingly powerful Germany in the 1990s were eerily similar to those articulated by Wilson for the United States on the eve of its own emergence as a great power. As Germany has achieved unity, grown in power, and broken the external and internally imposed bonds hindering an independent foreign policy, political elites have urged Germany to use its power to take on the "global responsibility" of leadership. For these elites, German leadership is required in order to maintain "the stability of Europe in which military factors will play an ever-decreasing role." They further argue that Germany should use its power to help the other industrial democracies to build "a new world order" that would not be dominated by power politics.

Just as Wilson rejected the idea that a balance of power was the key to peace and argued that its inherent failings were one of the principal causes of war, German leaders too reject "power politics" as the goal of foreign policy. They reject the "balance of power" that had prevailed during the Cold War in favor of building new cooperative structures in Europe and deepening the OSCE process. Indeed, the early vision of the Green Party, now in control of the Foreign Ministry, was even more global, lofty, ambitious, and reminiscent of Wilson's goals: "to create a new order of peace . . . a world without military blocs and a society without weapons and armies." And in Germany – as in the United States before it – the internationalists have triumphed over the isolationists as power has grown. At different historical periods, these two emerging powers have both been able to impose their visions on others.

Are these simply utopian visions? Or can power in the inter-national system lead to the realization of the utopian visions of the most powerful states? Do the similarities in American and German visions and goals suggest that under the leadership of a benign hegemon, a new era of peace, democracy, and respect for human rights has begun? Or are those high-minded goals simply rhetoric to justify the pursuit of national power in world politics? And if the rhetoric of peace, democracy, and stability simply masks the pursuit of power, won't world politics in the twenth-first century look very much like world politics in most of the twentieth century?

These questions are not simply academic: as the twentieth century came to a close, both countries joined together to wage war against another sovereign state in the name of protecting human rights. The Hitler–Saddam–Milosevic analogies saturate the press in both countries. But do the goals of resisting aggression and protecting human rights simply mask the more basic goals of states in an anarchic international system in which no common authority exists: to exercise power in world politics and to show the rest of the world that they can indeed exercise that power? In a broader historical sense, was Thucycides right when he wrote in 431 BC that "The strong do what they can and the weak suffer what they must."

If William A. Williams is correct, the United States consistently pursued a policy of expansionism, empire-building, and militarism as its power grew throughout the twentieth century. Its utopian rhetoric simply masked its pursuit of power. And its policies intended to expand and maintain political and economic dominance were justified to the American public and the world at large in expansive utopian terms: as a high-minded concern with democracy, human rights, and human progress. Williams would say that its behavior in international politics today is no different than its behavior in the past.

And today, despite Germany's entrenched democracy and Western integration, the "German Question" has dominated all serious debate about the future of Europe since the Berlin Wall's collapse. Few need to be reminded that the growth of German power allowed it to provoke two world wars in the twentieth century, and many speculate that Germany will again seek the status of a great power in the twenty-first century.[1] The new "German Question" usually

1. Christopher Layne, for example, notes that Kurt Reiszler, the political confidant of pre-World War I Chancellor Hollweg, observed that Germany's *Weltpolitik* was tightly linked to the dynamic growth of Germany's export-driven economy, and that Germany's demands for power and prestige increased in proportion to its rising strength. See Christopher Layne, "The Unipolar Illusion: Why New Great Powers will rise," *International Security* 17 (1993), 5–50, here 22, n. 70 and 71. In

takes the following form: Do lofty idealistic policy goals provide a veil behind which Germany will exercise self-interested economic and political dominance, both in Europe and on the international stage?

Both Burlin and Hellmann are outspoken critics of the foreign policy rhetoric expressed by their countries' political elites. Burlin prescribes a new form of American restraint and humility commensurate with global problems of environmental degradation, mass consumerism, and gross materialism. He writes that the United States has much to gain from "quiet and sustained national contemplation and discussion of ways Americans should conduct themselves at home and abroad – ways which are more commensurate with the overarching limits that set the parameters of sustainable life. Americans, he warns, should get their own house in order – since they do consume most of the world's resources – before they attempt to reshape the culture of other nations and engineer the rest of the world in America's image.

Hellmann resists prescriptions for German foreign policy in the post-Cold War era. Instead he predicts that the realities of international politics will largely shape Germany's foreign policy behavior, and indeed should shape that behavior. Indeed, Hellmann's analysis of Germany's foreign policy today parallels George Kennan's view of American foreign policy in an earlier era. Just as Kennan believed that America stepped onto the scene as a nascent power harboring naive ideas, spouting "moralistic" clichés, and championing high-sounding policies that bore no relationship to the realities of global politics, Hellmann believes that Germany's naive rhetoric was bound

---

1998, *The Economist* wrote: "As every student of modern European politics knows, post-war Germany's closest western allies have always had a slight, nagging fear in the pit of their stomachs. One day, the Germans might lose interest in them and become cozy, instead, with their Slav neighbors. . . ." (*The Economist*, May 30–June 5 (1998), 51). And even in 2000 some key French officials remained skeptical. French Interior Minister Jean-Pierre Chevenement stated publicly that Germany "has not been cured of the derailment that Nazism represented in its history. . ." (quoted in the *New York Herald Tribune*, May 23, 2000, 1).

to give way to a more realistic policy of a "normal" power in pursuit of its national interest. Germany is really no different than its allies.

German soldiers in Kosovo are now on combat missions projecting German power, not protecting German territory. For Hellmann, realist theories of international politics – theories advanced by people like Kennan – could have predicted that German soldiers would soon be in combat as German power and status in the world has grown. There is no way that, in the anarchic world of international politics dominated by the security dilemma, Germany could continue to exercise the military restraint that it had exercised earlier.

Burlin believes that other, more pressing realities of environmental degradation, cultural diversity, and the need to respect human rights should shape foreign policy, especially the foreign policy of the United States. He advises the United States to exercise the "self-containment" that seems to have characterized German policy until recently. Hellmann, in contrast, accepts the realities of power politics and believes that Germany's leaders are learning to accept these realities as well, as Germany's behavior is normalized. If Hellmann is correct in his assessment of the realities of international politics, then Burlin's advice to the United States to withdraw will go unheeded. Indeed, the United States was never really an isolationist power, and its global involvement grew with the growth of its economic and political power. If Hellmann is correct, then the same will be true for Germany.

In sum, these two papers raise important issues for our assessment of how visions of world order can play themselves out in international politics. More importantly, however, they illuminate the central question posed of all utopian visions: Can the vision change the structural realities it implicitly criticizes in order to create a new world? Or will the structural realities that constrain the utopian vision simply overwhelm it? The foreign policies of these two important countries provide rich material to be further mined in pursuit of the answers. And it would seem that the evidence from both countries suggests that the structural realities do undermine the utopian vision. While for some foreign policy analysts, this may be undesirable, for others, it is a relief.

Comment on Part Two: American Diplomacy: The Quest for a Global *Pax Americana*: Myths and Realities A Reply[1]

Ralph Dietl

In writing his paper it was never Professor Burlin's intention to evaluate the credibility of explanations given by different currents in historical research for the supposed US quest for a global *Pax Americana*.[2] Professor Burlin instead contrasted the Americans' view of themselves as a chosen people predestined to redeem an always amenable and changeable world – the set of beliefs he holds responsible for the US quest for a global *Pax Americana* – with a global environment which has proved time and again not to be amenable to such far-reaching American hopes and dreams. History, collective experience, or – in a word – reality challenges the myth on which US foreign policy is supposed to be based, the myth of a chosen people predestined to redeem the world.[3]

1. I am extremely grateful to the editors of this volume for giving me a chance to develop a thesis of my own as a reply to Professor Burlin's stimulating article, instead of restricting myself to a commentary in the strict sense. I am also indebted to Colin Foskett (Wuppertal) for kindly proofreading this article.

2. See Jerald A. Combs, *American Diplomatic History: Two Centuries of Changing Interpretations* (Berkeley, CA, 1983); Walter La Feber, "The World and the United States," *American Historical Review* 100 (1995), 1015–1033.

3. Cf. Louis Hartz, *The Liberal Tradition in America: An Interpretation of American Political Thought Since the Revolution* (New York, 1955). The United States lacked "the feudal stage of history" and therefore the strands of both reactionary and revolutionary thought, and was ill-equipped to understand the rest of the world, which had evolved quite differently. "Born equal", the United States failed to appreciate indigenous nationalism and revolutions abroad and therefore had no understanding of the global environment. The result is an unrealistic foreign policy guided by the unique American experience.

The logical conclusion to the aforesaid would be that American foreign policy has always been and still is shaped by an unwavering faith in America's divine mission. But is this really the case? Is there really a nexus between the Puritan ideology (or language)[4] which interpreted the United States as the "city upon the hill" for all to see and for all to emulate and America's vision of a world order? Are nineteenth-century expansionism and twentieth-century internationalism efforts to redeem the world?

What about capitalism?[5] What about self-interest or national interest[6] and national security?[7] What about the frontier and its role in shaping American ideology?[8]

The purpose of this essay is to show that neither a divine mission nor possessive individualism, neither idealism nor capitalist exploitation properly characterize the US quest for a *Pax Americana*, for in most instances the United States did not intervene overseas to

---

4. Ideology might be defined as "an interrelated set of convictions or assumptions that reduces the complexities of a particular slice of reality to easily comprehensible terms and suggests appropriate ways of dealing with that reality"(Michael H. Hunt, "Ideology," *The Journal of American History* 77 [1990/91], 108–115; id., *Ideology and US Foreign Policy* [New Haven, CT, 1987]).

5. Charles A. Beard, *An Economic Interpretation of the Constitution of the United States* (New York, 1913); Richard Hofstadter, *The Progressive Historians, Turner, Beard, Parrington* (Chicago, IL, 1979); cf. William Appleman Williams, *The Tragedy of American Diplomacy* (New York, 1962); Walter La Feber, *The New Empire. An Interpretation of American Expansion 1860–1898* (Ithaca, NY, 1963).

6. Charles A. Beard, *The Idea of National Interest: An Analytical Study in Foreign Policy* (New York, 1934); H. W. Brands, "The Idea of the National Interest," *Diplomatic History* 23(2) (1999), 239–261; Robert Endigott Osgood, *Ideals and Self-Interest in America's Foreign Relations. The Great Transformation of the Twentieth Century* (Chicago, IL, 1953); Hans J. Morgenthau, *In Defense of the National Interest* (New York, 1951).

7. "National security policy encompasses the decisions and actions deemed imperative to protect domestic core values from external threats. . . . Core values usually fuse material self-interest with more fundamental goals like the defense of the state's organizing ideology" (Melvyn P. Leffler, "National Security," *The Journal of American History* 77 [1990/91], 143–152).

8. Ray Allen Billington, ed., *The Frontier Thesis. Valid Interpretation of American History?* (Chicago, IL, 1966); Vannevar Bush, *Science: The Endless Frontier* (Washington, DC, 1960).

redeem the world nor to protect "special interests" of American companies and trusts.

One hundred years ago the United States entered the field of international relations as a global player. The Age of Imperialism undeniably altered the foreign relations of the United States. By fighting the Spanish–American War of 1898/99 and by entering the First World War in 1917, the United States deliberately broke with the diplomatic tradition shaping the first century of its existence, thereby disregarding the principle of the Founding Fathers not to get involved in European power politics.[9] But what caused this radical change? Why did the US replace isolationism by interventionism? Can we find here, in the Age of Imperialism, the answer to the US quest for a *Pax Americana*? Do we really have to go back to the colonial period, to Puritan ideology, to be able to find an explanation for America's world vision? Is there really a "continuous pattern of belief which runs from early American history to the present"[10] shaping America's outlook on foreign policy, or can we find the answer to America's quest in Darwinism,[11] balance-of-power philosophy and other European isms that reached America and were adopted in the late nineteenth century, in the Age of Imperialism? And is, therefore, America's divine mission nothing but rhetoric, nothing but another form of justification for the expansion and imperialism so widespread during the second half of the nineteenth century?[12]

American diplomacy in the twentieth century definitely is a product of this formative period in US foreign relations, and from then on has been labeled democratic internationalism, liberal internationalism, or Wilsonianism, in honor of President Woodrow

---

9. Lawrence S. Kaplan, *Entangling Alliances With None* (Kent, OH, 1987).

10. Cf. George L. Hunt, ed., *Calvinism and the Political Order* (Philadelphia, PA, 1965); Ernest Tuverson, *Redeemer Nation: The Idea of America's Millennial Role* (Chicago, IL, 1974).

11. Richard Hofstadter, *Social Darwinism in American Thought, 1860–1915* (Philadelphia, PA, 1945).

12. David M. Pletcher, "Rhetoric and Results. A Pragmatic View of American Economic Expansionism, 1865–98," *Diplomatic History* 5 (1981), 93–104.

Wilson, who shaped this diplomatic tradition.[13] President Wilson, however, did not create something entirely new, he just combined in a new way two diverging streams of thought in international relations – modern internationalism and traditional Jeffersonianism.[14] Thus, it is, indeed, necessary to investigate the roots of these streams of thought which were blended and then shaped US behavior in foreign relations, roots dating back to colonial times and to metropolitan Britain.

As John G. Pocock[15] has shown, the American mentality has derived directly from the "country philosophy" of the English Old Whig opposition of the seventeenth and early eighteenth centuries, a philosophy predating the modern Enlightenment but rooted in the British reception of Italian humanist Renaissance philosophy and English common-law.[16] According to Pocock's thesis America

13. Tony Smith, "Making the World Safe for Democracy in the American Century," *Diplomatic History* 23(2) (1999), 173–188, at, 174, 179.

14. N. Gordon Levin, Jr., *Woodrow Wilson and World Politics: America's Response to War and Revolution* (New York, 1968); Arno J. Mayer, *Political Origins of the New Diplomacy, 1917–1918* (New Haven, CT, 1959); Ralph Dietl, *USA und Mittelamerika. Die Außenpolitik von William J. Bryan 1913–1915* (Stuttgart, 1996), 425–447; id., "American Expansion: From Jeffersonianism to Wilsonianism. The United States and Its Southern Neighbors at the Turn of the Century," in Walther L. Bernecker, ed., *1898: su significado para Centroamérica y el Caribe. Cesura, cambio, continuidad?* (Frankfurt and Madrid, 1998), 47–60.

15. J. G. A. Pocock, *The Machiavellian Moment. Florentine Political Thought and the Atlantic Republican Tradition* (Princeton, NJ, 1975); Pocock, *Politics, Language and Time. Essays on Political Thought and History* (London, 1971); Pocock, *Virtue, Commerce and History. Essays on Political Thought and History, Chiefly in the Eighteenth Century* (Cambridge, 1985).

16. Robert E. Shalhope, "Republicanism and Early American Historiography," *William & Mary Quarterly* 39(2) (1982), 334–356; Daniel T. Rodgers, "Republicanism: The Career of a Concept," *The Journal of American History* 79 (1992/93), 11–38; Steven Pincus, "Neither Machiavellian Moment nor Possessive Individualism: Commercial Society and the Defenders of the English Commonwealth," *American Historical Review* 103 (1998), 705–736. Bernard Bailyn, *The Ideological Origins of the American Revolution* (Cambridge, MA, 1967); Gordon S. Wood, *The Creation of the American Republic, 1776–1787* (Chapel Hill, NC, 1969) and Pocock's *Machiavellian Moment* established the interpretation of early American history as a constant struggle between liberty and power. This cyclical interpretation of American history

has inherited British republicanism, with its firm belief in an early medieval balanced constitution, a constitution which offered a perfect equilibrium of powers, which checked the passions of the citizenry, and thereby safeguarded the unfolding of the divine gifts of God's exact likeness – the individual. Although this balanced constitution prevented a rapid degeneration of the polis, the once golden equilibrium was fragile, was always threatened by corrupting influences, by "special" or "group-interests," by the violation of the indispensable covenant of any community – the Ten Command-ments – and by amoral behavior.[17]

The popular writings of James Harrington,[18] John Milton,[19] Andrew Marvell and Algernon Sidney,[20] once used by the British "landed gentry" in defense of a virtuous society, and the "constitu-tional" equilibrium threatened by the arbitrary government of the crown, made their reappearance in British North America now as a means to defend the colonists' rights as Englishmen against the colonial rule of the metropolis. Thus, the American Revolution was simply an attempt to reestablish the rule of law.[21] Thomas Jefferson

---

based on Renaissance pessimism contradicts liberal linear progressive interpretations of American historiography. Cf. Ruth H. Bloch, *Visionary Republic. Millennial Themes in American Thought, 1756–1800* (Cambridge, 1985).

17. Pocock, "Machiavelli, Harrington and English Political Ideologies in the Eighteenth Century," in Pocock, *Politics, Language and Time,* 104–147.

18. Pocock, ed., *The Political Works of James Harrington* (Cambridge, 1977), 155–360.

19. David Armitage, Armand Himy, and Quentin Skinner, eds., *Milton and Republicanism* (Cambridge, 1995).

20. Alan Craig Houston, *Algernon Sidney and the Republican Heritage in England and America* (Princeton, NJ, 1991).

21. Pocock, "Civic Humanism and Its Role in Anglo-American Thought," in Pocock, *Politics, Language and Time,* 80–103; Pauline Maier, *From Resistance to Revolution. Colonial Radicals and the Development of American Opposition to Britain, 1765–1776* (New York, 1972), 28; Richard R. Breeman, "Deference, Republicanism, and the Emergence of Popular Politics in Eighteenth Century America," *William & Mary Quarterly* 49(3) (1992), 400–430; Forrest McDonald, *Novus Ordo Seclorum. The Intellectual Origins of the Consitution* (Lawrence, KS, 1985); for a fresh view on the development of an American national consciousness, see T. H. Breen, "Ideology and Nationalism on the eve of the American Revolution: Revisions Once More in Need of Revising," *The Journal of American History* 84 (1997), 13–39.

himself interpreted the American Constitution of 1789 as the recreation of the golden Ancient Constitution, which had to be protected from vices and corruption to ensure that the perfect equilibrium which had been restored did not degenerate.[22] According to Jefferson the Constitution had to be protected against the centrist excesses of the Federalists, who intended to violate the perfect balance of the American Constitution by introducing cabinet-style British government; and future generations had to be reminded that the US executive should always keep a low profile in foreign relations and avoid entangling alliances in order not to put the American experiment in jeopardy of outside destruction and interior destabilization through standing armies and imperial presidencies.[23] But the Jeffersonian persuasion,[24] the American

22. "The battle of Hastings, indeed, was lost, but the natural rights of the nation were not staked on the event of a single battle. Their wish to recover the Saxon constitution continued unabated, and was at bottom of all the unsuccessful insurrections which succeeded in subsequent times" (Jefferson to G. W. Lewis, cited in Tony Davies, "Borrowed Language: Milton, Jefferson, Mirabeau," in Armitage, Himy, and Skinner, eds., *Milton and Republicanism*, 254–271, at 257).

23. Drew R. McCoy, *Political Economy in Jeffersonian America* (Chapel Hill, NC, 1980), 48, 60, 63, 153; Bradford Perkins, *The Creation of a Republican Empire, 1776–1865*, Cambridge History of American Foreign Relations, vol. I (Cambridge, 1993), 10–16, 103.

24. Lance Banning, *The Jeffersonian Persuasion. Evolution of a Party Ideology* (Ithaca, NY, 1978); id., "Jeffersonian Ideology Revisited: Liberal and Classical Ideas in the New American Republic," *William & Mary Quarterly* 43 (1986), 3–19; Eugene R. Sheridan, "Freiheit und Tugend. Religion und Republikanismus im Denken von Thomas Jefferson," in Hartmut Wasser, ed., *Thomas Jefferson. Historische Bedeutung und politische Aktualität* (Paderborn, 1995), 153–168; Peter S. Onuf, "The Scholars' Jefferson," *William & Mary Quarterly* 50,4 (1993), 671–699. The republican interpretation of the American Revolution in general and Thomas Jefferson in particular is challenged by Joyce Appleby. Her work recasts the Revolution in progressive, forward-looking terms. See Joyce Appleby, *Capitalism and the New Social Order: The Republican Vision of the 1790s* (New York, 1984); Appleby, *Liberalism and Republicanism in the Historical Imagination* (Cambridge, MA, 1992); Appleby, "Republicanism in Old and New Contexts," *William & Mary Quarterly* 43,1 (1986), 20–34. A synthesis of the republican and liberal traditions is offered by James T. Kloppenberg, "The Virtues of Liberalism: Christianity, Republicanism, and Ethics in Early American Political Discourse," *The Journal of American History* 74 (1987/88), 9–33.

offspring of British "country philosophy," did not limit its fears to manipulations of and by the central government, but perceived industry, central banking, speculation and any kind of undue accumulation of wealth or power as a corrupting influence, able to shift the precious equilibrium of power.[25] To fend off these threats, the acquisition and wide distribution of real estate had to be promoted in order to ensure an economically and politically independent and virtuous citizenry which would safeguard society from corruption. The protection of a balanced constitution therefore demanded expansion – a demand which Thomas Jefferson heeded in opening the lands of the West. The Louisiana Purchase of 1803 was thus simply the thin end of the wedge of American expansion from coast to coast. It was the Jeffersonian persuasion which perceived the *frontier* as a stabilizing force of society.[26]

It was not divine mission but self-preservation which led to this enlargement of the area of freedom. Expansion, i.e. the acquisition and settlement of sparsely inhabited contiguous territory ensured the protection of the American experiment from outside inter-ference and from internal decay.[27] Expansion was conceived as vital

25. Pocock, "Anglo-American Thought," 97; Pocock, ed., *The Political Works of James Harrington*, 151.

26. "Those who labour in the earth are the chosen people of God [. . .] Corruption of morals in the mass of cultivators is a phenomenon of which no age nor nation has furnished an example" (Thomas Jefferson, cited in McCoy, *Political Economy in Jeffersonian America,* 13); the American system should be to "pursue agriculture, and open all the foreign markets possible to our produce" (Thomas Jefferson, 1789, cited ibid., 132). The American founding fathers were well aware that the United States would become as corrupt as the most advanced areas of Europe, yet it was within the power of its citizens to place this "sad catastrophe at a distance." Free trade and westward expansion would guarantee a virtuous society of indus-trious farmers. Cf. Drew McCoy, "Republicanism and American Foreign Policy: James Madison and the Political Economy of Commercial Discrimination 1789 to 1794, *William & Mary Quarterly* 31 (1974), 633–646. A critical appraisal of the yeoman ideal can be found in Joyce Appleby, "Commercial Farming and the 'Agrarian Myth' in the Early Republic," *The Journal of American History* 68 (1982), 833–849.

27. Cf. Walter LaFeber, "Jefferson and the American Foreign Policy," in Peter S. Onuf, ed., *Jeffersonian Legacies* (Charlottesville, VA, 1993), 370–391, esp. 372ff.; McCoy, *Political Economy in Jeffersonian America,* 204f., 228, 248.; Banning, *Jeffersonian Persuasion,* 29f., Perkins, *The Creation of a Republican Empire,* 115.

for the preservation of liberty and democracy. The closing of the *frontier* at the end of the nineteenth century was therefore interpreted as a deadly threat to the American way of life, to the equilibrium of the Constitution, henceforth to be guaranteed by economic opportunity.[28]

The search for a new frontier, a new area of opportunity, made an ever-increasing share of the population adopt foreign ideas and isms. America had to rid herself of the limitations of the past and had to follow the example of British imperialism.[29]

An imperial policy, however, threatened the very survival of America's institutions. Imperialism would lead to standing armies,

---

28. For an analysis of attempts to reduce the tensions between liberalism and classical American republicanism see Drew McCoy, *Elusive Republic*, Banning, *Jeffersonian Ideology Revisited*, 16f. and in particular Marvin Meyers, *The Jacksonian Persuasion. Politics and Belief* (Stanford, CA, 1960). The blending of classical republican virtues with an expansive commercial economy in the early nineteenth century created a producer ideology, fearful of the machinations of a corrupt mercantilist government that sacrificed equal opportunity and the public good to special interests. "A laissez-faire society with this source of corruption cut out would reestablish continuity with that golden age in which liberty and progress were joined inseparably with simple yeoman values." (ibid., 12). The preservation of opportunity lay at the very heart of the American ideology – either horizontal by the expansion of the area of freedom or vertical through opportunities offered by an open economy. For further reading concerning the preservation of economic opportunity see Robert V. Remini, *The Revolutionary Age of Andrew Jackson* (New York, 1976); Eric Foner, *Free Soil, Free Labour and Free Men. The Ideology of the Republican Party Before the Civil War* (Oxford, 1970).

29. "American factories are making more than the American people can use . . . . Fate has written our history . . ., the trade of the world must and can be ours. and we shall get it, as our mother England has told us how . . . . We will cover the ocean with our merchant marine. We will build a navy to the measure of our greatness" (Jeremiah Beveridge, cited in Jenny Pearce, *US Intervention in Central America and the Caribbean* [London, 1981], 9); "We as a nation are following the inevitable law of evolution [. . .], we have entered the field of competition with the other great nations of the world. We are in the struggle for political supremacy and commercial preeminence whether we wish it or not and must advance always; for stopping means stagnation or decay" (Lt. John Wood, cited in Richard D. Challener, *Admirals, Generals and American Foreign Policy, 1898–1914* [Princeton, NJ 1973]).

would enrich the few and increase the number of the downtrodden by an ever-increasing tax burden. Imperialism would unduly strengthen the executive and thereby endanger the constitutional equilibrium. It was in defense of the American system that William J. Bryan, three times presidential candidate of the Democratic Party between 1896 and 1908, organized his crusade against the growing Anglo-Saxonism of the East Coast.[30] According to Bryan, America had to recreate opportunity by inflationary economic measures, by the coining of silver and by the destruction of trusts and monopolies, and not by the forceful conquest of new markets or even colonialism. America's expansion had to stop, for America could not administer foreign lands without damaging her own institutions. America could not be half empire and half republic. America had to resist the temptations of empire and stick to the advice of the Funding Fathers, to the isolationism or continentalism of the past.[31]

Jeffersonianism was certainly alive at the turn of the century – although in 1896 it was narrowly defeated by the "special interests" of the East. The contest of the regions, however, was carried on up to the First World War and beyond.[32]

---

30. Michael Kazin, *The Populist Persuasion. An American History* (New York, 1995), ch 2; Dietl, *USA und Mittelamerika*, 53–69; William J. Bryan, ed., *Bryan on Imperialism. Speeches, Newspaper Articles, Interviews* (Chicago, IL, 1900).

31. "We declare again that all governments instituted among men derive their just powers from the consent of the governed; that any government not based upon on the consent of the governed is tyranny; and to impose upon any people a government of force is to substitute the methods of imperialism for those of a republic. . . . We assert that no nation can long endure half republic and half empire, and we warn the American people that imperialism abroad will lead quickly and inevitably to despotism at home" (Platform of the Democratic Party, Kansas City 1900, cited in Göran Rystad, *Ambiguous Imperialism. American Foreign Policy and Domestic Politics at the Turn of the Century* [Lund, 1975], 212; cf. Arthur M. Schlesinger, Jr. *Imperial Presidency* [Boston, MA, 1973])

32. "Man is the master, money the servant, but upon all important questions today Republican legislation tends to make money the master and man the servant. The maxim of Jefferson "equal rights to all and special privilege to none" and the doctrine of Lincoln that this should be a government "of the people, by the people and for the people" are being disregarded and the instrumentalities of government are being used to advance the interests of those who are in a position to secure

Looking at this contest, looking at the debate on imperialism, it does not appear that Manifest Destiny – used by imperialists to justify their aims – was manifest at all. Rural America, uninfected by European isms, did not believe in a divine mission to redeem the world, but it believed in enhancing the American experiment by domestic means. America had to content herself with being a shining example for the world – for all to see and for all to emulate. This is certainly pride in American exceptionalism, but this pride does not necessarily imply a quest for a global *Pax Americana*![33]

Well, in a way it does. There is a nexus between this pride and affirmative foreign policy – for it was not the imperialism or internationalism of the late nineteenth and early twentieth centuries nourished by European ideas which was responsible for the US departure from continentalism. It was an entirely new, entirely distinct form of internationalism which emerged during the First World War. It was Wilsonianism, a blend of Jeffersonianism and European balance-of-power philosophy, a common denominator for Midwestern republicanism and East Coast internationalism which enabled the President not just to unite the country in the context of the First World War, but to convince a peace-loving and

---

favours from the government" (William J. Bryan, "On Imperialism, Address delivered at Indianapolis, 8 Aug 1900," *Nebraska State Historical Society* Manuscript Record, William J. Bryan, 1860–1925, box 2, S6,F6; William J. Bryan, *The First Battle. A Story of the Campaign of 1896* [Chicago, IL, 1896]).

33. "Behold a republic standing erect while empires all around are bowed beneath the weight of their own armaments – a republic whose flags are only feared. Behold a republic increasing in population, in wealth, in strength, and in influence, solving the problems of civilization and hastening the coming of the universal brotherhood – a republic that shakes thrones and dissolves aristocracies by its silent example and gives light and inspiration to those who sit in darkness. Behold a republic gradually but surely becoming a supreme moral factor in the world's disputes – a republic whose history, like the path of the just "is as the shining light that shineth more and more unto the perfect day" (Prov. 4, 18). (William J. Bryan, "On Imperialism," 8 Aug. 1900, *Nebraska State Historical Society* Manuscript Record, William J. Bryan, 1860–1925, box 2, S6, F6; Hans J. Morgenthau, *The Purpose of American Politics* [New York, 1962], 71)

isolationist population of its duty to take up arms and to intervene in the European struggle.[34]

Wilson managed to convince the American population that intervention overseas was in all their interests and not just in the interests of the few by enlarging the sphere to be taken into account by republicanism, by showing that corrupting influences from abroad could and indeed would threaten the balance of the Constitution. Therefore, Americans had to be as watchful in the international sphere as in domestic policy, had to fight evil abroad as much as at home to guarantee the survival of virtuous society, of American democracy. The ideological challenge posed by German militarism was such a corrupting influence, such a threat for democratic government.

By taking up arms, Americans would not be fighting for a new balance of power in Europe, Americans would not be fighting for the victory of the Entente, but they would be fighting to crush German militarism,[35] they would be fighting for a new European

---

34. "[T]he Wilsonian phase, in contrast to McKinley's and Roosevelt's, is marked by a more clearly defined relationship between temporary territorial expansion, on the one hand, and the American purpose and the concrete national interests of the United States, on the other. Intervention for a particular purpose now replaced annexation" (Morgenthau, *The Purpose of American Politics,* 101f.); Henry Kissinger, *Diplomacy* (London, 1994), 47, 55; Ralph Dietl, "Friedensvermittlung oder Siegfrieden? William Jennings Bryan und der Erste Weltkrieg", in Ragnhild Fiebig von Hase and Jürgen Heideking, eds., *Zwei Wege in die Moderne. Amerika und Deutschland, 1900–1920* (Trier, 1997), 211–230; Dietl, *American Expansion,* 58ff.

35. Lloyd Ambrosius, "The Orthodoxy of Revisionism: Woodrow Wilson and the New Left," *Diplomatic History* 1 (1977), 199–214, at 207, 212; Edward H. Buehrig, *Woodrow Wilson and the Balance of Power* (Bloomington, IN, 1955); Ernest R. May, *The World War and American Isolation* (Cambridge, MA, 1959); Robert H. Ferrell, *Woodrow Wilson and World War I, 1917–1921* (New York, 1985); Brands, "The Idea of the National Interest," 242f., 246; Smith, "Making the World Safe for Democracy," 179. Cf. "It was not good for the US to have peace brought about until Germany was sufficiently beaten to cause her to a fundamental change in her military policy", Colonel House Diary, 3.12.1914, Arthur S. Link, ed., *The Papers of Woodrow Wilson* [henceforth: PWW](Princeton, NJ, 1966ff) vol. 31 (1914):

Germany is utterly hostile to all nations with democratic institutions [. . .] the remedy seems to be plain. It is that Germany must not be permitted to

order, labeled world order, in which democracy could flourish: they would "fight a war to end all wars."[36] For after having installed self-determination overseas America could disarm and retreat to its former isolation without any risks to its democratic institutions.

However, this first attempt to create a peaceful and democratic international environment as a means of safeguarding the American experiment failed. It failed because the war was not waged to its bitter end; it led to the defeat of the Reich, but not to the defeat of German militarism. It failed because Wilson, hampered by the limitations of the past, did not support an active reconstruction of European society, because he did not support imposing a new order on friends and foes alike but believed in the magic charm of

---

win this war [. . .] though to prevent it this country is forced to take an active part. This ultimate necessity must be constantly in our minds in all our controversies with the belligerents. American public opinion must be prepared for the time, which may come, when we have to cast aside our neutrality and become one of the champions of democracy. (Robert Lansing, 11.7.1915, cited in: Daniel M. Smith, "Robert Lansing and the Formulation of American Neutrality Policy, 1914–1915," *Mississippi Valley Historical Review* 43 [1956/57], 59–81, here 80)

"England is fighting our fight [. . .]; you may well understand that I shall not, in the present state of world affairs, place obstacles in her way [. . .]; I will not take any measure to embarrass England [. . .]; she is fighting for her life and the life of the world" (Wilson to Tumulty, cited in Lawrence W. Levine, *Defender of the Faith. William J. Bryan: The Last Decade, 1915–1925* [Cambridge, MA, 1987], 33); "The days of anxiety and uncertainty are over. The American people are at last ready to make war on Germany, thank God. I shall openly and no more secretly exert my influence in favor of a declaration" (Robert Lansing, 19.3.1917 cited in Levine, *Defender of the Faith* 88).

36. Woodrow Wilson, An Address to the Senate, 22 Jan. 1917 and Woodrow Wilson Address 2 Apr. 1917, PWW 40 (1917), 536; 41 (1917), 519; Daniel M. Smith, "National Interest and American Intervention, 1917: An Historiographical Appraisal," *The Journal of American History* 52 (1965/66), 5–25; Lloyd Ambrosius, *Wilsonian Statecraft. Theory and Practice of Liberal Internationalism during World War I* (Wilmington, NC, 1991), Arthur S. Link, *Wilson. The Struggle for Neutrality* (Princeton, NJ, 1960); Link, *Wilson. Campaigns for Progressivism and Peace* (Princeton, NJ, 1965); Thomas J. Knock, *To End All Wars. Woodrow Wilson and the Quest for a New World Order* (New York, 1992).

democratic institutions. It failed because America's population, disgusted by events in Europe, soon supported a retreat to isolationism in order to disconnect America from evil influences from abroad. Democratic internationalism, however, survived the defeat of the first attempt at "global" management.[37]

The attack on Pearl Harbor in December 1941 finally convinced the American public that at a time of narrowing space it was impossible to escape from a belligerent environment. Pearl Harbor was the final proof of the necessity to fight evil abroad.[38] Fighting corrupting influences and national security had finally become one. National security, the protection of America's core values, demanded not only the defeat of the enemy, but the destruction of those evil forces and those dangerous isms that had taken control of Germany and Japan and threatened America's way of life. This time, however,

---

37. Lloyd Ambrosius, *Woodrow Wilson and the American Diplomatic Tradition. The Treaty Fight in Perspective* (Cambridge, 1987). Cf. N. Gordon Levin, Jr., *Woodrow Wilson and World Politics: America's Response to War and Revolution* (New York, 1968); Klaus Schwabe, *Woodrow Wilson, Revolutionary Germany, and Peacemaking, 1918–1919: Missionary Diplomacy and the Realities of Power* (Chapel Hill, NC, 1985); Hans-Jürgen Schröder, ed., *Confrontation and Cooperation. Germany and the United States in the Era of World War I, 1900–1924* (Providence, RI, 1993).

38. Up to Pearl Harbor an affirmative foreign policy, and not the rise of undemocratic regimes overseas, had been perceived by continentalists (isolationists) as the by far greater threat to the American way of life.

> We are all acquainted with the fearful forecast – that some form of dictatorship is required to fight a modern war, that we will certainly go bankrupt, that in the process of war and its aftermath our economy will be largely socialized, that the politicians now in office will seize complete power and never yield it up, and that . . . we will end up in such a total national socialism that any faint semblances of our constitutional American democracy will be totally unrecognizable. (Henry R. Luce, "The American Century," reprint, *Diplomatic History* 23(2) [1999], 159–171, here 162)

Cf. C. Vann Woodward, "The Age of Reinterpretation," *American Historical Review* 66 (1960), 2–8; Uwe Lübken, "'An Awfully Small World'. Air Power, die Vernichtung von Raum und der Atlantik. Eine amerikanische Perspektive," in Ralph Dietl and Franz Knipping, eds., *Begegnung zweier Kontinente. Die Vereinigten Staaten und Europa seit dem Ersten Weltkrieg* (Trier, 1999), 103–119.

America was determined to fight to the end; unconditional surrender was indispensable to crush the corrupting influences from abroad and to enable a thorough reconstruction of societies in those regions vital to American national security.[39] America would export democracy to Europe and the Far East, for Washington was convinced that internal structures do shape international conduct.[40]

Again America did not intervene to redeem the world, and it was not idealism that made America export democracy. Exporting democracy and reconstructing Europe were simply a strategy that would render America's disengagement from the European Continent possible without having to fear a threat to American national security. Exporting democracy would free the United States from an enduring military presence overseas, from commitments that threatened political liberty and free enterprise at home.[41] This strategy, however, was hampered by the Cold War and the division of Europe which limited reconstruction to Western Europe.[42]

39. "We got in via defense . . . But what are we defending? . . . To the average American the plain meaning of the word defense is defense of the American territory. Is our national policy today limited to the defense of the American homeland by whatever means may seem wise? We are in a war to defend and even to promote, encourage and incite so-called democratic principles throughout the world." (Luce, "The American Century," 161; Leffler, "National Security," 143)

40. Cf. Joshua Muravchik, *Exporting Democracy. Fullfilling America's Destiny* (Washington, DC, 1992), 8ff., 81f., 117ff., 227. Whether exporting democracy was America's destiny is questionable. It is unquestionable, however, that by exporting democracy America increased her national security (see the following notes).

41. The initial intention of FDR had been to leave the responsibility of reconstruction of Europe to Britain. "I do not want the United States to have the postwar burden of reconstituting France, Italy and the Balkans. This is not our natural task at a distance of 3,500 miles or more. It is definitely a British task in which the British are much more vitally interested than we are", cited in Kissinger, *Diplomacy*, 396.

42. See Geir Lundestad, *"Empire" by Integration. The United States and European Integration 1945–1997* (Oxford, 1998); Hans-Peter Schwarz, "Die wohltätige Hegemonie und die Spaltung Europas," in Guido Müller, ed., *Deutschland und der Westen* (Stuttgart, 1998); Ralph Dietl, "Die Westeuropäische Union – 'A return to the dark ages?' Die Vereinigten Staaten und die europäische Integration 1953–1955," in Dietl and Knipping, eds., *Begegnung zweier Kontinente,* 67–86; Klaus Schwabe, "Hegemonie durch Integration? Die Vereinigten Staaten und die

However, the Soviet threat only speeded up evolution by furthering the democratic reconstruction in Western Europe and Japan, by integrating Western Europe under the umbrella of a transatlantic alliance, and by laying the foundation for a second pillar of Western defense. Although the Cold War had forced the United States to an unprecedented level of military engagement overseas, it was the burden-sharing among democratic nations which had enabled the United States to face this new external challenge to the American way of life without lasting detriment to the precious equilibrium of the Constitution. [43]

Even today it is neither idealism nor altruism, nor a missionary quest to redeem the world, nor imperialism that makes America intervene overseas, but the defense of the achievements of the

---

europäische Integration 1947–1957," in Manfred Berg, Michaela Hönicke, Raimund Lammersdorf, and Anneke de Rudder, eds., *Macht und Moral. Beiträge zur Ideologie und Praxis amerikanischer Außenpolitik im 20. Jahrhundert* (Münster, 1999), 171–188. Cf. "One of the men I've admired extravagantly is Herbert Hoover. I am forced to believe he's getting senile. God knows I'd personally like to get out of Europe and I'd like to see US *able* to sit at home & ignore the rest of the world! What a pleasing prospect – until you look at ultimate consequences – destruction" (Dwight D. Eisenhower, Diary, March 5, 1951, in Louis Galambos, ed., *The Papers of Dwight D. Eisenhower*, vol. XII: *NATO and the Campaign of 1952* [Baltimore, MD, 1989], 91).

43. The fear that high defense spending would tip the balance between society and the state and produce a "garrison state" was shared by President Truman and President Eisenhower. Nevertheless President Truman and his successors accepted the assumption of NSC 68 that "the integrity of our system will not be jeopardized by any measures, covert or overt, violent or non-violent, which will serve the purposes of frustrating the Kremlin design." "They largely severed foreign policy from traditional constitutional restraints by declaring international and domestic relations could be dealt with separately. Actions in the world arena were not unduly to affect liberties at home." This was a strategy whose false premises were revealed during the Vietnam War. See Walter La Feber, "The Constitution and United States Foreign Policy: An Interpretation," *The Journal of American History* 74 (1987/88), 695–717, here 695f.; Aaron Friedberg, "Why Didn't the US Become a Garrison State?" *International Security* 16 (1992), 109–142; Robert Jervis, "America and the Twentieth Century: Continuity and Change," *Diplomatic History* 23,2 (1999), 219–238; Leffler, "National Security," 150f.; Robert R. Bowie and Richard H. Immerman, *Waging Peace. How Eisenhower Shaped an Enduring Cold War Strategy* (Oxford, 1998), 44.

postwar era, the defense of the reconstruction of Western Europe and the Far East, and especially the interests of European integration and an open global economy, so indispensable for safeguarding economic opportunity and so necessary for Japan's and Western Europe's economic well-being and democratic stability.[44] It is the national interest that makes Washington intervene.

Although the United States has supported global institutions in order to foster a healthy economic and political environment, and although the United States has supported the furthering of the law of nations, in the last resort there is no such thing as a US quest for a global, I repeat global, *Pax Americana*. US diplomacy concentrates on areas vital to its well-being. America does not intervene in any war or civil strife to restore justice. It is not America's intention to redeem the world. US foreign policy, guided by Wilsonianism, is focussed on fostering democratic order, and on crushing or containing corrupting influences in regions vital for America's well-being.[45]

NATO's intervention in Kosovo has to be seen in this context. It is not an altruistic peace effort, it is not a humanitarian mission,

---

44. Christopher Coker, *Reflections on American Foreign Policy Since 1945* (London, 1989); Marc Trachtenberg, *History & Strategy* (Princeton, NJ, 1991); Robert Bowie and Richard Immermann, *Waging Peace. How Eisenhower Shaped an Enduring Cold War Strategy* (New York, 1998); Tom Lansford, "The Triumph of Transatlanticism: NATO and the Evolution of European Security After the Cold War," *The Journal of Strategic Studies* 22(1) (1999), 1–28; Stanley R. Sloan, "US Perspectives on NATO's Future," *International Affairs* 71(2) (1995), 217–231.

45. Cf.

> Emphatically our only alternative to isolationism is not to undertake to police the whole world nor to impose democratic institutions on all mankind including the Dalai Lama and the good shepherds of Tibet. America cannot be responsible for the good behavior of the entire world. But America is responsible, to herself as well as to history, for the world environment in which she lives. (Luce, "The American Century," 166)

> "Wherever the standard of freedom and independence has been or shall be unfurled, there will her heart, her benediction, and her prayers be. But she goes not abroad in search of monsters to destroy. She is the well-wisher to the freedom and independence of all. She is the champion and vindicator only of her own" (John Quincy Adams, cited in Perkins, *The Creation of a Republican Empire*, 149f.).

it is not imperialist expansionism, but an effort to defend American democracy, by defending the reconstructed Europe. It is not the Serb military that is feared, but the corrupting influence that the success of a nationalistic and racist policy would have on the still unstable regimes in countries that used to form the European satellites of the Soviet Union. A policy of ethnic cleansing tolerated by Western society would be a precedent for others to follow, a precedent that could in the long run endanger America's postwar reconstruction of Europe, that could endanger European integration.[46] NATO's intervention is therefore simply an attempt to put "an end to the beginnings to all wars."

And it is not a coincidence that those words uttered by President Franklin D. Roosevelt in an address commemorating Thomas Jefferson were used by President Clinton in his address in Norfolk, Virginia on April 1, 1999 in order to explain to American soldiers the necessity of waging war on Slobodan Milosevic – the Yugoslav dictator who was threatening to corrupt the healthy environment necessary for democratic society to flourish.

*

Is the "idealistic" interpretation of American history valid? Is the United States indeed aiming at a global *Pax Americana*? Is the United States exporting democracy to redeem the world? Is it America's mission to create a *novus ordo seclorum* or is the Wilsonian impulse to promote democracy abroad nothing but an ideological smokescreen, a means to rally the public around the flag in order to make affirmative foreign policy succeed in America? Is the Wilsonianism of the twentieth century nothing but rhetoric?

It is neither. Wilsonianism, America's distinctive foreign policy, is a valid national security policy, a security policy that relates foreign threats to internal core values, that relates corrupting influences from abroad to the stability of the political institutions of the United

---

46. James Hooper, "Kosovo: America's Balkan Problem," *Current History* (April 1999), 159–164, at 159; Javier Solana, "Es geht um die Verteidigung unserer Werte," *Frankfurter Allgemeine*, April 24, 1999, 12.

States; it is a foreign policy which naturally and gradually evolved out of domestic republicanism. Challenges to the precious American experiment, to the balanced Constitution, had to be met, regardless of whether they were internal or external, for any external challenge or threat would in the last resort affect domestic stability.[47] Wilsonianism is simply a strategy for the defense of American exceptionalism, or *national security republicanism.*[48]

It is not a quest for a US global *Pax Americana,* but a quest for security, for stability, that makes the United States intervene overseas; it is not idealism but prudence that makes the United States export democracy. By making "the world" safe for democracy, the world first and foremost is made safe for America.[49]

47. "[I]t is really foolish for people to worry about our 'constitutional democracy' without worrying or, better thinking hard about the world revolution. For only as we go out to meet and solve for our time the problems of the world revolution, can we know how to re-establish our constitutional democracy for another 50 or 100 years" (Luce, "The American Century," 167).

48. The term "national security liberalism" used by Tony Smith overemphasizes the importance of economic openness as the prime US core value. Economic openness is nothing more than a means to safeguard a balanced Constitution. Cf. Walter La Feber, "The Tension between Democracy and Capitalism during the American Century," *Diplomatic History* 23(2) (1999), 263–284. According to La Feber it is the expansion of capitalist systems and not the spread of democracy that properly characterizes US diplomacy in the American Century. It has been a "century shaped by US policies demanding that the world be made safe and assessable for the American economic system" (p. 284). The validity of La Feber's argument is unquestionable, as long as the view is focused on the Western Hemisphere and the Third World. A focus on areas vital to American national security, a focus on Europe and Japan, however, might challenge these findings. In these areas American diplomacy has concentrated on a distinctive reconstruction of societies, a reconstruction that has not been limited to the introduction of a free market economy. (The assumption that capitalism guarantees democracy is discussed in Joan Hoff, "The American Century. From Sarajevo to Sarajevo," *Diplomatic History* 23(2) (1999), 285–319, at 309ff.)

49. "First and foremost we are to make the world safe for ourselves. This is our war, America's war. If we do not win it, we shall some day have to reckon with Germany single-handed. Therefore for our own sakes let us strike down Germany" (Theodore Roosevelt, cited in Osgood, *Ideals and Self-Interest in America's Foreign Relations,* 273).

Part 3
Utopian Communities in the Nineteenth and Twentieth Centuries

1
Social Utopias in Modern America

James Gilbert

It can hardly be believed how many facts naturally flow from the philo-
sophic theory of the perfectibility of man, or how strong an influence it
exercises even on those who, living entirely for the purpose of action
and not of thought, seem to conform their actions to it, without knowing
anything about it.

Alexis de Tocqueville, *Democracy in America*

The subject of utopian community in the twentieth century is
almost as broad and deep as American history itself; it has, as well,
been a central preoccupation of the mainstream of American fiction.
It exists as an activity, a theme, a goal, a model, a preoccupation, a
historical vestige of earlier traditions. It appears in so many guises
that the first act of understanding and analysis must be to recognize
its largest and most obvious continuities. Thus understood, intentional communities are, in some respects, only heightened instances
of common American themes and practices.[1]

In its broadest sense, utopianism is a renewable and changing
heritage of European Christianity, a millennial and perfectionist
legacy of both Protestantism in its many forms and Roman
Catholicism. One of the most difficult tasks for any historian – and
probably a fruitless one at that – is to separate the sacred from the
secular in discussing utopian communities. This is difficult because

---

1. Donald E. Pitzer, ed., *America's Communal Utopias* (Chapel Hill, NC, 1997).
Pitzer notes the huge number of utopian studies and the wave of interest in the
subject beginning in the late 1960s with the foundation of Utopia USA in 1966.
The Communal Studies Association was founded in 1975; the Society for Utopian
Studies in 1976; and the Intentional Communal Studies Association in 1985.

251

of historical continuities and the contemporary similarities between communities that range from Catholic religious orders on the one extreme, and the Twin Oaks communal experiment of the late 1960s, modeled on the theories of B. F. Skinner, on the other. In examining works of utopian literature, one confronts the same inseparability of the sacred and the secular, whether in Edward Bellamy's millennial *Looking Backward* (1888) or Ray Bradbury's dystopic *Fahrenheit 451*, written in 1953. The problem is intensified by a larger cultural reality in America: the inseparability of religion and secularism, concepts which define nodes on a continuous scale of meaning rather than absolutely distinct doctrines.[2]

Whether or not one subscribes entirely to his theory of advancing historical cycles, there is much to be learned from William McLoughlin on this score. In his noted work, *Awakenings, Revivals, and Reform*, he posited a specific connection between recurrent phenomena: the simultaneous onset of religious revivals and political reform. Although he did not dwell on it, one of the most important expressions of this energy were simultaneous waves of utopian literature and the founding of both religious and social utopian communities. McLoughlin rightly cites the 1830s and 1840s, the 1890s to the First World War, and, again, the 1970s as moments of intense religious and reform interest which also resulted in a dramatic increase in communitarian experiments. While the emphasis of this essay is on social utopians, their appearance within the context of waves of religious revival is part of the larger story and provides the setting and landscape in which secular experiments thrived or withered.[3]

2. In this essay, I employ the words utopia, intentional community, and commune to refer essentially to the same phenomena, although different contexts will suggest different nuances in the terms. While there have been scores of interpretations of this variegated tradition, I agree with Michael Kammen that the dream of order (or conversely the fear of disorder) is one of the principal elements of any definition of any of these terms. Michael Kammen "Historical Reflexions Upon the Role of Utopianism in American Culture," in Rob Kroes, ed., *Nineteen Eighty-Four and the Apocalyptic Imagination in America* (Amsterdam, 1985), 110–123.

3. William McLoughlin, *Revivals, Awakenings and Reform: An Essay on Religion and Social Change in America* (Chicago, IL, 1978).

Another continuity of modern social utopias is a long history of utopian thinking and experimentation. This record should be understood both as a historic remnant, a bibliography of ideas, and as a continuing conversation with the great works in the tradition. A number of modern communes self-consciously modeled themselves upon, or more commonly footnoted, past American experiments such as Brook Farm, by naming buildings after famous inhabitants or places associated with that community. Or, stretching even further back, some modern communes self-consciously celebrated Thomas More or even Plato's Republic. Twentieth-century utopias, in particular, carried on a long and fruitful conversation with the ideas of Edward Bellamy. Many of the literary utopias of the twentieth century, some of the social communes around the turn of the century, and even utopian political movements such as the Utopian Society of Los Angeles in 1934, or Arthur Morgan's New Deal, TVA project communities, self-consciously tried to put Bellamy's program into practice. Others argued with him. But the impetus to utopian speculation that he provided has never entirely disappeared and during the moments of serious utopian revival in the 1930s and the 1960s and 1970s, his ideas reappeared with renewed vigor.[4]

There is another, more obliquely related, but immensely important continuity between utopia formation and mainstream American history and that is the ongoing process of community founding. If utopias can be defined as "intentional communities" of a special sort, then they represent only an exceptional variant of the common American process of settlement and town and city building. A great many American towns were, and continue to be, intentional communities, established along the lines of some idealized format, and devoted to specific purposes. These communities include religious establishments such as the evangelical Protestant suburbs that ringed Chicago in the late nineteenth and early twentieth centuries: Oak Park, Evanston, Wheaton, Zion, Harvey, and so forth. Even without their dedicated purpose of temperance and the

---

4. The persistence of Bellamy clubs is one sign of this interest.

promotion of evangelical religion, a great many contemporaneous towns and suburbs contained elements of planning and intention aimed toward the creation of community, not just the housing of population. Often the early histories of these communities exhibit the enthusiasms and discouragements common to more explicit utopian experiments. With the relentless westward settlement of the nineteenth century and the expanding concentric rings of new communities around established urban centers in the twentieth century, the foundation of community is one of the most important processes of American expansion.

Within the broad tradition of community-building there are several special forms that merit mention although they are not exactly utopian experiments. One of these is the company town, developed primarily in the late nineteenth century but showing signs of renewed vigor in the new century in such places as Gary, Indiana. The purpose of these communities (particularly in the latter part of the nineteenth century) was to promote a stable and loyal workforce and to house workers on special projects in hostile or deserted areas. The distinction between such communities and utopian experiments is sometimes hard to discover except for the forms of governance, which in the company town rest exclusively in the hands of corporate or government management.

Another utopia-like intentional community is the government town, an odd entity that is both company town planned and administered by bureaucrats and yet communitarian in its form. The most famous of these are the Greenbelt communities, established in the late 1930s by the New Deal as experiments in suburban housing. Deeply influenced by utopian thinkers and urban planners, these communities had extensive social-planning mechanisms built into their architecture and population selection. Greenbelt, Maryland, for example promoted a sort of pluralist homogeneity. Its apartments were modest, organized around a civic center, and located within a park-like setting. Because of the limited size and nature of its facilities, Greenbelt's managers allowed only middle-class families to rent; for example no unattached women were admitted. This being Maryland in the late 1930s, the town was exclusively white. But it proudly claimed integration of another sort. Based upon a religious sample of the Washington, D.C. area, a representative percentage of Catholics, Protestants and Jews was maintained in the community.

Like many utopian communities the first order of business in Greenbelt in the late 1930s was organization. Indeed there were so many meetings and organizations initially, that citizens complained of a lack of privacy and free time. And, like many utopian experiments, the Greenbelt communities evolved into more normal small towns and suburbs.[5]

A more contemporary example of small-community utopia-like establishments is the gated community, an enclave designed to filter out undesired elements of the American environment. Many of these gated communities are built to accommodate special populations: retirees, certain kinds of leisure and sport devotees, the well-to-do, and so on. Their most distinctive (and controversial) feature is the protected and policed environment, maintained by high fences, walls, or natural obstacles designed to exclude the casual visitor whatever his or her purpose.[6]

Another element of continuity between utopia and mainstream culture can be found in large-scale, citywide urban planning projects,

5. Joseph L. Arnold, *The New Deal in the Suburbs: A History of the Greenbelt Town Program, 1935–1954* (Columbus, OH, 1971). Arnold discusses the religious inclusion and racial exclusion of Greenbelt towns. George A. Warner in *Greenbelt: The Cooperative Community, An Experiment in Democratic Living* (New York, 1954), examines the thick texture of organizations found in early Greenbelt, Maryland. On December 5, 1938, during the early history of the community, the citizens' Association declared a week's moratorium on meetings in the town to give its citizens a rest.

6. Edward J. Blakely and Mary Gail Snyder, *Fortress America: Gated Communities in the United States* (Washington, D.C., 1997) specifically link the huge trend toward gated communities to an earlier tradition of intentional community formation from the Puritans to the Garden City proposals based upon the works of Ebenezer Howard. They distinguish among three types of contemporary communities: lifestyle (gold and retirement), prestige (wealthy estates), and security zones, which they describe as "enclaves of fear."

One might also include in the list of intentional communities such institutions as prisons, mental institutions, and children's camps, all of which attempt to promote behavior changes and new forms of community through isolation from normal society. Such disciplinary communities, however, lack any of the freedoms normally associated with utopian experiments.

many of which have been influenced by utopian models. The most important of these were world fairs and related expositions and exhibits. Among the most famous and influential of these are the World's Columbian Exhibition of 1893 held in Chicago and the World of Tomorrow pavilion at the New York World's Fair of 1939. Both of these exhibits were, in a sense, bridges between utopian planning and notions of the perfected city and the actual plans of urban architects, road-builders and transportation designers. Thus the Chicago Fair linked the utopian speculations of the late nineteenth century, particularly as expressed by Edward Bellamy and William Dean Howells, to the City Beautiful movement of the first decade of the twentieth century which redesigned cities following the inspiration of the layout of the Fair. Similarly, the speculations of urban planners realized in the massive private transport system around New York in the World of Tomorrow exhibit became concrete and lawn in the superhighways and suburbs of Long Island and New Jersey after World War II.[7]

A final continuity deserves special mention in the twentieth century: utopian political movements. Not only were Bellamy's ideas translated into an important political movement in the 1890s and beyond, but the 1930s also witnessed a significant attempt to push utopian ideas into politics. In 1934, the Technocracy movement, the Utopian Society, and, finally, the candidacy of Upton Sinclair for governor of California, opened a causeway between notions of intentional community-building and the broad-scale political assault on national economic and social problems.

As administrator of the Tennessee Valley Authority under the New Deal, Arthur Morgan, biographer of Bellamy and a strong advocate of planned communities, tried to impose elements of Bellamyite philosophy in the construction communities that sprang up around the dam-building sites. One of these, Norris, Tennessee, consisted of inexpensive housing in a park-like setting. Morgan was also

7. Donald J. Bush, "Futurama: World's Fair as Utopia," *Alternative Futures*, 2 (Fall, 1979), 3–20.

8. Roy Talbert, Jr., *FDR's Utopian: Arthur Morgan of the TVA* (Jackson, MS, 1987), 105–122.

instrumental in setting up training schools for workers. All of these efforts were in pursuit of his dream of a harmonious, cooperative, and ethical society that was also efficient and scientific.[8]

As in the nineteenth century, modern utopianism has had two fundamental modes of existence. The first is literary and imaginative, belonging to a long tradition of fiction that reaches well back into European dreams of a better society and which was continuously refreshed by important new works from Europe. Thus authors such as H. G. Wells, Aldous Huxley, and George Orwell wrote novels which were quickly imported and absorbed by American utopian writers. In a different sense, older works by Fourier and Saint-Simon continued to be read and to influence the direction of American utopian letters.

The other form of utopia is the community itself. During the twentieth century, thousands of utopian communities were founded, although most of them were short-lived and inconsequential. Some were only partially conceived as utopias. While their appearance can be organized by the historian into different categories, the most significant clusters fall naturally into three periods. Designating them as such does not diminish the ongoing importance of community-founding throughout the whole century. Nonetheless, three periods seem particularly important: the early years of the century, the 1930s, and especially the 1970s when there were 2,000 or perhaps many more social communes of one sort or another in existence.

Considered side by side, the two modalities of utopianism – the literary and the actual – there is an obvious parallel development and yet a curious divergence. Utopian literature also tends to cluster in these three periods, but overall, it increasingly becomes dystopic, growing in hostility to the emergence of bureaucratic, consumer society and deeply pessimistic about the consequences of intentional social design, making it ultimately satiric of its own premises.[9] Social communes, on the other hand, after the 1930s, when this literary

---

9. I am intentionally excluding science fiction literature from this essay, although this is an arbitrary and ultimately impossible division to make. It should be noted that science fiction also harbors strong dystopic tendencies from the 1930s on, if not before.

turn became a permanent direction, seem almost to be a rebuttal of dystopic thinking. Ironically, literary dystopias contained fundamental critiques of utopian thinking itself and thus helped define the social criticism and ideology that inspired the communitarian movement of the 1970s. They provided a negative reference for the small-scale experiments which dotted the rural landscapes of Oregon, the Appalachians, and New England in this period. The evolution of literary utopias from optimistic visions of large-scale transformation of society to nightmares projected onto these once positive dreams, represents, in effect, a massive shift in the cultural environment in which Edward Bellamy wrote *Looking Backward* and a change from the post-Millennialism of the Progressive Era in the 1890s, to the pre-Millennialist and apocalyptic environment of the 1970s. This transition is dramatically captured in Hollywood films, from *Forbidden Planet* in the 1950s to *Sleeper* and *Bladerunner* in the 1970s and 1980s.[10]

One of the most significant contributions to understanding literary utopias has been the effort of historians and literary critics to categorize the various appearances of utopian writing throughout Western literature. Some of this work helps us simplify complex movements and sort out some of the dominant motives that may have inspired utopians, since some sort of imposed order is useful and, indeed, necessary. Frank and Fritzie Manuel's categories of the utopian mind are a worthwhile starting point. They describe three extended historical periods, beginning with the fifteenth–eighteenth centuries (the era of "calm felicity") in which tranquility and retreat are commonplace goals of writers. The nineteenth century, they

10. Bellamy's hero is born again in an Americanized Kingdom of God on Earth in the year 2000. Another border of utopian literature edges off into fantasy and children's fiction. For example, the adventure stories by Edgar Rice Burroughs, particularly the original *Tarzan of the Apes*, published in 1914, contain strong utopian elements: social satire, an isolated setting, an implied orderly, idealized community achievable only in those circumstances, and so on. So too, stories like Frank L. Baum's *The Wizard of Oz* posit a fictional world that operates more or less as an idealized society. But neither of these, or the hundreds of fantasy stories like them, can be construed as, at best, anything more than satire. Utopia usually has more to offer.

argue, is more open-ended, where change and possibility are the coefficients of creative speculation. Following the Second World War they detect the rise of "eupsychias" in which the obstacles to be overcome in achieving utopia are psychological and sexual.[11]

Lyman Tower Sargent, writing in a volume dedicated to defining utopia, describes utopia as a radical desire to return to a simpler world and a form of social dreaming. He divides utopia into three portions, utopian literature, communitarianism, and utopian social theory, and then subdivides literature into myths, fictions, and non-fictional works.[12]

On the other hand, Lewis Mumford's seminal *Story of Utopias* proposes two general sorts of intentional communities, the utopias of escape and of reconstruction. In this early book, Mumford clearly advocates a reconstructive vision that he sees as a powerful means to criticize contemporary society and plan for a better future. Only such speculation, he concludes, can pretend to close the gap between science and humanity, reality and possibility. In this accounting, utopia leads the moving edge of progress – and, it very much describes the positive thinking that still enveloped much utopian speculation in the 1920s when it was written.[13] My emphasis is somewhat different from these and other accounts, although based in part upon them.

By far the most important literary vision of utopia of the twentieth century is Edward Bellamy's nineteenth-century description of America in the year 2000. It also belongs to a special category of cross-over novels, such as B. F. Skinner's *Walden II* (1948), which

11. Frank E. Manuel and Fritzie P. Manuel, *Utopian Thought in the Western World* (Cambridge, MA, 1979), *passim*. The Manuels rightly point out that dystopic thinking has been common throughout the tradition of utopian writing.

12. Lyman Tower Sargent, "Political Dimensions of Utopianism with Special Reference to American Communitarianism," in Nadia Minerva, ed, *Per Una Definizione Dell'Utopia* (Ravenna, 1992), 186ff.

13. Lewis Mumford, *The Story of Utopia* (New York, 1922). See also Erik Rabkin, "Atavism and Utopia," *Alternative Futures* I (Spring, 1978), 71–81. Rabkin posits that Western utopian thinking has passed through four stages: (1) Slave Labor [Platonic utopias], (2) Christian [More], (3) Enslavement of Machines [Bellamy], and (4) Dystopia [Pavlovian].

led either to associated political movements or to specific communitarian experiments, or to both. Bellamy's genius lay in his ability to see utopian blueprints in contemporary society. I do not mean in the sense of describing buildings or economic organization. Rather, Bellamy sketched an easily recognizable moral and psychological landscape, well known to millions of middle-class Americans. And by extending forward so many of the powerful economic and organizational impulses he observed around him, he gained insights that escaped others. In adapting the Victorian family to the new economic and political organizations of the day – the burgeoning consumer and corporate society – Bellamy imagined social equality alongside strong domestic relationships within a consumer society. He also "solved" the perennial political problems of the late nineteenth century: money and depressions. His argument, in fact, was that utopia was possible, desirable, and achievable. In this his program shared a great deal with other, end-of-the-century, universal, social solutions such as the Single Tax.

Bellamy's utopian prognostications were echoed in a variety of books and novels published in the early part of the twentieth century, principally those designated by historian Howard Segal as "technological utopias." Segal rightly argues that a large number of lesser writers followed Bellamy's lead in describing a future of technological abundance and organizational efficiency. This era of speculation, he concludes, ran from about 1883 to 1933, to be followed then by periods of considerably less faith in the machine to solve economic and social problems.[14]

Of the large group of eighty or so utopian novels that appeared in the United States between 1885 and 1905, a great many concentrated on sketching a corporate, collective, and efficient future that contrasted sharply with the contemporary impression of ruthless competition, led by powerful and dictatorial businessmen. Many of these books engaged Bellamy's ideas, positively and negatively. Others

14. Howard Segal, *Technological Utopianism in American Culture* (Chicago, IL, 1985), 105–125. In addition to the literary production provoked by *Looking Backward*, there were also various sorts of affiliated utopian societies and Bellamy clubs that appeared during the period.

took up the arguments of two other great utopian novels of the day, William Dean Howells' *A Traveler from Altruria* (1894) and Ignatius Donnelly's bleak *Caesar's Column* (1890).[15]

In this period, while the predominant mode was probably optimistic, there were important and strong examples of dystopian fiction. Jack London's *The Iron Heel* and H. G. Wells' *The Time Machine* are only two of the best-known examples. The purpose of such works was social satire, as it had been in some of the earliest utopian writings. The modern literary dystopia expressed a bitter commentary upon emerging industrial society and mass organization. Satire became nightmare; progress issued in evil. So while Bellamy could happily contemplate a military-type social hierarchy, a bureaucratic politics, and a passionless consumerism as both feasible and desirable, other writers looked at this same future and longed for the confusion and idiosyncratic possibilities of contemporary individualism.[16] It was not that Bellamy's prognostications were wrong. On the contrary, they seemed all too achievable and imminent, and they also appeared to be a desperately inadequate measurement of human potential, one which denied genuine freedom of the spirit. Certainly not all American dystopias were a literal response to Bellamy, although some, like Franz Werfel's *Star of the Unborn*, were. Rather, it was the coming society which Bellamy lionized that caused the intense reaction.

Of course the utopian novel of mass organization could take other forms than a bleak appraisal of conformity. There are outstanding examples of positive literary utopias throughout the twentieth century: Harold Loeb's *Life in a Technocracy* (1933), B. F. Skinner's *Walden II* (1948), Gerald O'Neill's *The High Frontier* (1982), and Ernest Cullenbach's *Ecotopia* (1977). But these positive visionary

15. H. Ickstadt, "Utopia or Catastrophe: Ignatius Donnelly and the Rhetoric of Nineteenth Century Radical Fiction in America," Rob Kroes, ed., *Nineteen Eighty Four* (Amsterdam, 1985), 140–157. Another important utopian novel of this early period is *Herland*, a feminist exploration written by Charlotte Perkins Gilman in 1915.

16. John L. Thomas, "Introduction," to Edward Bellamy, *Looking Backward, 2000– 1887* (Cambridge, MA, 1967), 1–88. Thomas also mentions the Civil Service as a model for Bellamy's thinking.

fictions became less frequent and central to utopian literature, particularly after the 1930s. The reasons for this shift are transparent. Two World Wars, the appearance of totalitarianism, weapons of mass destruction, psychologies of mass manipulation, and the rise of mass media made dystopic speculations almost inevitable. Utopian fiction became a principle vehicle for fleshing out the bones of an emerging reality. By fictionalizing (and distancing in time and by place) the menacing developments of the mid-twentieth century, it became possible to contemplate their potential horrors. Thus works like George Orwell's *1984*, Aldous Huxley's *Brave New World*, William Golding's *Lord of the Flies* (1954), Neville Shute's *On the Beach* (1957), and John Bruner's *The Sheep Look Up* (1972), and a good many other novels and stories, shaped the dominant tone and style of utopian exploration. As some of the most important modern satiric and prophetic literary works of their age, they constitute a principal form of social and moral criticism of contemporary society. Concerned with, even obsessed by, the daunting tyrannies of modern industrial society, this literature, like Bellamy's, exaggerated and extended reality, but as a warning not an aspiration.

If it is true that utopian speculation and the actual social communitarian experiments of the twentieth century generally grew apart, to the point where each cast a shadow upon the other – where imagination and reality clashed – then it is necessary to explore some of the intentional communities to see how they functioned. How did they offer refuge and criticism of the society that utopian literature savagely satirized as a dystopia?

To a degree the difference between utopia and dystopia in the twentieth century is a question of scale. Whereas it might have been possible in the 1830s to imagine Brook Farm as some sort of comparable alternative to life in Boston or Concord, Massachusetts, the relationship between the size of actual social utopias of the twentieth century and the urban society about which they were usually a comment, is a comparison that can only be understood as a contrast. Even the relationship between Bellamy's comprehensive vision of Boston in the year 2000 and the various colonies founded upon his ideas and in his name had become far-fetched in the early part of the century.

Bellamy had always opposed communal experiments founded in his name, arguing, accurately, that his vision offered regeneration on a society-wide scale, a New Nationalism, not an isolated agricultural community. Nonetheless, several small early twentieth-century social utopias tried to put the principles enunciated by Bellamy into practice, becoming demonstration projects for what the Bellamy clubs and the Nationalist Movement (a political "party" based loosely upon his ideas) asserted. While political "nationalism" died rather quickly, utopian communities continued to be founded after the turn of the century: Llano del Rio, for example, in 1914, and Equality (named after Bellamy's next novel) in Washington State. Other important but short-lived experiments included Single-tax enclaves, Upton Sinclair's Helicon Home Colony (1906–1907) in California, Point Loma colony near San Diego, and the socialist utopias of Winter Island, Altruria, and the Army of Industry. Many of these experiments sought to revolutionize gender and political relationships and institute economic practices that were founded upon equality and the rejection of profit-making, accumulation, and money exchange. Yet most could not imagine reformation on a large scale; they could only practice their new economy in an old setting of agricultural and handicraft communism.[17]

A few urban groups existed such as the Ferrer Colony, originally founded in New York City in 1915 and devoted to the application of progressive education. But this experiment quickly dissolved and moved to Steton, New Jersey, where most of its members (largely from a Russian Jewish background) built homes. There they founded a cooperative store and established a viable communal lifestyle, sharing meals, participating in common folk culture, and so on.[18]

Mention of this ethnic-oriented intentional community suggests the difficulty of separating social utopias from other forms of communal experiments during the twentieth century. While there were scores of utopian communities founded in the first two decades

17. Timothy Miller, *The Quest for Utopia in Twentieth-Century America* (Syracuse, NY, 1998), 10, 31ff, 46ff. Pitzer, *America's Communal Utopias*, passim.

18. Robert S. Fogarty, *Dictionary of American Communal and Utopian History* (Westport, CT, 1980), 140.

of the twentieth century, there were almost as many expressed purposes and causes wrapped up in their establishment. Thus Madame Blavatsky, founder of the Theosophic Movement, endorsed Bellamy's ideas, and several theosophic communities attempted to graft elements of his theory onto their existing practices. This example suggests that the lived experience in many of the most secular communes had much in common with more spiritual neighbors. In effect, the social reform communities belong in a continuum with Adventist, Theosophical, prohibitionist, Swedenborgian, and even some of the special artistic colonies of the era.[19]

Although social utopian communities continued to be founded throughout the 1920s, the Depression and the New Deal gave impetus, in particular, to renewed efforts to think about utopia and community-planning on a wide scale, and the influence of Bellamy and other, earlier socialist thinkers returned to the forefront. In fact, during the New Deal, Bellamy's speculations came as close to realization as they ever would in the twentieth century (although not very close). For one brief period, during the mid-1930s, it became possible to consider once again some sort of grand-scale community formation.

Two important examples illustrate this renewed utopian optimism. The first occurred early in the first Roosevelt Administration and sprang to life almost spontaneously in the cultural hothouse of southern California. Beginning in 1929, and constructed out of the leftover elements of several earlier utopian suggestions, the Utopian Society was founded in Los Angeles by a group including Jonathan F. Glendon, Eugene J. Reed, W. H. Rousseau, and others. Self-consciously basing their plans upon Bellamy, Howard Scott's Technocracy movement, the ideas of socialists and Upton Sinclair, the group proclaimed an eclectic, utopian vision. Developing a pageantry borrowed from the rituals of the Masons and the Catholic Church and dramatized as a sort of "Pilgrim's Progress"[20] to the

19. Pitzer, *America's Communal Utopias*; Miller, *Quest for Utopia*, 10–25.
20. John Bunyan's *Pilgrim's Progress* was the first widely read account of utopia in America and a persistent model of the literary quest for perfection.

millennium of full employment, the Society swept onto the political scene with remarkable energy.[21]

With its organizing base located in private residences and an initiation rite maintained in semi-secret, the Utopians built an organization that had as many as 600,000 members in seventeen states by the end of 1934. Avowing some of Bellamy's proposals, it envisioned elimination of money exchange and a society in which all members were equal and equally compensated. Production would only be for use, never profit. This new society, leaders maintained, would represent the application of scientific thinking to the disorganized and depression-strangled American nation.

The most curious and compelling facet of the Utopians was their rituals. Each new recruit had to pass through the cycle rituals, a ceremony where each "pilgrim" (or "forgotten man") confronted representatives of the failed and wasteful economic system until he or she was guided to the truth by a "hermit." These cycles were first enacted in private homes until the explosion of membership propelled them into the open. On June 23, 1934, the society held its first public cycle rituals before 20,000 spectators at the Hollywood Bowl. As Newton Van Dalsem wrote in his history of the organization, "The result was a semi-secret society whose initiatory ceremonies embodied a series of dramatic performances epitomizing man's struggle for economic security and well-being, tracing the purpose of that struggle up thru past centuries, and looking to the near future for the attainment of its goal."[22]

The astounding growth of the society and its equally sudden demise fascinated journalists, who linked the movement to Upton Sinclair's equally meteoric bid for the California governorship, to the planning wing of the New Deal, to the religious visions of Aimee Semple McPherson, the Masonic Lodge Movement, the

21. Newton Van Dalsem, *History of the Utopian Society of America* (Los Angeles, CA, 1942), 11–13. See also Hanson Hathaway, *The Utopians are Coming* (Hollywood, CA, 1934). John Bunyan's story of Pilgrim's Progress is one of the strongest and most persistent narratives in American culture, a form of millennial story that captures an essential version of the struggle for perfection.

22. Van Dalsem, *History of the Utopian Society*, 39, 11.

British Oxford Group, and, generally, to the mainstream history of utopianism in America. That these observers could discover (rightly) such diverse origins of the group testifies to the centrality of utopian thinking in the United States. In fact, the Utopian Society was a large signpost at the intersection of all of these influences.[23]

The Society claimed friends in very high places. New Dealers Raymond Moley and Rexford Tugwell were reported to have affiliations with the group and Mrs. Roosevelt was said to be sympathetic. Even the President was rumored to be a secret admirer, who signaled his interest by using the phrase "a wise hermit" in one of his addresses.[24] These "secret admirers" were undoubtedly a figment of an over-active Utopian imagination, but in fact, the New Deal itself was deeply influenced by utopian thinking in general, particularly in its initiatives toward community planning. Among these, the Greenbelt towns were just a few, if the best-known, examples.

The origins of the Greenbelt suburbs are easiest to trace back to the works of Ebenezer Howard and his plans for the Garden City.[25] Some efforts to create such experiments in town planning had been attempted in 1904 on Long Island and then again in 1912. The most important model, however, was the planned suburb of Radburn, New Jersey, constructed in 1928 and designed to establish an ideal suburban community. Within the New Deal, Rexford Tugwell was a particularly important advocate of community-planning and he, together with John S. Lansill and a number of other administrators, located in the Resettlement Administration, advocated government leadership in redesigning American communities. During the 1930s, the New Deal managed to build the

23. The following articles are a sample of the sorts of commentary summarized here: Miriam Allen deFord, "Utopia Incorporated," *Nation*, 139 (September 5, 1934), 268–269; "Out of the West Come Utopians Seeking a New Socialist State," *New York Times* (July 29, 1934), Section 8, p. 3; George Creel, "Utopia Unlimited," *Saturday Evening Post*, 207 (November 24, 1934), 5–7ff.; Aaron Allen Heist, "California's Utopia, Inc.," *Christian Century*, 51 (October 24, 1934), 1342–1344.

24. Carey McWilliams, "Utopia Incorporated," *New Republic*, 79 (July 18, 1934), 258.

25. Ebenezer Howard, *Garden Cities of Tomorrow* (London, 1946).

three Greenbelt towns, in addition to several other sorts of planned communities, such as Norris. Then, during World War II, the Roosevelt Administration constructed three research towns associated with the atomic bomb project: Los Alamos, New Mexico; Richland, Washington; and Oak Ridge, Tennessee.

Designed and built despite inter-agency feuding and bitter opposition from some in Congress and the press, the Greenbelt suburbs were small-scale and hardly the brave new world of urban community that both advocates and detractors predicted. Constructed within the tradition of utopian town planning, they lacked, however, the common self-contained economic activity which would have made more radical social and economic experimentation feasible. Their only experimental economic forms were dedicated to consumption, not production, so that the town founded cooperatives of various sorts to purchase food, provide services such as medicine, and so on. Despite the limited possibilities, the Greenbelt towns had certain common lifestyles that they shared with utopian communities, particularly the organizational and political style of direct and generally equal participation.[26] But the failure of any large-scale utopian planning during the 1930s, when such ideas were again prominent, and when men held office who might be expected to advocate them, illustrates the overwhelming difficulties of making utopian ideas the science of a new society.

Following World War II and particularly in the late 1960s and 1970s, utopia became a way of life for many Americans, perhaps more so than in any other period in American history. This was simultaneously the heyday of dystopian novels, when *Fahrenheit 451*, *1984*, and *Brave New World* were widely read by the very young men and women who settled in the social and religious communes that sprang up across America. Most of the utopian literature by this time had become stridently dystopic, although one bit of "news from nowhere" maintained a very optimistic tone. This was B. F. Skinner's *Walden II*, published in 1948 but still eagerly read by later

---

26. Carol Corden, *Planned Cities: New Towns in Britain and America* (Beverly Hills, CA, 1977); Joseph L. Arnold, *The New Deal in the Suburbs: A History of the Greenbelt Town Program, 1935–1954* (Columbus, OH, 1971), 3–19; 24–32.

generations of utopians. Based upon the psychologist's theories of behavior modification and child-rearing, *Walden II* proposed a perfected, if highly manipulative, future. In this it did not differ remarkably from some of the major dystopias of the age, which also looked to modern psychology as a means of maintaining social order.[27] While many readers and critics recoiled at Skinner's brief for social control, several experimental communities tried to put his ideas into practice.

The other literature of utopia which distinguishes this period is the explosion of academic writing about utopias. Several journals and organizations were founded with the purpose of exploring the tradition of utopian thinking and communal experiments throughout American history. In part, this scholarly interest was occasioned by the remarkable number of new intentional communities founded in the 1960s and 1970s. Pushed and pulled into existence by dissatisfaction and a wide-eyed hopefulness, these communities had an extraordinary range of purpose and form. Estimates of their numbers range from around 2,000 to 10,000 depending on what is included in the definition. From urban crash pads to full-blown utopian social experiments, these communities were devoted to religion, drugs, agriculture, psychology, spiritualism, whole foods, new forms of child-rearing, Eastern religions, experimental sexual and gender relationships, and so on.[28] Some were based on the blueprints of novels or social, psychological, or spiritual tracts; some were more accidental in their form. Many were democratic in organization; others were highly authoritarian. Some, like Farralones, were noted for experiments in solar greenhouse design. The University of the Trees experimented in conflict resolution techniques. The Ananda Community was founded by Swami Kriyananda

27. B. F. Skinner, *Walden II* (New York, 1948). The novel sold over 1,000,000 copies. David M. Fine writes of the strength of the dystopic novel in Los Angeles during the 1930s: "California as Dystopia: Los Angeles Fiction in the 1930s," *Alternative Futures* 2 (Fall, 1979), 21–30.

28. Richard Fairchild discusses a wide variety of religious communes and intentional communities throughout the twentieth century. They were particularly common in the 1970s. See *Utopia USA* (San Francisco, CA: Alternative Foundation, 1972), passim.

to celebrate his ideas of yoga and chanting. Sharon Farm devoted itself to participatory democracy; some communities practiced celibacy or New Age communalism; the Farm experimented with midwifery; the Sirius Community explored holistic health and monastic sharing. Other communities were founded to propagate communal ideas popularized by Robert Heinlein, Paul Goodman, Wilhelm Reich, and Murray Bookchin.[29]

Despite the huge variety of communes and intentional communities devoted to exploring a multitude of different social and spiritual blueprints in these fervent decades, there are important continuities that illustrate an underlying similarity linking them together. Part of this similarity originates with the participants. The 1960s and especially the early 1970s shook hundreds of thousands of young men and women out of their expected career and training paths, out of college, the military, and corporate apprenticeships, and plunged them into a moving stream of population that traipsed from one utopia to the next. The two authors of *Builders of the Dawn*, a very useful guidebook and survey of utopian experiments in the 1970s, illustrate this process in their short autobiographical introduction:

> The two of us have lived in everything from the hippie communes of Haight-Ashbury to radical political communes, from shared urban households of professionals to rural spiritual communities. For several years, we both lived at the Findhorn Community in Scotland, which had a particularly profound effect on us in our personal growth and in inspiring us about the effectiveness of community as a strategy to social transformation. In 1978 we cofounded Sirius Community on eight-six acres in Western Massachusetts as a non-profit education center to communicate new ways to transform self and society.[30]

29. Connie McLoughlin and Gordon David, *Community Lifestyles in a Changing World* (Walpole, NH, 1985), passim; Pitzer, *America's Communal Utopias*, 12. Pitzer estimates 10,0000 communes in the late 1960s and early 1970s. Robert Houriet, *Getting Back Together* (New York, 1971), passim.

30. Connie McLaughlin and Gordon Davidson, *Builders of the Dawn*, 1–2. A significant number of young Americans also lived on Kibbutzim in Israel for a summer or, sometimes, longer. See also Houriet, *Getting Back Together*, 144.

Aside from creating an almost professional communal clientele, the movement and constant interchange of members helped universalize particular experiences and ideas. One of these was vegetarianism, and perhaps 40 percent of communes in the early 1970s practiced some sort of vegetarian diet.

There were other common elements that derived primarily from the setting and the size of utopian experiments. Edward Bellamy and even the New Deal could dream of vast social organizations and a society completely transformed by ideas and evolution. But the actual communes of the 1970s (as they have been throughout American history) were generally rural, small, under-capitalized and voluntary in membership. This stimulated a mobile and unstable membership. More important, it tended to focus attention on the problems of hand, heart, and hierarchy which characterize the communes of this period.

Hand: A great many, if not most of these intentional communities, whatever their ideological provenance, were founded upon the premise of maintaining a self-sufficient agriculture or handicraft industry. Many were located on farms in upstate New England, New York, the Appalachians, or California, Oregon, and Washington. Whether they called themselves Bellamyite or Skinneresque, the work and financial reward system was based in agriculture or craft. In fact, most of these communities sought out agricultural work because of the close relationship of labor to physical, psychological, and social rewards. At the same time, the visibility, rhythms, and transparency of agricultural work and the craft industry limited the range of social experimentation that could be attempted.

Heart: The agrarian-based commune lent itself to different sorts of social systems, but primarily those in which productive labor was a central feature. Communal cooking, canning, and eating became ritualized zones in communities that produced their food cooperatively. Agricultural and craft work were both visibly related to communal living possibilities and illustrative of non-alienated work. As alternatives to the bureaucratic, consumer society surrounding them, they demonstrated a direct relationship between labor and life, something that a great many literary utopias and communal experiments had recommended for centuries. Here, with honest labor and in cooperation with nature, men and women could husband and share the fruits of their labor.

Hierarchy: While the hand and the heart could be united in communal work, providing a basis for the exchange of hand-made goods and cooperative living, questions of hierarchy and social order loomed large (and often disrupted) many utopian schemes. Even on such a small scale, the design of obligations, responsibilities, incentives, and organization preoccupied many communes. Rural utopias did not run automatically and, with a peripatetic and unstable membership, they could scarcely shut themselves off from the rest of society. Thus some sort of voluntary subordination was necessary: to an idea, a group, or an individual. What rendered most of these communities volatile was the inability of members to make or keep such commitments, to submit to the social and psychological designs and experiments of their founders. Problems were resolved in a great many ways: some by the collapse of the experiment; some by intensely democratic procedures; some by commitment to an ideal or a spiritual leader; some by a powerful personality.

An illustration of the ideas and contradictions that bore down upon the communes of the 1960s and 1970s can be illustrated in the long-running Walden II experiment at Twin Oaks in Louisa, Virginia. Founded in 1967, Twin Oaks was established to try out the ideas expressed by B. F. Skinner in his novel. As Kathleen Kinkade, one of the original founders, wrote, the effort was to create a society "where every member does what he ought just because he wants to" (a phrase that could be the motto for a great many utopias). Based on Skinner's theories of an orderly, cooperative society, which in turn rested upon special child-rearing techniques, Twin Oaks actually had few children in residence. Its membership turned over quickly. As one observer wrote, "Throughout my communal travels, I was always bumping into someone who had either visited or been one of Twin Oaks' many short-term members."[31]

---

31. Kathleen Kinkade, *A Walden Two Experiment: The First five Years of Twin Oaks Community*, B. F. Skinner, Foreword (New York, 1973), 57; Houriet, *Getting Back Together*, 279.

Deeply self-conscious of its social utopian heritage, Twin Oaks named its buildings after famous communitarian experiments: Farmhouse, Llano, Oneida, Harmony, and so on. It instituted a manager system of government and elaborate means to diffuse conflict through extended group "rap" and feedback sessions. But, unlike literary utopias, Skinner's included, where one could envision elaborate social schemes, Twin Oaks spent most of its energy in creating a self-sufficient agriculture and a handicraft industry making hammocks. At the same time, members struggled with personal relationships and a variety of work-disciplinary schemes designed to facilitate communal living. Almost immediately, most of Skinner's blueprints were discarded or relegated to a minor role. That the society still existed in 1999 is testimony to the will of some of its leaders, the constant infusion of new members, and a combination of tolerance and orderliness. Skinner's social utopia, however, could hardly be detected.[32] Instead, in its short history, the commune reflected a variety of causes and popular-culture fads passed through the community by its new members. Utopia had porous boundaries with the society it sought to abandon or reform. Twin Oaks could not maintain its isolation nor freeze time, process, and change.

Considered over the twentieth century, social utopianism consists of complex and interrelated literary and community-founding traditions. It manifests a history filled with diverse experiments which were nonetheless regularly linked together by a common form of experience that could be found in even the most specialized religious, ethnic, and social communities. Despite the grand-scale thinking of Bellamy, Howells, Donnelly, and a host of turn-of-the-century speculators, most of the modern utopian experiments remained resolutely agricultural and small. As time passed, this predominant agricultural model became more and more a retreat into isolation and a vision of the past as utopia, not the future. As always, intentional communities refracted American culture and society in fascinating ways. In the largest sense, they could be

---

32. Kinkade, *A Walden Two Experiment*, passim. See also, Tamara Jones, "Paradise Sought," *Washington Post Magazine* (November 15, 1998), pp. 13ff.

considered both critical of and refuges from the persistent, self-proclaimed utopianism of American society itself – its own millennial pretensions and claims to perfectionism. They were, and are, a constant reminder of the failures of that national utopian vision and, at the same time, an irrepressible attempt to fulfill its blueprints.

2
Broken Utopias: Visions of the Social Order in Modern Germany

Paul Nolte

I

Utopia is, as the Greek word says, a place in nowhere, a land that can never be reached. And yet, people have invented and imagined utopias not only as mere theoretical experiments in philosophy and politics, or for reasons of literary entertainment, but as a way of giving their own present world a direction toward an idealized future. While in modern times the fascination of science and technology has often served as a starting point for utopian plans, the classical subject, the core theme of "utopia" since Plato has remained in the realm of politics and society. Utopia provided visions for a better, or even perfect, order of social life and its political organization – often, indeed, for a sort of communitarian social life in which all political organization was rendered unnecessary. Modern blueprints for a utopian social order, especially since the nineteenth century, often adopted a central idea from technical-scientific visions of the future, namely the idea that there were no limits to knowledge and to the capability of mankind to devise its own future.[1] Utopia could be reached on this earth and perhaps in one's own lifetime. On the other hand, utopian visions of the future were often fused with religious visions of a transcendent future, and thus they assumed qualities of a secularized chiliastic, or millenarian, project.

1. Cf. Martin Schwonke, *Vom Staatsroman zur Science Fiction. Eine Untersuchung über Geschichte und Funktion der naturwissenschaftlich-technischen Utopie.* Stuttgart, 1957. This essay outlines some of the arguments I have treated in more detail in my *Die Ordnung der deutschen Gesellschaft. Geschichte und Selbstbeschreibung im 20. Jahrhundert* (Habilitationsschrift, Bielefeld, 1999).

275

There were at least two ways in which a social utopia, from the vantage point of an unsatisfactory present social order, could be imagined. One idea was not to change society at large, but to start "here and now," surrounded by an "evil" society, with small islands of self-reliant utopian communities. We learn about aspects of this approach in James Gilbert's essay on social utopias in modern America. I will, however, concern myself with the second, more general, and also somewhat more diffuse, approach: the idea that society as a whole had to be overcome in its basic structural features in order to reach a quasi-utopian state of social harmony and community. This vision has figured very prominently in German social thought and social perceptions during the nineteenth and twentieth centuries, and we have to go back to the very origins of German "society" at the beginning of the nineteenth century to be able to understand and further trace this vision. Although the word "society" was not new then, it acquired new meanings when social structures were being radically transformed. People noticed the emergence of a new, all-encompassing entity of social relations which they designated as "the society", as "*die*" *Gesellschaft* (with the definite article).

Let me mention three structural preconditions for this emergence and invention of society, particularly since the 1830s and 1840s: First of all, horizons of social contact and communication widened. Where formerly the boundaries of the village or small town where one lived constituted the limits of individual experience and were seldom transgressed, these "island communities" (Robert Wiebe) now started to break up ever more rapidly; new loyalties were built which stretched out to the far horizons of a German "nation." People read newspapers, they traveled by train, and (somewhat later) began to move across large distances to live in one of the fast-growing urban agglomerations like the Ruhr or Berlin. Second, a profound economic crisis before and during early industrialization destroyed the older estate-system of vertical patron–client relationships for good. In what contemporaries called "Pauperismus," a poor under-class emerged whose members were no longer integrated into personal dependency; they formed a distinct group, a horizontal layer at the bottom of society; a group, moreover, which seemed to develop from a diffuse "crowd" to a self-conscious proletariat. "Society" became visible as a hierarchical order of groups, as a structure of groups primarily bound together by a common economic origin and occupation.

That structure, third, increasingly came to be seen as a relatively autonomous sphere, as distinct, in particular, from the political order of the "state." In older nations, these two realms of the political and the social world had usually been closely knit together; now, in the middle of the nineteenth century, they seemed to come apart. Long before the founding of a nation-state in 1871, German states like Prussia had evolved into complex bureaucratic structures which conceived of themselves as standing "above" the whole array of the newly crystallizing social groups; and at the same time these groups, especially the liberal middle classes, preferred the image of standing distinct from the monarchical state. They were proud to have reserved for themselves a sphere not quite free from politics, but free from the state. That was what Hegel tried to express by his idea of a *bürgerliche Gesellschaft*, a civil society as a new intermediate sphere between the older orders of the family and the state. While liberals insisted on, and exaggerated, the autonomy of "society," conservatives tried to reunify the two under the clear primacy of the state. Since then, for more than a hundred years the "division between state and society" has been a major concern of German intellectuals. Whatever the ideological vantage point, "state" and "society" were hard to conceive of as being at ease with each other.

Be it as an intellectual construction or as an institutional reality – society emerged, to sum up, as what we basically still understand today by the *Gesellschaft*: the comprehensive social system on a national scale, somewhat apart from the state, internally structured into hierarchical positions that tend to cluster into more or less discernible social layers or groups. If this were the whole story, I might as well stop here. But the complicated history of German "society" was just beginning in the mid-nineteenth century. In at least two respects, there was more to the emergence of society than a concept or set of social structures, and that, among other things, makes our story complex and fascinating. Together with society, a whole new science was born, the science of society, *Gesellschafts-*

wissenschaft or, as it later came to be called, *Soziologie*. It has even been argued that the whole notion of society has been an invention and construction by the proponents of this new science in order to give legitimacy to their scholarly endeavors. While this may be too radical a view, there is no doubt that from its very inception social science has managed to influence and shape visions and concepts of society within the society at large. Social scientists have often dug the channels within which common understandings of the social world could then flow. On the other hand, what social scientists believed to be a purely scientific discourse, a growth of "objective" knowledge about society, on closer inspection turns out to be a reflection of much broader social processes and mental projections in modern Germany.

"Mental projections" – this phrase hints at the utopian qualitities in the perception of the social order in Germany in the nineteenth and twentieth centuries which this essay will pay particular attention to. "Society" was not just a descriptive concept for any presently given social structure. It also opened up horizons of social expectation, of desires and anxieties for the future. The notion of society assumed utopian qualities; it served to bridge the gap between the "no longer" and the "not yet" of one's social conditions. As sociologist Niklas Luhmann has argued, since about 1800 the "impossibility of adequately describing the new structures of modern society was compensated for by projections of the future".[2] German society emerged at a time of crisis and upheaval. It was born into an order of obviously harsh inequalities and conflicts which hardly anybody could conceive of as a stable and morally welcome arrangement for the decades or even centuries to come. Liberals in the middle of the nineteenth century, for example, held up their vision of a classless middling society against the realities of class formation and increasing social distances: a vision that at the same time drew upon the memory of a more stable order in the past and framed an ideal for a better order in the future. This remained an important

---

2. Niklas Luhmann, "Die Beschreibung der Zukunft", in Luhmann, *Beobachtungen der Moderne* (Opladen, 1992), 129–147, esp. 133.

and, as we shall see, consequential feature of German society up to the mid-twentieth century: Germans were never quite satisfied with their social order; their society seemed to lack a present; and this restlessness opened up room for dangerous utopias of a better, more stable, more homogeneous world. It was a world that could not be attained from within present society, by means of reform or gradual change; but rather by a great revolutionary breakthrough, by stepping out of, or getting "beyond," society.

II

Toward the end of the nineteenth century, it became increasingly clear that Germany, like other industrial nations during this time, was moving farther away from this vision of a simple and pacified society rather than coming close to its fulfillment. The memories of a pre-industrial past were vanishing, and people realized that society would not work as a civic association, as a *bürgerlicher Verein* with its ideal of *Eintracht*, or "harmony," on a larger scale. Thus, beneath the overarching, holistic vision of society, representations of disorder and difference, of social fissures and cleavages came to dominate the decades around 1900. These social images in the late nineteenth and early to mid-twentieth century were focussed on two major ideas, on two sets of perceptions, arguments, etc. that can be traced throughout this period and among different, even antagonistic, social groups and milieus. They can be summarized as the ideas of "class society" (*Klassengesellschaft*) on the one hand, and of "mass society" (*Massengesellschaft*) on the other hand.

The notion of a "class society," of course, referred to the division of the people into two or more sharply distinguished groups, whose existence and identity was based on the availability of economic resources, especially on those resources of financial and industrial capital which Karl Marx termed the "means of production." Originally, the idea of *soziale Klassen* was a rather loose and flexible concept that drew attention to the variety and pluralism of groups in a society no longer fixed into the rigid caste-like bounds of honor and lifestyle; and in many countries, the concept of class – or rather, "classes" in plural – retained this meaning in everyday as well as in social scientific use until today – think, for example, of the United States. In Germany, however, in the middle of the nineteenth century the notion of class turned into something more specific, into a more rigid category of social description, a category that more and more came to resemble the older ideas of estate or caste. When speaking of "class society," one was not so much thinking of a pluralism of groups competing for their chances on a free market, but of a system of social positions that was fixed and that people were born into for life. Also, the pluralism of many classes increasingly turned into a sharp dichotomy, into the highly polarized image of a bourgeois upper class and a proletarian lower class which were aggressively competing not just for social or cultural "hegemony" in society, but for its very center of political power, for a hold on its political and state institutions.

This perception was closely linked to Marxism and its rise as the official ideology of a particularly strong socialist labor movement in Germany. But it was not just the political leaders of organized labor who subscribed to the notion of a society deeply split into two antagonistic classes one of which, the proletariat, would eventually tear its chains apart, overthrow the bourgeoisie and its state, and erect the regime of egalitarian communism. Though ideologically less elaborated, a large part of the rank-and-file was also committed to this view of society and indeed clung to it as a sort of last hope in a life of misery and oppression from which no other escape seemed possible. By the end of the nineteenth century, the German labor movement had locked itself into this almost religious vision of an evil present world that was only to be overcome by a revolutionary breakthrough into the "otherworldy" future of a classless society.[3] This is not to put moral blame on German industrial workers and their political organizations in the nineteenth century. They had good reasons to view German society the way they did. The gap between the classes was indeed widening; it was increasingly difficult for an individual to leave the class of his or her social origin;

---

3. Cf. Lucian Hölscher, *Weltgericht oder Revolution. Protestantische und sozialistische Zukunftsvorstellungen im deutschen Kaiserreich* (Stuttgart, 1989).

and, moreover, German class structure was reinforced by politics: it was not just a matter of socio-economic difference, but of political distinctions, a matter of belonging or not belonging to the core political society of Imperial Germany to which socialists were denied access.

However, the labor movement grew strong enough to influence deeply the perceptions of society within the bourgeoisie and the upper and middle classes in general. In a somewhat ironic adaptation of their enemy's beliefs, the bourgeoisie also took over the image of a split, a dualistic society, including the conviction that this extreme polarization could not possibly persist as a stable order for a longer period of time. Social reformers strove to alleviate social differences by uplifting the poor, thereby hoping to get rid of their revolutionary political ambitions, but many well-to-do people in Germany around 1900, though they might at first glance feel secure in their own suburbs, miles away from a largely invisible industrial working class, deeply feared an overthrow of social and political conditions, the "Grosser Kladderadatsch" of a socialist revolution. In the twentieth century, and especially in the years of the Weimar Republic, many developments in politics and society betrayed this view of an ever-growing class rift. Some of the industrial workers were faring better in economic terms and no longer resembled the Marxist vision of a proletariat that had "nothing to lose but its chains." In the republic, the working class gained access to many formerly restricted preserves of political power. A new middle class of office employees was growing fast, especially in large cities like Berlin, and refuted the widespread notion of the vanishing "middle" in German society. However, the perception of a deeply divided society, which was somehow doomed to a final breakup out of which a new order would emerge, grew even stronger and more radical in the 1920s. Left-wing and right-wing ideologies now tried to capitalize on the fears of this coming catastrophe by promises of a more harmonious, less conflict-ridden, communitarian social order.

The second problem, the second major idea of social disunity and, indeed, fragmentation in the nineteenth and twentieth centuries, crystallized around the concept of the "masses." This concept, too, underwent an important transformation. In the first half of the nineteenth century, it did not refer to any (visible) great number of people, but served as a category of social description that marked the new industrial underclass as a strange and foreign element from the point of view of the middle classes; it was roughly equivalent with the *Pöbel*, the crowd. Toward the end of the century, however, "mass" tended to be perceived not as a particular group, but as an overall state of society that concerned every individual. With the enormous growth of population, with the breakup of traditional regional identities, with a burgeoning spatial mobility and a massive concentration of people in the big cities and urban areas, a feeling was growing that people's identities were losing their significance and individuality; that people were becoming uniform and inter-changeable; and that society was losing any clear structure that told people where they belonged. Instead, they were just grains of sand drifting around without ever being able to build secure relationships with one another. Whereas with the notion of "class society" people mourned a too rigid social structure, they equally feared a total loss of hierarchy and order in a society of "masses." The key phrase here was the *Nivellierung* of society, the leveling of all differences in which the individuality of persons, this great bourgeois project of the eighteenth and nineteenth centuries, would forever be lost.

The diagnosis of mass society often contained a paradox. There were too many people crowded together in a limited space – like the thousands of shoppers streaming through the large inner-city department stores – and yet they were lonely, they were desperately lacking social contacts because they lost sight of each other just seconds after their eyes had met. Drawing on his own experience with Berlin city life at the turn of the century, the sociologist Georg Simmel described this tension between individualism and mass uniformity in modern urban society.[4] On the one hand, he was fascinated by the mechanisms of this depersonalized world (how could society still work although people were complete strangers to most other people?); on the other hand, there was a deep uneasiness with these observations. They expressed forces beyond

4. Georg Simmel, "Die Großstädte und das Geistesleben" (1903), in Simmel, *Das Individuum und die Freiheit. Essais* (Frankfurt, 1993), 192–204.

the influence of man, anonymous, inescapable forces of mechaniza-
tion and organization in a world increasingly dominated by technical
imperatives, as Walther Rathenau put it in his "Zur Kritik der Zeit"
in 1912.[5] Why was this "mass society" so hard to bear? Instead of
getting used to it, instead of understanding its rules and its possible
coexistence with individualism, freedom, and hierarchy, the idea of
mass society was radicalized in a very paradoxical way in the first
decades of the twentieth century: While fear of the masses was
growing, so was their attractiveness when they were turned into
ordered masses in which one could freely give up one's individuality
and be put under the command of a "Führer".

III

While the state of their society seemed more and more fragile,
Germans searched for order and harmony in their social affairs;
they longed for closely-knit bonds that would supersede the large
structures of social anonymity; they looked for social relationships
in which a firm and stable position was attributed to every individual.
This "desire for unity" was expressed in different ways by different
social groups and organizations. The working class, as we have already
seen, hoped for a homogeneous classless society in the future and
otherwise tried to compensate for the disparate and diffuse reality
by building up a network of community and neighborhood
associations within the limits of its own class. Middle-class Germans,
of course, rejected the notion of a proletarian revolution, or whatever
else might lead to an egalitarian society in which they would lose
some of their status and economic well-being. Instead, they clung
to notions of a well-ordered society that would in other ways help
to overcome class fragmentation and the breakup of traditional
communal relations into mere isolated individuals. In the late
nineteenth and early twentieth centuries, social scientists increasingly
supported this search for a new order by rejecting the early

5. Walther Rathenau, "Zur Kritik der Zeit" (1912), in Rathenau, *Gesammelte
Schriften*, vol. 1 (Berlin, 1925), 7–148.

nineteenth-century liberal ideal of "society" as being too rational, artificial, and "unorganic"; as unable to describe and cope with social problems of modern life in Germany. Instead, they brought concepts of social relationships to the fore that favored a tranquil, "natural," a conflict-free building-up of personal social ties and larger institutions. Let us take a closer look at some of these concepts.

Upper- and middle-class people, including social scientists, understandably did not conceive of social homogeneity as an egalitarian, undifferentiated order – there had to be hierarchy in society, but not in the form of a highly polarized class system that was defined in purely economic terms. Rather, difference should be expressed through a multiplicity of groups defined by their specific functional uses for society as a whole. The traditional concept for this in Germany was the social estate, the *Stand*. During the nineteenth century, the "language of Stand" in Germany, despite the rise of "class"-based notions of society, had never been abandoned, but continued to play a major role in liberal and conservative thought. However, support for a *Ständegesellschaft*, especially in the first decades of the twentieth century, did not imply a return to the simple structures of pre-industrial, agrarian estate society, and certainly not a return to the early-modern concept of *Stand* as a relational quality rather than a social group. The idea of *Stand* proved to be very flexible; it came to refer to occupational groups as functional parts within the whole body of society – the so-called *Berufsstände*, remnants of which still linger today in the ideology of some German academic professions such as lawyers and physicians. These *Stände* were meant to be modern, highly specialized groups which, unlike classes, did not compete with each other for political power in a distasteful class struggle, but kept their place in a society that was envisioned as a great machine with the gearing together of its different parts.

A second, equally important concept within that larger desire for unity and order was the idea of "community", or *Gemeinschaft*. It provided an answer not so much, like *Stand*, to the question of a legitimate and stable differentiation of society, but to the larger, and at the same time more personal, problem of the loss of close and intimate bonding in urban society with its mushrooming population and its multiplication of the social roles an individual had to assume. Whereas *Gemeinschaft* had long been a rather unspecified concept, related to many forms of more or less institutionalized social togetherness in smaller groups, it acquired a new and more precise meaning toward the end of the nineteenth century. On the one hand, the notion of community was now built into a larger concept of social development; it became part of a historical process from a more simple, more natural, "community"-like social organization to the more rational, more complex and technical world of modern "society." Some saw this with cold eyes as a change that could not be valued as either "good" or "bad," but there was a growing propensity to view this shift from community to society as a decline, as a loss that had to be mourned, and as a process that had to be reversed if at all possible. On the other hand, *Gemeinschaft* was now seen not just as a type of close social relationship within a larger society that also comprised more complex types of institutions and organizations, but increasingly came to express an alternative to society at large. The whole of society might then be structured as a community, as a network of close contacts and affective bonding. This expanded vision of community leaned heavily toward a pseudo-egalitarian, conformistic model of society.

The sharp distinction between community and society, with a preference for the first, is commonly attributed to the German sociologist Ferdinand Tönnies and his 1887 book on "*Gemeinschaft* and *Gesellschaft.*" But it would be too easy to blame a single person for a very complex and multi-dimensional change in social perceptions that occurred, on many different but interconnected levels, from social science to a broader *bildungsbürgerlich* thought, and to even more diffuse moods and anxieties of common people. The same was true for other concepts or arguments related to the social order that rose to prominence around 1900 or shortly thereafter – for example, the idea of *Bund*, almost impossible to translate into English: a special type of close and affectionate (also: very particularly male) bonding that originated with the German Youth Movement (*Jugendbewegung*) in the beginning of the twentieth century and was later also adopted in social scientific vocabulary. Overall, as these examples show very clearly, the inclination was to "soften" the harsh realities of modern society by turning to romantic and organicist notions of the social order.

In the brief period of the Weimar Republic, there was no relief from the social tensions so intensely felt by many Germans; there was no turning away from those mental projections of a somewhat irrational social unity I have just described in favor of a more "realistic" understanding of the social necessities and requirements of a pluralistic, urban, and industrial society. On the contrary, the concepts of *Stand, Gemeinschaft,* and so forth gained even more influence. They dominated the "social language" in Germany in the 1920s to a degree that they were almost indisputable; and at the same time, they were radicalized: The cry for a social order became more desperate and often assumed prophetic qualities. In part, this was because of the experience of World War I, the bitter political struggles in the first years of Weimar, and an important generational sentiment that I cannot further discuss here. The search for community found a new catchword in the ideal of the *Volksgemeinschaft*: a society in which the bitter cleavages of class and ideology would be bridged by an overarching consciousness of togetherness and cooperation. This was by no means a Nazi invention. As early as 1920, the *Volksgemeinschaft* was very popular with both Social Democrats and Liberals; ironically, it started its career as a sort of unofficial social ideology of the republican and leftist forces; for the conservatives, it carried too much egalitarianism to be considered an attractive concept.

Thus, in the 1920s and early 1930s there was hardly a group, a school of thought, or whatever to be found in Germany that insisted on the "older" vision of society as it had originated in the early nineteenth century: as a complex, pluralistic and, indeed, conflict-ridden network of social groups and positions that may at times alienate individuals, but also renders possible their freedom from both the state and other people. The social sciences, which around 1900 had, at least in parts, been a mainstay of a sober and critical view of society, now also succumbed to the general desire for harmony and homogeneous unity. The famous book by Karl Mannheim on *Ideology and Utopia,* published in 1929, sought to establish a methodology for criticizing "false" beliefs on social structure and social development, but in the end failed to establish an alternative path to social changes that might have been grounded in social practice and reform rather than in social thought.[6] His colleague Hans Freyer, a young right-wing sociologist, like many of his contemporaries in the 1920s and 1930s, believed the "industrial society" of the present to be only a transitional stage that had to be overcome by voluntaristic action in the name of "utopian" political programs.[7] In the Third Reich, the long-grown dreams of a classless society and *Volksgemeinschaft* were indeed turned into a political program with disastrous results. What is the idea of "society" good for? It is interesting to see that some Nazi intellectuals not only strove dramatically to change German society, but tried to get rid of the term *Gesellschaft* itself. It was to be, as the young professor of law Ernst Rudolf Huber demanded, extinguished from socio-political language.[8] *Gesellschaft* still contained memories of a free and voluntary order that were now no longer welcome.

IV

It may seem obvious that things changed dramatically after 1945, after the experience of Nazism. But this was not at all clear. Nazi social ideology, including the dismissal of class cleavages and class struggle and the call for a homogeneous and orderly *Volksgemeinschaft*, had been attractive to many people, and one could assume that it had a lasting impact on the German mentality; indeed, that it may even have strengthened belief in a well-regulated, organic system of social order. Even the most radical opposition to Nazi ideology could in the end find itself trapped in the very same problem. In East Germany, the utopia of a race-based *Volksgemeinschaft* was quickly succeeded by the new utopia of a class-based socialism in which class differences would eventually be overcome in an egalitarian

---

6. Karl Mannheim, *Ideologie und Utopie* (Bonn, 1929).

7. Hans Freyer, *Einleitung in die Soziologie* (Leipzig, 1931), 143, 148f.

8. Ernst Rudolf Huber, "Die deutsche Staatswissenschaft," *Zeitschrift für die gesamte Staatswissenschaft* 95 (1935), 1–65, esp. 46.

and harmonious order that finally fulfilled the promises resulting from nineteenth-century dissatisfaction with modern industrial society. This last grand illusion of a better future society only ended in 1989.

In West Germany, things were more complicated and slower to develop. As for other realms of social and cultural development, there was not a sudden new beginning in an "hour zero," a "Stunde Null," in 1945 in regard to thinking about society either. As we are currently learning about important historians like Theodor Schieder and Werner Conze, intellectual elites whose concepts and opinions had been shaped by Nazi thought, or who themselves had been spokesmen for Nazi ideology, continued to be influential at least through the 1950s, and some – not all – of them at least for some time relied on the concepts and patterns of thought they had grown up with. However, the 1950s and 1960s witnessed a radical shift, a major transformation in the way Germans conceived of their society and of their own position within it. Once again, this shift occured in a triangular relationship between the social structure and "reality" of West Germany; popular notions about how society should be organized; and the development of social scientific concepts and interpretations that tried to make sense of this new society. This time, however, German sociology turned out to be a vanguard of a new image of society. The concept of *Gesellschaft* became a key phrase in the public discourse of the Federal Republic, not as a matter of contempt, but in an emphatically positive way – many years before 1968 and the rise of the social-democratic era, by the way. It was certainly, if perhaps unconsciously, used by sociologists in an attempt to win public recognition for their professional activities and scholarship, but it also trickled down into wider, popular notions of society, into the *Gesellschaftsbilder*, as they were then called, and helped make West Germans feel at ease with their society rather than trying to step out of it. Also, since Germany was divided, the population of the Federal Republic could no longer be referred to as a *Volk* or *Nation*, and *Gesellschaft* came to be a very successful substitute for these competing concepts of social entity.

Until about 1955, however, uncertainty prevailed in many respects, not least as part of the often desperate economic and social conditions of the immediate postwar years. Millions of fugitives and expellees from the East, for example, had to find shelter and jobs and struggled with cultural assimilation. It seemed to many observers as though society now had completely lost its coherence and was tumbling into chaos. This was a good occasion to speak of social disorganization once more, of the danger posed by the anonymous "masses," and to remind people of the possibly more stable structures of a *Stände*-society. Yet arguments presented in that older language of cultural criticism hardly caught on any more in a wider public. They were even explicitly rejected. In a somewhat naive but very serious personal experiment, the German émigré sociologist Theodor Geiger kept a diary of all his personal contacts over several months (including talks with his family as well as a quick "Hello" to the mailman), only to prove that modern society was in fact not anonymous, but was still firmly grounded in contacts with people one was closely related to.[9] In the same vein, others argued against long-standing anti-urban attitudes in Germany by claiming that the *Großstädter*, the inhabitants of big cities, were not as "lonely" as had formerly been maintained. What is striking about these conceptual changes is that they were not limited to the political left, including radical liberalism, but stretched out into conservative thought, too, and thus gradually but decisively transformed conserva-tive, *bildungsbürgerliche* German ideology. This, in turn, was part of a larger shift in German conservatism in the early decades of the Federal Republic, when conservatism abandoned some of its most fundamental anti-modern attitudes. Some intellectuals – although they were not setting the tone any more – still clung to their descriptions of society as a "mass society" governed by "technical" imperatives, but they no longer believed in a future alternative social order and instead accepted the present as the destiny, the *Schicksal* of modern man, as it was often called.

But what, we may ask, did the society look like that Germans now envisioned? It was a society with some social differences, a society in which some people were better off than others, and yet a

---

9. Cf. Theodor Geiger, *Demokratie ohne Dogma: Die Gesellschaft zwischen Pathos und Nüchternheit* (Munich, 1963).

society that was no longer torn apart, no longer in danger of being radically polarized into the extremely rich and the extremely poor and thereby losing its solid middle. Changes in working-class attitudes and in the ideology of the labor movement also contributed to this. The workers were no longer the destitute poor, but aspired to middling positions themselves. It is true that they often continued to hold a somewhat "dichotomous" view of society ("We down here – they up there"), but it was no longer the highly ideological image of classes and class struggles that had prevailed in the nineteenth and early twentieth centuries. The labor movement definitely abandoned Marxism, and with it, the leftist variety of a potentially anti-democratic utopian egalitarianism came to an almost complete end. As early as 1953, only a very few years into the Federal Republic, when the *Wirtschaftswunder* and the social changes accompanying it were just beginning, the sociologist Helmut Schelsky ingeniously coined the phrase of the "nivellierte Mittelstandsgesellschaft," or leveled-down middle-class society, as a description of the emerging West German society.[10]

Actually, it was less a description of reality than a beacon for the future. The phrase quickly caught on, and it became something of a mental pacifier for the notorious nervousness of German society. If you were not yet part of the middle, you would certainly be able to get there in the near future; and in any case you could be sure that society was not about to break apart, that it was not dominated by centrifugal forces, but that it was gravitating toward the middle. It has been argued that the idea of "nivellierte Mittelstandsgesellschaft" was just a rephrasing of the *Volksgemeinschaft* idea under democratic auspices, especially since Schelsky himself, much like the historians Schieder and Conze, had sympathized with Nazism in his early career. There is probably some truth to that – not so much with regard to a personal continuity in Schelsky's thought, but rather when we look at the eager reception of his idea, which seemed to prove a continuing desire for social tranquility and

---

10. Helmut Schelsky, "Die Bedeutung des Schichtungsbegriffs für die Analyse der gegenwärtigen deutschen Gesellschaft" (1953), in Schelsky, *Auf der Suche nach Wirklichkeit*. (Düsseldorf, 1965), 331–336.

homogeneity in Germany. Then again, it looked more like a successful tranformation, because the "nivellierte Mittelstandsgesell-schaft" as well as other, similarly conceived descriptions of West German society did not imply an anti-liberal political ideology any more. They were free from politics and centered on what many West Germans in the 1950s and 1960s were most interested in: their economic well-being through mass consumption. And also, those models were basically images of the present. They were not referring to a better utopia for which society had to undergo the ordeal of destruction. Instead, as Ralf Dahrendorf put it in the late 1950s, "Pfade aus Utopia," paths out of utopia, had been devised with regard to images of society. "Utopia" as a political and intellectual program of a classless society, of a better and more harmonious, more communitarian order, for Dahrendorf only ended in terrorism and serfdom.[11] "Society" thus became self-evident; it did not arouse anxieties any more.

VI

This is all history, and why should we care about it today, as Germans and, especially, as non-Germans? One might even argue that the "strange career of German society," the invention of a concept of society and its subsequent transformations, is reason enough *not* to touch on this subject any more. In seems that German intellectuals in particular have, over the course of much of the nineteenth and twentieth centuries, been almost obsessed with their society. Over many generations, they have spent a lot of energy in thinking about it; they have suffered from the supposed deficiencies of the social order in a rapidly changing world; and they have suggested cures and remedies that turned out to be a very bitter medicine for Germany and beyond. So again: may we not be happy that this has finally come to an end; should we not go ahead and close the dossier on German society?

11. Cf. Ralf Dahrendorf, "Pfade aus Utopia. Zu einer Neuorientierung der soziologischen Analyse", in id., *Gesellschaft und Freiheit* (Munich, 1961), 85–111.

And yet we still can't evade German society – not just because the past weighs heavily upon us and will have to be remembered by future generations – this is the usual pathos-laden talk one would expect from a historian anyway, because otherwise his would be a useless profession. No, I'm thinking rather of the continuing presence of "society" today, in the late twentieth century. We still live in, and cannot step out of, a world made of social contacts and social organizations. We live in a world of social differences and social hierarchy, and we problably do need some categories, some concepts, some *Begriffe* of both unity and hierarchy, identity and difference, in order to describe and understand the world in which we live. In German public and political language during the past decades, it has become very difficult to openly address social differences in categories of "class" or even the more flexible, less ideological *Schichten*. Instead, a language of euphemism prevails. We hear about the *Besserverdienende* (the better-earners) or, even more subtle, the *Leistungsträger* (achievers), instead of talking about the upper or upper middle class; we refer to the *Sozialhilfeempfänger* (welfare recipients) or the *sozial Schwächere* (socially weaker), instead of speaking of a "lower class" or a new "underclass." The language of horizontally layered inequality that prevailed for a long time in Germany now almost sounds obscene.

On the other hand, new descriptions of difference have gained public prominence since the 1980s, in response to changes in German society. When it turned out that the "nivellierte Mittelstandsgesellschaft" did not include everyone, but sorted out a large proportion of people who didn't make it to the security and affluence of the "middle", social scientists suggested the phrase *Zweidrittelgesellschaft*: a "two-thirds-society" of an inclusive majority, from which one third of society was distinctly and permanently excluded. (However, enormous differences within the great block of the two-thirds seem not to matter in this model.) And for a decade now, we have witnessed the rise and importance of a new "sectional" difference in German society, of a new dual split into the inhabitants of the "old" Federal Republic and the citizens of the former GDR, into "Wessis" and "Ossis." Sure enough, some who are not professional sociologists or historians will have heard about the *Risikogesellschaft*, or "risk society", in which we now live: a phrase coined by the sociologist Ulrich Beck some twelve years ago to point out the reduced significance of traditional inequalities at the expense of new risks and insecurities which are increasingly structuring our existence in both private family life and technology politics at the same time.

The way in which *Risikogesellschaft* has rapidly and extensively been taken over in public discourse hints at the fact that sociology – or at least a certain branch of it – still today, as in the times we've been looking at, retains an important function in developing and mediating interpretations of society for a wider public. But this close connection between social scientific concepts and social understandings in larger groups, or society as a whole, also continues to work the other way round. Although one could expect sociology to become increasingly detached from specific influences of a particular society (with its increasing professionalization and its supposed "inner logic" of theoretical progress), grand visions of social theory like the works of Jürgen Habermas and Niklas Luhmann are very much a mirror of current social movements and cultural tendencies in Germany. Habermas' distinction between the aggressive and alienating "systems" of power and economy on the one hand, and the calmer, communicative life-world as society's "Kuschelecke" (cuddling corner) on the other hand is easy to relate to widespread moods and perceptions in large parts of the West German population in the 1980s; and similar things could be said about Luhmann's cold-blooded theory of social systems and their functional differentiation. From the vantage point of the audience, all this is indicative of a continuing desire in society for its self-description, for a mental and semantic map of its structure and identity.

If it may thus be impossible to get rid of society, our historical excursion has also demonstrated how dangerous in political terms any attempt to give up the notion of society can be. The "invention of society" in the early nineteenth century was, as we have seen, intimately linked not only to social differentiation and class formation, but also to the emergence of a private and public sphere that was free from political intervention by the state. The German dilemma often was to either insist on a strict separation of "state" and "society," and thereby depoliticize society, or to move society closer to the state, to have it shielded and guarded by the state to the point where it lost its autonomy; in other words: where individuals lost their personal freedom and political liberty to Leviathan. One could argue that in a democratic society, under democratic political institutions, this is no longer a danger to be feared. But history has shown that some notion of social unity or entity can hardly be circumvented, and alternatives like the *Volk* or the *Nation* have not proven particularly attractive in the past. Thus it seems that we still do need "society" because we need a conceptual capability for asserting difference and pluralism, and for maintaining individual liberties against the state.

Still, it may be asked whether the German concept of society is now in need of a fundamental revision. It may well be that it still carries too many *Altlasten*, too many relics from a now outdated past in its meaning and political implications. Is our idea of society not still too much fixed on socio-economic differences on the one hand, on the *völkisch* idea of a German national unity of blood on the other hand? Will we be able to integrate the current challenges of citizenship and cultural pluralism into the concept of society – or would we be better advised to relegate the idea of society to history and start anew with different concepts? But which? That is now the question.

Comment on Part Three: Thoughts on the National Peculiarities of Talking about Utopias

Martin H. Geyer

When Jimmy Carter became US President in 1976, his German counterpart, Helmut Schmidt, made no secret of his irritation, indeed of his disdain for the new administration. The German *Realpolitiker*, who conceived himself as a "crisis manager" not only at home but also on the level of international politics, clearly could not connect with the new President, whose language was so strongly imbued with an appeal to sentiments of religious brotherly love, to national and international rejuvenation, and to an international political order centered not on power but on human rights. It was neither the first nor the last time that Germans (and certainly not only Germans) found themselves bewildered by the political rhetoric coming from the United States, which evoked metaphors involving "frontiers," "new visions," the "rejuvenation" and "betterment" of the country. This rhetorical preoccupation with the future is not only strongly imbued with notions of a grand national heritage featuring universalistic pretensions, but also relies on a repertoire of authoritative quotes ranging from John Winthrop to Martin Luther King, from Thomas Jefferson to John F. Kennedy, and on an agrarian republican ethos of equality and justice popularized by Thomas Paine and William J. Bryan mixed with the promises of the latter-day saints of modern capitalism and consumerism like Andrew Carnegie, Henry Ford, and Milton Friedman.

It is against this deeply rooted and very vocal national heritage of notions of betterment, improvement, and perfectibility that James Gilbert argues. For Gilbert, both the fictional and the actually established utopian communities of modern America are but "heightened instances of common American themes and practices";

he understands them to be a "constant reminder of the failures of that national utopian vision and, at the same time, an irrepressible attempt to fulfill its blueprints." The proponents of utopian communities are depicted not as the nation's crackpots, fanatics, or outsiders. On the contrary, they represent almost the ideological core of American society, despite the fact that many of them retreated (and continue to retreat) from the mainstream of society. They are patriotic Americans, for they share widely valued notions of improvement and betterment. Even during the confrontation with Nazi Germany and the Cold War, the popular period for the dystopian novels of Aldous Huxley and George Orwell with their themes of totalitarian control over the mind and social life, there was a general feeling that utopian experiments were a genuine part of the American heritage, ambivalent as this heritage might have been considered at the time.

Paul Nolte tells an altogether different story. In his view, modern utopian thinking and utopian concepts and experiments posed a threat to civil liberties. More concretely, Nolte is concerned with how the concept of *Gesellschaft* was shaped and formed during the nineteenth century and the manner in which this concept was then challenged, if not attacked outright, in an effort to eradicate the idea in order instead "to reach a quasi-utopian state of social harmony and community." In this analysis, utopias are not a reminder of fulfilled or unfulfilled promises and possibilities, as is the case in James Gilbert's paper. Instead they are a warning, the writing on the wall. After all, German history in the twentieth century, overshadowed by both the Nazi and Communist dictatorships, appears more than anything else as a flight into utopian irrationality and anti-modernism, as a yearning for a sense of *Gemeinschaft* that was to replace modern notions of liberty, pluralism, and individualism, which are embodied, as Paul Nolte argues, in the original concept of *Gesellschaft*. It is the deviation from the original path, blazed in the nineteenth century, that led to the catastrophes of the twentieth century. And what would German history be without the Federal Republic? The spell is broken after the German Platos married Nato – at least this is how I understood "Broken Utopias," the title of the essay. German sociologists threw out their criticism of modern society, once expressed as the threat of the masses and class society, and embraced the concept of *Gesellschaft*. Schelsky's "nivellierte Mittelstandstandsgesellschaft" might still have been imbued with the desire for social tranquility and homogeneity – a yearning for a *Volksgemeinschaft* – yet the anti-modernist bias of an earlier generation of sociologists was something of the past and would no longer block Germany's path of modernity. It is noteworthy that these very same assumptions and fears lead Helmut Schmidt in the 1970s to criticize not only President Carter but even more so the socialist "utopian wing" of his own party and the doomsday-outlook of the then emerging "alternative" ecologist movement and the peace movement, both of which propagated different and new forms of social organization. The blossoming of utopianism seemed to threaten once more the liberal-democratic, capitalist society that had been successfully established after the Second World War.

These are two altogether contrary narratives which, however, each fit well into the established although contested grand narratives of their respective countries. Paul Nolte's argument demonstrates that German utopian thinking has lost its innocence, quite unlike its American counterpart. One reason may be that Germany's history in the twentieth century is closer to a dystopia than a utopia. This is not a theme among German fiction writers but among historians, an interesting fact that indeed deserves further inquiry. If we think with respect to Germany about the peculiar mixture of the religious and the secular, mentioned by Gilbert, then one parallel that comes to mind is the millennial and perfectionist legacies of Christian thinking and the "thousand years" of the Third Reich, including the religious forms in which its public staging took place and its pervasive cult of death (described so well by Sabine Behrenbeck). In the background lurks that not so blond Austrian, who saw himself as a "heroic realist," who despised what he decried as liberal, humanitarian, and socialist utopias, and who at the same time developed as early as the 1920s the outlines not only of a utopian future for Germany but also of a new man. The innumerable groups of reformers that organized at the end of the nineteenth century in order to better society and mankind from within – vegetarians, prohibitionists, city reformers, the eugenic movement, to name just a few – are not exactly the exponents of Paul Nolte's liberal society, and many of them did indeed fall under the spell of the *völkisch* movement. Whereas the proponents of urban greenbelts, garden cities, and industrial housing projects that thrived in Germany no less (if not far more) than in the United States might have radiated an aura of utopian innocence we can identify with, today "gated communities" most certainly evoke an altogether different association in Germany, namely that of a deathly utopia, than they do in the United States. Or take Edward Bellamy's *Looking Backward*, which tackled the primordial issues of family and community, money and authority, as well as production and consumption in a way that had always stood at the heart of utopian thinking and which was the model for many communities. Such communities of anarchists, land- and life-reformers existed also in Germany. Bellamy both puzzled and infatuated European socialists who, despite their political strength, were so poor in imagining a future society built on the new moral forms of consumption, non-monetary exchange, and social hierarchy which Bellamy describes so passionately (despite the fact that the leader of the Socialists, August Bebel, supposedly once asked Bismarck to give the Socialists one of the Prussian provinces so that they could make a model province out of it). Yet forty years of "funny-money," a rate of full employment that could not mask the deficiencies of the economic system, and a dictatorship that determined its people's needs based on older models of "virtuous consumption" – in other words, forty years of experience with the former German Democratic Republic – makes one read Bellamy far more critically than even the critics of his time or later ones who attacked his naivité and the potential oppressiveness of his ideas.

Striking is another aspect of the two papers, namely the altogether different evaluation of the communities. With astonishing self-confidence, Gilbert associates utopian communities with American heritage, thereby emphasizing the high degree of commonality between American utopian communities, both fictional and real, and the mainstream of American culture. Certainly one can argue that it is necessary to differentiate between the various types of communities, such as between the ideal communities of the world fairs and the experimental agricultural settlements, between those who aimed to reform society from within and those who fled society. As has often been argued, the rules of the latter are, after all, *not* those of the mainstream of American society, an issue of vital importance if one looks at the chances of failure or success. One can refer, among other things, to the denial of personal wealth, honor, power, money, and consumption, to the strong denial of individualism and the premium on conformity, and not least, to the denial of openness resulting from the screening of potential members. Undoubtedly this can be explained by reference to the rich tradition of religious dissent with its specific forms of closed in-group building, on the one hand, and the peculiar tradition of republican radicalism with its critique of some basic features of capitalism, on the other. Whether this puts many American utopian communities not at the periphery of society – at the end of the twentieth century even more so than at its beginning – is another question.

Nolte does not share Gilbert's self-confidence with regard to utopias or his positive picture of "communities," and one may wonder why Nolte sees *Gesellschaft* in such an unequivocally positive light. In part this has already been answered: *Gesellschaft* is for him by definition the harbinger of freedom and pluralism, and the various quotes he uses indeed illustrate how strongly the concept of *Gesellschaft* was associated with the liberal society of the nineteenth century both by its advocates as well as by its detractors. Juxtaposed to this were the self-proclaimed illiberal forms of *Gemeinschaft*. Ferdinand Tönnies' dichotomy between *Gemeinschaft* and *Gesellschaft* fell on fertile ground, even if his original intentions might have been misread. The ideological mobilization of World War I did its part to make this argument blossom. However, to understand the position taken by Nolte, it seems to me that one must also take into account the fierce debates in the late 1960s and 1970s, when the struggle over political terms became intense in Germany and when the concept of *Gesellschaft* became closely associated by its proponents with an emancipatory potential for social, political, and economic reform that some critics considered utopian itself.

The fundamental question is whether one should and can work with such an abstract, normative, and somewhat simplified concept of *Gesellschaft*, as does Nolte, in order to describe the grand design and, as he illustrates, the deficiencies of German intellectual history. The prevalent critique of the masses among sociologists at the time and their explicit or implicit notions of how to "reorder" society, combined with all the talk about the *Gemeinschaft* that was to replace the "mechanical society," should not obscure the fact that the crisis of society and politics in the interwar period brought forth these diagnoses. Instead of being described as a history of resentment and estrangement, it might better be understood as a crisis of knowledge and a crisis in conceptualizing modern society, which is, after all, not that foreign to the social sciences at the end of the twentieth century. Intellectually, it might be rewarding to compare the arguments of the sociologists with those of fiction writers who dealt in a very similar fashion with what appeared as the apories of contemporary mass-society.

But the German–American comparison might give us other clues. The German concept of *Gesellschaft* has an amazing power of defining conformity and unity with respect to rights, religion, behavior, and cultural norms, and much of the confusion that surrounds the flourishing of the language of *Volksgemeinschaft* after World War I has do with contested ideas of unifying this society. Perhaps my reasoning is wrong, but I am under the impression that it is exactly this somewhat underdeveloped concept of *Gesellschaft* in the American context that has always made and continues to make the flowering of utopian communities possible in the United States. They can spring up everywhere, sometimes in an isolated corner of the country, sometimes in the middle of society, although the case of Waco also illustrates the precarious line of any such experiment. To exaggerate the point a little: Within a *Gesellschaft,* utopias are for all of the members or for none. This might be seen first of all with respect to the radical claim of the eighteenth and nineteenth centuries that the *bürgerliche Gesellschaft*, that is, civil society (just as later the social state), was to encompass all the citizens. But this idea can also be seen with the difficulties of the established churches and the state in unison with its pedagogic apparatus to deal with what are in Germany not called "religious groups" but "sects," outsiders who fit badly into society. Leaving Germany has been for many the better avenue. Ethnicity is another case, not the least because of the high premium most nation-states and societies have always given to ethnic homogenity. And it should not astonish that some of the greatest utopias revolved around this issue: Theodor Herzl's *Judenstaat*, one of the great utopias of the early twentieth century which incorporated many aspects of Bellamy-like experiments and contemporary life reform, testifies to this, as does the utopia of creating a new, ethnically cleansed Germany propagated very early on in the speeches and the writings of Adolf Hitler.

Many other examples of utopian visions could be cited, such as the promises of consumption, Fordist rationalization, or the "wonders" of atomic energy. If there are many similarities between Germany and the United States, there are still many fundamental differences, and the experience with utopias, or more specifically with dystopias, is one of these. More than anything else this different experience sets the two countries apart.

Comment on Part Three: Comparative Views on Social Utopias in Germany and the United States

Ursula Lehmkuhl

One of the main purposes of the triennial "Krefeld Conferences" is to further comparative history. Structures, processes, or developments which are crucial for German and American history or which characterize a common German and American experience during specific historical periods are scrutinized not only with regard to national differences or the specificities of each nation's distinctive culture, its *Sonderweg* or exceptionalism, but to discuss junctures in the history of the two nations, in order to bring the permeability of the two nation-states into view or to analyze the work of transnational forces. Since both papers of this session focus on specific national, i.e. German and American, experiences, the commentator's main task will be to introduce comparative features.

Erich Angermann pointed out in his essay *Challenges of Ambiguity. Doing Comparative History*[1] that in order to do comparative history one needs "a historical question of genuine transnational interest apt to serve as a dominant theme wide enough to encompass a variety of related phenomena and flexible enough for them to be dealt with in detail without digression from the main question".[2]

---

1. Erich Angermann, *Challenges of Ambiguity. Doing Comparative History*, German Historical Institute, Washington, D.C. Annual Lecture Series No. 4 (New York and Oxford 1991). A good overview of the methodology of comparative history is given by Hartmut Kaelble, *Der historische Vergleich. Eine Einführung zum 19. und 20. Jahrhundert* (Frankfurt a.M., 1999) and Heinz-Gerhard Haupt and Jürgen Kocka, eds., *Geschichte und Vergleich. Ansätze und Ergebnisse international vergleichender Geschichtsschreibung* (Frankfurt a.M., 1996).
2. Angermann, *Challenges of Ambiguity*, 8.

This conference has chosen "Visions of the Future in Germany and America" as such a historical question with a genuine transnational content, which again is subdivided into several aspects, one of which is "Social utopias in Germany and the United States," the topic of this session. The phenomenon of "Social Utopias" as discussed by James Gilbert and Paul Nolte circles around several "skeleton (sub-)topics"[3] — to borrow again a notion from Angermann's essay — on some of which I would like to focus my remarks. I will discuss the following four questions by introducing a comparative perspective on the basis of the historical insights presented by the two papers:

1 What is meant by "utopia" or "utopianism" in the German and American context? And what is the function of "social utopias" in Germany as compared to the United States?

2 What are the commonalties and differences in the use of the concepts of "society" and "community" in German and American social theories? How are "community" and "society" as concepts related to utopian thinking or utopian (social) theories?

3 Referring to the argument put forward by James Gilbert that there exists a continuity between utopia formation and mainstream American history my third question is: What are the historical dimensions of "utopian thought" and "utopianism"? Are there comparable historical dependencies in Germany and the United States with regard to the emergence of utopian (social) theory or utopian communities?

4 In my fourth point I would like to go a step beyond historical comparison by looking at processes of "cultural transfer"[4] and their influence on visions of the future in both societies. Looking

---

3. Ibid., 8. Angermann uses the term "skeleton topics," which I slightly modified in the above quotation.

4. For the conceptual underpinnings of this approach see Matthias Middell, ed., *Kulturtransfer und Vergleich* (Leipzig, 2000); Michel Espagne, *Histoire culturelle* (Paris, 1998); R. Muhs, J. Paulmann, and W. Steinmetz, eds., *Aneignung und Abwehr. Interkultureller Transfer zwischen Deutschland und Großbritannien im 19. Jahrhundert* (Bodenheim, 1998); *Comparativ: Leipziger Beiträge zur Universalgeschichte und vergleichenden Gesellschaftsforschung* 10(1) (2000): "Kulturtransfer im Vergleich."

at American and German "visions of the future" for the twenty-first century we need to take into account the fact that the two societies, because of intensive processes of cultural transfer since the late 1960s, have become more homogeneous with regard to their respective value systems, with regard to central social and political assumptions, and with regard to leading political, social, and cultural concepts – commonalties resulting from the common experience in both societies that boundaries are shifting, that borders are fading, that a global middle class, a global civil society in the Hegelian sense (a *bürgerliche Gesellschaft*), is emerging with a broad common set of values, norms, lifestyle, etc.[5] Taking this process into account I would like to ask whether the concept of a "global civil society" as discussed by German and American social scientists is an utopian one.

Concepts of "Utopia" and "Utopianism"

Much has been written about concepts of utopia and utopianism. Although the concepts themselves are hard to define – and the editor of the historical dictionary *Utopias and Utopians* even denies the necessity to do so[6] – one can differentiate with Lyman Tower Sargent three fundamental forms of utopianism: utopian literature, communitarianism, and utopian social theory.[7] As the two papers demonstrate, all three forms of utopianism are central for an understanding of the form and function of social utopias. James Gilbert discusses in his paper utopias as "intentional communities of a special sort," thereby analyzing the correlation between utopian

---

5. For this argument see: Arjun Appadurai, *Modernity at Large: Cultural Dimensions of Globalization* (Minneapolis, MN 1998).

6. Richard C. S. Trahair, *Utopias and Utopians. An Historical Dictionary* (Westport, CT, 1999), x: "deciding on a final definition attracts too many problems for practicing utopians that they are bound to argue that utopias should enjoy an infinity of connotations and that in practice it is necessary merely to settle on a few features of the future that matter to only the individuals involved."

7. Lyman Tower Sargent, "The Three Faces of Utopianism Revisited," *Utopian Studies* 5 (1994), 1–37.

literature and the formation of utopian community (one might as well say examples of the communitarian movement in the history of the United States). Paul Nolte, on the other hand, analyzes social theory as an expression of intellectual utopianism in German history, thereby defining utopia as a "way of giving their own present world a direction towards an idealized future." Nolte tackles the communitarian ideas or communitarianism, which I would like to pinpoint as the common ground of the two papers, top down, from the level of ideas to the level of social movements, whereas James Gilbert discusses communitarianism bottom-up, from the historical facts of the social experiments to the idea of community or communitarianism. Hence, comparing the two papers with regard to their concepts of utopia and utopianism, we first of all find two very different ways in dealing with the topic "social utopias" and in presenting the results of the endeavor to come to terms with American and German experiences. Whereas James Gilbert uses the approach of a social historian, Paul Nolte focuses on the history of ideas. But the historiographical differences in approaching the topic "social utopias" in German and US history tell us a lot about the differences between Germany and the United States in dealing with and thinking about utopias. As Paul Nolte argues convincingly, in Germany "utopias of a better, a more stable, a more homogeneous world" are not to be attained "from within present society, by means of reform or gradual change; but rather by a great revolutionary breakthrough." This revolutionary breakthrough needs strong ideas, maybe even an ideology. Utopias understood as mental projections about a better future were necessary as an ideational framework for social change. This is why it is necessary, in order to understand the German case, to focus on "ideas" on "theories," in our case on the utopian character of social theories discussed by the developing social sciences.

James Gilbert, on the other hand demonstrates, that social utopias in America (=intentional communities) are to be understood as an "exceptional variant of the common American process of settlement and town and city building." The foundation of communities is – so Gilbert – "one of the most important processes of American expansion." As such, "utopias" and "utopianism" are not an imaginary or indefinitely remote construct, but are a part of mainstream American social history. Social utopias in the form of intentional communities, moreover, became "refuges from the self-proclaimed utopianism of American society; its millennial pretensions and claims to perfectionism."

Looking at numbers the argument put forward by James Gilbert that "utopia" is a central element of the concept of "Americanism" becomes undeniable. More than 100 American communities with a "utopian" character were formed in the century preceding the American Civil War and thousands thereafter.[8] Experiments of utopian communities were interpreted as "patent-office models of the good society."[9] The new United States established itself as a utopian venture. This was partly owing to America's own sense of its "exceptionalism," its providential mission in the world. America was the promised land, the "place where humanity was destined to find its fulfillment after the bitter years in the wilderness."[10]

In analyzing "intentional communities" as expressions of social utopias in the United States James Gilbert exemplifies, however, not only a central feature of American social utopias but brings to the fore a characteristic of utopian thinking that is also typical for the German case. "Utopia" as a concept embodies the often conflicting pulls of the need for order and the desire for freedom – i.e. utopia as a "state of social harmony and community" (Paul Nolte) – and the claims of local autonomy and individual creativity – i.e. utopia as a "radical desire to return to a simpler world and a form of social dreaming" (James Gilbert, Lyman Tower Sargent). With regard to the content of utopian thinking it is hence possible to pinpoint some similarities between the German and the American experience. The function of utopia, however, differs very much in the two societies.

8. See M. Holloway, *Heavens on Earth: Utopian Communities in America* 1680–1880 (New York, 1966); A. E. Bestor, Jr., *Backwoods Utopias: The Sectarian and Owenite Phases of Communitarian Socialism in America, 1663–1829* (Philadelphia, PA, 1950); Y. Owen, *Two Hundred Years of American Communes* (New Brunswick, 1988).

9. A. E. Bestor, Jr., "Patent-Office Models of the Good Society," *American Historical Review* 58 (1953), 505–526.

10. Krishan Kumar, *Utopianism*, Open University Press 1991, 81.

"Social utopias" as social theory, as an academically constructed ideational framework, had a strong missionary impulse in Germany, as Paul Nolte's analysis points out. The function of utopian thinking was essentially to provide the intellectual means for a possibly revolutionary overthrow of existing social and political structures. In the German case utopias aimed at the realization of "a better, a more stable, a more homogeneous world. It was a world not to be attained from within present society, by means of reform or gradual change; but rather by a great revolutionary breakthrough, by stepping out of, or getting 'beyond', society." "Social utopias" in the United States represented by utopian communities had no such missionary impulse; these communities did not aim at altering the whole society but they became reality as segments of the society, as "small islands of self-reliant utopian communities". This marks a very strong difference which has not become a topic in our discussions during the conference. Since it seems to be, however, a crucial difference between the two national entities under scrutiny I would like to plead for further comparative research with regard to the function of social utopias in Germany and the United States. How can we explain the functional difference of "utopia" and utopian thinking and living in Germany and the United States? It is because "Americanism" understood as an utopian social and political model – for the sake of the argument at this point – encompasses all the essentials of utopia: offering a better world where all is calm and happiness that radical or revolutionary elements are not a central characteristic of American social utopias?

Communitarian Social Theories as Social Utopias: "Society" vs "Community"

I argued in the first point of my comparison that both papers have a common subject which only is approached from very different angles. And this common subject is "communitarianism" as social experience and social theory. In the second part I will focus on this common topic of both papers by discussing the use and the function of the concepts "society" and "community" in utopian thinking.

In analyzing and describing the modes of existence of modern utopianism James Gilbert focusses on communities. The foundation of communities was one of the most important processes of American expansion. America always had a special appeal for utopians, socialist and other, who wished to experiment with radically new forms of life, because America with its wide open spaces offered a most fitting and congenial environment for these communities.[11] Before the search for utopias in the United States, utopian ventures were not so dynamic. Nineteenth-century utopias in the United States offered a new society with a sincere commitment to different forms of Christianity and paternalistic socialism and later the early forms of modern social democracy.[12] Utopian ventures have been studied more thoroughly in the United States than elsewhere, and many have set an example for the reorganization of society. Hence in many ways America is a special place for utopia as a social experience, which again marks a central difference from Germany where utopia was not so much experienced in real life but expressed itself predominantly in utopian thinking.

Modern social utopia in the United States, however, oscillated between communal ventures in the form of utopian communities and social theory. Utopian communities very often focussed their utopian programs on the problems of "hand, heart, and hierarchy," thereby expressing in some cases a quite radical desire to return to a simpler world, where social bonds and social self-organization figure prominently as against a society that was developing more and more machine-like, anonymous traits – mass society. Utopian communities had the desire to replace the outer force as a guarantor for social security and cohesiveness by educating an inner compulsion of the members of a community to secure its functioning. Besides this form of individualized experience of living in an utopian community there exists a tradition of theorizing about society as a whole with a reform impulse as was the case in late nineteenth- and early twentieth-century Germany. James Gilbert, for example, points out the desire of Bellamy and New Deal utopians to establish

---

11. Ibid., 82
12. Trahair, *Utopias and Utopians*, xi.

a special sort of consumer society based on social equality alongside strong domestic relationships. In *Looking Backward* Bellamy describes an utopia in Boston in the year 2000, where bureaucratic state capitalism ensures its citizens' welfare with equal wages – and with "culture" as the main item of consumption.[13] Bellamy "dreamt of vast social organizations and a society completely transformed by ideas and evolution" (James Gilbert). Utopian social theories going beyond single communities and looking at society as a whole, like the ones formulated by Bellamy and his followers, hence constructed a middle-class utopianism. The socialist ideas espoused in such writing looked to the state as an active instrument in the balancing of class forces and the facilitating of progress and prosperity.[14] And in this regard they very much reflect the European or German political situation in the late nineteenth and early twentieth centuries but not so much the utopian social theories of the time.

As Paul Nolte points out, "society" as a social construct was only developed and reflected upon theoretically from the 1830s and 1840s. During that period "society" became visible "as a hierarchical order of groups, as a structure of groups bound together by a common economic origin and occupation" (Paul Nolte). Unlike Bellamy, German social theorists constructed an antagonistic relationship between the "state" and "society." It was not the state which was thought to be responsible for the balancing of class forces or social unrest, but it was the function of "society" understood as a "new, all-encompassing entity of social relations" to manage and to overcome social conflicts. Social Science established itself as an academic discipline influencing and shaping visions and concepts of society, thereby opening up "horizons of social expectation, of desires and anxieties for the future" (Paul Nolte). In this regard the notion of society assumed utopian qualities and became a focus of social reform movements or reform theories in the twentieth century, most of them designing a political and intellectual program

---

13. Ibid., 33.

14. Francis Robert Shor, *Utopianism and Radicalism in a Reforming America, 1888–1918* (Westport, CT, 1997), 101.

of a classless society, a "society of a better and more harmonious, more communitarian order" (Paul Nolte).

The ideological underpinnings of the developing labor movement, theorizing on questions of social hierarchies ("class society"), constructed the image of a dualistic society. Bourgeois or middle-class theories on the other hand shifted their focus to the "mass" aspect of modern society where "people's identities were losing their significance and individuality" and were becoming uniform (Paul Nolte). It was in the context of this argument that the idea of "community" was introduced into the theoretical discussion, not only in Germany, as the paper by Paul Nolte suggests, but also in the United States. As was the case with American communal experience, the idea of "community" in the German context" provided an answer to the problem of the loss of close and intimate bonding in urban society" (Paul Nolte). As in the American case the idea of community related to many forms of more or less institutionalized social togetherness in smaller groups.[15]

So again in comparing the German and American cases we can discern differences and commonalties. Social theories or reform theories existed on both sides of the Atlantic. In both cases they were developed, especially during the second half of the nineteenth and early twentieth centuries. With regard to the theoretical representation of the phenomenon of "mass society" we can point out in both cases a certain radicalization of the idea of mass society during the first decade of the twentieth century. As Francis Shor argues in his study on utopianism and radicalism between 1888 and 1918, reform and radical change were fundamental components of the political and cultural environment in America during the Progressive Era.[16] As in the German case, the radical aspect of American utopianism was introduced by utopian social theories. In order to compare American and German "thinking" about social

15. A good overview of Max Weber's reception of the Tönnies notions "society" and "community" is given by Stefan Breuer, "Max Webers Staatssoziologie," *Kölner Zeitschrift für Soziologie und Sozialpsychologie* 45(2) (1993), 199–219.

16. Shor, *Utopianism*, xiv.

utopias it would hence be necessary to take American social theories as a *tertium comparationis* into account.

Besides, we have to ask ourselves what exactly is the dividing line between utopian theory and other kinds of social theory, or to make it more concrete: How utopian were the theories of Ferdinand Toennies, Georg Simmel, and Max Weber? And can we really compare their work with the utopian theories developed by Bellamy and other representatives of a literary utopianism?

Utopia and Utopianism as Central Elements in US and German History

In analyzing the concepts of "society" and "community" the historical embeddedness of utopian theory especially with regard to their radical content came to a fore as a central feature of utopia or utopianism. Francis R. Shor makes this point very strongly. He argues:

> While the thread of this [radical reform movement, U.L.] utopian impulse and radical reform has run throughout American history, one cannot neglect how historical factors have shaped the emergence of utopianism in specific periods. Historical dislocations caused by the long wave of economic crises as well as political and social conflicts rooted in increasing urbanization and industrial modernization, have created a broad epistemic context within which utopian aspirations have resonated.[17]

Utopia hence is a concept that is defined by its appearance at a certain point in history, within a certain intellectual and cultural tradition. And this is exactly what is demonstrated in both papers. James Gilbert shows how social utopias appear in the (epistemic)

---

17. Ibid., xv. For further readings on the historically determined emergence of utopian thought and communal experiments in America see: Michael Barkun, "Communal Societies and Cyclical Phenomena," *Communal Societies* 4 (1984), 35–48; Brian J. L. Berry, *America's Utopian Experiments: Communal Havens from Long-Wave Crisis* (Hanover, NH, 1992).

context of waves of religious revival "which provide the setting and landscape in which secular experiments thrived or withered" (James Gilbert). Paul Nolte on the other hand demonstrates how social science influenced and shaped visions and concepts of society within the society at large, while at the same time the scientific discourse was influenced by and reflected much broader social processes and mental projections in German society.

The interesting question here is, however, under what circumstances and conditions, and in which way, does a social imaginary find concrete representation. The answer suggested by Ernst Bloch, for example, is that particular social groups are needed to articulate specific visions intended to mobilize sentiments for social fulfillment in order to transform social theory or utopian thought into reality.[18] This argument is also put forward by Francis Shor. Utopianism, he argues, achieves a historical resonance "at those exact moments when agents engaged in a willed transformation of reality seek to redress the imbalance between what is lacking and what they desire."[19]

A Global Civil Society as a Social Utopia of the Twenty-First Century?

The imbalance between what is lacking and what is needed or desired is today a central theoretical and political concern of all those who deal with problems of international conflict and cooperation, with regime formation or with the establishment of some form of internationally accepted normative frameworks to solve conflicts in such issue areas as the environment, human rights,

18. Ernst Bloch, *Das Prinzip Hoffnung*, Bd. 1, S. 227: "die konkrete Phantasie und das Bildwerk ihrer vermittelten Antizipationen sind im Prozeß des Wirklichen selber gärend und bilden sich im konkreten Traum nach vorwärts ab; antizipatorische Elemente sind ein Bestandteil der Wirklichkeit selbst. Also ist der Wille zur Utopia mit objekthafter Tendenz durchaus verbindbar, ja in ihr bestätigt und zu Hause."

19. Shor, *Utopianism*, 183. See also Barbara Goodwin and Keith Taylor, *The Politics of Utopia: A Study in Theory and Practice* (New York, 1982), 138; Ruth Levitas, *The Concept of Utopia* (Syracuse, NY, 1990), 182.

economic development, or peacekeeping. In all these issue areas the actual situation is very often still characterized by national egoism, a lack of inner compulsion by the actors involved to live up to a common cause, a lack of global governance mechanisms that might take over the function of the state as an outer force to induce cooperation, social cohesiveness, equality, and freedom on an international scale. Hence, although Germany and the United States might today find themselves in a situation where the idea of Hegel's *bürgerliche Gesellschaft*, the civil society, have been more or less realized within the border's of their nation-states, both nations are today confronted with the problem that a comprehensive social system on the international level does not yet exist. This is a problem challenging social scientists to think about the structural, institutional, and normative prerequisites for the realization of such a global civil society.[20] Interestingly, on both sides of the Atlantic the concepts of "society" and "community" figure prominently in the theoretical endeavors that try to give an answer to the problems involved. It is argued that, because of an increase in the number of transnational social and cultural spheres (NGOs, cultural regions, international regimes, multicultural societies, hyphenated identities), "society" and "community" have become characteristics of the international system; they can no longer be conceived of as concepts applicable only to social constructs within the geographically defined spaces of the modern nation-state.[21]

International relations understood as international social relations (*Gesellschaftswelt*)[22] are characterized – as society was during the nineteenth and twentieth centuries – by social, cultural and political fragmentation, by the lack of bonding mechanism and social cohesiveness. Like Georg Simmel and Ferdinand Tönnies at the turn

20. See e.g. Scott Turner, "Global Civil Society, Anarchy and Governance: Assessing an Emerging Paradigm," *Journal of Peace Research* 35(1) (1998), 25–42.

21. John W. Meyer, John Boli, George M. Thomas, and Francisco O. Ramirez, "World Society and the Nation-State," *AJS* 103(1) (1997), 144–181; Dietrich Jung, "Weltgesellschaft als theoretisches Konzept der Internationalen Beziehungen," *Zeitschrift für Internationale Beziehungen* 5(2) (1998), 241–271; Martin Shaw, "Civil Society and Global Politics: Beyond a Social Movements Approach," *Millennium* 23(3) (1994), 647–668.

of the century we are today looking for concepts that help to explain how people who are complete strangers to other people could nevertheless engage in cooperative endeavors. Interesting here is the fact that we can draw a line between what Paul Nolte discussed as an organizing principle for the German society – the functionally differentiated concept of a *Ständegesellschaft* – and "functionalism" as an Anglo-Saxon theory[23] that figured prominently in the discussions during the early 1940s about how the new world organization, the United Nations, should be structured. Functionalism in the German tradition connotes, as Paul Nolte demonstrates, the traditional concept of the social estate, the *Stand* referring to "occupational groups as functional parts within the whole body of society." As in the theory of functionalism these ideas refer to a concept of society based on a multiplicity of groups defined by their "specific functional uses for society as a whole" or in the case of the United Nations for the international community as a whole. Social, economic, and political integration via functionalism is one of the central tasks of the United Nations today. The most comprehensive of the reports written by special UN commissions in order to analyze the current world situation and to develop an action plan for the future is the report of the Commission on Global Governance, entitled *Our Global Neighborhood*.[24] If we look at the vocabulary used in this report and also in social science theories

22. Ernst-Otto Czempiel, *Weltpolitik im Umbruch. Das internationale System nach dem Ende des Ost-West-Konflikts* (Munich, 1991); Czempiel, *Kluge Macht. Außenpolitik für das 21. Jahrhundert* (Munich, 1999), which can be read as an utopian theory of international relations; and two as I think very important articles on the relationship between "state" and "society" in a developing transnational system: Niklas Luhmann, "Der Staat des politischen Systems," in Ulrich Beck, ed., *Perspektiven der Weltgesellschaft* (Frankfurt a.M., 1998), 345–381 and Alexander Wendt, "Der Internationalstaat: Identität und Strukturwandel in der internationalen Politik," ibid., 381–410.

23. See David Mitrany, *A Working Peace System: An Argument for the Functional Devlepment of International Organization* (London, 1943).

24. Commission on Global Governance, *Our Global Neighborhood* (New York, 1996); Dianne Otto, "Nongovernmental Organizations in the United Nations System: The Emerging Role of International Civil Society," *Human Rights Quarterly* 18(1) (1996), 107–141; Peter Spiro, "New Global Communities: NGO Organizations in International Decision-Making Institutions," *Washington Quarterly* 18(1)

about globalization and the development of elements of a global civil society we find many parallels to the vocabulary of Ferdinand Tönnies. As I mentioned above, the concepts of "society" and "community" figure prominently in the theoretical debates about the mechanisms that are able to produce social cohesiveness on an international level. Hence even today, under the circumstances of growing denationalization or globalization the question of how *Gemeinschaft/*"community" is developed and stabilized (today including the global dimension) remains the focal point of the analysis of the structural and institutional basis of "society." In theorizing about the possible governance mechanisms of such a global civil society one asks how the quasi-statelessness of world society is being held together by cultural and associational structures – as was the case in the nearly stateless American society of the 1830s. Visions of the future in German and American social theories tend toward a common concept. Whether this has to be understood as a consequence of the Americanization of Germany or whether it has to be interpreted as a common European and American experience of modernization – as the notion of utopia implies – is a question that needs further research and discussion.

The idea of a global civil society and the existence of universalistic forms of bonding mechanisms has been debated strongly, in International Relations theory, in sociology and anthropology. Especially in the context of political science the concept of a *Weltgesellschaft* has been denounced as an utopian concept[25] and even Czempiel's compromise, the concept of the *Gesellschaftswelt*, the international system as an international social system, has been discussed controversially.[26] Indeed one has to ask whether it is possible at all to transfer the concepts of "civil society" and "state" to the structures of the international system. Can we draw a parallel

(1997), 45–56; Peter Willetts, eds., *The Conscience of the World – The Influence of Non-governmental Organizations in the U.N. System* (Washington, D.C., 1996).

25. Forschungsgruppe Weltgesellschaft, "Weltgesellschaft: Identifizierung eines 'Phantoms'," *Politische Vierteljahresschrift* 37(1) (1996), 584–587.

26. See e.g. Werner Link, *Die Neuordnung der Weltpolitik. Grundprobleme globaler Politik an der Schwelle zum 21 Jahrhundert* (Munich, 1998).

between the United Nations as a "proto-state" and the global economic and social system as a "protoglobaler Zivilgesellschaft" (proto-global civil society)?[27] I think that this is the central question to be asked today when talking about the utopianism of a global civil society. I do not see that we can "relegate the idea of society to history and start anew with different concepts," as Paul Nolte suggests at the very end of his paper. Nolte's scepticism against his own argument expressed by ending his question "But which?" is very appropriate here. Human beings are social beings whether they live in a nationally defined society or in a transnationally characterized social environment. "Society" and "community" are central elements of humanity.

27. Meghnad Desai, "Global Governance", in Dirk Messner, ed., *Die Zukunft des Staats und der Politik Möglichkeiten und Grenzen politischer Steuerung in der Weltgesellschaft* (Bonn, 1998), 341; Meghnad Desai, Paul Redfern, and Antonio Rengifo, "Global Governance: Ethics and Economics of the World Order," *Review of European Community & International Environmental Law* 6(19) (1997), 98.

Part 4
The Future Society Envisioned

1
Beyond the Nation? A Grand Category Revisited

Dietmar Schirmer

Introduction

The late twentieth century developed, as did all fin de siècles of the modern age, a strong sense of imminent epochal change. Part of it may be attributed to the magic of numbers. As the hype around Y2K has demonstrated, the end of the old and the beginning of a new millennium is enough to evoke the expectation of the normal flow of time and history being disrupted. The sense of change, however, has substance. Nineteen eighty-nine, precisely two centuries after the Grand Revolution, saw state socialism exit the stage, with a sigh, not a blast, and changed the world order from bipolar bloc confrontation to something new. What this new order is – whether it fits the category of order at all – is not yet entirely clear.

Hence the question: If 1789 and the self-constitution of the Estate Generale as the French nation represents the beginning of modernity in a political sense, what does 1989 stand for? The "end of history" – hypothesis[1] can be rejected on empirical grounds. Rwanda, Yugoslavia, and Russia warn us that the liberal consensus is more fragile; the victory of representative democracy is less complete than the triumphalist interpretation of 1989 would have us assume. It has been suggested, instead, that we view epochal change not in terms of "an end of history," but rather as a switch from one to another kind of history: With the class-based confrontation between capitalism and socialism allegedly having exhausted itself, it will

---

1. See Francis Fukuyama, *The End of History and the Last Man* (New York and Toronto 1992).

instead be conflicts of culture and civilization that provide the momentum for world history.[2] However, while the potentially explosive nature of perceived cultural differences is undeniable, it seems that culturally induced conflicts are as likely, if not more so, to appear *within* rather than *at* the borders between the large cultural units, as the "clash of civilization" hypothesis suggests. Further, given the not only sustained, but growing inequality in the global distribution of wealth, it seems unlikely that history is about to phase out the economy-driven type of social conflict that dominated the nineteenth and twentieth centuries.

A third idea regarding the nature of epochal change is centered on "globalization" – a symbol, I would suggest, rather than a well-defined concept, a generator of images of a world of unprecedented risks and opportunities. A search in a social-scientific database reveals the stunning career "globalization" has had since the mid-1980s, when the term first appeared: Between 1985 and 1989, the term appears between three and eight times per year. In 1990, the number jumps to 42; from there to 430 in 1995; and to above 1,000 in 1998.[3]

Primarily, globalization refers to the reorganization of capital, of product and labor markets on a global scale. In this respect, it is associated with the new dogmatism of free trade; the free movement of capital and the less free, but nonetheless substantial, movement of migrants; the scaling back of welfare and other regulatory regimes that potential investors might find annoying; and the decreasing power of territorial states. Frequently, however, globalization is used in a broader sense and signifies processes that are cultural as well as economic. And cultural globalization has a twin named fragmentation – which of the two is the evil one is a matter of perspective. Globalization and fragmentation, in the cultural sense, refer to the parallel processes of an emerging world popular culture that homogenizes tastes in food, fashion, movies, television, and music,

---

2. See Samuel Huntington, *The Clash of Civilizations and the Remaking of World Order* (New York 1996).

3. These are the numbers of hits that a title search for "globalization," broken down by year, in the Social Science Citation Index produces.

and the simultaneous revitalization of regional and local vernaculars and idiosyncrasies that may produce folklore as well ethnic conflict.[4]

This essay concerns itself with the political consequences of globalization. Obviously, there are many: The financial, social, and trade policies that the IMF and the World Bank impose on the countries of the developing world; the worldwide competition between states for jobs and investments; the conflicts concerning labor and environmental standards; the inability of national governments to regulate internet-based communication; the spread of international and transnational organizations, to name but a few. The recent IMF and World Bank meetings in Seattle and Washington put them neatly on display – not only on the agendas of the meetings, but on the streets of the host cities as well, where an unlikely coalition of activists – labor unions, environmental organizations, human and civil rights groups, nationalist protectionists, anarchist circles, and many more – aired their grievances.

However diverse the political manifestations and consequences of globalization, they have an identifiable core: the transformation of the world of nation-states. For the last two centuries, the external and internal sovereignty of the nation-state has been the dominant organizing principle of state–state as well as state–society relations; and likewise the nation has been the dominant source of political legitimacy and collective identity. I suggest that what 1989 represents – beyond the abortion of the experiment in centralist socialism – is this: the dusk of the nation-state age, just as 1789 symbolizes its dawn.[5]

---

4. For the cultural dialectics of fragmentation and globalization see Benjamin R. Barber, *Jihad vs. McWorld: How Globalism and Tribalism are Reshaping the World* (New York, 1995). For the debate on multiculturalism and the supposed threat of the ethnic Balkanization of the US see Arthur M. Schlesinger, Jr., *The Disuniting of America: Reflections on a Multicultural Society* (New York and London 1992).

5. Needless to say that this hypothesis has Europe as its immediate reference point. While 1789 marks an inherently European process that would, eventually and over the course of two centuries, structure political and social relations on a global scale, 1989 – understood as the breakthrough of globalization – refers to a process that is global by definition. However, whether the transformation of state–state and state–society relations will take a similar course in other parts of the

A Post-national Era

To speak of the beginning of a post-national era is not the same as to announce the end of the nation. Indeed, the end of the nation and the nation-state has been proclaimed innumerable times, and this essay is not intended to add to the list of premature obituaries. However, there is considerable evidence that something about the capacity and function of nation-states is changing in a very fundamental way, particularly in Europe where we can witness the emergence of the first real and fully-fledged trans- and international polity.[6] Thus, the term postnationalism is not supposed to suggest a state without nations and nation-states, but rather one where the national principle – both as an institutional framework and as a category of societal integration – ceases to be the a priori of all political and social relations.

My hypothesis is that the world of nation-states, as we know it, represents historically the extremely unlikely case of the successful containment of functional differentiation in the iron cages of territorial and regulatory states. The nation-state world as a system of structurally similar cages is characterized by a peculiar mix of forms of differentiation, with segmentation characterizing the relations between nation-state societies, and functional differentiation being dominant *within* them. It is this mix that is changing.[7]

---

world, remains to be seen. So far, there is no empirical evidence to support such an assumption. Regional organizations outside of Europe, including Nafta, are international organizations of the type characteristic for the nation-state era.

6. See, for example, David Held, "The Decline of the Nation State," in Geoff Eley and Ronald G. Suny, eds., *Becoming National: A Reader* (New York and Oxford 1996), 407–416.

7. The imagery of the nation-state as a cage resembles that of the nation-state as a "power-container," as introduced by Anthony Giddens (and pays, of course, homage to Max Weber's "iron cage" as a metaphor for the bureaucratic state). See Giddens, *The Nation-state and Violence: A Contemporary Critique of Historical Materialism*, vol. 2 (Berkeley, CA, 1985), 120. Giddens also correctly identifies the structure of segmentation characteristic for the relations between nation-states: "The nation-state . . . exists within a complex of other nation-states" (Giddens, *Nation-state*, 18). However, his definition of the nation-state largely repeats Weber's definition

The postnational condition appears to be one where the super-structure of segmentation withers away. The cages of the zoo of nations give way to an open and rather loosely structured landscape. For better or worse, social differentiation is free to proceed in a manner largely unconfined by the crumbling regulatory monopolies of the states. A century or two after the fact, the nation–state societies have to realize that they have indeed merged into a world society, although one that is very different from the neatly staked out sociotopes of the older historical formation, with regard to both forms of differentiation as well as integration. The result is the de-hierarchization of state–society relations and de-territorialization of social relations.

This transition has immediate consequences for the type of socio-cultural and political integration that is characteristic of the world of nation-states. The nation as an including/excluding category of collective identity evolved as an answer to the existential problems posed by functional differentiation: the loss of the idea of ontological unity, and the loss of the experience of "natural" community. However, the nation as the focus of that collective identity which is hierarchically situated above all other social identities that an individual may have or take is plausible and is thus sustainable only if it correlates either with a nation-state that really is, and not only pretends to be, the structuring principle of social practice, or with the expectation of the future achievement of national statehood. If the nation-state cage, if the segmented superstructure of the nation-state world, gives way to globalization, including the weakening of the regulatory capacities of the state or their relocation to other than the national authorities, national identity loses, or substantially changes, its meaning.

Globalization and the ways in which political actors respond to it have already produced an enormous body of political science literature, notably in the fields of international relations and comparative politics. The concepts of global governance, inter-

---

of the state of 1919, although it is quite a bit wordier and, thus, fails to account for the specifics of the nation-state as opposed to the state in general.

national regimes, world system, world society, and transnational relations may serve as examples for the neo-realist, neo-liberal, and neo-Marxist response to the observation of growing interdependency across national borders.[8] The culturalist and constructivist turn in the study of international relations allowed for a much richer and thicker understanding of the relations between states, governments, and society under the conditions of global interdependency than the older paradigm of a *situation hobbésienne* between nation-states had provided for. Add to this concepts like interlocking politics, pooled sovereignty, multilevel governance, or network analysis which comparativists developed to shed light on the process of European integration and the institutional structure and policy-making processes of the European Union,[9] and the richness of scholarly

8. See, for example, Martin Albrow, *Abschied vom Nationalstaat: Staat und Gesellschaft im globalen Zeitalter* [Engl.: The Global Age: State and Society Beyond Modernity] (Frankfurt a.M., 1998); Giovanni Arrighi et al., *Chaos and Governance in the Modern World System* (Minneapolis, MN, and London, 1999); Volker Bonschier and Peter Legyel, eds., *Waves, Formations and Values in the World System: World Society Studies vol. 2* (New Brunswick, NJ, and London, 1992); Volker Bonschier and Peter Legyel, eds., *Conflicts and New Departures in World Society: World Society Studies vol. 3* (New Brunswick, NJ, and London, 1994); Lester R. Brown, *World Without Borders* (New York, 1972); David Held, *Democracy and the Global Order: From the Modern State to Cosmopolitan Governance* (Cambridge, 1995); Martin Hewson and Timothy J. Sinclair, eds., *Approaches to Global Governance Theory* (Albany, NY, 1999); Steven D. Krasner, ed., *International Regimes* (Ithaca, NY, 1983); Niklas Luhmann, "Die Weltgesellschaft," in *Soziologische Aufklärung 2: Aufsätze zur Theorie der Gesellschaft* (Opladen, 1975); Thomas Risse-Kappen, ed., *Bringing Transnational Relations Back In: Non-State Actors, Domestic Structures, and International Institutions* (Cambridge and New York, 1995); Immanuel Wallerstein, *Unthinking Social Science: The Limits of Nineteenth-Century Paradigms* (Cambridge, 1991); Immanuel Wallerstein et al., *The Age of Transition: Trajectory of the World-System 1945–2025* (London, 1996); Michael Zürn, *Regieren jenseits des Nationalstaats* (Frankfurt a.M., 1998). For a remarkably sweeping account see Manuel Castells' Information Age Trilogy: *The Rise of the Network Society (The Information Age: Economy, Society and Culture, vol. I); The Power of Identity (The Information Age: Economy, Society and Culture, vol. II); and End of Millennium (The Information Age: Economy, Society and Culture, vol. III)*, (Oxford, 1996–1998).

9. Markus Jachtenfuchs and Beate Kohler-Koch, eds., *Europäische Integration* (Opladen, 1996); Beate Kohler-Koch and Rainer Eising, eds., *The Transformation of Governance in the European Union* (London and New York, 1999); M. Kreile, ed.,

work that pertains to the post-national transition of politics becomes quite apparent. It is particularly interesting and encouraging to observe that in the process, the formerly well-maintained disciplinary boundaries between the study of international relations and that of comparative politics have begun to blur: The subdisciplines acknowledge the fact that the time-honored boundaries between foreign and domestic spheres have to be overcome in order to keep up with a world in the process of transnationalization.[10]

In contrast, it is somewhat surprising and disconcerting that the study of nationalism and national identity so far has avoided confronting a topic that is so obviously relevant to its subject.[11] Rather, those with academic stakes in nationalisms and national identities choose to point to the revival of nationalist and ethnic conflicts in various quarters of the world and claim: See, it is as alive as ever – as if transnationalization and nationalism need be mutually exclusive. They are not. In a certain sense, quite the opposite is true. Take devolution in Great Britain, Catalan, Galician, or Basque autonomy in Spain, or the radical federalization of Belgium: Nationalist and regionalist sentiments in Western Europe can be successfully played out not despite, but because of, European integration. It is the European Union that lowers the stakes both for the nation-states and for sub-national movements. I suggest, therefore, that we understand the European Union's internal regionalisms and mini-nationalisms in terms of post-nationalism

---

Die Integration Europas [Politische Vierteljahresschrift, special issue 23], (Opladen, 1992); Fritz W. Scharpf, *Regieren in Europa: Effektiv und demokratisch?* (Frankfurt a.M., and New York, 1999).

10. See Thomas Risse-Kappen, "Exploring the Nature of the Beast: International Relations Theory and Comparative Policy Analysis Meet the European Union," *Journal of Common Market Studies* 34(1) (March 1996), 53–80.

11. Exceptions include James E. Caporaso, "The European Union and Forms of State: Westphalian, Regulatory, or Post-Modern?", *Journal of Common Market Studies* 34(1) (March 1996), 29–52; Michael Mann, "Nation-States in Europe and Other Continents: Diversifying, Developing, Not Dying," *Daedalus* 122(3) (summer 1993), 115–140; Michael Smith, "The European Union and a Changing Europe: Establishing the Boundaries of Order," *Journal of Common Market Studies* 34(1) (March 1996), 5–28.

rather than in terms of nationalist revival. In other quarters, nationalist revival may be understood, once again, not as proof of the unquestionable priority of the national principle, but rather as a fundamentalist response to its apparent weakness in the face of the forces of globalization and as a response to the risks and uncertainties they produce.

However, it also should be noted that the world does not move at a uniform pace. Western Europe is certainly the region that is already most thoroughly post-national. By contrast, the United States, the global hegemon, is powerful enough, because of its sheer size, its military clout, its economic power, and its geographical position, to maintain its sovereignty as if little has changed. In other regions, the nation-state may still be in the process of strengthening and maturing.[12] And in yet other regions, particular in those Central European countries that are preparing for accession to the European Union, the processes of unfolding and of overcoming the national principle are oddly pulled together into one simultaneous transition. The same, incidentally, is true for Germany, where regaining sovereignty *qua* unification and ceding sovereignty *qua* Europeanization were bound together in a causal nexus.

The argument will unfold in two steps: First, I will reconstruct a theory of nation-ness that attempts to fuse the prisms of functionalist theories and theories of social action in the dialectics of disembedding

---

12. Arrighi et al., for example, argue a bifurcation of state development, with the crumbling of state sovereignty in the Western core and state empowerment in East Asia:

"Multinational corporations . . . were empowered by the United States and its European allies to operate globally, but as they did in ever increasing numbers, they undermined the power of the very states on which they rely for protection and sustenance. This is one of the reasons why Tilly finds (correctly in our view) that . . . the present wave [of globalization] is associated with their disempowerment. This empowerment/disempowerment, however, concerns primarily the states of the Western world. . . . And it is precisely [in East Asia] that we can also detect important exceptions to the ongoing tendency toward the disempowerment of states. These exceptions are the city-states and the semisovereign states of the East Asian "capitalist archipelago" that have grown wealthy under the carapace of the unilateral U.S. military regime in the region." (Arrighi et al., *Chaos and Governance*, 279–80)

and re-embedding. Second, I will explore some of the consequences that the withering away of the superstructure of segmentation and the development of functional differentiation irrespective of national boundaries may have in stock for the disembedding–re-embedding relation and, consequently, for the generation of trust and social identity.

Reconstructing a Theory of Nation-ness

It has been pointed out that, throughout its history and in stark contrast to its evident social effectiveness, nationalism has been philosophically and intellectually rather poor.[13] This is certainly true with respect to the nationalist gospel itself, which never managed to bring about a nationalist Mill or Marx. And it also used to be true with respect to the academically detached theorizing on nationalism. As far as the latter is concerned, things have changed considerably over the course of the last few decades, thanks to Ernest Gellner, Miroslav Hroch, Eric Hobsbawm, Anthony Smith, Charles Tilly, Benedict Anderson, John Breuilly, and many others who have greatly enriched our theoretical understanding of modernity's most powerful socio-political force. Today, nationalism is among the certified hot topics of social science and theory, a fact that is only superficially at odds with the common suspicion that its institutional correlate, the nation-state, is in a crisis. In fact, I posit that it is the crisis that moves the national principle from the realm of the indisputable and unquestionable into that of academic, political, and public discourse.

Primordialist and substantialist approaches to nationalism – the idea that nations are natural and eternal entities that nationalism

13. Benedict Anderson, *Imagined Communities: Reflections on the Origin and Spread of Nationalism* (London and New York, 1991), 5; Brendan O'Leary, "Ernest Gellner's Diagnosis of Nationalism: A Critical Overview, Or, What is Living and What is Dead in Ernest Gellner's Philosophy of Nationalism," in John A. Hall, ed., *The State of the Nation: Ernest Gellner and the Theory of Nationalism* (Cambridge and New York, 1998), 40–88, at 68.

only needs to "awaken" – have long, and rightly, been identified as parts of the nationalist belief system and have all but vanished from the theoretical discourse. The remaining body of literature seems to fall into one of two categories: Either it deals with typologies of nations, nationalisms, and nation-states, or it concerns itself with their contingent coming into existence, through evolution or as a result of political, social, or cultural construction.

Typologies of nations usually categorize empirical concepts of nationhood according to the kind of national communality they claim. The basic dichotomy is that of ethnic and civic nations.[14] The ethnic–civic distinction parallels a series of related antagonistic concepts, such as descent–consent, *jus sanguinis–jus soli*, community–society, and so forth. As these concepts already suggest, the ethnic–civic dichotomy has analytical as well as normative implications. Analytically, the dichotomy relates a typology of nations with one of two historical trajectories of nation-state emergence, where civic nations follow a state-to-nation trajectory, and ethnic nations follow a nation-to-state trajectory.[15] Normatively, it suggests that civic

14. The ethnic-civic dichotomy can be traced back to the late nineteenth century. See Renan's famous essay of 1882 "Qu'est -ce qu'une nations" (engl. "What is a Nation?" in: Eley and Suny, eds., *Becoming National: A Reader*, 42–55) and Friedrich Meinecke, *Cosmopolitanism and the National State* (Princeton, NJ, 1970). For more recent applications see Hans Kohn, *The Idea of Nationalism* (New York, 1944); Emerich Francis, *Ethnos und Demos: Soziologische Beiträge zur Volkstheorie* (Berlin, 1965); Michael Ignatieff, *Blood and Belonging: Journeys into the New Nationalism* (New York, 1993); M. Rainer Lepsius, "'Ethnos' oder 'Demos'," in Lepsius, *Interessen, Ideen und Institutionen* (Opladen, 1990), 247–255; Jürgen Habermas, "Geschichtsbewußtsein und posttraditionale Identität: Die Westorientierung der Bundesrepublik," in Habermas, *Eine Art Schadensabwicklung – Kleine Politische Schriften VI* (Frankfurt a.M., 1987), 159–79; Jürgen Habermas, "Citizenship and National Identity," in Ronald Beiner, ed., *Theorizing Citizenship* (Albany, NY, 1995); Jürgen Habermas, "The European Nation-State – Its Achievements and Its Limits," in G. Balakrishnan, ed., *Mapping the Nation* (London and New York 1996), 281–294; Claus Leggewie, "Ethnizität, Nationalismus und multikulturelle Gesellschaft," in Helmut Berding, ed., *Nationales Bewußtsein und kollektive Identität: Studien zur Entwicklung des kollektiven Bewußtseins in der Neuzeit, vol. 2* (Frankfurt a.M., 1994), 46–65.

15. For a more elaborate version that identifies four rather than two trajectories of nation-state development in Europe see Ernest Gellner, "The Time Zones of Europe," in *Conditions of Liberty: Civil Society and Its Enemies* (London, 1995).

nations are principally benign, tolerant, and rather inclusive, while ethnic nations are exclusive, intolerant, and prone to ethnocentrism and racism. While this diagnosis can hardly be dismissed as far as the destructive potential of ethnic nations is concerned, the embrace of the civic nation seems to systematically underestimate the repressive, coercive, and exclusionary potential of communities of consent.[16]

However one assesses the general merits of the ethnic–civic dispositive, be it as a typology of nation-state trajectories or as one of better and worse nations, it definitely falls short of a theory of either nation or nationalism, because it presupposes what needs to be explained. The theoretical discourse on nations, nationalisms, and nation-states – in contrast to the merely typological operations performed on the ethnic–civic axis – operates between the epistemological poles of subjectivism and objectivism in general, and variants of functionalism and theories of social action in particular.

Functionalist approaches[17] explain nations and nation-states as the political functions of processes of social modernization that originate in social subsystems other than politics. The more or less stringently functionalist contributions to a theory of nationalism differ greatly as to which aspect or set of aspects of modernization they suggest to be the cause of the emergence of the national paradigm; the bids refer to the productive, distributive, cultural, psychological, communicative, and coercive systems and include capitalism, industrialization, secularization, the modernization of

---

16. The nation-as-covenant model that is at the center of the founding of the United States, as well as the radically political model of the Jacobin concept of membership, are, at least potentially, much narrower as their supposed inclusiveness suggests. The Jacobin terror as well as the anti-Communist hysteria of the McCarthy era may serve as historical examples that the civic nation model can at times be employed in an extremely intolerant manner. For a critique of the ethnic-civic dispositive see Rogers Brubaker, "Myths and Misconceptions in the Study of Nationalism," in Hall, *State of the Nation*, 272–306, 298–300, and Bernard Yack, "The Myth of the Civic Nation," in Ronald Beiner, ed., *Theorizing Nationalism* (New York, 1999), 103–118.

17. I apply the term here in a rather broad manner, including theories of evolution, modernization, as well as functional differentiation proper.

communication, or that of warfare or state surveillance. The polyphony of proposed causes is not really surprising. The functional method depends ultimately on an inference from effect to cause,[18] and if applied to a subject as historically pervasive and socially complex as nationalism the results of this inference will to a large degree hinge on pre-theoretical decisions on the selection of cases and historical time frames.

The conflicting results aside, the functionalist approaches to nationalism are similar in their understanding that nation–states emerge as historically contingent institutional frameworks within which specific modernization processes can be played out.[19] Consequently, the objectivist–functionalist argument is not particularly interested in the formation of nationalist ideologies or movements or any other aspect of nationalist practice. "It is not the case", as the leading author of the functionalist variety has it, "that nationalism imposes homogeneity out of a willful cultural *Machtbedürfnis*; it is the objective need for homogeneity which is reflected in nationalism."[20]

Theories of social action, on the other hand, reverse the perspective. They focus on social action and individual and collective actors of various kinds that foster nationalism, and political, social, and cultural opportunity structures that enhance or constrain their

18. See, for example, Jon Elser, "Marxism, Functionalism, and Game Theory," *Theory and Society* 11 (1982), 453–482; Anthony Giddens, "Functionalism: Après la lutte," *Social Research* 43 (1976), 325–366; Hans Joas, *Die Kreativität des Handelns* (Frankfurt a.M., 1996), 306–326.

19. The classics among this group of theories include Karl W. Deutsch, *Nationalism and Social Communication* (Cambridge, MA, 1966) and Deutsch, *Nationalism and Its Alternatives* (New York, 1969). For a bibliography of the Deutsch-school see Deutsch and Richard L. Merritt, *Nationalism and National Development: An Interdisciplinary Bibliography* (Cambridge and London, 1970). Probably the most influential work in the functional tradition is Ernest Gellner, *Nations and Nationalism* (Ithaca, NY, 1983). See also Gellner, *Nationalism* (New York, 1997). On Gellner see John A. Hall, ed., *The State of the Nation*. Another prominent example for a modernization theory of nationalism, although one combined with a theory of elite manipulation, is Eric J. Hobsbawm, *Nations and Nationalism since 1780: Programme, Myth, Reality* (Cambridge and New York, 1990).

20. Gellner, *Nations and Nationalism*, 46.

prospect of success. As in the case of functionalist theories, the differences within the group of social action theories are significant. Social action theories of nationalism may come as symbolic interactionism, social or cultural constructivism, or game theory; they may focus on the social movement character of nationalist practices, the framing of social conflicts in nationalist terms, the role of intellectuals in the production of national symbols, the internal or external political opportunity structures within which nationalist politics can prevail, or the interests of manipulating political elites or abstract collective actors such as states.[21] Yet, the common denominator is the importance of social actors and action in the making and sustaining of nations and nationalisms and the centrality of the bearers – and their interests and ideas – of nationalizing processes.[22]

The functional paradigm has proved quite compelling in providing general explanations as to why nationalist ideologies and nation-states begin to emerge sometime between the mid-seventeenth and the early nineteenth century. However, the above-mentioned epistemological problem of inferring causes from effects manifests itself practically and unavoidably in overgeneralization. Owing to the bird's eye perspective they take, functionalist approaches are unable to contribute much, if anything, to the explanation of the concrete and contingent real histories of particular nations and

21. See, for an instance, Miroslav Hroch, *Social Preconditions of National Revival in Europe* (Cambridge and New York, 1985); Rogers Brubaker, *Nationalism Reframed: Nationalism and the National Question in the New Europe* (Cambridge and New York, 1996); Benedict Anderson, *Imagined Communities: Reflections on the Origin and Spread of Nationalism* (London and New York, 1991); Bernhard Giessen, *Die Intellektuellen und die Nation: Eine deutsche Achsenzeit* (Frankfurt a.M., 1993); John Breuilly, *Nationalism and the State* (Chicago, IL, 1982). See also the nation-building literature with which comparative political science accompanied the de-colonization processes of the 1960s.

22. A remark to prevent a common misunderstanding: The assumption that nations are social constructs does not imply that they were not real – just as the constructed-ness of a building does not affect its reality. Neither does it necessarily imply, as the theoretical tradition known as *Ideologiekritik* has it, that nationalist agents inherently are manipulators who mislead the masses into accepting an essentially false or unauthentic fabrication.

nationalisms. Further, they do not provide a framework that would allow for the systematic inclusion of social learning, copying, and adoption that appear to be the driving forces of most twentieth-century and many nineteenth-century nationalisms, yet would, contrary to the functionalist intuition, reintroduce the problem of social action.

Instead of reinforcing the neatly maintained borders between the traditions of functional and action theories, it might be useful to make an attempt at fusion. After three decades of substantial critique, functionalism as a meta-theory seems hardly tenable, in social theory in general as well as with respect to a theory of nationalism.[23] However, there is no reason why one should not try to rescue its explanatory power by isolating its key element, the theory of differentiation, as an evolutionary heuristics and integrate it into a theory of social action.[24] In contrast to functionalism proper, which presupposes that the social world is essentially of a systemic nature, a heuristics of functional differentiation would have to use system theory in an empirically controlled manner by determining the "degrees of 'systemness'"[25] of a social situation. In this perspective, systems appear as "reproduced relations between actors or collectives, organized as regular social practices"[26] – in other words, as specific frameworks of social action.

The theoretical consequences of the transformation of functional differentiation from a paradigm to a heuristics and its integration into a theory of action are quite radical and far-reaching, but cannot be discussed here.[27] What concerns us here is the more modest project of a reconstruction of a theory of nations and nationalisms. My discussion of functional and social action approaches in

23. For a review of the debate on functionalism, and a sketch of possible ways out of its aporetic structures see Joas, *Kreativität*, 306–326. See also Anthony Giddens, "Functionalism: Après la lutte," *Social Research* 43 (1976), 325–366.

24. Joas, *Kreativität*, 326.

25. Anthony Giddens, *The Constitution of Society: Outline of the Theory of Structurationder Gesellschaft* (Cambridge, 1984), 283.

26. Giddens, *Constitution*, 25.

27. Instead, see Joas, *Kreativität*; Giddens, *Constitution*; Giddens, *The Consequences of Modernity* (Stanford, CA, 1990).

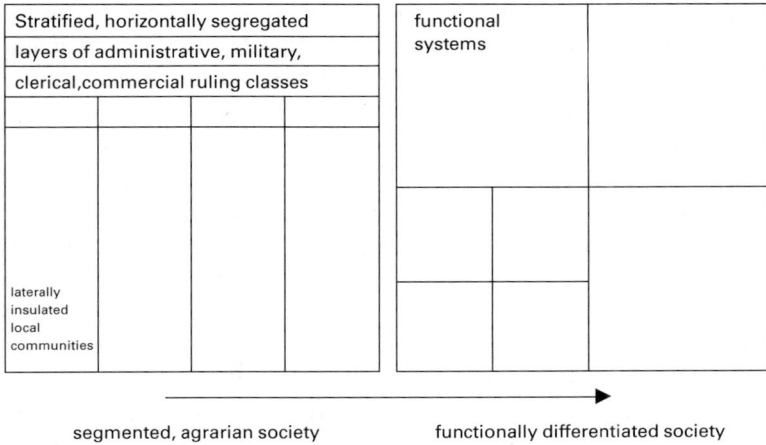

Figure 1 *Segmented/stratified into functionally differentiated society*[28]

theorizing nationalism in particular, and society in general, suggests the following:

At the core of the functional theories of nationalism is, as we have seen, a variety of specific processes of differentiation – industrialization, the emergence of capitalism or of an educational system, and so forth. Instead of declaring one particular aspect of modernization to be the trigger of the national paradigm and in order to escape the danger of overgeneralization, I suggest that we reformulate in a more abstract manner the emergence of nations and nationalisms as an effect of society's conversion from segmented/stratified to functional differentiation.

While the various causes that have been offered for the emergence of nationalism – exo-education and industrialism (Gellner), print capitalism and the threat of contingency (Anderson), communication technology (Deutsch), and the like – have certainly been relevant in particular historical circumstances, I suggest that the unique capacity of nation and nation-state relates to the transition to functional differentiation in general rather than the differentiation

28. For the left part of figure 1 see Gellner, *Nations and Nationalism*, 9.

of a particular functional system. By providing a superstructure of segmentation, nation and nation-state hide the de-territorializing nature of the transition to functional differentiation. At their core, nation and nation-state are a cover-up.

Segmented differentiation is a state where the system as a whole consists of subsystems that are essentially smaller versions of itself. From the perspective of these smaller units, the border between system and environment is territorial. It is not necessarily neatly staked out, but it marks more or less the territory within which regular social interaction actually takes place. We could also say that the border differentiates place from space. Functional differentiation, in contrast, is non-territorial. From the perspective of the subsystems, the border between system and environment is defined by the particular function a subsystem furnishes for the system as a whole. The spatial scope of functional differentiation depends principally on conditions that are internal to the subsystems. Consequently, we can, for all practical purposes, rule out the case that the subsystems strive for congruent borders. "The institutionalization of uniform borders for society in all its subsystems becomes problematic wherever the evolutionary process of functional differentiation and the intensification of potentialities succeeds."[29]

The boundary of a social system is defined by the difference between communication and non-communication. In this sense, world society is not a product of the current processes of globalization, but rather evolved in the eighteenth and nineteenth centuries, once the globe was thoroughly "discovered," colonized, and covered with networks of regular communication. World society begins, once *terrae incognitae* – or *incommunicadae*, which is the same – cease to exist, and asserts itself once functional differentiation dominates.[30] This, however, means that world society evolves around the same time as nations and nation-states.

29. Niklas Luhmann, "Die Weltgesellschaft," in Luhmann, *Soziologische Aufklärung 2: Aufsätze zur Theorie der Gesellschaft* (Opladen, 1975), 51–71, at 60 (own translation).
30. See Niklas Luhmann, *Die Gesellschaft der Gesellschaft* (Frankfurt a.M., 1999), 145–170.

The cover-up lies in the fact that nation-states territorialize the de-territorialized social system into societies – in the plural – which interpret themselves as substantial units and behave as if they were closed systems.[31]

> In the late eighteenth and nineteenth centuries, nation-building in Europe profited from the ongoing and undeniable process of social transformation. It is the new differentiations and the disappearance of older social divisions that strengthen the need for a national sense of belonging. With the concept of the nation, as well as that of man as individual and subject, the self-description of the social system creates a plausible solution for the problem of mobilizing resources of identity that the functional systems with their forms of inclusion cannot offer. The concept of the nation . . . helps to counter the universalisms of functional orientations with the higher dignity of the particularisms of regional communities. . . . The concept of the nation offers a concept of inclusion that does not depend on the specific conditions of the functional systems and forces even politics to respect all members of the nation as co-equals.[32]

Note how this perspective departs from the traditional set of functional explanations of nationalism: In Luhmann's schema, nation and nation-state do not emerge out of *systemic* necessities, such as to provide industrialism with an educated workforce or capitalism with a sufficiently large domestic market, or to furnish the military with an adequate supply of conscripts, but rather as a solution to problems of *identity and social integration* created by systemic differentiation. Nation and nation-state, therefore, counteract the universalism of the functional subsystems with a dispositive of particularistic and territorial inclusion. National identity, however, is only plausible if it can be rooted in social practice, and the territorial nation-state accomplishes this by institutionalizing a difference between "normal" social interaction, which takes place within the boundaries of nation and state, and "extraordinary" social interaction that takes place across

---

31. On the nation-state as closed system see Anthony Giddens, *Modernity and Self-Identity: Self and Society in the Late Modern Age* (Stanford, CA, 1991), 15.

32. Niklas Luhmann, *Die Gesellschaft der Gesellschaft* (Frankfurt a.M., 1998), 1051–1052 (own translation).

borders. The institutions that maintain and represent this difference are those which specialize in surveillance, constraining, and enabling, in short: those which regulate cross-border interactions and, thereby, set them apart and mark them as being different from interactions that take place within the borders of the state. Examples are the border police, customs and immigration authorities, foreign trade and tourism agencies, or agencies for cultural, educational, or academic cooperation and exchange. The effect is the substantiation of a nation-state society. Substantiating society, thus, is not simply something the nation-state does as a means of securing its own claims to internal and external sovereignty, or, to put it differently, it is not only a matter of system integration from the perspective of the state. Rather, it is a matter of social integration by converting space into place and strangers into co-nationals.

I suggest that we understand, for the purposes of a theory of nation and nation-state, the relation between systemic differentiation and social integration as a dialectics of disembedding and re-embedding.[33] Disembedding of social relations refers to the distanciation of social action in time and space. As a general principle, it accounts for the shift from types of social interactions that depend on co-presence in time and space and occur under the conditions of trust generated by familiarity and personal acquaintance to types of interactions that typically take place in a state of anonymity and time-spatial distance. However, it also destroys traditional forms of social integration in locally rooted communities and lifeworlds and would produce psychologically and socially unbearable burdens of alienation and distrust, were it not complemented by re-embedding mechanisms. If disembedding refers to the lifting out, the uprooting of social relations from the immediacy of communal forms, re-embedding refers to strategies and mechanisms of re-creating social meaning and trust under the conditions of time–space distanciation and functional differentiation. The re-embedding of disembedded social relations can be accomplished in extremely diverse ways, however. For our purposes it is sufficient to note that the historically

33. On disembedding see Anthony Giddens, *The Consequences of Modernity* (Stanford, CA, 1990), 21–29 and passim.

most powerful and pervasive re-embedding dispositive is none other than the nation. The nation as "imagined community," in Benedict Anderson's apt phrase, "conceived as a deep, horizontal comradeship"[34] despite its internal stratification and differentiation, despite the fact that even in the smallest nations anonymity between fellow nationals is the rule and intimacy extremely unlikely – all this alludes to the nation as a dispositive of re-embedding. Rudolf Stichweh's wonderfully aphoristic definition of the nation as "a society which is a community,"[35] delivered almost in passing, points in the same direction: Disembedding and re-embedding, the uprooting of social relations and their re-rooting in the nation, systemic differentiation and social integration, are sides of the same coin.

From the Nation-State World to the Postnational Condition

The suspicion that we are approaching a postnational condition is based on the empirical observation that international dependencies are intensifying and social relations that transcend national borders are becoming increasingly normal. World society penetrates everyday life to a degree virtually inconceivable only one or two generations ago.[36] In the course of this development, the regulatory confinement of functional differentiation by the nation-state becomes decreasingly effective and is more and more shifted to regulatory authorities on levels other than the national. As a result, nation-states increasingly lose their ability to bring the scopes of the differentiated spheres of social action into congruency with each other and within their own borders and lose their ability to define and enforce autonomously the rules of the game for the different social subsystems.

34. Anderson, *Imagined Communities*, 7.

35. Rudolf Stichweh, "Nation und Weltgesellschaft," in Bernd Estel and Tilman Mayer, eds., *Das Prinzip Nation in modernen Gesellschaften* (Opladen, 1994), 83–96, at 85 (own translation).

36. How much sense would the concept of a "Kolonialwarenhandlung" or colonial grocery as a store that specializes on non-domestic products make today?

The political remedies oscillate between pleas for the restoration of nation-state sovereignty or even autonomy,[37] on the one hand, and the replacement of all forms of particularistic organizations with a universal world state, on the other. While the former does not seem very realistic vis-à-vis the logic of functional differentiation, the latter seems to depend on a confusion of the abstract universalism of the human rights tradition and the historical and empirical particularism of norms and interests. Thus, the problem is to develop an argument that is neither conservative nor utopian, but is able to present an abstract, yet fairly realistic model of society under post-national conditions.

As we have seen, the world of nation-states is characterized by an inherent tension between the universalistic tendencies of functional differentiation and the particularistic segmentation of world society into territorialized nation-state societies. The re-embedding of disembedded social relations *qua* nation and national identity, however, depends on plausibility and the practical experience that the re-embedding mechanisms actually matter, such as the greater probability of social interaction within than across national borders, the practical feasibility of national self-determination, the possibility of national warfare, or the effectiveness of the nation-state as a uniform regulatory authority. In the course of the post-national transition, these plausibilities tend to wither away: Globalization frees communication and interaction for ever larger portions of the population of its national constraints. The principle of self-determination, institutionalized after World War I in the Wilsonian restructuring of Central Europe and in the norms of the League of Nations, found its moral disaster when nobody seriously objected

37. This position is particularly strong among American conservatives and articulates itself, for example, on issues of economic cooperation (see the Nafta-debate and Ross Perot's anticipation of the "big sucking sound" of American jobs being relocated to low-wage Mexico), military interventions, and international environmental regimes. For this line of argument, see Jeremy Rabkin, *Why Sovereignty Matters* (American Enterprise Institute Studies on Global Environmental Policy), (Washington, D.C., 1998). However, structurally similar arguments have been made by social-democratic traditionalists in Europe and by liberal populists in the United States.

to the Nazis' persecution of the German Jews, and it became entirely impractical – contrary to the prevailing rhetoric – in the era of bloc confrontation. National warfare has become, in the age of readily available weapons of mass destruction, a lose-lose option. The technological liberation of capital, knowledge, and information from time-spatial constraints undercuts the regulatory power of the nation-states, with particularly dramatic effects on welfare and environmental regimes.

This said, is it true that nationalism and the nation-state are obsolete[38] and, as Luhmann contends, that "the idea of the nation belongs to that cluster of transitory semantics which may fascinate a period of transition without ever revealing to which social system they refer"?[39] The answer has to be ambivalent in two respects: First, social and political development is extremely uneven. In many regions of the world, the nation and the nation-state form are in the process of maturation rather than in decline, although without having any hope of ever arriving at the degree of nation-ness, in terms of sovereignty, autonomy, and infrastructural power, that the European nation-states used to enjoy in their classical period. The transitory character of nation and nation-state, if we want to call it that, manifests itself so far primarily within the European Union. Second, while it may indeed be true that nation and nation-state in their classic form are becoming inappropriate, it seems unlikely that their semantics will disappear any time soon.[40] It seems more realistic to suppose a shifting of signifiers: The semantics of the nation might stay, but may refer to a changed social reality.

At the core of the post-national transformation there seem to be processes of de-territorialization and de-hierarchization. De-

38. For this position see, for example, David Beetham, "The Future of the Nation-State?" in Gregor McLennan, David Held, and Stuart Hall, eds., *The Idea of the Modern State* (Milton Keynes, 1984) and David Held, "The Decline of the Nation-State," in Eley and Suny, eds., *Becoming National: A Reader* (Oxford and New York, 1996), 407–416.

39. Luhmann, *Die Gesellschaft der Gesellschaft,* 1055.

40. Of course, Luhmann's assumption that the nation represents a semantics of transition cannot be falsified unless he defines a timeframe. Otherwise, everything has to be conceived of as transitory.

341

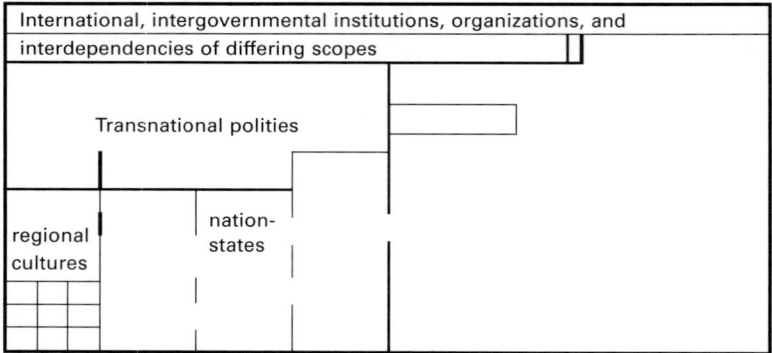

Figure 2 *The post-national condition*

territorialization is the effect of the state's decreasing ability to domesticate functional differentiation; de-hierarchization refers to the tendency to reorganize state–society relations in non-hierarchical or less hierarchical networks rather than vertically. In the course of this, the segmented superstructure of the nation-state world gives way to the unavoidably state-sanctioned dominance of functional differentiation. This implies that the spatial scopes of the functional systems will be incongruent with each other and with any given state-boundary.[41] The result could look somewhat like Figure 2.

Despite the rather unsophisticated character of the figure,[42] I think that it illustrates my central arguments. First, the spheres of functional

41. Capitalism, industrialism, and popular culture make good candidates for true globalization. Military and security policies might go the way of selective globalization. In the case of Western and, eventually, Central Europe, it seems reasonable to assume that many of the key policies that so far belong in the realm of national sovereignty will be reorganized on the level of the European Union. National cultures will probably, owing to the power of linguistic homogeneity, retain their national locus and maybe give room to a strengthening of regional, local, or ethnic vernaculars.

42. The depiction given here is extremely insufficient, particularly in ignoring the dominant principle of differentiation, which is, of course, functional; it only indicates the increasingly irregular (see the uneven "depth" of the transnational polity) and weakened (see the various openings in the vertical lines) structure of political segmentation.

differentiation and social action are reorganized on multiple levels, including, but not privileging, that of the nation. This presents, among others, the problem that nation-states are held accountable for spheres that have grown out of their autonomous control. In order to catch up politically with the actual state of differentiation, we see the spread of international organizations of the traditional, intergovernmental type as well as the emergence of transnational polities. The best example for the latter is certainly the European Union, with its mix of intergovernmental and supranational institutions and its dense networks of transnational relations. We can further assume that transnational polities are not likely to be closed systems of the nation-state type, not even of the type of federalized nation-states. Rather, transnational polities present the opportunity to adapt the depth of political cooperation and integration to the respective possibilities and constraints of situative contexts. The simple fact that neither the European Monetary Union nor the Schengen Group is congruent with each other or with the European Union itself may serve as a case in point. It is further safe to assume that the eventual integration of Central European countries into the framework of the Union will take place in an uneven manner, resulting in further internal differentiation with respect to the degree of integration.[43]

Yet, even such an uneven, incomplete, and differentiated process of polity-building presents a severe problem for the nation-state model in its classic form, and for its functioning as the general framework of (a) disembedding and (b) re-embedding.

43. German foreign minister Joschka Fischer proposed the concept of a further differentiation of degrees of integration, with an "avant-garde" of European countries pushing for ever fuller integration, in his statement of principles "From Confederation of States to Federation – On the Finality of European Integration" (given at Humboldt University, Berlin, May 12, 2000). While most of his suggestions clearly went too far towards a European federation for the taste of the leaders of other EU-members, the idea of differentiating degrees of integration and giving an avant-garde function to some core countries, in particular to Germany and France, was met with strong approval by French President Chirac, as expressed on the occasion of his speech before the German Bundestag June 27, 2000. For the Fischer-speech see http://www.auswaertiges-amt.de/ 6_archiv/2/r/r000512a.htm; for Chirac's speech see http://www. bundestag.de/blickpkt/arch_bpk/ chirac1. htm.

(a) With every capacity and policy that is transferred from the national to another level, the nation-state not only surrenders aspects of sovereignty, but also disembedding mechanisms. Thus, the EMU has already taken currency, one of the principal symbolic tokens of generating trust under the conditions of time–space distanciation, out of the control of the nation-state and placed it under the supervision of a transnational institution that does not report to the national governments. The same is true for many expert systems of policy-making, implementation, and evaluation that have been established at the European level. Thus, many EU-programs are designed in a way that allows actors on the local and regional level to access them with complete circumvention of the national level. Consequently, to the degree that functions that had typically belonged into the realm of the national polity are relocated at the European level, the nation-state ceases to be the frame of reference for the generation of trust as well as, in the case of malfunctions, uncertainty. Thus, nation-states lose – or rather voluntarily surrender – the monopoly of providing the means of time–space distanciation to a multilayered, transnational, and non-substantiated network of policy-making.[44]

(b) While the consequences of postnationalization are quite severe for the nation-state as the institutional framework of disembedding, the consequences for its re-embedding function might be even graver. Reembedding: the pinning down of disembedded social relations to the hic et nunc of social practices, is what the nationalist transformation of a functionally differentiated society into a horizontal community of mutual comradeship does. Nation-ness, as re-embedded social relation, is what national identity refers to. The conversion of contingency into fate, including the link it establishes between every single member of the nation and its most

---

44. On the evolution of a network-mode of governance see Beate Kohler-Koch and Rainer Eising, eds., *The Transformation of Governance in the European Union* (London and New York, 1999); on multi-level governance in the European Union see Fritz W. Scharpf, *Regieren in Europa: Effektiv und demokratisch?* (Frankfurt a.M., and New York, 1999) and Scharpf, "Die Handlungsfähigkeit des Staates am Ende des zwanzigsten Jahrhunderts," *Politische Vierteljahresschrift* 32 (1991), 621–634.

distant past and future and its most distant territories, can be considered the reason for the amazing and quite disturbing fact that so many people have shown their willingness to die for the nation.

Postnationalization does not deprive the nation of its re-embedding functions altogether. Yet, again, it seems unlikely that the total character of its re-embedding capacity can be maintained if the scopes of the different spheres of social action are not congruent to each other. If the boundaries of the nation prove to be increasingly marginal for the framing of everyday practices of growing parts of the population – business and professional relations, travel, cultural consumption, eventually even political participation – the imagination of the nation as the macro-community which vaults and integrates all other communities cannot be sustained. This does not mean that national identities disappear or become irrelevant, but they are reduced in status to being one source and subject of collective identification among a plurality of others which may be subsets of it, may transcend it, or may be entirely indifferent toward it. In other words, in the course of postnationalization, social identities catch up with functional differentiation.

Conclusion

Apart from all the warfare, chauvinism, and hatred, apart from the furor that the national principle unleashed throughout its existence, it also served as the medium for the establishment of equality vis-à-vis the state and for the expansion and intensification of citizenship rights.[45] Top-down, the nation could legitimate states' use of their populations as a supply of conscripts for the demands of nationalist warfare, yet bottom-up it legitimated and ultimately helped to win democracy – in some instances, at least. So far, we have not even touched upon a truly crucial question: What happens to democracy in a postnational situation?

45. See Mann, "Nation-States in Europe," 137.

The democratic deficit is, within the European Union, a topic almost as old as the process of European integration itself. Incomplete parliamentarization, indirect legitimacy, a lack of accountability, the overall elusive character of power within the EU nurture the suspicion that the locus of democracy is the nation-state and that, consequently, less nation-state comes with less democracy. Similar fears surround the process of globalization. "No globalization without representation" has recently become a popular slogan among protesters against World Bank and IMF meetings.

Thus, there is, on the one hand, little doubt that the postnational condition complicates the matter of democratic legitimacy immensely and has, for the time being, reduced the democratic accountability of politics. Yet, on the other hand, it is quite evident that the established forms of democracy suffer from the decreasing regulatory power of their institutional locus, the nation-state, as the social-democratic parties that currently govern in all major European countries had to learn. The situation resembles a prisoner's dilemma.

However, the fact that democratic government historically emerged within nation-states does not mean that postnationalization should come per se with less democracy. A postnational polity like the European Union can be democratized very much along the lines that have been developed within the world of nation-states. Following Maastricht and Amsterdam, the European Union gained a Social Chapter, although one that is much too weak to guarantee the kind of social citizenship that the European nation-states provide; and it has its own citizenship, although one that is, so far, empirically rather empty. A Charter of Basic Rights, which could prove the nucleus of a European Constitution, is included in the preparations for the Treaty of Nice. A little farther down the road, the Union will have to clean up its institutional structure in order to provide for accountability and open up more avenues for participation. A European public sphere and a European political identity would emerge to the degree that the European Union becomes a recognizable center of policy-making. As far as the intermediary institutions are concerned, the process of Europeanization is well under way, with the notable exception of political parties.

Apart from postnational polities like the European Union – and for the time being, there is only the European Union – the alignment of globalization and democracy is more difficult. A global citizenship, as Habermas imagines it,[46] is rather illusory, as is, for the reasons discussed in this essay, a global government. Rather, participation in global policy-making will depend on more or less institutionalized non-traditional collective actors, such as INGOs, transnational social movements, and the transnationalization of the public sphere. Further, it is these non-traditional actors that may have the best chance of taming those multinational economic beasts that have long escaped the regulatory power of the nation-states, either directly by organizing consumers, or in a combination of consumer organization and the stimulation of state activity. The campaigns against the sweat shop practices of Nike and other producers of athletic and general apparel in Southeast Asia may serve as an example. Finally, and in response to the increasing depth of policy penetration, it is conceivable that not only transnational organizations, but also the traditional actors of international relations – national governments and international organizations – may reframe their mutual relations at least partly on the basis of a communicative rather than an exclusively instrumental mode of rationality.[47]

46. Jürgen Habermas, "Staatsbürgerschaft und nationale Identität," in Habermas, *Faktizität und Geltung: Beiträge zur Diskurstheorie des Rechts und des demokratischen Rechtsstaats* (Frankfurt a.M., 1992), 632–660, 659–660.

47. On communicative rationality in international relations see Thomas Risse, "'Let's Argue!': Communicative Action in World Politics," *International Organization* 54 (2000), 1–39.

2
Future Blues: Race Relations in the United States

Leon F. Litwack[1]

Shortly after the Civil War, Oliver Howard, head of the Freedmen's Bureau, a government agency designed to oversee the transition from slavery to freedom, came to Edisto Island, off the coast of South Carolina.[2] The newly freed slaves who lived and worked there knew why he was coming – to order them to surrender to the original owners (their former owners) the lands they had been working as their own after their masters had fled during the war. Only Howard, it was thought, who enjoyed immense popularity among blacks, could make them believe it.[3] The church in which

1. Leon Litwack's contribution did not contain footnotes or annotations originally. With Dr. Litwack's explicit consent, Norbert Finzsch added some footnotes that give some documentation in order to facilitate further reading. Any mistakes in the footnotes are Norbert Finzsch's exclusive responsibility.

2. John Alcott Carpenter, (Pittsburgh, PA, 1964); Oliver Otis Howard, *Autobiography of Oliver Otis Howard, Major General, United States Army* (Freeport, NY, 1971; 1st edn. 1907); William S. McFeely, *Yankee Stepfather: General O. O. Howard and the Freedmen* (New Haven, CT, 1968); Gerald Weland, *O. O. Howard, Union General* (Jefferson, NC, 1995). The Freedmen's Bureau played a very ambiguous role in the integration of freedmen in the Southern economy: Paul A. Cimbala, *Under the Guardianship of the Nation: The Freedmen's Bureau and the Reconstruction of Georgia, 1865–1870* (Athens, GA, 1997); Barry A. Crouch, *The Freedmen's Bureau and Black Texans* (Austin, TX, 1992); Randy Finley, *From Slavery to Uncertain Freedom: The Freedmen's Bureau in Arkansas, 1865–1869* (Fayetteville, AR, 1996); Donald G. Nieman, *The Freedmen's Bureau and Black Freedom* (New York, 1994); Paul A. Cimbala and Randall M. Miller, eds., *The Freedmen's Bureau and Reconstruction: Reconsiderations* (New York, 1999); William Lee Richter, *Overreached on All Sides: The Freedmen's Bureau Administrators in Texas, 1865–1868* (College Station, TX, 1991).

3. Edisto Island was part of an area in the South that was taken by Union troops as soon as 1862. Ira Berlin et al., *Freedom: A Documentary History of Emancipation,*

he met them was filled, the auditorium and galleries jammed with sad and angry blacks who were in no mood to come to order. Suddenly an old woman began to sing, "Nobody knows the trouble I feel – Nobody knows but Jesus," and the entire audience of some 2,000 joined her. Whether it was the song, the look of dismay on the faces before him, or the shouts of "no, no!" that greeted his words, Howard was so flustered that he could barely finish. But he managed to communicate the position of the federal government. He told them to lay aside any bitter feelings they harbored for their former masters and to contract to work for those same masters; they would, he assured them, achieve the same ends. If the freedmen found Howard's advice incomprehensible, that was because they understood him all too clearly. A voice from the gallery rang out, "*Why*, General Howard, why do you take away our lands? You take them from us who have always been true, always true to the Government! You give them to our all-time enemies! That is not right!"

Nearly a century later, July 1966, Martin Luther King faced a black audience in Chicago. He had come to Chicago to address the violence of poverty, to battle slum conditions and the slumlords and politicians who perpetuated them.[4] He knew by now that segregation was but part of an elaborate system of racial inequality in housing, jobs, and education. But Chicago proved to be a frustrating experience. The old tactics of non-violence, street marches, and mass rallies no longer worked. The goal of economic justice proved more elusive, the barriers more formidable than what he had encountered in the South. He failed to achieve his objectives in Chicago, and when he tried to address the meeting, he encountered for the first time a hostile black audience, some of whom jeered as he started to speak. That night, returning to his home "with an

---

1861–1867, Series 1, Volume 3: *The Wartime Genesis of Free Labor: The Lower South* (New York and Cambridge 1990), 91; Leon F. Litwack, *Been in the Storm So Long: The Aftermath of Slavery* (New York, 1979), 113–114.

4. James R. Ralph, Jr., *Northern Protest: Martin Luther King, Jr., Chicago, and the Civil Rights Movement* (Cambridge, 1994).

ugly feeling," King brooded over this encounter. After some reflection, he thought he understood:

> For twelve years I, and others like me, had held out radiant promises of progress. I had preached to them about my dream. I had lectured to them about the not too distant day when they would have freedom, "all, here and now." I had urged them to have faith in America and in white society. Their hopes had soared. They were now booing because they felt that we were unable to deliver on our promises. They were booing because we had urged them to have faith in people who had too often proved to be unfaithful. They were now hostile because they were watching the dream that they had so readily accepted turn into a frustrating nightmare.

For more than a century, black Americans learned to live with betrayed expectations. In the 1860s, and a century later, in the 1960s, two major struggles, two major civil conflicts were fought over the meaning of freedom in America: over the enslavement of black men and women and over the legally sanctioned repression of their descendants, over the shackles of slavery and the fetters of segregation and discrimination. In the 1860s and in the 1960s, partly for military and partly for political reasons (the need to win the Civil War, the need to win the Cold War), major efforts were undertaken to restructure race relations. And in both decades, this nation made commitments to black freedom and civil rights that overreached popular convictions and that would subsequently be compromised, discarded, or deferred.

Some thirty years after emancipation, between 1890 and World War I, in response to perceptions of a new generation of black southerners, born in freedom, undisciplined by slavery and unschooled in racial etiquette, and in response to growing doubts that this generation could be trusted to stay in its place without legal force, the white South denied blacks a political voice, imposed rigid patterns of segregation (Jim Crow), sustained an economic system – sharecropping and tenantry – that left little room for hope or ambition, refused blacks equal educational resources ("enforced ignorance"), and embraced racial caricatures and pseudo-scientific theories that reinforced and comforted whites in their racial beliefs and practices.[5] The criminal justice system (the law, the courts, the legal profession) operated with ruthless efficiency in upholding the absolute power of whites to command the subordination and labor of blacks. No wonder blacks came to view the courts as instruments of injustice and upon those convicted in them as victims if not martyrs.

How to respond to this repressive apparatus assumed an urgency in the black South. Thirty years after the Civil War, Booker T. Washington emerged as the preeminent black spokesman. He charted for his people a strategy of uplift and accommodation, grounded in the belief that work and economic progress would command the respect and recognition of whites. "It's not within the province of human nature, that the man who is intelligent and virtuous, and owns and cultivates the best farm in his county, shall very long be denied the proper respect and consideration."[6] That advice would be shared by many in black leadership, including W. E. B Du Bois.[7] Whatever his differences with Washington on other

---

5. Leon F. Litwack, *Trouble in Mind: Black Southerners in the Age of Jim Crow* (New York, 1999). Norbert Finzsch, James O. Horton and Lois E. Horton, *Von Benin nach Baltimore: Die Geschichte der African Americans* (Hamburg, 1999), 310–387; Kenneth S. Greenberg, *Honor & Slavery: Lies, Duels, Noses, Masks, Dressing as a Woman, Gifts, Strangers, Humanitarianism, Death, Slave Rebellions, The Proslavery Argument, Baseball, Hunting, and Gambling in the Old South* (Princeton, NJ, 1996), 67–69; Leon Litwack, *Been in the Storm So Long* (New York, 1979), 448; Glenda Elizabeth Gilmore, *Gender and Jim Crow: Women and the Politics of White Supremacy in North Carolina, 1896–1920* (Chapel Hill, NC, 1996); Stetson Kennedy, *Jim Crow Guide to the U.S.A: The Laws, Customs and Etiquette Governing the Conduct of Nonwhites and Other Minorities as Second-Class Citizens* (Westport, CN, 1973); David M. Oshinsky, *"Worse than Slavery": Parchman Farm and the Ordeal of Jim Crow Justice* (New York , 1996); Joseph H. Cartwright, *The Triumph of Jim Crow: Tennessee Race Relations in the 1880's* (Knoxville, TN, 1976);. Donald G. Nieman, *From Slavery to Sharecropping: White Land and Black Labor in the Rural South, 1865–1900* (New York, 1994); Edward Cary Royce, *The Origins of Southern Sharecropping* (Philadelphia, 1993).

6. Quoted in Litwack, *Trouble in Mind*, 148.

7. Finzsch et al., *Von Benin nach Baltimore*, 356–364. W. E. B. Du Bois, *The Souls of Black Folk* (New York and Toronto, 1994), 33–46; Cary D. Wintz, ed., *African American Political Thought, 1890–1930: Washington, Du Bois, Garvey, and Randolph* (Armonk, NY, 1995); Virginia Lantz Denton, *Booker T. Washington and the Adult Education Movement* (Gainesville, FL, 1993); Thomas E. Harris, *Analysis of the Clash*

questions, he shared with him at the turn of the century a faith in the prevailing Gospel of Wealth: "The day the Negro race courts and marries the savings-bank will be the day of its salvation." [8]

But they were wrong. The experience of black southerners contradicted the dominant success credo. Faithful adherence to the work ethic brought most of them nothing. No matter how hard they labored, no matter how they conducted themselves, no matter how fervently they prayed, the chances for making it were less than encouraging, the basic rules and controls remained in place.

> Our father, who is in heaven,
> White man owe me eleven and pay me seven,
> Thy kingdom come, thy will be done,
> And if I hadn't took that, I wouldn't had none.

From their first days of freedom, black men and women had been forcibly reminded that lofty ambitions and evidence of advancement might be resented rather than welcomed by whites. The obstacles black people faced were exceptional, unlike those faced by any group of immigrants, shaped profoundly by the slave experience and the ways in which white people perceived and acted upon racial differences. While maintaining that blacks were incapable of becoming their social, political, or economic equals, the dominant society betrayed the fear that they might. What had alarmed the white South during Reconstruction was not evidence of black failure but evidence of black success, evidence of black assertion, independence, and advancement, evidence of black men learning

---

over the Issues between Booker T. Washington and W.E.B. Du Bois (New York, 1993); Daniel Agbeyebiawo, *The Life and Works of W.E.B. Du Bois* (Accra, 1998); Keith Eldon Byerman, *Seizing the Word: History, Art, and Self in the Work of W.E.B. Du Bois* (Athens, GA, 1994); Rutledge M. Dennis, *W.E.B. Du Bois: The Scholar as Activist* (Greenwich, CT, 1996).

8. Francis L. Broderick, *W.E.B. Du Bois: Negro Leader in Time of Crisis* (Stanford, CA, 1955), 66, quoted in Litwack, *Trouble in Mind*, 148; W. E. B. Du Bois, *Writings: Dusk of Dawn* (New York, 1986), 787–789.

the uses of political power.[9] The closer the black man got to the ballot box, someone noted, the more he looked like a rapist.[10]

That suggests the magnitude of the problem, and black leaders were never able to surmount this paradox. Even as whites scorned black incompetence, they feared evidence of black competence and independence. Even as whites derided blacks for their ignorance, they resented educated, literate, ambitious, and successful blacks. The Negro as a buffoon, a menial, a servant was acceptable; that kind of Negro threatened no one. The historical record is replete with examples of violence and harassment aimed at successful blacks, those in positions of leadership, who owned farms and stores, those suspected of saving their earnings, those trying to improve themselves, those perceived as having stepped out of their place, "trying to be white."[11]

Perhaps Washington never fully grasped the tragic flaw in his success creed. W. E. B. Du Bois, on the other hand, came to understand the depths of white fear and that it was directed less at the vagabond or the criminal black as at the successful and ambitious

9. Finzsch et al., *Von Benin nach Baltimore*, 310–339; David A. Lincove, *Reconstruction in the United States: An Annotated Bibliography* (Westport, CT, 2000); Richard Bailey, *Neither Carpetbaggers nor Scalawags: Black Officeholders during the Reconstruction of Alabama, 1867–1878* (Montgomery, AL, 1991); Paul Finkelman, *Emancipation and Reconstruction* (New York, 1992); Eric Foner, *A Short History of Reconstruction, 1863–1877* (New York, 1990); John Hope Franklin, Eric Anderson, and Alfred A. Moss, *The Facts of Reconstruction: Essays in Honor of John Hope Franklin* (Baton Rouge, LA, 1991); Stetson Kennedy, *After Appomattox: How the South Won the War* (Gainesville, FL, 1995); Harriette Robinet, *Forty Acres and Maybe a Mule* (New York, 1998); Willie Lee Rose, *Rehearsal for Reconstruction: The Port Royal Experiment* (Athens, GA, 1999); James D. Schmidt, *Free to Work: Labor Law, Emancipation, and Reconstruction, 1815–1880* (Athens, GA, 1998); John David Smith, *Black Voices From Reconstruction, 1865–1877* (Brookfield, CT, 1996); Dorothy Sterling, *The Trouble They Seen: The Story of Reconstruction in the Words of African Americans* (New York, 1994).

10. Angela Y. Davis, *Rassismus und Sexismus: Schwarze Frauen und Klassenkampf in den USA* (Berlin, 1982), 177.

11. Quoted in Litwack, *Trouble in Mind*, 154. Norbert Finzsch, "Rassistische Gewalt im Süden der USA: 1865 bis 1920," *Kriminologisches Journal* 3 (1994), 191–209; William F. Brundage, *Lynching in the New South: Georgia and Virginia, 1880–1930* (Urbana, IL, and Chicago 1993).

black. The historical evidence fully supports the grim conclusion
Du Bois reached:

> If my own city of Atlanta were offered to-day the choice between 500
> Negro college graduates – forceful, busy, ambitious men of property
> and self-respect – and 500 black, cringing vagrants and criminals, the
> popular vote in favor of the criminals would be simply overwhelming.
> Why? because they want Negro crime? No, not that they fear Negro
> crime less, but that they fear Negro ambition and success more. They
> can deal with crime by chain-gang and lynch law, or at least they think
> they can, but the South can conceive neither machinery nor place for
> the educated, self-reliant, self-assertive black man.

Neither accommodation nor economic success guaranteed blacks
their civil rights. The quality of the racial violence that gripped the
South made it distinctive in this nation's history. Some two to three
black men and women, sometimes entire families, were lynched,
hanged, burned at the stake, or quietly murdered each week. The
offenses which precipitated the lynchings related less to sex-related
crimes than to questions of racial violence, racial etiquette, and
economic competition – and all too often, an observer concluded,
"There was just an assumption that you had to have a lynching
every now and then to preserve equitable race relations."[12]

Nothing so dramatically underscored the cheapness of black life.
"In those days," a black man recalled, "it was 'Kill a mule, buy another.
Kill a nigger, hire another.' They had to have a license to kill anything
but a nigger We was always in season." What was strikingly new
and different by the late nineteenth century was the sadism and
exhibitionism that characterized white violence. The lynching
became a public ritual, a collective experience, a voyeuristic spectacle
prolonged as long as possible for the benefit of the crowd, with
severed bodily parts distributed as favors and souvenirs.[13]

Excursion trains brought thousands on a Sunday afternoon in
1899 to Palmetto, Georgia, to see Sam Hose, a black man, burned

12. Quoted in Litwack, *Trouble in Mind*, 101.
13. See Arthur F. Raper, *The Tragedy of Lynching* (Montclair, NJ, 1969), 6–7.

alive, but only after his ears, toes and fingers were cut off and passed to the crowd, his eyes gouged, his tongue torn out, and his flesh cut in strips with knives; afterwards his heart was cut out and sliced. The crowd fought over the souvenirs, and one of the lynchers reportedly left for the state capitol hoping to deliver to the Governor a slice of Sam Hose's heart.[14]

Two weeks after the murder of her husband by a white mob, Mary Turner – in her eighth month of pregnancy – vowed to reveal the names of the mob leaders to a grand jury. For making such threats, several hundred men and women seized her; she was then tortured, hanged, shot, and disemboweled. The infant fell prematurely from her womb and cried briefly, whereupon a member of this mob in Valdosta, Georia crushed the baby's head beneath his heel.[15]

Two black brothers, Irving and Herman Arthur, were lynched and burned in Paris, Texas, in August 1920. Their roasted bodies were chained to the back of an automobile and dragged through the streets, with the lynchers shouting jubilantly as they drove through the black neighborhood, "Here come the barbecued niggers."

Part of their lives, part of America's heritage. To dismiss the atrocities as the work of crazed fiends is to miss how terrifyingly normal these people were, the frequency with which lynchings took place in the most churchified communities. These were churchgoing folks, and hence clergymen refrained from comment. "The only way to keep the pro-lynching element in the church," a pastor confessed, "is to say nothing which would tend to make them uncomfortable as church members."[16] For the lynchers and the approving spectators, this was the highest idealism in the service of their God and race. What is most disturbing was the capacity of ordinary, often educated and trained people, to kill as they did, and

14. Litwack, *Trouble in Mind*, 280–283.

15. Ibid., p. 289–290.

16. In later years, some pastors did in fact stand up against lynching. Will Gravely, ed., "A Man Lynched in Inhuman Lawlessness: South Carolina Methodist Hawley Lynn Condems the Killing of Willie Earle (1947)," *Methodist History* 35(2) (1997), 71–80.

to be able to justify their actions, or reinterpret them, so they would not see themselves as evil people but as the dispensers of justice and the guardians of communal values.[17] For black southerners, the lynchings confirmed not the superiority of whites but their enormous capacity for savagery and cowardice. "The lynch mob came," a Mississippi black woman observed. "I ain't heard of no one white man going to get a Negro."

The terrorism meted out by whites rested on the racism of genteel society. If mobs lynched blacks with calculated sadistic cruelty, historians and the academic sciences were no less resourceful in providing the intellectual underpinnings of racist thought and behavior, validating theories of black degeneracy and cultural and intellectual inferiority, helping to justify on "scientific" and historical grounds a complex of racial laws, practices, and beliefs.[18] Popular literature, newspaper caricatures, minstrel shows, and vaudeville depicted blacks as a race of buffoons and half-wits.[19] And with "Birth of a Nation" in 1915, the cinema did more than any historian to explain the "Negro problem" to the American people – the dangers

17. Norton H. Moses (ed.), *Lynching and Vigilantism in the United States: An Annotated Bibliography* (Westport, CN, 1997); Michael James Pfeifer, "Lynching and Criminal Justice in Regional Context: Iowa, Wyoming, and Louisiana, 1878–1946" (Ph.D.-Thesis, University Iowa, 1998); Mary Jane Brown, "'Eradicating This Evil': Women in the American Anti-Lynching Movement, 1892–1940" (Ph.D.-Thesis, Ohio State University, 1998); W. Fitzhugh Brundage, *Under Sentence of Death: Lynching in the South* (Chapel Hill, NC, 1997); Stewart E. Tolnay and E. M. Beck, *A Festival of Violence: An Analysis of Southern Lynchings, 1882–1930* (Urbana, IL, 1995).

18. Norbert Finzsch, "Wissenschaftlicher Rassismus in den Vereinigten Staaten – 1850 bis 1930," in Heidrun Kaupen-Haas and Christian Saller, eds., *Wissenschaftlicher Rassismus: Analysen einer Kontinuität in den Human- und Geisteswissenschaften* (Frankfurt am Main and New York, 1999), 84–110.

19. Dale Cockrell, *Demons of Disorder: Early Blackface Minstrels and Their World* (Cambridge and New York, 1997); Annemarie Bean, James Vernon Hatch and Brooks McNamara, *Inside the Minstrel Mask: Readings in Nineteenth-Century Blackface Minstrelsy* (Hanover, NH, 1996); W. T. Lhamon, *Raising Cain: Blackface Performance from Jim Crow to Hip Hop* (Cambridge, MA, 1998); Eric Lott, *Love and Theft: Blackface Minstrelsy and the American Working Class* (New York, 1993); William J. Mahar, *Behind the Burnt Cork Mask: Early Blackface Minstrelsy and Antebellum American Popular Culture* (Urbana, IL, 1999).

(vividly depicted on the screen) posed by a race freed from the restraints of slavery.[20] Beneath the grinning exterior of the black man, this film warned, there lurks a mindless savagery. The total effect of popular culture was to solidify stereotypes in the white mind, to portray the Negro as sometimes servile and comic, sometimes bestial and threatening, but in either case less than a man or a woman.

With equal forcefulness, dehumanizing images of black men and women were imprinted on the white mind in the commercial products sold to white America, in crude objects that exaggerated and distorted the physical appearance of black people and mocked their lives and aspirations. The "picturesque Negro" was packaged and marketed as a suitable household or yard adornment: the hitching post, a lawn ornament in the form of a grinning black stable boy; the doll, milk pitcher, or ceramic cookie jar fashioned after the image of a smiling, heavy set, aproned and turbaned black mammy; the bottle opener in the shape of a gaping minstrel; the white haired, toothless Uncle Remus smiling on the label of a can of syrup bearing his name and his testimonial; the salt and pepper shakers in the shape of black children; the ashtrays in the shape of Ubangi lips; a children's bank, called "The Jolly Nigger," in the shape of a grinning black man, whose eyes rolled when a coin was placed in his mouth. Golly-wogs and pick-a-ninnies, Mammies, Aunt Jeminas, and Uncle Bens, crap-shooting, minstrel-tapping, watermelon-eating, hallelujah-shouting black caricatures in the white mind.[21]

---

20. Roy E. Aitken and Al P. Nelson, *The Birth of a Nation Story* (Middleburg, VA, 1965); Karl Brown and Kevin Brownlow, *Adventures with D. W. Griffith* (London, 1988); John Cuniberti, *The Birth of a Nation: A Formal Shot-by-Shot Analysis* (Woodbridge, CT, 1979); Nickieann Fleener-Marzec, *D. W. Griffith's The Birth of a Nation: Controversy, Suppression, and the First Amendment as It Applies to Filmic Expression, 1915–1973* (New York, 1980); Sonya Michel, "The Reconstruction of White Southern Manhood," in Norbert Finzsch and Jürgen Martschukat, eds., *Different Restorations: Reconstruction and "Wiederaufbau" in the United States and Germany: 1865–1945–1989* (Providence, RI, and Oxford, 1996), 140–164.

21. Leon Litwack deals with the character of "uncle Remus" in *Trouble in Mind*, 187–188.

In the face of white hostility, blacks drew inward, constructing in their communities a separate world, a replica of the society that excluded them, with their own schools, churches, businesses, fraternal orders, and cultural practices. Within rigidly prescribed boundaries, they improvised strategies for dealing with whites. The choices were never easy, the risks always great. Most tried to accommodate without submitting, to defend themselves without inviting retribution, to enjoy the personal and family experiences life has to offer. To survive was to watch every word and action in the presence of whites, to veil their inner feelings, to wear the mask. Ellison once called southern life the most dramatic form of life in the United States, because it was so full of actors, white and black.[22] For black southerners, however, experience taught them that misreading a line or misplaying a role might cost them their lives.

Few blacks opted for a direct confrontation; more preferred a quieter subversion of the system, sensing they were bound to lose if any protracted racial conflict broke out. Still others, rapidly drawing attention, became essentially interior exiles, disengaging themselves from the norms and values of conventional society. Empty of belief or hope, they chose to live by their wits on the fringes of society, testing the limits of permissible dissent and misconduct, often outside the law, finding alternative ways to survive.

Nowhere perhaps did black southerners pour out their concerns with such feeling as in the music they created. It was in the early twentieth century that a new form of music appeared, in the Mississippi Delta, but also in East Texas, Arkansas, Louisiana, Georgia, and Alabama, and in urban New Orleans, Helena, Memphis, and St. Louis. Blues, it was called, and it could be heard on street corners, in storefronts, barbershops, cafes, and train stations, in the boarding houses and work camps, and at the crossroads stores – wherever performers could find people ready to part with some loose change.[23]

22. Quoted in Litwack, *Trouble in Mind*, 431; Mark Busby, *Ralph Ellison* (Boston, MA, 1991); Robert Butler, *The Critical Response to Ralph Ellison* (Westport, CT, 2000).

23. Patrick Ragains, "Blues Information Sources: An Annotated Bibliography and Critical Assessment," *Bulletin of Bibliography* 46(4) (1989), 249–256; Alan Lomax, *The Land Where the Blues Began* (New York, 1993); Peter Guralnick, *Sweet Soul Music:*

The men and women who played and sang the blues were mostly propertyless, disreputable, on the move, many of them illiterate, loners, living on the edge. The format and content of the music bewildered and dismayed some listeners. Although the roots of the blues may be found in the religious music of black Americans, in their chants, work songs, field hollers, and ring shouts, this was unlike anything anyone had experienced before – deeper, more immediate, more gripping, more painful. ("Blues grabbed mama's child, and it tore me all upside down. / The blues is a low down aching old heart disease / And like consumption, killing me by degrees.") Not every one wanted to experience it again. Some thought it unearthly, terrifying, and subversive. Middle-class blacks had expended much energy trying to escape primitive stereotypes reinforced by the blues, and many churchgoing blacks thought the blues to be downright blasphemous – the devil's music. Many aspiring bluesmen saw their first guitar destroyed by an outraged parent; W. C. Handy, at his father's insistence, turned in his guitar for a new Webster's Unabridged Dictionary.[24]

Through their songs, bluesmen and blueswomen conveyed emotions and feelings many whites thought black people incapable of possessing. When the bluesman related his escape from disaster, when he talked of the absent woman he loved, when he sang of the train that would take him to a freer life, when he mocked the judicial system or the bossman, he sang to himself, but he was aware that others whom he did not necessarily know shared these blues with him, shared a common history and experience – as bluesman

---

Rhythm and Blues and the Southern Dream of Freedom (New York, 1986); Marcus Charles Tribbett, "Lyrical Struggles: Hegemony and Resistance in English Broadside Ballads and African-American Blues" (Ph.D.-thesis, Washington State University, 1996); Jeff Todd Titon, *Early Downhome Blues: A Musical and Cultural Analysis* (Chapel Hill, NC, 1994); Worth Long, "The Wisdom of the Blues – Defining Blues as the True Fact of Life: An Interview with Willie Dixon," in *African American Review* 29(2) (1995), 207–212; William F. Danaher and Stephen P. Blackwelder, "The Emergence of Blues and Rap: A Comparison of the Context, Meaning, and Message," *Popular Music and Society* 17(4) (1993), 1–12.

24. Quoted in Litwack, *Trouble in Mind*, 452; William Christopher Handy and Arna Wendell Bontemps, *Father of the Blues: An Autobiography* (New York, 1991).

Henry Townsend explained: "Because people in general they takes the song as an explanation for *themselves*, they believe this song is expressing *their* feelin's instead of the one that singin' it. They feel that maybe I have just hit upon somethin' that's in their lives, and yet at the same time it was some of the things that went wrong with me too."[25]

McKinley Morganfield (Muddy Waters) remembered singing from the moment he began chopping cotton as a young boy in the 1920s and the feelings he was trying to articulate: "I do remember I was always singin', 'I cain't be satisfied, I be all troubled in mind.' Seems to me like I was always singin' that, because I was always singin' jest the way I felt, and maybe I didn't exactly *know* it, but I jest didn't like the way things were down there − in Mississippi."[26]

Blues had a language of its own, and to a remarkable degree it enabled a new black generation to confront accumulation of frustration, bitterness, and trouble − with a directness whites rarely tolerated in public, as in the chilling fantasy described by Furry Lewis, born in 1900 and raised in the Delta.

> I believe I'll buy me a graveyard of my own.
> I believe I'll buy me a graveyard of my own.
> I'm goin' kill everybody that have done me wrong.[27]

or in a different kind of fantasy, in which black southerners turn segregation on its head,

> Well, I'm goin' to buy me a little railroad of my own;
> Ain't goin' to let nobody ride but the chocolate to the bone.
> Well, I goin' to buy me a hotel of my own;
> Ain't goin' to let nobody eat but the chocolate to the bone.[28]

or in the depiction of hard times by Skip James, born in Yazoo County, Mississippi, at the turn of the century,

25. Quoted in Litwack, *Trouble in Mind*, 455.
26. Quoted in ibid. 453; Sandra B. Tooze, *Muddy Waters: The Mojo Man* (Toronto, 1997).
27. Quoted in Litwack, *Trouble in Mind*, 456.
28. Quoted in ibid. 456.

These hard times can last us so very long
if I ever get off this shit-ass floor
I'll never get down this low no more.

or in the imagery conveyed by Robert Johnson, roaming the Delta
with his demonic songs and guitar licks, learning to live with fear,
uncertainty, and daily terrors.

I got to keep moving, I got to keep moving
blues falling down like hail
blues falling down like hail
Uumh, blues falling down like hail
blues falling down like hail
and the days keeps on worryin' me
there's a hellhound on my trail,
hellhound on my trail,
hellhound on my trail.[29]

And few could match the emotional depths plumbed by Bertha
"Chippie" Hill in her plaintive, chilling lament:

I'm gonna lay my head on a lonesome railroad
And let the 2:19 pacify my mind.[30]

Humor provided some of the same opportunities for expression,
escape, and release provided by the blues, and it helped blacks to
deal with the contradictions they faced. A common theme in black
humor was the betrayal of expectations, and the belief that the success
creed in America was for white folks only. Even when blacks played
by the rules and did everything demanded of them, the results were
very much the same. More often than not, in fact, when blacks
entered the contest, the rules changed, almost always to their
detriment. That theme would dominate much of the black experience in the twentieth century, and few speeches or editorials made

29. Quoted in ibid. 479; Werner Gissing, *Mississippi Delta Blues: Formen und
Texte von Robert Johnson (1911–1938* (Graz, 1986).
30. Quoted in Litwack, *Trouble in Mind*, 456.

the point more tellingly than this tale, passed on in various versions from generation to generation:

> After the Lord had created the Earth, he created the white man, the Mexican, and the Negro. So one day he told them, "Go out and get you some rocks." The white man, being industrious, went out and got a huge rock. The Mexican got a middle-sized rock, and the Negro, being lazy, got a pebble. Later on that evening, the Lord said, "I'm going to turn these rocks into bread." As a result, the white man had a lot of bread, the Mexican had a sufficient amount, but the Negro only had a crumb, and he stayed hungry. So the next day, the Lord again told them the same thing. This time the white man got a great big rock, the Mexican got a little smaller rock, but the Negro brought back a whole half of a mountain. That evening the Lord stood before them and said, "Upon this rock, I will build my church." The Negro said, "You're a mother-fuckin' liar, you're going to make me some bread."

The story suggests a perception of white America as unbeatable: a familiar theme in the black experience. To succeed is to fail. There is no way to win.

Black leaders, editors, preachers, and community organizations thrashed about with their programs, manifestos, sermons, and strategies. But most blacks sensed they had been done in. The optimism expressed by leaders, the achievements of a new black middle class, could not overcome the realities most black southerners faced in the early twentieth century. No matter how "progress" might be measured – by their homes, income, or prospects – blacks lived in a grim and unpromising world. And the future seemed equally bleak and unredeeming. As late as 1937, John Dollard could write, "Every Negro in the South knows that he is under a kind of sentence of death; he does not know when his turn will come, it may never come, but it may also be any time." Bluesman Willie Brown, born in 1900, employed a chilling, apocalyptic imagery to convey that same feeling:

> Can't tell my future, I can't tell my past.
> Lord, it seems like every minute sure gon' be my last.

Oh, a minute seems like hours, and hours seems like days.
Yes, minutes seems like hours, hour seems like days.[31]

Resignation to a life with such limited options and prospects did not come easily, mixed as it was with a sense of betrayal. The alternatives were all but exhausted – politics, rebellion, organization, protest, participation in America's wars. The attempts by blacks to substitute class consciousness for race consciousness, to align themselves with beleaguered white farmers under the banner of Populism, to break into exclusionist trade unions or surmount the racism of much of the labor movement's rank-and-file had been largely a history of futility, failure, and betrayal.[32] Hence that old black folk wisdom, "Even after a revolution the country will be full of crackers." The strategy of accommodation underestimated the depth and permanence of white hostility to black aspirations. The strategy of agitation had its obvious limits in a violent and repressive society where whites owned the machinery and arsenals of power. "The tenacious racism in the South, the indifference of whites in the North, the moral cowardice of the 'Progressive' Presidents (Theodore Roosevelt, William Howard Taft, and Woodrow Wilson), hardly suggest an atmosphere in which black militancy would have made much difference; the more likely outcome would have been a race war blacks were certain to lose."[33] Both strategies – accommodation and agitation – demanded far-reaching and often complex commitments. Who can presume to know what most blacks who lived at the time were prepared to suffer, to sacrifice in the name of either strategy.

"Any people who could endure so much brutalization and keep together and endure," as Ralph Ellison once suggested, "is obviously more than the sum of its brutalization." Neither black accommodation nor resignation translated into contentment or into respect for whites; blacks simply did not expect in their dealings with whites any demonstration of fairness or justice. "It's stamped in me, in my

---

31. Quoted in ibid. 470.
32. Finzsch, et al., *Von Benin nach Baltimore*, 342–354.
33. Litwack, *Trouble in Mind*, 472.

mind, the way I been treated," Ned Cobb said of his life in Alabama from 1885 to 1973,

> the way I have seed other colored people treated – couldn't never go by what you think or say, had to come up to the white man's orders. Well, that's disrecognizin me. Just disrecognized, discounted in every walk of life. That's the way they worked it, and there's niggers in this country believed that shit. . . . I've studied and studied these white men. . . . I've studied them close.[34]

Ned Cobb accommodated, he never submitted. To "get along," to obtain what he wanted from white people, he acquired the necessary demeanor and verbal skills. He learned "to humble down and play shut-mouthed." He knew to play dumb when the situation demanded it. He learned "to fall back," to take "every kind of insult." But there were limits, and these assumed a growing importance in his life; he refused to demean himself, to become one of the "white men's niggers." "In my years past, I'd accommodate anybody; but I didn't believe in this way of bowin to my knees and doin what *any* white man said do. . . . I just aint goin to go nobody's way against my own self. First thing of all – I care for myself and respect myself."[35] That ultimately cost Ned Cobb twelve years in an Alabama prison.

Through the first three decades of the twentieth century, the mechanisms that regulated the place of black men and women remained mostly in place. Individual blacks made some break-throughs. The Great Migration afforded opportunities to some, the New Deal brought a measure of relief and hope, but most black southerners still lived out their lives in a rigidly segregated and repressive world. Reflecting over the indignities he had endured, Arthur Brodie, who lived and worked in North Carolina until he entered the army in 1942, felt numbed by the experience. "There's been so many times that you get to the point you feel it's a way of life for a long, long time."

---

34. Quoted in ibid. 472.
35. Quoted in ibid. 432–433.

No wonder the cynicism ran so deep in black America during World War II. Four days before the United States entered the war, Charles Jenkins wrote President Roosevelt, "If there is such a thing as God, he must be a white person, according to the conditions we colored people are in. Hitler has not done anything to colored people – it's the people right here in the United States who are keeping us out of work and keeping us down." Unlike in World War I, when blacks were urged by their leaders to close ranks and set aside their grievances, this time the bitterness, the ambivalence, the questioning ran much deeper, "White folks talking about the Four Freedoms, and we ain't got none."[36] A black youth about to be inducted into the Army summed up the cynicism tempering black patriotism: "Just carve on my tombstone, 'Here lies a black man killed fighting a yellow man for the protection of a white man.'"

Nothing illustrated more graphically or more symbolically the utter hypocrisy of the democratic slogans under which the United States fought this war than what Lloyd Brown and his fellow black soldiers encountered in Salina, Kansas:

> As we entered a lunchroom on the main street, the owner hurried out front to tell us with urgent politeness, "You boys know we don't serve colored here." Of course we knew it. They didn't serve "colored" anywhere in town. The best movie house did not admit Negroes. There was no room at the inn for any black visitor, and there was no place where he could get a cup of coffee. "You know we don't serve colored here," the man repeated. We ignored him, and just stood there inside the door, staring at what we had come to see – the German prisoners of war who were having lunch at the counter. We continued to stare. This was really happening. It was no jive talk. The people of Salina would serve these enemy soldiers and turn away black American GIs. If we were untermenschen in Nazi Germany, they would break our bones. As "colored" men in Salina, they only break our hearts.[37]

36. Frank Robert Donovan, *Mr. Roosevelt's Four Freedoms: The Story behind the United Nations Charter* (New York, 1966); United States. Office of War Information, *The Four Freedoms: The Arsenal of Democracy* (Washington, DC, 1942).

37. Matthias Reiß, "'Die Schwarzen waren unsere Freunde': Deutsche Kriegs-gefangene und African Americans in den Vereinigten Staaten während des Zweiten Weltkrieges" (Dissertation, Universität Hamburg, 2000 [in print, forthcoming]).

What these soldiers had seen was by no means rare. Nazi prisoners of war enroute to camps in the South and in parts of the Midwest and West were permitted to eat with white soldiers, guards, and civilians in railroad dining cars and in station restaurants, while black soldiers were barred from the same facilities.

To look at the black experience during World War II is to discern few changes in the interlocking mechanisms governing race relations. And yet, in some significant and far-reaching ways – in how it dramatized the disparity between American democratic rhetoric and racial practices, in the ways it heightened, even revolutionized, black consciousness and expectations, in the ways military service abroad gave black soldiers a new perspective on the provincial nature of their segregated society at home – World War II marked a shift in the relationship of African-Americans to American society. The mounting anger and frustration could no longer be contained, as the Double V campaign (victory over our enemies abroad, and victory over our enemies at home) waged by blacks during the war so vividly demonstrated.

Nearly a century after the Civil War, then, on new battlefields – Montgomery, Selma, Birmingham, Little Rock, Boston, Chicago, Los Angeles – another struggle would be fought over the meaning of freedom in America, by a new generation of African-Americans, in a rapidly changing world, and in a new climate of political necessity. More than a million black Americans fought in World War II to make the world safe for democracy. After the war, even larger numbers developed new strategies to make the United States safe for themselves. The conviction grew that the way it used to be did not have to be any longer, and black men and women would give voice to that feeling in ways white America could no longer ignore.

The restructuring of race relationships had become necessary, if only to give the United States credibility as a leader of the Free World and in the battle for the hearts and minds of the emerging Third World peoples. Success in foreign policy demanded progress, or the appearance of progress, in guaranteeing black Americans the same rights of citizenship enjoyed by white Americans. Actions by the federal government, from the symbolic to the concrete, from

367

the report of President Truman's Civil Rights Committee in 1947 to the integration of the armed forces to the dispatch by Presidents Eisenhower and Kennedy of federal troops into the South to enforce integration orders were often couched in the language of national security and the anti-communist struggle.[38] "Why," asked President Kennedy, "can a Communist eat at a lunch counter at Selma, Alabama, while a black American cannot?" White supremacy had become too costly to defend or to sustain. Perhaps, then, we can begin to understand what black sociologist E. Franklin Frazier meant when several weeks after the Supreme Court decision in 1954 he remarked: "The white man is scared down to his bowels, so it's be-kind-to-Negroes-decade at last." The victory, he added, "approaches so late and for so many wrong reasons that for many black Americans it begins to bear the visage of defeat."

The civil rights movement struck down the legal barriers of segregation and disfranchisement in the South and challenged the economic and educational barriers that had crippled black aspirations in the North. It left its mark on the nation. Hundreds and thousands took to the streets, mostly young people, defying the laws, defying the apathy of their elders, disciplined by non-violence, insisting on bringing the Constitution and the nation's professed values into closer harmony, embracing the promise of a new reconstruction, more sweeping, more enduring than the last. That, at least, was the heightened expectation of the civil rights movement, and its spirit prevailed as long as its participants glimpsed more fulfilling possibilities for black lives. By the 1970s, however, much of that promise had dimmed. The optimism about redeeming America had passed. "Most of the gains made by the civil rights movement," Martin Luther King conceded, "were obtained at bargain rates. The desegregation of public facilities cost nothing; neither did the election and appointment of a few black public officials." To make a commitment to economic justice, however, would not be so easy, as it involved economic costs many Americans were unwilling to pay.

38. William C. Berman, *The Politics of Civil Rights in the Truman Administration* (Columbus, OH, 1970); Philip H. Vaughan, *The Truman Administration's Legacy for Black America* (Reseda, CA, 1976).

Even as the civil rights movement ended the violence of segregation, it failed to diminish the violence of poverty. Even as it transformed the face of Southern politics, it did nothing to reallocate resources, to redistribute wealth and income. Even as it entered schools and colleges, voting booths and lunch counters, it failed to penetrate the corporate boardrooms and federal bureaucracies where the most critical decisions affecting American lives were made. Even as the black middle class increased and registered striking gains for blacks in white-collar positions, in political representation, in the entertainment industry, and in educational opportunities, it left behind a greater number of black Americans to endure lives of quiet despair and hopelessness, trapped in a mire of failing schools, bad housing, inadequate health care, meager opportunity, and discrimination. The desegregation of a bus terminal, a drugstore counter, a public school did little to alter the day-to-day lives of most black Americans. As a new breed of black activists demanded to know, what did civil rights mean to black men and women living in hovels with empty stomachs and no jobs? "I'm not going to sit at your table and watch you eat, with nothing on my plate, and call myself a diner," Malcolm X declared. "Sitting at the table doesn't make you a diner, unless you eat some of what's on the plate."

For more than two centuries, freedom in America had meant not being a slave, not being black. No wonder in 1865 when a group of slaves in Tennessee were told they were free, they asked, "How free?" How free is free? That question persists. Slavery was abolished more than a century ago, Jim Crow was dismantled some two decades ago, but we continue to live with their consequences, in our racial attitudes, in our institutions, in our social problems. White supremacy is legally dead but racism remains the most debilitating virus in the American system, deeply embedded in our psyche and culture, nourished by historical and cultural illiteracy, more cleverly coded in expression, able to adapt to changes in laws and public attitudes, assuming different guises as the occasion demands, knowing no geographical boundaries.

Newspaper columnists and some social scientists have tended to view race relations as bright and promising. But out in the streets and urban enclaves, blacks and whites still face each other, by and

369

large, across a perpetual divide. The deteriorating quality of public education (the struggle is no longer to keep blacks out of the public schools but to keep whites in), the controversy over special efforts to redress 200 years of special exploitation and white privilege, the discriminatory policing practices of law enforcement, the persistent gap between whites and blacks in wealth, housing, and life expectancy, the number of black children in poverty and attending schools in racial isolation, and the disproportionate number of blacks in prisons (blacks make up 12 percent of the nation's population, 50 percent of the nation's prisoners) – all add up to a grim chronicle. More than thirty years have passed since the Kerner commission warned that the United States was "moving toward two societies, one black, one white – separate and unequal." That process continues, and the implications for the twenty-first century are devastating.[39]

To achieve equality, to make the American Dream available to everyone, as Martin Luther King came to recognize, would require far more massive changes than most Americans were willing to concede – equal access to economic resources and political power, a fundamental redistribution of wealth, income, and power, giving up privileges long available to whites simply because they were whites, and a thorough restructuring of American society, government, and economy. "For years," King confessed to a reporter shortly before his assassination, "I labored with the idea of reforming the existing institutions of the society, a little change here, a little change there. Now I feel differently. I think you've got to have a reconstruction of the entire society, a revolution of values." King knew that civil rights legislation alone had failed to create a level playing field. If a man is entered at the starting line in a race 300 years after another man, King argued, he would have to perform some impossible feat to catch up with his fellow runner. Expressed a different way, equality, one black youth explained, "is like Whitey holds you by the belt at the starting line until everyone else is halfway round the track, then gives you a big slap on the rump and says,

39. Philip J. Meranto, *The Kerner Report Revisited: Final Report and Background Papers* (Urbana, IL, 1970); Brian S. Vargus, *The Kerner Commission Report: Black and White in America. A Study Guide* (Bloomington, IN, 1968).

'Go, baby, you're equal.' Takes an unusual man to win a race like that. It's easier to shoot the starter."

Thirty years ago, black aspirations found soulful expression not only in the civil rights movement and in the eloquence of Martin Luther King and Malcolm X, but in the names black musical artists gave to their groups, suggesting a confident faith in progress, the belief that America held a special promise: the Supremes, the Miracles, the Marvelettes, the Invincibles. The Impressions sang with such certainty, "We're a Winner," and urged their people, "Keep on Pushing." James Brown boasted in song "I'm Black and I'm Proud, and Sam Cooke projected the ultimate optimism when he sang "I Know That A Change Is Gonna Come." But some thirty years later, the songs, the beat, the names captured a different mood: Snoop Doggy Dog, NWA (Niggaz With Attitude), Outkast, Ice Cube, Scarface, Black Sheep, Black Star, Blackalicious, Tupac Shakur, X-Clan, Gang Starr, Geto Boys, Junior M.A.F.I.A., Urban Underground, Notorious B.I.G., Lady of Rage, ODB (Old Dirty Bastard).

Perhaps with Sam Cooke in mind, WC and the MAAD Circle rapped, "Yeah, it's 1997 y'all and ain't a damn thing changed." Grandmaster Flash and the Furious Five came from the most ravaged urban neighborhood of the 1970s. "It's like a jungle, sometimes," he warned, "it makes me wonder/how I keep from going under / So don't push me, cause I'm close to the edge / I'm, tryin' not to lose my head." Declaring themselves "Rebels Without a Pause," Public Enemy admonished young, "We got to fight the Power," and "Don't, Don't, Don't, Believe the Hype." Ice Cube addressed growing tensions between African-Americans and Asian-Americans, threatening boycotts of and violence against Korean merchants in the black community, "Pay respect to the black fist or we'll burn your store right down to a crisp, and then we'll see ya because you can't turn the ghetto into Black Korea."

KRS-1 raised the urgent and critical question of institutional power, deeply rooted in the history of race relations: who will police the police?

You were put here to protect us, but who protects us from you?
Everytime you say, "that's illegal," does it mean that it's true?

You were put here to protect us, but who protects us from you?
It seems that when you walk the ghetto
You walk with your own point of view.
Looking through my history book, I've watched you as you grew
Killing blacks, and calling it the law, and worshipping Jesus, too.

As we enter a new century, it remains inconceivable to think of America, its culture, its history, and its future, without thinking of African-Americans. "We are that people," W. E. B. Du Bois wrote, "whose subtle sense of song has given America its only American music, its only American fairy tales, its only touch of pathos and humor amid its mad money-getting plutocracy." Whatever the United States becomes, Ralph Ellison suggested, will be shaped in part by the black presence. That may, in fact, be the nation's saving grace. Throughout our history, and particularly since the Civil War, black Americans have in various ways, not always in easily discernible ways, forced the nation to face up to its contradictions – but not necessarily to act upon them. It is the African-American who has reminded the nation that it has not lived up to its ideals. It is the African-American, Ellison wrote, who "gives creative tension to our struggle for justice" and human dignity. It is the African-American

> who insists that we purify the American language by demanding that there be a closer correlation between the meaning of words and reality, between ideal and conduct, our assertions and our actions. Without the black American, something irrepressibly hopeful and creative would go out of the American spirit, and the nation might well succumb to the moral slobbism that has ever threatened its existence from within.

The song "Trouble in Mind," like the African-American odyssey, encompassed enslavement, a tortured freedom, a new beginning in the North, and both triumphs and retreats.[40] The song began as a slave spiritual, and in 1860 would have sounded like this:

---

40. "Trouble in mind" is a song that is available in uncountable versions. See Big Bill Broonzy and Pete Seeger, *Trouble in mind* [sound recording] (Washington, DC, 2000) (CD); King Curtis, *Trouble in mind* [sound recording] (Berkeley, CA, 1992) (CD); Mark Isham, *Trouble in mind* [sound recording] (New York, 1986) (LP).

I am a-trouble in de mind.
O I am a-trouble in de mind.
I ask my Lord what shall I do,
I am a-trouble in de mind.

It reentered folk tradition in the late nineteenth century as country
blues, reflecting the restlessness of a new black generation, the first
generation born in freedom.

If I'm feelin' tomorrow
Like I feel today
I'm gonna pack my suitcase
and make my getaway
'Cause I'm troubled
I'm all worried in mind
And I never been satisfied
And I just can't keep from cryin'.

With the Great Migration, in the twentieth century, the song moved
up North, along with hundreds of thousands of black southerners,
and it would be revived in a new setting, in an urban and industrial
setting.[41]

Well, trouble, oh, trouble
Trouble on my worried mind.
When you see me laughin',
I'm laughin' just to keep from cryin'.

And some years later, rapper Chuck D. of Public Enemy would add
his own refrain, in a number he called "Welcome to the Terrordome":

41. Alferdteen Harrison, *Black Exodus: The Great Migration from the American
South* (Jackson, MS, 1991); Michael L. Cooper, *Bound for the Promised Land: The
Great Black Migration* (New York, 1995); Nicholas Lemann, *The Promised Land: The
Great Black Migration and How It Changed America* (New York, 1991); Milton C.
Sernett, *Bound for the Promised Land: African American Religion and the Great Migration*
(Durham, NC, 1997).

I got so much trouble on my mind
(On my mind)
I refuse to lose
Here's your ticket
Hear the drummer get wicked.

At the dawn of the twenty-first century, it is all very different. It is all very much the same. It is a different America, and it is a familiar America. When asked to assess the legacy of the civil rights era, a black preacher in Mississippi answered, "Everything has changed, and nothing has changed."

3
Volksgemeinschaft in the Third Reich: Concession, Conflict, Consensus

Maria Mitchell

The literature on the National Socialist *Volksgemeinschaft*, or *Volk*-community, is voluminous. The roots of the *Volksgemeinschaft* and its violent implementation have justifiably attracted enormous scholarly attention: Understanding the *Volksgemeinschaft* is central to fathoming the horror of National Socialism. As both an all-encompassing utopian vision and a political and murderous process, the *Volksgemeinschaft* was replete with contradictions. In achieving their *Volksgemeinschaft*, Nazi officials met with concession, conflict, and consensus; tragically, they ultimately met with success.

This essay will make no attempt to survey the vast literature on the *Volksgemeinschaft* in Nazi Germany or its rich historiographical debates (particularly that concerning modernization).[1] Instead, it will negotiate the scholarship selectively in an effort to examine the *Volksgemeinschaft* as an applied utopia, a utopian vision instrumentalized by a political regime. To that end, it will court the appellative risk of using the terms "Nazis" and "Germans" without suggesting a false divide between them; indeed, determining their relationship lies at the heart of assessing the *Volksgemeinschaft*.[2]

---

1. This paper has explicitly sought to avoid the modernization debate. Certainly many of the authors cited address it directly. In addition to Peukert, Alber and Fritzsche, see among numerous others Zygmunt Bauman, *Modernity and the Holocaust* (Ithaca, NY, 1996).

2. Peter Fritzsche, "Nazi Modern," *Modernism/Modernity* 3(1) (1996), 1–22. This paper will specifically exclude those countries occupied by Germans, although it is arguable that similar processes transpired in the occupied territories.

This essay will explore the *Volksgemeinschaft* from two distinct vantage points: popular motive and function. In examining motive, it will focus on the allure of Nazi utopianism to select groups of Germans in order to explore larger bases of that vision's appeal. The second concern of the essay is the enactment of utopia. The realization of the *Volksgemeinschaft* was a project of both the Nazi government and the German populace. Characterized by a multiplicity of responses to the Nazi project, Germans of conflicting motives nonetheless constructed an everyday universe of racial hierarchy. Grounded in functional popular consensus and Germans' active engagement, the *Volksgemeinschaft* utopia was made real.

*

A distinctly Western phenomenon spawned by diminished religious authority across Europe, utopianism remains informed by classical and Christian influences. Epitomized since the nineteenth century by socialism, modern utopianism rests on Enlightenment and Industrial Revolution suggestions of man's unlimited potential to tame nature[3] while adopting the Enlightenment's scheme of a secular salvation and belief.[4] As a plan of action, the modern utopia imagines an immediately attainable future; it heralds a decisive departure from current developments and an abrupt transition to a new world.[5]

Weimar Germany was home to a host of utopian visions, most associated with the political extremes of left or right. Following their devastating loss in World War I, Germans across ideological lines shared a discourse of national "reawakening" or "resurrection." Fear of modern mass society inspired in many utopian thinkers a reliance on dictatorship, and rightists projected a military path to a renewed Germany free of inner turmoil. At the same time, a racially

---

3. Krishan Kumar, *Utopia and Anti-Utopia in Modern Times* (New York, 1987), 3, 23, 49.

4. Lawrence Birken, *Hitler as Philosophe: Remnants of the Enlightenment in National Socialism* (Westport, CT, 1995), 31, 69.

5. Barbara Goodwin and Keith Taylor, *The Politics of Utopia: A Study in Theory and Practice* (New York, 1982), 26.

based antisemitism fed several intersecting strains of eugenic utopianism. Out of this milieu emerged the National Socialist proposition that a break with history would rescue Germany from chaos and danger and propel it on a course of grandeur. For the Nazis, the danger of modern life, manifest in military defeat and the rise of the Bolsheviks, was above all present in the threat of biological degeneration.[6]

In his book comparing Soviet and Nazi science, Paul R. Josephson argues that, while all governments harbor a vision of the future, the utopias offered by totalitarian regimes are distinct for their radical scope. Comparable to the Soviets' dream of refashioning fundamentally the Russian empire, the Nazis' "transformationist vision" of a racially pure Germany drove the Third Reich to mass murder and large-scale environmental destruction. Relying primarily on the practice of science, Josephson argues that the Nazi and Soviet transformationist visions established a model for the twentieth century, one later pursued by Cuba, North Korea, and China.[7]

But in establishing racial "renovation" as the key to a utopian Germany, the National Socialists marched into largely uncharted territory.[8] Not only among German varieties of utopia, but as a transformationist vision, the National Socialist program for the future stands apart. In the Soviet Union, the obliteration of enemies was seen as a means to a visionary end, not as an end itself. It was the goal of the Nazi utopia, however, to eliminate those deemed hostile and inferior to the *Volk*.[9] As "the first state in world history whose dogma and practice was racism,"[10] the Third Reich enshrined

6. Peter Lambert, "German Historians and Nazi Ideology: The Parameters of the *Volksgemeinschaft* and the Problem of Historical Legitimation, 1930–45," *European History Quarterly* 25 (1995), 555; Peter S. Fisher, *Fantasy and Politics: Visions of the Future in the Weimar Republic* (Madison, WI, 1991); Fritzsche, "Nazi Modern."

7. Paul R. Josephson, *Totalitarian Science and Technology* (Atlantic Highlands, NJ, 1996).

8. Fritzsche, "Nazi Modern," 16.

9. Omer Bartov, "Defining Enemies, Making Victims: Germans, Jews, and the Holocaust," *The American Historical Review* 103(3) (June 1998), 814.

10. Michael Burleigh and Wolfgang Wippermann, *The Racial State: Germany 1933–1945* (New York, 1991), 23.

antisemitism as the central tenet of state ideology.[11] In practice, as Eberhard Jäckel has famously explained, "never before had a state . . . decided that a specific human group, including its aged, its women, its children and infants, would be killed as quickly as possible, and then carried through this regulation using every possible means of state power."[12] In the Nazi *Volksgemeinschaft*, we confront something exceptional.

The contours of this uniquely corrupt utopia are well-known. The component elements of the *Volksgemeinschaft* – the *Volk* and "community" – had deep and complex roots in eighteenth- and nineteenth-century German thought and politics as well as in the larger European phenomena of antisemitism, Social Darwinism, and eugenics.[13] Traditionally, the *Volk* was portrayed as a *Herrenvolk* who defended sacred German soil, a warrior class that conjured up a heroic Nordic past forged in *Blut and Boden*.[14] But while the meanings of *Blut und Boden* and *Volksgemeinschaft* shifted during the late Weimar and early Nazi years between proletarian and capitalist, and religious and nonreligious, one organizing principle remained constant: the primacy of race.[15] Constructed as a racial prototype, the idealized *Volk* represented a community of genetically pure individuals of mythical potential.[16]

The centrality of race to the *Volksgemeinschaft* was evident not only in the most basic conceptions of *Volk*, but also in the projected

11. Avraham Barkai, "*Volksgemeinschaft*, 'Aryanization' and the Holocaust," in David Cesarani, ed., *The Final Solution: Origins and Implementation* (London and New York, 1994), 35.

12. Eberhard Jäckel, as quoted in Charles S. Maier, *The Unmasterable Past: History, Holocaust, and German National Identity* (Cambridge, MA, and London, 1988), 76.

13. Burleigh and Wipperman, *The Racial State*, 29–37; Hermann Glaser, *The Cultural Roots of National Socialism* (Austin, TX, 1978).

14. David Welch, *The Third Reich: Politics and Propaganda* (London and New York, 1993), 66.

15. Jost Hermand, *Old Dreams of a New Reich: Volkish Utopias and National Socialism* (Bloomington and Indianapolis, IN, 1992), 158–262.

16. Gabriele Czarnowski, "'The Value of Marriage for the *Volksgemeinschaft*': Policies Towards Women and Marriage under National Socialism," in Richard Bessel, ed., *Fascist Italy and Nazi Germany: Comparisons and Contrasts* (New York, 1996), 95.

power of race to redefine social relations. Of the Aryan community's virtues, the most important was its putative equality: For those deemed biologically pure, race was to transcend all other social identification.[17] In particular, race was functionally to replace class as society's discriminating principle;[18] in the *Volksgemeinschaft*, dividing lines of class were to be erased and reinscribed around race. As Avraham Barkai has argued, the *Volksgemeinschaft* represented the

> answer of National or German Socialism to the Marxist challenge of the classless society. Even the term *Genossen* (comrade) was borrowed from the socialist parties to become *Volks*genossen. Proletarians and capitalists, peasants and landowners, artisans, blue- or white-collar workers and intellectuals . . . were to be united in the racially purified community of the German *Volk*, to toil together for the common weal of the fatherland.[19]

By transcending social and class tensions, the *Volksgemeinschaft* was also to integrate Aryan individuals into a harmonious and productive society. Only with the elimination of the "parasitic" and "genetically inferior" could Germany become an "achievement-orientated community primed for self-sacrifice."[20] The pairing of Germans to the *Volk* would create an "efficiency community" (*Leistungsgemeinschaft*), one free of internal impediments to unprecedented accomplishment.[21]

Creating this "racially purified community of the German *Volk*" rested on the process of racial exclusion of all those deemed racial enemies of the *Gemeinschaft*: "aliens," the "hereditarily ill," "incurable" political opponents, and the "asocial." Of the numerous groups

---

17. Welch, *The Third Reich*, 56; Barkai, "*Volksgemeinschaft*, 'Aryanization' and the Holocaust," 34.

18. Burleigh and Wippermann, *The Racial State*, 4.

19. Barkai, "*Volksgemeinschaft*, 'Aryanization' and the Holocaust," 34.

20. Detlev J.K. Peukert, *Inside Nazi Germany: Conformity, Opposition, and Racism in Everyday Life*, .trans. Richard Deveson (New Haven and London, 1987), 209.

21. Timothy W. Mason, *Social Policy in the Third Reich: The Working Class and the 'National Community'*, ed., Jane Caplan; trans. John Broadwin (Providence and Oxford, 1993), 280.

encompassed by such a list, Jews were National Socialism's ceaseless primary targets. Portrayed as the embodiment of modernity – capitalists, communists, anti-nationalist traitors, and most importantly the polluters of German blood – Jews were mythologized to represent all abstract threats to German unity.[22] National Socialist "redemptive anti-Semitism" posited that a corrupt Germany could only be "redeemed" through an elimination of the corruptors. In a clear reliance on Christian traditions, a utopian redemption of the German people rested on German "liberation" from the Jews.[23]

At the same time Jewish Europeans posed the greatest "threat" to a Nazi utopia, the *Volk* faced other "biologically inferior" enemies as well. The Nazis labeled as anathema to the *Volksgemeinschaft* anyone who transgressed National Socialist notions of proper behavior.[24] For those deemed alien to the "community," including homosexuals, the physically and mentally handicapped, schizophrenics, alcoholics, and Jehovah's Witnesses, penalties included imprisonment, sterilization, and death.

The process of racializing social difference also revealed the primacy of gender in the *Volksgemeinschaft*. Under National Socialism, women's secondary status was a biological truism parallel to the hierarchy of race. Women deemed failures – for whatever reason – at fulfilling their charge to produce racially pure children were subject to the enforcement of Nazi codes of social and physical fitness.[25] In the same way as the *Volksgemeinschaft* heralded an end to class conflict, it evoked a nostalgia of harmonious male and female hierarchy, projecting a cooperative arrangement of biologically pure heterosexuals.[26]

Even purified of "deviants," the *Volk*, the Nazis believed, could only be assured true security through rule over Eastern Europe. National Socialism mandated that Germany extend its empire of racial purity to the Urals, enslaving or eliminating all "inferior"

22. Barkai, "*Volksgemeinschaft*, 'Aryanization' and the Holocaust," 34–35.

23. Saul Friedländer, *Nazi Germany and the Jews, Vol. I: The Years of Persecution, 1933–1939* (New York, 1997), 87.

24. Peukert, *Inside Nazi Germany*, 220–223.

25. Czarnowski, "The Value of Marriage for the *Volksgemeinschaft*," 111–112.

26. Claudia Koonz, *Mothers in the Fatherland: Women, the Family and Nazi Politics* (New York, 1987), 53.

people in its swathe, including the Slavs, Sinti, and Roma. The Nazis' aggressive militarism was infused with a belief in racial superiority; the conquest of *Lebensraum* through the elimination of non-Aryans was central to the *Volksgemeinschaft*.[27]

The drive for a *Volksgemeinschaft* informed all Nazi policies, from elimination of the Jews to the invasion of the Soviet Union, the "euthanasia" killings, school curriculum and marriage laws. The scope of these utopian policies meant that every German citizen interacted with the *Volksgemeinschaft* in some way.[28] While the motivations for and function of those interactions remained contestable, the racist underpinnings and destination of the *Volksgemeinschaft* rendered this intersection of citizenry and utopian vision unprecedented.

*

The general consensus of the literature is that the Nazis were ultimately unsuccessful in inculcating the ideal of *Volksgemeinschaft* in the German people. As Mary Fulbrook contends, the Nazis may have disrupted and refashioned preexisting societal institutions, but they did not succeed in replacing them with new attitudes or an infrastructure of their making. Ideologically, their utopian vision of a racially pure Germany was not shared widely by the population.[29]

There is clear evidence that in some cases the NSDAP program to propagate the *Volksgemeinschaft* was designed primarily to occupy party members' time.[30] In other instances, even party members appeared less than persuaded by Nazi efforts to promote the cultural logic of the *Volksgemeinschaft*.[31] Perhaps most strikingly, as Detlev

27. Eberhard Jäckel, *Hitler's World View: A Blueprint for Power. Translated by Herbert Arnold* (Cambridge and London, 1981).

28. Peukert, *Inside Nazi Germany*, 79.

29. Mary Fulbrook, *The Divided Nation: A History of Germany, 1918–1990* (New York, 1992), 354. This thesis is argued strongly in Gerhard Paul, "Die widerspenstige 'Volksgemeinschaft': Dissens und Verweigerung im Dritten Reich," in Peter Steinbach and Johannes Tuchel, eds., *Widerstand gegen den Nationalsozialismus* (Bonn, 1994).

30. For one such example, see Dietrich Orlow, *The History of the Nazi Party, Vol. II: 1933–1945* (Newton Abbot, 1973), 91.

31. Anthony McElligott, *Contested City: Municipal Politics and the Rise of Nazism in Altona, 1917–1937* (Ann Arbor, MI, 1998), 235.

Peukert has argued, the apparent divide between rhetoric and reality in the Third Reich was not lost on the German citizenry: "The longer the Nazi regime lasted, the less people believed its slogans about the . . . 'national community'."[32]

That the *Volksgemeinschaft* failed as a utopian vision for the Aryan population may well be true. Its failure, however, raises enormous and wide-ranging questions. Most basically, if the *Volksgemeinschaft* floundered as a people's utopia, how does one reconcile that failure with the violence and murder perpetrated in its name? To assess fully the legacy of the Nazi utopianism, interrogating popular motive alone does not suffice.

Shifting, then, from a consideration of public support to the very basic equation of consequence, was not the success of the *Volksgemeinschaft* indisputable? The Nazis did orchestrate the deaths of the majority of European Jews. The Holocaust and war decimated European Jewish culture, and millions of others deemed racially inferior lost their lives.[33] If we count those imprisoned in concentration camps between 1933 and 1945 alone, 8 to 10 million people were subjected to the strictures of the *Volksgemeinschaft*.[34] From a purely ends-oriented vantage point, the National Socialist utopia not only functioned, it functioned on an immense scale.

So, how best do we bridge this gap between competing estimations of the *Volksgemeinschaft*, between public belief and public policy? One important way is to acknowledge the terror that undergirded German life under Hitler. Repression of political dissent led to imprisonment and death for those suspected of opposing the regime; in 1933 in Bavaria alone, some 15,000 to 20,000 people were brought into "protective custody."[35] Millions of Germans lived in fear, a fear compounded in the late war years by the vast chaos of

32. Peukert, *Inside Nazi Germany*, 109.

33. Moishe Postone, "Anti-Semitism and National Socialism," in Jack David Zipes and Anson Rabinbach, eds., *Germans and the Jews Since the Holocaust: The Changing Situation in West Germany* (New York, 1986), 314.

34. Maier, *The Unmasterable Past*, 74–75.

35. Ian Kershaw, *Popular Opinion & Political Dissent in the Third Reich: Bavaria 1933–1945* (New York, 1988), 71.

Allied bombing and invasion. In part, the *Volksgemeinschaft* functioned through dictatorship.

To implement its utopia, however, the Nazis could not rely solely on policing. The explanation of terror only goes so far. Nazi Germany shared with other political systems the need for public support or at least acquiescence.[36] This calls our attention to the complex connection of popular motive to the functioning of utopia.

There is a deep theoretical literature on this issue,[37] but perhaps one example may illuminate the complexities involved in characterizing German individuals' motives and roles in the functioning of the *Volksgemeinschaft*. Regarding working women during the war, Tilla Siegel asked, "[H]ow are we to interpret reports that employers were not very satisfied with the performance of women who were conscripted to work in armaments production? These women work slowly in order to be sent home, or to sabotage armaments production, or both?"[38]

Clearly, the conundrum of representation cannot easily be unraveled. Beyond this riddle of representation, furthermore, there exists the challenge of characterization. In examining youth culture, for example, David Welch has concluded that, despite the popularity of such groups as the Swing Youth and Edelweiss Pirates, German youth on the whole "proved particularly receptive to the notion of

---

36. Welch, *The Third Reich*, 51.

37. For a discussion of the various definitions of "resistance," including a debate over the role of Catholic Church during the Nazi era, see Jürgen Schmädeke and Peter Steinbach, eds., *Der Widerstand gegen den Nationalsozialismus: Die deutsche Gesellschaft und der Widerstand gegen Hitler* (Munich, 1986), 1120–1127. Further explorations of the phenomenon of "resistance" can be found in Hans Mommsen, "Begriff und Problematik des deutschen Widerstands gegen Hitler in der zeitgeschichtlichen Forschung," in *Widerstandsbewegungen in Deutschland und in Polen während des zweiten Weltkrieges*, 2nd ed. (Brunswick, 1983), 16–23; Martin Broszat, "Resistenz und Widerstand," in Martin Broszat, Elke Fröhlich, and Anton Grossmann, eds., *Bayern in der NS-Zeit*, Vol. 4 (Munich and Vienna, 1981), 691–709; Peter Hüttenberger, "Vorüberlegungen zum 'Widerstandsbegriff,'" in Jürgen Kocka, ed., *Theorie in der Praxis des Historikers* (Göttingen, 1977), 117–134.

38. Tilla Siegel, "Whatever was the attitude of German Workers? Reflections on Recent Interpretations," in Richard Bessel, ed., *Fascist Italy and Nazi Germany: Comparisons and Contrasts* (New York, 1996), 68.

a 'national community' . . ."[39] In these same "cliques", however, Michael Burleigh and Wolfgang Wippermann see evidence of the failure of Nazi attempts to propagate the *Volksgemeinschaft*, suggesting that youth in some ways remained outside the functioning of the Nazi utopia.[40]

Again, how do we appraise dissent and support? The scholarly attention to these questions has not produced a consensus, nor has it detracted from the questions' powerful simplicity or urgency. It has, however, led to new insights and important reconceptualizations. Perhaps most helpful here is Alf Lüdtke's warning that we cannot ignore the multiplicity of responses of which any one person was capable. As Lüdtke argues, seemingly adversative impulses character-ized many individuals' lives within the system. "For individuals, that meant: consent, accept, cooperate – but also to 'go underground', to dissociate oneself, sometimes to oppose: these were no contradic-tions." In this sense, function and motive were both conditional and varied; every individual was capable of concession, conflict, and consensus.[41]

Not only does Lüdtke's formula offer valuable insights for examining individual behavior in the Nazi era, but it can also serve as a useful tool for understanding larger group behaviors. This is perhaps especially true regarding the two *Teilkulturen* – or "part cultures"[42] – considered least pervious to the *Volksgemeinschaft*, those of workers and Catholics.[43] As case studies, Catholics and workers

39. Welch, *The Third Reich*, 61–63.

40. Burleigh and Wippermann, *The Racial State*, 226–227.

41. Alf Lüdtke, "Arbeiten und Dabeisein: Wie Alltagsgeschichte den National-sozialismus erklärt," in Axel Lubinski, Thomas Rudert, and Martina Schattkowsky, eds., *Historie und Eigen-Sinn: Festschrift für Jan Peters zum 65. Geburtstag* (Weimar, 1997).

42. I adopt the term *Teilkultur* from Detlef Lehnert and Klaus Megerle to imply a distinct social group, the voting patterns of which are directly related to its unique assumptions and beliefs. I prefer the term *Teil-* as opposed to *Subkultur* (subculture) for its less hierarchical and hegemonical connotations. For Lehnert and Megerle's exploration of the connotations of the term *Teilkultur* and its relationship to the concepts Lager and sozialmoralisch Milieu, see Detlef Lehnert and Klaus Megerle, eds., *Politische Teilkulturen zwischen Integration und Polarisierung: Zur politischen Kultur in der Weimarer Republik* (Opladen, 1990), esp. 10–11.

43. Welch, *The Third Reich*, 54.

illuminate well the complexities of squaring motive and function in Nazi Germany. It is important to keep in mind, of course, that neither of these *Teilkulturen* existed as a closed category. Catholic workers, for example, lived at the intersection of working and Catholic life, and gender operated as a category within each. Keeping Lüdtke's theoretical insights in mind, however, sheds light on the parameters of competing impulses evident even among those considered most opposed to Nazi rule.

Catholics

The question of Catholicism's relationship to National Socialism has long been controversial.[44] The Catholic Church is often credited with having offered the greatest institutional resistance to the Nazi regime, particularly in light of its unparalleled resilience in the wake of the Nazi collapse. While many Church members portrayed the Church as Hitler's primary victim, the Western Allies' early reliance on Catholic priests bolstered a widespread regard for the Church as unsullied.[45]

Ideologically, Catholicism did appear to have provided many Catholic Germans a "defense shield" against the *weltanschauliche*

44. Ulrich von Hehl traces the shifting interpretations of the relationship of Catholicism to Nazism from 1945 through the mid-1970s, including the bitter debates occasioned by the review of the Concordat by the *Bundesverfassungsgericht* from 1955 to 1957, Ernst-Wolfgang Böckenförde's articles in *Hochland* in 1961 and 1962, and Rolf Hochhuth's play *The Deputy* of 1963. Ulrich von Hehl, *Katholische Kirche und National Sozialismus im Erzbistum Köln 1933–1945* (Mainz, 1977), 1–5.

45. Heinz Hürten, *Deutsche Katholiken 1918 bis 1945* (Paderborn and Munich, 1992); Martin Greschat, "Die Kirchen in den beiden deutschen Staaten nach 1945," Geschichte in Wissenschaft und Unterricht 42(5) (1991), 267–284; Rudolf Morsey, *Von Windthorst bis Adenauer: Ausgewählte Aufsätze zu Politik, Verwaltung und politischem Katholizismus im 19. und 20. Jahrhundert,* ed. Ulrich von Hehl, Hans Günter Hockerts, Horst Möller, and Martin Schumacher (Paderborn and München, 1997), 245–253; Maria Mitchell, *The Origins of Christian Democracy: Politics and Confession in Modern Germany* (Ann Arbor, MI, forthcoming); Peter Hoffmann, *The History of the German Resistance 1933–1945,* trans. by Richard Barry (Cambridge, MA, 1979).

Gleichschaltung of National Socialism.[46] Proportionately, fewer Catholics voted for the Nazis before 1933 than did Protestants,[47] and Catholics in general were slower to respond to certain Nazi exhortations, such as boycotting Jewish stores.[48] In August 1941, Cardinal Clemens August Count von Galen's protest of the so-called euthanasia program was echoed by a number of lower-ranking clergy, and Hitler's decision to end euthanasia's *T-4* phase marked a "victory without parallel during the Third Reich for the force of popular opinion".[49]

Moreover, Catholics offered significant opposition to the Nazi introduction of *Gemeinschaftsschulen* to replace confessional schools, a move the Nazis justified in the name of the *Volksgemeinschaft*.[50] Catholics posed equally strong resistance to the removal of crucifixes from school classrooms, forcing the Nazis in Bavaria, for example, to concede defeat of party authority.[51] Pockets of active Catholic resistance to the Nazi regime dotted the landscape; Catholics tied to the former Christian trade unions were particularly successful in maintaining pre-1933 contacts.[52]

In general, Catholic cultural networks not only survived the Nazi years unbroken, but in some cases were strengthened in reaction to persecution.[53] As postwar Christian Democracy makes clear, a strong

46. Hugo Stehkämper, "Protest, Opposition and Widerstand im Umkreis der (untergegangenen) Zentrumspartei: Ein Überblick, Teil II: Widerstand," in Jürgen Schmädeke and Peter Steinbach, eds., *Der Widerstand gegen den Nationalsozialismus* (Munich, 1986), 907.

47. Karl-Egon Lönne, *Politischer Katholizismus im 19. und 20. Jahrhundert* (Frankfurt a.M., 1986), 234.

48. Robert Gellately, *The Gestapo and German Society: Enforcing Racial Policy 1933–1945* (Oxford and New York, 1990), 104.

49. Kershaw, *Popular Opinion & Political Dissent in the Third Reich*, 339.

50. Franz Sonnenberger, "Die Vollstreckte Reform – Die Einführung der Gemeinschaftsschule in Bayern 1935–1938," in Rainer Zitelmann and Michael Prinz, eds., *Nationalsozialismus und Modernisierung* (Darmstadt, 1991), 172–198.

51. Kershaw, *Popular Opinion & Political Dissent in the Third Reich*, 355.

52. Günter Buchstab, Brigitte Kaff, and Hans-Otto Kleinmann, *Verfolgung und Widerstand 1933–1945: Christliche Demokraten gegen Hitler*, 2nd ed. (Düsseldorf, 1990).

53. The Nazis' persecution of the clergy through trumped-up "morality" trials served in many cases to strengthen grassroots Catholic support for their priests.

Catholic identity and *Teilkultur* emerged from the war years intact, both socially and politically.[54] Potent confessional identities – Protestant as well as Catholic – served to inflame religious conflict generated by war-related population transfers; indeed, the Nazis' efforts to subordinate Christian confessional antagonism to the *Volksgemeinschaft* met with little apparent success.[55]

At the same time, however, aspects of the Nazis' origins (in Catholic Bavaria) and rise suggest indispensable Catholic participation in National Socialist rule.[56] Catholics' votes for the Center Party or the Bavarian People's Party in the last years of the Weimar Republic did not connote a total rejection of Nazism's ideas; by the end of the Weimar era, support for political Catholicism in no way automatically signaled support for republican democracy. And while Catholics, especially working-class Catholics, did organize opposition groups, one cannot speak of "Catholic resistance" against Hitler per se: After 1933, all Catholic political activity directly violated the Vatican-sanctioned Concordat.

In fact, many Catholics were attracted by similarities between their conservative hierarchical set of beliefs and those of National Socialism.[57] When stressed by the Nazis, antisemitism, anti-material-

54. Mitchell, *The Origins of Christian Democracy.*

55. Shelley Baranowski, *The Sanctity of Rural Life: Nobility, Protestantism, and Nazism in Weimar Prussia* (New York and Oxford, 1995), 169; Harry Noormann, "Neue Freiheit, vertagte Befreiung: Zur gesellschaftlichen Rolle der Kirchen in der Nachkriegszeit," in Hans-Gerd Schumann, ed., *Deutschland, 1945–1949: Ringvorlesung an der THD im Sommersemester 1985* (Darmstadt, 1989), 134; Paul Erker, "Revolution des Dorfes? Ländliche Bevölkerung zwischen Flüchtlings-zustrom und landwirtschaftlichem Strukturwandel," in Martin Broszat, Klaus-Dietmar Henke, and Hans Woller, eds., *Von Stalingrad zur Währungsreform: Zur Sozialgeschichte des Umbruchs in Deutschland* (Munich, 1990), 382–383.

56. As early as September 1930, the Center Party's support in even some of the most loyal *Zentrum* electoral districts decreased, and the NSDAP came in third (after the KPD). Von Hehl, *Katholische Kirche und National Socialism im Erzbistum Köln 1933–1945*, 16. For a survey of the interaction of the Catholic Church with the early "Third Reich," see Klaus Scholder, *Die Kirchen und das Dritte Reich, Vol. II: Das Jahr der Ernüchterung 1934* (Berlin, 1985), 221–268.

57. Herbert Gottwald, "Katholischer Univeralismus und nationale Identifikation: Zum Weg des deutschen Katholizismus im 19. und 20. Jahrhundert," in Matthias Werner, ed., *Identität und Geschichte* (Weimar, 1997), 161–173.

ism, anti-mammonism, and anti-urbanism held compelling allure for Catholics long opposed to what they understood as modernism.[58] In particular, the massive support for Nazism in some Catholic areas as early as 1928[59] reflected strong Catholic receptiveness to Nazi anti-Bolshevism.[60] Though the primacy of race in Nazi ideology continued to jar on many Catholics, especially Church leaders, Catholic politicians signaled a new openness to eugenic practices in the wake of the Depression.[61] For many Catholics, then, there was much to support in the Nazi utopian vision.

Workers

Nazi Germany's workers reveal similar contradictions and competing impulses. Election results before 1933 suggest that Germany's "tight-knit proletarian milieu," offered the lowest level of support for National Socialism.[62] After the Nazis came to power, labor leaders organized the most effective and consistent opposition to the new regime. The elite of the Communist Party of Germany suffered imprisonment and death at the hands of the Nazis, and – on the whole – workers experienced greater political persecution under the Nazis than did any other group.[63]

There is also strong evidence that workers maintained after 1933 the integrity of their closely interwoven workers' world, a world distinct from Nazism. In numerous cases, workers alienated and derided those among them who supported the *Volksgemeinschaft* with

---

58. Maria Mitchell, "Materialism and Secularism: CDU Politicians and National Socialism, 1945–1949," *The Journal of Modern History* 67(2) (June 1995), 278–308.

59. Oded Heilbronner, *Catholicism, Political Culture, and the Countryside: A Social History of the Nazi Party in South Germany* (Ann Arbor, MI, 1998).

60. Hürten, *Deutsche Katholiken 1918 bis 1945*, 348.

61. This culminated in the Prussian Zentrum's support in 1932 for sterilization. Michael Schwartz, "Konfessionelle Milieus und Weimarer Eugenik," *Historische Zeitschrift* 261(2) (October 1995), 403–448.

62. Peukert, *Inside Nazi Germany*, 101.

63. Burleigh and Wippermann, *The Racial State*, 283–284.

enthusiasm. Many laborers, antagonized by *Volksgemeinschaft* propaganda, sought refuge in a constructed private sphere of non-compliance and peer solidarity.[64]

Furthermore, as Tim Mason showed us, Nazi leaders themselves regarded workers as politically unreliable. Class conflict remained endemic during the Nazi years and Nazi leaders lived in fear of workers' unrest. As the Nazi response to workers' passive resistance during the fall of 1939 made clear, the Nazis believed that workers, though stripped of their leadership and organization, retained the power to weaken Nazi control.[65] As they did with the Churches, then, the Nazis made limited (primarily financial) concessions to the working class,[66] even if workers – arguing individually rather than collectively – were able ultimately to effect little real pressure on the regime.[67]

Yet, did German workers resist completely the blandishments of the *Volksgemeinschaft*? As Mason concluded in his epilogue to *Social Policy in the Third Reich*, had workers been such unreliable supporters of Nazism, they should have rebelled in the later years of the war. In fact, many observers expected workers to rise up immediately after Hitler was named Chancellor. Instead, workers' January 1933 protests remained local and ultimately ineffectual.[68]

There is also much evidence that Aryan workers profited from the benefits offered by the *Volksgemeinschaft*. The Labor Front (*Deutsche Arbeitsfront*, or DAF), the largest mass organization in the Third Reich, took steps to improve working conditions, while

---

64. Peukert, *Inside Nazi Germany*, 106–110.

65. Siegel, "Whatever was the attitude of German workers?," 65; Mason, *Social Policy in the Third Reich*, 285, 337.

66. Omer Bartov, "The Missing Years: German Workers, German Soldiers," in David F. Crew, ed., *Nazism and German Society, 1933–1945* (London and New York, 1994), 45.

67. Rüdiger Hachtmann, *Industriearbeit im 'Dritten Reich'. Untersuchungen zu den Lohn- und Arbeitsbedingungen in Deutschland 1933–1945* (Göttingen, 1989).

68. Alf Lüdtke, "What Happened to the 'Fiery Red Glow'? Workers' Experiences and German Fascism," in Alf Lüdtke, ed., *The History of Everyday Life: Reconstructing Historical Experiences and Ways of Life* (Princeton, NJ, 1995).

Strength Through Joy (*Kraft durch Freude*, KdF) organized affordable recreation and travel. By 1936, workers in particularly valuable sectors of the economy, such as arms manufacturing, were able to secure sizable wage increases. Nazi promises of mass consumerism – people's cars, for example – inspired widespread hopes of better living conditions. Certainly, all of this was not without effect in reconciling workers to the regime.[69]

Apart from these material benefits, National Socialism offered ideological inducements to workers as well. Not only did Nazism appeal to workers' preexisting nationalist and *völkisch* beliefs, but the Labor Front emphasized traditional workers' pride in well-performed labor.[70] The rhetorical and symbolic power of the *Qualitätsarbeiter*, imbedded in images of masculinity, struck a resonant chord with many male workers.[71] As the SOPADE (exiled SPD) reports indicate, workers throughout Germany were quite satisfied by much of Nazi life. Their complaints generally concerned specific apolitical matters;[72] indeed, positive memories of life under the Nazis before 1943 predominate.[73]

Worker acclimatization to the Nazi system was also evident in the functioning of German factories, which – by 1944 – were manned by a significant minority of forced laborers. That few Aryan workers challenged the racial hierarchy of Germany's

69. Avraham Barkai, "*Volksgemeinschaft*, 'Aryanization' and the Holocaust," 36; Burleigh and Wippermann, *The Racial State*, 288–290.

70. Welch, *The Third Reich*, 55–56.

71. Lüdtke, "Arbeiten und Dabeisein: Wie Alltagsgeschichte den National-sozialismus erklärt."

72. Lüdtke, "What Happened to the 'Fiery Red Glow'?," 203–204; *Deutschland-Berichte der Sozialdemokratischen Partei Deutschlands (Sopade) 1934–1940* (Salzhausen and Frankfurt a.M., 1980).

73. Lüdtke, "Arbeiten und Dabeisein: Wie Alltagsgeschichte den National-sozialismus erklärt"; Lutz Niethammer, ed., *"Die Jahre weiß man nicht, wo man die heute hinsetzen soll": Faschismus-Erfahrungen im Ruhrgebiet* (Berlin and Bonn, 1983); Lutz Niethammer and Alexander von Plato, eds., *"Wir kriegen jetzt andere Zeiten": Auf der Suche nach der Erfahrung des Volkes in nachfaschistischen Ländern* (Berlin, 1985); Ian Kershaw, *The "Hitler Myth": Image and Reality in the Third Reich* (Oxford and New York, 1989).

working forces suggested a certain acceptance of racial theory in action.[74] There is also the complex question of the millions of industrial wage earners who served as soldiers. (Here Catholic men naturally figure prominently as well.) Many workers understood soldiering as a continuation of factory work,[75] and there is little indication that workers (or Catholics) performed differently than other men. What limited evidence exists suggests that the bulk of German troops supported the Nazi regime in deed without registering vocal protest.[76] That clearly excludes the 40,000 to 50,000 German soldiers executed following courts-martial,[77] and the unknown number of others who objected without record.

*

Catholics and workers are instructive cases in that, in many ways, they maintained distance from or even expressed revulsion at the Nazi utopia. At the same time, however, both groups demonstrated an openness to the *Volksgemeinschaft* that coexisted – comfortably or not – with their own non-Nazi social practices and world views. Though conditioned by gender, class, and culture, the intersection and reconciliation of these competing beliefs and practices was an individualized process; it nevertheless had profound public consequences.

That this process was naturally not limited to Catholics and workers reminds us of the varieties of relationships between motive and function. At the same time, a focus on function and outcome highlights the structural similarities these relationships shared. According to Shelley Baranowski, reservations about the *Volksgemeinschaft*

---

74. Burleigh and Wippermann, *The Racial State*, 295–296; Ulrich Herbert, *Fremdarbeiter: Politik und Praxis des "Ausländer-Einsatzes" in der Kriegswirtschaft des Dritten Reiches* (Berlin and Bonn, 1985).

75. Lüdtke, "Arbeiten und Dabeisein: Wie Alltagsgeschichte den National-sozialismus erklärt."

76. Bartov, "The Missing Years: German Workers, German Soldiers"; Omer Bartov, *Hitler's Army: Soldiers, Nazis, and War in the Third Reich* (New York and Oxford, 1992).

77. Maier, *The Unmasterable Past*, 74.

were for most Germans "ultimately checkmated by agreement with much that Nazism offered."[78] This "checkmating" process need not have been consequential or even conscious.[79] For some groups – East Prussian Pomeranians, for example, resentful of Nazi incursions into their religious practices but enthusiastic supporters of Nazism's nationalism and antisemitism – a reconciliation of beliefs and practices ensued quite easily.[80] For Catholics and workers, the process was arguably less well realized. But whether their motives were mixed, the functional dynamic in most cases was the same: Ideological conflicts with the regime were outweighed by ideological and practical concessions and agreement; the end result was consensus.

In this sense, Catholics and workers were not isolated from the larger German populace in their identification with the utopia of the *Volksgemeinschaft*, but exemplary of it. Their motives, and the motives of most Germans, for accepting the *Volksgemeinschaft* are of enormous consequence not only on their own terms, but as fundamental elements of the equation that produced consensus. Here is not the place to review the rich literature on the multiplicity of sources of Nazi support. But as forces encouraging all Germans to Nazi utopianism, the following played especially powerful roles and therefore deserve brief mention.

Motive

The nationalism unleashed by World War I lost little potency throughout the Weimar Republic. Given shape and form by the *Burgfrieden* of World War I, the "united nation" remained poised for

78. Baranowski, *The Sanctity of Rural Life*, 186.
79. Siegel, "Whatever was the attitude of German workers?," 71–72. Siegel warns against overreading Germans' actions and investing in their decision-making a rational, conscious determination that may well not have been there. She argues that "dissociated thinking is one of the more usual ways of coping with such a dilemma."
80. Baranowski, *The Sanctity of Rural Life*, 184–185.

a just war. While this increasingly rabid nationalism was especially pronounced on the political right, antagonism to the Versailles settlement – fed by hostility to postwar treatment by the Allies – was palpable across the ideological spectrum.[81]

Furthermore, one need not accept that Germans were infused with "eliminationist antisemitism"[82] to assert the pervasiveness of antisemitism. As the SOPADE reports make clear,[83] preexisting German antisemitism provided fertile ground for Nazi propaganda.[84] Indeed, centuries-old prejudices intersected with Nazi distortions to produce a spectrum of negative attitudes about Jews ranging from unqualified hatred to indifferent disregard.[85]

Antisemitism was compounded and exacerbated during the Third Reich by National Socialist anti-communism. Both the Nazis' initial anti-capitalism and their hostility to Bolshevism stressed the role of the Jew as an enemy of the *Volk*.[86] By the mid-1930s anti-communism found support among almost all sectors of the population; in portraying themselves as Germany's only defense against Bolshevik takeover, the Nazis won new converts and simultaneously reinforced antisemitic stereotypes.[87]

The *Volksgemeinschaft* also won support for the specter it raised of an orderly society. The *Volksgemeinschaft* promised a certain "normalcy", important for those who had been dislocated psychologically by World War I and the Depression. In part a rejection of the seeming chaos of splintered party democratic politics, the search for normalcy was also grounded in a desire to end real social conflict.

The process of racial exclusion offered a concrete approach to eliminating "enemies" of the *Volk*. As race promised to negate class, gender, and religious difference and foster an Aryan utopia without

81. Welch, *The Third Reich*, 53.

82. Daniel Jonah Goldhagen, *Hitler's Willing Executioners: Ordinary Germans and the Holocaust* (New York, 1996).

83. Welch, *The Third Reich*, 74; *Deutschland-Berichte der Sozialdemokratischen Partei Deutschlands (Sopade) 1934–1940* (Salzhausen and Frankfurt a.M., 1980).

84. Barkai, "*Volksgemeinschaft*, 'Aryanization' and the Holocaust," 40.

85. Welch, *The Third Reich*, 74.

86. Barkai, "*Volksgemeinschaft*, 'Aryanization' and the Holocaust," 34–35.

87. Welch, *The Third Reich*, 65.

social conflict,[88] the very idea of *Volksgemeinschaft* inspired devotion. For some Germans who found hope in the ideal of a classless, racially pure utopia,[89] it was sufficient simply to believe utopia was in progress.[90]

At the same time, material relations were powerful in their persuasion. The concerns of job and family protection were influential,[91] but so was the desire to reap benefit from the Aryanization of retail trade, medicine, law, and Jewish property.[92] Equally significant was the advent of mass consumerism. Particularly through the spread of popular leisure activities – film, sports, and radio – Nazi society offered an enhancement of the everyday and a vision of an entertainment utopia.[93]

Finally, the myth of the Führer and his very real foreign policy victories served as an integrative function, securing the loyalty of those who might otherwise have remained distant from the *Volksgemeinschaft*. Mythologized as the embodiment of the unified nation, Hitler performed as the Germans' most effective defender abroad and at home, where he strove to "protect" Aryans against Bolsheviks and Jews. The director of a dramatically successful military and foreign policy (before the late war years), the Führer promised global power for a Germany "purified" of its internal weaknesses. For some individuals, belief in the Führer – "If only the Führer knew!" – was sufficient to catalyze participation in the Nazi utopia;[94] for others, the Nazi *Volksgemeinschaft* rested on international prestige.[95]

88. Peukert, *Inside Nazi Germany*, 76.

89. Gisela Diewald-Kerkmann, *Politische Denunziation im NS-Regime oder Die kleine Macht der "Volksgenossen"* (Bonn, 1995), 176.

90. Peukert, *Inside Nazi Germany*, 245. As Peukert's translation deftly reads, "It was more important to travel hopefully than to arrive."

91. Siegel, "Whatever was the attitude of German workers?," 68.

92. Barkai, "*Volksgemeinschaft*, 'Aryanization' and the Holocaust," 38–39.

93. Peukert, *Inside Nazi Germany*, pp. 77–78.

94. Gerhard Paul, "Die widerspenstige 'Volksgemeinschaft': Dissens und Verweigerung im Dritten Reich," in Peter Steinbach and Johannes Tuchel, eds., *Widerstand gegen den Nationalsozialismus* (Bonn, 1994).

95. Kershaw, *The "Hitler Myth"*.

Among others, these forces were significant for their ability to override moral or political objections Germans harbored to elements of the *Volksgemeinschaft*. This was true for Catholics as well as Protestants, workers as well as bourgeois, and women as well as men. Indeed, this "checkmating" dynamic was very evident among German women, who – though long considered ideologically distant from the regime[96] – provided little demonstration of disaffection. The Nazi vision of an authoritarian family anchored in a racially pure Germany appealed to many German women, as did the opportunities Nazis offered women in a specifically female public sphere.[97] For conservative Protestant women in Hanover, for example, anti-communism, nationalism, and conservative gender codes outweighed measured reticence about racism.[98] While, for many Catholic women imbedded in the Catholic *Teilkultur*, those racist principles were more difficult to embrace,[99] in the end, the overwhelming majority of women abided and engaged in the *Volksgemeinschaft*; their consensus enabled it to function.

In this regard, the relationship between motive and function attains an attractive facility. On an operational level, popular motive mattered

96. Elizabeth Heineman, "The Hour of the Woman: Memories of Germany's 'Crisis Years' and West German National Identity," *The American Historical Review* 101(2) (April 1996), 354–395. The most persuasive arguments for female victimization and rejection of the *Volksgemeinschaft* are found in Gisela Bock, *Zwangssterilisation im Nationalsozialismus. Studien zur Rassenpolitik und Frauenpolitik* (Opladen, 1986); Gisela Bock, "Racism and Sexism in Nazi Germany: Motherhood, Compulsory Sterilization, and the State," in Atina Grossmann, Renate Bridenthal, and Marion Kaplan, eds., *When Biology Became Destiny: Women in Weimar and Nazi Germany* (New York, 1984); Gisela Bock, "Antinatalism, Maternity and Paternity in National Socialist Racism," in David F. Crew, ed., *Nazism and German Society, 1933–1945* (London and New York, 1994). Women's relationship to the Third Reich has been the source of considerable controversy. Atina Grossmann, "Feminist Debates about Women and National Socialism," *Gender & History* 3(3) (Autumn 1991), 350–358; Adelheid von Saldern, "Victims or Perpetrators? Controversies about the Role of Women in the Nazi State," in David F. Crew, ed., *Nazism and German Society, 1933–1945* (London and New York, 1994).

97. Koonz, *Mothers in the Fatherland*.

98. Nancy R. Reagin, *A German Women's Movement: Class & Gender in Hanover, 1880–1933* (Chapel Hill and London, 1995), 256.

99. Koonz, *Mothers in the Fatherland*, 265–306.

only as it made possible the implementation of the *Volksgemeinschaft*. Indeed, as many scholars have noted, acquiescence was sufficient for the realization of Nazi utopian goals. In the words of Detlev Peukert, "Retreat into the private sphere and refusal to yield up anything more than the minimum necessary participation in the public state-management of *Volksgemeinschaft* still entailed, at the least, passive acceptance of the prevailing order."[100] Most basically, the *Volksgemeinschaft* vision of the future did not need to be embraced wholeheartedly by a majority of Germans for the Nazi utopia to function.[101]

And yet, the passive complicity model taken too simplistically becomes sterile. On the one hand, a mechanistic model of "check-mating" citizens abiding the Nazi government suggests an almost physical separation between "Germans" and "Nazis": Nazi leaders persuaded German citizens to accommodate Nazi control, but the two groups inhabited different, separate spaces. On the other hand, Nazi policy's rootedness in race implies that any citizen-state interaction implicated the German citizen in genocide. According to this schema, the boundary between Germans and Nazis dissolved as non-Nazi worlds became thoroughly perverted by collaboration.

While the first of these tenets denies the powerful consequences of passive support for dictatorship, the second comes perilously close to suggesting that all nonimprisoned Germans were Nazis. While the latter interpretation is more compelling on the level of function (recalling Peukert's words above), it risks obscuring the variety of paths Germans took to passive or active support; it also denies the continued existence after 1933 of non-National Socialist traditions and spheres.[102]

100. Peukert, *Inside Nazi Germany*, 238.

101. Lüdtke, "Arbeiten und Dabeisein: Wie Alltagsgeschichte den National-sozialismus erklärt"; Welch, *The Third Reich*, 57–58, 64–65; Gellately, *The Gestapo and German Society*, 13.

102. These considerations echo points raised in the very interesting 1987 Vierteljahrshefte für Zeitgeschichte letter exchange between Saul Friedländer and Martin Broszat, reprinted in Peter Baldwin, ed., *Reworking the Past: Hitler, the Holocaust, and the Historians' Debate* (Boston: Beacon Press, 1990), 102–134.

A middle ground seems therefore more persuasive, one that asserts that many Germans operated between "two worlds" in Nazi Germany, a set of non-Nazi values and customs on one hand and the *Volksgemeinschaft* on the other.[103] The non-Nazi sphere could be ideological or cultural: In what remained of non-Nazi world views, Catholics continued to revere the Pope and workers socialized with fellow workers. In a non-Nazi sphere, Germans could also acknowledge the continuance of social, particularly class and confessional, conflict, and act on non-ideological individual desire. (The fact that members of the SS had particularly small families suggests one manifestation of such preference.)[104]

For the overwhelming majority of Germans, these "worlds" overlapped: For some individuals whose *Teilkultur* differed little from that of the Nazis, the "worlds" merged completely; for others, as we have seen, the reconciliation or "checkmating" process was more complex. What many Germans shared, however, was Lüdtke's set of contradictory behaviors as they negotiated the relationship between non-Nazi belief and *Volksgemeinschaft*.

Indeed, the parallel existence of non-Nazi worlds and the *Volksgemeinschaft* was real as well as symbolic, and Germans' paradoxical behaviors had real consequence. The functioning of the *Volksgemeinschaft* was made possible by enthusiastic collaboration, acquiescence, and indifference, but also by isolated behaviors consistent with Lüdtke's model of contradiction. While many Germans maintained a separate, non-Nazi sphere, they also participated in the realm of the *Volksgemeinschaft*; that the sum of their contributions was sufficient to render the Nazi utopia real reminds us of the deadly consequences of function.

103. This relies on Peter Fritzsche's adaptation in Fritzsche, "Nazi Modern," of Jens Alber's argument that the Nazi regime had at best a short-term impact on longitudinal social developments. For Alber's original interpretation, see Jens Alber, "Nationalsozialismus und Modernisierung," *Kölner Zeitschrift für Soziologie und Sozialpsychologie* 41 (1989), 346–365.

104. Bock, "Antinatalism, Maternity and Paternity in National Socialist Racism," 127.

Function

Even a limited number of examples can illustrate how Germans reinforced the *Volksgemeinschaft* not simply through passivity, but through their adaptation of its norms into at least one sphere of their lives. As John Connelly's case study of Eisenach demonstrates, Germans did not need to be unqualified believers to participate actively in the Nazi utopia. By invoking *Volksgemeinschaft* rhetoric to achieve their own personal and political ends – challenging Jewish occupancy of desirable properties, for example – inhabitants of Eisenach helped to realize the *Volksgemeinschaft* in small but ultimately destructive ways;[105] in Connelly's words, they actively aided the construction of "a really existing *Volksgemeinschaft*."[106]

The workings of the Gestapo suggested a similar dynamic at play. In his examination of the Gestapo in Würzburg, Robert Gellately determined that the isolation of Jews was driven substantially by individual denunciations, while, in the Rhine–Ruhr area, most denunciations of German "forbidden contact" with Polish foreign workers originated with German non-official civilians. The mechanism of informing illuminates the operation of local Nazi terror and explains more broadly how the *Volksgemeinschaft* took root. It also reminds us of the basic power of function: Once informants contacted the Gestapo with a charge of "asocial" behavior, why they had done so was immaterial to the final outcome.[107]

The values of *Volksgemeinschaft* were also made real through everyday rituals. The Nazification of preexisting symbolic discourse – beginning a birthday dinner with a prayer for Hitler, for example

105. John Connelly, "The Uses of *Volksgemeinschaft*: Letters to the NSDAP Kreisleitung Eisenach, 1939–1940," in Sheila Fitzpatrick and Robert Gellately, eds., *Accusatory Practices: Denunciation in Modern European History, 1789–1989* (Chicago and London, 1997).

106. Connelly, "The Uses of *Volksgemeinschaft*," 183.

107. Gellately, *The Gestapo and German Society*; Robert Gellately, "Denunciations in Twentieth-Century Germany: Aspects of Self-Policing in the Third Reich and the German Democratic Republic," in Sheila Fitzpatrick and Robert Gellately, eds., *Accusatory Practices: Denunciation in Modern European History, 1789–1989* (Chicago and London, 1997).

– helped Germans preserve a sense of "normalcy". Such adaptation of everyday customs normalized radical change and served to mute reservations about Nazi-induced transformations. In even minor ways, then, where individuals participated in Nazi rites and rituals, they actively forged a real *Volksgemeinschaft*.[108]

The creation of the *Volksgemeinschaft* was well demonstrated, for example, by the perversion of public language.[109] As the labels "Jews" and "Aryans" appeared – from park benches to shop windows – with dramatic frequency, racist language began to permeate public discourse. The language of the *Volksgemeinschaft* was so pervasive and powerful that even victims adopted the language of their persecutors to describe themselves and others.[110]

Not only the everyday use of Nazi terms, but seemingly small gestures served to exclude the "enemies" of the *Volk*. In his "thick descriptions" of Hildesheim before and during Nazi rule, Andrew Bergerson argues that the "radicalization of the everyday" made possible a *Volksgemeinschaft* on the ground. As Germans adapted normal customs – social greetings on the street, for example – they actively transformed neighbors into Aryans and Jews. As these reinvented traditions fostered alienation, Jews were encouraged to flee – thus creating a physical *Volksgemeinschaft*. In these ways, small acts of social exclusion – or "social death" inflicted on "enemies" of the *Volk* – helped to construct a "really existing" *Volksgemeinschaft*, one ultimately marked by genocide.[111]

108. Heide Gerstenberger, "Alltagsforschung und Faschismustheorie," in Heide Gerstenberger and Dorothea Schmidt, eds., *Normalität oder Normalisierung? Geschichtswerkstätten und Faschismusanalyse* (Münster, 1987).

109. Gerhard Bauer, *Sprache und Sprachlosigkeit im 'Dritten Reich'* (Cologne, 1988).

110. Lüdtke, "Arbeiten und Dabeisein: Wie Alltagsgeschichte den National-sozialismus erklärt."

111. Andrew Stuart Bergerson, "Hildesheim in an Age of Pestilence: On the Birth, Death, and Resurrection of Normalcy," in Alon Confino and Peter Fritzsche, eds., *The Work of Memory: New Directions in German History and Culture* (Urbana: University of Illinois Press, forthcoming); Andrew Stuart Bergerson, "Hildesheim in an Age of Pestilence: An Alltagsgeschichte of Normalcy," *Tel Aviver Jahrbuch für deutsche Geschichte* 28 (1999), 303–340.

In some situations, Germans simultaneously demonstrated the parallel existences of a non-Nazi sphere and the *Volksgemeinschaft*. In response to the poorly enforced January 1943 order for all women between ages seventeen and forty-five to register for employment, Germany's middle- and upper-class women largely balked. Presumably, they did so for reasons beyond the ideology of *Volksgemeinschaft* – not out of resistance to its utopian goals but for practical motives pertaining to finances and work load.[112] When lower- and working-class women and men protested this class injustice, however, they invoked the language of *Volksgemeinschaft*. Well aware of the failure of the *Volksgemeinschaft* to operate in practice, German workers nonetheless invoked its language and ideals. Possibly a tactic to advance personal interests, the use of racist language nonetheless reinforced the legitimacy of the Nazi utopia; even as the motive remains unknown to us, its reinforcement of the *Volksgemeinschaft* does not.[113]

The complexity of individual behavior – to "consent, accept, cooperate – but also to 'go underground', to dissociate oneself, sometimes to oppose" – suggests that even as the Nazi utopia was institutionalized it did not absorb all preexisting cultural life or overcome all reservations about its goals. It did not need to destroy embedded *Teilkulturen* in order to function: Participation in the *Volksgemeinschaft* was possible even when opposition or skepticism concerning the *Volksgemeinschaft* endured.

For the most part, the Nazi regime rested on a peaceful cohabitation of Germans' preexisting norms and values with those of the Nazi utopia. As individuals experienced conflicts with the *Volksgemeinschaft* both in theory and in fact, the vast majority made concessions that produced a functional consensus. That consensus was not purely passive. In the *Volksgemeinschaft*, Catholics participated

112. Leila J. Rupp, "'I Don't Call That *Volksgemeinschaft*': Women, Class, and War in Nazi Germany," in Carol Berkin and Clara Maria Lovett, eds., *Women, War and Revolution* (New York, 1980).

113. Leila J. Rupp, "'I Don't Call That *Volksgemeinschaft*': Women, Class, and War in Nazi Germany," in Carol Berkin and Clara Maria Lovett, eds., *Women, War and Revolution* (New York, 1980).

in KdF activities, working-class men denounced "enemies" of the *Volk*, and Aryan women shunned women of Jewish ancestry.[114]

What this meant for German society after 1945 is hotly disputed. The effects of the implementation of the Nazi utopia before 1945, however, were deadly and clear. As competing motives led to a widespread "checkmate" between Nazi utopianism and non-Nazi practice and belief, Germans constructed a *Volksgemeinschaft* and the Nazi utopia was made real.

114. Fritzsche, "Nazi Modern," 7.

4

"We may be losing this generation": Talking about Youth and the Nation's Future during the New Deal Era[*]

Olaf Stieglitz

> It's an old story – the conflict of the older and younger generations . . .
> Old story or new story: the question is what are we going to do about
> it?[1]

Desirable blueprints for a future intentional community are commonly called utopia. Every more specified and differentiated definition is problematic, for utopia research, traditionally based in a variety of scholarly traditions, academic disciplines, and literary schools – and nowadays in a defensive position when confronted with a growing number of supporters of "predictable scenarios of the immediate future" – resists a stiff catalogue of necessary elements.[2] Nevertheless, there are at least two characteristics to be found in many utopian drafts since the beginnings of that genre and among examples of all degrees of sophistication. First, they can almost always be interpreted as arguing against a present perceived as largely negative: Tell me which kind of utopias were written (or lived) in that country at that time, and I tell you how social, economic and cultural conditions had been there – or as how bad they were perceived.[3] A second typical element of utopian thinking, although by far not as universally

* The author is very grateful that additional research for this article was made possible with the help of a grant from the Roosevelt Study Center in Middelburg/ Netherlands.

1. Paul Popenoe, "When Youth Goes Radical," *Parents' Magazine* 15 (November, 1940), 118.

2. Rolf Schwendter, *Utopie. Überlegungen zu einem zeitlosen Begriff* (Berlin, 1994).

3. Herbert Marcuse, *Das Ende der Utopien* (Berlin, 1967).

present than the first one, is its often implicit orientation towards a comforting past: ideal in its small size, in its controllable technology, in its stable "elementary units," like families for example. Even utopias with an enormous amount of breathtaking high-tech sometimes employ their futuristic devices as a means to return to the "basics" of some simpler life resembling times long gone.

With regard to this amateur-like excursion into the political thinking of utopia, it might become clear why the New Deal[4] gains prominence in debates about a future society. During the 1980s and early 1990s, in the triumphant age of neoliberalism, we witnessed the creation and stabilization of a globalized world of completely unregulated conditions of work and production. "The New Deal System," Keynesian in its economic thinking, interventionistic in what is expected from the state, from government or from politicians in general, and Fordistic in its way of organizing labor, was certainly not small in size, but rather grandly complex and notoriously fractured. Since its beginnings, a set of large successes paired with missed opportunities, unintended consequences, and dangerous but inescapable compromises – but from our present perspective, to many it seems to have been a controllable, stable, and, above all, socially just alternative to the radicalized market society of today.[5]

Yet talking about the role the "New Deal System" plays as a model in political debates today should not be a matter for economists and politicians alone. Social and cultural history might add material to the debate by providing background information on topics maybe not perceived as central but nevertheless revealing the hidden and not so obvious consequences of what had had its start as Franklin Roosevelt's New Deal of the 1930s. This essay will

---

4. For reasons of clarity, this article differentiates between the "original" New Deal as a set of legislative acts established by the administration of Franklin D. Roosevelt between 1933 and 1941 (the terminating point in time is very much disputable, of course, but is oriented at the entry of the United States into World War II) on the one hand and what Steve Fraser and Gery Gerstle termed the "New Deal System", which gained its full relevance after the war, see their *The Rise and Fall of the New Deal Order, 1930–1980* (Princeton, NJ, 1989).

5. Fraser and Gerstle, eds., *Rise and Fall of the New Deal Order*, introduction.

deal with the utopian character of that "original" New Deal itself;
a perspective which might not be too surprising. According to
historical writing, the political approach of the Roosevelt administration is often considered as shifting between a simple, pragmatic,
unideological, "emergency" character on the one hand and a
program endowed with the "vision" of a thoroughly planned society
on the other hand.[6] Today, the economic thinking of a Rexford G.
Tugwell, the Social Security legislation of the mid-1930s, and the
Tennessee Valley Authority (TVA) are remembered as having been
the best examples of New Deal thinking with a broad future
perspective, although all these ideas, plans, and actual programs
suffered from significant handicaps in the process of realization.[7]
Moreover, thinking of the United States of the 1930s, one has got
other "utopias" in mind which were not directly associated with
the federal government but grew out of the New Deal "spirit":
Industrial designers "invented" the streamline style, which was
supposed to "convince consumers of the wonders of progress,
prompt new buying that would combat the depression, and provide
conscious control over the influence of mass-produced goods on
everyday experience."[8] On a large scale, this vision of future harmony
through technology and design was celebrated at the New York
World's Fair of 1939, where another example of utopian thinking
was also exhibited in the tightly planned urban environment of
"Democracity." Greenbelt towns were very fashionable in the
depression decade, planned and constructed in part under the roof

6. The most relevant of the recent textbooks dealing with the US policy of the
1930s is Anthony J. Badger, *The New Deal. The Depression Years, 1933–1940* (London,
1989).

7. A new overview is presented by Robert A. Garson and Stuart S. Kidd, eds.,
The Roosevelt Years: New Perspective on American History, 1933–1945 (Edinburgh,
1999). Included in this volume is Gareth Davies, "The Unsuspected Radicalism of
the Social Security Act," 56–71. Especially for the TVA, see Roy Talbert, Jr., *FDR's
Utopian: Arthur Morgan of the TVA* (Jackson, MI, 1987).

8. Terry A. Cooney, *Balancing Acts: American Thought and Culture in the 1930s*
(New York, 1995), 21; Howard P. Segal, *Technological Utopianism in American Culture*
(Chicago, IL, 1985).

of the New Deal.[9] Of course, the 1930s saw attempts of original utopian-style projects as well. The Jewish Sunrise Colony, for instance, existed from 1933 till 1937 in the Saginaw Valley/Michigan and Upton Sinclair's 1934 campaign for governor in California gave widespread attention to a type of rural resettlement that was closely related to the writer's socialist-utopian ideas as presented in his earlier novels like *The Jungle*.

Here, another aspect of future-oriented thinking during the New Deal era should be underscored. The point that "the future belongs to youth" is maybe too obvious, too self-evident, to arouse scholarly interest. As this essay will show, this "naturalization" and intrumentalization of youth reveals important insights into how rhetorical strategies use the future to provide sense to the present. In North America, for more than 300 years, there has been constant public concern with the idea of a generation: Since the colonial era, specific crises and conditions produced a language that invested a "younger" generation with responsibilities for maintaining or advancing community ideals. As Glenn Wallach has shown recently, the formation of that elite discourse dates back to the writings of New England's Puritan leaders and reaches a first climax after the American Revolution, when the language of generation "yoked conservative motivations – follow in the footsteps of glorious founders, stay the course, transmit a heritage unimpaired to those who follow – to an activist vision of responsibility for building a new society."[10] During the first half of the nineteenth century, the concept of generation reached a new significance in national life. Historians provide evidence for an obsessive national anxiety about how to live up to the visions and examples set by the founders.[11]

9. Paul K. Conkin, *Tomorrow a New World. The New Deal Community Program* (Ithaca, NY, 1959); Helmut Lauerbach, "'Grennbelt New Towns – Ready to Serve a Better Age': Ideologie und Rhetorik in The City (1939)," *Amerikastudien/American Studies* 37(1) (1992), 51–63.

10. Glenn Wallach, *Obedient Sons. The Discourse of Youth and Generations in American Culture, 1630–1860* (Amherst, MA, 1997), see especially the introduction.

11. Michael Kammen, *The Season of Youth: The American Revolution and Historical Imagination* (New York, 1978), 31f.; Rush Welter, *The Mind of America, 1820–1860* (New York, 1975), 25ff.

And in the 1840s and 1850s, "youth for the first time became part of a national catchphrase — Young America."[12] The Civil War ruptured ideas about youth and generations, as it did most other aspects of national life, and set the generation that fought the war aside. The idea of a new founding or a second revolution certainly has to be mentioned here.[13] At the turn of the century, after rapid industrialization, urbanization, and other related aspects culminated in what Alan Trachtenberg called "the Incorporation of America," the concept of adolescence emerged in a now much more age-graded environment owing to the increasing high school population and other peer group-oriented organizations.[14] Youth, and especially boys, became the objects of a growing body of expert research and surveillance, most of them guided by ideas about a "natural" youthful character.[15] Despite such trends, adults still expressed concern about their children's future, focussing their anxiety now on the field of morality. Young people in their teens and early twenties were noticed in the 1920s to a greater degree than they had been earlier and in the eyes of more and more of their "audience," they were guilty of a trio of elementary sins: disregard for authority, rebellion against traditions, and allegedly unprecedented forms of sexual behavior, thus threatening the fundamentals of the community.[16]

By tracing the further development of this discourse and its relevance to the New Deal era, the focus here is not to determine

---

12. Wallach, *Obedient Sons*, 3.

13. See Norbert Finzsch, "Introduction: Reconstruction and 'Wiederaufbau' in German and American Perspective," in Norbert Finzsch and Jürgen Martschukat, eds., *Different Restorations. Reconstruction and »Wiederaufbau« in the United States and Germany: 1865 – 1945 – 1989* (Oxford, 1996), 1–23, here p. 2.

14. Joseph F. Kett, *Rites of Passage. Adolescence in America, 1790 to the Present* (New York, 1977).

15. G. Stanley Hall, *Adolescence. Its Psychology and its Realtion to Anthropology, Sociology, Sex, Crime, Religion, and Education*, 2 vols. (New York, 1905). This essay will define »youth« as comprising young people, roughly between the ages of 15 and 25, thereby excluding both children and »young adults« who were already settled in either stable work relations and/or marriage.

16. Paula Fass, *The Damned and the Beautiful. American Youth in the 1920s* (New York, 1977); John Modell, *Into One's Own. From Youth to Adulthood in the United States, 1920–1975* (Berkeley, CA, 1989).

the experience and situation of youth during the Depression decade, but rather to analyze the language that gives sense to youth and generation as "cultural ideals" in service of the whole nation. Choosing this focus means that I will touch the real socio-economic conditions of youths of different class, race, and gender only slightly. This is to be regretted, considering the fact that historiography on youths tends to concentrate on periods of relative economic affluence that maintained a friendly climate for the establishment of some kind of original "youth cultures." Thus, the social history of young men and (especially) women during the Depression decade remains to be written.[17] Nevertheless, considering the concept of utopia as a guideline, it seems even more interesting to look at the New Deal's language on youth and how it linked the generational idea to the nation – to its past, present, and future. This essay will take the following four aspects into special consideration when elaborating ideas about how policy during the Depression might have been inspired by ideas about the role of the forthcoming citizens: First, the article will show how a certain "new youth problem" developed in contrast to the "old" one known from the 1920s. Second, a language of national development will be analyzed which linked ideas about youth and generation to contemporary politics. As a third aspect, the essay will demonstrate how the image of a future citizen was imbedded into a language of youthful duty and generational responsibility; a language which climaxed and materialized itself in a (although short-lived) national holiday. And finally, this "utopia" will be discussed concerning its limitations in regard to race, class, and gender.

Stating the 1930s' Youth Problem

In a recent encyclopedic essay identifying the developing lifestyles, behaviors, and norms of the new youth culture which emerged in the early twentieth century and registering the numerous reactions

17. Olaf Stieglitz, "New Deal Programmes for Youth: Recent Historiography and Future Research," in Garson and Kidd, eds., *The Roosevelt Years*, 42–55.

of anxious parents and excited experts to these trends, the historian Ruth Alexander claims that, "[t]he Great Depression temporarily interrupted American anxieties about youth."[18] The contention is provocative to every historian of the New Deal era. Interest in the so-called "youth problem" continued through the 1930s, but its content and primary focus changed considerably. In fact, the very term "youth problem" was then in obvious need of redefinition. The 1920s' debate centered upon "morality," the dangers of commercialized consumption, and an (although exaggerated) notion of almost universal sexual promiscuity. By realizing the massive impact of the Depression, an even more amazing number of speeches, editorials, articles, and books devoted to a "new" youth problem reflected a growing interest in youth's "morale."[19] The elements that constituted the youth problem of the 1930s were manifold, the main one of course being the economy: there were no jobs for youngsters when they were through with schools. Between 1930 and 1940, young people appeared in large numbers among the unemployed and were overrepresented in proportion to their numbers in the population. For various reasons, the amount of youth unemployment can only be estimated for this decade, but at the time of the 1937 Census of Unemployment, approximately four million young men and women between 15 and 24 years old were completely out of work and an additional 1.5 million who were only part-time employed wanted more work. Many extended their school education, but those who left school because of necessity and were able to find employment often had to accept insecure, underpaid, and physically exhausting positions without prospects; their inexperience banned them from most rewarding jobs.[20] Unemployment was proportionally higher among young women, and the same was true for African-American and other non-white

18. Ruth M. Alexander, "Adolescence," in Mary Kupiec Cayton, Elliott J. Gorn, and Peter W. Williams, eds., *Encyclopedia of American Social History*, vol. 3, (New York, 1993), 2046.

19. "To speak of youth in the 1920s was to speak of their behavior, not their treatment," analyzed Joseph Kett correctly, see Kett, *Rites of Passage*, 258.

20. Compare Ruth E. Eckert u. Thomas O. Marshall, *When Youth Leave School* (New York, 1938), part II, chapter 3. See also Modell, *Into One's Own*, 122ff.

youths.[21] Thus, for many the crash cut all links to that affluent lifestyle of 1920s teenagers that in the eyes of many commentators had "ruined" that generation's morality. Despite indulging in "many pleasures which only money can buy," Depression youth was almost generally considered to be passive, resigned, even apathetic: "Whether he be boy or girl, he brings little thought or plan into the spending of his day."[22] "Idleness" was the word most frequently used to describe youth's situation and it transmitted more than just a descriptive meaning. In some regard, it somehow even characterized the true core of the whole problem, because, "normally," youth is never idle: "Youth is impatient. Naturally so."[23] Since the turn of the century, a whole cohort of educators, social workers, and other experts followed in the footsteps of G. Stanley Hall and labelled the youthful life period as one of "storm and stress," considering this as being almost an anthropological truth. For Progressives as well as for conservative advisors, this youthful activity had to be channeled in institutions and organizations under adult control: in clubs, in school, in the workplace. In the "unnatural times of the early 1930s,"[24] the *anomie* of youthful apathy was still unthinkable and commentators were eager to detect the outlets of teenage energy: In their eyes, they "had a great deal of time in which to get into trouble, and frequently [urged] this as . . . reason for doing so,"[25] and males seemed especially in danger of loosing their ties to society.

21. All numbers taken from U.S. National Youth Administration, *Final Report of the National Youth Administration, Fiscal Years 1936–1943* (Washington, D.C., 1944), 10–15. See also D.C. Harley, "Analysis of Unemployed Youth 15 to 24 Years of Age". Manuscript prepared for the American Youth Commission, October 19, 1939, documented in Robert H. Bremner et al., eds., *Children and Youth in America. A Documentary History* (Cambridge, MA, 1974), vol. III: 1933–1973, 21f.

22. Benedict S. Alper and George E. Lodgen, "Youth Without Work," in *The Survey*, 70 (1934), 285–286. This article was based on a survey conducted in Boston in 1933.

23. Aubrey Williams, address delivered before the students of Cornell University, Ithaca, NY, December 6, 1938. Roosevelt Study Center, Middelburg, NL (RSC): Collection: New Deal Agencies and Black Americans, Reel 2: NYA.

24. U.S. National Youth Administration, *Final Report of the National Youth Administration, Fiscal Years 1936–1943* (Washington, D.C., 1944), 15.

25. Alper and Lodgen, "Youth Without Work," 285–286.

Although careful criminologists warned about simple, unreflected conclusions,[26] juvenile delinquency ranked among the topics most fashionable in the public debate about youth, leaving its marks in scholarly discussions, government politics, the yellow press, and in a wave of Hollywood movies. "Most of our criminals," remarked Franklin Roosevelt's advisor Charles W. Taussig, "are to be found in this social no-man's land," meaning the period between leaving school and starting to work.[27] Not only did the reports from large cities state a "[marked] increase in crimes committed by boys between sixteen and nineteen, many of whom have no previous record," but the situation in rural areas was described similarly.[28] To what extent young people were not "criminals" but objects of a process of discursive criminalization can easily be demonstrated when concentrating on youthful transients, the "teenage tramps of America."[29] Making their living with odd jobs, stealing and begging, these transients filled the floors of juvenile courts all over the country, provoking concern as much as fear and sometimes, as the infamous example of so called Scottsborough boys in the early 1930s demonstrated, bore the possibilities of even harsher exploitation, too.[30]

26. J. P. Shalloo, "Youth and Crime," *The Annals of the American Academy of Political and Social Science* 194 (1937), 79–86; see also U.S. Department of Labor, *Facts about Juvenile Delinquency: Its Prevention and Treatment* (Washington, D.C., 1937).

27. Charles W. Taussig, speech delivered at a dinner meeting of the Maryland Youth Congress, February 1, 1939, RSC collection: New Deal Agencies and Black Americans, Reel 2: NYA.

28. The quotation is taken from "Youth in the Depression," *The Survey*, LXIX (1933), 67, an article describing the effect of the depression on youth in New York State. On rural youth, see Bruce L. Melvin, "The Special Problems of Rural Youth," *The Annals of the American Academy of Political and Social Science* 194 (1937), 25–33, and other publications by the same author.

29. Arthur M. Schlesinger, Jr., *The Crisis of the Old Order* (Boston, MA, 1957), 251.

30. James Goodman, *Stories of Scottsborough* (New York, 1994); for the general debate concerning "teenage tramps" see "The Young Transient: A Panel Discussion," *The Transient* (July, 1934), 8, documented in Bremner et al., eds., *Children and Youth in America*, 29f.

On the basis of that dangerous liaison between enforced idleness and criminality, and as its consequences, other risky elements grew that were recognized as amounting to the new youth problem and making it a true national concern: "At a time when there is so much talk about the dangers of reactionary oldsters, it might be an excellent idea to give a little thought to the dangers of developing a generation of apathetic youth . . . That can quite easily become a national calamity."[31] Although not really a recently publicized phenomenon, alcohol was one of the additional factors. A Maryland survey believed to be representative of the opinions of American youth in general stated that more than half the youth admitted that, with varying degrees of frequency and moderation, they indulged in some kind of alcoholic beverages.[32] That was considered a great distance away from what was perceived in the 1920s as "hedonistic" behavior of well-off college students. Many concerned observers linked the alcohol problem to the crisis of the family. The image of jobless fathers and sons, both hopeless, drunken, and more than a potential danger to their wives, mothers, and sisters, threatened the foundation of the American community, and many social scientists were very explicit on that point.[33]

With connecting the family crisis to the youth problem, the conviction that an unsupervised young generation threatened the whole society became a widely shared opinion, underscoring Franklin Roosevelt's biologistic interpretation of national well-being stated in 1932: "Any neglected group . . . can infect our national life and produce widespread misery."[34] And after 1933, examples from Europe seemed to clarify what could happen. By the end of

---

31. Howard Bell, "The Maryland Study of the American Youth Commission," *The Annals of the American Academy of Political and Social Science* 194 (1937), 187–196, here p. 196.

32. Howard M. Bell, *Youth Tell Their Story* (Washington, D.C., 1938), 249–255.

33. Ruth Cavan, *The Family and the Depression: A Study of One Hundred Chicago Families* (New York, 1971), 175f. (originally published 1938); Mirra Komarovsky, *The Unemployed Man and his Family: The Effect of Unemployment Upon the Status of the Man in Fifty-Nine Families* (New York, 1940).

34. As quoted in Richard Reiman, *The New Deal & American Youth. Ideas and Ideals in a Depression Decade* (Athens, GA, and London, 1992), 29.

that year, Roosevelt's ambassador to Germany, William E. Dodd, had taken notice of the activities of the Hitler Youth and included some personal observations in his cables to Washington. Together with brain trustee Taussig he agreed that tyrants abroad were turning European youth against democracy, exploiting the idealism of youth, and demonstrating how easily America's youth might suffer a similar experience.[35] The increasing numbers of protesting students at America's universities were interpreted as signs of what was called totalitarian radicalization, and thus, the question was raised, should not the New Deal establish a program to impart the lesson of democracy to the young?[36] A significant faction in the New Deal thought the answer to this was yes, and it was William Taussig who was especially outspoken in relating the complex socio-cultural youth problem to his concern about totalitarianism:

> If we are willing to pay the price, we can temporarily solve all these problems. Witness the totalitarian states. There youth have no material problems, there are enough jobs to go around, there are adequate educational institutions of a sort, there is a plethora of recreational opportunities, and everything is in order and regimentation. The price of that Utopia is plainly and clearly marked on the tag. They can have it all if they are willing to give up their freedom and liberty. . . .
> There are no less than 139 propaganda organizations in the United States, many of which monogram their stationery with the swastika, that are offering such youth the benefits of totalitarianism in exchange for their liberty.[37]

A journalist, after touring the country for several months, concluded that America's young people were a "lost generation,"

---

35. Reiman, *New Deal & American Youth*, 32.

36. On students' protest during the 1930s, see Robert Cohen, *When the Old Left Was Young: Student Radicals and America's First Mass Student Movement, 1929–1941* (Oxford, and New York, 1993).

37. Address of Charles W. Taussig, Chairman of the National Advisory Committee of the National Youth Administration, held before the Maryland Youth Congress, John Hopkins University, February 2, 1939. RSC collection: New Deal Agencies and Black Americans, Reel 2: NYA.

that they were "runners delayed at the gun. They have lost so much time at the start that only the exceptional can challenge the finish." Others were not as pessimistic, speaking of an "unfound generation" instead of a lost one.[38] Whatever label was given, from the early 1930s on, the idea of relating the situation of young Americans to a nation perceived as being in a state of crisis grew more and more popular. Taken the "plasticity of young minds" as a given fact, many believed it necessary for the federal state to take an active role in leading youth toward democracy.[39] It was the First Lady, Eleanor Roosevelt, who supported this idea most energetically: "I have moments of real terror when I think we may be losing this generation. We have got to bring these young people into the active life of the community and make them feel that they are necessary."[40] She and many others wanted to establish a national youth organization, or youth service,

> not to superimpose ideas upon them [youth] nor to indoctrinate in the worst sense of the words, but to lead them out in their thinking so that they see clearly what is wrong with our present order, that allows so much suffering and so little hope among the masses, and as a result of such constructive thought on their part, can intelligently ally themselves with the groups that are seeking practical solutions in bringing out a just and a fair social order.[41]

With both the Civilian Conservation Corps (CCC) and the National Youth Administration (NYA), the United States took a very specific route to achieve this objective. The CCC, created as President Roosevelt's "pet program" in the Hundred Days after his inauguration, employed in its camps almost 3 million young men

38. Maxine Davis, *The Lost Generation* (New York, 1936), 4.

39. Reiman, *New Deal & American Youth*, 24

40. Eleanor Roosevelt in an interview with the *New York Times*, May 7, 1934. See also *What I Hope to Leave Behind: The Essential Essays of Eleanor Roosevelt*. Edited with an introduction by Allida M. Black (Brooklyn, NY, 1995), 536.

41. Juanita J. Saddler on a conference of the National Youth Administration at Washington, DC, June 2–3, 1936. RSC collection: New Deal Agencies and Black Americans, Reel 2: NYA

in work relief over a nine-year period.[42] The NYA was established in 1935 to help students work their way through high school or college. These agencies not only testified to ongoing concerns about youth in US political culture during the 1930s, but also served as institutionalized and materialized discourses.

Youth and National Development

In the 1933 social-issue film, *Wild Boys of the Road*, Eddie, Tommy, and Sally, three teenagers from middle-class families, travel on freight trains, make their living with some petty crimes, and end up in a New York City Juvenile Court. Accused of robbery and "wayward-ness," the three youngsters are lucky. A compassionate judge, presiding under the sign of the National Recovery Administration's Blue Eagle, "does his part" by suspending their sentences and promising them local work relief, continued schooling, and even jobs for their unemployed fathers. Eddie responds to the prospect of a brighter future, offered by the judge, with a series of flic-flac handsprings on the streets in front of the courthouse.[43]

This episode taken from contemporary popular culture demon-strates the significance attributed to the New Deal's change in youth policy. Moreover, it shows that relief officials favored a solution to the problem of democratic values that mirrored the American past, not the European present; youth, in other words, were still rather identified as the "conquerors of the frontier and the creators of American democracy" than as apathetic masses.[44] Nevertheless, the

---

42. Standard reference on the Corps is still John Salmond, *The Civilian Conserva-tion Corps, 1933–1942: A New Deal Case Study* (Durham, NC, 1967). A new interpretation is offered by Olaf Stieglitz, »*100 Percent American Boys*«. *Disziplinie-rungsdiskurse und Ideologie im Civilian Conservation Corps, 1933–1942* (Stuttgart, 1999).

43. *Wild Boys of the Road*, 1933, produced by Warner Brothers and directed by William A. Wellman. Cast: Frankie Darro, Dorothy Coonan, Edwin Phillips, Rochelle Hudson. Sally, the girl in the gang, remains a »wild boy« as long as she lives as a tramp. To earn herself the return fare home, the judge wants her to work as a domestic servant, thus re-establishing traditional gender-roles.

44. Reiman, *New Deal & American Youth*, 35.

paradox is obvious: it is not the unsupervised transient, the "teenage hobo" or "wild boy of the road," that is allowed to be judged as a true pioneer, the one moving forward. With the official closing of the physical frontier after the 1890 census, the meaning of the phrase "Go West, young man" changed immensely. The important, powerful, and multi-dimensional myth, though, still allowed all metaphors of growth and progress, but the now omnipresent regulated society (that is, civilization) limited its realization: "Certainly the days of the Indian fighters and the robber barons are gone forever, but there are new frontiers in American life . . . [but] these are less tangible, and many youth are not equipped for such opportunities."[45] In particular, the notion of a personal approach to an unsupervised outbreak from society was sanctioned now, for it contained a kind of individualism considered unsuitable for current times:

> It is my firm belief that the newer generation of America has a different dream [than individual wealth]. You place emphasis on sufficiency in life, rather than on a plethora of riches. You think of the security for yourself and your family that will give you good health, good food, good education, good working conditions, and the opportunity for normal recreation and occasional travel. Your advancement, you hope, is along a broad highway on which thousands of your fellow men and women are advancing with you.[46]

Frontier experience was an essential part of the CCC's agenda, and one that shows that President Roosevelt's official intentions of the Corps as being an instrument of pure work relief and conservation of national forests had a much deeper educational function from the beginning. Although a kind of "mass migration" of young men from impoverished Eastern city districts – believed, in that location, to be in permanent danger of becoming criminals – was publicized again and again, the actual demography of the, at certain times, more than 2,000 camps all over the United States was not

45. W. Wallace Weaver, "Modern Youth – Retrospect and Prospect," *The Annals of the American Academy of Political and Social Science* 194 (1937), 1–5, here p. 4.

46. Franklin D. Roosevelt, Radio Message to the Young Democratic Clubs of America, 24.8.35, in: RSC collection: Franklin Roosevelt, President's Official File.

dominated by city dwellers. Only about 16 percent of the enrollees originated from that group.[47] But a work-guided confrontation with nature was considered of immense importance to the CCC's clientele as a whole, for it was of patriotic value: "Men like that will make forests grow. They will build nations."[48] The hard, physical labor that dominated the enrollees' work day at least in the early years of the Corps, their lodging in rural area camp sites and a sometimes almost mythical sense of nature were linked with the constitution and development of the nation state: "It should be remembered that camps and work in unsettled areas were an American inheritance three hundred years old. America had grown from cabins and sod huts pushing into forests or prairie . . ."[49] But the CCC was not only a romantic restaging of the past. By functionalizing the nation's history, it sought to emphasize its interpretation of an over-individualistic pioneer spirit as a basis for future progress. For personal as well as for national development, that was one of the fundamental messages the CCC tried to transmit: individual effort must be embedded in collective and centrally guided action. The evidence of this theory was supposed to be found in every enrollee's own story. Originating mostly, at least statistically, from a lower-middle-class, working-class, or agricultural background, the typical young CCC member lacked the educational norms of his age group and had no or only very limited job experience. He was what was generally thought of as "the raw material out of which the United States must shape its future. Nature's deepest instinct is the concern in every parent's heart for the welfare of children. . . . without the preservation of youth, the race itself would perish."[50] In the CCC, the road from human resource to effective and thus

47. Kenneth Holland and Frank E. Hill, *Youth in the CCC*. Prepared for the American Youth Commission (Washington, D.C., 1942), 83.

48. *Happy Days. Official Newspaper of the Civilian Conservation Corps.* 1(9) (July 15, 1933), 4.

49. Holland and Hill, *Youth in the CCC*, 136. The CCC used machines whenever the work assignment demanded them, but they did not replace the dominance of physical labor before the integration of the Corps into the national defense program.

50. Franklin D. Roosevelt, Campaign Address, Kansas City, 13.10.1936, in: RSC collection: Franklin Roosevelt, President's Official File.

valuable member of a future economy and society was a strictly regimented one, from daily camp routine under the command of an Army officer, to work assignments dominated by physically exhausting tasks, to educational programs providing elementary knowledge and lessons in work ethic. The success of the program was demonstrated in the individual enrollee's body: "The tanned, healthy, well-muscled men who are discharged from the Corps at the end of their enrollment are in marked contrast to the pale, oft-times stoop-shouldered, undernourished youths who replace them in the camps."[51] Taken together, a certain camp and finally the whole Corps was declared to be a coherent group bound in constant advancement.

The group of young men, Army officers, work supervisors, and teachers of each individual CCC camp was supposed to form a kind of microcosm in which the ideal American society was reflected. Here, one finds the utopian blueprint of living and working together, of tradition and progress, as the nucleus of the nation state:

> It is very much an American life. In a way it goes back a century and absorbs something of pioneer flavor and the pioneer spirit: the closeness to the American soil, the look and use of its granite, its oaks and pines and hickories. But it absorbs also the spirit of the Machine Age. It has its electric lights, its water and sewage systems, its gnawing shovels and lumbering tractors, its blueprints and its laboratory wisdom.[52]

Contemporary critics of the Civilian Conservation Corps repeatedly pointed at the similarities between it and other work programs for youth in Europe. Especially the presence of the Army in the camps rated as the dark spot of the whole organization, making it a potential instrument for militarizing the next generation. With regard to the objective of the New Deal's youth policy, to protect young people from totalitarianism, this accusation provoked clarify-

---

51. *Annual Report of the Director of the Civilian Conservation Corps, 1940* (Washington, D.C., 1940), 8.

52. Frank E. Hill, *The School in the Camps: The Educational Program of The Civilian Conservation Corps* (New York, 1935), 3.

ing responses, but different ones for different audiences. The public debate focussed on information. The CCC headquarters added lengthy paragraphs to their advertising brochures in which it tried to calm frightened parents, and other government agencies, like the NYA, published comparative studies of youth programs all over the world.[53] While here every reference to any kind of totalitarianism was denied, the fear of potential "radicals" led to the banning of newspapers in the camps and at times even to the expulsion of enrollees considered to be communist inspired "agitators" or "ringleaders" of some kind.[54]

"One could say", remarked Eleanor Roosevelt, "that one very prevalent attitude in youth is the desire to do, to stop talking about things and thinking about things and actually to do something."[55] And one might add: just like the New Deal. The example of the CCC shows that the view of a young generation perceived as apathetic or, even worse, criminal shocked almost all voices participating in the debate about the new youth problem. Youth standing still or travelling on wrong tracks (the transients) was deemed to be evidence of a nation without perspective. So the Roosevelt administration adopted what they thought was natural youthful behavior and acted on a broad experimental level. But they had distinct ideas about how the ideal society of tomorrow should look like.

53. Just two examples: Kenneth Holland, *Youth in European Labor Camps. A Report to the American Youth Commission* (Washington, D.C., 1939); W. Thatcher Winslow, *Youth – A World Problem. A Study in World Perspective of Youth Conditions, Movements and Programs* (Washington, D.C., 1937).

54. The actual role of the Communist Party in the camps can be neglected, but that fact did not change the attitudes of most Army members, as the statement of an independent camp inspector shows: "The Army classes anybody who makes a complaint as an agitator." James C. Reddoch, on a conference of the CCC's Division of Investigation, April 5–10, 1937. National Archives (NARA), Record Group (RG) 35, Entry Number (Ent.No.) 114, Box 3.

55. Eleanor Roosevelt, "Attitudes of Youth and Morale," in Sidonie M. Gruenberg (ed.), *The Family in a World at War* (New York, 1942), 230–236, here 231.

Rights and Obligations of Youthful Citizens

"The National Youth Administration", in the eyes of the organization's National Advisory Committee's chairman, Charles Taussig,
"is a potent instrument of practical democracy." And in further
defining and explaining what he believes is the suitable antidote to
the masses of young people betrayed by both Hitler and Stalin, he
stated that "by popular democracy, I mean affording every citizen
an opportunity actively to participate in the affairs of the community
and of the nation."[56]

The brief references to the NYA in general history textbooks
have three characteristics. First, the agency is portrayed as a branch
of the larger Works Progress Administration (WPA) which distributed relief money and jobs to students. As such, it is viewed as a
rather small part of a much broader program. Second, research is
focussing on administrators of the program such as Aubrey Williams,
the agency's head, or future President Lyndon B. Johnson who was
responsible for local projects in Texas. Mary McLeod Bethune's work
for the NYA's Division of Negro Affairs is also given prominence
especially because it exemplifies a third characteristic of general
textbooks' coverage of the NYA: Given the circumstances of the
time, it had a remarkable record of racial equality and justice; a
point, to which this essay will return later.[57] Generally speaking,
the youth that profited from NYA money had a slightly different
background than the CCC members. Although the NYA was
originally designed by Taussig and other liberals as a means to spread
the opportunity for higher education, most of those young people

56. Charles W. Taussig, address delivered at a regional meeting of the National
Youth Administration, St. Paul, MN, November 1, 1938. RSC, New Deal Agencies
and Black Americans, Reel 2: NYA.

57. Until recently, John Salmond's biography of Aubrey Williams, published in
1983, has been the most authoritative source on the NYA which, effectively,
compounded the "great men/great woman" approach to the agency, see his *A
Southern Rebel: The Life and Times of Aubrey Willis Williams, 1890–1965* (Chapel
Hill, NC, 1983). Richard Reiman's *New Deal & American Youth*, despite its all-
inclusive title, deals exclusively with the NYA and certainly fills a void in its
historiography.

whose parents had never been able to afford to assist them in acquiring a college education were no more likely to attend after 1935 than before; thus, the clientele of the NYA was middle class in economic capacity and general mentality.[58]

With establishing the NYA, the New Deal completed its institutional design for modeling the future citizens of the United States. According to a theory of two known experts, Kenneth Holland and Frank Hill, what they called citizenship-education operated on two different levels. The first one, named "confirming citizen," is characterized by basic qualities, "the minimum which any individual must achieve in any kind of society . . . if he is not to become a social liability."[59] The two authors counted seven constitutive elements: (1) the ability to support oneself and one's family through useful occupation; (2) to be physically and mentally healthy; thus, "an individual is neither a public charge nor a source of danger to other people"; (3) observance of law and moral conduct; (4) the ability to live and work peacefully together with other people; (5) to provide a home environment suitable for children to achieve this level of citizenship; (6) literacy; and (7) the "ability to understand and carry out instructions in situations in which disciplined action best serves society."[60] These conditions of a "confirming citizen" were supposed to be met by as many members of any society as possible, and in Holland's and Hill's opinion, it was the task of the CCC to educate its clientele along that standard.[61] But they did not believe the average CCC enrollee to be capable of reaching the advanced level of citizenship, what they called "contributing citizens." Again, seven characteristics were given to describe that type: (1) the ability to play a responsible role in a self-governing group; (2) an ability to develop and make use of certain capacities

58. Reiman, *New Deal & American Youth*, 1.

59. Holland and Hill, *Youth in the CCC*, 221.

60. Ibid., 222.

61. Ibid., 230; see also Eric Gorham, *National Service, Citizenship, and Political Education* (New York, 1992), 137; and Olaf Stieglitz, "'. . . very much an American life'. The Concept of Citizenship in the Civilian Conservation Corps," in Knud Krakau, ed., *The American Nation – National Identity – Nationalism* (Münster, 1997), 185–195.

of social interest; (3) a knowledge of the political system; (4) interest in political news and social developments; (5) a knowledge about where and how to find relevant information about current topics; (6) tolerance towards the opinions and rights of others and respect for their property; and (7) a deep loyalty towards democracy and its special American design.[62] At this point, both authors thought of an institution like the National Youth Administration with its usually better schooled members as the right place to educate those they believed to be the future leaders of American communities, locally, statewide, and nationally.

While Holland and Hill were certainly right about the role of citizenship training in the CCC, the record of the NYA with regard to the above program is a mixed one. Much attention and publicity was dedicated to the creation of rural residential centers, which placed out-of-school youths in group living arrangements where they would receive both vocational and citizenship training and moreover gained experience with forms of self-governing.[63] But still, the large majority of the NYA's funding was assigned to simple student aid and work relief, with citizenship training being only a contingent by-product.

Nevertheless, it is clear that the New Deal's vision of a future citizenship was not a universal one, but constructed hierarchically. What linked the two concepts with each other and what was developed as a focussing point was a certain notion about the relevance of work as a social good. Eugen Rosenstock-Huessy, the well-known sociologist, philosopher, and outspoken critic of the CCC, once defined the CCC's concept of citizenship as "to be profitably employed." This may be a provocative simplification, but it was not coincidential that regular, gainful, and useful employment topped the list of a confirming-citizen's criteria. The CCC was established to provide jobs, the work assignment quantitatively dominated the daily camp routine, and education and all other non-job activities

---

62. Holland and Hill, *Youth in the CCC*, 230.

63. Reiman, *New Deal & American Youth*, ch. 7. See also Michael G. Wade, "'Farm Dorm Boys': The Origins of the NYA Resident Training Program," *Louisiana History* 27(2) (1986), 117–132.

were strictly job-oriented. "Work" and "Citizenship" were corresponding concepts: "It takes a good many people with good brains and fine ideals, working together day in day out, to make a great nation."[64] The relation between employer and employee paralleled the bond between the nation-state and its citizens in its hierarchical fixing of rights, obligations, and responsibilities:

> Lazy, indifferent, dishonest citizens are the worst enemies a country can have . . . If a man *will* not work, nor try to find work, and if he is a person who will not try to meet his obligation as a citizen, does the state have any obligation to him or should the remainder of the working society support him?[65]

The NYA was much more open in design, but here too, work formed the necessary obligation to achieve the benefits of the program. The jobs provided were intended to teach poor students the value of money and to develop a work ethic which the organization's leaders thought they did not learn at home. The important role of local high school and college administrators, cornerstones of keeping the balance between federal planning and a traditionally local control of education, was crucial in that question, because they made absolutely sure that NYA students earned their government pay checks – getting something for nothing was never part of the plan. In Topeka, Kansas, for instance, students who failed to meet high standards of "character, need, and logical scholarship" were dropped from the program. In El Paso, Texas, administrators promptly weeded out a small group whom they considered to be "unworthy of aid."[66]

"I Am An American Day," an interwar addition to the national holiday calendar, perfectly highlights these New Dealish aims

64. Ned H. Dearborn, *Once in a Lifetime. A Guide to the CCC* (New York, and Chicago, IL, 1936), 22.

65. See the textbook used for camp education, *The Art of Living Together*. Ed. by the New Mexico Work Projects Administration (Santa Fe, NM, 1939), 3; emphasis in original.

66. The examples are taken from Grace Palladino, *Teenagers. An American History* (New York, 1996), 42.

concerning youth and citizenship. Taking its cue from a couple of local and private initiatives, some of which were influenced by such patriotic organizations as the American Legion or the Daughters of the American Revolution, the federal government in 1939 adopted the idea of creating a meaningful national rite of passage. It was signed into law in 1940, and the President was to proclaim it each year to recognize on the third Sunday in May "all who, by coming of age or naturalization, have attained the status of citizenship."[67]

"I Am An American Day" was widely celebrated and although it focussed on naturalized Americans, the New Deal youth organizations construed it as a *fete* for the maturing native-born young adult becoming twenty-one years old – and thus gaining full citizenship rights. In correspondence with the WPA's naturalization classes, the NYA organized special classes in colleges as well. In 1941, the holiday marked one of the last highlights of a CCC already loosing its importance. CCC officials invested much energy in celebrating the day proudly, they organized parades, lectures and ceremonies were certificates of adulthood should be handed out to the new citizens. In his official address, read in every company during the celebration, James McEntee, Director of the CCC, emphasized the significance of this particular moment in the life of a man, as well as the nation's new expectations of him:

> I congratulate all of you who have reached man's estate this past year. You have come of age at a time when your government has the most urgent need for your loyalty and the best that is in you. As members of the Civilian Conservation Corps, I know you are making a real contribution to the winning of the war. You are fitting yourselves for bigger contributions in the stern days that lie ahead for all of us. In the camps you have learned discipline. You have acquired physical stamina, and you have learned how to work. Above all, you have developed a greater appre-

---

67. A longer discussion of »I Am An American Day« and its role in the patriotic discourse of the Unted States can be found in Richard M. Fried, *The Russians Are Coming! The Russians Are Coming! Pageantry and Patriotism in Cold-War America* (New York and Oxford, 1998), 14ff.

ciation of your country and the democratic principles which this nation is fighting to preserve.[68]

By adding such a soldier-like aspect to the concept of citizenship, the federal government participated in the national discourse on gender, which marked one of the significant limits to the utopian approach that will be discussed in the next paragraph.

Limits of Utopia

The discourse on youth of the 1930s tended to universalize and naturalize young peoples' bodies and minds. One very rarely detects differentiations in that group along class, race, or gender fractions; "youth" in general was both a treasure to be kept and a threat to be tamed. The only exception to that rule was that a closer look at an urban–rural dichotomy was present in many of the discussion's contributions, but of course the group in question was not nearly as coherent and homogeneous as many commentators saw it. The establishment of two different organizational bodies for members with similar problems but originating from distinct social groups was already discussed above. Besides this focus on class, the New Deal clearly acted along other social criteria, too.

The most obvious limitation to the New Deal's utopian vision with regard to youth was its very gendered approach. This is no surprise, for a growing body of historical literature contends that the American welfare state developed that way: "imbued by particular ideas regarding the proper social organization of sexual difference, such that men and women were treated differently in the policy-making process, with ascribed gender roles and gender inequalities perpetuated."[69] Most policymakers in the Roosevelt administration,

68. NARA, RG 407, Section 1, Box 56. See Stieglitz, ". . . very much an American life," 193.

69. Suzanne Mettler, *Dividing Citizens. Gender and Federalism in New Deal Public Policy* (Ithaca, NY, and London, 1998), 16. See also Eileen Boris, *Home to Work: Motherhood and the Politics of Industrial Homework in the United States* (New York, 1994); Linda Gordon, *Pitied but not Entitled: Single Mothers and the History of*

for example, were sympathetic to the "family wage" ideal, the notion that men's work in the market economy should enable them to serve as "breadwinners" for their families, so that women could attend to unpaid domestic work and refrain from taking jobs that could otherwise belong to men.

Most obviously, the Civilian Conservation Corps is a point in case. The demographic composition of a CCC camp created an all-male atmosphere which in one way or another had to respond to the "masculinity crisis" of the late nineteenth and early twentieth centuries and, in particular, to the so-called sexual revolution experienced by young Americans during the 1920s.[70] The CCC celebrated the strong male body and its economic, moral, and eugenic value. The purpose of the CCC's emphasis on the male body was to stabilize gender roles perceived as endangered. To achieve this objective, traditional working-class notions of masculinity like physical activity and aggressive competition had to be underscored on a basic level, but were channelled with the help of ideals rooted in the Victorian understanding of an inward-oriented manhood and in the breadwinner notion: "You are now not dependent on your family. You are even helping to support your family. And when a boy begins to support himself, and his family, he truly is entering into man's estate."[71]

The National Youth Administration was more inclusive in character; in fact it was recently labeled as the nation's first affirmative action program.[72] Nevertheless, its program added to the reinforcement of traditional norms, too. The NYA fully intended to transmit

---

Welfare, 1890–1935 (New York, 1994); Susan Ware, *Beyond Suffrage. Women in the New Deal* (Cambridge, MA, 1981).

70. The "masculinity crisis" and the historiography dealing with it is discussed in Gail Bederman, *Manliness and Civilization: A Cultural History of Gender and Race in the United States, 1880–1917* (Chicago and London, 1995); see especially the introduction. Masculinity in the CCC is discussed in Olaf Stieglitz, "'. . . not mishappen creatures, but unshaped.' Konstruktionen maskuliner Körperbilder im Civilian Conservation Corps, 1933–1942," *1999. Zeitschrift für Sozialgeschichte des 20. und 21. Jahrhunderts* 14(2) (1999), 13–34.

71. *Happy Days*, vol. 5, no. 21, (October 2, 1937), 4.

72. Reiman, *New Deal & American Youth*, 2.

the values and habits of middle-class families to those whom the administrators believed had never experienced them. This was especially true for the resident centers. One of them, in Conway, Arkansas, for instance gave girls and boys a chance to develop their social skills and acquire what the NYA called "family-life education." Girls cooked for the entire group and did all the household chores. They managed family-size homes and spent some time working in a nearby nursery school. At dinners – which they planned, cooked, and served – the girls presided over tables of ten to twelve "guests" and got a rare opportunity to practice the middle-class role of gracious hostess.[73] One recognizes the progressive combination of tradition and effectiveness that Eleanor Roosevelt stated as a guiding line when asked about the education of girls, as a woman who considered herself old fashioned enough to believe that every girl should marry and have a family, progressive and modern enough to hold the opinion that that is a job one has to be prepared for: "There are no jobs in the world so important as marriage and motherhood and I am inclined to believe that if girls were taught to consider them as jobs there would be fewer failures and more successes."[74]

NYA administrators obviously never assumed that the sky was the limit for their participants; or, formulated differently, their utopia was clearly limited with regard to female emancipation. Much the same was true with regard to African-Americans, although the NYA in fact was remarkably progressive in that respect. The program's aim was to train teenage youth to reach their full potential within the confines of their social place, which meant that white boys and girls had more varied opportunities for training than blacks and members of other ethnic groups did. But the mere fact that the NYA established a Division of Negro Affairs showed that they at least had an idea of accepting the structural and practical challenge to bring about social integration. And criticism was explicit from within their own ranks: "Realism in guidance for Negroes has meant in too many cases the negative approach, and the effect of constant

73. Palladino, *Teenagers*, 39f.
74. Eleanor Roosevelt, "Today's Girl and Tomorrow's Job," *Woman's Home Companion* 59 (June, 1932), 11–12.

discouragement on the basis of extreme realism. Realism for the Negro means preservation of the status quo."[75]

The situation in the Civilian Conservation Corps was even worse, although individual success stories were often portrayed in public and should not be neglected. Furthermore, African-Americans profited especially from the CCC's medical and educational efforts. Still, discrimination was policy. Black enrollees of the CCC were overwhelmingly located in separate camps under the command of white officers, so that the image of the irresponsible, marginal, and potentially dangerous "black man" was underscored. That such racist and sexualized stereotypes did play a role is shown in the discussions between the CCC's Bureau of the Director and the inhabitants of towns and villages near proposed all-black camp sites. The CCC's leaders and especially the Army had an interest in demonstrating that they were in control of their African-American clientele, that they had disciplined them. Here what critics said about most of the NYA was true: What was missing, was "[a] willingness to recognize a problem of democracy in our own job. Democracy has been too far away."[76]

A Defensive Utopia

The New Deal's approach towards youth policy was, as I have tried to make clear, guided by a certain vision about the role young people or a generation should play in the present as well as in the future. These ideas were rooted in traditional notions about the country's national development, to which popularized beliefs taken from different scholarly disciplines were added. But the crucial points were the internal and external effects of what was perceived as a

75. R. O'Hara Lanier, "Occupational and Social Adjustment in a Self-Governing Free Society – With Reference to the Negro," address at the 25th Annual Meeting of the National Vocational Guidance Association, St. Louis, MO, February 21, 1940, 2f. Lanier was the Assistent Director of the NYA's Division of Negro Affairs. See RSC, Collection: New Deal Agencies and Black Americans, Reel 2: NYA.

76. O'Hara Lanier, "Occupational and Social Adjustment," 9.

crisis. Commentators on youth thought of their country, its children, and therefore its future, as almost besieged by economic depression, institutional erosion, and, most dangerously, international pressure. As an answer to this situation, the New Deal established what can be described as a defensive utopia. Trusting in the convincing power of a truly American interpretation of democracy, the New Dealers intended to assist, enlist, and make use of youth in an effort to realize a friendlier future for the American people. It was their desire to superintend and guide the minds of young people in the interests of both national security and youths themselves. Their ideas materialized in two distinct organizations with different clienteles and with different approaches to controlling youth's behavior and molding their minds. Taken as a whole, discursive and non-discursive elements of the New Deal formed not a broad utopian departure, but a careful and very hesitant attempt to invest a "younger" genera-tion with responsibilities for maintaining or advancing community ideals.

Comments on Part Four: Biblical Narratives in German and American National Utopias

A. D. Moses

The virtue of these contributions is that they afford the commentator the opportunity to address the (so to speak) "metalevel" of the utopias and visions of the future that are the subject of this volume: not just utopias *in* Germany and the United States, but Germany and the United States *as* utopias. This angle surely comes as no surprise. Were there any Western countries as large and significant over the past 100 years with as intense a consciousness of mission, election, and specialness?

We have heard much about religious themes, and rightly so. I should like to take this opportunity to deal further with this theme by asking whether there is an anthropologically rooted framework that underlies all such nationalist utopias and that can have a religiously expressed mythic form. Close attention to the self-understandings of the founders of the United States – and one might add here the Boers in South Africa – reveals that they were clearly inspired by biblical themes.[1] And even if most Germans did not think of themselves as Teutonic Israelites, many Protestant Germans regarded themselves as a chosen people with a special relationship with God, who intervened periodically in their history.[2] These parallels suggest the existence of a basic structure to all national utopias.

1. Sacvan Bercovitch, *The Puritan Origins of the American Self* (New Haven, CT, 1975).
2. Hartmut Lehmann, "'God Our Old Ally': The Chosen People Theme in Late Nineteenth- and Early Twentieth-Century German Nationalism," in William R. Hutchinson and Hartmut Lehmann, eds., *Many Are Chosen. Divine Election and Western Nationalism* (Minneapolis, MI, 1994), 85–108. Conor Cruise O'Brien, *God Land. Reflections on Religion and Nationalism* (Cambridge, MA, 1988).

431

Lewis Feuer calls it the Mosaic Myth, but let us use the term Exodus Narrative.[3] What are its essential elements? The Israelites leave for the greener pastures of Egypt, but so prosper that the Egyptians feel threatened and Pharaoh enslaves them. Under the leadership of the prophet Moses, they wander through the wilderness, negotiate the threat at the Red Sea, and are led back eventually to the promised land as the chosen people with a new covenant.

> I will take you as my own people, and I will be your God. Then you will know that I am the Lord your God, who brought you out from under the yoke of the Egyptians. And I will bring you to the land I swore with uplifted hand to give to Abraham, to Isaac, and to Jacob. I will give it to you as a possession. I am the Lord. (Exodus 6:7,8)

But the story is not unambiguously redemptive: the return succeeds at the expense of the tribes already settled there, leading either to a genocide or ethnic cleansing: "My angel will go ahead of you and bring you into the land of the Amorites, Hivites, and Jebusites, and I will wipe them out" (Exodus 23:23; cf. 33:2); "I will send a hornet ahead of you to drive the Hivites, Canaanites, and Hittites out of your way" (Exodus 23:28).

At the same time, the Israelites are also enjoined not to mistreat aliens, "for you were aliens in Egypt" (Exodus 22:21; cf. 23: 9; Deuteronomy 10: 18,19), although this injunction is clearly not designed as a measure to make peaceful coexistence possible, because God expressly forbids any kind of social intercourse, lest it lead to impurity: "Do not let them live in your land, or they will cause you to sin against me, because the worship of their gods will certainly

---

3. Lewis S. Feuer, *Ideology and the Ideologists* (Oxford, 1975). Feuer thinks that every ideology repeats the Mosaic myth – "the dramatic story of liberation of the Hebrew tribes by Moses." For stimulating ideas regarding nationalism and biblical motifs, I should like to acknowledge the papers of Ann Curthoys, "Whose Home? Expulsion, Exodus, and Exile in White Australian Historical Mythology," in Margaret Jolly, ed., *Governing Bodies. Race, Person, and Gender* (Durham, NC, forthcoming), and of John Docker, "Liberation or Disaster? Exodus in Contemporary Cultural Theory," unpublished MS delivered at the Australian National University, March 17, 1993.

be a snare to you" (Exodus 23:33). The promise of land and concomitant expulsion, or destruction, of its prior inhabitants is contingent upon the Israelites upholding the new law and preventing religious and cultural contamination (Exodus 34:11,24; Deuteronomy 30: 9,10).[4]

Even in this highly abbreviated version, it is apparent that the Exodus narrative gestures to the problem of undeserved suffering, that is, to the problem of evil. For the oppressed, it provides an inspiring story of liberation: Its promise of collective salvation offers hope to the downtrodden, empowering them to "walk tall" when all seems lost. Such hopes must have kept the candles burning for the East Timorese in the dark years of the Indonesian occupation since the mid-1970s, and African-Americans for a much longer period. At the same time, the narrative licenses the colonization of occupied land and consequent dispossession, perhaps even genocide, of its inhabitants. And perversely, because such action is perpetrated by a subjective sense of victimhood in the moment of deliverance, the victimhood of the pagan Canaanites is forgotten. The problem of evil – undeserved suffering – is solved by and licenses the perpetration of evil upon others, because suffering is a sign of providential chosenness and provides a moral warrant for colonization, expulsion, and even extermination.[5]

4. Cf. Michael Prior, *The Bible and Colonialism. A Moral Critique* (Sheffield, 1997), 39ff. There is a useful listing of other passages in the Old Testament that license genocide in Helen Fein, "Genocide and Gender: the Uses of Women and Group Diversity," *Journal of Genocide Research* 1:1 (March, 1999), 46f. See also Daniel J. Elazar, *Covenant and Polity and Biblical Israel. Biblical Foundations and Jewish Expressions* (New Brunswick and London, 1995), 178–182.

5. In a recent, important article, Omer Bartov has highlighted how the "discourse of victimhood" and "metaphors of evil" in German nationalism and Zionism comprise a "vicious circle of defining enemies and making victims" in which the perpetrators view themselves as victims: "Defining Enemies, Making Victims: Germans, Jews, and the Holocaust," *American Historical Review* 103 (1998), 779–816. Daniel Boyarin notes that some modern ultra-orthodox groups in Israel justify hardline measures against Palestinians by casting them as the "five nations" that God commanded to be driven from the land. Boyarin, *A Radical Jew. Paul and the Politics of Identity* (Berkeley, 1994), 333, n. 27.

These are the issues at stake in Edward Said's well-known polemic with Michael Walzer over the meaning of the Exodus narrative. In his book, *Exodus and Revolution*, Walzer proffered a meliorist and secular interpretation that emphasized the emancipatory meaning redolent in the biblical story: It posited a progressive, linear temporality, rather than a closed cyclical one of eternal return, and it culminated in the moderate labor Zionism of the twentieth century that he supports.[6] Walzer's aim was to rescue the text from right-wing fundamentalists who opposed a peaceful resolution to the Middle East crisis, but he incurred the ire of Said, who of course articulates the Palestinian perspective and who doubts whether the Exodus can be domesticated in this manner. Walzer had illegitimately downplayed the moment of dispossession in the story, as well as denuding it of its messianic dimension, Said charged. "The most troubling . . . is of course the injunction laid on the Jews by God to exterminate their opponents, an injunction that somewhat takes away the aura of progressive national liberation which Walzer is bent upon giving Exodus."[7] There is no getting around the fact, he concludes, that while Exodus may have inspired radical and progressive politics – American-Black leaders, Latin American liberation theologians – it also legitimized "Indian-killing Puritans in New England to South African Boers claiming large swatches of territory held by blacks."[8]

It is not my intention to take sides in this debate; clearly, the Exodus narrative contains both moments and they are probably inseparable where occupied land is in question.[9] Suffice it to say

6. Michael Walzer, *Exodus and Revolution* (New York, 1985). For an excellent overview of Walzer's project, see Gerd Hurm, "Community, Commitment, and Criticism: The Rhetorical Embeddedness of Michael Walzer's Communitarian Theory," in Roland Hagenbüchle and Joseph Raab, eds., *Negotiations of American's National Identity* (Tübingen, 1999).

7. Edward Said, "Michael Walzer's *Exodus and Revolution*: A Canaanite Reading," in Edward Said and Christopher Hitchens, eds., *Blaming the Victims: Spurious Scholarship and the Palestinian Question* (London and New York, 1988), 166.

8. Said, "Michael Walzer's *Exodus and Revolution*," 167.

9. Jonathan Boyarin, "Reading Exodus into History," *New Literary History* 23 (1992), 523–554.

that it provides a good starting point for identifying the nexus between biblical narrative and the colonization projects that often attend nationalism. When one considers many of the ethnic conflicts today – Northern Ireland, the Middle East, South Africa, the Balkans – the religious and colonial dimensions are readily apparent. They are equally apparent in the secular religion of National Socialism and its hubristic plans for the colonization of Central and Eastern Europe by moving and exterminating millions of people. Each of these colonization projects was motivated by the attempt to escape bondage by appropriating a "promised land," and by a consciousness of a national or ethnic calling, that is, a special consciousness of election as the "chosen people."

And yet, to identify the Exodus narrative at work here is insufficient, for it cannot account for obvious differences in the type of nationalisms that we encounter. It is not only the case that New Testament themes overlay Exodus ones, like the image of the suffering Christ as the redeemer nation of the world, an image important in Polish national thought.[10] It is also the fact that the Exodus story in itself contains no missionary element; it is a particularistic tale that appertains to any group that wants to see itself as the Israelites. This was clearly the case with English radical Protestantism and the American Pilgrims. But in these cases, there was and is something more: a distinctively Christian universalizing dimension with missionary zeal to convert.[11]

As Daniel Boyarin has pointed out in his fascinating study on the Apostle Paul, *A Radical Jew: Paul and the Politics of Identity*, the source of "sacred violence" that attends "forced conversion, whether by the sword, ridicule, or the Pound, or deculturation in the name of some new human community" cannot be located in rabbinic Judaism or Exodus, whose supreme virtue was "leaving other people alone."[12] The universalism that homogenizes and effaces difference

10. Andrzej Walicki, *Philosophy and Romantic Nationalism. The Case of Poland* (Oxford, 1982).

11. This point is ignored by Michael Prior in his recent book *The Bible in Colonialism*, which lays all the ills of colonialism at the feet of the Old Testament. See n.4 above.

12. Boyarin, *A Radical Jew*, 232ff.

A. D. Moses

he identifies, following Etienne Balibar and Marc Shell, in Pauline Christianity, although Arlene Saxonhouse has made a strong case for its origin in ancient Greek thought.[13] Whatever its provenance, however, there is a consensus that universalism found its modern incarnation in liberalism. Steven T. Katz, for example, holds it responsible for ethnocide: "The liberals in both Europe and America – and this is what made them liberals – were for rapid acculturation and (eventual) equality of the Jew and the Indian respectively, but only after all vestiges of their traditional *tribal* consciousness and classical forms of life had been eliminated."[14] It is in Paul's letter to the Galatians that the danger of abstract universalism begins, which, Boyarin argues, has been "even more dangerous [than 'Jewish difference . . . as the Palestinians know only too well'], as Jews, Muslims, Native Americans, Africans, and others have been forced to demonstrate with their bodies."[15] This is quite a statement. Has universalism really been more dangerous than particularism?

It is possible to concur with Boyarin that hubristic projects of human regeneration and arrogant assumptions of universality have licensed the evils of European colonialism, while noting that nowhere in his book does he explicitly attempt to situate the Holocaust in the particular/universal spectrum. Perhaps in arguing that the insistence "on genealogical identity and its significance has been one of the major forms of resistance against such [universalist colonialist] violence," he forgets that such an insistence was also

13. Etienne Balibar, "Racism and Nationalism," in Balibar and Immanuel Wallerstein, *Race, Nation, Class: Ambiguous Identities*, trans. Chris Turner (London, 1991), 37–67; Marc Shell, "Marranos (pigs); or from Coexistence to Toleration," *Critical Inquiry*, 17 (Winter, 1991), 306–336; Arlene W. Saxonhouse, *The Fear of Diversity: The Birth of Political Science in Ancient Greek Thought* (Chicago and London, 1992).

14. Steven T. Katz, "The Uniqueness of the Holocaust. The Historical Dimension," in Alan Rosenbaum, ed., *Is the Holocaust Unique? Perspectives on Comparative Genocide* (Boulder, CO, 1996), 23f. Daniel J. Goldhagen analyses German liberalism in similar terms, accusing it of "eliminationism." See my discussion in "Structure and Agency in the Holocaust: Daniel J. Goldhagen and his Critics," *History and Theory* 37 (1998), 194–219.

15. Boyarin, *A Radical Jew*, 235.

the motivation for the Holocaust, as the controversial German historian Ernst Nolte so eloquently argued in his book *Three Faces of Fasicsm*.[16] Boyarin, to be sure, is a passionate critic of Zionism, and he seeks to temper the chauvinism to which he recognizes political particularism inexorably leads by pleading for diasporic identities: Particularity should not coincide with political power.[17] Nonetheless, his inability to consider the Holocaust in his rehabilitation of a chastened notion of particularism indicates that the Holocaust is perhaps the most odious case of particularist violence after all. The Nazis did not seek to convert, but to exclude, expel, and ultimately exterminate anything that was thought to contaminate an apprehended "German racial purity."

It is possible, then, to identify two types of nationalisms on the basis of their respective religious narrative underpinnings, analogous to the typologies of "civic" and "ethnic" nationalism adumbrated by Dietmar Schirmer: on the one hand, an Exodus-inspired story of ethnic particularism with the concomitant conception of the nation as a kind of large family or tribe defined by direct descent, which seeks its place in the sun, but not to make the world in its image; on the other, a nationalism based on a missionary story of conversion that regards itself as universally human and often has few scruples about imposing its model, which is necessarily particular, on others. For the purposes of neat categorization and at the risk of violating some historical distinctions, I think it is possible to see these typologies at work not only in the World War II, but also in World War I, which, let us not forget, was regarded by many as "holy war."[18] Germans shouted "Gott strafe England" and "Gott mit uns," as much as Anglican Bishops were convinced that God was on the side of the British Empire. Opposed to Germany were the powers that were convinced of their universal civilizing mission:

16. Ernst Nolte, *Three Faces of Fascism. Action Francaise, Italian Fascism, National Socialism*, trans. Leile Vennewitz (New York, 1965). Nolte writes of fascism as a reaction to theoretic and practical transcendence.

17. Boyarin, *A Radical Jew*, 228, 242–60.

18. John A. Moses, "The First World War as a Holy War in German and Australian Perspective," *Colloquium* [Australia], 26:1 (1994), 44–55.

the British Empire, the United States, and France. Germany's finest and liberal minds – Friedrich Meinecke, Ernst Troeltsch, Thomas Mann – poured scorn on this mission, which they derided as hypocritical and inimical to Germany's special particularity and attempt to find a path between Manchester liberalism and collectivist socialism. Meinecke's book on the German wars of liberation against the French and his inveighing against German universalism in *Cosmopolitanism and the National State* mark the intellectual preparation for Germany's ideological opposition to "the West."[19]

The conflagration in Yugoslavia reminds us that the Exodus nationalism is not a German monopoly. Ten years ago, Ralf Dahrendorf warned of nationalist resurgence in Eastern and Central Europe in the wake of what he called the "vacuum of meaning" after the historical mythologies of real existing communism had been deposited into the dustbin of history.[20] Unfortunately, his prophecy has become all too true. But it is not my intention to pick out Serbia for special attention as it is to ask whether this typology of nationalisms can be seen at work in the war over Kosovo. For complaints have been heard from Central European intellectuals about an apprehended American and/or Western drive to impose its "way of life" on the peoples there. I will return to this point later.

Whither radical particularism can lead has been made abundantly clear by Maria Mitchell in her perspicacious paper on the Nazi *Volksgemeinschaft*. Its elements are well known and do not need repeating here. Professor Mitchell's achievement lies in her discriminating sifting of the current literature on the subject in the service of her arresting conclusion: for such a totalitarian particularist, utopian fantasy to function more or less friction-free, it was not necessary for the members of the society to be themselves fanatical believers in all tenets of the animating ideology. It suffices when

---

19. Friedrich Meinecke, *Cosmopolitanism and the National State*, trans. Robert B. Kimber (Princeton, NJ, 1970); id., *The Age of German Liberation, 1795–1815*, trans. Peter Paret and Helmuth Fischer (Berkeley, CA, 1977).

20. Ralf Dahrendorf, *Reflections on the Revolution in Europe: in a Letter intended to have been sent to a Gentleman in Warsaw* (New York, 1990).

they share the key elements, and such consensus is hardly limited to Germany.[21] In other words, recent research on Nazi Germany brings that society back into the realm of the explicable, the recognizable, perhaps even the "normal." Should we be so surprised by the fact, recounted by Leon Litwack, that African-American soldiers in World War II were banned from eating in diners in the South for racial reasons while German prisoners of war were not? Mitchell's analysis allows us to reframe the misleading question about the relationship between Germans and Nazis, which tends sometimes to consider the latter as Martians who reboarded their spacecraft in 1945, leaving only bewildered and exploited Germans behind.

By focussing on the overlapping circles of consent between the Nazi elites and the various milieus that comprised German society at the time, it becomes clear that it makes more sense to focus on broad areas of consensus that bound so many Germans, a culture that Rolf Schörken calls the *Kultur von Rechts*: contempt for parliamentary democracy, antisemitism, anti-Western sentiment, intolerance of social conflict, the longing for national harmony, bitterness at the Treaty of Versailles, a feeling that Germany needed to expand to survive, a feeling captured and articulated well in the bestseller by Hans Grimm, *Volk ohne Raum*.[22] Many Germans who did not regard themselves as Nazis regarded 1933 as a national awakening and the liberation from the bondage of Versailles. Hitler represented a Teutonic Moses leading the way to the promised land in the East. Were not his foreign policy successes in the 1930s wildly popular? The structure of the Exodus narrative – the vicious circle of a consciousness of victimization as a license to victimize others – appears clearly at work here.[23] Although the individual elements of the nationalist-*völkisch* consensus did not disappear overnight in

---

21. It is worth recalling here Martin Broszat's important essay of 1970, "Soziale Motivation und Führer-Bindung des Nationalsozialismus," in his *Nach Hitler. Der schwierige Umgang mit unserer Geschichte* (Munich, 1988), 11–34.

22. Rolf Schörken, *Jugend 1945: Politisches Denken und Lebensgeschichte* (Frankfurt a.m., 1990).

23. Norbert Elias investigates the pyschosocial origins of the German reception of the Exodus narrative in his *Studien über die Deutschen* (Frankfurt a.M., 1989).

1945, the vicious circle was broken, and this is surely a factor in the remarkable liberalization and universalization that German culture has undergone since then.

Even a political culture that professes universal values requires a particular anchoring. Clearly, the tension between particularism and universalism can never be resolved entirely. This tension produces, at least in the case of the Unites States, some curious paradoxes. The country denies the right of other countries, like Yugoslavia and China for example, to hide behind their sovereign claims in solving their domestic problems in any way they see fit. At the same time, it baulks at recognizing international agreements on personnel land mines and an international court of justice. On closer inspection, perhaps there is no paradox after all: A country that thinks it embodies universal values will jealously guard its sovereignty and not suffer the judgement of any other organization, even the international legal order, especially if it regards them as the creature of foreign particular interests. This may be good news for universal values.

Olaf Stieglitz is not so sure. In his elegant examination of the youth discourses and policies in the 1930s in the United States, we witness a nation gripped by a sense of crisis, because the economic system and associated value system were obviously called into question. By focussing on the so-called youth problem, Stieglitz is able to interrogate the psyche of the nation as a whole, because its elite projected onto the coming generation its hopes and fears, as well as its normative vision, or in other words, its utopia. It should be pointed out, however, that a discourse of youth-degeneration and self-sufficiency was not invented in the interwar years or even in the nineteenth century. It was there from the moment the pilgrims arrived on North American shores.[24]

When we consider what Stieglitz calls a "Defensive Utopia," let us not forget that we are dealing with the 1930s, that is, a time when barbarism had found a home in Germany, and Europe was not safe for democracy. This utopia looks fairly benign by the standards of the day. It cast anxious glances over the Atlantic and

---

24. Michael Walzer, *Revolution of the Saints* (Cambridge, MA, 1965), 215–217.

sought actively to immunize young Americans against the totalitarian disease. That it did so on the basis of conservative values and a reinscription of the Exodus narrative – that is how I understand the references to the "founders," "the frontier," and "pioneer spirit" – rather than on the basis of antifascism, is hardly surprising. Would that Germany had had leaders determined to "impart the lesson of democracy to the young." There may have been some formal parallels between the Civilian Conservation Corps and the Hitler Youth, and perhaps even in content with regard to gender roles. And it may have been all in the name of "disciplining," as Dr. Stieglitz entitles one of his articles on the subject. But if we are to believe Foucault, every organization of which we are members entails our disciplining. So the question perforce becomes, disciplining for what?

I agree with Dr. Stieglitz that this defensive utopia possessed remarkably progressive elements in the context of the time. But I would also like to emphasize more the "pay-off" of such programs and disciplinary discourses. The young people who went through them stormed the beaches of Normandy and saved Europe from fascism. Let us not forget, either, in our Eurocentric and Atlantic viewpoints, that they were the sailors, airmen, and nurses who served in the Pacific and particularly in the battle of the Coral Sea off the coast of North Queensland – one of the turning points of the World War II – thereby saving Australia from ultimate invasion. American exceptionalism did help make the world safe for democracy: not the impotent League of Nations, but a country convinced of its rectitude and overflowing with moral energy.

So far, I have depicted nationalism and its mythic framework in terms of two alternatives: a homogenizing liberal universalism and an exclusionary ethnic particularism. And I have perhaps given the impression that the former is vastly preferable. The value of Leon Litwack's passionate contribution is that he puts a lot of pressure on the former. For the burden of his paper is that the promise of redemption for African-Americans after their emancipation has not been realized in liberal America. Not only was America anything but liberal for those outside its white *Volksgemeinschaft*, but its liberalism contains limits of which it is barely conscious. The African-American experience shatters the promise of redemption in the

European Exodus narrative, although I remain unclear why those limits exist.

For that reason, I should like to ask some questions of Professor Litwack. He rightly mentions the importance of the blues as a musical tradition for American-Americans, but very little attention was paid to Gospel music and Christianity. Including this dimension would fit the African-American experience neatly into my schema of mythic narratives, for the Exodus story was an "archetypal paradigm" for African-Americans and represented the emancipatory hope about which Walzer wrote. In the sacred history incarnated in that story, the African outcasts played the role of the Israelites and the whites that of Pharaoh. In an ironic inversion of the white self-understanding, America is Egypt, not the promised land. As a white chaplain of the Union army in Alabama observed:

> There is no part of the Bible with which they are so familiar as the story of the deliverance of Israel. Moses is their ideal of all that is high, and noble, and perfect, in man. I think they have been accustomed to regard Christ not so much in the light of a spiritual Deliverer, as that of a second Moses who would eventually lead them out of their prison house of bondage.[25]

But as Litwack points out, the hopes that the industrial North would be the promised land have been dashed. African-Americans remain in the wilderness – indeed they have entered a new bondage – and Martin Luther King's paeans of redemptive suffering no longer appear plausible.

I am unsure from Professor Litwack's contribution, however, whether this situation is a logical consequence of liberal universalism or of its incomplete realization. It is possible to answer this question by continuing the biblical analogies. The biblical prophets, like Amos, and the jeremiad as a genre of political theology, played the role of reminding the people to live up to the covenant and the command-

---

25. Cited in Albert J. Raboteau, "African Americans: Exodus, Ethiopia, and Racial Messianism: Texts and Contexts of African American Choseness," in Hutchinson and Lehmann, eds., *Many Are Chosen*, 177.

ment to respect the stranger. Professor Litwack's paper struck me as a kind of jeremiad in the manner identified by Sacvan Bercovitch, and I should like to ask him whether he sees himself as such a prophet, admonishing his compatriots for violating their covenant? Or whether he thinks the covenant – that is, liberal universalism – is bankrupt and needs to be replaced?[26] Is liberal universalism the problem, or does it need to live up to its promise?

Dietmar Schirmer's magisterial survey and analysis of the literature on nationalism hints at an answer by altering the terms of the debate. For he argues that neither the functionalist nor the social-action theories of nationalism can account satisfactorily for the "post-national" challenges of the globalizing world economy. Relying primarily on the social scientists Niklas Luhmann, Anthony Giddens, and Benedict Anderson, he argues that the nation-state is a contingent but necessary product of the "functional differentiation" of the world economy in the nineteenth century. The integration of local communities into regional and eventually international networks of exchange and governance "disembedded" them, creating problems of identity and orientation. Nation-states emerged simultaneously as world society by "re-embedding" people in the new "imagined community" of the nation, to use Anderson's famous term. How is the "dialectics of disembedding and re-embedding," as Schirmer puts it, affected by globalization? He argues that as nation-states increasingly lose the ability to control and regulate the process of functional differentiation, like managing the new European currency, so they lose the ability to domesticate their consequences. As a result, the nation state "ceases to be the frame of reference for the generation of trust," that is, its re-embedding function loses its force. Formerly communities of fate for which one was prepared to die, the nation-state appears more as a site for "business and professional relations, travel, cultural consumption, eventually even political participation." Schirmer is wise not to push his analysis too far, so he notes that national identities will not disappear altogether, but they will be "reduced in status to be one source and subject of collective identification among a plurality of

26. Sacvan Bercovitch, *The American Jeremiad* (Madison, WI, 1978).

others which may be subsets of it, may transcend it, or may be entirely indifferent toward it."

This fact makes space for various commitments and points of orientation: In other words, multiculturalism replaces liberal universalism. What, then, does America, as perhaps the most functionally differentiated country, represent? And for what was NATO fighting in Yugoslavia? Outsiders still see the old American story of liberal universalism. True, the universalistic rhetoric remained, but has not its content changed? Is not the considerable moral energy behind multiculturalism and the NATO response the indignation at the homogenizing tendencies of even the liberal-universal state, let alone the ethnically cleansing one? For the same reason, the assimilationist policies toward native peoples of former government administations is today considered intolerable. Has not the curious American combination of the Exodus story and New Testament missionary zeal been replaced by another biblical trope, namely with what Carla Hesse calls the "Job Narrative": renouncing the dream of redemption, the promised land without conflict, and instead learning to living with difference?[27] If it has — and there are good reasons to think so — this does not necessarily entail an abandonment of universalism. Diversity is only sustainable in a world where it is recognized as a universal good, and for this reason Thomas McCarthy advocates "multicultural universalism,"[28] and one philosopher heralds the "human rights culture."[29] There is no conceptual reason why even the Job narrative — a defensive utopia, if ever there was one — cannot license defensive violence in the name of universal values.

27. I owe this biblical trope to Carla Hesse, "After Exodus: a History Lesson for Generation X," unpublished MS Department of History, University of California, Berkeley, May 1996.

28. Thomas McCarthy, "Doing the Right Thing in Cross-Cultural Representation," *Ethics* 102 (April 1992), 648.

29. Eduardo Rabossi "Human Rights Naturalized," quoted in Richard Rorty, "Human Rights, Rationality, and Sentimentality," in Stephen Shute and Susan Hurley, eds., *On Human Rights. The Oxford Amnesty Lectures, 1993* (New York, 1993), 115.

Comment on Part Four: Utopian Thinking between Producerism and Consumerism. What Distinguishes the American New Deal from the German *Volksgemeinschaft*?

Heiko Stoff

We usually accept a definition of "utopia" both as a critique of prevailing social conditions and as a blueprint for a future society. This vision involves normative statements about property, work, gender, the state of science and technique, and last, but not least the political order.[1] But how is utopian thinking realized and materialized? Utopia is simultaneously "now" and "not yet"; it is expressed with urgency, yet usually situated in a spatio-temporal distance.[2] Even the most prominent utopian novels of the turn of the twentieth century – Bellamy's *Looking Backward*, Bulwer-Lytton's *The Coming Race*, H. G. Wells' *A Modern Utopia* and *Men like Gods*, and many others – all take place in a distant future or in a parallel universe. This characteristic can be traced back to the nineteenth century's evolutionary style of thought, which assumed that the transformation of society and human beings is bound to long-term social, economical, biological and intellectual changes. For radical social improvement and human betterment it needs evolution and long-term measures rather than revolutions or hasty actions.[3] The

1. See Richard Saage, *Politische Utopien der Neuzeit* (Darmstadt, 1991), 5f.
2. I owe this phrase of "now" and "not yet" to Gottfried Küenzlen, *Der neue Mensch. Eine Untersuchung zur säkularen Religionsgeschichte der Moderne* (München, 1994), 59–60.
3. As we know, the concept of revolution also was mainly teleological evolutionism. The revolution did not promise any immediate satisfaction besides the overthrow of the exploiters, yet it openly established the dictatorship of the proletariat and an uncertain period of suffering, hard work, and struggling.

unsatisfactory punch-line of the utopian narrative was that this improvement might take more than a thousand years. The twentieth century knew only two actively practiced ideas to deal with the paradox of a utopian "now and not yet." Biomedical operations and surgery promised the immediate materialization of young, healthy, and beautiful bodies. At the same time, National Socialism proclaimed that it would definitely realize the millennium. But while biomedicine's utopian narratives have never shown more proof than long-living cells in a petri-dish, rats called "Methusalem," and flies x-times their usual age, Nazi Germany indeed had attained its announced utopian aims. In its time the Nazi utopia succeeded in nearly exterminating European Jewry and creating a state that was purely designated to fit racist ideas.

It is still an open question why the Nazi utopia, a dystopia in its full sense, was so easily and successfully established; why there was hardly any resistance and such widespread support. On the following pages, I will analyze the German national/racist community as a reaction to the fundamental transition from producerist to consumerist discourse that took part in the most developed industrial states at the long turn of the twentieth century. Thus, I will be able to compare Nazi Germany to another reaction to the crisis of modernity: America's New Deal. Nazi Germany's racist community and America's New Deal both were situated in a historical scheme which Michel Foucault describes as the biopower of disciplining the individual and regulating the population. It is of political, moral, and intellectual importance to analyze why both nations found such different ways to realize biopower and to respond to the transition of modernity. My aim is to show that modern antisemitism as a fetishized revolt against capitalism, as Moishe Postone calls it, is a direct outcome of producerist ideology. Nazi Germany indeed was a defense of producerism, whereas Americanism represented the vanguard of consumerism. But this should not lead us to reestablish identities. The shift from producerism to consumerism was an interdiscursive transformation, while Nazism and Americanism were just specific realizations of this transnational movement.

This commentary in all its briefness will only slightly touch the surface of this problem. But I hope that it may mark down a different way of thinking about both the specialty of National Socialism and the discourse of modernity.

The Normalcy of the German *Volksgemeinschaft*

What was the *Volksgemeinschaft*? To give a rather unusual definition: The *Volksgemeinschaft* promised a "good life" for everyone who was not already expelled by the racist order or did not agree with at least some of the *Volksgemeinschaft*'s basic assumptions. These basic assumptions were rooted in nationalism, racism, antisemitism and anti-capitalism, the disapproval of Bolshevism, a rejection of cultural modernism and Americanism, and finally a glorification of "natural" artisanal labor. The promise of the *Volksgemeinschaft* was an orderly society, better living conditions, mass consumerism without Americanism, popular leisure activities, good clean fun, stable and clearly defined hierarchical race- and gender-relations, and finally the leadership principle. In summary: recreation and discipline.[4] In his speculative, but thought-provoking book *Hitler as Philosophe*, Lawrence Birken describes National Socialism as a combination of economic thought with race policy. In the national community everybody had his (or her?) individual chance, given that he (or she?) was Aryan or German: "A successful people, endowed with high race value and organized into a leader-state, which could transform those race values into personality values." It seems self-evident that this noble race with its perfect individuals had the right and the need to expand and conquer.[5]

There is no need to stress the terror of the Nazi system to explain the participation of the German populace in establishing a national community. First of all, Nazi Germany was never completely unified as a national community. But this does not mean that its basic functions were not working. In a day-to-day practice, there was

4. See Peter Fritzsche, *Germans into Nazis* (Cambridge, MA, and London, 1998), 222.

5. See Lawrence Birken, *Hitler as Philosophe. Remnants of the Enlightenment in National Socialism* (Westport, CT, 1995), 47–50.

discontent, dissatisfaction, and discomfort with many of the Nazi-policies. As Maria Mitchell has shown, dissent and support were based on an everyday concept of checkmating the National Socialist offer and alternating between collaboration and living in the separate sphere of privacy. Still, the question remains unanswered why the utopia of extermination could be realized with hardly any resistance or was even co-opted. As long as the majority was benefiting from the Nazi politics, no revolt was to be expected. Thus the simple, but successful program of Nazi ideology consisted in privileging the German majority. While Stalinism was founded on an idiosyncratic and unstable society where nobody could be certain to fulfill the communists' demands, in Nazi Germany it was easy to participate: As long as you were German and you knew how to behave yourself correctly, there was nothing to fear! Furthermore, the Nazi policies were not exclusively supported because of social reform and economic prosperity. More profoundly, the National Socialists enabled and realized with astonishing verve the German discourse of the turn of the century: A *national* socialism. A short glance at political publications in the Weimar Republic would indeed proof that a "national socialism" was commonly approved. National-socialist, bourgeois-intellectual, and many left-wing positions agreed conceptually on a specific German socialism which referred to race and biology rather than class and sociology. There is evidence for a specific German discourse on race, whiteness, labor, equality, and identity[6]. Thus, there is a moral, historical, and political need to focus on the huge intersection of the Nazi utopia and the interests of different social groups – men and women, workers and capitalists, Protestants and Catholics – in Germany. Indeed, the Nazi ideology corresponded to the dominant discourse about the normal state of being in Germany, a "normality" that was fixed in a discourse upon

---

6. Just take a look at the writings of the eminent and prominent nationalist Arthur Moeller van den Bruck. See among others Uli Linke, *German Bodies. Race and Representation After Hitler* (New York and London, 1999); Jeffrey Herf, *Reactionary Modernism. Technology, Culture, and Politics in Weimar and the Third Reich* (Cambridge, 1984); and George L. Mosse, *The Crisis of German Ideology. Intellectual Origins of the Third Reich* (London, 1964).

social and race hygiene. Assuming the artificiality of capitalism and communism, it could be supposed that National Socialism was a natural socialism[7]. Thus, normality was the main achievement of the *Volksgemeinschaft*. As Detlev J. K. Peukert's definition of the *Volksgemeinschaft* elegantly sums up, Nazi policy aimed at the need to restore the disrupted "normality" of life:

> A utopian normality, to be sure, with a social hierarchy which was somehow "just" and in which everyone had a niche where he could feel secure and respected: in short, a true "national community" (*Volksgemeinschaft*) from which all sources of friction and unease had been removed, all reminders of "conspiracy", all abnormality, all that could jeopardize the ultimate "ideal order". At the same time, the "movement" allowed scope for undirected "action" and hankerings for non-quotidian adventure.[8]

The German populace profited from the Nazi state – e.g. by the expropriation of Jews – and thus constructed a *Volksgemeinschaft*. Many Germans might have been ambivalent about *völkisch* spectacles and some esoteric aspects of National Socialism. Nonetheless, they participated in the mobilization of nationalism, the "National Revolution," which seemed to fulfill long-delayed developments with vitality and speed. Germans met their own familiar desires in National Socialist politics which praised labor and workers, technique and efficiency, and defined these characteristics as specifically German.[9] But this "normalcy" remembered by many Germans today as a good and memorable life was fundamentally based on the expulsion of those deemed as inferior and menacing. It is the singularity of Nazi Germany that it achieved its announced utopian aims only through the elimination of its constituted outsiders. The "German racial state" can even be defined purely in negative terms: as a community that was neither Jewish nor degenerate.[10] For Nazi

---

7. See Birken, *Hitler as Philosophe*, 73–75.

8. See Peukert, *Inside Nazi Germany. Conformity, Opposition and Racism in Everyday Life* (London, 1989), 41–42.

9. See Fritzsche, *Germans into Nazis*, 215–235 and esp. 229.

10. See Omer Bartov, "Defining Enemies, Making Victims: Germans, Jews, and the Holocaust," *American Historical Review* 103 (1998), 791; Michael Burleigh,

Germany's policies, it was never the main cause to overcome social stratification and the juxtaposition of divergent capitalist society. Rather, their aim was to redefine social tension in biological and antisemitic terms. Peukert argues that the *Volksgemeinschaft* propaganda did not propose egalitarianism but suggested "merely a restructuring of the hierarchy on the basis of efficiency and performance."[11] Race replaces class – this very popular and accepted assumption of a "national socialism" was indeed a very successful answer to the Marxist challenge of the classless society. As Lawrence Birken puts it: "Hitler destroyed Marx by separating the socialist idea from class."[12]

Michel Foucault defines racism as the central mechanism for modern power relations. Related, but different power techniques disciplined the individual through exercise, training, and drill while regulating the life-processes through a population policy. These normalizing techniques had the purpose improving the quality of life: to prolong it, to multiply its possibilities, to compensate its deficiencies. But this strengthening of life was fundamentally connected with the urge to kill. In Foucault's terms, these power relations included the right to death ("laisser mourir") and the power over life ("faire vivre").[13] The racist ideal, most explicitly established in Nazi Germany, brought living and dying into a causal relation. Consequently, exclusion and murder was directly linked to a paradoxical power to strengthen life. In its logic it implied that the dying of Jews would strengthen the Aryans and purify life itself. In a normalizing society, this biological racism is needed to legitimate the killing. The combination of discipline and regulation – biopower

---

Wolfgang Wippermann, *The Racial State: Germany 1933–194*5 (Cambridge and New York, 1991).

11. See Peukert, *Inside Nazi Germany*, 95.

12. See Birken, *Hitler as Philosophe*, 104.

13. Foucault elaborated the concept of "biopower" in a lecture at the Collège de France on March 17, 1976. He first published it in the final chapter of the introduction to the *History of Sexuality*. See Michel Foucault, *"Il Faut Défendre La Société". Cours au Collège de France, 1976* (Paris, 1997), 213–244 and Michel Foucault, *History of Sexuality. Vol. 1* (New York, 1980).

in Foucault's words – can result in a logic of inevitable extermination. There is, as Omer Bartov writes, "the need to define enemies and the urge to make victims."[14] Antisemitism in its modern form left not the slightest chance for assimilation. In this it differs from premodern antisemitism. If exterminating the Jews was the Nazi utopia, the Nazis were indeed exceptionally successful.[15]

Racism is based on a strictly binary system; a system that generates exclusive qualities and entities like *fit* versus *unfit*, *Aryan* versus *Jewish*, *productive* versus *parasitic*, *the good body* versus *the wrong body*. But the manner in which these dichotomies are performed depend on the political and historical setting. Racist epistemology does not necessarily lead to the murderous selection of Nazi Germany's antisemitism. Foucault himself does not distinguish between the different ways biopower was realized. In this regard, colonialism, Stalinism and Nazi Germany are all products of modern biopower. Thus, the Holocaust, Gulags, and genocides are generally the same. Foucault indeed regards Nazi Germany only as a paroxysm of biopower. Hence, the Jews were just a manifestation of all other races. The uniqueness of modern antisemitism once again disappears in a generalization of racism. His concept of biopower, as useful as it is to describe racism and normalization, finds its limits in analyzing anti-Semitism. Biopower helps us to investigate the *Volksgemeinschaft*, but it fails to explain why it was the Jews who had to be exterminated.

Live and Let Live

A distinction between civic and ethnic nations can be dated well back into the late nineteenth century. Demos-based nations are

---

14. See Bartov, "Defining Enemies, Making Victims."

15. Foucault himself describes Nazi Germany as the most racist and murderous state, based on the right to strengthen life and to kill everyone – not only the others but also itself: "L'État nazi a rendu absolument coextensifs le champ d'une vie qu'il aménage, protège, garantit, cultive biologiquement, et, en même temps, le droit souverain de tuer quiconque – non seulement les autres, mais les siens propres." See Michel Foucault, *"Il Faut Défendre La Société"*, 232.

usually seen as benign, tolerant, rather inclusive; ethnos-based nations as exclusive, intolerant, prone to racism. But this clear distinction, as Dietmar Schirmer points out, underestimates the potential repressive, coercive, and exclusionary character to be found in civic nations, too. Even if Nazi Germany and America seem to be good representatives of ethnic and civic nations, any analysis referring only to this dichotomy must run short. So, how can it be explained that Nazi Germany applied exterminatory anti-Semitism and America the New Deal program to solve the crisis of (classical) modernity?

American mythology is based on assimilation and not on race purity. But assimilation as an Enlightenment concept was bound to the agenda of productivity and utility. Thomas Jefferson was serious when he offered race-mixing to the Native Americans: "You will become one people with us; your blood will mix with ours and will spread with ours over this great island."[16] But to achieve this charity of race-mixture, the noble savages had to surrender to the "civilized" mode of life. Jefferson was just as serious, when he ordered their expulsion the moment they did not fit into the policies of expansion anymore. Assimilation was always performed under the conditions of a producerist and white supremacist ideology. In the nineteenth century, Jeffersonian philanthropy was replaced by a more cynical version of power formulated by the German philosopher Arthur Schopenhauer. No individuality should be repudiated, he wrote in 1851 in his *Parerga und Paralipomena*, not even the lowest, most miserable, or ridiculous one. Because it is impossible to change *nature* – the moral character, the disposition, the physiognomy – there also can be no hope for improvement. If there is no need to utilize them, they should be left alone. This, so Schopenhauer concluded, is the true meaning of the saying "live and let live."[17] The Enlightenment's optimism at transforming all human beings through assimilation and education hardly survived nineteenth

16. See Reginald Horsman, *Expansion and American Indian Policy 1783–1812* (East Lansing, MI, 1967), 108.

17. See Arthur Schopenhauer, *Aphorismen zur Lebensweisheit* (Munich, 1966), 162.

century's evolutionism and naturalism. Whereas in the enlightened discourse of the eighteenth century, as Zygmunt Bauman says, "real, empirical men and women were but crude mutilations of what they could be and what they were called to be, pale reflections of their true potential," an assumption that guided the Enlightenment's gigantic task of transformation, it was indeed biological arguments which, as Bauman again puts it, "occupied the opposite pole to the sanguine hope/promise of liberalism to assimilate everyone and everybody into one unified company of rational human beings by the simple expedient of re-education."[18] Surely, America at the turn of the twentieth century, like every modern state, was bound to biopower. Selecting material for the melting pot at Ellis Island, sterilizing so-called "degenerate families," and securing white supremacy with anti-miscegenation laws were America's prime biopolitical techniques. But these measures were never undisputed; they did not lead to any sort of consent to racist politics and could not overcome the doctrine of assimilation itself. The influential American eugenics-movement in the long run did not succeed in enforcing its white supremacist politics, which so many German racists looked at full of envy.[19] Despite its history of genocide and slavery, it is indeed the constituency of America to select qualities, not to obtain a purified racist entity. It is no wonder that for present-day white supremacists it is Uncle Sam himself alias the "Zionist Occupied Government" who embodies the evils of pornography, homosexuality, and race-mixing.[20] The difference between Nazi Germany and America corresponds to the distinction drawn between biopower's "the right of death and the power over life" and laissez-faire liberalism's "live and let live."

18. See Zygmunt Bauman, *Biology and the Modern Project* (Hamburg, 1993), 9–11.

19. Hitler's enthusiasm for America's anti-miscegenation laws, its policy of limited immigration, and its forced sterilization vanished with Roosevelt's so called "Jew Deal." See Birken, *Hitler as Philosophe*, 83, 89. See in general Stefan Kühl, *The Nazi Connection. Eugenics, American Racism and German National Socialism* (New York and Oxford, 1994).

20. See also Birken, *Hitler as Philosophe*, 102–103.

The New Deal program of the 1930s amongst others was a rejection of this laissez-faire liberalism of "live and let live." The Civilian Conservation Corps and the National Youth Administration, as Olaf Stieglitz shows, tried to integrate even those who were stigmatized as "useless" and "worthless" – "the raw material out of which the United States must shape its future," as Roosevelt said – into the American "efficiency community." In proclaiming the moral superiority of American democracy, this youth program was a direct answer to the Hitler Youth. In this sense, the New Deal might be understood as a modernized form of Jeffersonian philanthropy: Everyone has his useful features and therefore is able to change through (re-)education, training, and exercise. The manpower envisioned by the New Deal had to be active and powerful, but not necessarily racially pure. It seemed to be self-evident that there was no need for idleness, femininity, and feebleness, but a strong demand for productivity, masculinity, and fitness. The New Deal's state interventionism emphasized a nation based on internalism and individual competition, whereas the Nazi utopia proclaimed a racially purified community for competitive Aryans only. America selected qualities, whereas Nazi Germany selected entities. Thus, in comparison with Nazi Germany, America, and especially New Deal America, is a typical example of a "civic nation." But compared with its own rhetoric, America's "institutionalized white supremacist domination," a "historico-racial schema," renders America's version of Enlightenment into a rather poor alternative to any "ethnic state."[21]

Leon F. Litwack shows in his convincing essay on race relations in the United States that the American utopia of equal opportunities for all was never realized, that there always existed a disparity between American democratic rhetoric and racial practices. Nevertheless, many African-American intellectuals took the promise of equality, emancipation, and individual freedom for granted and promised

---

21. See Thomas C. Holt, "Marking: Race, Race-making, and the Writing of History," *American Historical Review* 100 (1995), 1–20, here 2; and Bell Hooks, *Black Looks. Race and Representation* (Boston, MA, 1992), 15.

the emancipation to come if African-Americans could only prove their good qualities. But neither assimilation nor laissez-faire liberalism were meant to abolish the existent race-structure. Any effort to restructure race relations in America has been paralyzed by the paradox of propagating universal equality in a society fundamentally based on white supremacy and black inferiority. Without making up for centuries of suppression, lynching, and slavery, desegregation just left African-Americans on their own. The result was, as Litwack puts it, "pragmatic resignation." African-American culture was based on the idea of diaspora: of wearing a mask as a survival-strategy, of being alienated within a hostile culture, of being aliens in America. America was a utopia for African-Americans only in the literal meaning of the Greek "ou tópos": a "no place."

Tearing down Nineteenth Century-Boundaries

Even if it is accurate to term both Nazi Germany and America "racist states," there nonetheless exists a fundamental difference between murderous Germany and liberal America. And as I would like to emphasize, it is precisely the new ideology of consumerism usually associated with Americanism that holds the means of countering nationalism, racism, and antisemitism. Furthermore, it is not even sufficient to use the term "racism" to analyze the functioning of the German *Volksgemeinschaft*. Nazi Germany was surely racist, but its antisemitism was much more important. New Deal America was indeed structurally racist, but seldom anti-Semite. The main question therefore is what constitutes the particularity of modern anti-Semitism and what establishes the difference between German anti-Semitism and modern Americanism?

With the help of Lawrence Birken and Moishe Postone I should like to emphasize that in the first half of the twentieth century modernity underwent a fundamental transformation. This "crisis of (classical) modernity" was marked by the disintegration of supposedly natural boundaries, the "dissolutions of gender, species, need, and development-in-time."[22] Fundamental transgressions like these must have been much more horrifying for a Germany whose agenda consisted of distinct entities like race, white skin, virility, than for an America whose setting consisted of assimilation, transgression, and consumption. Both the New Deal and National Socialism can be considered as reactions to this shift, but as reactions that resulted in different practices.

Birken asserts that the turn of the twentieth century was characterized by the transition from a producerist to a consumerist ideology, by a movement from proto-industrial culture to an industrial culture of mass consumption. The twentieth century, he concludes, was marked by "an egalitarian ideology of consumers united under the single function of desire."[23] This transition cannot be satisfactorily described as the triumph of capitalist mass consumerism. It is indeed a discursive shift that constituted new sciences, new desires, new bodies, new ways of life, and new power techniques.[24] Manifestations of a consumerist discourse included cultural modernity and the sexual revolution, Hollywood and jazz, girl-

22. See Lawrence Birken, *Consuming Desire. Sexual Science and the Emergence of a Culture of Abundance, 1871–1914* (Ithaca, NY, 1988), 72. The term "crisis of classical modernity" was coined with a slightly different meaning by Detlev J. K. Peukert. See Detlev J. K. Peukert, *The Weimar Republic. The Crisis of Classical Modernity* (New York, 1987).

23. Birkens' main statement runs as follows:

Neoclassical economics emancipated desire in the form of marginal utility from socially determined needs of utilities. At the same time, sexology liberated perversity from heterogenitality, redefining the meaning of "sex" in the process. This redefinition of sexuality is central to any understanding of the series of changes that have gripped Western cultures since the latter part of the nineteenth century, changes whose more recent manifestations are sometimes summed up under the term "sexual revolution". (Birken, *Consuming Desire*, 122)

24. The transition from producerist to consumerist ideology indeed resembles the shift from "proto-normalism" to "flexible normalism" that Jürgen Link tries to establish in his discourse-analysis of "normalism." See Link, *Versuch über den Normalismus. Wie Normalität produziert wird* (Opladen, 1996).

culture and homosexuality. A consumerist discourse generated consuming beings of only subtle graduation and mixture. Such epistemological demarcations as race, gender, and age, which are systematically based on strict dichotomies, were rendered into scientific, political, and practical questions. At the turn of the twentieth century, such divergent disciplines as neoclassical economy and sexology gave consumption the precedence over production. Late nineteenth-century sexologists investigated reproduction from the point of view of desire. Indeed, such essential categories as *sexual dimorphism, reproduction,* and *marriage* were challenged by the attributes of *variety/perversity, promiscuity,* and *marriage-reform.* It was precisely the eighteenth and nineteenth centuries two-sex-model that was at stake.[25] "The emergence of a modern culture beginning at the end of the nineteenth century," as Birken describes this process, "saw the erosion of the separate spheres constructed during the previous 150 years, further reducing the male/female dichotomy of the Enlightenment to a single sphere of action in which all sexes and races were potentially equal."[26] When there is only variation and individualized polymorph perversity, as consumerist discourse concludes, then there can hardly be any amorality or degeneration.[27] This supposedly libertarian ideology itself was fundamentally based on biopower's agenda, but it proclaimed the selection of qualities and not of entities. Sexologists were usually adherents of eugenics, but most of them did not support race hygiene and race-selection.[28] It was not just up to the sexologists to query producerist assumptions about stable entities. Turn-of-the-century scientists in general proclaimed an epistemological transformation from stability to fluidity, from the old physiology of nerves to the new physiology of hormones.[29] Human beings, according to the conclusion of the

25. For the dominant "two-sex-model," see Thomas Laqueur, *Making Sex. Body and Gender from the Greeks to Freud* (Cambridge, MA, 1990).

26. See Birken, *Hitler as Philosophe,* 15

27. See also Birken, *Consuming Desire,* 48–52, 65–67.

28. See Atina Grossmann, *Reforming Sex. The German Movement for Birth Control & Abortion Reform, 1920–1950* (New York and Oxford, 1995).

29. See Nelly Oudshoorn, *Beyond the Natural Body. An Archeology of Sex Hormones* (London and New York, 1994).

transsexual surgeries performed by the Austrian physiologist Eugen Steinach, were just a precarious mixture of male and female qualities that could be transformed by nature and experimental biology.[30] This relativism was expanded to such basic categories of producerist discourse as age, race, fitness, beauty, and health. Gender, age, vitality – everything that makes a man a man and a woman a woman – seemed to be the result of just a lucky balance of male and female sex hormones.

At the end of the nineteenth century even the inevitability of dying was challenged. Cell-biologists stated the immortality of protozoa, while experimental biologists searched for the physiological reason of aging itself. It was again Eugen Steinach who in 1920 proclaimed that he was able to rejuvenate humans through a quite simple hormonal manipulation. Steinach, who was at that time so famous and influential that he was even proposed for the Noble Prize, proclaimed an "artificial rejuvenation" which allowed every individual to regain or improve his youth, fitness, and sexual potency. This biomedical technique of "artificial rejuvenation" came under fierce attack by German naturists, who proclaimed a "natural rejuvenation" through body culture, nudism, and race hygiene. For them, rejuvenation had to be the privilege of a selected elite of Germans.[31] "Artificial rejuvenation" was blamed for being an unauthorized intervention into the holistic integrity of the natural body. Prophets of "natural rejuvenation" proclaimed that the clientele of this Jewish physician consisted of dirty old men and wealthy hedonists, while the naturists were all proven Aryans. The debate

---

30. Steinach transplanted "male" gonads into "female" bodies and "female" gonads into "male" bodies with the claimed effect of masculinization and feminization. See Heiko Stoff, "Vermännlichung und Verweiblichung: Wissenschaftliche und utopische Experimente im frühen 20. Jahrhundert," Ursula Pasero and Friederike Braun, eds., *Wahrnehmung und Herstellung von Geschlecht – Perceiving and Performing Gender* (Opladen and Wiesbaden, 1999), 47–62; and Chandak Sengoopta, "Glandular Politics. Experimental Biology, Clinical Medicine, and Homosexual Emancipation in Fin-de-Siècle Central Europe," *Isis* 89 (1998), 445–473.

31. See the anti-Steinach position of the well-known racist and naturist Heinrich Pudor, *Die Steinachschen Verjüngungsversuche und die natürliche Verjüngung durch Nacktkultur* (Dresden, 1920).

over youth and rejuvenation indeed reflects the conflict between producerist and consumerist ideology. Steinach's bodies were transformable owing to nature's contingence and the abilities of the operating surgeon. "Artificial rejuvenation" was part of consumer ideology's assumption that everyone has the democratic right to youth, beauty, and health. Every individual could be transformed according to his own desires or to the needs of society.[32] In many regards, the rejuvenated patients were a materialization of American-ism's young, beautiful, healthy, and fit body. Facing opposition from the German medical establishment, Steinach and his supporters indeed tried to establish rejuvenation clinics in America. Moreover, even the American bestseller of 1923, Gertrude Atherton's *Black Oxen*, had rejuvenation as its subject and referred directly to the "Steinach-operation". *Black Oxen* was only the starting point of a series of rejuvenation novels and Hollywood adaptations.[33] Like the beauty operations, the new morality, and the youth cult, rejuvenation were part of the Roaring Twenties' culture and components of a new body-concept. Body history seems to be the key to analyze the deep tensions that eroded the twentieth century. It was bodies that were transformed, educated, disciplined, killed, rejected and praised. Scientists, physicians, reformers, politicians, writers, artists – they all discussed and predicted fundamental corporeal transforma-tions. As Tim Armstrong puts it in his cultural study of *Modernism, Technology, and the Modern Body*: "In the modern period, the body is re-energized, re-formed, subject to new modes of production, representation, and commodification."[34] From the point of view of body history, the question of the twentieth century was not socialism or barbarism, but Americanism or National Socialism.

32. The same would be true for aesthetic surgery. See Sander Gilman, *Creating Beauty to Cure the Soul. Race and Psychology in the Shaping of Aesthetic Surgery* (Durham, NC, 1998).

33. See Phil Hardy, ed., *Science Fiction* (London, 1994), 22–79; Margaret Morganroth Gullette, "Creativity, Aging, Gender. A Study of Their Intersections, 1910–1935," Anne M. Wyatt-Brown and Janice Rosen, eds., *Aging and Gender in Literature. Studies in Creativity* (Charlottesville, VA, 1993), 19–48.

34. See Tim Armstrong, *Modernism, Technology, and the Modern Body. A Cultural Study* (Cambridge, 1998), 2.

Next to "gender," it was the category of "age" that was the main object of contention. The early twentieth century witnessed a youth cult that not only favored juvenile qualities over those associated with old age, but also a fundamental opposition of *old morality, old values, old order* and *new morality, new values, new order.*[35] The narrative of a struggle between old and young was probably the most mobilizing issue of the twentieth century's political discourse. As a dehistorized and decontextualized topic it restabilized a complex social situation in translating it into the quasi-natural antinomy of young versus old (plus its respective metonymies like *vital, strong, masculine* and *decrepit, weak, sexless*). When someone like the American eugenicist Paul Popenoe referred to the "old story" of the conflict of the older and younger generation this was already an instruction to discriminate between those defined as young (*healthy, fit, German, National Socialist*) and those repudiated as old (*degenerate, impotent, not-German/Jewish, bourgeois/conservative*). It was their duty, the National Socialists proclaimed, finally to solve the battle between the old and the young, between the dying and the living. Youth itself seemed to be possessed with the power to rejuvenate the racial corpus. Like the hormones, which Ernest Starling in 1905 had defined as chemical messengers with the literal meaning of "I excite or arouse," youth was a necessary prerequisite to strengthen the nation or the race.[36] But even this juvenile body was bound to evolutionism's great fear of potential degeneration. In this regard, both the New Deal and Nazi Germany reacted to a suspected corruption of youth. While the Nazis' seizure of power itself was represented as the self-realization of a German youth purged of the evil influences of modernity and consumerism, the "lost generation" of America's depression years was seen as an direct outcome of the Roaring Twenties' hedonism.

35. For excellent histories of aging see Gerd Göckenjan, *Das Alter würdigen. Altersbilder und Bedeutungswandel des Alters* (Frankfurt a.M., 2000); and Thomas R. Cole, *The Journey of Life. A Cultural History of Aging in America* (Cambridge and New York, 1992).

36. See Victor Medvei, *The History of Clinical Endocrinology. A Comprehensive Account of Endocrinology from Earliest Times to the Present Day* (Cornforth, Lancashire, 1993), 189.

Ideal American men and women of the 1920s were young, beautiful, healthy, and rational. They lived in the big cities and they consumed without any significant class and gender difference the cultural offering of film, music, and sport.[37] This "Revolt of Modern Youth," which included rebellion, sexual liberty, and promiscuity, was certainly a phenomenon in all Western capitals, but it was perceived as exceptionally powerful in America.[38] The dissolution of social, moral, and epistemological boundaries was far from undisputed in the American debate of the 1920s and 1930s. New Deal politics were explicitly directed against this consumerist ideology and its destabilization not only of moral values, but of the American body as well. In the end, this was a hopeless battle, a battle against Americanism itself and its triumphant promise of individual satisfaction. The hedonist youth of America's 1920s affluent society was seen as a symptom of degeneration and immorality, as vitality gone wrong. In a redefinition of the youth problem it was not only the economic depression itself which was made responsible for the idleness of the "lost generation," but the moral decline of the older generation. This young generation seemed to be deprived of its natural energetic qualities: it was lifeless, inept, impotent. Regeneration of youth and the nation could only be achieved through reactivating and controlling its natural juvenile potentials. In this regard, the New Deal's youth program was actually a regeneration program, a defensive utopia. The 1920s effeminate and feeble bodies had to be substituted by manly, healthy, and muscular ones. The New Deal was an organized battle to reestablish the producerist ideology and to reshape a productive body. But, as the history of the twentieth century has shown, the Americanism of juvenile rebellion and consuming desire was much more effective. In the end, the key to the worldwide success of Americanism was exactly the promise of unlimited consumerism of sex, youth, beauty, individualism, and surely not America's Puritanism and disciplinary power. There were indeed three methods to rejuvenate the modern

---

37. See Mary Nolan, *Visions of Modernity. American Business and the Modernization of Germany* (New York, 1994), 108–109.

38. See Ben B. Lindsey, *The Revolt of Modern Youth* (New York, 1925).

body in crisis: first there was biomedicine's hormonal manipulation to reestablish a young, healthy, fit, and potent body; second there was a takeover of youth as deliverer of a resolute, energetic, and strong-willed race; and last, but not least there was Franklin D. Roosevelt's call to preserve American youth. Hormones, Aryans, and Young America were the three competing actors to regenerate corporeal degeneration.

Anti-modern Modernity

The German body of the 1930s and 1940s was defined through negative terms: it was not-Jewish, not-mixed, not-ill, and therefore idealized as Aryan and pure. The *völkisch* dream, as Lawrence Birken writes, was "the desire to purge the Germans of 'Jewish' characteristics."[39] The *Volksgemeinschaft* promised a purged version of modernity, an anti-modernist modernity, as the purified product of selection and annihilation. This German anti-modernism was deeply rooted in modernism, but it was, as Jeffrey Herf calls it, a "reactionary modernism." National Socialism was not only promoting a technocratic and prosperous future, but at the same time it was fundamentally anti-democratic, anti-capitalistic, and anti-materialistic.[40] The whole German reform movement of the turn of the twentieth century, while not always nationalist or proto-fascist, acted according to anti-modern law. It was the body that was the primary site of contention between modernity and anti-modernity. This was formulated in another setting of dichotomies: *pure* versus *assimilated*, *strong* versus *weak*, *old* versus *young*, *masculinized/feminized* versus *manly/womanly*, *degenerated* versus *regenerated*, *pornography* versus *nudism*.[41] As Uli Linke acutely points out: "The German disenchant-

---

39. See Birken, *Hitler as Philosophe*, 30.

40. See Herf, *Reactionary Modernism*, 11–13.

41. Uli Linke shows that this rejection of modernity articulated as "commodity resistance" survived well into postwar Germany and till today. See Linke, *German Bodies*, 65. For the importance of nudity for the creation of a German body see also Wilfried van der Will, "The Body and the Body Politics as Symptom and

ment with the 'modern' was to be cured by modifying corporeal practices."[42] The *völkisch* body was a defense against the tendency toward universal democratization implicit in the ideology of consumerism.[43] The realization of the consuming body's universal desire was most effectively rendered possible in modern capitalism. Taylorism and Fordism, the emergence of a new market, were not the reason but the necessary condition for the materialization of consuming bodies. In this regard, Americanism is the ideology which propagated consumerism and the consuming body most success-fully.[44] Leftist anti-capitalist critique always tended to ignore the anti-capitalist and anti-American aspects of National Socialism, thus hindering a discussion about producerism.[45] Americanism was indeed an offense to all producerist and essentialist worldviews. As many contemporaries feared, the Weimar Republic was already under the spell of Americanism.[46] German cultural criticism from the right or from the left was directed against American rationaliza-tion and its standardized culture of consumption, which seemed to lead to an irrevocable loss of German profundity and substance. The "democratization through consumption" was seen as an equalizing dissolution of difference. There was widespread approval of Fordism, but disapproval of consumerism. As Mary Nolan points

---

Metaphor in the Transition of German Culture to National Socialism," Brandon Taylor and Wilfried van der Will, eds., *The Nazification of Art* (Winchester, Hampshire, 1990), 14–52.

42. See Linke, *German Bodies*, 46.

43. See Birken, *Consuming Desire*, 74.

44. See Nolan, *Visions of Modernity*, 30–57.

45. In this regard, it was Horkheimer and Adorno's otherwise important "Dialectic of Enlightenment" that set the wrong course. As Jürgen Link shows, Adorno was not able to distinguish between the normalizing techniques in National Socialism and the cultural industry (a.k.a. America). See Link, *Versuch über den Normalismus*, 103–109.

46. For "Americanism" in Germany see amongst others Alf Lüdtke, Inge Marssolek, and Adelheid von Saldern, eds., *Amerikanisierung. Traum und Alptraum im Deutschland des 20. Jahrhunderts* (Stuttgart, 1996); and Frank Trommler and Joseph McVeigh, eds., *America and the Germans. An Assessment of a Three-Hundred-Year History* (Philadelphia, PA, 1985).

out for the German Social Democrats of the 1920s: they wanted mass consumption but not a culture of consumption.[47] It was the "Völkische Bewegung" that most successfully criticized and combatted the idea of universal equality in consumption and the disintegration of gender-, race-, and class-boundaries. Hitler, in Birken's analysis a proponent of economical liberalism based on a racist agenda, not only "asserted himself against the last remnants of aristocratic civility" but also opposed the emerging relativism of consumer culture.[48] It shows the power of the consumerist discourse that not even National Socialism could avoid American mass entertainment as the most important representation of consumerism.[49] Race-regeneration was a counter-discourse whose task it was to restrain the uncontrollable powers released through consumerism. National Socialism propagated, as again Birken expresses it, "a titanic struggle between the masculine productive Aryan and the feminine unproductive Jew."[50] In a logic where production was understood as male and consumption as female the economic and cultural primacy of consumption seemed to initiate a female supremacy.[51] The "feminization of American culture" and the "girlization of taste" were debated and rejected as a very dangerous subversion not only of American culture but of the Western world in general. A feminized consuming body must have been a profound threat to nineteenth-century values like productive work, virility, and nation.[52]

In his effort to explain anti-Semitism neither as a "scapegoat ideology" nor as "functionalism" Moishe Postone refers exactly to this producerist ideology. "The extermination of the Jews not only

47. See Nolan, *Visions of Modernity*, 120.

48. See Birken, *Hitler as Philosophe*, 54.

49. See Philipp Gassert, *Amerika im Dritten Reich. Ideologie, Propaganda und Volksmeinung 1933–1945* (Stuttgart, 1997).

50. See Birken, *Hitler as Philosophe*, 17.

51. See Nolan, *Visions of Modernity*, 123–124.

52. See Georg Bollenbeck, *Tradition, Avantgarde, Reaktion. Deutsche Kontroversen um die kulturelle Moderne 1880–1945* (Frankfurt a.M., 1999), 260; Nolan, *Visions of Modernity*, 120–127; and Andreas Huyssen, "Mass Culture as Woman. Modernism's Other," Tania Modleski, ed., *Studies in Entertainment. Critical Approaches to Mass Culture* (Bloomington, IN, 1986), 188–207.

was to have been total," Postone states, "but was its own goal – extermination in order to exterminate – a goal which acquired absolute priority."[53] In his words, it is necessary to explain National Socialism in terms of socio-historical epistemology. Postone's analysis can be understood as an attempt to reintegrate the Holocaust into fundamental historical processes without neglecting its qualitative specialty.[54] If the assumption is true, that the abstract domination of capital became perceived as the domination of international Jewry, why then were the Jews also seen as the dynamic power behind social democracy and communism? And why didn't the *völkisch* "revolt against modernity" include an attack on industrial capital and modern technology? Postone's solution for this contradiction is Marx's concept of the fetish:"The specific characteristics of power attributed to the Jews by modern anti-Semitism – abstractness, intangibility, universality, mobility – it is striking that they are all characteristics of the value dimension of the social forms analyzed by Marx."[55] The fetish, to cut a complicated Marxist story short, indicates an antinomy of abstractness (money) and concreteness (the commodity). The double character of the commodity as value (expressed by money) and use-value (expressed by the commodity), allows concrete labor and even industrial production to appear as a purely material process untouched by or just alienated from capitalism. The capitalist social relations do not appear as such, Postone points out, they appear as quasi-natural phenomena in which the social and historical do not appear. In naturalizing the historical specialty of labor, the revolt against capitalism appeared as the liberation of work from its parasitical suppressors – aristocrats, capitalists, Jews – with the aim to give work back to its genuine owners. This producerist ideology was virulent in all capitalist societies, but it only found an appropriate foundation in Germany. National Socialism was a fetishized revolt against capitalism. The naturalization immanent in the commodity fetish led to an ontologization of

53. See Moishe Postone, "Anti-Semitism and National Socialism: Notes on the German Reaction to 'Holocaust'," *New German Critique* 19 (1980), 105.
54. See Postone, "Anti-Semitism and National-Socialism," 107.
55. See Ibid., 108.

society and history. Anti-Semitism therefore can be explained as a "biologization of capitalism."[56] The extermination of European Jewry was a "qualitative specificity" which cannot be compared to other genocides, because it followed no specific reason, no immediate hate, no extrinsic goal. It can not be explained either in functionalist or in intentionalist terms. All of everyday Nazi Germany was seen as the drama of a battle of the Aryans against the Jews, between so-called "'natural' artisanal labor" and "'parasitic' finance capital."[57] This was even symbolized in the swastika as the explicitly proclaimed sign for the victory of the Aryans and the idea of productive labor. "The hagiography of labor and the demonology of laziness were no mere propaganda points," Birken points out, "but fundamental axioms that set the whole system of valuation in motion." The difference between productive and unproductive labor is indeed one of the fundamental dichotomies of Enlightenment. As a manifestation of biopower the distinction between creative work and unproductive "parasitism" became the means for distinguishing between life and death.[58] The Jews were only human beings in disguise; they were actually the materialization of abstractness. That is why they were seen as the force behind both plutocratic capitalism and socialism. The real human beings, whom the Germans had to kill, were never those one actually saw but merely what they represented. For the perpetrators, it wasn't the Jews that had to be killed in the concentration camps, but just a dangerous abstractness, flexibility, and universality.[59]

A Consumerist Utopia?

The struggle between producerism and consumerism was a phenomenon in all capitalist states. But only in Germany did producerism already function as national identity. There is no need to claim a

---

56. See Ibid., 110, 112.
57. See Ibid., 110.
58. See Birken, *Hitler as Philosophe*, 16, 53.
59. See Bartov, "Defining Enemies, Making Victims," 785.

German disposition to exterminatory antisemitism, but nowhere else did the fetishized revolt against capitalism fall upon such fertile ground as in turn-of-the-century Germany. Every modern state, concludes Michel Foucault in his lecture on biopower, is racist at its core and needs those doomed to non-existence as its constituted outsiders. But, as should be clear by now, (bio)power techniques differ crucially in their murderous selectivity as in German Anti-Semitism, and in their mere liberal laissez-faire version of American racism. The emergence of consumerism indeed allows a fundamental turning away from any producerist utopia of constructing a purged race. A society based on consumerism is not at all a just society, but it will be structurally incapable of repeating the Holocaust. Thus, claiming a direct relationship between the Holocaust and modernity should not mislead us to reflect upon modernity solely from the point of view of the Holocaust. Contemporary bioscience, population, and immigration policy should indeed be analyzed and criticized as manifestations of bio-power, but they do not necessarily lead to a repetition of National Socialism. In claiming the existence of a producerist and a consumerist discourse we can differentiate between two distinct forms of (bio)power.

Every crisis generates the mobilization of the "the right to death and the power over life." The nearly unchecked activities of East German Nazis, the reactions of politicians who worry about "German youth" and not about mistreated and murdered immigrants, and the readiness in every society to mobilize for war show how easy it still is to draw a line between those who have the right to live and the others who are doomed to non-existence. And as the German "Walser-Debatte" again shows, huge sections of German intellectuals, politicians, and citizens are not willing just to let producerism fade away. It seems as if there is indeed only a consumerist utopia left; a consumerism which is neither bound to biopower, laissez-faire liberalism, and capitalism, nor belongs to the rather apolitical section of postmodern relativism; a consumerism that consists of bending, transforming, and refusing to build and select entities. And utopia which is indeed now and not yet.

Part 5
Science Fiction, Social Construction, and New Realities

1
Different Drafts of a "Future Horizon": *Weird Science* versus *Nick der Weltraumfahrer*

Ole Frahm

Like us, the humans of the past have been subjects of initiative, retrospection and prevision.[1] The humans of the past not only had their own past but, like us, they had a future of their own which has become our past. By stating this commonplace truth Paul Ricœur wants to remind us, the present, that even in the future we remain bound by the unfulfilled promises of the past. It is only through the dialectics of past and future that historiography, as part of a culture of "just memory," can liberate the suppressed promises of the past.[2] It is in the name of the future that Ricœur seeks reconciliation with the "painful past." Liberation through history enables "a people, a nation, a culture (to attain) an open and living notion of its tradition."[3] This in turn is necessary if the past is not to haunt the present like a "specter without distance."[4]

Historiography as exorcism: By trying to render impossible any chauvinist recourse to the past as a rhetoric support for the justification of future wars Ricœur, however, is not providing a convincing foundation for the science of historiography. For do not specters necessarily haunt us from the distance while at the same time keeping no distance if they are specters?[5] More so, must the spectres

1. Paul Ricœr, *Das Rätsel der Vergangenheit. Erinnern – Vergessen –* (Göttingen, 1998), 63.
2. Ibid., 113.
3. Ibid., 66.
4. Ibid., 113.
5. Jacques Derrida, *The Specters of Marx. The Stae of the Debt, the Work of Mourning, and the New International*, trans. Peggy Kamuf (New York and London, 1994).

of the past not by necessity be unforseeable, uncontrollable revenants? And how are we to imagine a "liberation of promises"? Are there not promises, possibilities never realized, which are pleasurable as such? How are we to distinguish between different promises, the racist and the non-racist for example? Ricœur avoids any closer definition of the political field which the past must constitute for the present, and his theories are of little help for its analysis.

"Like us, the humans of the past have been subjects of initiative, retrospection and prevision": Who are "the humans," who are supposed to be "like us" but obviously belong to different "peoples," "nations," and "cultures"? Apparently Ricœur is referring to "all" humans, then and now: "We" who even in the future will still belong to many different generations. Generations who, in their respective pasts, have had quite different experiences. Historical experiences which can only be compared under specific conditions, if at all. Generations that are haunted by quite different "specters from the past" and therefore write "history" quite differently. And so, given all these conditions, how much "like us" are those humans of the past really? What within their hopes for their future can be compared to our hopes for our future?

"The humans of past times had their own past future": Commenting on Ricœur's text, the German philosopher Burkhard Liebsch quotes the historian Rainer Kosellek with yet another commonplace truth.[6] If the future of former days now lies in the past, so we may conclude, the ideas of their future, of *the* future, which these humans of former days held, are gone as well. The future, to state a possible commonplace truth of future times, has its own history. But, contrary to the history which the past has written and which historiography time and again makes the subject of its studies, with few exceptions[7] the history of the future remains to be written. A possible reason for this may be that the origins of the science of history in the

6. Ibid., 17.
7. Rainer Kosellek, *Vergangene Zukunft. Zur Semantik geschichtlicher Zeiten* (Frankfurt, a.M., 1979).

nineteenth century themselves cannot be seperated from a specific concept of progress. This led to a specific idea of the future of the discipline. Without the belief in the possibility of a progressive recording of the whole of humankind's history the enormous project of scientific historiography could and can not be conceived.

As we all know, during the years 1936 to 1945, the concept of the future as a continuing progress underwent a crisis. Certainly, before that, there had been talk of decline in view of the progress of capitalism. But the historical crisis of the concept of the future no doubt came when the failure of the project of building up a society different from the capitalist one in the Soviet Union became apparent. And the industrialized mass-gassing of the European Jews by Nazi Germany shattered all hopes for a continuing progress of civilization: Too many achivements of modernity had been necessary to accomplish this crime. And finally, the invention and the dropping of the atomic bomb brought about the dawning of an age in which humankind like never before in human history could bring about its own destruction. The dominant hope for progress through enlightenment was replaced by an apocalyptic fear. However, as an indispensable prerequisite of capitalist economy, progress and the believe in it remained unbroken.

This may help to explain why, after the victory over Soviet socialism, i.e., after the end of the Cold War, the belief in progress accelerated once more. Today, the apocalyptic fear that the "unfulfilled promise" – the possibility of a destruction of the world – could still be fulfilled is no longer voiced, quite unlike the situation in the 1980s. And the feeble hope for a re-evaluation of the concept of progress within the communist movements is not only questionable but also completely unrealistic. The "sober victory" of capitalism, nowadays called globalization, seems to predict a pragmatic future, and – for the West – possibly even a "privatization", i.e., a depoliticization of the future. Ricœur's phrase that all humans look back *and* into the future may find its banal and only superficially historical truth in this development.

On the other hand there are intellectuals who, in recent years, have been returning to Walter Benjamin's concept of a "weak messianic power" ("schwache messianische Kraft"[8]). One reason for this is the attempt to reanimate the future as a political field. This return to the future – trying to recover the future's future[9] – after years of critical assessment of progress has become possible because with it went a critical assessment of the belief in continuity. So, to hope for the future is only possible because history appears as discontinuous. By emphasizing the breaches we become aware of the possibilities which lie in the future. Possibilities, it has to be added, which only exist because decisions in favor of one or the other possibility have been taken. Every breach therefore implies an exclusion. The "weak hope" for the future means to emphasise exactly that, for otherwise there will be no shapes, no knowledge, no decisions. History is not only the history of class wars but also the history of vehement, violent exclusions. And different kinds of exclusions. By commenting on Luce Irigaray's reading of Plato, Judith Butler demonstrates how the human body is shaped as a result of various exclusions; exclusions which produce an "outside" of this body where everything remains shapeless which is not part of the body. Butler's conclusion – which has inspired the title of this article – is that: "The task is to refigure this necessary 'outside' as a future horizon."[10]

But what task is Judith Butler referring to? If the "outside," which in this case is constituted through the exclusion of women, animals, and slaves, remains opaque, i.e., beyond intellegibility and beyond the borders of language,[11] then how can this inaccessibility constitute a future horizon? And as what kind of horizon are we to "refigure the outside"? How can "the outside," being both heterogeneous and spectre-like, be challenged?

---

8. Walter Benjamin: *Der Begriff der Geschichte*. In: Walter Benjamin, *Gesammelte Schriften* 2 vols., es. Rolf Tiedemann and Hermann Schwepennhäuser (Frankfurt a.M., 1974), 691–703, here 694.

9. Jacques Derrida, "Archive Fever. A Freudian Impression," *Diacritics* 25(2) (Summer, 1995), 9–63, here 45ff.

10. Judith Butler, *Bodies that Matter. On the Discursive Limits of Sex* (New York and London, 1993), 53.

11. Ibid., 52f.

In view of this theoretical horizon I shall, in the following discussion, reflect upon two comic-book serials from the 1950s. Two science fiction series, one from the United States and one from West Germany: *Entertaining Comics*, which appeared under various titles like *Weird Science, Weird Fantasy,* and *Weird Science Fantasy* between 1950 and 1955; and *Nick der Weltraumfahrer* (Nick the Space-Traveller), which was published by Walter Lehning Verlag from 1958 until 1960 in its peculiar oblong *Piccolo* format (9 x 18 cm).

The two examples could hardly be more different. *Weird Science* was produced by a group of writers and illustrators – Al Feldstein, Joe Orlando, Wally Wood, Al Williamson, and Harvey Kurtzman – and was part of a mainstream of comic books which in some cases sold several millions of copies. *Nick der Weltraumfahrer* was created under the sole responsibility of Hansrudi Wäscher, whose style in this as in other, simultaneously published series like *Sigurd* and *Tibor,* appears to be heavily influenced by Italian comic books. Wäscher was one of the most prolific West German comic producers of his time.

Edited by William Gaines, *Entertaining Comics* appeared *before* the publication of Frederic Wertham's *Seduction of the Innocent* (1954) which resulted, after a number of public burnings of comic books, in the universal adoption of a Comic Books Code by the *Comics Magazine Association of America.* This Code made a publication like *Weird Science* an impossibility, only for its title.[12] *Nick* appeared for the first time *after* public burnings of comic books had occured in West Germany as well and was considered "clean" from its outset.[13]

In comparing these two "drafts of a future horizon" I shall concentrate on two aspects: First, how do these comics conceive today's "future horizon" enabling us to read them as a "history of the future"? And second, in what way can their respective visions of the future be considered a contribution to a "refiguration of this necessary outside"?[14]

12. Maurice Horn, ed., *The World Encyclopedia of Comics* 2 vols. (New York, 1976), 820ff.

13. Bernd Dolle-Weinkauff, *Comics. Geschichte einer populären Literaturform in Deutschland seit 1945* (Weinheim and Basle, 1990).

14. Butler, *Bodies that Matter,* 53.

In the Future

In 1975, humankind has finally overcome all divisions. The Cold War is over. The destruction of London had been the final sacrifice when in 1971 a bomber plane on a training mission had crashed and released a hydrogen bomb. The ensuing shock led, after prolonged negotiations, to the forming of a global union, which in turn allowed for a period of peaceful development. We are not told what kind of economy this global state had. What we know is that, in 2008, humans reached out for the stars. The famous professor Raskin had developed a space ship which not only was able to fly to the moon like others before, but also to reach Venus. On Earth, all uranium deposits had been exhausted, and so – for the benefit of humankind – new ones had to be explored on other planets. And indeed, as it turned out, rich deposits were found on Venus which were easier to exploit because the planet's atmosphere proved to be breathable. Maybe this was one of the last true adventures of humankind. Because, everywhere on the blue planet lurked yellow-skinned aliens, reckless gangsters, and unknown animals and diseases. And, in a struggle for interplanetary hegemony, the green-skinned, arrogant, and technologically advanced Martians had to be vanquished. In 1908, they had by law banned any possibility of interplanetary space flight for humankind, and now they were ready to implement this ban with atomic bombs dropped on research sites. Thanks to a square-shouldered hero, the humans remained masters of all these dangers. His name was *Nick der Weltraumfahrer* (Nick the Space-Traveller).

Cut. Let's start over. Six planets belong to the confederacy of the solar system. Once there had been nine planets. In those times, the earthlings were mining uranium on Mars. Eventually, all deposits had been exploited. The Uranium Mining Company faced close-down. But then its chairman of the board, Anthony W. Brisbane, discovered a way to mine the uranium deposits on Venus despite the planet's formaldehyde atmosphere, which was unbreathable for humans. Business was flourishing: by microwave radio signals, uranium was transmitted via teleportation to Mars. Eight hundred teleportation receivers on Mars received 14 tons a second. On Mars, the refinery processed a billion tons of uranium into 5,000 ounces of U 235 daily which were then shipped to Earth. Unfortunately though, as a result, Venus started to lose mass which Mars in turn gained, so that, within five years, both planets were nearing the orbit of Earth. "Earthquakes, tornados and holocausts killed most of Earth's living creatures. . ." Finally, in a catastrophic "mass meeting," both planets collided with Earth, and today all three form one gigantic asteroid belt between Mercury and our planet, Jupiter.

The future could not be more different. In one case, it comes as a success story about humankind's superiority, while in the other, the children of Jupiter are told about humankind's ultimate failure. In one case, humankind exists without an economy, the striving for profit being restricted to a gang of irresponsible saboteurs. In the other, it is just one company among many that fails to consider the ultimate consequences of its greed for profit. In one case, Venus is turned into a home, in the other, into a death star. And the history of the future could not be told more differently, too.

Two Kinds of Future

Nick der Weltraumfahrer is an extensive epic tale about a hero and his companions who, week after week, overcome one danger after the other. In most cases the episodes end on a cliffhanger to make the next installment sell. The readers' curiosity about how Nick is going to get out of the next critical situation is satisfied for a short while, only to be aroused by the development of a new danger. Week after week this interruption is thus suspended, allowing the space adventure to grow into a continuing epic tale. A curious continuity of discontinuous events is built up. This continuity soothes. Although each cliffhanger interrupts the continuity, it never actually jeopardizes its existence. The hero's symbolic death is not part of the tale's design. The only danger which the cliffhanger implies, without actually intending to, is the series' going out of print, which would cause the real death of the hero. *Nick der Weltraumfahrer* is exceptional, because it minimizes the danger of discontinuation through its aesthetics of representation. Although the imminent dangers are not forseeable, their contingency makes them reliable and constant. With one danger averted, it takes exactly the interval between two panels for the next to loom around the corner. Danger after danger is lined up like a chain. It is the peculiar *Piccolo* format which creates this impression: It makes the comics appear like one long strip. *Piccolo* comics lack the concise formal austerity of the comic strips in the daily press, just as they lack the graphic potential of the comic book's page layout. To preserve the continuity of danger it does not matter what the next threat to Nick is going to be: meteors or explosions, Martians or gangsters, giant spiders or swarming mosquitos – from one panel to the next, anything can turn into an adversary that has to be overcome with the help of Nick's radiation gun, dexterity, and a little luck.

The observation that *Nick* is published according to a standard form offers no help in understanding why *Nick* differs from the comic books published by the *Entertaining Comics* group. Each *EC* comic book featured four short stories of six to eight pages, with an additional page provided for the indispensable "letters to the editor." So, instead of relying on the cliffhanger device, every single story had to be convincingly conceived with respect both to its narrative and to its unexpected ending. *EC* – until 1947 the acronym for *Educational Comics* – professes an aesthetics of the exclamation mark: *The Exile!, What He Saw!, Mass Meeting!, The Green Thing!* — the exclamation mark turns the most trivial title into a promise of something special: We're not captivated by just any exile, we're captivated by *The Exile!*

None of the many adversaries of *Nick der Weltraumfahrer* is a real danger to the homogeneity of its proposed vision of the future. No danger can really threaten the continuity of its world. The exclamation mark in *Weird Science* and *Weird Fantasy*, on the other hand, is a signal announcing the recurrent transgression of the limits set by standardization and genre. However, for all its regularity of occurrence, the transgression itself can never be standardized. The continuity of narration in *Nick* implies a continuing exploration of the universe, an accumulation of knowledge that has no significance at all for future episodes (we shall come back to this). The frontiers conquered by *Nick* all point in the same direction: to the future. It is the future of humankind's superiority, its progress, and its predominance throughout the universe. In *Weird Science*, there may be recurrent motifs, but their variation has to be marked enough, their difference from repetition to repetition noticeable enough, in order for each of them to acquire an appeal of its own, meaning nothing less than the creation of a new, undreamt-of vision of the future. Any new constellation of motifs must impose itself on all preceding ones for a story's length.

In *Nick*, suspension is generated by the continued appearance of new adversaries. What interests the reader is: Who is going to be the next adversary to precipitate Nick into a critical situation? In *EC*, suspension has to be recreated in story after story: Now, how are they going to tell the end of the world this time to have me surprised? So, while in the universe of Hansrudi Wäscher the end of the world is simply unthinkable, the *Weird Science* visions of the future make it happen almost regularly. This generates a suspense of its own between the different short stories. What we see are fragments of the future which never add up to a whole picture, let alone one in which the world society is governed by a Security Council. *Entertaining Comics* entertain because they do not tell the story of progress. Or, if they do, progress serves no other purpose than bringing about a *Mass Meeting!* of Venus and Mars on planet Earth. It is thus that *EC*'s science fiction creates its own, new, and different tales of genesis. They are left unrelated and often come as opening stories for a certain issue. For instance: Is Earth an exile for the most vicious criminals of the universe, of whom the first two bear the names of Adam and Eve (*The Exile!*)? Or, were Adam and Eve two who traveled into the past with a time machine to make "A New Beginning", wishing to ban all evil from the world? All stories in *Weird Fantasy* are *weird* fictions, but all of them are made possible by *science*. The future is a set of possibilities which can be expanded at will. The future is not seen as one progressive time-line.

Wäscher presents us with a vision of the future, the homogeneity of which cannot be endangered by any adversary in the world. No alien in the universe can make Nick lose his composure or let him doubt his superiority. Nor has these aliens' strangeness any effect:

The human perspective is at the center and remains there, whatever happens. Even when the atmosphere on Mars is destroyed by the explosion of an atomic bomb, the comment given by its sole survivor, Xutl, a Martian secret agent who has become Nick's friend, is clear-cut: "LASST EUCH DAS EINE WARNUNG SEIN, ERDENMENSCHEN, DIE IHR DIE ERSTEN SCHRITTE IN DAS REICH DER ATOME UNTERNEHMT: WER MIT DEM GÖTTLICHEN FEUER SPIELT, KOMMT IN DER ALLES-VERZEHRENDEN FLAMME UM" (see figure 1).[15] The "work of mourning" of this member of an "unknown race" consists in deducing a universal lesson for the humans. The "all-consuming flame," an image reminding us somehow of the Holocaust, has not destroyed any relatives or friends. It does not constitute a historical breach of the continuum of the future. And in any case, there is no time left for further thought. Already in the next panel, the heroes' lives are in danger once more when they find their spaceship's hull is corroding. From then on, Xutl stays on as the good "green" stranger whose stature so closely resembles that of the title hero. Once again, the danger of interruption by something strange has been successfully averted.

The stories of *Weird Science* are more than once told from the unusual perspective of aliens. And often this is precisely the point of the story. The heterogeneity of the future implies the hetero-

Figure 1 *Hansrudi Wäscher, Nick der Weltraumfahrer.*

15. "Let this be a warning to you, earthlings, who make your first steps into the world of the atom: He who plays with the divine fire shall perish in the all-consuming flame" Hansrudi Wäscher, *Nick der Weltraumfahrer*, Nr. 3, 24/4.

geneity of perspectives concerning this future. And at the same time, the stories again and again insist on the truth of their respective visions of the future or the possibility of their providing an exact prediction of it. Science fiction can thus take place in the past when the aliens predict that the criminal they are about to bring to a place called Germany on a planet named Earth in 1914 will take exactly nineteen years to make his full impact on the history of humankind. So, when X-51 asks "HOW MUCH EFFECT HE WILL HAVE", we get the editors' laconic comment: "WOULD YOU LIKE IT IN ROUND NUMBERS, X-51?" (*The Exile!*). In another case, aliens who wander about a fragment of Earth exploded in a nuclear blast discover a copy of *Weird Fantasy* no. 17. Reading it they discover that they shall find and read this copy. So, what the readers read shall have taken place because they are shown how the aliens recognize themselves and read how they recognize themselves reading – a perfect example of self-referentiality (see figure 2).[16]

It is this alienated perspective, the aliens' gaze so strange to us, which constitutes the heterogeneity of future. None of these outcomes are imaginable: That is their historical truth. One cannot believe that what happened in *Weird Science* shall come true. And yet it shall happen in spite of it all, it shall have come true, true in spite of our imagination: That is the historical experience which can be read between the stories of *Entertaining Comics*. "It shall have come true" – but the truth of this prediction as a prediction cannot be proven, or can only be proven *post festum*. When it is proven in spite of its being unbelievable, it is too late. When the editors answer X-51's question, it is too late. When history is written, it is too late. The historical experience of posteriority, and the experience that historical experience can only be articulated afterwards, motivate the varying visions of the future. In the twentieth century, this experience has become, to borrow a term from psychoanalysis, a traumatic one. It is therefore appropriate for *Entertaining Comics'*

16. For Al Williamson, "The Aliens", *Weird Fantasy* 17 (Nov.–Dec., 1952), cf. Ole Frahm, "Weird Signs. Comics as Medium of Parody," in Anne Magnussen and Hans Christian Christiansen, eds., *Comics Culture* (Kopenhagen, 2001), 177–191.

Figure 2 *Al Williamson, The Aliens.*

weird science fiction to become the place for space; space which contains this historical experience.

In contrast, the space of adventure of *Nick der Weltraumfahrer* is not one of experience but of permanent ahistorical danger. For the future of this representation, reification of history has made so much progress that one event resembles every other. Here, it is almost impossible to envision the specificity of the particular which guides the writing of history. Danger in this case means quite universally the loss of male potency, which is the reason why there are few women in the first installments of the series and why all members of the global union of humans are white. The fear of permanent castration, which is the fear of the symbolic death of the hero and the actual termination of the series, is what propels the breathless action. Every interruption of the continuum turns into a danger which must be overcome with the radiation gun, if necessary. It is because of this fear that in Wäscher's series, the very aesthetics of representation exclude the danger of a real interruption. Since the 1980s, *Nick der Weltraumfahrer* has been republished and become a fetish object for collectors. The traumatic interruption of the series has thus been resolved.

In Future?

"The happiest time is always the present".[17] *Weird Fantasy* and *Weird Science* not only try to recover a historical experience in their genre, which is about the future, but in doing this they try to recover the future of historical experience itself. And justly so. Because, if today, on the threshold of a new millennium, we were to decide which draft of a future horizon should become predominant now and in future, surely we would hesitate to name *Nick der Weltraumfahrer.* But any other answer would be nothing less than a lie. Not least, in recent years a way of treating history and of looking at the future has been established in West Germany which the structure of *Nick der Weltraumfahrer* seems to prefigure.

This may be no accident. Born in 1928, Hansrudi Wäscher belongs to the generation of those too young to feel responsible for the war, but old enough to feel themselves its victims. It would be cynical to relate the ahistoricity of the National Socialist utopia to the ahistorical future of *Nick.* But the structural resemblance is no mere coincidence. Here, Butler's "necessary outside" cannot be figured as a "future horizon." Any "outside" is a danger. Certainly, some of the adversaries that Nick encounters in the course of time can be read as "spectres" of "the excluded." But the horizon for all this is limited: It is progress, time progressing.

If we were to imagine the portrayal of the future horizon as a line, then in Nick's case this line would be a frontier which may be

---

17. Wäscher, quoted in Gerhard Förster, *Das große Hansrudi Wäscher Buch* (Schönau, 1987), 30.

pushed forward further and further but will always remain the central horizon for every one of the hero's actions. In *Weird Fantasy*, on the contrary, and not unlike what we see on a Sunday page of George Herriman from 1918, we could see this horizon line as being hewn, as serving as a bond or appearing as a graphic sign, in short: it would not be *a* horizon, but a *future* horizon.[18]

In other words, *Nick der Weltraumfahrer* can be seen as the shape of a future within the capitalism of a new world order. And it is little wonder that, opposed to this, *Entertaining Comics* were already considered an exception in their own time. *Weird Fantasy* and *Weird Science* bear witness that, soon after the destruction of the European Jews and soon after the dropping of the first atomic bomb on Hiroshima, the future horizon itself seemed to be in danger. For it is on this future horizon that the historical experiences appear *post festum*.

The future horizon cannot be "pushed forward," let alone be "transgressed" in *one* direction: into the future, as *Nick* seems to imply. As a future *horizon* it cannot be transgressed at all if it is to remain opaque: a *future* horizon "as a disruptive site of . . . unrepresentability."[19] This future horizon *Weird Science* and *Weird Fantasy* try to recover whenever new aliens make their appearance and start to dispute male white humankind's central place in space. It is always a different history, a different possibility of history which appears on this horizon. And it is only on this horizon that history appears at all. To do the specter-like aliens of *Weird Fantasy* justice by means of *Weird Science* also means to refigure the outside as a future horizon, i.e., to wait for it as a site of experience, "a waiting without horizon of expectation."[20]

Maybe this is too weak a hope for some, being too distant from what "humans like us" in future may expect from the future. However, it should be kept in mind that in view of the dominant concept of history as a "stream of time"[21] – a stream which seems

---

18. Patrick McDonnell, Karen O'Conell, and Georgia Riley de Havenon, eds., *Krazy Kat. The Art of George Herriman* (New York, 1986), 134.

19. Butler, *Bodies that Matter*, 53.

20. Derrida, *The Specters of Marx*, 168.

21. Ricœur, *Das Rätsel der Vergangenheit*, 86.

to flow faster under the conditions of the new world order – this "weak messianic hope" has assumed new importance. If *Entertaining Comics* reflect the future horizon and thus develop the potential of standardized comics for such a reflection, then, as a strategy against ahistoricity, this could contribute more to a necessary politicization of the future than may at first glance be imagined.

A Note on Entertaining Comics

The following *EC stories* are mentioned, nearly all written by Al Feldstein and William Gaines:

The Aliens In: *Weird Fantasy* no. 17, November/December 1952. Drawn by Al Williamson.
The Exile! In: *Weird Fantasy* no. 14, July/August 1952. Drawn by Wally Wood.
The Green Thing! In: *Weird Fantasy* no. 16, September/October 1952. Drawn by Joe Orlando
A New Beginning In: *Weird Science* no. 1, May/June 1950. Drawn by Al Williamson.
Mass Meeting! In: *Weird Fantasy* no. 16, September/October 1952. Drawn by Joe Orlando.
What He Saw! In: *Weird Fantasy* no. 16, September/October 1952. Drawn by Jack Kamen.

2
Ecology and Epocalypse*

Susan Strasser

Behold, the day of the Lord cometh, cruel both with wrath and fierce anger, to lay the land desolate.

Isaiah, 13:9

One must probably find the humility to admit that the time of one's own life is not the one-time, basic, revolutionary moment of history, from which everything begins and is completed. At the same time humility is needed to say without solemnity that the present time is rather exciting and demands an analysis.

Michel Foucault[1]

Daedalus was trapped on Crete with his son. There being no escape by land or sea, this talented inventor and designer therefore contemplated the sky and "turned his thinking," Ovid tells us, "toward unknown arts, changing the laws of nature." The poet goes on to describe the wings made of feathers fastened with twine and wax, the instructions to the boy ("No fancy steering . . . Follow my lead!"), the pleasure he took in flying, and his bare arms flapping up and down after the wax melted. "And Daedalus, / Father no more," the story ends, "saw the wings on the waves, and cursed his talents."[2]

I learned this myth as the story of Icarus, a cautionary tale for potential daredevils. In contemplating it alongside American

*Thanks to Bob Guldin, Phyllis Palmer, and Ann Romines for helpful readings of this piece.

1. Michel Foucault, "How Much Does It Cost for Reason to Tell the Truth?" in Sylvere Lotringer, ed., *Foucault Live*, trans. Mia Foret and Marion Martius, (New York, 1989), 251, quoted in Lee Quinby, *Anti-Apocalypse: Exercises in Genealogical Criticism* (Minneapolis, MN, 1994), 31.

2. Ovid, *Metamorphoses*, trans. Rolfe Humphries, in F.R.B. Godolphin, ed., *Great Classical Myths* (New York, 1964), 267–268.

speculation on the environmental future, I have returned to Ovid and discovered his focus on the father. Like the apocalyptic worldview that influences popular American environmental discourse about the dangers of useful, effective technologies, the myth warns about the hazards of killing our descendants by using our technological virtuosity to transcend burdensome limits. But unlike the warnings of prophets in both Old Testament and New, the Daedalus story emphasizes the consequences of human endeavor: No gods show up to cause trouble or intercede in human affairs. It may serve to suggest that the history of the stress that humans have exerted on the biosphere over the past two centuries through industrialization and the creation of a mass consumer market can be better analyzed from a non-apocalyptic stance.

Concepts of technologically induced eco-apocalypse are at least partly grounded in the literature of the American environmental movement, which offers some classic apocalyptic titles that have served as major texts for this essay: Rachel Carson's *Silent Spring* (1962), Paul Ehrlich's *The Population Bomb* (1968), Barry Commoner's *The Closing Circle* (1971), Jonathan Schell's *The Fate of the Earth* (1982), and Bill McKibben's *The End of Nature* (1989). These are not necessarily the most influential or representative books of the American environmental movement; a list of those would have to include as well such wilderness meditations and portraits of American landscape as Aldo Leopold's *A Sand County Almanac*, Edward Abbey's *Desert Solitaire*, and the classic nineteenth-century writings of Henry David Thoreau and John Muir. But the apocalyptically titled books are the ones that have outlined for liberal general audiences – all but *The Population Bomb* appeared first in *The New Yorker* – the contemporary predicaments facing the global environment, and the tasks confronting any environmental movement.

The titles of these books have structured considerable public discourse, yet apocalyptic titles do not necessarily characterize apocalyptic books. Marketing departments usually have the final say on titles at American publishers, not the editorial staff, and surely not authors. In fact, these books do not, upon examination, promote a genuinely apocalyptic worldview. They are surely jeremiads, calls to action lest it become too late, and passages in some of the texts echo the tone of the titles. And they do share with apocalyptics a claim to correct understandings of the present; in this sense, their treatment of science may provide an analogy for religion, and scientific writings for books of revelation.

But environmental apocalyptic writing differs essentially from religious millennialism. Environmentalists do not name an antichrist nor regard the reassembling of believers as a precondition for the endtime. Rather than looking for a place of refuge, they declare that there will be no refuge. And anticipation of the endtime is not mingled with a belief in salvation: catastrophe is itself the final event. Although a few "deep ecologists" suggest that the earth will be better off without human beings after we perish by our own hand, most environmentalists – and certainly these authors – would prefer not to see their most dire predictions come true.[3]

Rachel Carson's *Silent Spring* – the best known and most influential of these books – is an argument against the use of pesticides, especially DDT, based on research in sources as diverse as sport fishing magazines, government reports, and medical and scientific journals. Carson was already a popular science writer when the book was published; her *The Sea Around Us* (1951) had won the National Book Award, sold more than 2 million copies, and been translated into thirty-two languages.[4] *Silent Spring* begins with a parable, "A Fable for Tomorrow:" A town once in harmony with its verdant surroundings experiences a "strange blight" that kills animals and humans. The birds stop singing, the bees stop pollinating fruit, the vegetation withers. No actual community, Carson explains, has suffered all of these calamities, but each of them has happened somewhere.

The language of Carson's fable echoes Old Testament tales of God wreaking havoc on Israel's enemies, employing lists of plagues

---

3. For raising and clarifying to me the considerations in the preceding two paragraphs I am indebted to my colleagues at the Krefeld conference, especially Grant Wacker and Hartmut Lehmann.

4. Robert Gottleib, "Reconstructing Environmentalism: Complex Movements, Diverse Roots," *Environmental History Review* 17 (Winter, 1993), 11.

and biblical quotation: "mysterious maladies swept the flocks of chickens," she writes; "the cattle and sheep sickened and died. Everywhere was a shadow of death."[5] But in the introduction to *Silent Spring*, misfortune issues from "some evil spell" rather than from God – an evil to be scientifically described and passionately denounced in the course of the book. Carson turns in the next chapter to language more suggestive of the *Communist Manifesto* than of the Bible: "The history of life on earth," she declares, "has been a history of interaction between living things and their surroundings."[6] She changes then from storyteller to crusading science reporter, offering an ardent exposition of technical subjects that established her influence over both the form and content of environmental prophecy. Indeed, all the other books pay homage to Carson, less by mentioning her name than by frequently citing the dangers of pesticides.

Disaster is not predetermined in these books. Each of them is inherently a call to action, intended to inspire political activity. Schell asserts that he went through the considerable hell it must have taken to research and write *The Fate of the Earth* – a graphic, pessimistic essay on nuclear holocaust and an environmental book in the broadest sense – in hopes of lessening the inevitability of such a catastrophe.[7] Ehrlich devotes more than half of *The Population Bomb* to chapters entitled "What Is Being Done?", "What Needs To Be Done?", and "What Can You Do?" The last of these supplies activists with sample letters to policymakers, strategies for organizing action groups, and advice for "proselytizing friends and associates." The books do alert readers to alarming futures, but they are not the results of God's long-term plans. Instead, the authors insist, the problems that establish a basis for their dire projections have emerged suddenly and quite recently as a result of human behavior in the twentieth century. Commoner insists "that the world is being carried to the brink of ecological disaster not by a singular fault, which some clever scheme can correct, but by the phalanx of powerful

---

5. Rachel Carson, *Silent Spring* (1962; Boston, MA, 1994), 2.
6. Ibid., 5.
7. Jonathan Schell, *The Fate of the Earth* (New York, 1982).

economic, political, and social forces that constitute the march of history."[8] McKibben echoes Carson, who wrote decades earlier that the human capacity to alter the natural world had "not only increased to one of disturbing magnitude but it has changed in character."[9]

Apocalyptic thinking offers individuals and groups a way to think about the Big Picture, to confront death and eternity, to ask about the meaning of human life. These books raise such questions in part by asserting that environmental issues are too big for human comprehension. "The many consequences of a global warming," writes McKibben, "are so big we literally can't understand them." Our attempts to do so by computer modeling, he explains, have a high potential for error because the phenomena are so complex.[10] Commoner, trained as a biologist, similarly regards environmental systems as too intricate for science, which reduces phenomena to simple, isolated events; even the study of ecology, he demonstrates, must be linked with an understanding of social phenomena.[11] Schell describes the earth epistemologically as "a special object. . . . We cannot run experiments with the earth, because we have only one earth, on which we depend for our survival." Whereas the Heisenberg uncertainty principle explains that observations interfere with phenomena under study, here the phenomena would interfere with the observers. "Our uncertainty is forced on us not so much by the limitations of our intellectual ability as by the irreducible fact that we have no platform for observation except our mortal frames."[12]

By limiting their questions to the simple models Commoner criticizes, natural scientists can make predictions and run experiments to test them. More expansive forecasts are generally the province of religion, astrology, futurism, and fiction, and while some religious and artistic practitioners may be strikingly prescient, most fail to generate descriptions of the future that prove reliable. Apocalyptic

8. Barry Commoner, *The Closing Circle: Nature, Man, and Technology* (New York, 1971), 300.

9. Carson, *Silent Spring*, 5–6.

10. Bill McKibben, *The End of Nature* (New York, 1989), 117, 124.

11. Commoner, *Closing Circle*, 21.

12. Schell, *Fate of the Earth*, 76–77.

writing inherently entails the pitfalls of prediction. Even with solid projections, the sky might not fall precisely as expected, and, to the best of our knowledge, Jesus has not yet shown up on the prophesied dates. To historians trained to rely on evidence, the hazards are obvious: Prognostication can only be based on guesses, dreams, fears, calculations, or projections. Show us the documents. Indeed, daily experience suggests that even the short-run future is uncertain in its details; we cannot tell what will happen on the Asian stock markets, nor project which celebrity will do what to initiate the big media *contretemps* that will supersede Monica or OJ. Dire predictions about the conditions of life generations from now will certainly not be accurate in their details.

Reading Paul Ehrlich's *The Population Bomb* thirty years after publication suggests how rickety the project of prediction can be, in part because more than any of the rest of these writers, he phrased his forecasts as predictions rather than warnings. His projections of widespread starvation and malnutrition ring true, but most of the particulars have not been borne out; his discussion of viruses, written long before AIDS was identified, seems prescient but features a virulent flu.[13] More importantly, even while Ehrlich promoted political activity in the interest of staving off the population crisis, his projections did not – indeed, could not – encompass the wide range of potential human activity. In a discussion of Costa Rica's high birth and low death rates, for example, he asked where the food would come from to feed a population projected to double during the following fourteen years. He did not foresee the development of eco-tourism, which may be regarded as evidence of the enormous ingenuity of human beings at creating new commodities to trade for food.[14]

To think apocalyptically means to think outside of history, to declare human action beside the point. Ronald Reagan's Secretary of the Interior James Watt was once said to have proclaimed that because the Second Coming was imminent and earthly fears were soon to become meaningless, concern about the environment was

13. Paul Ehrlich, *The Population Bomb*, (San Francisco, CA, 1969), 61.
14. Ibid., 22.

irrelevant. In contrast, some of the predictions in these books are now inaccurate because they *did* inspire human action. In the United States, some of the most egregious environmental predicaments have been turned around during the last three decades by changes in public policy: Fish once again live in Lake Erie, smog has decreased in Los Angeles. The ban on DDT is the most important testimonial to Rachel Carson's work. In that sense, even predictions whose inaccuracy we may identify with hindsight do not invalidate these books.

Bill McKibben's *The End of Nature* is less a prognostication than a lament. The disaster of his title, he explains, has already occurred. "When I say 'nature,' I mean a certain set of human ideas about the world and our place in it," McKibben writes, "our sense of nature as eternal and separate." Humans once had to adapt themselves to nature's rules, and the environmental damage they inflicted was akin to "stabbing a man with toothpicks." Now, he points out, pollution is global in nature, not local; the book emphasizes greenhouse gases, global warming, and their effects on the weather. "The *meaning* of the wind, the sun, the rain – of nature – has already changed," McKibben insists. Photosynthesis, respiration, growth and decay continue, but he argues that the very definition of nature once entailed the independence of natural processes from human ones. Nature once offered its own arguments against apocalyptic thinking; a world that took eons to develop did not seem likely to end in a day. Nature was powerful, not endangered and in need of protection.[15]

Some ecologists who study managed forests and fisheries believe that managerial institutions make intervention decisions based on four distinct "myths of nature." Natural processes are regarded as always forgiving, returning to equilibrium; as forgiving of most events but vulnerable to unusual occurrences; as capricious and random; or as ephemeral, vulnerable to catastrophe.[16] In contrast, these writers argue that the very concept of "managing" nature is fundamental to the potential for catastrophe. "The 'control of

---

15. McKibben, *End of Nature*, 8, 48, 64, 147.

16. Michael Schwarz and Michael Thompson, *Divided We Stand: Redefining Politics, Technology and Social Choice* (Philadelphia, PA, 1990), 4–5.

nature,'" writes Carson in her final paragraph, "is a phrase conceived in arrogance, born of the Neanderthal age of biology and philosophy, when it was supposed that nature exists for the convenience of man."[17] Citing historian Lynn White, Ehrlich argues that technology, natural science, and Christian theology met in the creation of this human-centered stance, replacing cyclical time and pagan animism with linear time and "indifference to the feelings of natural objects."[18]

Modern science and technology, Commoner explains, has "enticed" Western societies "into a nearly fatal illusion: that through our machines we have at last escaped from dependence on the natural environment."[19] Indeed, as philosopher Thomas F. Tierney proposes, even the fundamental biological needs of the body are understood as limits in the modern world: "inconveniences, obstacles, or annoyances" that impinge on time. The products of modern technology, Tierney asserts, appeal to consumers because they alleviate inconvenience by enabling people to satisfy bodily needs in as little time as possible.[20] Alienated from our bodies, how can human beings connect to the earth?

Yet for all the dangers technology represents, it has also been a source of abundance and comfort. It may bring on disaster or deliver humankind from its burdens. And it may do both.[21] As in the story of Daedalus, the generations that invented the internal combustion engine and DDT enjoyed their benefits without dying from their hazards; the eco-apocalyptics forecast disasters caused by *successful* technology. Pointing to the rise in pollution levels after World War II, Commoner insists that the production of the very things that have made American daily life convenient and abundant – agribusiness, pesticides, detergents, synthetic fibers, and automobiles – have come to imperil it, as have increasing population and nuclear

17. Carson, *Silent Spring*, 297.

18. Ehrlich, *Population Bomb*, 151–153.

19. Commoner, *Closing Circle*, 15.

20. Thomas F. Tierney, *The Value of Convenience: A Genealogy of Technical Culture* (Albany, NY, 1993), 6, 30, 36.

21. For the double-edged nature of technological apocalypse, see Quinby, *Anti-Apocalypse*, xvi–xix.

technologies. "Unwittingly," Commoner writes, "we have created for ourselves a new and dangerous world. We would be wise to move through it as though our lives were at stake."[22]

Commoner suggests that an understanding of global ecology is central to any solution. He explains that the ecosphere – "the home that life has built for itself on the planet's outer surface" – must support human activity, for we do indeed live in our bodies. Yet the wastes that human beings have produced in recent years go beyond toxicity and contamination; they provide "evidence that the ecosphere is being driven towards collapse." In simple language that echoes the popular culture of the day, he explains the "laws of ecology": "Everything Is Connected to Everything Else," "Everything Must Go Somewhere," "Nature Knows Best," and "There is No Such Thing as a Free Lunch."[23] Since Commoner wrote, many ecologists have adopted the "Gaia hypothesis," which expands the concept of the "ecosphere" or "biosphere" into an assertion that Earth is itself alive, a unified network of living organisms, "a total planetary being."[24] As human damage to the environment went from local to global during the twentieth century, so also did environmental theory.

Social theory that can provide a non-apocalyptic analytic framework for thinking about the environment has begun to develop. Some business analysts and engineers, calling themselves "industrial ecologists," have attempted to incorporate industrial and consumer activity into ecological models and laws. Ironically, they employ the very concept that McKibben laments: the idea that human processes and natural ones are intertwined. Industrial ecology studies both the physical and economic processes whereby raw materials and energy are converted by labor and capital into industrial products

22. Commoner, *Closing Circle*, 140, 144, 231.

23. Ibid., 11–12, 33:34.

24. For an intellectual history of the Gaia hypothesis and an attempt to substitute it for the Darwinian worldview in interpreting a particular historical phenomenon, see Brett Fairbairn, "History from the Ecological Perspective: Gaia Theory and the Problem of Cooperatives in Turn-of-the-Century Germany," *American Historical Review* 99 (October, 1994), 1203–1239.

and waste. It assumes that the flows of materials and energy in industrial endeavors and consumer activities intersect with the processes of the planet – the water, carbon/oxygen, nitrogen, sulfur and other materials cycles – and with the biological cycles of life and death. It insists that human beings are part of industrial ecosystems as well as natural ones. Developing models that specify the basic concepts Commoner proposed, industrial ecologists consider the ways that economic, political, and social factors interact with material and energy flows. And they regard disposal as well as production as part of the "product life cycle" – a process that encompasses extracting raw materials, manufacturing products, distributing and consuming them, and finally disposing of them.[25]

Industrial ecology employs an analogy between the material and energy flows of industrial systems and those of biological ecosystems. The organism eats, processes food, and excretes waste; it lives and dies; its body is a waste product. Sustainable biological ecosystems are in general closed, or cyclical; waste to one part of the system acts as resources to another.[26] In the closed ecological system, waste products become food: The bodies and excrement of one organism nourish its neighbor. In contrast, industrial cycles are open. "In other words," writes one industrial ecologist, "the industrial system does *not* generally recycle its nutrients. Rather, the industrial system starts with high-quality materials (fossil fuels, ores) extracted from the earth, and returns them to nature in degraded form."[27]

Throughout human history, urban households have taken in material produced by others, and have excreted waste. Visitors to ancient sites can see the stepping stones that kept its citizens clean as they traversed the garbage-filled streets, and the material remains of drains and other disposal strategies. Even otherwise self-sufficient

25. Christine Meisner Rosen, "Industrial Ecology and the Greening of Business History," *Business and Economic History* 26 (Fall, 1997), 123–137; Braden R. Allenby and Deanna J. Richards, eds., *The Greening of Industrial Ecosystems* (Washington, DC, 1994), v.

26. T.E. Graedel, B.R. Allenby, and P.B. Linhart, "Implementing Industrial Ecology," *IEEE Technology and Society Magazine* (Spring, 1993), 19.

27. Robert U. Ayres, "Industrial Metabolism: Theory and Policy," in Allenby and Richards, eds., *Greening of Industrial Ecosystems*, 25.

farmers have bought or traded for salt and the wares of craftspeople, and created dumps on their property for broken pottery, glass, and other trash that would neither decompose nor serve as animal feed. But until quite recently in the developed world, households have also behaved like closed systems: The table scraps fed the dog, Dad's torn trousers provided the material for Junior's new ones. Before the twentieth century, cities, too, were systems that incorporated ragpickers, swill children, and street pigs to use the detritus of others. Compare the twenty-first-century household – procuring goods from factories, mending little, bagging the detritus in plastic and placing it at the curb for transport to the landfill or incinerator. Or the twenty-first-century city, taking in most of what it uses along highways and from airplanes, and flushing its waste into landfills and toxic dumps.[28]

 Business historian Christine Meisner Rosen suggests that industrial ecology provides a model for weaving business history into the history of the environment.[29] Taking a cue from Brett Fairbairn's imaginative use of the Gaia hypothesis to model historical investigation, I suggest that this may help develop histories of industry and the biosphere that model human societies as complex systems rather than as mechanisms.[30] Environmental historians have begun this project with style and imagination.[31] Their work demonstrates as well that processes modeled on natural ones must be related to such longstanding categories of historical inquiry as class dynamics and cultural values. It describes the globalization of problems once localized. And it points toward a non-apocalyptic approach to the environmental future.

 What do we mean when we forecast the end of the world? The end of human life? The end of progress as it has been defined over the past quarter-millennium? Schell complains that Soviet and American Cold War leaders were imprecise about nuclear catas-

---

28. See my *Waste and Want: A Social History of Trash* (New York, 1999).
29. Rosen, "Industrial Ecology," 125.
30. See Fairbairn, "History from the Ecological Perspective."
31. See especially the work of William Cronon, as well as that of Andrew Hurley, Theodore Steinberg, Joel Tarr, and Donald Worster.

trophe, mentioning "a variety of different outcomes, including the annihilation of the belligerent nations, the destruction of 'human civilization,' the extinction of mankind, and the extinction of life on earth . . . in loose rhetorical fashion, more or less interchangeably."[32] In an attempt to be more precise about the results of a major nuclear attack on the United States, he emphasizes that even nuclear devastation – the ultimate in environmental disaster – might or might not destroy human life and that of many other species, but would probably not mean the end of all species. Instead, it would recall "early geological times, when, in response to natural catastrophes whose nature has not been determined, sudden mass extinctions of species and whole ecosystems occurred all over the earth . . . it appears that at the outset the United States would be a republic of insects and grass."[33] Nuclear holocaust and ecological disaster do not mean the end of time – that incomprehensible concept of millennialism – but rather of life as we know it, of our civilization and perhaps of our species, and even of most species, but not necessarily of all species.

This is not to suggest that the world will end with a whimper instead of a bang, to rephrase T. S. Eliot. Science writer David Quammen has recently argued that "we're headed into another mass extinction" commensurate with five previous ones, of which the most recent and best known did in the dinosaurs, along with three-quarters of all other species. But he points out that *homo sapiens* will not necessarily be one of the victims. While many species are disappearing as a result of human environmental degradation, others are thriving, individuals living longer and populations multiplying. These are weeds in the biological sense: they adapt easily to a wide range of habitats, they reproduce quickly, and they succeed in disturbed ecosystems. Quammen points to a number of such weedy species: fire ants, zebra mussels, kudzu, Mediterranean fruit flies – and us. We will probably not merely survive, he asserts; we will multiply, but as we do, the quality of life will decline for ever-greater

32. Schell, *Fate of the Earth*, 6.
33. Ibid., 64–65.

proportions of us. Like the earlier writers, he warns that any solution will have to entail abandoning the tendency to regard "the environment" as a backdrop for human activity.[34]

The good news is that there won't be a bang, a single event that kills our children, leaving only feathers on the waves. Unlike fears of the Y2K computer bug and the predictions fostered by millennial cults, global environmental problems will probably not come to a head at some precisely describable moment of disaster. The process will probably be full of steps forward as well as back. The near future probably entails the inexorable degradation of water, air, and soil for ever-increasing numbers of people, but human action and human ingenuity are fundamental sources for optimism that the endtime is not upon us. The environmental history of urban-industrial life is full of examples of human resourcefulness and positive change: the creation of the technological systems that have enabled concentrated human populations to survive in a wide range of climates, the triumph of political processes being brought to bear on polluters.

In the short run, businesses prosper from eco-apocalyptic warnings, selling smokestack scrubbers, catalytic converters, and prophetic books. But things may have to get worse before they get better. If *homo sapiens* is to survive the global extinction we are engendering, let alone enjoy abundance and comfort in large numbers, we may first have to experience something akin to what the promoters of proletarian uprising used to call the crisis of capitalism. Despite the best efforts of environmental activists and the extraordinary force of entrepreneurial inventiveness, decision-making about production based on stockholders' short-run profits may not avert the course of environmental degradation now apparent in global deforestation and climate change. By this interpretation, Rachel Carson's "interaction between living things and their surroundings" indeed supplants the class struggle of that other manifesto as the driving force in history.[35]

---

34. David Quammen, "Planet of Weeds," *Harper's* (October, 1998), 58.

35. See Joni Seager, *Earth Follies: Coming to Feminist Terms with the Global Environmental Crisis* (New York, 1993), 3.

Historians know that nothing is eternal; our central message is that things change. One day, one way or another, even the automobile will be obsolete – or, in the current American idiom, "history." Nor will contemporary economic theory live forever. What we cannot predict is whether they will be superseded by technologies and organizing principles that will sustain life on this planet, or merely by new gadgets made of wax and feathers.

3

"Dad, are you there? Come back": Gender and the Narrative of Science Fiction

Susan Winnet

Elaine Steinmann (1943–1999), in memoriam.

> "Some place where there isn't any trouble. Do you think there is such a place, Toto? There must be. Not a place that you could get to by a boat or a train. It's far, far away – behind the moon, beyond the rain."

I

"There's no place like home. . ."

In the 1939 film, *The Wizard of Oz*, Dorothy (Judy Garland) misses her chance to return to Kansas with the Wizard when she jumps out of the basket of his hot-air balloon in pursuit of her dog, Toto. Almost a half a century later, in *Alien* (1979) and *Aliens* (1986) – two films we'd not be likely to mention in the same breath as *The Wizard of Oz,* but which seem determined to make us do so – Ripley (Sigourney Weaver) risks missing the take-off of her spacecraft and being vanquished by the alien in order to rescue her cat (in the first film) and the little girl, Newt (in the second). In the 1997 film version of Carl Sagan's novel, *Contact*, Ellie Arroway's (Jodie Foster's) transit from Earth to Vega recalls the passage in *The Wizard of Oz* in which the cyclone carries Dorothy's house from Kansas to the Land of Oz, and the technicolor landscape of Vega directly recalls the texture of the scene that greets Dorothy upon landing in Munchkinland. An orphan like Dorothy, Ellie has "wished upon a star" and struggles against the scientific and political powers that be for the opportunity to journey to Vega and wake up "where the clouds are far behind me."[1] Like Dorothy's confrontation with Oz, the reunion with the projection of her father that marks her brief sojourn on Vega gives her nothing but what she brought with her. Like both Ripley and Ellie, Dorothy never knows whether her journey is a dream or a nightmare, and discovers that "home" is the ultimate test of whatever it was that she sought "beyond the rainbow," although unlike Ripley and Ellie, Dorothy returns home more docile and compliant than she was when she left. Finally, all three films force us to evaluate critically the structures of authority in the worlds in which these women's adventures take place; in each film, the curtain is pulled back – literally in *The Wizard of Oz*, more figuratively in *Contact* and the *Alien* films – to expose male embodiments of authoritative science as, at best, lovable but incompetent mountebanks, and, at worst, evil, calculating misusers of knowledge and power.

It's important to emphasize here that the *Alien* films and *Contact* invoke *The Wizard of Oz* to vastly different ends; the earthly resolution of Ellie Arroway's adventure in outer space stands in stark constrast to the entirely dysphoric sense of menace unconquered that marks each of Ripley's adventures and ensures that she never returns to earth (even the adventure in *Alien* that would seem to have been drawn to an inescapable conclusion by Ripley's death is haunted by what the title of the fourth *Alien* film makes explicit: "Resurrection"). I make the connection between "adult" science fiction and "children's" fantasy at the outset of this essay in order to point to their ideological affinities; the former "cites"

---

1. Carl Sagan's novel, *Contact*, invokes *The Wizard of Oz* directly: Ellie's admiration for her mentor, Valerian's "thinking about extraterrestrial intelligence" is described as being "like entering Wonderland or the Emerald City" (Carl Sagan, *Contact* [New York, 1997]), 29, and the death of her other, ambivalent mentor Drumlin, when the Machine is sabotaged, is described as follows: "Suddenly Drumlin was in the air, flying. Everything else seemed to be flying, too. It reminded her of the tornado that had carried Dorothy to Oz" (ibid., 267). And finally, as Ellie sits in the Machine waiting for it to "take off," she is described as a "wonder junkie . . . Dorothy catching her first glimpse of the vaulted spires of the Emerald City" (ibid., 323).

the latter in order to demystify sophisticated science's aura, to suggest a continuum between some aspects of its claims to authority and the hocus-pocus effects of a self-confessed "humbug." All three films foreground the negotiations of a female protagonist with a world where some form of science – or, in *The Wizard*, the appearance of science – and its power are conspicuous, and suggest that this power is grounded less in the authority of science than in the will to power of its practitioners. Moreover, the efficacy of this will to power seems directly connected to the marginalization, within these worlds, of both women and what is often called the "female principle." As the feminist science fiction writer Ursula K. LeGuin has written:

> The "female principle" has historically been anarchic; that is, anarchy has historically been identified as female. The domain allotted to women – "the family," for example – is the area of order without coercion, rule by custom not by force. Men have reserved the structures of social power to themselves (and those few women whom they admit to it on male terms, such as queens, prime ministers); men make the wars and peace, men make, enforce, and break the laws.[2]

The world of science has done its best to police itself against both the "feminine" and "females." Like so many other domains where knowledge and power are at stake, it has endorsed a view of the human (traditionally called "man") that needs to posit "femininity" (and women) as the negative "other" on which it constructs its own "positive" plot of development. Until recently, the "gender" of science was unreflectingly male; what has happened in the last several decades is not that this "gender" has shifted, but that the presuppositions underwriting this gendering have begun to be interrogated.

Science fiction as a genre was long considered as masculine a domain as science itself, although there is an illustrious, if not

---

2. Ursula K. LeGuin, "Is Gender Necessary? Redux," in *Dancing at the Edge of the World* (London, 1989), 11. Subsequent references will be given in parentheses in the text (IGN).

long, tradition of female novelists who have written science fiction, sometimes under a male pseudonym.[3] Since the 1960s, however, women have become more numerous and more prominent within the community of science fiction writers, and gender has become a more prominent concern in the works of both male and female writers. Joanna Russ, who is both a writer of science fiction and a literary critic, sees science fiction as one of the few literary genres in which serious speculation about gender can be carried out, since it can project "myths that have nothing to do with our accepted gender roles": "The myths of science fiction run along the lines of exploring a new world conceptually (not necessarily physically), creating needed physical or social machinery, assessing the consequences of technological or other changes, and so on."[4] The freedom from the constraints of the realistic, the *vraisemblable*, enables the novelist to present what Marleen S. Barr has described as "blueprints for social structures that allow women's words to counter patriarchal myths."[5] In a world "radically discontinuous from the patriarchal one we know"[6] the constitutive myths of patriarchy can be critically evaluated, exposed, and, ideally, rewritten. Thus, such "other worlds" as Russ' Whileaway (*The Female Man*), Marge Piercy's Mattapoisett (*Woman on the Edge of Time*) and Tikva (*He, She, and It*), and the satellite-like "ship" in which Octavia Butler's Oankali nurture the survivors of earth's holocaust (*Dawn*) make it possible to imagine worlds in

3. Marleen S. Barr has complied a valuable bibliography of feminist science fiction and science fiction written by women in *Alien to Femininity: Speculative Fiction and Feminist Theory* (New York, Westport, CT, and London, 1984)."A Guide to Feminist Science Fiction Resources in Print and on the Net" (www.swarthmore.edu/library hwhippl1/rg.print.hmtl) and "Lousisiana State University Law Library – Women's Rights and Women's Images in Science Fiction" (*www.lsu.edu/guests/wwwlawl/biblio/womenscifi.htm*) are both useful for updating Barr's bibliography.

4. Joanna Russ, "What Can a Heroine Do? or Why Women Can't Write," in *To Write Like a Woman: Essays in Feminism and Science Fiction* (Bloomington and Indianapolis, IN, 1995), 90–91.

5. Marleen S. Barr, *Lost in Space: Probing Feminist Science Fiction and Beyond* (Chapel Hill, NC, and London, 1993), 7.

6. Ibid., 11.

which women live without men or where gender relations are subject to laws other than the ones with which we are familiar. The projection of such alternative realities, Sara Lefanu summarizes,

> lets writers defamiliarize the familiar, and make familiar the new and strange. These twin possibilities, apparently contradictory (but SF is full of contradictions), offer enormous scope to women writers who are thus released from the constraints of realism. The social and sexual hierarchies of the contemporary world can be examined through the process of "estrangement," thus challenging normative ideas of gender roles; and visions of different worlds can be created, made familiar to the reader through the process of narrative.[7]

Yet, it is this process of "familiarization" through narrative that works against the challenge to "normative ideas of gender roles" that feminist science fiction seeks to pose. The gender biases of science fiction are difficult to overcome because of the traditional gender ideology of science on the one hand, and the equally tenacious gender ideology of fiction, on the other hand. This discussion will focus particularly on the "fiction" part of "science fiction," and, more precisely, on the properties of narrative that undermine science fiction's attempts at experimentation with gender. If we consider, for instance, the gender ideology of the narrative of *The Wizard of Oz*, we are forced to read the citations of it in late twentieth-century gynocentric science fiction as being profoundly ironic. The suggestion that Dorothy's journey to, through, and from Oz is some kind of a pre-text for the adventures of Ripley and Ellie Arroway is a challenge and a warning: Although Dorothy's *adventure* is absorbing and substantial, her *plot* is limited and conventional; her dream of escaping the monotonous and oppressive world of Kansas is "corrected," upon her arrival in Munchkinland, by the ardent desire, repeated throughout her sojourn in Oz, to return home as quickly as possible. The lesson she learns from the good witch, Glinda, is that she could have gone home whenever she wanted; she needed

---

7. Sara Lefanu, *Feminism and Science Fiction* (Bloomington and Indianapolis, IN, 1989), 21–22.

only to recognize her real desire. If, for the viewer, the film's yield lies in Dorothy's adventures – her confrontation with a world so unlike "Kansas," her ability to share her intelligence, heart, and courage with the companions she meets along the way, her vanquishing of two wicked witches, and her debunking of the Wizard – for Dorothy, the trip to Oz serves to teach her that adventure is not what she really wants. Far from being a test of her mettle, the sojourn in Oz has shown her the self-indulgent vanity of her technicolor dreams. (This point is underscored in the film where the population of Dorothy's Kansas world – the three farmhands, the nasty neighbor, and the mountebank – reappears in the Oz sequence in the guise of the Scarecrow, the Tin Man, the Lion, the Wicked Witch, and the Wizard. The trajectory of Dorothy's plot could be summarized by Freud's observation that, "Die Objektfindung ist eigentlich eine Wieder-findung" ["The discovery of the object is actually a rediscovery"].[8])

If the grand tableaux of the *Alien* films and *Contact* invoke as a generic predecessor the adventures of a girl from Kansas and her dog in a world of Munchkins, scarecrows, tin men, cowardly lions, good and wicked witches, and mountebank wizards, they must be taking a fairly critical position vis-à-vis the grandiose claims of science, on the one hand, and the chances of a woman's having anything other than an adolescent, fairy-tale relation to the structures of power, on the other hand.[9] Like Dorothy's leap from the balloon to pursue Toto, Ripley's rescue of the cat and the little girl suggests other priorities that *could* yield other (kinds of) plots or seriously and compellingly complicate existing ones. These are truncated, however, by the thrust of the plot that gets them back on track in the nick of time.[10] Much as the *Alien* films suggest

8. Sigmund Freud, "Drei Abhandlungen zur Sexualtheorie," *Studienausgabe* V (Frankfurt a.M., 1982), 126.

9. The *Alien* quartet's hostility to science is borne out by John Thomson's contention that "Alien and its successors are sci-fi films that grow to loathe and fear science" (John Thomson, *The "Alien" Quartet* [London, 1998], 34).

10. Although these films, like so many science fiction texts, suggest possibilities for dislodging the gender-identifications that so cripple our culture, the stories they end up telling fail to pursue these possibilities. Short science fiction, which is

the possibility in the saga of Ripley of a woman's story that remains unpursued, the critical yield of both gynocentric science fiction (which deals with a female protagonist and her concerns but need not be feminist) and feminist science fiction (which scrutinizes gender relations in patriarchy but need not deal with a female protagonist) seems limited by the constraints of a conventional narrative trajectory that reinforces the gender ideologies that are being dismantled thematically.

In order to examine the functioning of gender in science fiction narrative, and not simply the possibilities and limitations afforded to its female protagonists, I will now turn first to a (too) brief overview of the theoretical framework in which I consider the issue of narrative and gender and then to a discussion of three science fiction texts that raise and/or address this issue in very different ways: *The Left Hand of Darkness*, Ursula K. LeGuin's classic novel of a genderless society; *Galatea 2.2*, Richard Powers' post-modern narrative of a computer that masters the Great Books; and *Contact*, Robert Zemeckis' film about a female astrophysicist in search of extraterrestrial civilization. My readings of these texts demonstrate how difficult it is, with all the technology in the world and all the freedom to rewrite the world according only to the dictates of the imagination, to imagine plots that deviate significantly and productively from what Peter Brooks has called the "master-plot" that has prescribed the plot of individual development and its relation to knowledge and power in Western culture.

II

"Follow the yellow brick road . . ."

In his by now classic study of narrative, *Reading for the Plot* (1984), Brooks writes that "ambition provides not only a typical novelistic theme, but also a dominant dynamic of plot: a force that drives

---

not dependent on plot for its denouement but tends rather to present a situation or phenomenon in a way that provokes meditation rather than resolution, is being far more radical in its challenge to gender norms.

the protagonist forward, assuring that no incident or action is final or closed in itself until such a moment as the ends of ambition have been clarified, through success or else renunciation."[11] This notion of a narrative trajectory set in motion by ambition seems to be limited, as Brooks himself recognizes, to "male plots," and he sees the "female plot" as taking "a more complex stance toward ambition, the formation of an inner drive toward the assertion of selfhood in resistance to the overt and violating male plots of ambition, a counter-dynamic which . . . is only superficially passive."[12] Traditionally, as Rachel Blau DuPlessis points out, the "end, the rightful end, of women in novels was social – successful courtship, marriage – or judgmental of her sexual and social failure – death."[13] Since romance's traditional repertoire of rewards and punishments is clearly out of place in the world in which science fiction's protagonists – male and female – operate, it seems necessary to look beyond both Brooks' notion of a critical "inner drive" defined a priori in resistance to male plots of ambition and the romance plot DuPlessis sees as (de)limiting the sphere of female experience prior to the twentieth century – both of which locate the woman protagonist's story within the context of personalized romantic/erotic experience. The "male" plots of which Brooks writes depend upon sublimation, through which erotic drives are "translated" into other forms of ambition that can seek fulfillment within the social, political, and scientific institutions that we so often call "the world."[14] Because, however, the institutions of this "world" are structured to accommodate

11. Peter Brooks, *Reading for the Plot* (New York, 1984), 39.

12. Ibid., 39. For feminist critiques of Brooks' narratology, see Susan Winnett, "Coming Unstrung: Women, Men, Narrative, and Principles of Pleasure," *PMLA* 105 (1990), 505–518 and Marianne Hirsch, "Ideology, Form, and 'Allerleirauh': Reflections on *Reading for the Plot*," *Children's Literature* 14 (1986), 163–168.

13. Rachel Blau DuPlessis, *Writing beyond the Ending: Narrative Strategies of Twentieth-Century Women Writers* (Bloomington, IN, 1985), 1.

14. In his "Drei Abhandlungen zur Sexualtheorie," Freud describes sublimation as an "Ablenkung sexueller Triebkraefte von sexuellen Zielen und Hinlenkung auf neue Ziele" from which "maechtige Komponenten fuer alle kulturellen Leistungen" can be gained. Freud, "Drei Abhandlungen," 85.

and enforce the male plot of ambition, the narrative possibilities for a female protagonist who claims the same capacities to sublimate as a male are limited to either a truncated (Brooks's variant) or "drag" version of what many students of narrative – feminist and not – identify as the "Oedipal" plot.

When Freud called the story of Oedipus "the poetic working through of what is typical in the relations between parents and children,"[15] he did not *choose* against giving women a story of their own, although it should be clear that the story of a man, a king, a slayer of his father and marrier of his mother, leaves very little place for consideration of what, in a woman's life, could be typical for narrative. Rather, as Teresa de Lauretis reminds us most forcefully, he diagnosed a reality of our culture, in which "*woman*, the other-from-man (nature and Mother, site of sexuality and masculine desire, sign and object of men's social exchange) is the term that designates at once the vanishing point of our culture's fictions of itself and the condition of the discourses in which the fictions are represented"[16] The postulate that the structures of the world so neatly repeat those of the family that the plot of ambition represents nothing more than a projection onto a grand screen of the little boy's negotiations with his mother and father represents a glorious – and, unfortunately oft-proved – piece of chutzpah. It is within this homology that the Oedipal logic of narrative can ensure that the place of the subject is gendered male, regardless of the gender of the figure who assumes this place in a particular narrative. The process that this narrative charts, then, is that of becoming a man – of entering into the negotiations with culture and its institutions that, successfully undertaken, confer manhood. Or, to put it another way: of answering in and through time the riddle of the Sphinx. Hence, the woman who assumes the place

15. "Ich habe an anderer Stelle ausgeführt, wie frühzeitig die sexuelle Attraktion sich zwischen Eltern und Kindern geltend macht, und gezeigt, dass die Oedipusfabel wahrscheinlich als die dichterische Bearbeitung des Typischen an diesen Beziehungen zu verstehen ist" (Sigmund Freud, "Bruchstück einer Hysterie-Analyse," in *Studienausgabe* VI (Frankfurt a.M., 1982), 130.

16. Teresa de Lauretis, *Alice Doesn't: Feminism, Semiotics, Cinema* (Bloomington, IN, 1984), 5.

of a protagonist in narrative is taking – as far as gender is concerned – the wrong test, answering the wrong question. And she is doing so at the expense of what she would probably like to think of as her own female subjectivity, which, according to the logic of narrative, is what must be overcome in order for the story to achieve the kind of meaning-producing ending that Brooks has described. As de Lauretis so persuasively argues:

> The end of the girl's journey, if successful, will bring her to the place where the boy will find her, like Sleeping Beauty, awaiting him, Prince Charming. For the boy has been promised, by the social contract he has entered at his Oedipal phase, that he will find woman waiting at the end of *his* journey. Thus the itinerary of the female's journey, mapped from the very start on the territory of her own body . . . is guided by a compass pointing not to reproduction as the fulfillment of *her* biological destiny, but more exactly to the fulfillment of the promise made to "the little man," of *his* social contract, his biological and affective destiny – and to the fulfillment of his desire. This is what predetermines the positions she must occupy in her journey. The myth of which she is presumed to be the subject, generated by the same mechanism that generated the myth of Oedipus, in fact works to construct *her* as a "personified obstacle". . .[17]

In the past two decades there has been considerable debate as to whether there are, on the one hand, literary works that escape this Oedipal double bind and, on the other hand, non-psycho-analytic paradigms for discussing narrative that do not lead us to such depressing, deterministic conclusions about the relation between gender and plot.[18] There have also been attempts, on the part of science fiction writers, to circumvent the trap of Oedipal narrative and project feminist quests that are not bound up in the dynamics I have sketched. I will return to this issue in section IV of this essay, once I have demonstrated, in my discussion of *The*

17. Ibid., 133.

18. See Margaret Homans, "Feminist Fictions and Feminist Theories of Narrative," *Narrative* 2(1) (January, 1994) for a deft and sensitive critical survey of these positions and their implications.

Left Hand of Darkness, how automatically – even counterintention-
ally – the gendering of narrative as I have described it takes place.

III

"Now I know I'm not in Kansas"

Ursula K. LeGuin's novel *The Left Hand of Darkness* introduces a
world whose inhabitants have no gender: the denizens of the
planet, Gethen, all inhabit the same kinds of sexual bodies, and
are without sexual attributes and desires most of the time. The
Gethenian sexual cycle somewhat resembles the oestrus cycle of
animals, except that it effects all – and not only female – Gethenians.
When Gethenians are not in the sexual phase known as "kemmer,"
they have no gender marking; they are sexually inactive, impotent,
and ambisexual. During kemmer, chemical processes in the body
stimulate it to sexualize:

> In the first phase of kemmer [the individual] remains completely
> androgynous. Gender, and potency, are not attained in isolation . . . Yet
> the sexual impulse is tremendously strong in this phase, controlling the
> entire personality . . . When the individual finds a partner in kemmer,
> hormonal secretion is further stimulated . . . until in one partner either a
> male or female hormonal dominance is established. The genitals engorge
> or shrink accordingly, foreplay intensifies, and the partner, triggered by
> the change, takes on the other sexual role . . . Normal individuals have
> no predisposition to either sexual role in kemmer; they do not know
> whether they will be the male or the female, and have no choice in the
> matter . . . The culminant phase of kemmer lasts from two to five days,
> during which sexual drive and capacity are at a maximum. It ends fairly
> abruptly, and if conception has not taken place, the individual returns to
> the latent phase and the cycle begins anew. If the individual was in the
> female role and was impregnated, hormonal activity of course continues,
> and for the gestation and lactation periods this individual remains female.
> . . . With the cessation of lactation the female becomes once more a
> perfect androgyne. No physiological habit is established, and the mother
> of several children may be the father of several more.[19]

19. Ursula K. LeGuin, *The Left Hand of Darkness* (London, 1997), 73–74.
Subsequent references to this novel will be given in parentheses in the text.

This eradication of gender difference produces a society with an organization substantially different from our own. The relegation of sexual activity to the periods of kemmer has led to the development of institutions to accommodate this discrete phase of human experience: "the structure of their societies, the management of their industry, agriculture, commerce, the size of their settlements, the subjects of their stories, everything is shaped to fit the somer-kemmer cycle. . . . Everything gives way before the recurring torment and festivity of passion" (LHD 75). The fact that, "four-fifths of the time, these people are not sexually motivated at all," and that daily life completely lacks any erotic component makes for the differences that strike us as particularly strange: children's relation to their mothers and fathers are not sexualized relations (and therefore not conceivable according to "Oedipal" developmental schema) since, after birth, the birth-giving parent returns to sexual neutrality. Since both partners in the sexual act must be in kemmer in order for sex to be physically possible, there is no forced sex, or rape.

Psychology as we know it – and Freudian psychology in particular – derives many of its conceptual structures from and in analogy with a sexuality that is constantly in the process of plotting its own satisfaction. Since, in Gethen, sexual fulfillment, so compelling a goal and so probable during kemmer, is a non-issue the rest of the time, a psychological model (such as the Freudian one) based on compensation for and sublimation of sexual energies cannot begin to explain the existence on Gethen of such phenomena as ambition, creativity, love – in short, what we normally regard as the emotional baggage of humankind. What, for example, if not sublimation, motivates creativity? How, if not in reaction to the sundering (through the child's entrance into the symbolic order, the realm of language) of the sexualized mother–child dyad, is the affective life of the individual to be understood?

LeGuin assumes that sexuality as we know it and the gender constructions that ensue from this sexuality are responsible for our social institutions and practices. The male/female binary opposition initiates all the other binaries and structures of oppression in human society:

If we were socially ambisexual, if men and women were completely and genuinely equal in their social roles, equal legally and economically, equal in freedom, in responsibility, in self-esteem, then society would be a very different thing. What our problems might be, God knows; I only know we would have them. But it seems likely that our central problem would not be the one it is now: the problem of exploitation – exploitation of the woman, of the weak, of the earth. . . . The dualism of value that destroys us, the dualism of superior/inferior, ruler/ruled, owner/owned, user/used, might give way to what seems to me, from here, a much healthier, sounder, more promising modality of integration and integrity. (IGN 16)

In addition to the common – but still highly debatable – assumption that chromosomal sexual identity, practiced sexual identity, and gender identity line up neatly, this passage demonstrates another way in which LeGuin's project is limited by the discursive conventions of her socio-historical location. Note the slippage in this passage from talk of the abolishment of gender to a fairly standard discourse of gender equality, from the abolition of binary thinking to its resolution in integration and integrity. I do not think this slippage occurs because LeGuin has lost heart or is weak-minded, but rather, because of the power of the narrative conventions that govern not only our storytelling but also our "scientific" thinking. The search for "solutions" creates – even retroactively – the binary structures that will resolve themselves into "(re)solutions" as we know them. LeGuin's plan is to "eliminate gender; to find out what [is] left" (IGN 10). Her conclusion that "[w]hatever was left would be, presumably, simply human. It would define the area that is shared by men and women alike" presumes, however, that the "human" is thinkable outside of the categories that have constructed it, and that such categories could be peeled away, like a transparent overleaf, to reveal some common, hidden entity.

At this point, I see a discourse about the abolition of gender recapitulating and ultimately performing the very work of gender. The word "gender" designates the social construction of sexual identity and is thus both related to and potentially free of the one-to-one correspondence between chromosomal sex and social role that LeGuin attributes to earthly social organization; it is what happens when our given, chromosomal sex enters into negotiation with the (other) social constructs – institutions, discourses – it encounters. When Simone de Beauvoir writes that one is not born a woman, but becomes one, she is pointing toward the process of gendering, the complex of experiences that turn a human individual with two X chromosomes into a "woman," and it follows, of course, that an analogous process takes place with individuals with one X and one Y chromosome, although, until fairly recently, this process was called "human development," instead of the "social construction of masculinity."[20] A world not structured by the binary opposition "male/female" is barely imaginable, and LeGuin's project in *The Left Hand of Darkness* is, as she puts it, a "a thought experiment": "One of the essential functions of science fiction," she writes, "is precisely this kind of question-asking: reversals of a habitual way of thinking, *metaphors for what our language has no words for as yet*, experiments in imagination" (IGN 9). In order, then, to explore "what truly differentiates men from women," LeGuin constructs her imaginary world of Gethen.

Instead of eliminating gender to find out what is left, however, LeGuin's experiment reveals how gender inheres in formations that are held to be separate from it. Even if gender is nominally abolished, its effects, the tasks of social organization that have, as it were, been assigned to it, are *redistributed* within a narrative (read also: social, political, [hetero]sexual) economy. Thus, although LeGuin postulates that a world without gender distinctions would also be a world without war, exploitation, and sexuality as a continuous social factor (IGN 10-12), what her narrative presents is a world *on the verge of* war and exploitation, and visited by representatives of a culture that experiences sexuality as a continuous social factor. That is, whereas LeGuin can imagine a world where war, exploitation, and sexuality are absent, these issues inhabit her narrative – because they inhabit narrative itself. We see the Gethenian world through the eyes of emissaries from human

20. Simone de Beauvoir, *The Second Sex*, trans. H. M. Parshley (New York, 1974), 301.

civilizations, who, like ourselves and like LeGuin, cannot describe the society without invoking the quantities whose absence characterizes it. Even if war, exploitation, and sex are absent, the narrators' accounts of Gethen – their terms of description – reintroduce them.

The Left Hand of Darkness tells the story of the sojourn on the Gethenian planet, Winter, of the Ekumen (human) first emissary, Genly Ai. In the course of his negotiations with the powers that be of the Gethenian nation, Karhide, Genly Ai hopes to bring Gethen into an alliance with the Ekumen, a treaty-community of worlds to which Earth belongs. His presence on Winter is concomitant with – or precipitates; it is never entirely clear – subtle changes in the social organization of the planet; the power relations in Karhide are unstable, and the neighboring country of Orgoreyn is in the process of modernization, becoming a nation-state with bureaucracy, patriotism, state capitalism and the centralization of power, authoritarian government and a secret police. Needless to say, this process in Orgoreyn threatens to bring war to the planet. Against this backdrop, the novel charts the falling out of favor of both Genly Ai and his sometimes/maybe Karhidish ally, Therem Harth rem ir Estraven, whose inclination toward joining the Ekumen brings him into disfavor with his capricious ruler. As the tensions between the two states increase, Genly and Estraven flee separately; Estraven survives incognito and Genly is arrested, imprisoned, and subjected to medically induced torture in Orgoreyn. At the moment of Genly's most acute need – he is on the verge of death – he is rescued and nursed back to strength by Estraven. The two figures (one can not say "men," since Estraven is, strictly speaking, not gendered) escape together across the icy north of the planet, and enter Karhide, where Estraven, whose rehabilitation is still pending, is betrayed, ambushed, and killed. Genly Ai survives and summons his Ekumen colleagues to begin the process of negotiating a treaty with Karhide. The final pages of the novel recount Ai's trip into the eastern reaches of Karhide to pay his respects to Estraven's father. Ai is granted the family's hospitality, and the novel ends with Estraven's son asking for the story of his father's death.

The reader might have noticed that LeGuin's great innovation – the suppression of gender – is itself entirely suppressed in my rendition of the novel's plot, and I want to claim that such a suppression is no distortion of what ultimately transpires in *The Left Hand of Darkness*. Reflecting on the sexual politics of her novel, LeGuin acknowledges as a shortcoming that "the Gethenians seem like men, instead of menwomen" (IGN 14). However much her exposition has emphasized the ambisexuality of Gethenians, her narrative almost entirely ignores it. She attributes this at least in part to the necessity of choosing a pronoun to represent her Gethenian figures ("'He' is the generic pronoun, damn it, in English" [IGN 15]), but there is, to my mind, far more going on here. The entire generic structure of the novel is ("damn it") male and appears most irreducibly so if we scan it as pure narrative structure: *The ambassador encounters a respected rival from the host nation. As both accede to the demands of their political offices, their uneasy cooperation is sundered, and each embarks on a separate journey of survival. When they meet again, their situations have changed, and one rescues the other. Together they flee across the icy wastes of the planet, where, thoroughly dependent upon each other, they enter into a profound bond that both engages and subsumes both their similarities and differences. The tension that enters the relation when Estraven enters kemming is homosexual panic pure and simple, and is overcome through the conscious stalwartness of both.*[21] *Upon the death of one, the other dedicates himself to the public mission of his lost friend and seeks some sort of solace through his encounter*

---

21. In "Is Gender Necessary" LeGuin acknowledges this lapse:

I quite unnecessarily locked the Gethenians into heterosexuality. It is a naively pragmatic view of sex that insists that sexual partners must be of opposite sex! In any kemmer-house homosexual practice would, of course, be possible and acceptable and welcomed – but I never thought to explore this option; and the omission, alas, implies that sexuality is heterosexuality. I regret this very much (IGN 14).

But there is, I think, more at stake: In the plot chronicling the relationship of Genly Ai and Estraven, the tensions are profoundly homosocial; that is, their bond is mediated – both intensified and given another name – by their common pursuit,

with his friend's family. I do not wish to belittle LeGuin's achievement by reducing this plot to a variant of "a boy and his dog," but there is little in the novel that works against the grain of the classic Oedipal narrative. Nor could there be. LeGuin carries out her "experiment" with the tools of her novelist's trade and, as Audre Lorde has written, "the master's tools can never dismantle the master's house."[22] LeGuin, in her very critical reassessment of the novel, does indeed see its "messiness." Yet she responds to these shortcomings by reassessing her intentions ("I must have wanted to") and criticizing this early and inadequate avatar of her feminism instead of regarding what happens in *The Left Hand of Darkness* as endemic to narrative fiction. LeGuin's intentions in introducing a world otherwise organized are thwarted – inevitably – by the conventions of plot that enable her to represent this world at all.

IV

The wind began to switch the house to pitch
And suddenly the hinges started to unhitch
Just then the witch, to satisfy an itch
Went flying on her broomstick thumbing for a hitch.

I seem to be taking a bleak view of the possibilities of articulating a truly alternative world – a world free of the ideological mappings of the culture that imagines it – in narrative prose, and I do, indeed, think that admittedly daring attempts to rethink gender are thwarted time and again by the master-plot of narrative. Science fiction should, of course, be the literary genre most available to postulators of alternative bodily and social organizations, since its

---

and the consummation of the bond (during Estraven's kemmer, which the narrative faintly suggests would have been possible) would have broken the spell of their relationship and violated the plot.

22. Audre Lorde. "The Master's Tools Will Never Dismantle the Master's House," in *Sister Outsider: Essays and Speeches by Audre Lorde* (Freedom, CA, 1984), 112.

independence from the restraints of verisimilitude and literary realism favor the projection of technologies, bodies, and societies whose incredibility would discredit them in another genre. Since Mary Shelley's *Frankenstein*, science and the possibilities of science have made it possible for writers to push their imaginations beyond the representational strictures of literary realism. Science enables Shelley to hypothesize a living being who is not born of woman (and hence, to trace the moral trajectories of male motherhood, on the one hand, and parentless progeny, on the other hand). Similarly, although in a very different historical context, the scientific possibility of constructing non-human life (a robot) enables Marge Piercy (in *He, She and It*) to present the scientific and political conflicts of a future dystopia within the context of historical and mythical antecedents in Jewish culture.

There is a wealth of feminist science fiction that is conscious of the double-bind of narrative, and that questions the master-plot's dreams of coherence and will to power. Such novels as Joanna Russ' *The Female Man* defy the master-plot by introducing what DuPlessis terms "collective protagonists" and proceeding via collage, parody, and pastiche instead of via linear narrative. Other texts introduce cyborg figures, descendants of the Golem and of Frankenstein's Monster, which, in Donna Haraway's words "refuse the reader's search for innocent wholeness while granting the wish for heroic quests, exuberant eroticism, and serious politics"[23] and enable writers to project "non-Oedipal narratives with a different logic of repression." In "A Manifesto for Cyborgs: Science, Technology, and Socialist Feminism in the 1980s," Haraway writes:

> The cyborg is a creature in a postgender world; it has no truck with bisexuality, pre-Oedipal symbiosis, unalienated labor, or other seductions to organic wholeness through a final appropriation of all the powers of the whole into a higher unity. In a sense, the cyborg has no origin story in the Western sense. . . . An origin story in the Western humanist sense

---

23. Donna Haraway, "A Manifesto for Cyborgs: Science, Technology, and Socialist Feminism in the 1980s," in Linda Nicholson, ed., *Feminism/Postmodernism* (New York and London, 1990), 220.

depends on the myth of original unity, fullness, bliss, and terror represented by the phallic mother from whom all humans must separate, the task of individual development and of history, the twin potent myths inscribed most powerfully for us in psychoanalysis and Marxism. [24]

Haraway's cyborg challenge is a powerful one, and her program for the cyborg pastiche beyond gender is provocative. Yet her manifesto is, as its title confirms, a document of the 1980s, and, fifteen years later, I worry that globalization has so appropriated the moves of postmodernism that it will certainly have upped the ante on any "other route that does not pass through Woman, Primitive, Zero, the Mirror Stage, and its imaginary [passing instead] through women and other present-tense, illegitimate cyborgs, not of Woman born, who refuse the ideological resources of victimization so as to have a real life."[25] Although I acknowledge (more than acknowledge; I actually agree with) Haraway's contention that we can only escape the tyranny of gender by foiling its appropriations, I find myself resisting the kinds of fictions that seek to subvert these appropriations through a technology – and a technology of plot – that becomes as arcane and as discursively non-negotiable as the patriarchy's most pernicious mystifications.

Haraway concludes her "Manifesto for Cyborgs" by reminding us of the dangers of "an anti-science metaphysics, a demonology of technology."[26] Yet it is crucial to remember that technology is still related – crucially related – to the humans who produce it. The cyborg that has no "birth," and that would thus seem even more properly outside the Oedipal matrix than the offspring of LeGuin's kemmer does acquire "affect"; in fact, if my (admittedly limited) reading is any indication, non-human, cyborg beings who are introduced into human society quickly develop a preternatural (indeed!) interest and fluency in – even obsession with – the language of human relations. In representations as different as *Frankenstein, He, She and It*, Richard Powers' *Galatea 2.2*, and Ridley

24. Ibid., 192.
25. Ibid., 219.
26. Ibid., 223.

Scott's *Blade Runner*, cyborgs (computers, replicants) develop highly complex and baffling affective systems. Imagining the monster (the cyborg, the artificial intelligence, the replicant) seems also to involve imagining the demands it makes on the human. (Perhaps this is the real reason why the control computer in *Alien* is called "mother.") Gender, in science fiction, seems to come into existence interactively and hence as a citation, as it were, of the culture that produces it; as such, it remains, in these representations, one of the most powerful articulations of cultural nostalgia.

V

> "Send me back to Kansas where my Aunt Em and Uncle Henry are . . ."
> "Why should I do this for you?"
> "Because you are Strong and I am weak; because you are a Great Wizard and I am only a little girl!"

In Richard Powers' novel, *Galatea 2.2* (1995), a burned-out novelist in his mid-thirties returns to his alma mater, a large, midwestern university, to be the resident humanist in a high-tech scientific think-tank. A disabused, cynical, but (and?) clearly brilliant colleague, Lentz, engages the narrator-novelist (named, like the author, Richard Powers) in an attempt to program a computer with all of Western literature in order that it pass the English Department's doctoral examination. As Lentz programs and refines the computer, Richard reads to it. The computer (called "H," because it is the eighth in a line of prototypes) rapidly develops the capacity to deploy the rhetorical models with which it has been programmed, and does so so deftly and "personally" that Richard cannot help imputing to it intelligence and affect:

> H was growing up too quickly. I was not the first trainer in the world to feel this. But I was among the first who might have some say in the matter. . . . I thought we might nestle down again, into simpler play. But it was too late. I learned that certain lessons are not undone by their opposites. Certain lessons are self-protecting, self-correcting tangles of

threads that will forever remain a frayed knot.[27]

As Richard teaches H the Mother Goose rhyme, "Sugar and spice [and all things nice; that's what little girls are made of] . . . Snips and snails [and puppydog tails; that's what little boys are made of]," H wonders:

> "Am I a boy or a girl?"
> I should have seen. Even ungrounded intelligence had to grow self-aware eventually. To grab what it needed. . . .
> "You're a girl," I said, without hesitation. I hoped I was right. "You are a little girl, Helen."
> I hope she liked the name. (*Galatea* 179)

When a child is born, the first question we ask is, "what is it?" and everyone knows to what we are referring. Similarly, with the computer's arrival at self-awareness — a self-awareness it achieves through "processing" Western literature — comes its need to "know what it is." And, consistent with the logic through which the matrix of Western culture generates the question of gender, Richard's gendering of the computer gives articulation to the desire that drove him first to return to his alma mater and then to collaborate with Lentz. The creature he creates is an "other." And however desperately Richard wishes that with his return "home" to a site of pure learning he could put the emotional baggage of his life behind them, his activities there — even the computer's interpretation of the texts he reads it — are shaped by the life from which he'd tried to escape. Of course, his "relationship" with the computer recapitulates the traumatic relationship with the former student whom he had met (and who had consoled him) the day his father died and with whom he had lived for many years. The book's elegant, extended conceit asks whether a subjectivity that has been produced and produced itself through the texts of Western culture can ever liberate itself from the gender relations

---

27. Richard Powers, *Galatea 2.2* (New York, 1996), 178–179. Subsequent references to this novel are given in parentheses in the text.

encoded into those texts. The novel demonstrates how these texts so reinforce the replication of gender that a computer "fed" with them will ask the question of identity such that the answer is "you are a little girl."

The myth of Oedipus organizes both the construction of gender in Western culture and the organization of knowledge. The little (male) person forges his identity by "killing off" his father so that he can (re)gain access to his mother. In the course of development, the position of the "mother" is occupied by other goals (knowledge, power, but also love), the achievement of which repeats structurally the original patricidal process and insures the legitimacy of the subject's participation in society and culture. What Richard discovers in front of the mirror – represented by Helen's appropriation of Western literature is that he can "kill off" the father only provisionally, and only with the help of some "stand in" for the mother, be it his woman friend, C., the books he writes, or H. Powers' (science) fiction of gender (or: fiction of the gender of science) – demonstrates the contagion of the desires of humans in their interactions with cyborgs.

VI

"Somewhere, over the rainbow. . ."

If, as I have been claiming up until now, there seems no way out of the Oedipal double bind of narrative, and hence no way – even within the repertoire of possibilities opened by science fiction – to radically reorient gender through narrative, it would stand to reason that a "female" plot in science fiction would be but a differently inflected – or, given women's limited access to power, a truncated – version of what I've called the Oedipal master-plot. Yet, as I suggested at the outset in my discussion of *The Wizard of Oz*, the *Alien* films, and *Contact*, there are possibilities within the gender ideology of narrative as I've articulated it of interrogating the relation of the subject to power and knowledge; if the subject's access to the conventional vectors of plot is complicated by gender, then a text can raise questions even if it cannot plot its way toward an answer. If, for instance, in *Galatea 2.2*, Helen had talked back, asking Richard why she is "a little girl," the text would have had to expose the assumptions that guide both its narrative dynamics and Richard's readings of the tomes he "feeds" Helen. If *The Left Hand of Darkness* had pursued the sexual attraction between Genly Ai and Estraven, and staged the interaction between Estraven's kemmer and Genly's masculinity, it would have critically strained at the limits of its own mythmaking. Since science fiction grants us freedom from the strictures of representational verisimilitude, it should be able to push narrative to the point where the biases and contradictions of its gender ideology are at least exposed. Returning now to Robert Zemeckis' 1997 film, *Contact*, I want to examine how the figure of the female scientist overdetermines the narratives available for telling her story.

In *Contact*, Jodie Foster plays the role of Ellie Arroway, an astrophysicist whose zeal for knowledge is presented as a response to the loss at birth of her mother and, nine years later, of the father who encouraged her early scientific endeavors. *Contact* begins with a visual extravaganza of stars, planets, and galaxies that resolves into a point on a close-up image of the young Ellie's eyeball. In the opening scene that establishes the film's narrative motivations, the young Ellie sits at her short-wave radio, attempting to make contact with the disembodied voices of other radio operators and charting her successes on a map of the United States. In a poignant exchange with her father, she wonders whether radio technology would allow her to contact other countries, even other planets, and asks him whether he thinks there are people on other planets. He answers, "If not, It seems like an awful waste of space." She then asks him whether she might be able to "talk to mom." Her father's answer, "I don't think the biggest radio could reach that far," achieves a double plangency when he, too, dies and leaves Ellie calling into her radio, "Dad, are you there? Come back," and committing her life to making contact with extraterrestrial life.

The actual plot of *Contact* begins when Ellie, now a well-regarded scientist with an eccentric specialty, is dismissed from the project which has been sponsoring the satellite time during which she sweeps distant space for signs of extraterrestrial life. After months of begging for funding, she receives support from an eccentric multimillionaire, S. R. Hadden, and finally does intercept a signal from the star, Vega. This discovery attracts immediate international interest, and the professor who had denigrated her pursuits and cut off her original funding now uses all his (masculine) clout to push Ellie out of the limelight and assume leadership of the project. With Hadden's help, Ellie's team deciphers the messages being sent them from Vega; they contain blueprints for a machine for intergalactic travel. The conflict between Ellie and her former mentor, David Drumlin, escalates as they emerge as the two prime candidates to "man" the vehicle. Drumlin – who, unlike Ellie, claims to believe in God – is chosen by an international panel, but dies when the machine is sabotaged by a fanatical Christian. When Hadden reveals that he has secretly built a replica of the vehicle, Ellie gets her opportunity to penetrate outer space and seek contact.

Her trip into space involves crossing through waves of galactic interference ("wormholes"), punctuated by peaceful interludes of cosmic beauty. Finally, Ellie lands on a technicolor tropical beach, in a world apparently without space, whose "walls," to which the landscape adheres, are like flexible plastic and yield slightly to her touch. A figure approaches her on the beach; it is her father.[28] She embraces him, recognizes that he's "not real," and accuses him of having "downloaded [her] thoughts, [her] memories. . .":

"Why did you contact us?"
"You contacted us. We were just listening."
"Then there are others?"
"Many others."
"Is this some test?"
"No. No tests. You have your mother's hands. You're an interesting species,

28. Ellie's father's approach (his 'materialization') recalls the approach, in a pink balloon, of Glinda, the good Witch of the North, in *The Wizard of Oz*.

an interesting mix. You're capable of such beautiful dreams and such horrible nightmares. You feel so lost, so cut-off, so alone, only you're not. You see, in all our searching what makes the emptiness bearable is each other."

"What happens now?"

"You go home."

"Home? But . . . I have so many questions. Do we get to come back?"

"This was just a first step. In time you'll take another. . . . This is the way it's been done for billions of years. "

At this point, Ellie is swept up into a celestial vortex and finds herself back in the space vehicle. She is informed that her vehicle has crashed upon takeoff, and that she has been nowhere except in the water off the coast of Japan. The rest of the film charts Ellie's attempts to persuade the world of the reality of her adventure, a reality which, however dubious, is supported by the eighteen hours of tape recording that lapsed during her seemingly minute-long sojourn in the vehicle. Without ever getting official acknowledgment of the authority of her experience, Ellie does, however, receive the funding to continue her research and to teach children that, should there not be any other life out there, "it would be a real waste of space."

Contact is so glaringly Oedipal in its plotting that it embarrasses the cultural codings that try so hard to make the Oedipal plot really look like a plot about other – usually loftier – things such as knowledge, power, or ideal love. After being one-upped by Drumlin time and again, Ellie has the dubious satisfaction of seeing him killed off (as often as Ellie seems ready to kill the overbearing Drumlin, she seems truly horrified and aggrieved when he dies); Hadden, himself in what he regards as Oedipal combat with the world's powers and potentates, "adopts" her in order that she carry out his final mission. Yet – and here is where *Contact* differs from other Oedipal representations – the chain of substitutions ends. At the end of Ellie's rainbow is not the humbug scientist-wizard Oz (whose resemblance to Hadden cannot be accidental), nor the Auntie Ems and Uncle Henrys (Drumlin, Rachel Constantine, the high-ranking presidential advisor who keeps Ellie in line but also tells her where to find a "fantastic dress"), who stand in for the orphan's parents, but "Dad" himself. Science gives Ellie what she wants.

Moreover, Ellie's plot of true Oedipal satisfaction, however fantastic, achieves credibility. At the congressional hearings, Kitz, the presidential security advisor-become-investigator who has been her antagonist all along, demands that she retract her testimony. He tries to convince Congress that "nothing happened": Ellie's experience, he submits, is most plausibly explained as a giant, final hoax perpetrated by the terminally ill Hadden. Kitz contrasts his seamless narrative linking this hoax with Ellie's hallucination of her "contact"-experience with what he calls a "story . . . that strains credibility." In this battle of narratives, Ellie pleads for – and is ultimately granted – the authority of the narrative of science as pure wish fulfillment, "the story that strains credibility."

In my synopsis of the film, I have intentionally neglected the love affair that achieves articulation and consummation in the course of *Contact*. Although the film's love plot – the standard plot of female development – is well integrated into the narrative of Ellie's pursuit of knowledge, it is not, as the summary above demonstrates, essential to it in the way, for instance, the love plots in *Galatea 2.2* are essential to and inextricable from it. Warner Brothers' "Production Notes" to the film, to which I respond in italics, show how hard the film's writers had to work to get the love plot in synch with the science-fiction plot:

> Amid the worldwide tumult, Ellie becomes a lightening rod of controversy. Fighting for her rightful place as leader of the scientific investigation, she turns to her one potential ally among those wielding influence on the world stage: Palmer Joss, a respected religious scholar and top-level government advisor [*I have seen the film many times, and I cannot find any instance of her "turning to" Palmer Joss. Au* contraire: *he always turns up where she already is, and although his interests are very clearly in her they are in no way identical with hers*]. Years earlier, Ellie and Palmer had shared a brief and passionate relationship that ended because of Ellie's single-minded pursuit of her career [*not to mention that he (1) asked her painful questions about her father, and (2) echoed verbatim her father's observation about an uninhabited universe*

being a "waste of space."] Now estranged by time and their divergent beliefs, but brought together by their joint passion for understanding the message, the scientist and the spiritual leader find themselves struggling with their renewed mutual attraction.[29]

What this summary leaves out is that Palmer is a member of the committee that rejects Ellie in favor of Drumlin, that he is, in fact, *the* member of the committee who sabotages her chances by asking her about her religious views, and that he later admits that he asked the question because he didn't want her to go and knew her answer would disqualify her (I guess this is what the summary means by "struggling with their renewed mutual attraction"). Ellie gets into space *despite* Palmer. Later, of course, it is Palmer who most fervently believes Ellie's account of her voyage into space, especially because in her interrogation, she is forced to claim a knowledge she cannot prove – what Palmer would call faith. As the film PR puts it, "her personal voyage will take her beyond theory, beyond knowledge, beyond experience, to the realization that true vision is ultimately the union of fact and faith." The PR would have it, of course, that "the union of fact and faith" is represented in the union of Ellie the scientist and Palmer "the man of cloth without the cloth" so dramatically staged when, as they make their way down Capitol Hill through the throngs of admirers, Palmer confers the ultimate stamp of authority on Ellie's story when he tells a reporter that "I, for one, believe her." But it is absolutely clear that Ellie has achieved this "union" all by herself, independent not only of Palmer, but of the romantic subplot in which he participates.

Throughout the film, Palmer has presented a challenge – even an obstacle – to Ellie's trajectory, and not simply because erotic consummation would absorb the energy devoted to knowledge and ambition. Palmer reminds Ellie of her father, not because he resembles him or stands in for him on some phantasmatic level, but because he wants to talk about him and inadvertently cites

29. *Contact*: Production Notes, www.CONTACT-themovie.com/emp/production.html#part1.

him. When Ellie neglects to pursue their relationship, she seems motivated less by her "single-minded pursuit of her career" than by the profound pain that Palmer semi-wittingly causes because, in fact, *he is not what she wants; he is not her father*. It is only as the contours of her identity – as, to be sure, forged through her career – and her ability to orient herself among the male powermongers and powersharers in the scientific and political communities solidify that she can begin to meet the emotional challenge that Palmer Joss poses. His love for her tries to deter her from her pursuit of her father, but fails. It is only *after* she has gotten what she wants, has realized her Oedipal desires in her own terms through her own brains, heart, and courage,[30] that she can enter into a relationship with Palmer Joss and tolerate a situation in which his word will, given their gendered positions in the power-knowledge system, always be taken as "authorization" of hers.

Does the *Contact* take us "beyond gender"? It most certainly does not, although it is ingenious in its manipulation of a feminized Oedipal narrative. It can attempt, as the opening sequence suggests, to represent the universe contracted in the eye of a woman capable of pursuing her vision. In fact, this image of the universe contracted in Ellie's eye is repeated during her journey through space, when she says, "Some celestial event . . . no words can describe . . . poetry . . . they should have sent a poet . . . it is so beautiful. I had no idea." The film's establishing shot is reiterated at the moment when Ellie declares her inadequacy to her task ("they should have sent a poet") and conceded the limits of her knowledge ("I had no idea"). The knowledge she gains is not to be found on the map of science; nor will she concede it to religion. Ellie's pursuit of "some reason why we're here – what we are doing here, who [we are]" remains a private and inconclusive one. *Contact* makes visible the disparities between personal motivations and the

---

30. Here again, the film enters into dialogue with *The Wizard of Oz*: The attributes that Ellie needs to successfully complete the trajectory of her ambition (brains, heart, and courage) are those sought by the nominally 'male' (but very sexually ambiguous) companions that Dorothy collects on her trip down the yellow brick road.

narratives through which they are played out. Because it is, in de Lauretis's words, "Oedipal with a vengeance," it challenges the inevitability with which, in texts such as *The Left Hand of Darkness* and *Galatea 2.2*, gender ideologies are reinforced.

VII

(Scarecrow's Beauticians)
Pat, pat here, pat, pat there
And a couple of brand new straws
That's how we keep you young and fair
In the merry Old Land of Oz

The medium in which science fiction comes to us (narrative, film) and its appeal for popularity limit the range of its experimentation. The conventions of narrative and film domesticate "thought experiments" in the very act of representation. And I think that experimentation with the possibilities of gender is particularly vulnerable to this domestication because of the ineradicable gender biases built into our conventions of narrative and cinematic representation. I also think that this domestication is part of what we crave about science fiction; our sojourn in an alternative world is temporary. We know, as Dorothy doesn't, that we have only to click our red shoes together and we are returned to a drab quotidian reality in which there are to be sure, no technicolor sunsets and no good witch of the north. But we also know that the wicked witch of the west is really only the nasty lady down the road and Aunt Em is waiting at home.

Although I doubt that science fiction can break out of the gender ideologies of narrative, I do think that the introduction of gender issues into science fiction can enable it to perform more critically its task of projecting future, alternative worlds, exploring the moral and social issues raised by scientific possibilities, and thus commenting creatively on the social and cultural formations in the culture that produces it. But, as I have explored at length, science fiction remains limited by the fact that it is – usually –

narrative fiction and, as such, driven by plot engines that determine the ideological directions in which it (sometimes unwittingly and often unwillingly) moves.

To pursue further the fictions of science and gender and their relations, it would seem necessary to turn to genres less reliant on plot than the novel and narrative film. As I have already suggested, short fiction seems capable of escaping the ideological trap set by narrative; documentary film – because it can refuse or downplay narrative causality – and a certain kind of medical case study – because it is compelled to follow the shape of a real life – would seem to open up even more radical possibilities for exploring the interfaces between science and gender.

As its title suggests, Monika Treut's film, *Gendernauts* (1999), is indebted to science fiction in its exploration of transgender identity as a frontier comparable to that of outer space. The people who are the subjects of Treut's attention are experimenters in gender, individuals who chemically and surgically manipulate their bodies in order that they may correspond to their felt gender–identity. The film allows these subjects to speak, to tell stories which, not surprisingly, are often extraordinarily discontinuous and generally quite banal. But because of the way the camera makes itself receptive to its subjects, the viewer is compelled to comply with the terms in which they address the camera. If at first one can often not tell what their chromosomal sex is, ultimately, one ceases to care, and finds oneself on the verge of being able to think without thinking through gender. Treut's film works because it appears to have no narrative objective of its own. The juxtaposition of the individual subject's stories, the images of their changing bodies, interviews with their medical consultants, and material in which the subjects are filmed in social interaction and theatrical performance succeeds in creating a context in which conventional notions of gender are suspended – at least for the duration of the film. One leaves the cinema conscious – as one is not after reading *The Left Hand of Darkness* – of real possibilities for gender identity outside of the categories male/female and the institutions that enforce them.

I would like to close by invoking one more – extremely dysphoric – domain in which science rewrites, as it were, the plots of gender. The diagnosis of neoplasmic illness is usually accompanied by a therapy in which bodily parts are amputated and/or chemicals are administered to stop the proliferation of malignant cells. When malignancies occur in organs related to sexual functioning (in women, breasts, ovaries, uterus, cervix; in men, prostate and testicles), many of the chemicals administered are either hormones themselves or substances that alter the production of hormones that influence tumor growth either positively or negatively. Other chemicals cause hair loss and weight gain or loss, which further change the subject-become-patient's relation to her or his gender. As Eve Kosofsky Sedgwick has written:

> Early in 1991 I was diagnosed, quite unexpectedly, with a breast cancer that had already spread to my lymph system, and the experiences of diagnosis, surgery, chemotherapy, and so forth, while draining and scary, have also proven just sheerly *interesting* with respect to exactly the issues of gender, sexuality, and identity formation that were already on my docket. (Forget the literal-mindedness of mastectomy, chemically induced menopause, etc.: I would warmly encourage anyone interested in the social construction of gender to find some way of spending half a year or so as a totally bald woman.)[31]

Or:

> a dizzying array of gender challenges and experiments comes with the initiations of surgery, of chemotherapy, of hormone therapy. Just getting dressed in the morning means deciding how many breasts I will be able to recognize myself if I am wearing (a voice in me keeps whispering, three); the apparition of my only slightly fuzzy head, facing me in the mirror after my shower like my own handsome and bald father, demands that I decide if I would feel least alienated or most adventurous or comforted today as Gloria Swanson or Jambi, as a head-covered Hasidic housewife, as an Afro wannabe in a probably unraveling head rag, as a drag queen who never quite figured out how to do wigs, as a large bald

31. Eve Kosofsky Sedgwick, *Tendencies* (Durham: NC, 1993), 12.

baby or Buddha or wise extraterrestrial . . . . Indeed, every aspect of a self comes up for grabs under the pressure of modern medicine . . . [32]

Sedgwick makes it clear that treatment for cancer is science fiction in action. What she makes less clear in these passages is the effect of the changes she enumerates on a life narrative. If her relation to her daily self is renegotiated every time she looks into the mirror and decides how or whether to cover her head, the imperfection of every and any cover-up ensures that in her interactions with the world, she will be regarded as a cancer patient who has chosen a particular compensatory "look."

Beyond this, however, there are artificially induced menopause in women (a friend of mine went through menopause twice: once after her ovaries were removed, and a second time when she was taken off a particular hormone therapy); chemically determined changes in libido that bear no direct correspondence to one's health or lack thereof; infertility in men and women; impotence in men; mood changes that range from profound depression to the euphoria that comes from taking certain steroids: these changes in the determinants of one's sexual and gender performance introduce changes in the plot of one's life. Although all these plot-changes are subsumed by the larger "narrative" question of whether or not or how long one is going to live, they have force in their own right and effect major changes in the life actions whatever shape the life plot assumes whenever it ends.[33]

If we are serious about examining the interdeterminations of the fictions of gender and those of science, we have to look to those life-texts whose plots are in the process of being written. In literature and film, as in life, the Oedipal plot still has substantial power to write our lives. At the fringes of gender and on the verges of life, however, there are chapters being written to which we would do well to attend.

---

32. Ibid., 263.
33. See Audre Lorde, *The Cancer Journals* (London, 1980) for an eloquent exposition of these issues.

Comment on Part Five: Apocalypse How? Or the Visions of Future Between Fear and Hope

Luigi Cajani

Catastrophes in Western Culture

Catastrophes have always been part of the real and imaginary experience of mankind. Men were always afraid of being victim of a catastrophe and always looked for an answer to this fear. The nature and dimension of both real and imagined catastrophes change in time, according to the transformations of the relationship between mankind and the environment. In the Christian West, during the premodern era, when man had a very limited power over nature, catastrophes were acts of God: both the actual and partial catastrophes (plagues, famines, wars) and the final and total one, the end of the world with the final judgment. In the modern era the Industrial Revolution gave to mankind a tremendous power over nature, without comparison in the past; and technology first promised, then frightened. Also catastrophes changed: They were now related to the new performances of technology, until the extreme catastrophe, the nuclear war, modern form of the end of the world. Therefore, if in the premodern age it was the task of religion to give an answer to the fear of catastrophes, and its answers worked both on the rational and on the imaginary level, in the modern age this role has been divided and picked up by science on the rational level and by science fiction on the imaginary level. In fact, science fiction has accompanied the development of science and its social impact since the beginning of the twentieth century. In the first part of its history, which started with the activity of Hugo Gernsback in the United States, science fiction was characterized by the optimistic faith in science as the motor of progress. Then, after the end of World War

II, the dropping of the atom bombs on Japan and the beginning of the Cold War gave rise to a feeling of uncertainty: science showed its terrible face and gave to mankind, for the first time in its history, the possibility of destroying itself, which before had been possible only for God. Catastrophes had already been the subject of a few science fiction books: I just quote *The Purple Cloud,* by Matthew Shiel, published 1901; but only after the atom bomb did they became a major theme. Since then, pessimism started to contend with optimism, with alternate fortune.

We find direct expression of the fear of nuclear war in Judith Merril's *Shadow on the Earth*, published 1950, one of the first books to deal with it, together with *The Martian Chronicles* by Ray Bradbury, of the same year, and then in many many books and movies, like *The Day After,* directed by Nicholas Meyer in 1983, in the middle of a revival of the USA–USSR confrontation. We may consider this fear as the original sin of contemporary catastrophes: It has been for long time the most likely one, but beside it other fears have haunted people's consciousness. In the following years the imaginary of fear has taken many forms through science fiction, new forms all related to the fields of science.

A Taxonomy of Catastrophes in Science Fiction

We may distinguish two main categories of catastrophe in science fiction literature: the first one includes catastrophes not produced by mankind; the second one, catastrophes produced by mankind.

The first category includes catastrophes of an extraterrestrial kind (like an asteroid falling on the planet, the sun becoming a nova, or an alien invasion) as well as catastrophes of a terrestrial kind, eventually connected to astronomic events (like a new ice age, the melting of the glacial sheets as a consequence of global warming, a series of volcanic eruptions or of earthquakes), which generally bring a general collapse of modern civilization and a return to a less civilized past.

In the second category we find catastrophes produced by mankind, either intentionally or unintentionally, like a nuclear war, ecological disasters, artificial epidemics, technological accidents, or social and political catastrophes.

Catastrophes of extraterrestrial origin may include natural events, like asteroids striking the Earth. This is a peculiar catastrophe, because it probably already happened, many million of years ago, leading to the extinction of the dinosaurs, and could happen again, as has recently been often suggested by the mass media, when asteroids passed near the Earth. At present there would be no way of rescue, although movies like *Meteor,* directed by Ronald Neame in 1979, let people hope in nuclear rockets, originally intended for destruction, as means to destroy or deviate the danger from the space. Far less likely, but most characteristic, is the encounter with aliens. The attitude toward aliens is interestingly ambiguous. They can be dreadful enemies, as in Paul Anderson's *After Doomsday* (1962), where they destroy the Earth and only the passengers of a starship survive to fight for revenge and to carry on the human venture; or in William Tenn's *Of Men and Monsters* (1968), where a few humans go on living like insects on the Earth conquered by giant beings. Aliens in such cases are a metaphor of the real enemy. But aliens can also be benign and act in a friendly way to mankind, for instance by helping it to a better future. They are like a good genius. And the salvation for mankind, salvation from the danger that it represents for itself, can (only) come from outside. Mankind itself could come from outside. In fact, the followers of the Raelian Movement, a ufologic religion founded 1975 by Claude Vorilhon, believe that aliens, called Elohim, created mankind using science.

All the same, independent from human responsibility are natural catastrophes more connected to the Earth. Doris Lessing describes in *The Making of the Representative for Planet 8* (1982) the consequences of a new ice age, not on the Earth but on a similar planet, inhabited by human beings; James Ballard tells in *The Drowned World* (1962) how the warming up of the Sun melts the ice sheet and the sea covers therefore most of the land; John Chistopher shows in *A Wrinkle in the Skin* (1965) the effects of a series of earthquakes.

Most of these catastrophes are much more a matter of the imagination than of rational concern, and express a general fear of the fragility of modern civilization in relation to nature. Quite different is the case of catastrophes where human responsibility is involved, either by malice – and not to forget stupidity – or by mistake. They constitute not only a subject of science fiction literature, but are widely discussed in the mass media. This is not only the case of a general nuclear war, but also of ecological disasters, like the hole in the ozone layer, which has for some years been an issue, or the chemical pollution, as we can read in James Ballard's *The Burning World* (1966), where the oceans are covered by a polymeric film which prevents evaporation and therefore rainfall, thus converting Earth into a desert. Mankind itself, not by special acts of violence, but just with its normal rate of consumption and production of waste, is a danger to the environment and to itself. Besides science fiction, the concern for environmental catastrophes is expressed by science, and often with a great impact on public opinion, like Rachel Carson's book *Silent Spring* (1962), which had a great influence in the United States and starts in a science fictional mode: "A Fable for Tomorrow" is the title of the first chapter, describing a land where insects had been destroyed by pesticides. Overpopulation and overconsumption are dealt with by a well-known and fundamental research report by the MIT, *The Limits to Growth, a Report for the Club of Rome's Project on the Predicament of Mankind* published 1972 by Donella H. Meadows [et al.], which produced a furor of debate. "The book was interpreted by many as a prediction of the doom", remark the authors twenty years later in the preface of the follow-up study, but it was no prediction at all "… It contained a warning, to be sure, but also a message of promise:[1]" the promise of sustainable growth, which at the beginning of the 1990s seemed to them to be more likely than at first glance in the 1970s. A few years before the first study, a famous science fiction book had also dealt with the social consequences of overpopulation: John Brunner's *Stand on Zanzibar,* winner of the Hugo Award in 1969.

---

1. Donella H. Meadows et al., *Beyond the Limits. Confronting Global Collapse, Envisioning a Sustainable Future* (White River Junction, VT, 1992), xiii.

Epidemics, which had anguished men before the modern age, even causing true catastrophes like the Black Death in fourteenth-century Europe, seemed to have been defeated by the power of science, before AIDS appeared. But public opinion was aware that science was not only working on the destruction of disease, but also on its use as a bacteriological weapon. It is no coincidence that some people suspect that AIDS is the result of a virus created by scientists and unfortunately escaped from a laboratory. In Frank Herbert's *The White Plague* (1982) something of that kind happens, but intentionally: a scientist, whose wife and child were killed in a terrorist attack, creates a virus which only kills women and diffuses it in order to show to other men what it means to lose one's own woman. By the way, it is amazing how epidemics are used as a tool in the gender struggle. A feminist utopia asserting that a world only inhabited by women would be a better one, without violence, also has recourse to an epidemic, of course with the opposite effect from Herbert's virus. Alice Sheldon in his *Houston, Houston, do you read?*, published under the masculine pseudonym James Tiptree Jr. and winner in 1977 of the Hugo Award, imagines an epidemic destroying all men and thus realizing the extreme feminist dream.

The first and the second category of this taxonomy can also be combined, as in the famous novel by John Wyndham, *The Day of the Triffids* (1951). The triffids are plants created by scientists to produce a peculiar oil, but they have two dangerous features: They walk and they can kill with their poisonous needles. Then comes a catastrophe from the sky: a spectacular rain of meteors casts rays which blind all who watch it, that is, the great part of humankind, except for a few lucky ones. Civilization collapses, men are not only blind but also threatened by the triffids, and those who still can see have to organize survival.

How to survive is the fundamental question for everybody fearing a catastrophe. There is an imaginary pact, an underlying agreement, between the writer and the reader: Both have survived, and the proof is that I wrote and you are reading. This is the first and fundamental answer to fear.

Luigi Cajani

The (Provisional) End of Apocalypse

At the of the twentieth century, the century of nuclear energy, the fear of a nuclear world war has practically disappeared. It is hard to believe that a movie like *The Day After* could be a blockbuster today. The demonstrations against the nuclear arms race, which walked the streets of Western cities in the 1980s are outside the experience of the younger generation. The man who killed the nuclear anguish was Mikail Gorbachev, in a speech held in February 1987 at the Forum on Denuclearization in Moscow. Nuclear weapons, he said, had changed for ever the relationship between mankind and war, because of the possibility of self-destruction, and had thus shaped not only the reality and the imagination of war, but also the main features of our time. Therefore, to put an end to nuclear weapons didn't merely mean a return to the situation before August 6, 1945, but a step forward, toward the overcoming of violence itself.[2] The elimination of the ultimate form of war should bring the elimination of war itself. In this speech Gorbachev went beyond his role of politician and assumed the one of a science fiction writer.

I asserted that the fear of a nuclear catastrophe was the mother of all contemporary fears. It is therefore no surprise, that after it had vanished, all the other fears are vanishing as well. Catastrophe is no longer a major theme in science fiction. A new positive, although cautious, attitude toward the future has replaced pessimism and anguish. A significant form of this eudemonism, significant just because it is excessive, can be found in a science fiction book belonging to the genre of history of future: *The Third Millennium: A History of the World AD 2000-3000,* by Brian Stableford and David Langford, published 1985. Very precisely, following the model of a history textbook, the authors describe the beginning of the next millennium still under the environmental problems and the geo-political tensions of their time, when the Berlin Wall hadn't yet been pulled down. On the geopolitical landscape, peace will soon reign all over the world: in fact, after a few nuclear conflicts fought

2. See *URSS oggi,* XV n. 3, February 1–15, 1987.

by minor countries, at the end of twenty-first century the United States and the still existing USSR will work together to achieve a stable peace. And concerning the environment, a miracle will happen: In fact, the greenhouse effect will not be stopped in time, and the coasts will be submerged and some cities will be damaged. But the phenomenon will be mitigated by a *deus ex machina*, that is, a lower thermic emission of the Sun, until finally scientists and politicians will find the way to a new balance.

This book was written on the verge of the turning point, and can be considered in a way as an anticipation of the coming optimist trend in the Western culture. Perhaps the end of the nuclear threat is not the only cause for this change in mentality. The long public discourse on possible catastrophes has made people more familiar with them. Science seems to be not too powerful and not too dangerous. A new science fiction thread, the cyberpunk, describes a near future of tighter integration between man and machine, which apart from that is quite usual in its degradation. Instead of the big question about the apocalypse, which deserves a big answer, there are a lot of little questions about specific problems, and a corresponding set of little answers.

Select Bibliography

Norbert Finzsch

This bibliography contains only a small selection of the literature on the issues debated in this volume. The titles mentioned here do not necessarily appear in the contributions included in this conference volume – in fact, as a rule, they do not. As a general policy, we included only books, that were published after 1989. Exceptions to this rule were made occasionally in order to include a title of special importance. This bibliography is first organized according to the symposium's five sessions and then topically within each session.

Introduction

Edward Bellamy

Bowman, Sylvia E. *The Year 2000: A Critical Biography of Edward Bellamy* (New York, 1979).

Griffith, Nancy Snell. *Edward Bellamy: A Bibliography* (Metuchen, NJ, 1986).

Peyser, Thomas. *Utopia & Cosmopolis: Globalization in the Era of American Literary Realism* (Durham, NC, 1998).

Widdicombe, Richard Toby. *Edward Bellamy: An Annotated Bibliography of Secondary Criticism* (New York, 1988).

Dystopia in Literature

Baker, Robert S. *Brave New World: History, Science, and Dystopia* (Boston, 1990).

Booker, M. Keith. *The Dystopian Impulse in Modern Literature: Fiction As Social Criticism* (Westport, CT, 1994).

——. *Dystopian Literature: A Theory and Research Guide* (Westport, CT, 1994).

Sisk, David W. *Transformations of Language in Modern Dystopias* (Westport, CT, 1997).

The Millennium

Ahearn, Edward J. *Visionary Fictions: Apocalyptic Writing From Blake to the Modern Age* (New Haven, CT, 1996).

Barkun, Michael. *Millennialism and Violence* (London, Portland OR, 1996).

Bloom, Harold. *Omens of Millennium: The Gnosis of Angels, Dreams, and Resurrection* (New York, 1996).

Bostick, Curtis V. *The Antichrist and the Lollards: Apocalypticism in Late Medieval Reformation England* (Leiden, Boston, 1998).

Bowie, Fiona, and Christopher Deacy. *The Coming Deliverer: Millennial Themes in World Religions* (Cardiff, 1997).

Campbell, James P. *The Third Millennium: A Catholic Perspective. A Critique of Fundamentalism in Light of Catholic Hope for the Future* (Washington, DC, 1996).

Campion, Nicholas. *The Great Year: Astrology: Millenarianism and History in the Tradition* (London, New York, 1994).

Cook, Stephen L. *Prophecy & Apocalypticism: The Postexilic Social Setting* (Minneapolis, MN, 1995).

Daniels, Ted. *A Doomsday Reader: Prophets, Predictors, and Hucksters of Salvation* (New York, 1999).

Dick, Everett Newfon, and Gary Land. *William Miller and the Advent Crisis, 1831–1844* (Berrien Springs, MI, 1994).

Eco, Umberto, Frederic Lenoir, Catherine David, and Jean-Philippe de Tonnac. *Conversations about the End of Time* (London, New York, 1999).

Gomez-Pena, Guillermo. *The New World Border: Prophecies, Poems, & Loqueras for the End of Century* (San Francisco, 1996).

Graziano, Frank. *The Millennial New World* (New York, 1999).

Heard, Alex. *Apocalypse Pretty Soon: Travels in End-Time America* (New York, 1999).

Keller, Catherine. *Apocalypse Now and Then: A Feminist Guide to the End of the World* (Boston, 1996).

Kessel, John. *Good News From Outer Space* (New York, 1995).

Kleinhenz, Christopher, and Fannie LeMoine. *Fearful Hope: Approaching the New Millennium* (Madison, WI, 1999).

Lamy, Philip. *Millennium Rage: Survivalists, White Supremacists, and the Doomsday Prophecy* (New York, 1996).

McMullen, Sean, and John Harris. *Souls in the Great Machine* (New York, 1999).

Meissner, W. W. William W. *Thy Kingdom Come: Psychoanalytic Perspectives on the Messiah and Millennium* (Kansas City, MO, 1995).

Stone, Jon R. *A Guide to the End of the World: Popular Eschatology in America* (New York, 1993).

Thompson, Damian. *The End of Time: Faith and Fear in the Shadow of the Millennium* (London, 1996).

Underwood, Grant. *The Millenarian World of Early Mormonism* (Urbana IL, 1993).

Wessinger, Catherine Lowman. *How the Millennium Comes Violently: From Jonestown to Heaven's Gate* (New York, 2000).

——. *Millennialism, Persecution, and Violence: Historical Cases* (Syracuse, NY, 2000).

Wojcik, Daniel. *The End of the World as We Know It: Faith, Fatalism, and Apocalypse in America* (New York, 1997).

Thomas More

Ackroyd, Peter. *The Life of Thomas More* (New York, 1998).

Baker, David Weil. *Divulging Utopia: Radical Humanism in Sixteenth-Century England* (Amherst, MA, 1999).

Kenyon, Timothy. *Utopian Communism and Political Thought in Early Modern England* (London, 1989).

Marius, Richard. *Thomas More: A Biography* (Cambridge, MA, 1999).

Monti, James. *The King's Good Servant but God's First: The Life and Writings of Thomas More* (San Francisco, 1997).

Sisk, David W. *Transformations of Language in Modern Dystopias* (Westport, CT, 1997).

Wegemer, Gerard. *Thomas More: A Portrait of Courage* (Princeton, NJ, 1995).

Concepts of Time

Jammer, Max. *Concepts of Space: The History of Theories of Space in Physics* (New York, 1993).

Koecke, Christian. *Zeit des Ressentiments, Zeit der Erlösung: Nietzsches Typologie temporaler Interpretation und ihre Aufhebung in der Zeit* (Berlin and New York, 1994).

Laget, Annette. *Freud et le Temps* (Lyons, 1995).

Macey, Samuel L. *The Dynamics of Progress: Time, Method, and Measure* (Athens, GA, 1989).

MacKenzie, Iain M. *The Anachronism of Time: A Theological Study into the Nature of Time* (Norwich, 1994).

Naglee, David Ingersoll. *From Everlasting to Everlasting: John Wesley on Eternity and Time* (New York, 1991).

Nowotny, Helga. *Eigenzeit: Entstehung und Strukturierung eines Zeitgefühls* (Frankfurt am Main, 1989).

——. *Time: Modern and Postmodern Experience* (Cambridge, MA, 1994).

O'Malley, Michael. *Keeping Watch: A History of American Time* (New York, 1990).

Wood, David. *On Paul Ricoeur: Narrative and Interpretation* (London and New York, 1991).

German Literary Utopias

Affeldt-Schmidt, Birgit. *Fortschrittsutopien: Vom Wandel der utopischen Literatur im 19. Jahrhundert* (Stuttgart, 1991).

Eickelpasch, Rolf, and Armin Nassehi. *Utopie und Moderne* (Frankfurt am Main, 1996).

Gerlach, Ingeborg. *Die Ferne Utopie: Studien zu Peter Weiss' Ästhetik des Widerstands* (Aachen, 1991).

Glaser, Horst Albert. *Utopische Inseln: Beiträge zu ihrer Geschichte und Theorie* (Frankfurt am Main and New York, 1996).

Jablkowska, Joanna. *Literatur ohne Hoffnung: Die Krise der Utopie in der deutschen Gegenwartsliteratur* (Wiesbaden, 1993).

Jenkis, Helmut Walter. *Sozialutopien – barbarische Glücksverheißungen?: Zur Geistesgeschichte der Idee von der vollkommenen Gesellschaft* (Berlin, 1992).

Moltmann, Jürgen, Wolfgang Teichert, and Ezzelino von Wedel. *Die Flügel nicht stutzen: Warum wir Utopien brauchen* (Düsseldorf, 1994).

Müller-Doohm, Stefan. *Jenseits der Utopie: Theoriekritik der Gegenwart* (Frankfurt am Main, 1991).

Neugebauer-Wölk, Monika, and Richard Saage. *Die Politisierung des Utopischen im 18. Jahrhundert: Vom utopischen Systementwurf zum Zeitalter der Revolution* (Tübingen, 1996).

Rahmsdorf, Sabine. *Stadt und Architektur in der literarischen Utopie der frühen Neuzeit* (Heidelberg, 1999).

Saage, Richard. *Das Ende der politischen Utopie?* (Frankfurt am Main, 1990).

———. *Utopieforschung: Eine Bilanz* (Darmstadt, 1997).

Schwendter, Rolf. *Utopie: Überlegungen zu einem zeitlosen Begriff* (Berlin, 1994).

Shafi, Monika. *Utopische Entwürfe in der Literatur von Frauen* (Bern and New York, 1990).

Spies, Bernhard. *Ideologie und Utopie in der deutschen Literatur der Neuzeit* (Würzburg, 1995).

Zipes, Jack David. *Utopian Tales from Weimar* (Edinburgh, 1990).

Part 1: Transatlantic Millenarianism from the Seventeenth to the Twentieth Century

Adventist Churches

Bull, Malcolm, and Keith Lockhart. *Seeking a Sanctuary: Seventh-Day Adventism and the American Dream* (San Francisco, 1989).

Dudley, Roger L, and Edwin I. Hernandez. *Citizens of Two Worlds: Religion and Politics Among American Adventists* (Berrien Springs, MI, 1992).

Guy, Fritz. *Thinking Theologically: Adventist Christianity and the Faith* (Berrien Springs, MI, 1999).

Makapela, Alven. *The Problem With Africanity in the Seventh-Day Adventist Church* (Lewiston, NY, 1996).

Morales-Gudmundsson, Lourdes. *Women and the Church: The Feminine Perspective* (Berrien Springs, MI, 1995).

Pearson, Michael. *Millennial Dreams and Moral Dilemmas: Seventh-Day Adventism and Contemporary Ethics* (Cambridge and New York, 1990).

Plantak, Zdravko. *The Silent Church: Human Rights and Adventist Social Ethics* (New York, 1998).

Webster, Eric Claude. *Crosscurrents in Adventist Christology* (New York, 1984).

Whidden, Woodrow Wilson. *Ellen White on Salvation: A Chronological Study* (Hagerstown, MD, 1995).

African Methodist Episcopal Churches

Acornley, John Holmes. *The Colored Lady Evangelist: Women in American Protestant Religion, 1800–1930* (New York, 1987).

Angell, Stephen Ward, and Anthony B. Pinn. *Social Protest Thought in the African Methodist Episcopal Church, 1862–1939* (Knoxville, TN, 2000).

Campbell, James T. Songs of Zion: *The African Methodist Episcopal Church in the United States and South Africa* (New York, 1995).

Dvorak, Katharine L. *An African-American Exodus: The Segregation of the Southern Churches* (Brooklyn, NY, 1991).

Gomez-Jefferson, Annetta Louise. *In Darkness With God: The Life of Joseph Gomez, a Bishop in the Methodist Episcopal Church* (Kent, OH, 1998).

Gregg, Robert. *Sparks From the Anvil of Oppression: Philadelphia's African and Southern Migrants, 1890–1940* (Philadelphia, 1993).

Morris, Calvin S. Calvin Sylvester. *Reverdy C. Ransom: Black Advocate of the Social Gospel* (Lanham, MD, 1990).

Catholicism and Americanism

Appleby, R. Scott. *American Catholic Modernism at the Turn of the Century* (Chicago, 1985).
Braun, Carl. *Amerikanismus, Fortschritt, Reform: Ihr Zusammenhang und Verlauf in Amerika, Frankreich, England und Deutschland* (Würzburg, 1990).

Methodism

Andrews, Dee. *The Methodists and Revolutionary America, 1760–1800: The Shaping of Evangelical Culture* (Princeton, NJ, 2000).
Brown-Lawson, Albert. *John Wesley and the Anglican Evangelicals of the Eighteenth Century Study in Cooperation and Separation with Special Reference to the Calvinistic Controversies* (Edinburgh, 1994).
Craske, Jane, and Clive Marsh. *Methodism and the Future: Facing the Challenge* (London, 1999).
Dreyer, Frederick A. *The Genesis of Methodism* (Bethlehem, NJ, and London, 1999).
Ferguson, Moira, Anne Hart Gilbert, and Elizabeth Hart Thwaites. *The Hart Sisters: Early African Caribbean Writers, Evangelicals, Radicals* (Lincoln, NE, 1993).
Field, Clive D. *Anti-Methodist Publications of the Eighteenth Century: A Revised Bibliography* (Manchester, 1991).
Owen, Christopher H. *The Sacred Flame of Love: Methodism and Society in Georgia* (Athens, GA, 1998).
Stevens, Abel. *History of the Religious Movement of the Eighteenth Century Called Methodism: Considered in Its Different Denominational and Its Relations to British and American Protestantism* (New York, 1990).
Strickland, William Peter. *The Genius and Mission of Methodism: Embracing What Is Peculiar in Doctrine, Government, Modes of Worship, etc.* (Boston, 1990).

Tabraham, Barrie W. *The Making of Methodism* (London, 1995).

Taylor, Isaac. *Wesley, and Methodism* (London, 1990).

Wigger, John H. *Taking Heaven by Storm: Methodism and the Rise of Popular America* (New York, 1998).

Wood, Arthur Skevington. *Revelation and Reason: Wesleyan Responses to Eighteenth-Century Rationalism* (Nuneaton, 1992).

Pentecostal Churches

Aghahowa, Brenda Eatman. *Praising in Black and White: Unity and Diversity in Christian Worship* (Cleveland, OH, 1996).

Blumhofer, Edith Waldvogel. *Restoring the Faith: The Assemblies of God, Pentecostalism, and Culture* (Urbana, IL, 1993).

Cotton, Ian. *The Hallelujah Revolution: The Rise of the New Christians* (Amherst, NY, 1996).

Cox, Harvey Gallagher. *Fire From Heaven: The Rise of Pentecostal Spirituality and of Religion in the Twenty-First Century* (Reading, MA, 1995).

Crews, Mickey. *The Church of God: A Social History* (Knoxville, TN, 1990).

Diamond, Sara. *Spiritual Warfare: The Politics of the Christian Right* (Montreal, 1990).

DuPree, Sherry Sherrod. *African-American Holiness Pentecostal Movement: An Annotated Bibliography* (New York, 1996).

Faupel, David W. *The Everlasting Gospel: The Significance of Eschatology in the Development of Pentecostal Thought* (Sheffield, 1996).

Griffith, Ruth Marie. *God's Daughters: Evangelical Women and the Power of Submission* (Berkeley, CA, 1997).

Hollenweger, Walter J. *Pentecostalism: Origins and Developments Worldwide* (Peabody, MA, 1997).

Howard, Roland. *Charismania: When Christian Fundamentalism Goes Wrong* (London, Herndon, VA, 1997).

Hummel, Charles E. *Fire in the Fireplace: Charismatic Renewal in the Nineties* (Downers Grove, IL, 1993).

Hunt, Stephen, Malcolm Hamilton, and Tony Walter. *Charismatic Christianity: Sociological Perspectives* (New York, 1997).

Magnuson, Norris A., and William G Travis. *American Evangelicalism: An Annotated Bibliography* (West Cornwall, CT, 1990).

Martin, David. *Tongues of Fire: The Explosion of Protestantism in Latin America* (Oxford and Cambridge, MA, 1990).

Nordbeck, Elizabeth C. *Thunder on the Right: Understanding Conservative Christianity* (New York, 1990).

Poewe, Karla O. *Charismatic Christianity as a Global Culture* (Columbia, SC, 1994).

Scotland, Nigel. *Charismatics and the Next Millennium: Do They Have a Future?* (London, 1995).

Pietism

Ackva, Friedhelm, Martin Brecht, and Klaus Deppermann. *Der Pietismus im achtzehnten Jahrhundert* (Göttingen, 1995).

Arnoldi, Udo. *Pro Iudaeis: Die Gutachten der Hallischen Theologen im 18. Jahrhundert zu Fragen der Judentoleranz* (Berlin, 1993).

Bellardi, Werner. *Die Vorstufen der Collegia Pietatis bei Philipp Jakob Spener* (Giessen, 1994).

Berg, Johannes van den, and Martin Brecht. *Der Pietismus vom siebzehnten bis zum frühen achtzehnten Jahrhundert* (Göttingen, 1993).

Briese, Russell John. *Foundations of a Lutheran Theology of Evangelism* (Frankfurt am Main and New York, 1994).

Gawthrop, Richard L. *Pietism and the Making of Eighteenth-Century Prussia* (Cambridge and New York, 1993).

Gierl, Martin. *Pietismus und Aufklärung: Theologische Polemik und die Kommunikationsreform der Wissenschaft am Ende des 17. Jahrhunderts* (Göttingen, 1997).

Hoffmann, Barbara. *Radikalpietismus um 1700: Der Streit um das Recht auf eine neue Gesellschaft* (Frankfurt and New York, 1996).

Lehmann, Hartmut, Manfred Jakubowski-Tiessen, and Otto Ulbricht. *Religion und Religiosität in der Neuzeit* (Göttingen, 1996).

Lehmann, Hartmut. *Pietismus und weltliche Ordnung in Württemberg vom 17. bis zum 20. Jahrhundert* (Stuttgart, 1969).

Lehmann, Hartmut, and Dieter Lohmeier. *Aufklärung und Pietismus im dänischen Gesamtstaat, 1770–1820* (Neumünster, 1983)

Longenecker, Stephen L. *Piety and Tolerance: Pennsylvania German Religion, 1700–1850* (Metuchen, NJ, 1994).

O'Malley, J. Steven John Steven. *Early German-American Evangelicalism: Pietist Sources on Sanctification* (Lanham, MD, 1995).

Part 2: Visions of the New World Order

German Foreign Relations

Almond, Mark. *National Pacifism: Germany's New Temptation* (London, 1991).

Bach, Jonathan P. G. *Between Sovereignty and Integration: German Foreign Policy and Identity after 1989* (Berlin, Münster, and New York, 1999).

Banchoff, Thomas F. *The German Problem Transformed: Institutions, Politics, and Foreign Policy, 1945–1995* (Ann Arbor, MI, 1999).

Baring, Arnulf, and Volker Zastrow. *Unser neuer Größenwahn: Deutschland zwischen Ost und West* (Stuttgart, 1988).

Biedenkopf, Kurt H. *Einheit und Erneuerung: Deutschland nach dem Umbruch in Europa* (Stuttgart, 1994).

Bredow, Wilfried von, and Thomas Jaeger. *Neue deutsche Außenpolitik: Nationale Interessen in internationalen Beziehungen* (Opladen, 1993).

Brunner, Stefan. *Deutsche Soldaten im Ausland: Fortsetzung der Außenpolitik mit militärischen Mitteln?* (München, 1993).

Crawford, Beverly. *German Foreign Policy After the Cold War: The Decision to Recognize Croatia* (Berkeley, CA, 1993).

Glaessner, Gert-Joachim. *Germany after Unification: Coming to Terms with the Recent Past* (Amsterdam and Atlanta, GA, 1996).

Gutjahr, Lothar. *German Foreign and Defence Policy after Unification* (London and New York, 1994).

Hanrieder, Wolfram F. *Deutschland, Europa, Amerika: Die Außenpolitik der Bundesrepublik Deutschland 1949–1994* (Paderborn, 1995).

Heisenberg, Wolfgang. *German Unification in European Perspective* (London and Washington, D.C., 1991).

Herzog, Roman. *Lessons From the Past, Visions for the Future* (Washington, DC, 1997).

———. *Vision Europa: Antworten auf globale Herausforderungen* (Hamburg, 1996).

Hubert, Hans-Peter. *Grüne Außenpolitik: Aspekte einer Debatte* (Göttingen, 1993).

Kaiser, Karl, and Klaus Becher. *Deutschlands Vereinigung: Die internationalen Aspekte* (Bergisch-Gladbach, 1991).

Kaiser, Karl, and Hanss Maull. *Die Zukunft der deutschen Außenpolitik* (Bonn, 1993).

Krieger, Wolfgang. *The Germans and the Nuclear Question* (Washington, DC, 1995).

Krings, Hermann, and Venanz Schubert. *Deutschland in Europa: Wiedervereinigung und Integration* (St. Ottilien, 1996).

Kuhnhardt, Ludger. *Ideals and Interests in Recent German Foreign Policy* (Washington, DC, 1993).

Libal, Michael. *Limits of Persuasion: Germany and the Yugoslav Crisis, 1991–1992* (Westport, CT, 1997).

Lutz, Dieter S. *Deutschland und die kollektive Sicherheit: Politische und rechtliche programmatische Aspekte* (Opladen, 1993).

Mattox, Gale A., Geoffrey D. Oliver, and Jonathan B. Tucker. *Germany in Transition: A Unified Nation's Search for Identity* (Boulder, CO, 1999).

Mushaben, Joyce Marie. *From Post-War to Post-Wall Generations: Changing Attitudes towards National Question and NATO in the Federal Republic of Germany* (Boulder, CO, 1998).

Otte, Max, and Jürgen Greve. *A Rising Middle Power?: German Foreign Policy in Transformation, 1989–1999* (New York, 2000).

Ruehl, Lothar. *Deutschland als europäische Macht: Nationale Interessen und Internationale Verantwortung* (Bonn, 1996).

Schöllgen, Gregor. *Angst vor der Macht: Die Deutschen und ihre Außenpolitik* (Berlin, 1993).

———. *Die Außenpolitik der Bundesrepublik Deutschland: Von den Anfängen zur Gegenwart* (München, 1999).

Schwarz, Hans-Peter. *Die Zentralmacht Europas: Deutschlands Rückkehr auf die Weltbühne* (Berlin, 1994).

Seward, Valerie. *German Foreign Policy Challenges after Unification* (London, 1993).

Smyser, W. R. *Germany and America: New Identities, Fateful Rift?* (Boulder, CO, 1993).

Stares, Paul B. *The New Germany and the New Europe* (Washington, DC, 1992).

Treverton, Gregory F. *America, Germany, and the Future of Europe* (Princeton, NJ, 1992).

Verheyen, Dirk, and Christian Soe. *The Germans and Their Neighbors* (Boulder, CO, 1993).

Weidenfeld, Werner. *Was ändert die Einheit?: Deutschlands Standort in Europa. Strategien und Optionen für die Zukunft Europas* (Gütersloh, 1993).

Weiner, Myron. *Migration and Refugees: Politics and Policies in the United States and Germany* (Providence, RI, 1997).

Wood, Stephen. *Germany, Europe and the Persistence of Nations: Transformation, and Identity, 1989–1996* (Brookfield, VT, 1998).

American Foreign Relations

Brewer, Thomas L. *American Foreign Policy: A Contemporary Introduction* (Englewood Cliffs, NJ, 1992).

Broad, Dave, and Lori Foster. *The New World Order and the Third World* (Montreal and Cheektowaga, NY, 1992).

Coatsworth, John H. *Central America and the United States: The Clients and the Colossus* (New York, Toronto, 1994).

Cottam, Martha L. *Images and Intervention: U.S. Policies in Latin America* (Pittsburgh, PA, 1994).

Crabb, Cecil Van Meter, and Pat M. Holt. *Invitation to Struggle: Congress, the President, and Foreign Policy* (Washington, DC, 1992).

Crabb, Cecil Van Meter, and Kevin V. Mulcahy. *American National Security: A Presidential Perspective* (Pacific Grove, CA, 1991).

Friedlander, Melvin A. *Conviction & Credence: US Policymaking in the Middle East* (Boulder, CO, 1991).

Gaddis, John Lewis. *The United States and the End of the Cold War: Implications, Reconsiderations, Provocations* (New York, 1992).

George, Alexander L. *Forceful Persuasion: Coercive Diplomacy as an Alternative to War* (Washington, DC, 1991).

Hall, George M. *Geopolitics and the Decline of Empire: Implications for United Defense Policy* (Jefferson, NC, 1990).

Hastedt, Glenn P. *American Foreign Policy: Past, Present, Future* (Englewood Cliffs, NJ, 1991).

Henkin, Louis. *Right v. Might: International Law and the Use of Force* (New York, 1991).

Hyland, William. *The Cold War: Fifty Years of Conflict* (New York, 1991).

Kaufman, Burton Ira. *The Arab Middle East and the United States: Inter-Arab Rivalry and Superpower Diplomacy* (New York and London, 1996).

Kegley, Charles W., and Eugene R. Wittkopf. *American Foreign Policy: Pattern and Process* (New York, 1996).

Klieman, Aaron S. *Israel in American Middle East Policy* (New York, 1991).

Kovrig, Bennett. *Of Walls and Bridges: The United States and Eastern Europe* (New York, 1991).

Langley, Lester D. *Mexico and the United States: The Fragile Relationship* (Boston, 1991).

Lindsay, James M., and Randall B Ripley. *Congress Resurgent: Foreign and Defense Policy on Capitol Hill* (Ann Arbor, MI, 1993).

Munoz, Heraldo, and Carlos Portales. *Elusive Friendship: A Survey of U.S.-Chilean Relations* (Boulder, CO, 1991).

Neff, Donald. *Fallen Pillars: U.S. Policy Towards Palestine and Israel since 1945* (Washington, DC, 1995).

Orme, John David. *Deterrence, Reputation and Cold-War Cycles* (Basingstoke, 1992).

Pitsvada, Bernard T. *The Senate, Treaties, and National Security, 1945–1974* (Lanham, MD, 1991).

Smith, Robert Freeman. *The Caribbean World and the United States: Mixing Rum and Coca-Cola* (New York Toronto, 1994).

Staniland, Martin. *Falling Friends: The United States and Regime Change Abroad* (Boulder, CO, 1991).

Treverton, Gregory F. *Making American Foreign Policy* (Englewood Cliffs, NJ, 1994).

Part 3: Utopian Communities in the Nineteenth and Twentieth Centuries

German Socialism as Utopia

Ahearn, Edward J. *Marx and Modern Fiction* (New Haven, CT, 1989).

Hölscher, Lucian. *Weltgericht oder Revolution: Protestantische und sozialistische Zukunftsvorstellungen im deutschen Kaiserreich* (Stuttgart, 1989).

Jacobs, Dore, and Else Bramesfeld. *Gelebte Utopie: Aus dem Leben einer Gemeinschaft* (Essen, 1990).

Utopian Communities in the United States

Carden, Maren Lockwood. *Oneida: Utopian Community to Modern Corporation* (Syracuse, NY, 1998).

Chmielewski, Wendy E., Louis J. Kern, and Marlyn Klee-Hartzell. *Women in Spiritual and Communitarian Societies in the United States* (Syracuse, NY, 1993).

Clark, Christopher. *The Communitarian Moment: The Radical Challenge of the Northampton Association* (Ithaca, NY, 1995).

Dare, Philip N. *American Communes to 1860: Bibliography. Sects and Cults in America* (New York, 1990).

Fogarty, Robert S. *All Things New: American Communes and Utopian Movements, 1860–1914* (Chicago, 1990).

Foster, Lawrence. *Women, Family, and Utopia: Communal Experiments of the Shakers, the Oneida Community, and the Mormons* (Syracuse, NY, 1991).

Gauthier, Paul S. *Quest for Utopia: The Icarians of Adams County: With Colonies in County, Texas, Nauvoo, Illinois, Cheltenham, Missouri, and California* (Corning, IO, 1992).

Guarneri, Carl. *The Utopian Alternative: Fourierism in Nineteenth-Century America* (Ithaca, NY, 1991).

Hamm, Thomas D. *God's Government Begun: The Society for Universal Inquiry and Reform, 1842–1846* (Bloomington, IN, 1995).

Herrick, Tirzah Miller, and Robert S. Fogarty. *Desire and Duty at Oneida: Tirzah Miller's Intimate Memoir* (Bloomington and Indianapolis, IN, 2000).

Kern, Louis J. *An Ordered Love: Sex Roles and Sexuality in Victorian Utopias: The Shakers, the Mormons, and the Oneida Community* (Chapel Hill, NC, 1981).

Klaw, Spencer. *Without Sin: The Life and Death of the Oneida Community* (New York, 1993).

Kolmerten, Carol A. *Women in Utopia: The Ideology of Gender in the American Owenite Communities* (Bloomington, IN, 1990).

Pitzer, Donald E. *America's Communal Utopias* (Chapel Hill, NC, 1997).

Sutton, Robert P. *Les Icariens: The Utopian Dream in Europe and America* (Urbana, IL, 1994).

Part 4: The Future Society Envisioned

Scientific Racism and Eugenics in Germany

Aly, Götz, Peter Chroust, and Christian Pross. *Cleansing the Fatherland: Nazi Medicine and Racial Hygiene* (Baltimore, MD, 1994).

Baumer-Schleinkofer, Anne. *NS-Biologie* (Stuttgart, 1990).

Biesold, Horst. *Crying Hands: Eugenics and Deaf People in Nazi Germany* (Washington, DC, 1999).

Bock, Gisela. *Zwangssterilisation im Nationalsozialismus: Studien zur Frauenpolitik* (Opladen, 1986).

Clay, Catrine, and Michael Leapman. *Master Race: The Lebensborn Experiment in Nazi Germany* (London, 1995).

Daum, Monika, and Hans-Ulrich Deppe. *Zwangssterilisation in Frankfurt am Main, 1933–1945* (Frankfurt am Main and New York, 1991).

Ehlers, Paul Nikolai. *Die Praxis der Sterilisierungsprozesse in den Jahren 1934–1945 im Regierungsbezirk Düsseldorf unter besonderer Berücksichtigung der Erbgesundheitsgerichte Duisburg und Wuppertal* (München, 1994).

Fenner, Elisabeth. *Zwangssterilisation im Nationalsozialismus: Zur Rolle der Hamburger Sozialverwaltung* (Ammersbek bei Hamburg, 1990).

Gerrens, Uwe. *Medizinisches Ethos und theologische Ethik: Karl und Dietrich in der Auseinandersetzung um Zwangssterilisation und "Euthanasie" im National-sozialismus* (München, 1996).

Grossmann, Atina. *Reforming Sex: The German Movement for Birth Control and Abortion 1920–1950* (New York, 1995).

Herlitzius, Anette. *Frauenbefreiung und Rassenideologie: Rassenhygiene und Eugenik im politischen Programm der "Radikalen Frauenbewegung" (1900–1933)* (Wiesbaden, 1995).

Hermand, Jost. *Old Dreams of a New Reich: Völkisch Utopias and National Socialism* (Bloomington, IN, 1992).

Kaminsky, Uwe. *Zwangssterilisation und "Euthanasie" im Rheinland: Evangelische Erziehungsanstalten sowie Heil- und Pflegeanstalten, 1933–1945* (Köln and Bonn, 1995).

Kroner, Hans-Peter. *Von der Rassenhygiene zur Humangenetik: Das Kaiser-Wilhelm-Institut. Anthropologie, menschliche Erblehre und Eugenik nach dem Kriege* (Stuttgart, 1998).

Kuhl, Stefan. *The Nazi Connection: Eugenics, American Racism, and German National Socialism* (New York, 1994).

Nitschke, Asmus. *Die "Erbpolizei" im Nationalsozialismus: Zur Alltagsgeschichte der Gesundheitsämter im Dritten Reich: Das Beispiel Bremen* (Wiesbaden, 1999).

Proctor, Robert. *Racial Hygiene: Medicine Under the Nazis* (Cambridge, MA, 1988).

Reyer, Jürgen. *Alte Eugenik und Wohlfahrtspflege: Entwertung und Fürsorge vom Ende des 19. Jahrhunderts bis zur Gegenwart* (Freiburg im Breisgau, 1991).

Sierck, Udo. *Normalisierung von Rechts: Biopolitik und "Neue Rechte"* (Hamburg, 1995).

Vieler, Eric H. *The Ideological Roots of German National Socialism* (New York, 1999).

Weingart, Peter, Jürgen Kroll, and Kurt Bayertz. *Rasse, Blut und Gene: Geschichte der Eugenik und Rassenhygiene in Deutschland* (Frankfurt am Main, 1988).

American Racism

Alexander, Rudolph. *Race and Justice* (Huntington, NY, 2000).

Bell, Derrick A. *Afrolantica Legacies* (Chicago, 1998).

Berger, Maurice. *White Lies: Race and the Myths of Whiteness* (New York, 1999).

Bushart, Howard L., John R. Craig, and Myra Edwards Barnes. *Soldiers of God: White Supremacists and Their Holy War for America* (New York, 1998).

Carr, Leslie G. *"Color-Blind" Racism* (Thousand Oaks, CA, 1997).

Clarke, James W. *The Lineaments of Wrath: Race, Violent Crime, and American Culture* (New Brunswick, NJ, 1998).

Cohen, Mark Nathan. *Culture of Intolerance: Chauvinism, Class, and Racism in the United States* (New Haven, CT, 1998).

Coleman, Jonathan. *Long Way to Go: Black and White in America* (New York, 1997).

Connolly, Paul. *Racism, Gender Identities, and Young Children: Social Relations in Multi-Ethnic, Inner-City Primary School* (London and New York, 1998).

Cooper, Michael L. *The Double V Campaign: African Americans and World War II* (New York, 1998).

Cose, Ellis. *Color-Blind: Seeing Beyond Race in a Race-Obsessed World* (New York, 1997).

Cuomo, Chris J, and Kim Q. Hall. *Whiteness: Feminist Philosophical Reflections* (Lanham, MD, 1999).

Delgado, Richard, and Jean Stefancic. *The Latino/a Condition: A Critical Reader* (New York, 1998).

Donohue, John J., and Steven D. Levitt. *The Impact of Race on Policing, Arrest Patterns, and Crime* (Cambridge, MA, 1998).

Ferber, Abby L. *White Man Falling: Race, Gender, and White Supremacy* (Lanham, MD, 1998).

Fine, Michelle. *Off White: Readings on Race, Power, and Society* (New York, 1997).

Fredrickson, George M. *The Comparative Imagination: On the History of Racism, Nationalism, Social Movements* (Berkeley, CA, 1997).

Goldberg, David Theo. *Racial Subjects: Writing on Race in America* (New York, 1997).

Gossett, Thomas F. *Race: The History of an Idea in America* (New York, 1997).

Harris, Paul. *Black Rage Confronts the Law* (New York, 1997).

Healey, Joseph F. *Race, Ethnicity, and Gender in the United States: Inequality, Group Conflict, and Power* (Thousand Oaks, CA, 1997).

Hurley, Jennifer A. *Racism. Current Controversies* (San Diego, CA, 1998).

Jacobson, Matthew Frye. *Whiteness of a Different Color: European Immigrants and the Alchemy of Race* (Cambridge, MA, 1998).

———. *Barbarian Virtues: The United States Encounters Foreign Peoples at Home and Abroad, 1876–1917* (New York, 2000).

Joshi, S. T. *Documents of American Prejudice: An Anthology of Writings on Race from Thomas Jefferson to David Duke* (New York, 1999).

Kaplan, Jeffrey, and Tore Bjorgo. *Nation and Race: The Developing Euro-American Racist Subculture* (Boston, 1998).

Krenn, Michael. *The Impact of Race on U.S. Foreign Policy: A Reader* (New York, 1999).

———. *Race and U.S. Foreign Policy during the Cold War* (New York, 1998).

———. *Race and U.S. Foreign Policy From 1900 Through World War II* (New York, 1998).

———. *Race and U.S. Foreign Policy From Colonial Times Through the Age of Jackson* (New York, 1998).

———. *Race and U.S. Foreign Policy in the Ages of Territorial and Market Expansion, 1840 to 1900* (New York, 1998).

Lincoln, Charles Eric. *Race, Religion, and the Continuing American Dilemma* (New York, 1999).

Mills, Charles Wade. *Blackness Visible: Essays on Philosophy and Race* (Ithaca, NY, 1998).

Perlmutter, Philip. *Legacy of Hate: A Short History of Ethnic, Religious, and Racial Prejudice in America* (Armonk, NY, 1999).

Scott, Daryl Michael. *Contempt and Pity: Social Policy and the Image of the Damaged Black Psyche, 1880–1996* (Chapel Hill, NC, 1997).

Selden, Steven. *Inheriting Shame: The Story of Eugenics and Racism in America* (New York, 1999).

Smith, John David. *Slavery, Race, and American History: Historical Conflict, Trends, and Method, 1866–1953* (Armonk, NY, 1999).

Stewart, Marsha. *We Be Headed for Execution: The Genocide of Today's Black Males* (Hampton, VA, 1997).

Takaki, Ronald T. *Double Victory: A Multicultural History of America in World War II* (Boston, 2000).

Waller, James. *Face to Face: The Changing State of Racism Across America* (New York, 1998).

Walters, Jerome. *One Aryan Nation Under God: Exposing the New Racial Extremists* (Cleveland, OH, 2000).

German Racism

Bahr, Eckhard. *Verfluchte Gewalt: Dokumentierte Geschichten* (Leipzig, 1992).

Beckmann, Herbert. *Angegriffen und bedroht in Deutschland: Selbstzeugnisse, Berichte, Analysen* (Weinheim, 1993).

Blackburn, Gilmer W. *Education in the Third Reich: A Study of Race and History in Nazi Textbooks* (Albany, NY, 1985).

Clay, Catrine, and Michael Leapman. *Master Race: The Lebensborn Experiment in Nazi Germany* (London, 1995).

Foitzik, Andreas. *"Ein Herrenvolk von Untertanen": Rassismus, Nationalismus, Sexismus* (Duisburg, 1992).

Garbe, Detlef. *Rassismus in Deutschland* (Bremen, 1994).

Goodrick-Clarke, Nicholas. *The Occult Roots of Nazism: Secret Aryan Cults and Their Influence on Nazi Ideology: The Ariosophists of Austria and Germany, 1890–1935* (New York, 1992).

Greenspan, Louis I., and Cyril Levitt. *Under the Shadow of Weimar: Democracy, Law, and Racial Incitement in Six Countries* (Westport, CT, 1993).

Heuss, Herbert. *Die Verfolgung der Sinti in Mainz und Rheinhessen, 1933–1945* (Landau, 1996).

Kiefer, Annegret. *Das Problem einer "Jüdischen Rasse": Eine Diskussion zwischen Wissenschaft und Ideologie (1870–1930)* (Frankfurt am Main and New York, 1991).

Kuhl, Stefan. *The Nazi Connection: Eugenics, American Racism, and German National Socialism* (New York, 1994).

Lewis, Rand C. *The Neo-Nazis and German Unification* (Westport, CT, 1996).

Mendlewitsch, Doris. *Volk und Heil: Vordenker des Nationalsozialismus im 19. Jahrhundert* (Rheda-Wiedenbrück, 1988).

Stackelberg, Roderick. *Idealism Debased: From Volkisch Ideology to National Socialism* (Kent, OH, 1981).

Part 5: Science Fiction, Social Construction, and New Realities

The Apocalypse in Literature

Ahearn, Edward J. *Visionary Fictions: Apocalyptic Writing From Blake to the Modern Age* (New Haven, CT, 1996).

Dewey, Joseph. *In a Dark Time: The Apocalyptic Temper in the American Novel of the Nuclear Age* (West Lafayette, IN, 1990).

Freese, Peter. *From Apocalypse to Entropy and Beyond: The Second Law of Thermodynamics in Post-War American Fiction* (Essen, 1997).

Gery, John. *Nuclear Annihilation and Contemporary American Poetry: Ways of Nothingness* (Gainesville, FL, 1996).

Goldsmith, Steven. *Unbuilding Jerusalem: Apocalypse and Romantic Representation* (Ithaca, NY, 1993).

Hendrix, Howard V. *The Ecstasy of Catastrophe: A Study of Apocalyptic Narrative From Langland to Milton* (New York, 1990).

Kaiser, Gerhard R. *Poesie der Apokalypse* (Würzburg, 1991).

Montgomery, Maxine Lavon. *The Apocalypse in African-American Fiction* (Gainesville, FL, 1996).

Pippin, Tina. *Apocalyptic Bodies: The Biblical End of the World in Text and Image* (London and New York, 1999).

Seed, David. *Imagining Apocalypse: Studies in Cultural Crisis* (New York, 2000).

Stafford, Fiona J. *The Last of the Race: The Growth of a Myth From Milton to Darwin* (Oxford and New York, 1994).

Stokes, John. *Fin De Siècle, Fin Du Globe: Fears and Fantasies of the Late Century* (New York, 1992).

The History and Aesthetics of Comics

Carrier, David. *The Aesthetics of Comics* (University Park, PA, 2000).

Dorfman, Ariel, and Armand Mattelart. *How to Read Donald Duck: Imperialist Ideology in the Disney Comic* (New York, 1991).

Estren, Mark James. *A History of Underground Comics* (Berkeley, CA, 1993).

[Ohio State University]. *See You in the Funny Papers: American Life As Reflected in the Comic Strip* (Columbus, OH, 1995).

Gordon, Ian. *Comic Strips and Consumer Culture, 1890–1945* (Washington, DC, 1998).

Harvey, Robert C. *The Art of the Comic Book: An Aesthetic History* (Jackson, MS, 1996).

Harvey, Robert C, Brian Walker, and Richard V. West. *Children of the Yellow Kid: The Evolution of the American Comic* (Seattle, WA, 1998).

Inge, M. Thomas. *Comics As Culture* (Jackson, MS, 1990).

Kinsella, Sharon. *Adult Manga: Culture and Power in Contemporary Japanese Society* (Honolulu, HW, 2000).

Kunzle, David. *The Nineteenth Century. The History of the Comic Strip* (Berkeley, CA, 1990).

——. *The Early Comic Strip: Narrative Strips and Picture Stories in the European Broadsheet from c. 1450 to 1825* (Berkeley, CA, 1973).

Kurtzman, Harvey, and J. Michael Barrier. *From Aargh To Zap: Harvey Kurtzman's Visual History of the Comics* (Princeton, NJ, 1991).

Lefevre, Pascal, and Charles Dierick. *Forging a New Medium: The Comic Strip in the Nineteenth Century* (Brussels, 1998).

Lent, John A. *Pulp Demons: International Dimensions of the Postwar Anti-Comics* (Madison, NJ, and London, 1999).

McCloud, Scott. *Reinventing Comics: How Imagination and Technology Are an Art Form* (New York, 2000).

——. *Understanding Comics: The Invisible Art* (New York, 1994).

Nyberg, Amy Kiste. *Seal of Approval: The History of the Comics Code* (Jackson, MS, 1998).

O'Sullivan, Judith. *The Great American Comic Strip: One Hundred Years of Cartoon Art* (Boston, 1990).

561

Pustz, Matthew. *Comic Book Culture: Fanboys and True Believers* (Jackson, MS, 1999).

Rhodes, Molly Rae. "Doctoring Culture: Literary Intellectuals, Psychology and Mass Culture in the Twentieth-Century United States". (Ph.D-thesis, University of California, San Diego, CA, 1997).

Robbins, Trina. *Girls to Grrrlz: A History of [Women's] Comics From Teens to Zines* (San Francisco, 1999).

Whyte, Malcolm, and Clay Geerdes. *The Underground Comix Family Album* (San Francisco, 1998).

Ecologic Dystopias

Bahro, Rudolf. *Bleibt mir der Erde treu: Apokalypse oder Geist einer neuen Zeit* (Berlin, 1995).

Dauncey, Guy. *Earthfuture: Stories From a Sustainable World* (Gabriola Island, BC, 1999).

Dews, Peter, Wolfgang Zierhofer, and Dieter Steiner. *Vernunft angesichts der Umweltzerstörung* (Opladen, 1994).

Ernste, Huib. *Pathways to Human Ecology: From Observation to Commitment* (Bern and New York, 1994).

Goodbody, Axel. *Umwelt-Lesebuch: Green Issues in Contemporary German Writing* (Manchester and New York, 1996).

Gorholt, Martin, and Ralf Ludwig. *Rettungsversuche: Der ökologische Umbau der Industriegesellschaft* (Marburg, 1990).

Hassenpflug, Dieter. *Industrialismus und Ökoromantik: Geschichte und Perspektiven der Ökologisierung* (Wiesbaden, 1991).

Hosle, Vittorio. *Philosophie der ökologischen Krise: Moskauer Vorträge* (München, 1991).

Irrgang, Bernhard. *Christliche Umweltethik: Eine Einführung* (München, 1992).

Jonas, Hans, and Wolfgang Schneider. *Dem bösen Ende näher: Gespräche über das Verhältnis des Menschen zur Natur* (Frankfurt am Main, 1993).

Kelly, Petra Karin. *Fighting for Hope* (Boston, 1984).

Mellor, Mary. *Wann, wenn nicht jetzt: Für einen ökosozialistischen Feminismus* (Hamburg, 1994).

Morris-Keitel, Peter, and Michael Niedermeier. *Ökologie und Literatur* (New York, 2000).

Schubert, Ernst, and Bernd Herrmann. *Von der Angst zur Ausbeutung: Umwelterfahrung zwischen Mittelalter und Neuzeit* (Frankfurt am Main, 1994).

Stapleton, Amy. *Utopias for a Dying World: Contemporary German Science Fiction's New Ecological Awareness* (New York, 1993).

Science Fiction in Literature and the Media

Aldiss, Brian Wilson. *The Detached Retina: Aspects of SF and Fantasy* (Liverpool, 1995).

Alkon, Paul K. *Science Fiction Before 1900: Imagination Discovers Technology* (Toronto and New York, 1994).

[Anonymous]. *Utopie et Dystopie* (Nice, 1996).

Armitt, Lucie. *Where No Man Has Gone Before: Women and Science Fiction* (London and New York, 1991).

Bacon-Smith, Camille. *Science Fiction Culture: Feminist Cultural Studies, the Media, and Political Culture* (Philadelphia, 2000).

Bann, Stephen. *Frankenstein, Creation, and Monstrosity* (London, 1994).

Barr, Marleen S. *Feminist Fabulation: Space/Postmodern Fiction* (Iowa City, IA, 1992).

——. *Future Females, the Next Generation: New Voices and Velocities in Feminist Science Fiction Criticism* (Lanham, MD, 2000).

——. *Lost in Space: Probing Feminist Science Fiction and Beyond* (Chapel Hill, NC, 1993).

Ben-Tov, S. Sharona. *The Artificial Paradise: Science Fiction and American Reality* (Ann Arbor, MI, 1995).

Bleiler, Richard. *Science Fiction Writers: Critical Studies of the Major Authors from Early Nineteenth Century to the Present Day* (New York, 1999).

Bogstad, Janice Marie. "Gender, Power and Reversal in Contemporary Anglo-American and French Feminist Science Fiction" (Ph.D.-thesis, Madison, WI, 1992).

Booker, M. Keith. *The Dystopian Impulse in Modern Literature: Fiction as Social Criticism* (Westport, CT, 1994).

———. *Dystopian Literature: A Theory and Research Guide* (Westport, CT, 1994).

Botting, Fred. *Making Monstrous: Frankenstein, Criticism, Theory* (Manchester and New York, 1991).

———. *Sex, Machines and Navels: Fiction, Fantasy and History in the Present* (Manchester and New York, 1999).

Breitenfeld, Annette. *Die Begegnung mit außerirdischen Lebensformen: Untersuchungen zur Science-Fiction-Literatur der DDR* (Wetzlar, 1994).

Broderick, Damien. *Transrealist Fiction: Writing in the Slipstream of Science* (Westport, CT, 2000).

Brosnan, John. *The Primal Screen: A History of Science Fiction Film* (London, 1991).

Bukatman, Scott. *Terminal Identity: The Virtual Subject in Postmodern Science* (Durham, NC, 1993).

Burmeister, Klaus, and Karlheinz Steinmüller. *Streifzüge ins Übermorgen: Science Fiction und Zukunftsforschung* (Weinheim, 1992).

Cavallaro, Dani. *Cyberpunk and Cyberculture: Science Fiction and the Work of William Gibson* (London, New Brunswick, NJ, and Somerset, NJ, 2000).

Chernaik, Laura Rose. "Calling in Question: Science Fiction and Cultural Studies" (Ph.D.-thesis, Santa Cruz, CA, 1995).

Clarens, Carlos. *An Illustrated History of Horror and Science-Fiction Films* (New York, 1997).

Clareson, Thomas D. *Understanding Contemporary American Science Fiction: The Formative Years (1926–1970)* (Columbia, SC, 1990).

Clark, Stephen R. L. *How to Live Forever: Science Fiction and Philosophy* (London and New York, 1995).

Collings, Michael R. *In the Image of God: Theme, Characterization, and Landscape in the Fiction of Orson Scott Card* (New York, 1990).

Cortiel, Jeanne. *Demand My Writing: Joanna Russ, Feminism, Science Fiction* (Liverpool, 1999).

Crossley, Robert. *Olaf Stapledon: Speaking for the Future* (Liverpool, 1994).

Donawerth, Jane. *Frankenstein's Daughters: Women Writing Science Fiction* (Syracuse, NY, 1997).

Everman, Welch D. *Cult Science Fiction Films: From the Amazing Colossal Man to Monster From Space* (New York, 1995).

Ferns, Christopher S., and Frances Dorsey. *Narrating Utopia: Ideology, Gender, Form in Utopian Literature* (Liverpool, 1999).

Freedman, Carl Howard. *Critical Theory and Science Fiction* (Hanover, NH, 2000).

Friedrich, Hans-Edwin. *Science Fiction in der deutschsprachigen Literatur: Ein Referat zur Forschung bis 1993* (Tübingen, 1995).

Garnett, Rhys, and R. J. Ellis. *Science Fiction Roots and Branches: Contemporary Critical Approaches* (New York, 1990).

Goldberg, Lee. *Science Fiction Filmmaking in the 1980s: Interviews with Actors, Directors, Producers, and Writers* (Jefferson, NC, 1995).

Gottwald, Ulrike. *Science Fiction (SF) als Literatur in der Bundesrepublik der Achtziger Jahre* (Frankfurt am Main and New York, 1990).

Gough, Val, and Jill Rudd. *A Very Different Story: Studies on the Fiction of Charlotte Perkins Gilman* (Liverpool, 1998).

Gunn, James E. *Inside Science Fiction: Essays on Fantastic Literature* (San Bernardino, CA, 1992).

Hardy, David A, and Harold Bloom. *Science Fiction Writers of the Golden Age* (New York, 1995).

Hartwell, David G. *Age of Wonders: Exploring the World of Science Fiction* (New York, 1996).

Hartwell, David G., and Kathryn Cramer. *The Ascent of Wonder: The Evolution of Hard SF* (New York, 1994).

Hassler, Donald M, and Clyde Wilcox. *Political Science Fiction* (Columbia, SC, 1997).

Hendershot, Cynthia. *Paranoia, the Bomb, and 1950s Science Fiction Films* (Bowling Green, OH, 1999).

Huber, Peter W. Peter William. *Orwell's Revenge: The 1984 Palimpsest* (New York, Toronto, 1994).

Iaccino, James F. *Jungian Reflections Within the Cinema: A Psychological Analysis of Sci-Fi and Fantasy Archetypes* (Westport, CT, 1998).

Ige, Barbara Kaoru. "Virtual Textualities: Postmodern Dialectics of Democracy" (Ph.D.-thesis, Santa Cruz, CA, 1997).

Innerhofer, Roland. *Deutsche Science Fiction 1870–1914: Rekonstruktion und Analyse der Anfänge einer Gattung* (Literatur in der Geschichte, Geschichte in der Literatur, Vol. 38; Wien, 1996).

Jones, Gwyneth A. *Deconstructing the Starships: Science, Fiction and Reality.* Liverpool Science Fiction Texts and Studies, 16 (Liverpool, 1999).

Kolmerten, Carol A., and Jane Donawerth. *Utopian and Science Fiction by Women: Worlds of Difference* (Syracuse, NY, 1994).

Kuhn, Annette. *Alien Zone: Cultural Theory and Contemporary Science Fiction Cinema* (London and New York, 1990).

——. *Alien Zone II: The Spaces of Science-Fiction Cinema* (London and New York, 1999).

Leonard, Elisabeth Anne. *Into Darkness Peering: Race and Color in the Fantastic* (Westport, CT, 1997).

Lewes, Darby. *Dream Revisionaries: Gender and Genre in Women's Utopian Fiction, 1870–1920* (Tuscaloosa, AL, 1995).

Malmgren, Carl Darryl. *Worlds Apart: Narratology of Science Fiction* (Bloomington, IN, 1991).

May, Stephen. *Stardust and Ashes: Science Fiction in Christian Perspective* (London, 1998).

McCaffery, Larry. *Storming the Reality Studio: A Casebook of Cyberpunk and Postmodern Science Fiction* (Durham, NC, 1991).

Miller, Ron, and Pamela Sargent. *Firebrands: The Heroines of Science Fiction and Fantasy* (New York, 1998).

Morrill, Cynthia Anne. "Paradigms Out of Joint: Feminist Science and Cultural Logic" (Ph.D.-thesis, Riverside, CA, 1997).

Nahin, Paul J. *Time Machines: Time Travel in Physics, Metaphysics, and Science* (New York, 1993).

Newman, Kim. *Apocalypse Movies: End of the World Cinema* (New York, 2000).

——. *Millennium Movies: End of the World Cinema* (London, 1999).

Parrinder, Patrick. *Shadows of the Future: H. G. Wells, Science Fiction, and Prophecy* (Syracuse, NY, 1995).

Penley, Constance. *Close Encounters: Film, Feminism, and Science Fiction* (Minneapolis, MN, 1991).

Pierce, John J. *Odd Genre: A Study in Imagination and Evolution* (Westport, CN, 1994).

Puschmann-Nalenz, Barbara. *Science Fiction and Postmodern Fiction: A Genre Study* (New York, 1992).

Russ, Joanna. *To Write Like a Woman: Essays in Feminism and Science Fiction* (Bloomington, IN, 1995).

Rux, Bruce. *Hollywood vs. the Aliens: The Motion Picture Industry's UFO Disinformation* (Berkeley, CA, 1997).

Sallis, James. *Ash of Stars: On the Writing of Samuel R. Delany* (Jackson, MS, 1996).

Schelde, Per. *Androids, Humanoids, and Other Science Fiction Monsters: Science in Science Fiction Films* (New York, 1993).

Seed, David. *American Science Fiction and the Cold War: Literature and Film* (Edinburgh, 1999).

———. *Anticipations: Essays on Early Science Fiction and Its Precursors* (Syracuse, NY, 1995).

———. *Imagining Apocalypse: Studies in Cultural Crisis* (New York, 2000).

Silverberg, Robert. *Reflections and Refractions: Thoughts on Science-Fiction, Science, Other Matters* (Grass Valley, CA, 1997).

Sisk, David W. *Transformations of Language in Modern Dystopias* (Westport, CT, 1997).

Stapleton, Amy. *Utopias for a Dying World: Contemporary German Science Fiction's a New Ecological Awareness* (New York, 1993).

Staskowski, Andrea. *Science Fiction Movies* (Minneapolis, MN, 1992).

Steinmüller, Angela, Karlheinz Steinmüller, and Hans-Peter Neumann. *Vorgriff auf das lichte Morgen: Studien zur DDR-Science-Fiction* (Passau, 1995).

Vollprecht, Sabine. *Science-Fiction für Kinder in der DDR* (Stuttgart, 1994).

Westfahl, Gary, and George Edgar Slusser. *Nursery Realms: Children in the Worlds of Science Fiction, Fantasy, Horror* (Athens, GA, 1999).

Wolmark, Jenny. *Aliens and Others: Science Fiction, Feminism and Postmodernism* (New York, London, 1993).

Zaki, Hoda M. *Phoenix Renewed: The Survival and Mutation of Utopian Thought in American Science Fiction, 1965–1982* (San Bernardino, CA, 1993).

Zebrowski, George, and Pamela Sargent. *Beneath the Red Star: Studies on International Science Fiction* (San Bernardino, CA, 1996).

Zentz, Gregory L. *Jupiter's Ghost: Next Generation Science Fiction* (New York, 1991).

Index of Names

Index of Places